The African Union: Legal and Institutional Framework

The African Union: Legal and Institutional Framework

A Manual on the Pan-African Organization

Edited by
Abdulqawi A. Yusuf and Fatsah Ouguergouz

LEIDEN • BOSTON
2012

Cover illustration: design by Mr. François Malœuvre.

Library of Congress Cataloging-in-Publication Data

The African Union legal and institutional framework : a manual on the pan-African organization / edited by Abdulqawi A. Yusuf and Fatsah Ouguergouz.
 p. cm.
 Includes index.
 ISBN 978-90-04-22100-0 (hardback : alk. paper) 1. African Union. 2. Africa--Politics and government--1960- 3. Pan-Africanism. 4. African cooperation. I. Yusuf, Abdulqawi. II. Ouguergouz, Fatsah, 1958-
 KQE721.A37 2012
 341.24'9--dc23

2011052658

ISBN 978 90 04 22100 0 (hardback)
ISBN 978 90 04 22772 9 (e-book)

Copyright 2012 by Koninklijke Brill NV, Leiden, The Netherlands.
Koninklijke Brill NV incorporates the imprints Brill, Global Oriental, Hotei Publishing, IDC Publishers, Martinus Nijhoff Publishers and VSP.

All rights reserved. No part of this publication may be reproduced, translated, stored in a retrieval system, or transmitted in any form or by any means, electronic, mechanical, photocopying, recording or otherwise, without prior written permission from the publisher.

Authorization to photocopy items for internal or personal use is granted by Koninklijke Brill NV provided that the appropriate fees are paid directly to The Copyright Clearance Center, 222 Rosewood Drive, Suite 910, Danvers, MA 01923, USA.
Fees are subject to change.

This book is printed on acid-free paper.

PRINTED BY DRUKKERIJ WILCO B.V. - AMERSFOORT, THE NETHERLANDS

TABLE OF CONTENTS

Editors and Contributing Authors ix-xii

PREFACE xiii-xvi
Jean Ping
Chairperson of the African Union Commission

INTRODUCTION 1-6
Abdulqawi A. Yusuf & Fatsah Ouguergouz

PART I. From the Pan-Africanist Movement to the African Union

1. Brief Historical Overview of Steps to African Unity 9-23
   Mohammed Bedjaoui

2. The Transition from the Organisation of African Unity to the African Union 25-52
   Tiyanjana Maluwa

3. The African Union: Principles and Purposes 53-75
   Stéphane Doumbé-Billé

PART II. Structure and Organs of the African Union

4. The Assembly, Executive Council and Commission 79-94
   Joram M. Biswaro

5. The Pan-African Parliament 95-117
   Sani L. Mohamed

6. The African Court of Justice and Human Rights 119-142
   Fatsah Ouguergouz

7. The Peace and Security Council 143-158
   Roland Adjovi

8. The Economic, Social and Cultural Council of the African Union 159-183
   Mohamed S. Amr

PART III. Economic Integration, Development and Good Governance

9. The African Economic Community 187-202
   Makane M. Mbenge & Ousseni Illy

10. The New Partnership for Africa's Development (NEPAD) 203-229
    Edward Kannyo

11. The Regional Economic Communities 231-249
    Stephen Karangizi

12. The Prohibition of Unconstitutional Change of Government 251-274
    Muna Ndulo

13. The African Charter on Democracy, Elections and Governance 275-290
    Hélène Tigroudja

14. The African Convention on the Prevention and Combating of Corruption 291-301
    Mpazi Sinjela

PART IV. Peace and Security

15. The Role of the Union in Conflict Prevention and Resolution 305-333
    Mesmer L. Gueuyou

16. The Right of Forcible Intervention in Certain Conflicts 335-353
    Abdulqawi A. Yusuf

17. Peacekeeping Operations: The Examples of Burundi and Sudan 355-374
    Mutoy Mubiala

18. The African Union's Relationship with the United Nations in the Maintenance of Peace and Security 375-413
    Djacoba L. Tehindrazanarivelo

PART V. Human Rights

19.	The African Charter on Human and Peoples' Rights *Michelo Hansungule*	417-453
20.	The Protocol on the Rights of Women in Africa *Rachel Mayanja*	455-476
21.	The African Charter on the Rights and Welfare of the Child *Chris M. Peter & Ummy A. Mwalimu*	477-493
22.	The Convention Governing the Specific Aspects of Refugee Problems in Africa *Osita C. Eze †*	495-518

APPENDICES

A.	Sirte Declaration (1999)	521-524
B.	Constitutive Act of the African Union (2000)	525-542
C.	Protocol on Amendments to the Constitutive Act of the African Union	543-548
D.	Links to the African Union Organs, Agencies and Instruments	549-552

INDEX 553-576

EDITORS AND CONTRIBUTING AUTHORS

Roland Adjovi (Benin)
Professor at Arcadia University, The College of Global Studies (Glenside, Pennsylvania, U.S.A.) and Academic Director of the Arcadia Center for East African Studies in Arusha (Tanzania).

Mohamed Sameh Amr (Egypt)
Professor of Public International Law, Faculty of Law, Cairo University (Egypt).

Mohammed Bedjaoui (Algeria)
Member of the *Institut de Droit International*, former President of the International Court of Justice, former State Minister, Minister of Foreign Affairs of Algeria.

Joram Mukama Biswaro (Tanzania)
PhD, Ambassador of the United Republic of Tanzania to Ethiopia, and Permanent Representative to the African Union and the United Nations Economic Commission for Africa (E.C.A.), Addis Ababa (Ethiopia).

Stéphane Doumbé-Billé (Cameroon)
Lecturer at the Université Jean Moulin – Lyon 3 (France); Director of the international Law Centre and Director of the *Observatoire de l'intégration juridique et politique africaine*.

Osita C. Eze † (Nigeria)
Professor of Law, Former Director-General of the Nigerian Institute of International Affairs in Lagos (Nigeria).

Mesmer Luther Gueuyou (Cameroon)
PhD, Attorney at Law, Nanterre's Bar (France), Assistant Counsel at the International Criminal Court.

Michelo Hansungule (Zambia)
Professor of Human Rights Law, Centre for Human Rights, Faculty of Law, University of Pretoria (South Africa).

Ousseni Illy (Burkina Faso)
Ph.D. in Law, University of Geneva, and Post-doctoral researcher at Oxford University (U.K.) and Princeton University (U.S.A.).

Edward Kannyo (Uganda)
Associate Professor at the Rochester Institute of Technology (New York, U.S.A.).

Stephen Karangizi (Uganda)
Director, African Legal Support Facility (ALSF); and formerly Deputy Secretary General (Programmes) and General Counsel of the Common Market for Eastern and Southern Africa (COMESA).

Tiyanjana Maluwa (Malawi)
H. Laddie and Linda P. Montague Professor of Law, Pennsylvania State University, Dickinson School of Law (U.S.A.).

Rachel Mayanja (Uganda)
Former U.N. Assistant Secretary-General and Special Adviser to the United Nations Secretary-General on Gender Issues and Advancement of Women.

Makane Moïse Mbenge (Senegal)
Lecturer at the Faculty of Law, University of Geneva and at the Institute of Graduate International and Development Studies, Geneva (Switzerland).

Sani L. Mohamed (Nigeria)
Ambassador of the Federal Government of Nigeria to Egypt.

Mutoy Mubiala (DRC)
Staff member of the United Nations High Commission for Human Rights, Geneva (Switzerland).

Ummy Ally Mwalimu, MP (Tanzania)
Deputy Minister, Community Development, Gender and Children in the Government of the United Republic of Tanzania.

Muna Ndulo (Zambia)
Professor of Law, at the Cornell Law School and Director of the Cornell University's Institute for African Development, Ithaka (New York, U.S.A.).

Fatsah Ouguergouz (Algeria)
Judge at the African Court of Human and Peoples' Rights (Arusha, Tanzania) and Associate Editor of the *African Yearbook of International Law*.

Chris Maina Peter (Tanzania)
Professor of Law at the School of Law, University of Dar es Salaam (Tanzania) and Member of the United Nations Committee on Elimination of All Forms of Racial Discrimination.

Jean Ping (Gabon)
Chairperson of the Commission of the African Union.

Mpazi Sinjela (Zambia)
Former Dean, WIPO Worldwide Academy and Professor at the Faculty of Law of the University of Lusaka (Zambia).

Djacoba Liva Tehindrazanarivelo (Madagascar)
Doctor of international law (IUHEI, Geneva, Switzerland), Adjunct Professor at Boston University Geneva Program (Switzerland), and Lecturer at the Institute for Human Rights, Catholic University of Lyon (France).

Hélène Tigroudja (Algeria)
Professor at the Université d'Artois – Directrice du Centre Ethique et Procédure, Faculté de droit de Douai (France).

Abdulqawi A. Yusuf (Somalia)
Judge at the International Court of Justice (The Hague, The Netherlands); Member of the Institut de Droit International; and General Editor of the *African Yearbook of International Law*.

PREFACE

It is with a feeling of pleasure and pride that I accepted to write a preface to this outstanding piece of work on the African Union, an institution I have had the pleasure of serving since 2008. To write the preface for a book is a privilege for whoever accepts the task. The author of a preface thus finds himself associated with a publication without having contributed to the long and painstaking work required for its production. It is, therefore, gratification that is not really commensurate with the contribution made by its recipient. Writing a preface remains, nevertheless, a daunting privilege.

It is a challenge that requires one to capture the essence of a book and attempt to reproduce it in just a few sentences. While the exercise does not, in any way, commit the writer with regard to the opinions expressed by the author/s of the book in question, it nevertheless presupposes the existence of some degree of intellectual complicity with them. It is, finally, an overall appreciation of a work which, irrespective of any such complicity, must remain as objective as possible and avoid all excesses.

With reference to this book, I was able to resolve the three problems mentioned above with great ease. The first reason for this is that the publication deals with topics I am relatively familiar with but which I have never been able to address with the requisite detachment because of my responsibilities at the African Union. The second reason, which I consider central, has to do with the excellent quality of the contents of this publication. *The African Union: Legal and Institutional Framework – A Manual of the Pan-African Organization* is indeed one of those rare publications which, though written by experts, presents relatively complex concepts and issues to lay persons in simple but concise terms. It is the compilation of twenty-two chapters by eminent African jurists each of whom undertakes scientific analysis of the different instruments that constitute the legal and political framework of the functions, objectives and operational mechanisms of the African Union. I hasten to add, as this is an issue of considerable importance when dealing with a joint publication, that in spite of the number and diversity of its authors, its style is homogenous and seamless. It is therefore a book whose manuscript I read with great pleasure.

The objective of the *Manual* is to popularize the new law of the Pan-African Organization. Under the aegis of the African Foundation for International Law, this significant attempt at reflecting about the African Union will contribute towards a better understanding of this unique institution and the way in which it effectively functions.

The African Union is the latest institutional expression of a long-standing quest for political and economic unity of the African continent. It is the current concretization of Pan-African ideals for the economic, social and cultural progress of the peoples of Africa. Its creation represents the most significant political change in relations among African States in the past fifty years. Contrary to the Constitutive Charter of its predecessor – the Organization of African Unity – the Constitutive Act of the African Union lays down a new set of principles which, if effectively implemented, can position the Pan-African Organization at the forefront of the worldwide struggle for security, human rights and good governance. The founding principles of the African Union will also enable it to contribute to efforts at the international level especially in the areas of security, economic development, foreign trade, health, environment, unconstitutional change of government, the fight against impunity and terrorism. This underlines the significance of the mission of this organization in the development and self-realization of the peoples and individuals of the African continent.

The objective of the *Manual* is to offer clear and concise insight into the origins, principles, objectives, structure, organs and mandate of the new Pan-African Organization and, in so doing, to contribute towards a better understanding of the nature and functioning of an institution which is destined to reflect the deep aspirations of the peoples of the African continent at the dawn of the 21st century.

Consisting of twenty-two chapters divided into six main parts, it deals with different aspects of the origins, structure, activities and external relations of the African Union. It pays particular attention to organs of the African Union, the role of this latter in the area of peace and security (including some case studies), economic development and respect for human rights. The *Manual* has the further advantage of dealing with issues related to the legal framework for economic integration, good governance and development with particular attention to the African economic community, NEPAD and the African Peer Review Mechanism, three institutions set up by African states with the aim of enhancing their own economic, social and political development. While these institutions are still relatively unknown, an entire chapter in this publication is devoted to each of them. It is also to be noted, with appreciation, that this book includes an analysis of the relationship between the African Union and the United Nations Organization on the one hand and, on the other, with other sub-regional institutions for economic integration that have been set up in various parts of the continent.

The emphasis on the rich content and quality of this publication does not imply, however, that I necessarily share all the views expressed by the different authors on the issues they address. It could not be otherwise considering the great diversity of the topics discussed, their complexity and the position of a privileged observer, or even a full-fledged participant, that I have held in the African Union since 2008.

Written by specialists for non-specialists, the *Manual* will meet the needs of all those, even the most demanding, looking for tools to help them in the analysis of the African Union. Diplomats, decision-makers, parliamentarians, academicians, students, researchers, journalists, staff members of the African Union and of other African or non-African international organizations, non-governmental organizations, as well as the wider public as a whole, will therefore appreciate the publication of this piece of work. This initiative by the African Foundation for International Law is the more welcome because it fills a major vacuum. Since its inception in July 2002, the African Union has never been the subject of a comprehensive scientific analysis, both precise and exhaustive. Without doubt, the publication of this piece of work will reduce the feeling of frustration among those whose professional or academic activities or perhaps even intellectual curiosity could not allow to be contented with the piecemeal, and sometimes partial, information published here and there on the African Union.

I note, with satisfaction, that this valuable tool for the understanding of the African Union which is being launched in English today is in the process of being translated into French so as to reach the wider public for whom it is intended. I hope it will be subsequently translated into the other languages of the African Union for it deserves to be distributed as widely as possible.

Dr. Jean Ping
Chairperson of the African Union Commission

INTRODUCTION

Abdulqawi A. Yusuf & Fatsah Ouguergouz

A. The Subject-Matter of the Manual

This work is an introduction into the origins, law and institutions of the African Union (AU). It examines the evolution, structures, legal standards and operational activities of this Pan-African organization, which replaced ten years ago the Organization of African Unity (OAU). The AU did not, however, simply replace the OAU in name, or through some minor amendments to the Charter of the latter. It actually constitutes in many ways a complete break with its predecessor organization. The objectives and principles underlying the Constitutive Act of the AU represent a radical shift from those of the OAU Charter not only in terms of promoting African economic and political integration, but also in the advancement of peace and security as well as the rule of law, good governance, human rights and democracy in the continent. Indeed, while the OAU Charter was mainly focused on decolonization and the safeguarding of State sovereignty, the Constitutive Act of the AU mandates the organization to pursue collective action on behalf of the peoples of the continent and to ensure protection of human rights and respect for democratic principles. As such, it may be characterized as the present-day repository of the ideals of the Pan-African movement aimed at the political, economic, social and cultural advancement of the peoples of Africa.

Moreover, the Constitutive Act of the AU, in contrast to the Charter of its predecessor – the OAU, establishes a new set of principles that, if implemented in practice, could substantially contribute to the realization of the African people's quest for human security, development, human rights, and good governance. Although we are still far away from the concretization of the aspirations reflected in the objectives and principles enshrined in the Constitutive Act, the very fact that all African States now subscribe to these principles is a major victory for the peoples of Africa in their struggle for peace, unity, good governance, and socio-economic development.

In addition to the right of intervention of the AU in a Member State to prevent war crimes, genocide and crimes against humanity, the Constitutive Act contains a number of principles, which might be considered groundbreaking in the context of the evolution of the new "Public law of Africa". Thus, it provides for the right of Member States to request intervention from the Union in order to restore peace and security, the promotion of gender equality, respect for democratic principles, human rights, the rule of law and good governance, respect for the sanctity of human life, condemnation and rejection of impunity and political assassination, acts of terrorism and subversive activities, and enunciates the condemnation and rejection by the AU of unconstitutional changes of government. These principles can serve as a foundation stone not only for the construction of African unity, but also for the promotion of peace, political stability, democratic and human rights values throughout the continent. The extent, to which they have so far been implemented, as well as their prospective application, both at the continental level and in the domestic jurisdictions of the Member States of the AU, is analysed in various chapters of the Manual.

The Constitutive Act of the AU, together with the conventions and charters concluded among African States, under the auspices of the OAU and the AU, herald the emergence of a " public law of Africa" which provides a normative framework for the realization of the political, social and economic objectives of the Pan-African movement. A multitude of institutions, placed under the African Union or otherwise affiliated to it, are tasked with the implementation of this public law. However, although the AU came into being in 2001, there is so far no comprehensive work which addresses the institution, its organs and structures, the scope of its operations, its legal framework and the normative standards underpinning its objectives and functions or those underlying the conventions, charters and protocols it has enacted or inherited from its predecessor, the OAU.

It is the aim of this work to fill that void. The work has been conceived as a Manual, and not as a scholarly treatise, so as to serve as a basic introduction to the institutional and legal framework of the AU and its affiliated organizations. It is meant to offer a concise and clear picture of the nature and workings of a continental institution aimed not only at promoting peace and unity in Africa, but also at ensuring human security, development, human rights protection and good governance for the peoples of Africa.

B. The Contents of the Manual and its Contributors

As an introductory work on the African Union and the new "public law of Africa", which it helped generate, the Manual is aimed at a large readership of scholars, diplomats, policymakers, legislators, students and the wider public to bring into common knowledge the legal framework governing this unique African institution and the manner in which it operates in practice.

It consists of twenty-two chapters clustered under five main parts dealing with the various aspects of the structure, activities and legal framework of the African Union. Part I deals with the background and evolution of Pan-African institutions, the transition from the OAU to the AU and the objectives and principles underlying the new organization. Part II is devoted to an analysis of the institutional framework of the AU with particular emphasis on the role, functions, and decision-making procedures of its most important organs, namely the Assembly, the Executive Council, the Commission, the ECOSOCC, the Peace and Security Council, the Pan-African Parliament and the African Court of Justice and Human rights. Part III examines the normative framework for economic integration, good governance and development focusing in particular on the African Economic Community, the Regional Economic Communities (RECs), the NEPAD and the Peer Review Mechanism established under the latter to secure the conditions for African States to promote their own economic, social and political development. It also analyses the experience so far acquired by the AU in the implementation of the prohibition of unconstitutional change of government in its Member States, as well as the scope and content of the African Charter on Democracy Elections, and Governance, and the African Convention on the Prevention and Combating of Corruption.

Part IV on peace and security relates to the role of the AU in conflict prevention and resolution, the right of the Union to intervene in internal conflicts, and contains case studies on its recent efforts aimed at the maintenance of peace and security in Burundi, Sudan and other African Countries affected by internal conflicts. It also examines the African Union's relationship with the United Nations in the maintenance of Peace and Security in the continent. Part V deals with the normative and institutional framework established by the AU, and its predecessor – the OAU, for ensuring respect for human rights in the continent, and examines in particular the African Charter on Human and Peoples Rights and its Protocol, the Protocol on the Rights of Women in Africa, the African Charter on the Rights and Welfare of the Child, and the Convention Governing the Specific Aspects of Refugee Problems in Africa.

Work on the Manual started in 2005 in the context of the research activities of the African Foundation for International Law. Thanks to a generous grant from the Organisation Internationale de la Francophonie, the Foundation was able to convene a meeting of the prospective contributors in Alexandria (Egypt), from 16 to 18 December 2005. Most of the chapters of the Manual are based on the initial outlines submitted and oral presentations made at that meeting. Unfortunately, the finalization of some of the individual chapters and the translation of others from French to English, and from English to French, were affected by many unforeseen events that contributed to a considerable delay in the final editing and publication of the Manual. Nonetheless, we are very pleased that this important project could finally be brought to a successful completion, firstly, in this English-language edition of the Manual to be followed in the near future by a French-language one.

The contributors to the Manual are prominent African scholars of international law, international relations, the law of international organizations and specialists in the affairs of the African Union and sub-regional African organizations. They come from all sub-regions of the continent, and practice their professions both inside and outside the continent. They include three Algerians, one Beninese, one Burkinabe, two Cameroonians, one Congolese (DRC), one Egyptian, one Malagasy, one Malawian, two Nigerians, one Senegalese, one Somali, three Tanzanians, three Ugandans and three Zambians. [The Chairperson of the AU Commission has been kind enough to write the preface to the Manual].

It is with great regret that we have to mention here the passing away of one of the contributors to the Manual, Prof. Osita Eze of Nigeria, in April 2011. Prof. Eze was the former Director-General of the Nigerian Institute of International Relations, and a well-known legal scholar, whose outstanding contributions will be missed by all those working in the field of international law.

C. A Work in Progress

In view of the dynamic evolution of the African Union and its legal and institutional framework, and the continuing quest for a better and more advanced integration among African countries, any academic work on the African Union at this stage of its history can only be considered as a work in progress or a mirror image of the continuously-evolving state of the organization itself. Therefore, it is hoped that this first edition of the Manual will be followed in the future by others that will continue to complete and update the study of the legal and institutional framework of the African Union as the construction of this Pan-African organization advances, and as it puts into place new norms and standards of the emerging " public law of Africa" which is bound to shape not only inter-State relations in the continent, but also the manner in which the affairs of the State are conducted within the individual Member States of the Union. Such work will also be in partial fulfilment of the mission of the African Foundation for International Law, which is devoted to the advancement of African perspectives of international law and the analysis of Africa's ongoing contribution to the evolution and development of international law.

We cannot conclude this introduction without expressing our gratitude, on behalf of the African Foundation for International Law, to the Organisation Internationale de la Francophonie and to its Secretary-General, H.E. Abdou Diouf, for their unceasing support to the project of the Manual absent which this work would not have been completed. We also wish to thank all the contributors to the Manual for their patience as well as for their understanding of the manner in which the various chapters they authored had to be modified in order to bring them into line with each other and with the overall character of the work.

PART I. FROM THE PAN-AFRICANIST MOVEMENT TO THE AFRICAN UNION

CHAPTER 1.
BRIEF HISTORICAL OVERVIEW OF STEPS TO AFRICAN UNITY

Mohammed Bedjaoui

1. Introduction

Pan-Africanism has its pedigree, its advocates and its organizational achievements. The purpose of this paper is not a rigorously scientific review of Africa's march towards unity, which is more of a dream than reality at present. That would be beyond my scope. Instead, I shall attempt a modest review of some of the most significant milestones of the making of Africa, which was originally inspired by a visionary pan-African doctrine, advocated from time to time, to this day, by impatient proponents of unity.

This making of Africa occurred through the establishment of regional and sub-regional groupings, the result of a pragmatic forging of loose links into a continental organization established in 1963 and reformed in 1999 into a more integrated structure. In this regard, it can be noted that Africa has formed a remarkable number of regional and sub-regional bodies, some stillborn, others active only on the sidelines, while others have distinguished themselves by laudable efficiency.

A brief historical overview as defined above would benefit from an introductory look at the ideas of African intellectuals and statesmen who have etched on the collective memory of their peoples their passion for the integration and institutionalised union of the continent.

2. Discussing ideas between dream and reality

"The long, long night is over! Colonial and subject peoples of the world – unite!" Thus, like a banner snapping in the breeze, did Kwame Nkrumah, future President of the Gold Cost, now Ghana, address the oppressed men and women of all continents in 1947.

(a) The pan-African doctrine or ideology

Generally speaking, African integration processes have been strongly marked by an ideology called "pan-Africanism". This major movement, which first appeared in the Caribbean at the end of the 19th Century, had its roots in the slave trade and racial discrimination. Initially, it was a show of pride and recovery of injured dignity, of solidarity between members of the Black Diaspora and glorification of the motherland, Africa. It was first essentially racial and cultural. Subsequently, in the 1950s, it evolved and gained a political dimension. From the Antilles, it gradually gained ground in Africa and emerged as a political movement involved in the struggle against colonialism and for the socio-economic development of the African continent.

The definitions of the movement were many and varied on account of the sociological complexity of the phenomenon. Some authors defined it as an ideology. Others said it was a political doctrine whose goal was the African Renaissance.

By way of example, according to Hubert Kampang, pan-Africanism can be defined as

> "the ideology of democracy and human rights in an African federal framework ... (whose purpose is)... a government of Africans by Africans, which respects racial and religious minorities who wish to live in Africa with the black majority."[1]

---

[1] Kampang H., *Au-delà de la Conférence nationale pour les Etats-Unis d'Afrique*, Paris: L'Harmattan, p. 159.

Pan-Africanism is therefore a political and cultural movement that considers Africans, wherever they are, as a united whole and fosters solidarity amongst peoples of African origin.

(b) Founders and militants of pan-Africanism

The concept of pan-Africanism is supposed to have been formulated for the first time in 1900 during a conference in Westminster Hall in London. Convened by the West Indian Henry Sylvester Williams, this conference, which could be considered the first pan-African gathering, denounced the looting of the ancestral lands of the peoples of Southern Africa and the Gold Coast (Ghana) by the Europeans.

Some leaders and key intellectual figures influenced the movement. Particularly distinguished were four people, all from the Caribbean: Edward Wilmot Blyden, Antenor Firmin, Henry Sylvester Williams and Benito Sylvain.

Edward Wilmot Blyden (1832-1912) is considered to be the father of the modern pan-Africanist movement and the initiator of both the *Back to Africa* drive and Negritude. The other emblematic figures include Marcus Garvey (Jamaica), who in 1920 notably recommended the return of Africans in the diaspora to the "motherland". He influenced many other famous pan-Africanists such as Kwame Nkrumah. He was the Black Moses. William Burghart Dubois (United States of America) was, for his part, the first theorist of pan-Africanism and was the driving force behind the fist pan-African congress and eponymous movement. Henry Sylvester-Williams, Kwame Nkrumah, Fela Kuti, Malcom X, Steve Biko, Patrice Lumumba, Cheikh Anta Diop, Julius Nyerere, and others also left their mark in this category.

1937 saw the establishment of the International African Service Bureau, an organization to help Africans wherever they were. Its mystical objective was the unity of the black race.

(c) First pan-African congresses ... outside Africa

The Pan-African Conference organised in London in July 1900 was an important event that crowned the process of awareness that had begun in the 19th Century. Two people made a significant contribution to this event: Henry Sylvester Williams and Benito Sylvain. Representatives from the Caribbean drafted the statutes and defined the objectives of a new pan-African association. An "Address to the Nations of the World" was sent to the powers of the time, namely Great Britain, France, Germany and the United States.

Subsequently, the very first Pan-African Congress was held in Paris in 1919. At the conference, Dr. Dubois claimed the right to self-determination for Black people. This was a new development.

The second and third pan-African Congresses were held in London in 1921 and 1923 and the fourth in New York in 1927. They advocated rights for Black people equal to those of the white races, and freedom of expression. These first four congresses were dominated by bourgeois intellectuals and reformers, mainly from the United States of America and Europe.

The sixth congress took place in Manchester in October 1945 after the Second World War. For the first time, Africans from Africa, including Kwame Nkrumah, took part. The congress was distinguished by innovation, firstly in the unprecedented participation of African militants such as Georges Padmore and Jomo Kenyatta, and also because it was a milestone in the history of decolonisation. The proceedings focussed particularly on the crisis of colonialism and the growth of nationalism. Probably also for the first time, the ideas of pan-Africanism and nationalism were closely allied.

In its political manifestation, pan-Africanism therefore underwent profound changes, becoming a powerful tool for liberation from colonial dominance and the consolidation of independence. It was also considered to be the appropriate means of securing the unity of independent African states.

Kwame Nkrumah, who devoted a great deal of effort to the liberation of his country, is among those who defined the foundations of African unity, from the political, economic and cultural standpoint. He fought for the liberation of the African continent and the realisation of his dream for a united and independent Africa, considering in 1961 that:

> "Divided we are weak; united, Africa could become one of the greatest forces for good in the world.... I believe strongly and sincerely that with the deep-rooted wisdom and dignity, the innate respect for human lives, the intense humanity that is our heritage, the African race, united under one federal government, will emerge not as just another world bloc to flaunt its wealth and strength, but as a Great Power whose greatness is indestructible because it is built not on fear, envy and suspicion, nor won at the expense of others, but founded on hope, trust, friendship and directed to the good of all mankind."[2]

Against this backdrop of widespread mobilisation and evolution of pan-Africanism, Africa hosted its first pan-African conferences.

(d) Pan-African meetings in Africa

The most important African congresses took place in Accra, Brazzaville, Casablanca, Monrovia and Addis Ababa.

The first conference of independent African States, held in April 1958 in Accra, Ghana, condemned imperialism and colonialism and expressed support for independence movements. It noted the wish of participating countries to pursue a joint foreign policy based on the triumvirate of independence, sovereignty and territorial integrity. At this conference, Kwame Nkrumah called for the independence of African countries still under colonial domination, took steps to support nationalist movements in Africa, and advocated greater unity among African countries through the strengthening of economic and cultural ties.

A permanent secretariat, based in Accra, was placed in charge of fostering pan-African solidarity and the future establishment of the United States of Africa.

The second conference of independent States took place in August 1959 in Monrovia, Liberia and the second conference of

---

[2] Nkrumah K., *I Speak of Freedom: A Statement of African Ideology*, London: William Heinemann Ltd, 1961, pp. xi-xiv.

African peoples in Tunis in January 1960. These conferences notably proclaimed the right of colonised peoples to self-determination.

In November 1959, representatives of African trade unions met in Accra and formed the All-African Trade Union Federation (AATUF).

The third conference of African States, organised in Addis Ababa, Ethiopia in June 1960, distinguished itself by calling for a boycott of the Union of South Africa and its support for the Provisional Government of the Algerian Republic (GPRA).

Many other meetings took place in 1959-1960. They dealt with common African problems and how to solve them, and again called for a boycott of the Apartheid regime.

The Conference of Casablanca, Morocco, took place from 3 to 7 January 1961. Describing themselves as progressives, the participants drafted a political charter intended to guide the work of the Casablanca Group. The group was short-lived, ceasing to exist in 1962.

The Conference of Monrovia, Liberia, was held from 8 to 12 May 1961. At the initiative of Nigeria, this meeting brought together countries that claimed to be moderates, contrary to the progressive Casablanca Group. The principle of establishing an inter-African and Madagascan advisory organization was adopted but never implemented.

In general, all these meetings were characterised by important areas of convergence. This was the case, for example of the emphasis placed on the fragility of the newly acquired independence, the need to preserve freedoms, and the equally necessary advancement of the continent towards economic, social and cultural development.

(e) Sub-regional groupings prior to the Addis Ababa summit of 1963

The aspiration to a union of the countries that had gained their independence or were about to become independent was expressed by some of them, as illustrated by the following examples:

(i) The Conakry Declaration was signed in April 1959 between Ghana and Guinea and was intended to establish the Guinea-Ghana Union. It reaffirmed support for African unity. The organization never saw the light of day.

(ii) The Mali Federation was created in January 1959 by Senegal, Dahomey (Benin), the Sudan (Mali) and Upper Volta (Burkina Faso), but ceased to exist as from 1960.

(iii) The Conseil de l'Entente or the Sahel-Benin Union was composed of the four republics of Upper Volta (Burkina Faso), Niger, Dahomey (Benin) and Côte d'Ivoire, and was the first step to real Sub-regional Union of African States. This Union included, in particular, a Council of Heads of State. A customs union was established and political, economic and military coordination developed.

(iv) The Customs Union of Equatorial Africa was created in January 1959 when the four republics of the former French Equatorial Africa (Central African Republic, Chad, Gabon and Congo Brazzaville) decided to form a united front to deal with a number of economic issues.

(v) The East Africa Federation was created in June 1963 between the Republic of Tanganyika, Uganda and Kenya.

(vi) Senegambia was created when geographical and ethnic factors led the Gambia and Senegal to form a union for economic and cultural cooperation.

The varied fortunes of these sub-regional groupings reflect the obstacles to the attainment of the pan-African ideal, which may be said to have included at the time an exaggerated sense of nationalism, attachment to newfound sovereignty, tribal peculiarities, linguistic differences, and economic disparities.

For example, it is interesting to note that a number of sub-regional organizations were dissolved: the Permanent Consultative Committee of the Maghreb (1964), the Conference of Heads of State of Equatorial Africa (1959), the African and Madagascan Union for Economic Cooperation (UAMCE), the African and Madagascan Organization for Economic Cooperation (OAMCE), the Union of Central African States (UEAC, 1968), The Union of Central African Republics (URAC, 1960), and The African and Mauritian Organization (OCAM, 1966).

(f) The Addis Ababa Summit of 1963

At this meeting, the differences between the Casablanca (Ghana, Guinea, Mali, Libya, Egypt, Morocco and Algeria) and Monrovia (Cameroon, Liberia, Nigeria, Togo) Groups were again expressed. Thus, ideological schisms concerning the form and nature of a continental union characterised the negotiations, whose outcome was frustrating for those who wanted pan-African unity at all costs.

It would seem that the aspiration to continental unity was, and still is, largely shared, at least as an ideal. However, disagreements among African countries (progressives and moderates), ideological differences and other obstacles will continue to impede the quest for pan-Africanism, as visualised by its founding fathers, for a long time.

The espousal of pan-Africanism was not in itself a problem, but the concretisation of this aspiration engendered ideological differences between countries. These differences are still irreconcilable. They were evident in all the sub-regional groupings established between 1958 and 1963, and during the establishment of the Organization of African Unity, which sounded the death knell for Nkrumah's dream of unity and saw his project relegated to the rank of utopia.

3. The triumph of pragmatism: the establishment of the Organization of African Unity

In fact, two concepts clashed with respect to the concretisation of pan-Africanism: continentalism and regionalism. Regionalism won the day in Addis Ababa in 1963.

For Nkrumah, a Union of African States would contribute to the continent's freedom and would foster opportunities for economic development. Consequently, he advocated supranationalism (a federal government at continental level with supranational powers). But for the majority of African heads of state at the time, the expression of pan-Africanism was not supposed to extend beyond ordinary cooperation. Thus, they preferred it to be without any impact on national sovereignty. In fact, as noted before, the various regional and sub-regional groupings that were created in the 1960s are a clear reflection of this trend.

Following the Addis Ababa summit, a Charter of the Organization of African Unity (OAU) was adopted. This document was the result of a hard-fought compromise between the so-called moderate countries, which favoured gradual African unity, and the progressive countries, which advocated the immediate creation of a pan-African federation. It was obvious in 1963, and still is, that the majority of African countries were not remotely inclined to give up one iota of sovereignty to a continental organization. This opposition can be explained by the recent accession to independence of African countries and their intention to build nation-states.

The establishment of the Organization of African Unity in 1963 in Addis Ababa therefore enshrined a fairly risk-averse form of pan-Africanism, which was quite different from the all-encompassing original idea. Due to the prevailing environment, although designed as a forum for cooperation, the Organization of African Unity mainly focussed on the anti-colonial struggle.

Subsequently, crucial development issues were addressed by the Treaty of Abuja, which established an African Economic Community (AEC). This continental treaty was signed in 1991 by African countries. Its aim was to institute, in the long term, an African Common Market. However, in spite of the entry into force of the Treaty in 1994, and the holding of a first summit in June 1997 in Harare, the African Economic Community appears to have remained an idea, now incorporated into the Constitutive Act of the African Union.

Having been initiated in the 1960s, regional and sub-regional integration increased in the 1970s. These groupings, which were generally based on the geographical proximity and linguistic similarities of their member countries, sought the same objectives, particularly the coordination of socio-economic programmes and policies.

The number of sub-regional organizations thus established is proof of the sincerity of the wish of African countries to unite. However, as shown above, the resultant unions have been disappointing, if not outright failures.

4. The road from unity to the African Union

A few decades after the establishment of the Organization for African Unity, the need for greater unity at continental level became evident in light of the achievements of the Organization of African Unity and the upheavals caused by globalisation, considered in its broadest sense.

During the 1990s, new pan-African theories and proposals came into being. They expressed the continuing differences as to the choice of continental organization and its powers (federal union with supranational powers; a rejection of federalism and advocacy for a simple continental forum).

(a) Pan-Africanism à la Khadafi: the United States of Africa

Having finally become disenchanted with pan-Arabism, the Libyan leader seemed to have found another cause in pan-Africanism. He took the initiative to revive this movement and during the extraordinary summit organised in Sirte, Libya, in September 1999, he proposed to African countries a return to the ideal of pan-Africanism advocated by Kwame Nkrumah, and the creation of the United States of Africa.

During the summit, he submitted a document establishing a supranational organization, the United States of Africa, strongly influenced by the American federal system and the European model.

From the ideal of the United States of Africa to the concept of African government, the Libyan leader was espousing the unionist ideal. Since then, he has called for the attainment of the objective of "the political and socio-economic integration of the continent" as enshrined in the Constitutive Act of the African Union, and continued to submit proposals for an African unity government.

His project was always based on a number of ideas, which include equality among Member States, authority in the hands of the people, the commitment of Member States to implement the policy of the union on pain of sanctions to be decided by the "African Congress", granting the Union powers to defend the continent, "collective self-reliance" within the union for defence, economic and cultural matters, respect for human rights and civil and political freedoms, social justice, balanced development, popular socialism, etc.

At the institutional level, the Libyan leader proposed the establishment of an "African Congress" whose members would be elected for four-year terms and which would decide by absolute majority on foreign policy, defence, economic issues, finance, external trade and civil and consular matters; an African Council, which would be the supreme executive body, reporting to the Congress and empowered to propose federal laws by an absolute majority; a Federal Executive Council, fifteen specialised Federal Commissions which would be subject to the Union; a Federal Supreme Court; an African Monetary Fund; an African Central Bank; and an African Investment Bank.

This draft constitution for a united Africa embodied in a federal government and an African Common Market suffered the same fate as the previous ones. It was rejected by a majority of African countries, which preferred to opt for the African Union project.

In fact, having considered the recurrent obstacles and constraints posed by "globalisation", African leaders came to an agreement on the need to create a more efficient grouping, an organization that would be more in keeping with the times and that would, in the long term, foster the socio-economic and political integration of the African continent.

Here, too, Africa was plagued by deep-rooted differences. There were supporters of a new grouping and those who considered that the Organization of African Unity needed to be maintained while conceding that it needed to be strengthened so as to become a relevant instrument that could take up the various challenges of globalisation.

A compromise was finally found during the extraordinary summit of the Organization of African Unity held in Sirte (Libya), in September 1999, in the form of the Sirte Declaration establishing the African Union (9 September 1999).

The drafting of the Constitutive Act engendered the same differences between the proponents of a Federal Union and the opponents of supranationalism. Another compromise was found, and consensus was reached on the Constitutive Act of the African Union with an Executive Council, an advisory parliament, and specialised organs.

(b) The African Union Treaty: the search for a new beginning

The African Union Treaty was adopted on 11 July 2000 in Lomé, Togo. This marked significant progress for the African multilateralism that had been developing for decades. In particular, the treaty provided for the dissolution within a year of the Organization of African Unity, which would be replaced by the African Union.

The Constitutive Act of the African Union rests on two pillars. The first is an aspiration which has, over time, evolved into something other than what its proponents intended - the realisation of African unity through a continental organization. The second pillar springs from the realisation that existing organizations have shown their limitations in terms both of the realisation of pan-Africanism and of the management of Africa's problems.

The treaty was signed in Lomé on 12 July 2000 by twenty-seven African countries (Togo, Algeria, Zambia, Gabon, Libya, the Sahrawi Arab Democratic Republic (SADR), Equatorial Guinea, Ghana, Burkina Faso, Mali, Benin, Djibouti, Madagascar, the Central African Republic, Malawi, Burundi, Sierra Leone, Niger, Senegal, Ethiopia, Lesotho, Gambia, the Sudan, Guinea Bissau, Cape Verde, Chad and Liberia). The Organization of African Unity was dissolved.

5. The African Union, or incomplete pan-Africanism

In 2004, the Libyan leader again submitted to the African Union his vision for an African Federal Union. He was supported by the then chairperson of the African Union Commission, Professor Alpha Konaré, for whom the African Union was "an organization for regional integration" whose purpose was to establish the "United States of Africa".

During the African Union summit in Abuja in January 2005, Libya proposed that the positions of African Minister of Defence, Foreign Affairs, Communications and Trade be established. A Committee of Heads of State and Government was formed to examine the proposals.

Meeting in Uganda on 13 June 2005, this "Committee of Seven" (Uganda, Senegal, Botswana, Ethiopia, Niger, Chad and Tunisia) agreed on four options:
- creating appropriate and favourable conditions for the appointment of ministers;
- appointing a distinguished person to lead the integration process;
- designating a minister from amongst the ministers of African governments as coordinator of policies and programs in each specific sector;
- strengthening the powers of the current African Union Commissioners.

After its second session in Sirte in July 2005, the Committee made the following recommendations to the summit:
- to create ministerial positions at continental level for 11 sectors, the ministers acting under the authority of the Chairperson of the African Union Commission;
- to consider two options for the status of the Commissioners, either to maintain their positions while changing their powers, or to abolish these positions and replace them with elected ministers;
- to charge the future Minister of Finance with examining means of eliminating customs levies and harmonising tariffs between Member States.

These proposals were no more successful than previous ones and were rejected during the Sirte summit of July 2005. The Committee of Seven, now composed of Algeria, Gabon, Kenya, Nigeria, Uganda and Senegal, was charged with studying all the proposals and ideas already discussed, as well as those arising from further consultation, and submitting a report thereon to the Khartoum summit in January 2006.

For its part, Nigeria, as Chair of the African Union, had taken the initiative to organise a regional conference on "Africa and the challenges of a changing world order: the benefits of an African Union Government", in Abuja on 12 and 13 November 2005. This meeting brought together a number of countries as well as civil society representatives, among others, and concluded that this sensitive and complex issue should be broached pragmatically.

Seized of the issue, the summit of Heads of State and Government of January 2006 in Khartoum, the Sudan, had in particular requested the African Union Commission to monitor the implementation of the work plan and framework for action contained in the report, taking into account Libya's contribution and all other relevant ideas, and to submit a consolidated document, together with a road map, to the Assembly at its ordinary session in Banjul, the Gambia, in July 2006.

During the discussion of this controversial issue, the two major schools of thought that had emerged during previous summits again prevented the development of a consensus. Thus, on one side, the supporters of the "Union Government" approach, mainly represented by Libya and Senegal, were unable to secure the adoption of the report of the Committee of Seven entitled African Union Government for a United States of Africa. On the other side the countries opposed to the proposal rejected it, as they had equally rejected the proposal from Senegal to adopt at least in principle the constitution of an African government.

In the absence of an agreement, the seventh African Union Assembly held in Banjul, the Gambia in July 2006, confined itself to taking note of the report and asked the Commission to convene an extraordinary session of the Executive Council to discuss this issue.

Subsequently, at the Sharm-El-Sheikh Summit of 2008 and at various meetings of the Executive Council in Addis Ababa and in Tripoli (Libya), the possibility of transforming the Commission of the African Union into an "African Union Authority" was considered and further developed without arriving at a final decision on the matter.

6. Conclusion: African unity: between myth and reality

"African Unity" is evidently not a powerful uniting force and pan-Africanism must continue to overcome many recurrent obstacles such as linguistic and cultural differences, the weight of multifarious links with the former colonial masters, the reluctance of countries when it comes to pooling their wealth, the attachment to a brand new national sovereignty, etc.

At present, the construction of African continentalism seems an arduous task. It still comes up against many obstacles, and for various reasons the Libyan leader was unable to succeed where Kwame Nkrumah failed.

CHAPTER 2.
THE TRANSITION FROM THE ORGANIZATION OF AFRICAN UNITY TO THE AFRICAN UNION

Tiyanjana Maluwa

1. Introduction

Africa was not part of the move to multilateral institutions that unfolded at the international level at the turn of the last century, for the obvious reason that the emergence of this phenomenon occurred shortly after another, more debilitating and less civilizing, international phenomenon: the European colonization of African peoples and territories. Thus, with the exception of four States which had either never been colonized (Ethiopia and Liberia) or had become formally independent (Egypt) or were regarded as autonomous dominions of the colonial empire (South Africa), the colonized African territories were not represented in the League of Nations, the first truly international organization in the history of humankind. Africa's participation in the move to multilateral institutions had to wait for the establishment of the United Nations (UN) in 1945, and the emergence of the erstwhile colonies into independent States in the early and mid-1960s.

The rise of independent African States from the ashes of colonialism was accompanied by two developments. The first was the more or less automatic admission of these new States to UN membership. Secondly, the establishment of a continental organization whose membership was open to all independent sovereign African States as a forum for the pursuit of common objectives, including the promotion of the unity and solidarity of African States, the defence of their sovereignty, territorial integrity and independence, and the eradication of all forms of colonialism from Africa. The creation of the Organization of African Unity (OAU) on 25 May 1963 in Addis-Ababa, Ethiopia, was undertaken within the context of Article 53 of the UN Charter, which allows for such regional arrangements and agencies. It can thus be said that if African States were not "present at the creation" of the movement to international institutions at the turn of the twentieth century, by mid-century a significant number of them had emerged and were able not only to join the United Nations-which was itself barely two decades old-but to found their own regional organization. The story of the OAU has been told elsewhere and needs no repeating here.

The aim of this Chapter is to contribute to the debate over the transformation of the institutional framework for African inter-state cooperation and coordination from the OAU to its successor, the African Union (AU). It seeks to chart and analyze the transition from the former body to the latter, and to explore some of the cardinal issues that motivated this transformation.[1] In examining this transformation and transition from the old to the new organization, it may be instructive to contrast this experience with another phenomenon that some scholars have observed since the end of the cold war: namely, the degree to which "traditional" international organizations have adapted to deeply changing political and factual circumstances without formally amending their own constitutional structures or functions.

One of the pertinent questions that must be addressed here is: why did the OAU Member States opt to establish a new entity altogether to replace an organization that had served the continent well for over three and half decades instead of merely reforming it, through appropriate amendments to the Charter, to enable it to meet the new challenges?

---

[1] In this discussion, I have partly drawn from some of my earlier work, for example: "Re-imagining African Unity: Some Preliminary Observations on the Constitutive Act of the African Union," *African Yearbook of International Law* 9 (2002), pp. 3 et seq.

It may briefly be noted here that, in fact, the OAU Assembly initiated a process to review the Charter in 1979, taking into account the need to incorporate changes necessitated by the experiences that the organization had witnessed in the decade and half since its inception. The proposed review did not proceed as envisaged. In the seventeen years of its existence the OAU Charter Review Committee[2] met only a few times and did not adopt any concrete proposals for amendment or reform for consideration by the OAU policy organs. The transition from the OAU to the AU that was to occur a little more than two decades later thus followed a different trajectory: a radical rupture with the old legal and institutional order established by the OAU Charter and the creation of a new order under the Constitutive Act of the AU, rather than a formal amendment to the structure and functions of the former organization. In brief, then, this discussion aims to explore the cardinal aspects of, and motivating factors behind, the transition from the OAU to the AU. My aim is to offer an assessment of the legal and political significance of the Constitutive Act, and to provide a brief account of the political and contextual dynamics behind the transition from the old to the new; and, in doing so, to give some broad reflections on the significance of the adoption of the Constitutive Act for the project of African integration.

2. The Organization of African Unity: A Brief Excursus

The Pan-Africanist project of forging closer unity between African States as well as between African peoples within the continent and in the African Diaspora has a long history. It is a subject that has attracted considerable interest, and has partly been the focus of the discussion in the preceding Chapter of this volume.[3] Pan-Africanism

---

[2] The Charter Review Committee was established by the Assembly by Decision AHG/Dec.111 (XVI) at its Sixteenth Ordinary Session held in Monrovia (Liberia), from 17 to 20 July 1979. The Committee (initially composed of fourteen members, later expanded to twenty-right but subsequently reduced to fifteen) held its first session in Mogadishu (Somalia), from 7 to 12 April 1980. It met six times between 1980 and 1996, when it held its last session in Addis Ababa (Ethiopia), from 9 to 15 May 1996.

[3] See Chapter 1 of this volume.

is not simply a movement bringing together people of African origin, but an ideology that has left a strong imprint on African political thinking and sensitivities, and covering cultural, political and economic dimensions. I will not attempt to tread on this terrain in this discussion, save to note that the establishment of the OAU in 1963 represented the crystallization, in institutional terms, of this movement, at least as far as the quest for African continental unity was concerned.

One major task that Pan-Africanism set for itself-reflected in the OAU Charter-was the complete liberation of the continent from colonialism, racism and apartheid. Indeed, it was this task that gave rise to the need for unity: the sense of a shared responsibility by the newly emergent thirty-odd African States and a shared history of suffering from the combined experience of the transatlantic slave trade and colonial subjugation, oppression and exploitation. While there was general agreement among these States on the need for African unity, the form and nature of that unity were, however, sources of serious disagreements. One group favoured deep and immediate political union with a unitary continent-wide government; a second advocated a loose association of States; while a third group preferred an approach that emphasized regional unity as a first step towards continental unity.[4] These differences in approach reflected tensions between those who espoused a radical or revolutionary path to African unity, on the one hand, and those that favoured cautious and pragmatic, or even slow, evolutionary processes, on the other.

In the event, the organization that emerged from the Addis-Ababa conference was a loose association of sovereign African States, a compromise between what have been described as the two modernist concepts of international organizations: that of the management-oriented, functionalist and progressive international organization charged with the management of common problems; and that of an international organization as the classical agora, a public realm in which international issues can be debated and, perhaps,

---

[4] These groups were known, respectively, as the "Casablanca group", led by Egypt, Ghana and Guinea, the "Monrovia group", led by Liberia and Nigeria, and the "Brazzaville group" led by Congo and Tanzania.

decided.⁵ The former is usually an organization invested with certain limited executive power and enjoying a measure of supranational authority, a good example being the European Union; the latter is essentially a platform or forum where States can meet, exchange ideas, and discuss their common future, not necessarily with a view to solving problems.⁶ With its emphasis on the related principles of sovereign equality of the Member States, respect for the sovereignty, territorial integrity and independence of States and non-interference in the internal affairs of States, the OAU was clearly intended to be a loose organization for voluntary cooperation between African States, with no supra-national authority. As such, the OAU fell squarely within the typology of international organizations described in most of the traditional scholarly work in the field of international organizations: namely, international organizations as entities pursuing "common or converging national interests of Member States"⁷; or entities whose primary purpose is to resolve cross-border issues that cannot otherwise be addressed domestically.⁸

The OAU's greatest achievement lay in its role in spearheading the liberation and decolonization of the continent, the struggle against apartheid and racist minority rule in Southern Africa, forging a common socioeconomic agenda, and affirming a common African identity.⁹ Yet, as many scholars and commentators have stated over the years, the OAU had a mixed, if not dismal, record in respect of its other declared objectives. It failed to achieve much in advancing the

---

⁵ See, generally, Boutros-Ghali B., *L'Organization de l'Unité Africaine*, Paris: A. Colin Collection U, Series *Institutions Internationales*, 1969; Cervenka Z., *The Unfinished Quest for Unity, Africa and the Organization of African Unity*, New York: Freidman, 1977; Amate C.O.C., *Inside the OAU: Pan-Africanism in Practice*, New York: St Martin's Press, 1986

⁶ See Klabbers J., "Two Concepts of International Organization", *International Organisations Law Review* 2 (2005), pp. 282-283.

⁷ Feld W., Jordan R., and Hurwitz L., *International Organizations: A Comparative Approach*, 3rd ed., 1994, p. 10.

⁸ Archer C., *International Organizations*, 2nd ed., 1992, p. 48.

⁹ The major achievements of the OAU have been recognized and enumerated in a somewhat self-congratulatory declaration adopted by the first ordinary session of the Assembly of Heads of State and Government of the African Union on 10 July, 2002, AU Doc. ASS/AU/Decl.2 (I): the Durban Declaration in Tribute to the Organization of African Unity and on the Launching of the African Union.

socio-economic development of the continent or in deepening the unity and integration of African peoples. Its record in resolving the vicious circles of poverty, conflict and human rights violations was generally dismal.

These failures have been compounded by other, largely external, factors. By the beginning of the last decade of the twentieth century, developments in other regions of the world, especially the collapse of the Soviet Union, the end of the cold war and the relentless advance of globalization and global capitalism had begun to impact upon the African continent in ways that had not been anticipated. For many among the members of the OAU itself, the organization had become moribund and irrelevant, in the face of the changed circumstances of the world. As the Interim Chairperson of the Commission of the African Union was to observe later:[10]

> "The world had changed, the continent had changed but the organizational vehicle at the regional level remained pretty much the same, with prisms and methods that could not cope with emerging challenges. The commitment to change this situation fostered the birth of the African Union."

This commitment to change must be understood within the context of two specific factors. First, the fact that the efforts to review the OAU Charter had not moved with the anticipated speed and effectiveness. As indicated above, between 1980 and 1996, when it was last convened, the OAU Charter Review Committee had met only six times.[11] Inertia and an apparent lack of a sense of urgency on the part of the committee had driven some Member States to scepticism about any chance of achieving a meaningful review of the Charter. Second, the phenomenon of globalization, which gained currency in the immediate post-Cold War years, had begun to concentrate the collective minds of OAU Member States on the need to reposition the organization in the international scheme of things. In other words, there was an acceptance of the need to review the work of the OAU

---

[10] Amara Essy (then Interim Chairperson of the Commission of the African Union) in an address to the African Diaspora Forum in Washington, DC, December 2002. See, Report on the First African Union Western Diaspora Forum, Washington, DC, 17-19 December 2002.

[11] See note 2 *supra*.

and to put in its place a new mechanism or institutional structure, and to reorient its objectives in order to reinvigorate the project of African integration.[12] This new institutional structure is the AU.

3. Adoption of the Constitutive Act of the African Union

The Constitutive Act of the AU ("the Constitutive Act")[13] was adopted unanimously by the Assembly of Heads of State and Government of the OAU ("the Assembly") meeting in its thirty-sixth ordinary session in Lomé, Togo, on 11 July 2000. Subsequently, at its fifth extraordinary session held in Sirte, Libya, on 2 March 2001, the Assembly "proudly" declared the establishment of the AU. The Constitutive Act entered into force on 26 May 2001, following its ratification by two-thirds of the Member States of the OAU, as provided for in its Article 28.[14] Upon its entry into force, the Constitutive Act abrogated and superseded the OAU Charter, in accordance with Article 33(1). However, in terms of the same provision, the Charter, and thereby the OAU, remained operational for a transitional period of one year, following a decision adopted to that effect by the Assembly at its thirty-seventh ordinary session in Lusaka, Zambia, on 10 July 2001.[15] Thus, the thirty-eighth ordinary session of the Assembly held in Durban, South Africa, on

---

[12] The first collective response by African countries to the changes taking place in the world following the collapse of the Berlin Wall in 1989 is encapsulated in the Declaration on the Political and Socio-Economic Situation in Africa and the Fundamental Changes Taking Place in the World, adopted by the OAU Assembly of Heads of State and Government in July 1990 at its Twenty-sixth Ordinary Session in Addis-Ababa (Ethiopia). The project for the continental economic integration of Africa was given a formal legal basis with the adoption of the Treaty establishing the African Economic Community in 1991. The focal points for regional integration in Africa are the various Regional Economic Communities (RECs), some of which were established prior to the adoption of the treaty, which are perceived by the Treaty establishing the African Economic Community as its "building blocks" (Article 6).

[13] See text of the Constitutive Act on the Website of the African Union.

[14] All the former fifty-three OAU Member States are parties to the Constitutive Act and thus AU Member States. This leaves Morocco as the only African state that is not a member of the AU.

[15] OAU Assembly of Heads of State and Government, 37th Ord. Sess., OAU Doc. AHG/Dec.160 (XXXVII), para. 15.

8 July 2002, was the last summit of the OAU. This summit marked the demise of the OAU after 39 years of existence, and was immediately followed by the inaugural session of the new organization, which was held at the same venue on 9-10 July 2002.

The adoption of the Constitutive Act marked a significant milestone in the history of the African integration. In adopting a new treaty intended to supersede the OAU Charter, and replace the OAU itself with a new successor organization, it also marked the end of the tepid OAU Charter review process. As was indicated above, the efforts to revise the OAU Charter never came to successful fruition.[16] There never was a strong urge or enthusiasm among the Member States for any meaningful review of the charter. This is not as such surprising: the history of the UN system, for example, shows consistently the reluctance of Member States to open constitutions of international organizations to formal amendments (except, perhaps, for increasing the membership of executive bodies). Furthermore, the adoption of the Constitutive Act represented a critical moment in the long process of reconstructing and consolidating African unity and the historic quest for a politically integrated and unified Africa. At the same time, however, the adoption of the Constitutive Act gave rise to many questions, relating both to the substantive aspects of the proclaimed objectives of the African Union, in particular the project of African integration, and to the modalities and processes for carrying them out. Some of these questions revolved around the following issues: first, the extent to which the African Union would offer a substantive and qualitative difference from the current institutional framework of the OAU, and whether it truly ushered in a new entity that was not merely a reincarnation of the OAU under another name; and, second, the extent to which the establishment of the African Union represented an aspect of Africa's collective response to the twin-challenges of globalization and the "new regionalism", as had been claimed by African leaders themselves. Other questions relate to the relevance of the Constitutive Act and the African Union in confronting the equally important and

---

[16] See, note 2 *supra*.

urgent challenges of strengthening democracy, collective security and human rights in Africa.

An engagement with these issues goes some way towards addressing the question: what is the nature of integration entailed in the idea of the African Union? Indeed, what is the basic institutional premise of the African Union: is it a supranational institution or merely an intergovernmental organization, as was the OAU which it is replacing? While this short discussion cannot pretend to present detailed accounts of these integration narratives or respond critically to the questions they raise, it is apt to point out, at least, that these narratives remind us that part of the task involved in explaining the recent developments relating to the establishment of the African Union has to do with the problem of definition. As some of the discussions in this book suggest, there is a whole range of questions that require definitional clarity and elucidation. For example: is integration an economic or political phenomenon? If it is an economic phenomenon, what levels of interdependence need to be achieved among a group of national economies for them to be described as "integrated"? And does economic integration imply political integration? Or, conversely, does political integration create the space for economic integration to flourish? And what does the notion of political integration itself entail?

3.1. Background to the Adoption of the Constitutive Act: The Historical and Politico-Legal Context

The adoption of the Constitutive Act was preceded by a declaration adopted on 9 September 1999 by the fourth extraordinary session of the Assembly held in Sirte, Libya ("the Sirte Declaration").[17] The session had been convened at Libya's request

---

[17] EAHG/Decl. (IV) Rev. 1.
The relevant part of the declaration provides as follows:
"[8.] Having discussed frankly and extensively on how to proceed with the strengthening of the unity of our continent and its peoples, in the light of those proposals, and bearing in mind the current situation on the continent, we DECIDE TO:

"[to] discuss ways and means of making the OAU effective so as to keep pace with the political and economic developments taking place in the world and the preparation required of Africa within the context of globalization so as to preserve its social, economic and political potentials."[18]

In fact, when it considered the Libyan request and invitation to host the extraordinary session at its thirty-fifth ordinary session in Algiers, Algeria, on 14 July 1999, the Assembly had viewed this objective as an aspect of Africa's collective response to the phenomenon of globalization. Not surprisingly, various speakers at the Algiers summit, and subsequently in Sirte, reiterated the need to reposition the OAU in the international scheme of things, reorient its objectives and put in its place a new mechanism in order to reinvigorate the project of African integration in response to the forces of globalization. In brief, there was a perceived need for new forms of institutionalization to advance this project.

The idea of reviewing and reforming the political, legal and institutional bases of the OAU has a long history. The idea of a politically and territorially united Africa, first advocated in the early 1960s by Ghana's first president, Kwame Nkrumah, necessarily challenges Africans to re-think the whole question of the inviolability of the boundaries inherited at independence by the post-colonial

---

i) Establish an African Union, in conformity with the ultimate objectives of the Charter of our continental Organization and the provisions of the Treaty Establishing the African Economic Community.
ii) Accelerate the process of implementing the Treaty Establishing the African Economic Community, in particular:
a) Shorten the implementation periods of the Abuja Treaty.
b) Ensure the speedy establishment of all the institutions provided for in the Abuja Treaty, such as the African Central Bank, the African Monetary Union, the African Court of Justice and, in particular, the Pan-African Parliament. We aim to establish that Parliament by the year 2000, to provide a common platform for our peoples and their grass-root organizations to be more involved in discussions and decision-making on the problems and challenges facing our continent.
c) Strengthening and consolidating the Regional Economic Communities as the pillars for achieving the objectives of the African Economic Community and realizing the envisaged [Union]."

[18] OAU Assembly of Heads of State and Government, 35th Ord. Sess., OAU Doc. AHG/Dec.140 (XXXV).

African States. In this sense, therefore, the adoption of the Constitutive Act is but an aspect of the historic quest for a united Africa, whose origins can be traced back to the pioneers of the Pan-Africanist movement in the pre-independence era: Marcus Garvey, George Padmore, Kwame Nkrumah, Nnamdi Azikiwe and Julius Nyerere, among others. Moreover, as pointed out above, part of the political context within which the adoption of the Sirte Declaration and, subsequently, the Constitutive Act should be understood is the challenge posed by the phenomenon of globalization, and Africa's response to it.

The last two and half decades, and especially the period following the collapse of the Soviet Union, have witnessed something of a revival in regionalism in various regions of the world, including Africa. This period has seen an increase in African economic integration schemes and institutions, referred to as Regional Economic Communities (RECs), which are regarded as the "building blocks" of the African Economic Community (AEC), established in 1991 under the Abuja Treaty.[19] The older RECs, such as the Economic Community of West African States (ECOWAS), the Southern African Development Community (SADC) and the Common Market for Eastern and Southern Africa (COMESA), have in recent years been joined by two new such regional organizations: the East African Community (EAC) and the Community of Sahel-Saharan States (more commonly known by the acronym CEN-SAD).[20] All these were

---

[19] The Abuja Treaty established the African Economic Community (AEC) as an integral part of the OAU (Article 98). The Treaty, which entered into force on 12 May 1994, has not been abrogated by the Constitutive Act. However, its provisions shall have precedence over any inconsistent or contrary provisions of the Treaty (Article 33(2) of the Act). See Chapter 9 of this Manual.

[20] There are seven AU-recognized Regional Economic Communities: Arab Maghreb Union (AMU), Common Market for Eastern and Southern Africa (COMESA), Community of Sahel-Saharan States (CEN-SAD), Economic Community of Central African States (ECCAS), Economic Community of West African States (ECOWAS), Intergovernmental Authority on Development (IGAD) and Southern African Development Community (SADC). It should be noted that the membership of these RECs does not necessarily and completely coincide with membership of the geographical regions into which OAU Member States are divided: Central Africa, East Africa, North Africa, Southern Africa and West Africa. Furthermore, there is also a considerable degree of overlapping membership between the different organizations, with some countries belonging

intended to be the basis on which the linear progression of African integration envisaged under Article 6 of the Abuja Treaty, from free trade areas to a continent-wide common market, would proceed. The ultimate goal of continent-wide integration was supposed to be achieved in stages, over a period not exceeding thirty-four years. The very first stage was to have focused on the strengthening of the existing RECs and the establishment of new ones in regions of Africa where they did not already exist. According to the proposed timetable, the RECs were expected to develop gradually and progressively into free-trade areas, customs unions and, through horizontal co-ordination and harmonization, eventually evolve into a common market embracing the whole continent. The process originally envisaged under the Abuja Treaty brings into focus some aspects of the questions hinted at earlier-and addressed more properly in other contributions in this Manual-such as: is the end point of economic integration a customs union, a common market, or full economic and monetary union? What types and levels of common institutionalization are associated with an integrated economic space? Does this economic integration imply political integration?

In any event, the OAU's own approach to African integration did not faithfully follow the logic of the Abuja Treaty, nor has the process changed dramatically since the inception of the AU. Moreover, these RECs are neither progressing towards the goal of creating the AEC at the same pace, nor with the same procedures, processes or determination. Indeed, the candid observation made by the AEC's own Economic and Social Commission a few years ago, regarding the progress being achieved by the RECs, remains valid today. It observed:[21]

---

to as many as three different RECs, and some RECs drawing their membership from at least three different OAU geographical regions. Among other sub-regional groupings which have not yet sought or acquired the status of OAU-recognized RECs are: Economic and Monetary Community of Central Africa (CEMAC), Economic and Monetary Union of West Africa (UEMAO), Economic Community of Great Lakes Countries (ECGLC), East African Community (EAC) and Southern African Customs Union (SACU). See Chapter 9 of this *Manual*.

[21] AEC Economic and Social Commission, First Session, 11-12 June 1996: "Strategy and Approach to the Implementation of the Treaty establishing the African Economic Community," (OAU Doc. AEC/ECOSOC 3(I) Rev.1)

"[There is] no clear evidence that they have long-term continental integration in view, [although] trade liberalization is in the forefront and there seems to be an acceptance of the need for rationalization and programme harmonization [in most places]".

Although some aspects of these questions have been eloquently debated in the academic literature on regional integration in Africa, it is to be lamented that none of these questions were addressed as such in Sirte, nor has there been a serious engagement with these issues at the highest political level since. Beyond the broad platitudes about the need to enhance African political unity and integration, there has not been a deep discussion among political leaders in Africa of the idea of the African Union, of the very meaning of the "union" entailed in this project and of its economic, legal, and political implications for the continent. Some leaders regard it as the panacea for all of Africa's economic and political problems, while yet others still view it as the thin end of the wedge towards the creation of a "United States of Africa."[22] It was against this background, characterized by a lack of

---

[22] For example, Muammar Ghaddafi of Libya has never disguised his desire for the immediate establishment of a "United States of Africa", modelled on that of the United States of America, with a unitary government and a continental army under a single command, along the lines first advocated by Ghanaian President Kwame Nkrumah in the early 1960s. These proposals were first elaborated in one of the documents that Libya circulated at the Sirte summit in 1999 (see note 1 *supra*, p. 17, No. 24). Although theses proposals were initially emphatically rejected by other African leaders, Ghaddafi has doggedly persisted in making this call and has continued to present agenda items for discussion at subsequent AU summits aimed at securing, if not an immediate commitment from other African leaders, at least incremental steps towards the establishment of the "United States of Africa". These proposals, which have been officially supported by some countries such as Senegal, have included, for example, the creation, within the AU structures, of positions of "ministers" in the areas of trade, transport, foreign affairs, defence, etc. and the re-designation of the position of the position of Chairperson of the AU Commission as "prime minister." In response, the AU Assembly of Heads of State and Government decided to set up a Committee of Seven Heads of State and Government to study these various proposals. The Committee presented its initial report to the sixth ordinary session of the Assembly held in Khartoum, Sudan, from 23 to 24 January 2006. At that summit the Assembly consequently adopted a resolution in which, for the first time, it expressly "[reaffirms] that the ultimate goal of the African Union is the full political and economic integration of the continent leading to the United States of Africa". See Decision

strategic clarity and the slow pace of implementation of the Abuja Treaty programme, that the call was made in the *Sirte* Declaration to accelerate the project of African integration by short-cutting the tortuous path mapped out in the Abuja Treaty and establishing a new institution, the African Union. The need for the harmonization and strengthening of the RECs, as well as the acceleration of the implementation of the Abuja Treaty and the creation of the African Union, turned precisely on the question of how to enhance Africa's performance in the new global economy so as to ensure sustained growth and the improved welfare of its peoples.[23]

(b) From the Old to the New: the Transition to the African Union

In terms of the Sirte Declaration, the Constitutive Act was to be in conformity with the ultimate objectives of the OAU Charter and the provisions of the Abuja Treaty. However, the declaration did not specify the model or form the African Union was to assume. So, a number of preliminary questions immediately presented themselves. What was intended by this declaration: the creation of a new institution to exist alongside the OAU and AEC? A fusion of the two with the new organization? Or the replacement of the OAU only, while keeping the AEC intact? And, what was implied in the very choice of the designation "African Union"? Was it to be the equivalent of the European Union, for example, with its institutions and organs modelled on those of the latter? It cannot be denied that in the minds of most people, including some African political leaders, the African Union is not only inspired by the European Union, but the processes and outcome of African integration must also follow the logic and trajectory of European integration.[24]

---

on the Report of the Committee of Seven Heads of State and Government Chaired by the President of the Federal Republic of Nigeria: AU Doc. Assembly/AU/Dec.99 (VI).

[23] See Sirte Declaration, note 17 *supra*.

[24] Although most African political leaders have been at pains to insist that the African Union is not simply intended to be a carbon copy of the European Union, it cannot be denied that, in reality, the institutional make-up of the African Union (for example, the Commission, the Permanent Representatives' Committee, the Court of Justice and the Pan-African

These questions lay at the heart of the extensive debates that were conducted during the two meetings of legal experts and parliamentarians held to examine a Draft Treaty Establishing the African Union and a Draft Protocol to the Treaty Establishing the African Economic Community relating to the Pan African Parliament, which had been prepared by the OAU General Secretariat, in Addis Ababa, Ethiopia (17 to 20 April 2000), and Tripoli, Libya (27 to 29 May 2000).[25] The final draft legal text adopted by the second experts' meeting in Tripoli was submitted to a ministerial meeting, which was convened immediately thereafter, also in Tripoli, from 31 May to 2 June 2000. The ministerial meeting adopted a draft Constitutive Act of the African Union which was subsequently formally submitted to the OAU Council of Ministers and to the Thirty-Sixth Ordinary Session of the OAU Assembly in Lomé, Togo, for further consideration and eventual adoption. The draft Constitutive Act submitted to the Assembly for consideration and adoption at the Lomé summit was essentially the outcome of these experts' and ministerial meetings, with very few textual changes.[26] Most of the critical issues relating to the objectives and principles, institutional structure, and the powers and functions of the principal organs of the new body had largely been settled in the ministerial deliberations in Tripoli and Lomé itself. Consequently, there was very

---

Parliament) has been purposefully modelled on the latter's institutions and organs. However, it should also be noted that, apart from the Permanent Representatives' Committee, the other organs were already envisaged under the Abuja Treaty, as future organs of the African Economic Community to be set up subsequently by separate protocols.

[25] For reports of these meetings, see: "Report of the Meeting of Legal Experts and Parliamentarians on the Establishment of the African Union and the Pan-African Parliament,"17-20 April 2000, Addis Ababa (Ethiopia), OAU Doc. CAB/LEG/23.15/6/VOL/IV; "Report of the Second Meeting of Legal Experts and Parliamentarians on the Establishment of the African Union and the Pan-African Parliament," 27-29 May 2000, Tripoli (Libya), OAU Doc. SIRTE/Exp/Rpt (II).

[26] For reports of these meetings, see: "Report of the Meeting of Legal Experts and Parliamentarians on the Establishment of the African Union and the Pan-African Parliament," 17-20 April 2000, Addis Ababa (Ethiopia), OAU Doc. CAB/LEG/23.15/6/VOL/IV; "Report of the Second Meeting of Legal Experts and Parliamentarians on the Establishment of the African Union and the Pan-African Parliament," 27-29 May 2000, Tripoli (Libya), OAU Doc. SIRTE/Exp/Rpt (II).

little debate at the summit. Not surprisingly, the Constitutive Act was adopted by the Assembly on 11 July 2000 more speedily than even the most optimistic advocates of the project of the African Union had anticipated. Moreover, the caution that had been voiced by some of the leaders in Sirte only eleven months earlier hardly resurfaced in Lomé.

In fact, by the time the fifth extraordinary summit of the OAU Assembly was convened, again in Sirte, on 1-2 March 2001, to launch the African Union, a dramatic change had occurred in the disposition of all OAU members to the proposed African Union. By the close of the summit, all the fifty-three Member States had signed the Constitutive Act. The last few countries to do so actually signed it in the course of the summit itself.[27] In so doing, even those countries that had earlier categorically opposed the idea of establishing the African Union, such as Kenya, or had merely expressed grave reservations and caution, for example Botswana and Uganda, had now come on board. The conversion of President Jerry Rawlings of Ghana and President Yoweri Museveni of Uganda to the project of the African Union was probably the most astounding: having opposed the proposal and lectured their peers about the dangers of ill thought-out and rushed economic and political integration in Africa at the Sirte summit, they both turned out to be among the most ardent advocates of the proposed African Union in Lomé. What had changed?

The most generous explanation would be that continuing debates, consultation and reflection between the September 1999 and July 2000 on the proposal for the establishment of this new institution had led to a change of mind among most of the political leaders. But, in truth, there was very little discussion, both within the rarefied circles of the political elites, governments and ruling regimes or in public discourses generally, in almost all these countries. Indeed, one criticism that has repeatedly been made by commentators is that despite the promise made in one of the principles of the Constitutive Act relating to the "participation of African peoples in the activities of the Union"[28] so as to make the new institution a real

---

[27] Angola, Botswana, Cameroon, Congo, Democratic Republic of Congo, Eritrea, Guinea, Kenya, Mauritania, Swaziland and Uganda.
[28] See Article 4(c) of the Constitutive Act.

"community of peoples," the African citizenry was hardly involved in the process of conceptualizing and establishing the African Union. The only debate and discussion that took place occurred among the political leaders themselves.

As was stated above, the fifth extraordinary summit was convened with a view to formally launching the African Union. In terms of Article 28, the entry into force of the Constitutive Act required the deposit of instruments of ratification by two-thirds of the OAU Member States (that is, thirty-six countries), but by the time the summit was opened, only twenty-two instruments of ratification had been deposited with the General Secretariat.[29] However, this did not prevent the Assembly, following a highly spirited debate, from deciding to "proudly declare the establishment of the African Union," whilst recognizing that the actual entry into force of the Constitutive Act, and thus the legal birth of the new organization, would only be achieved subsequently once the necessary ratifications had been secured. In adopting this decision, the African leaders intended to do two things: first, to send out a political message, that the establishment of the African Union was an irreversible fact which was unanimously supported by all the members of the OAU; second, to reiterate the need to respect the legal requirements for the entry into force of the Constitutive Act, and thus the formal legal birth of the African Union, as provided for in Article 28.

The fifth extraordinary session of the OAU Assembly had been expected to mark the formal transition from the OAU to the AU. But the apparent distinction implied in the decision adopted on 2 March 2001, between the "political" birth of the African Union and its "legal" birth, to follow only subsequently, was problematic. An analogy was made with the creation of the OAU itself back in 1963: although the OAU Charter was adopted on 25 May 1963, it only entered into force on 13 September 1963, after the required

---

[29] The decision to hold this extraordinary summit resulted from an impromptu invitation that Ghaddafi extended to the OAU Assembly at the closing ceremony of the Lomé summit, following the signing of the Constitutive Act. Once the dates had been fixed and agreed upon following consultations with all the Member States, the summit had to go ahead notwithstanding the fact that the required number of ratifications for the entry into force of the Constitutive Act had not yet been secured.

number of ratifications had been achieved, in accordance with Article XXV of the Charter. Yet, it was assumed by the founding members, and it has always been accepted, that 25 May 1963, marked the birth of the OAU, and the date is celebrated as such. Indeed, it has been pointed out that the OAU started operating as an organization, with an interim secretariat, immediately following the adoption of the Charter, and before its entry into force. As I have argued elsewhere, the analogy does not seem to be appropriate in the case of the Sirte decision, given the different political context and exigencies surrounding the circumstances of the establishment of the two institutions.[30] In any case, I argue that even if it is accepted that the "political" birth as opposed to the "legal" birth of the African Union needed to be located at a particular juncture, the analogous date should have been 11 July 2000, when the Constitutive Act was adopted in Lomé.

4. New Normative Principles for New Institutional Challenges

The Constitutive Act consists of a preamble and thirty-three dispositive articles. These provisions are examined in the other essays in this volume in the specific contexts of the subject-matter addressed. I will only offer a few observations on some broad institutional and normative issues and their implications for the transition from the OAU to the AU.

The Constitutive Act enumerates a rather expansive list of 14 objectives and principles that go well beyond those enshrine in the OAU Charter. These objectives and principles are fairly expansive, and need not be recounted individually here. To begin with, it may be noted that the objectives of the African Union go beyond the rather limited objectives that are to be found in Article II of the OAU Charter. The objectives, or purposes, stipulated in the OAU Charter were limited to the following: the promotion and achievement of the unity and solidarity of African States; the coordination and intensification of cooperation and efforts to achieve a better life for African peoples; the defence of the sovereignty,

---

[30] See note 1 *supra*, p. 23.

territorial integrity and independence of African States; the eradication of colonialism; and the promotion of international cooperation within the context of the UN Charter and the Universal Declaration of Human Rights. To these, the Constitutive Act adds new ones for the new organization, for example: the acceleration of the political and socio-economic integration of the continent; the promotion and defence of African common positions on issues of common interest; the promotion of peace, security and stability of the continent; the promotion of democratic principles and institutions, popular participation and good governance; the promotion and protection of human and peoples' rights in accordance with the African Charter on Human and Peoples' Rights and other relevant instruments; the promotion of sustainable development at the economic, social and cultural levels; and the advancement of research in all fields, in particular science and technology, and the eradication of preventable diseases and the promotion of good health on the continent. Also included among the new objectives are the establishment of the necessary conditions for the continent to play its rightful role in the global economy and in international negotiations, and the coordination and harmonization of policies between the various African RECs. The last-mentioned objective is viewed as a necessary condition for the "gradual attainment of the objectives of the Union."

But of more significance, perhaps, is that Article 4 incorporates new, radically expanded principles with potentially far-reaching implications. These may be roughly classified into two categories. The first category consists of principles that are now more or less generally recognized in international law, for example, the prohibition of the use of force among Member States; peaceful coexistence among Member States and their right to live in peace and security; and respect for democratic principles, human rights and the rule of law, and good governance. The second category of principles reflects the new thinking and approaches among African States on how to coordinate common responses to present-day political and socio-economic challenges: the principles of participation by African peoples in the activities of the organization; the establishment of a common defence policy for the African continent; the right of the African Union to intervene in Member States under certain conditions where war crimes, genocide and crimes against humanity have been committed; the right of Member States request intervention from the African Union in order to restore peace and security; the promotion of self-reliance; the promotion of gender equality; the promotion of social justice so as to ensure balanced economic development; and the condemnation and rejection of unconstitutional changes of government.

The question that arises is what is the added value in this long catalogue of principles of the AU? There can be no doubt that, within the African political and cultural context and experience, the inclusion of principles in such a constitutive legal instrument relating to issues of gender equality, good governance, democratization, humanitarian intervention, war crimes and crimes against humanity, social justice, rejection of unconstitutional changes of government, and so on, would have been unthinkable a decade or so earlier. In view of the high value placed upon the commitment to respect democracy, human rights, and the rule of law in African politics today, it is appropriate to make a few remarks on this.

In addition to its inclusion in the Constitutive Act, the commitment to democracy, respect for human rights and the rule of law is also one of the fundamental principles upon which the New Partnership for Africa's Development (NEPAD), adopted in 2001 as an integral part of the AU, is based. Indeed, with regard to the principle relating to respect democracy, human rights, the rule of law, and good governance, the African Union has been hailed as joining an ever increasing number of regional organizations that have recently decided to incorporate "democracy clauses" in their constituent texts. Examples of such organizations include: The Organization of American States (OAS),[31] the Common Market of the South (Mercosur) and the European Union.[32] These developments support what some scholars have characterized as an "emerging right

---

[31] The OAS Charter was amended by the Protocol of Washington of 14 December 1992 to provide for this principle.

[32] The amendment effected by the Treaty of Amsterdam of 1997 to the Treaty of Rome (Article 309) provides for suspension of certain membership rights of countries in persistent breach of the principles of democracy, human rights and the rule of law.

to democratic governance", as part of the modern lexicon of international human rights.[33]

Another new principle that represents a radical shift from the OAU Charter, and linked to the commitment to democracy, the rule of law and good governance, is that relating to the condemnation of unconstitutional changes of government. This principle, enshrined in Article 4(p), is articulated again in Article 30 of the Constitutive Act, which provides for suspension of participation in the activities of the AU of any government of a Member State that comes to power through unconstitutional means. This does not mean that the African Union should be expected to use force to reverse military *coup d'état* in Member States, as ECOWAS did in Sierra Leone in 1998, but that governments coming to power through such means will no longer have a place at the African diplomatic table. This provision only strengthened and codified decisions previously adopted by the OAU policy organs, starting in 1997, to impose sanctions on governments that violated democratically established constitutional authority and to require such regimes to restore constitutional order speedily. On 30 May 1997, the OAU Council of Ministers adopted a decision, subsequently endorsed by the Assembly, to exclude the military regime that had come to power in Sierra Leone through a *coup d'état* only five days previously from participating in the OAU ministerial and summit meetings taking place in Harare, Zimbabwe.[34] To be sure, the adoption of this resolution was unprecedented; as an institution, the OAU had for the previous three and half decades not only avoided condemning and excluding governments that came to power unconstitutionally through military putsches, but on occasion had permitted the leaders of such regimes to host OAU meetings and

---

[33] See, for example, Franck T., "The Emerging Right to Democratic Governance," *American Journal of International Law* 86 (1992), pp. 46 *et seq.*

[34] See OAU Doc. CM/Rpt/LXVI. Subsequent decisions on non-participation of unconstitutional governments in OAU meetings were adopted in Algiers by the Council and the Assembly, respectively, in July 1999: see OAU Docs. CM/Dec.483 (LXX) and AHG/Dec.141; and in Lomé, where the Assembly adopted the Declaration on the Framework for an OAU Response to Unconstitutional Changes of Government, OAU Doc. AHG/Decl.5 (XXXVI).

assume the rotating annual chairmanship of the organization.[35] A perverse and absolute adherence to the twin principles of sovereignty and non-interference in the domestic affairs of Member States, regarded as sacred under the OAU Charter, prevented the organization collectively, or Member States individually, from condemning or excluding such regimes. In more recent times, this new principle has been invoked at various times to prevent governments that have come to power through unconstitutional means in the Central African Republic, Comoros, Ivory Coast, Guinea-Bissau and Niger from participating in the AU. The Harare decision was even invoked by the OAU as justification for the exclusion from participation by the government of Marc Ravalomanana in Madagascar in the last summit of the OAU and the inaugural summit of the AU because of the alleged constitutional irregularity of the manner in which that government assumed power following the disputed presidential election results in that country.[36]

I have argued elsewhere that the real test of the commitment of African States to these new, apparently radical, principles lies in their responses to the instances of actual disregard for democracy and violations of human rights that continue to characterize the political behaviour of some of their leaders, including those who may have come to power through the democratic process. I have also argued that the commitment to democracy will, in part, be measured by the extent and sincerity with which they abide by the Declaration Governing Democratic Elections in Africa, adopted by the last

---

[35] The most celebrated example was the decision to allow the military dictator of Uganda, and one of Africa's most notorious human rights violator, to host the 1975 OAU summit in Kampala and thereby assume the chairmanship of the organization.

[36] See the decision adopted by the AU Assembly at its inaugural summit on 10 July 2002: AU Doc. ASS/AU/Dec.7 (I). At the time, Madagascar had not yet ratified the Constitutive Act and was thus technically not yet a member of the new organization and, consequently, not bound by its decisions or the obligations entailed in membership of the new body. The decision to exclude it from participating in the inaugural session was, therefore, legally superfluous. On the other hand, there were a number of countries that participated in the inaugural session even though they had not yet ratified the Constitutive Act.

ordinary session of the OAU Assembly in Durban.[37] The Declaration sets out, *inter alia*, the agreed principles of democratic elections, the responsibilities of Member States, and the rights and obligations under which democratic elections are conducted.[38] Although, as a declaration, it lacks mandatory binding authority unlike, say, the decisions of the Assembly,[39] its legal significance cannot be discounted since it was intended both to provide a guiding framework and to harmonize the positions of the Member States, as well as to complement the earlier OAU decisions on unconstitutional changes of government mentioned above. It is only the conformity of the practice of the Member States to the principles set out in the Constitutive Act and in the Declaration on Democratic Elections in Africa which could justify the claim that the AU has joined the concert of regional organizations that have incorporated "democracy clauses" in their constituent texts.

At the time of this writing, the AU has demonstrated either a reluctance or an indifference to invoke its right of humanitarian intervention in accordance with Article 4 (h) of the Constitutive Act in certain situations such as the Darfur region of Sudan or where such circumstances are considered to exist. This does not inspire confidence in the commitment and ability of the AU to live up to the promises of a new culture that places respect for human rights, democracy, the rule of law and good governance enshrined in the Constitutive Act at the heart of the organization's principles. It also raises the following questions: does the AU truly represent a qualitative change and transition from the old to the new? Is the AU indeed ready to go beyond lip service and apply the new normative framework provided by the Constitutive Act and other related legal instruments to face the current and future challenges facing the continent?

---

[37] See Maluwa T., "The Constitutive Act of the African Union and Institution-Building in Postcolonial Africa," *Leiden Journal of International Law* 16 (2007), pp. 165-166. This section of the essay partly draws from this discussion.

[38] See OAU Doc. AHG/Decl.I (XXXVIII).

[39] See Rule 33 of the Rules of Procedure of the Assembly for the differences between regulations, decisions, directives, recommendations, declarations, etc.

In order to appreciate fully the extent to which the normative framework of the Constitutive Act differs from that of the OAU Charter, it is also instructive to note the principles which have not been replicated from the older text. Four cardinal principles are implicated here.

First, the principle of respect for the sovereignty and territorial integrity of each State and for its inalienable right to independent existence, enunciated in the Charter, has now been subsumed into the principle relating to the respect of borders existing on achievement of independence (Article 4(b) of the Constitutive Act). This is the well-known principle of *uti possidetis*.[40] The principle has been praised as a manifestation of a pragmatic approach to the problem of the arbitrary colonial balkanization of Africa and of the general denial of the legitimacy of intra-African post-colonial boundary claims and wars. At the same time, it has also been criticized as a principle that legitimizes, so to speak, the structural illegitimacy of the African State. It has indeed been observed that the sanctification of the inherited colonial boundaries in Africa is partly to blame for the failure of the post-colonial African States to reconfigure themselves in order to attract the widespread adherence of their constituent sub-State groups, and hence for the emergence of ethnic conflicts within some of these States between antagonistic ethnic communities forcibly bunched together due to the exigencies of colonial boundary-making, or attempts by some dissatisfied ethnic groups to secede from the post-colonial State. The fact that African countries have re-affirmed this principle in the Constitutive Act is itself an indication that, whatever may be the ultimate dream of a politically united or unified continent, for the present the African Union is viewed as an organization of independent and sovereign States that will continue to exist within their respective inherited colonial boundaries. There is no provision in the Constitutive Act that suggests any cession or surrender of sovereignty to the African Union by its members. Clearly, the African Union is predicated on intergovernmentalism, and is not conceived as a neofunctionalist supranational institution. This is

---

[40] See Resolution on Border Disputes Among African States: OAU Doc. AHG/Res. 16 (I), adopted on 21 July 1964. See also *Frontier Dispute, Judgment, I.C.J. Reports 1986*, p. 554.

far removed from the notion of a federal, or even a confederal State which the proponents of the United States of Africa might have wished for. In this sense, it does not represent a radical departure from the institutional framework of the OAU.

Second, the principle provided for in Article III (6) of the OAU Charter, relating to the absolute dedication to the total emancipation of the African territories which are still dependent, makes no appearance in the Constitutive Act. When the OAU was first established, only thirty-two African countries enjoyed independent statehood, and the struggle against colonialism was regarded as one of the fundamental objectives of the newly established organization. Indeed, this struggle lay at the root of the Pan-Africanist project which led to the establishment of the OAU.

Finally, the seventh principle in Article III of the OAU Charter, which relates to the policy of non alignment with regard to all blocs, also reflects the political realities of the Cold War era in which the organization was born. In today's world, in which the old divisions into two opposing power blocs between the communist East and the capitalist West have largely disappeared, or become politically irrelevant, the policy of non-alignment no longer carries any resonance. Its inclusion in the Constitutive Act would have been an historical anachronism.

5. Concluding Observations

I would conclude this reflection by recalling two of the questions posed at the outset: to what extent was the adoption of the Constitutive Act a manifestation of the desire of African States and peoples to create a new institutional framework representing a substantive departure from the OAU? And to what extent does it represent a distinct African effort to contain the challenge of globalization, in the manner in which similar claims have been made for the European Union?

It is apt to recall that in his report to what had been expected to be the last ordinary session of the OAU Assembly in Lusaka in

July 2001, the OAU Secretary General made the pertinent observation that:[41]

> "[It] is important to point out that when African leaders decided to establish the African Union when they adopted the *Sirte* Declaration and, subsequently, the Constitutive Act, they did not aim at establishing an organization which was going to be a continuation of the OAU by another name."

The African Union is supposed to represent a new political, legal and institutional order for Africa, and not an instance of merely pouring old wine into new bottles. As such, it holds out a lot of promise for the citizens of Africa as providing a new framework within which to pursue the decades-old project of deepening their unity and cohesion in the economic, political and social spheres. It cannot be denied that the establishment of the AU, based on the shared vision encapsulated in the objectives and principles contained in the Constitutive Act, provides a new beginning for Africa. But, as with all such new beginnings, the proof of the pudding is in the eating: unless African States exhibit the political will and commitment to implement these objectives and principles faithfully, the advent of the African Union could still turn out to be a false dawn for Africa. Yet, it would be a mistake to ignore the historical antecedents and context in which the AU has been established. These antecedents and context point towards an ideal that has a longer history and is widely shared by most Africans: that of forming a stronger and more cohesive institution to enable them to confront the challenges of the twenty-first century. This explains why, despite the initial misgivings, cynicism and outright hostility in some quarters, and despite the deplorable lack of grassroots involvement in the initial debates, the idea of the AU now appears to have been positively embraced by both the political leadership and common citizenry in almost all countries.

The Constitutive Act is hardly the charter for the politically integrated Africa that some African political leaders or commentators have made it out to be, or may have wished for. Moreover, the Constitutive Act is not a programme of action, in the sense that

---

[41] OAU Doc. AHG/Dec.160 (XXXVII).

the Abuja Treaty is, but simply an organizational framework which is intended to provide the parameters for the future political integration of the continent, a long term objective that has recently been formally reaffirmed by African political leaders. A global reading of the text suggests that the emphasis in the Constitutive Act is on economic integration and coordination of the socio-economic agenda of the continent. But, even this is predicated on a gradualist approach requiring certain levels of institutionalization. The accelerated implementation of the stages of integration envisaged under the Abuja Treaty may, in practical terms, not advance the African integration project in the way that the most ardent advocates of the AU generally assume, and cannot certainly be regarded as a sure-footed strategy in Africa's efforts to contain the consequences of globalization, notwithstanding the rhetorical claims of some African political leaders. The African Union is not, of course, a panacea for all of Africa's economic and political problems. Yet, the gradualist approach of consolidating economic integration, as a way of firming up the foundation for subsequent political integration, is both the most rational and realistic. Experience from other regions of the world, especially Europe, has amply demonstrated that regional integration is a long and complex process. This experience is instructive, and Africa would ignore it at its own peril.

The project of reconstructing and consolidating African unity has not yet resulted in the political union of the continent, the establishment of the AU to replace the OAU represents a modest, but important, advance in the long-standing efforts to establish an integrated African economic and political space. Only time will tell whether the legal and institutional framework established under the Constitutive Act provides the African continent and its people with a durable foundation for enhanced political cooperation and economic integration. Despite its acknowledged failures, the OAU, over a period of almost four decades, provided Africans with a framework for the coordination of their shared political objectives, at least as regards some of the cardinal and overarching concerns of the past decades: decolonization, the fight against apartheid and racist minority rule, and as a vehicle for forging a common socio-economic agenda. It also made an admirable contribution to post-colonial institution-building and international law-making.[42] But the problems that Africa continues to face today, for example deepening poverty and economic decline, HIV-AIDS and other pandemic diseases, the challenges of globalization and continued threats to peace and security and the full enjoyment of human rights by all, require new approaches, strategies and institutional frameworks. African States must empower the AU to make it a credible institution that can enable them to confront these enduring problems in an effective manner. Unless this happens, the AU will, indeed, amount to nothing more than a continuation of the OAU by another name. The transition to a new dawn and a new Chapter in the long quest for closer African unity, and the project of African integration, will thus be further delayed.

---

[42] See Maluwa T., "International Law-Making in Post-Colonial Africa: the Role of the Organization of African Unity," *Netherlands International Law Review*, 49 (2002), pp. 81 *et seq*.

CHAPTER 3.
THE AFRICAN UNION: PRINCIPLES AND PURPOSES

Stéphane Doumbé-Billé

1. Introduction

The Constitutive Act of the African Union (AU)[1] is wholly geared towards the principles and purposes of the new organization, amply demonstrating the role and importance that these two aspects play in defining the goals of the new pan-African organization established to replace the Organization of African Unity (OAU). This substitution does not represent a complete break with the past, in that the new Act does not disregard the "principles and purposes" set forth in the OAU Charter and the Treaty instituting the African Economic Community (AEC), mentioned in paragraph 2 of the Preamble. That said, the legal formulation of the principles and purposes, largely in paragraphs 3 and 4 of the new treaty, replaces that in Articles II and III of the OAU Charter. Even a brief comparison of the two texts reveals clear differences in both drafting and content.

With regard to drafting, even a cursory examination reveals differences in form between the two sets of provisions. In contrast to the terse drafting of the Charter, which contains five purposes (plus one, the coordination and harmonisation of policies) and seven principles, the Constitutive Act, with its seventeen purposes and eighteen principles, is longer, and therefore somewhat repetitive in more or less diverse formulations. Most importantly, its more

---

[1] The Constitutive Act of the African Union was adopted in Lomé, Togo on 11 July 2000 and article 1 of the Protocol on amendments to the Constitutive Act adopted in Maputo (Mozambique), 11 July 2003.

expansive nature means that it is prone to some omissions. This is in fact what happened: it was realised after the Constitutive Act was adopted that some provisions were missing or necessitated to be supplemented. Thus, the Protocol adopted in Maputo, Mozambique on 11 July 2003 "on Amendments to the Constitutive Act of the African Union" remedies these defects, though not entirely, by further lengthening and detailing the purposes and principles and by fleshing out existing clauses and adding new ones. It should be noted that the Protocol on Amendments to the Constitutive Act itself contains a numbering error at the new article 3, which actually adds a new point (i) to the one already existing in the initial version, and which should in fact be an (o), in order to restore continuous numbering. A decision should be adopted by the Assembly of the Union to rectify a material defect. This should be sufficient to repair the error, and might read thus: "at article 3 of the Constitutive Act, the (i) shall read (o)." Subsequently, any consolidated version of the Act would merely reflect the accurate numbering of the clauses. In the purposes, three "new" paragraphs are added to Article 3. Instead of being numbered (i), (p), and (q), they should be numbered (o), (p), and (q), thus correcting the text here. In the principles, an addition is first made to article 4(h).

The change in the content of the provisions is equally significant in that it introduces qualitative changes. The change from five plus one to seventeen purposes and from seven to eighteen principles is more than just an increase in quantity. The content of the Constitutive Act on purposes and principles is clearly denser, reflecting not only the process leading to the initial goals, but also a desire to address new requirements. It also reveals a desire to change with the times, so that the Constitutive Act is underpinned with a strong emphasis on the priorities of the new phase, in terms of residual shortcomings and prospective challenges.

These changes in perspective are not limited to the purposes and principles. The entire Constitutive Act seems to be characterised by a desire for evaluation and receptiveness to new developments in Africa and the world at large. Unsurprisingly, however, this desire is best reflected in the purposes and principles, which constitute the *raison d'être* of the institutional renewal embodied in the creation of a new continental organization as a comprehensive replacement for an existing one. Admittedly, the expected effects of this institutional change, particularly with respect to the exact nature of the African Union and its real capacity for action, have implications for the scope of these principles and purposes themselves. Analysing the purposes and principles as the solid rock on which the new organization stands, we find that the purposes are characterised by particular ambitions (Section 2), and that the principles have undergone profound changes to give full expression to the organization's multi-faceted existence (Section 3).

2. Rather Ambitious Purposes

This is the impression obtained upon analysis of the objectives of the Union. It is true that Article 3 of the Constitutive Act as amended by the Maputo Protocol of 11 July 2003 is only an enumerative clause. In this regard, it is not different from Article II of the OAU Charter, which also addresses the objectives. The drafting is also nearly identical in both instruments,[2] except that they are purposes of the Union in one case and objectives of the Organization in the other. Article 3 lists in alphabetical order a series of seventeen objectives from (a) to (q). This might seem a great many, especially in light of what are supposed to be objectives, and therefore must by definition be limited by the general nature of the purposes intended and pursued by an institution. The brevity of Article II of the OAU Charter was striking. It should also be noted that in the drafting of this Article, which apparently contained too many numerous general purposes, the articulation of the objectives was followed by a second paragraph in the form of an action clause under which "the Member States shall coordinate and harmonize their general policies" in a number of fields, which are also listed.

While this method had its merits, it was discarded in favour of direct numbering. The new Article 3 of the AU Act presents the purposes as they should be with no specific limit to the Union's scope for action. Admittedly, on closer inspection, the delimitation of

---

[2] "The (…) shall have the following purposes:"

paragraph 2 of Article II of the Charter required some improvement. This is not only because it was restrictive – at least apparently so – but also because such an approach was clearly too ambitious given the technical and legal resources which the Charter provided to the Organization. It might therefore be considered that this general desire for harmonisation and coordination was primarily a manifestation of the regionalist zeal that permeates the Charter. Ultimately, it merely introduced a fundamental ambiguity into the objectives by vesting the continental organization with attributes that it could not, by its very nature, sustain, because of the central role still accorded to States in the adopted formulation.

By contrast, the adopted purposes in the AU Act are characterised by this ambition, which must be achieved by firstly codifying the traditional objectives and secondly by adopting a more audacious outlook. These approaches are examined below.

2.1. An Indispensable Pruning of the Traditional Objectives

To make a clean break from the former structure of the Organization, the Act clarifies the components of the Organization by distinguishing between those which are obsolete and must be dispensed with, and those which may be reworked and/or maintained in the new version.

Most noteworthy is the deletion of objective (d) of Article II on the eradication of all forms of colonialism. This is not insignificant in light of the historical conditions under which the OAU was established, and reflects a desire to address other kinds of problems whose resolution no longer requires the new Union to act as a liberation movement. As shown in the preceding Chapters,[3] the OAU Charter focused on the complete and total liberation of all African peoples from the yoke of colonialism.

With the passing of time, the political liberation of colonial lands and peoples has ceased to be a direct objective of the new Union. Since colonial domination within the meaning of the Charter has essentially disappeared, the Preamble of the Constitutive Act merely

---

[3] Cf. Part I, Chapters 1 and 2.

recalls "the heroic struggles waged by our peoples and our countries for political independence, human dignity and economic emancipation." It also considers

"that since its inception, the Organization of African Unity has played a determining and invaluable role in the liberation of the continent, the affirmation of a common identity and the process of attainment of the unity of our Continent…"

Some purposes of the OAU Charter have been maintained in full in the AU Act or not amended to any great extent. This is the case for objective (b) of Article 3 of the Act, which aims to "Defend the sovereignty, territorial integrity and independence of its Member States." This is the same wording as purpose (c) of Article II of the OAU Charter. Even if it does not so indicate in the Preamble, it is understood that an inter-state organization follows the universal model of the United Nations – that is, that it is based both on the principle of sovereign equality among States (Article II(1) of the Charter) and the principle enshrined in United Nations General Assembly resolution 2625 (XXV) of 24 October 1974 on the "Declaration on Principles of International Law concerning Friendly relations and Co-operation among States in accordance with the Charter of the United Nations," under which

"States shall refrain in their international relations from the threat or use of force against the territorial integrity or political independence of any State, or in any other manner inconsistent with the purposes of the United Nations."

Objective 3(b) is still relevant, not only in the context of foreign aggression, but above all in the context of (too) many internal conflicts in Africa, which place its various elements in jeopardy, consequently weakening or even leading to the disappearance or fragmentation of existing States in light of new claims. Whether in the Comoros, Darfur, or Côte d'Ivoire, there are many examples of situations where the Organization has been able to do no more than take note of new situations – and sometimes, however grudgingly, endorse them. Recalling this objective is therefore welcome, solidly founded as it is on the principle of the inviolability of the borders inherited from colonialism as a functional expression of viable territorial frameworks for the international existence of African States.

Equally important is objective 3(e) of the Act, whose goal is to "Encourage international cooperation, taking due account of the Charter of the United Nations and the Universal Declaration of Human Rights." This is exactly the same as objective (e) of Article II of the OAU Charter, unsurprisingly, especially given the more explicit and precise submission to the universal framework, as signified by the word "due." The relevance of the objective of international cooperation does not only lie in the realisation of the necessity of the objectives pursued through international cooperation in the Charter. As noted above, it is cooperation with a given purpose, i.e. the implementation at the regional level of general policies coordinated and harmonised in clearly defined fields.

The justification for retaining the earlier versions of these objectives, which may appear as a sign of renewed realism, is the need for international cooperation, in the face of the aggravation of previously identified problems and the emergence of new ones of unexpected seriousness, to assist in solving specific problems, particularly those of a socio-economic nature, while guaranteeing respect for basic rights. This approach is more consistent with the provisions of Article I (3) of the UN Charter and tends to make the Union – to paraphrase the UN Charter – a genuine regional centre for the harmonisation of the efforts of Member States to achieve their common objectives. It also shows the extent to which the referenced texts serve as a framework for action by the new Union, which is thus required to be more dynamic in coming to grips with development issues and the protection of basic human rights.

Other purposes set out in the OAU Charter have been maintained, but sometimes with more or less extensive amendments in order to reflect the new objectives of the Union. This is the case for purpose (a) of Article II of the OAU Charter, whose intent was to "promote the unity and solidarity of the African States." The new Article 3(a) of the AU Act amends this formulation slightly, expressing the intent to "[a]chieve greater unity and solidarity between the African countries and the peoples of Africa." This nuance is doubly important. Firstly, the intention of achieving greater unity and solidarity in the new institutional framework seems like a cruel admission of failure on the part of a continent beset by conflicts of various types, some of which are seen as arising from petty wrangling and a generalized lack of will to act due to a degree of indifference to the problems of others which do not directly affect national life.

In this respect, it is worth advocating, if not the unity that lent its name to the previous organization, at least some effort to attain unity through the continued pursuit of this objective. Greater unity does not preclude conflicts, but it can make them exceptional, as they should be. It is equally worth advocating greater solidarity from States which see their neighbours faced with various difficulties without proffering any assistance. The wording of Article 3(a) is therefore clearly more realistic, in that what does not exist cannot be strengthened. However, an attempt can be made to achieve it to the extent possible, gradually testing the limits of the necessary unity and solidarity. This, in fact, is the new idea: it is through such testing that awareness is gained of what unites Africans, and not through proclamations that are more sterile than effective.

Secondly, Article 3(a) makes a subtle distinction between African countries and peoples, where there had previously been a reference only to States. This is a new sign of the realism underpinning the new objectives. This distinction is certainly a reflection of the pan-Africanism discussed in previous chapters, which might at first escape notice. The pan-African ideal is based on a sense of common belonging which was initially thought capable of moving mountains. After nearly a third of a century of existence, however, this "State pan-Africanism" also turned out to be impotent, because the fever of unity and solidarity did not sweep across the various lands and social groups. The distinction is based on the general perception that States have lost the Promethean aspect with which they were originally vested, and that all countries and peoples must therefore be committed to achieving unity and solidarity.

The same applies to objective (b) of Article II of the OAU Charter, whose intent was "[to] coordinate and intensify their cooperation and efforts to achieve a better life for the peoples of Africa." At first glance, there is no equivalent objective in Article 2 of the OAU Act. But a closer look at the objectives reveals possible similarities with objective (k), which seeks to "raise the living standards of African peoples." The link between the two objectives is obvious. It is true that the wording used in the Charter has a connotation of assistance which now appears dated in view of the economic situation of the people. The new formulation in the Act makes this objective strictly economic, which is not without implications for the changes in national economic systems towards greater economic and social progress on a popular level.

2.2. Adopting a More Audacious Outlook

This outlook characterises the newly enshrined purposes, which did not exist in the OAU Charter. They are, in fact, undeniably the most numerous and innovative. They confront the new organization with the challenges of the age, on whose resolution an African renaissance depends in a globalized world. In this context, objective (c) seems to be the lodestone of the Act, in that it aims to accelerate political integration, in conjunction with objective (i), which encourages the establishment of "the necessary conditions which enable the continent to play its rightful role in the global economy and in international negotiations." Objective (i) should also be considered in conjunction with objective (l) because the desired integration depends on the prior coordination and harmonisation of the various existing regional economic communities. This is a long and difficult process which developed significantly since 2007, when an in-depth examination of the issue was carried out during the Accra summit. But it is only through real and profound integration that African countries can confront the challenges of the contemporary world, express their own viewpoint and make their voice heard in international circles. This objective is therefore so broad as to justify in itself the new appellation of the Organization as a Union. In this regard, it gives concrete orientation to the new objectives, which can be classified for convenience into two main categories: socioeconomic, on the one hand; and political, diplomatic and strategic, on the other.

2.2.1. Socioeconomic Objectives

This heading may include objectives (j) and (n), although they do not carry equal weight. Promoting sustainable development and integrating African economies, as set out in (j) seems to be a contextual objective to be pursued in two ways: scientific and technical research (m), and the promotion of health and the fight against endemic diseases (n).

It should, however, be highlighted that, in contrast to the "constitutions" of most other regional organizations, the objective of socioeconomic and cultural activity is placed within the framework of sustainable development, as the relevant international texts of the past few years have been recommending since the 1992 Rio Conference, which placed this issue firmly at the centre of international cooperation. While not actually naming them, the wording of the Act nonetheless reflects the "pillars" of sustainable development. Both environmental protection and recognition of cultural diversity are referred to implicitly, and economic integration is seen as helping in their attainment. The same applies to what may be described as specific objectives, such as promoting scientific and technical research and the health of the populations, where the Act refers even more specifically to the eradication of "preventable" diseases. This is a somewhat curious expression at a time when international efforts are actually geared towards combating all kinds of diseases, even if, for some, there has been no breakthrough in treatment. It probably refers to endemic diseases that are preventable by public health policies, as opposed to pandemics such as HIV/AIDS.

2.2.2. Political, Diplomatic and Strategic Objectives

These objectives are the most numerous, and it would be well to attempt to distinguish between them at this juncture.

(i) Taken broadly, the political objectives are (g), (h), (o) and (q). They aim to promote political and democratic governance, to promote and protect human and peoples' rights, to guarantee the participation of women in the decision-making process and to involve the African diaspora in the organization's objectives. These objectives are as innovative as they are ambitious, and the substantive provisions of the Act seek to give them substance under conditions that are analyzed in detail in the relevant Chapters of this book. Here too, it all seems to boil down to one key objective, namely political and democratic governance. The issue of representation is thus at the centre of the search for real legitimacy. African political societies must therefore become democratic political societies, in which there is a balance between the exercise of power by public authorities and the guarantee of citizens' rights. This assumes – probably presupposes – that the participation of all so-called sensitive categories (women, diaspora Africans) is provided for in accordance with rights recognized at the regional and global levels;

(ii) The objectives considered as diplomatic and strategic are those set out in points (d), (f) and (p). In fact, they can be classified under two series of objectives: on the one hand, the "communitarization" of certain issues which require either a common position (d) or common policies (p); and on the other hand, the promotion of peace, security and stability in Africa (f).

With the stated objective of "communitarization" of the organization's activities in specific fields, the Act formally turned its back on the old horizontal concept of inter-State relations in favour of a more vertical approach. As the following development shows, in particular with regard to the organs of the organization and their powers, this is a decisive but very ambiguous choice, and thus a potential source of crisis within the organization. The purpose is, to the extent possible, to establish "common positions" on various matters that appear to be issues of common interest. In fact, this is not in itself innovative. On some key developments, such as the general acceptance of sustainable development during the preparatory conferences of the Rio conference, the former OAU adopted a common African position. The purpose of objective (d) is to formalise and regularise this sporadic practice.

The perspective of objective (p), to "develop and promote common policies on trade, defence and foreign relations to ensure the defence of the continent and the strengthening of its negotiating positions", is entirely different. This is a final stage of "communitarization", in which, formally, States are now expected to yield to the organs of the organization, and particularly the Commission. The first ten years of the Union have displayed the limited scope of such an ambition, as the wherewithal for its realisation does not appear to be forthcoming in the Union's headlong rush into the new idea of a "United States of Africa."

Promoting peace, security and stability on the continent (f) is a strategic objective of the organization. The OAU's record on this score is one of its glaring failures, despite its efforts, to establish a conflict prevention system. As shown in Part IV of this *Manual*, the African Union has institutionalised the modalities for attaining this objective. However, the results are still somewhat mixed.

3. An In-Depth Revision of the Principles

As impressively as in the case of the objectives, Article 4 of the Act, supplemented by the 2003 Maputo Protocol on amendments, sets out a series of eighteen principles. While this number may seem surprisingly large, it should not overshadow the equally clear ambition to carry out an in-depth revision of the very basis of future action, so as to devise new ethics for a pan-African organization which had often laboured unjustly under a negative image. In this respect alone, the progress is impressive relative to the principles previously enshrined in the OAU Charter, which were more succinct, but had nothing to do with the multi-faceted activities of the organization in largely new fields, for which the seven principles of Article III – the mere "vital minimum" for an organization (the OAU) which has often been stymied in its efforts – did not provide for an adequate legal basis.

Admittedly, due to their very number, not all the principles carry equal weight, and we should not underestimate the doubt that their number might raise as to the scope of the distinction in the Act between objectives and principles, given the similitude among some of them. This is the case for principle (d) on the establishment of a common defence policy, and the same certainly applies to principle (n) on the promotion of social justice. Both appear to be objectives rather than real principles whose legal content is open to debate. One might also wonder what legal weight can be attached to affirmations such as the principle of participation of African peoples in the activities of the Union (c) or collective self-reliance within the framework of the Union (k).

Raising these questions does not in any way diminish the symbolic power inherent in the desire to introduce amended principles more in accordance with the challenges faced by Africa and the action required to tackle them. In this regard, while their scope remains highly uncertain, the new principles constitute an undeniable improvement.

3.1. An Undeniable Improvement

To characterize these principles as an undeniable improvement does not seem inaccurate in that the Act broadly maintains the principles inherited from the OAU, but extends them considerably through a series of particularly innovative principles.

3.1.1. Maintaining the Principles Inherited from the OAU

As noted above, Article III of the OAU Charter laid down seven principles whose strength was based on the fact that "[t]he Member States, in pursuit of the purposes stated in Article II, solemnly affirm them." These were the principles of sovereign equality of all Member states, non-interference in the internal affairs of States; respect for the sovereignty and territorial integrity of each State and for its inalienable right to independent existence; peaceful settlement of disputes by negotiation, mediation, conciliation or arbitration; unreserved condemnation of all forms of political assassination and of subversive activities on the part of neighbouring States or any other States; absolute dedication to the total emancipation of the African territories which are still dependent; and political affirmation of non-alignment with all blocs.

It must be admitted that these are essentially political principles, whose purpose is chiefly to protect and/or consolidate African statehood, whose international existence, when it was first affirmed, might have appeared constantly under threat or disputed. Subsequently however, the context in which the organization operated changed rapidly, and other threats loomed larger than those of destabilization (which in the end proved relatively limited), the political emancipation of the last colonised territories (which rapidly came to fruition).

Thus, of the seven principles of the OAU, at least two – principles (6) and (7) – turned out to be outdated and at odds with the Organization's activities. However, the other five – principles (1), (2), (3), (4) and (5) – have stood the test of time and events. This is hardly surprising in that these are in fact traditional principles of international law enshrined in existing international instruments, which the Charter merely copied on account of the role they play in maintaining peaceful coexistence between States.

Not surprisingly, Article 4 of the AU Act also maintains these principles as a basis for the Union's functioning. Although classified differently, these are (a), (g), (b), (e) and (r).

Since the African Union is an inter-State organization, the principle of sovereign equality of States is pre-eminent in the reaffirmation in Article 4(a). Appearing in Article 2(1) of the UN Charter, it is also one of the principles of international law recalled in resolution 2625 (XXV) of the UN General Assembly of 24 October 1970, the "Declaration on Principles of International Law on Friendly Relations and Co-operation among States in Accordance with the Charter of the United Nations" (preamble, points f and point 1, 6th principle). According to the explanatory note of the resolution, this is an umbrella principle, whose components are the sovereign equality of States; the rights inherent in full sovereignty; respect for the personality of other States; the inviolability of the territorial integrity and political independence of States; the free choice of political, economic, social and cultural systems; the compliance in good faith with obligations; and living in peace with neighbouring States.

The principle of non-interference in the internal affairs of another Member state is set out in Article 4(g). This is also one of the principles affirmed in the Article 2(7) of the United Nations Charter, which limits its scope through a reservation clause regarding the enforcement measures provided for in Chapter VII of the Charter, which provides for action by the Security Council in case of threats to the peace, breaches of the peace, and acts of aggression. As reaffirmed in resolution 2625, this has the effect of prohibiting all forms of interference and coercion, including the use of force against a State.

Respect for the sovereignty and territorial integrity of every State, and its inalienable right to an independent existence, was not, of course, formulated in this manner. However, this concept is enshrined in Article 4(b) of the AU Act, on "respect of borders existing on achievement of independence." The actual purpose is to ensure respect for the territorial integrity of States according to the borders inherited from the colonial era, which is a variant of the principles affirmed by the United Nations of the prohibition of the "threat or use of force against the territorial integrity or political independence of any State" (resolution 2625, preamble). In the resolution, this principle prohibits the

> "violat[ion of] the existing international boundaries, the violation of international lines of demarcation, instigating, assisting or participating in acts of civil strife or terrorist acts in another State or occupying it militarily."

The principle of peaceful settlement of disputes is set out in Article 4(e). This is one of the goals of the United Nations, whose Charter advocates in Article 1 "bring[ing] about by peaceful means [...] adjustment or settlement of international disputes or situations which might lead to a breach of the peace." This is also the second "principle of international law" in resolution 2625, which calls on Member States to seek

> "early and just settlement of their international disputes by negotiation, inquiry, mediation, conciliation, arbitration, judicial settlement, resort to regional agencies or arrangements or other peaceful means of their choice."

The AU Act does not entirely reflect either Article II(4) of the OAU Charter, which briefly set out the modes of settlement, or resolution 2625, which reflects the wording of Article 33 of the United Nations Charter. Article 4(e) merely advocates peaceful resolution "through such appropriate means as may be decided upon by the Assembly."

The total condemnation of political assassinations and subversive activities against a State by its neighbour or by any other State is not set out as such in the new principles. The section of the OAU Charter regarding assassinations was expunged, and the provision relating to subversion was almost "forgotten." Fortunately, this was "recalled" in the Protocol to amend the Act, which adds a paragraph (r) to the list of principles: "prohibition of any Member State from allowing the use of its territory as a base for subversion against another Member State." Here also, the drafters of the Act "divided" the principle of non-interference in the internal affairs of a State, which upon closer exanimation is clearly only a variant of what is set out in UN GA resolution 2625. In the resolution, this principle provides that no State shall

> "organize, assist, foment, finance, incite or tolerate subversive, terrorist or armed activities directed towards the violent overthrow of the regime of another State, or interfere in civil strife in another State."

3.1.2. Introducing Innovative principles

The principles are without a doubt one of the major innovations of the Act, to which the new principles bring real added value in comparison with the principles enshrined in the OAU Charter. From this perspective, the originality of the AU Act is not so much in prioritising this new generation of principles over the traditional ones relating to inter-state cooperation which it inherited, but in placing the traditional requirements of coexistence on an equal footing with those of common interests. It is interesting to note that the areas it covers include the security and stability of Member States, thus fostering the application of traditional principles which now reflect international custom.

It was probably a feeling for new developments in international relations that led the drafters of the Act to "subdivide" a number of principles, such as those of non-recourse to the use of force in international relations and non-intervention in the internal affairs of a State, so as to bring out the aspects most relevant to current coexistence issues (subversion, terrorism, respect for boundaries, etc.) or to introduce new wordings (peaceful coexistence between States and the right to live in peace and security, the promotion of collective independence, the Union's right to intervene in a Member State, prohibition from using the territory of the State in a manner detrimental to another State, etc.). Thus presented, the new principles can be classified into three main categories: the principles of integrated action by the Union; political and democratic principles; and socio-economic principles.

The principles of integrated action by the Union are seven in number. They are the establishment of a common defence policy (d); prohibition of the use of force or threat to use force (f); the right of the Union to intervene (h); peaceful co-existence of Member States and their right to live in peace and security (i); the right of Member States to request intervention from the Union (j); promotion of collective self-reliance (k); and restraint by Member States from entering into any treaty or alliance incompatible with the principles and objectives of the Union (q). However, not all are of equal importance, some being more specific affirmations of broader principles.

The principle of prohibition of the use of force is an example of such a broader principle under which a first group of at least three other principles can be classified: in part because of another link to the principle of the sovereign equality and interdependence of all the Member States of the Union (a); the principle of peaceful coexistence of States and their right to live in peace and security (i); also in part, the right of the Union to intervene in case of "serious threat to legitimate order" (amended principle h); and the principle of the right of Member States to request intervention from the Union in order to restore peace and security (j). In the first case, this is a positive application of the principle, whose aim is to consolidate political independence, the right to self-determination and to freedom. The other two cases are exemptions from or exceptions to the general principle of prohibition of the use of force. While this issue is discussed in other Chapters, it is clear in light of the lessons learnt from NATO's intervention in Kosovo that Security Council authorisation will be indispensable to give the necessary weight to a recommendation of the Union's Peace and Security Council.

A second group of principles which includes the principles of establishing a common defence policy (d), the principle of the promotion of collective self-reliance within the Union (k) and the abstention by Member States from entering into any treaty or alliance incompatible with the principles and objectives of the Union corresponds to the objective of the development and promotion of common policies. This group of principles represents significant progress relative to the defunct OAU. Their end is to make the Organization a real Union, although its exact nature is not defined. Certainly, there is a strong inclination to view the union from the same perspective as the archetypal example of our era, the European Union. One might even question whether the separate principle of the establishment of a common defence policy is truly justified given the form of the new Article 3(p) of the Protocol on Amendments to the Constitutive Act, which lists defence, trade and foreign relations among the common policies to be established. It is clear, however, that the idea of specific common policies requires a common perception of powers justifiable only in the context of an integrated organization for cooperation – especially as Members States' recognition of their self-reliance within the Union attests to the limits of their functional independence, arguing for the organization of a new level of regional solidarity above the sovereignty of African States. Is this perception correct? Similarly, it is worth noting the intent to ensure the primacy of the AU Act over treaties and agreements signed by States, which are expected to contribute to the attainment of the objectives and principles of the Union. However, the question remains as to whether criteria and/or indicators of conformity or compliance will be defined, or whether the Commission will be vested with the authority necessary to ensure that they prevail.

In the area of political and democratic principles, too, the Act represents significant progress, reflecting greater coherence within the Organization, at least on a formal level. For too long, democracy and human rights have been the weak link of the pan-African organization, which lagged far behind the Council of Europe and the Organization of American States. We have already noted the extent to which this policy and the resulting discretion were justified by the consolidation of the State, despite the OAU's adoption of a great many regional instruments, particularly with regard to the protection of rights. However, at the dawn of a new institutional era, the results in this area have been mediocre: an African convention on human and peoples' rights was adopted only in 1981, and entered into force barely ten years ago, in 1986; an African Charter on the Rights and Well-Being of the Child was adopted in 1990 and entered into force in 1999, on the eve of the institutional change; and an additional protocol to the Human Rights Charter establishing an African Court of Human and Peoples' Rights was adopted in 1998 and entered into force under the new organization.

In this context, the Act represents a complete upheaval – almost a revolution – in an Africa characterised socially and politically by authoritarian regimes and the occasional dictatorship, whose leaders claimed legitimacy on the basis of a personalisation of power subject to considerations beyond the knowledge of the people, whose participation was generally limited to "electing" these leaders by overwhelming majorities. This state of affair would be amusing were it not a poignant reflection of the tragedies experienced by African societies. With the new principles in this category, it might be said that political society has finally returned to Africa, restoring the "power-freedom" balance.

Despite their apparent novelty, these principles are not in fact new. They derive almost all their legitimacy from the Universal Declaration on Human Rights, as enriched by the progress made by the international community in this area, particularly in the condemnation of impunity wherever it occurs, subject to the subsequent reservations of national and international jurisdictions and in the fight against terrorism and acts of violence of illegal armed combatants, often in the context of armed conflicts not of an international character, as is the case for many African conflicts. Together with the "great leap forward" of the adoption of the Rome Statute creating the International Criminal Court, and resolution 1368 (2001) of the Security Council on 12 September 2001 making terrorism a threat to peace and security, the two 1966 United Nations Covenants on Civil and Political Rights and on Economic, Social and Cultural Rights reflect, not only the gradual recognition of new rights, but also the intent to institute international democracy based on the preservation of the integrity of human beings, respect for human rights, legitimate participation in political society and the guarantee of measures to put an end to impunity of any kind, particularly within the framework of the arbitrary exercise of power.

These political and democratic principles include those of participation of African peoples in the activities of the Union (c); promotion of gender equality between men and women (l); respect for democratic principles, human rights, the rule of law and good governance (m); promotion of social justice (n); respect for human life and condemnation and rejection of impunity (o); and condemnation and rejection of unconstitutional changes of government (p).

The "segmentation" approach adopted by the drafters of the Act should again be noted given the obvious relationship between many of these principles. In any event, one of the principles is sufficiently broad to subsume all the others, namely principle (m), which can readily encompass principles (c), (l), (o) and (p). Its generality is obvious from its title, reflecting the inclusion of new needs in line with international standards. This may be seen as a consequence of the policy of conditionality instituted by international donors in order to impose changes that Africans have rejected for too long – but this is not the only reason. As numerous resolutions of the UN General Assembly and Security Council show, it is also necessary for the dialogue between civilisations, which is the basis for a culture of peace and sustainable development of the peoples of the world. While the development of these principles is analysed in Parts III and V of this *Manual*,[4] some observations are in order here.

The general principle of "respect for democratic principles, human rights, the rule of law and good governance" is really an umbrella principle, encompassing all the other political and democratic principles. One might even consider it as an objective rather than a principle. In fact, it is a political benchmark for the Assembly of the Union, the Executive Council, the Commission, the Pan-African Parliament and the future financial institutions of the Union to monitor respect for specific principles that might arise from it, rather than an actual reference point for possible monitoring in the African Commission of Human and Peoples' Rights, the African Court of Human and Peoples' Rights, or any other African court, such as the future Court of Justice or a national court. Nonetheless, its importance should not be underestimated, as attested by the adoption

---

[4] Cf. Chapters 12 to 14 and 19 to 21.

on 30 January 2007 in Addis Ababa of an independent guarantee mechanism: the African Charter on Democracy, Elections and Governance, which is currently open for signature, ratification, approval or acceptance by Member States.

The principle of "participation of the African peoples in the activities of the Union" is closely linked to the political and democratic principles. It is indeed the most remarkable expression of a democratic society based on a social contract that fosters social acceptance of rules and strengthens the members' adherence to the social project. According to traditional constitutional principles, such political participation is guaranteed through representation by elected officials who are supposed to express the will of the people. In the Union, this representation is provided through a pan-African parliament which the Act institutes as an organ of the Union in Articles 5(c) and 17. Under Article 17(1), this institution "ensure[s] the full participation of African peoples in the development and economic integration of the continent." This is why there is no additional protocol to the Act on this point, only a reference in Article 17(2) to the Protocol to the Treaty instituting the African Economic Community, which was adopted in Sirte, Libya, on 2 March 2001. Chapter 5 of Part II of this *Manual* deals with the pan-African Parliament.

The principle of promoting social justice also aims for "balanced economic development". It seems at first glance to be a concrete expression of the objective of "greater solidarity" set forth in Article 3(a) of the Act. Social justice in any case seems to be viewed as a corollary to the quest for economic integration, to avoid unbalanced development adversely affecting the more disadvantaged people as a result of imbalances arising from economic integration. The adoption of common policies could certainly foster the development of such social justice, which would in any case seem to be an essential aspect of the Act's objective of sustainable development.

The principle of "[c]ondemnation and rejection of unconstitutional changes of governments" is also a fundamental aspect of the democratic principles. It aims to strengthen the legitimacy of African political regimes by ensuring that they are henceforth subject to the will of the people and the "law of the ballot box." The purpose is to end once and for all the use of "strong-arm tactics" (*coups d'état, pronunciamentos* and other military takeovers) which have so often characterised certain African regimes, chronically undermining their representativeness and national and international authority, with serious implications for constitutionality, national independence and the countries' compliance with international obligations. In this regard, the acceptance of such a rule by all Heads of State, first as part of the decisions taken during the 2002 Lomé Summit and subsequently in the form of a principle in the Constitutive Act of the new organization, represents undeniable progress in light of previous experience. Chapter VIII of the new African Charter on Democracy, Elections and Governance (Articles 23 to 26) deals precisely with "[s]anctions in case of unconstitutional change of government."

The principle of "respect for the sanctity of human life, condemnation and rejection of impunity and political assassination, acts of terrorism and subversive activities" should be read together with principle (r), reintroduced by the protocol to amend the 2003 Act on the prohibition of use of the territory of a State as "a base for subversion against another Member State." This principle has two aspects: firstly, the sanctity of human life, which the Universal Declaration on Human Rights has helped to impose; and second, condemnation and rejection of impunity and political assassination, acts of terrorism and subversive activities. The enshrinement of the first aspect in the Act, though traditional, is nonetheless welcome – even though the value of human life is still paradoxically disregarded in the continent." In this regard, the "reaffirmation" in the preamble of the ACHPR of the "adherence to the principles of human and peoples' rights and freedoms contained in the declarations, conventions and other [international] instruments" might have been sufficient for the protection of this "right to life", particularly Article 6 of the International Covenant on Civil and Political Rights. In relation to the second aspect, Africa could not remain outside the international drive to provide for international punishment of the acts set out in the principle, such as crimes of genocide, war crimes and crimes against humanity. In its own way, Africa has also "outlawed" warlords, dictators of any ilk and the creation of conservative, antidemocratic forces seeking to reduce the people they wish to control to a "savage society" which is purportedly their "natural state", under the paternalistic or mocking gaze of other societies.

The principle of "promoting equality between men and women" is also one of these. It is a specific, and very traditional, aspect of Article 3 of the African Charter on Human and Peoples' Rights (ACHPR), which enshrines the principles of the equality of all under the law and equal protection for all under the law; and the principle of equality between men and women under Article 13(3) of the Charter on the equal use of public goods and services. This principle is in fact based on the principle of prohibition of discrimination based on sex under Article 28 of the ACHPR[5] and the Additional Protocol to the ACHPR on the rights of women adopted under the auspices of the new organization in Maputo on 11 July 2003, which entered into force on 25 November 2005, particularly Articles 2 (elimination of discrimination against women), 6 (equal rights and partners in marriage), 7 (equal rights in case of cessation of marriage in any form), 8 (equal access to justice and equal protection before the law), 12 (non-discrimination and equal opportunity and access in the sphere of education and training), 13 (equal economic rights, in particular equal access to employment and equal remuneration), 16 (the right to adequate housing), and 21 (right to inheritance).

3.2. Uncertain Scope?

Without prejudice to the other chapters in this *Manual* concerning the actual scope of the rules set forth in the AU Constitutive Act on the basis of the stated principles, it is appropriate to pose some brief questions. It is obvious that the Union, as conceived in the Act, is a dynamic, ongoing process. Some principles are beginning to be applied through implementing instruments. The Addis Ababa Charter on democracy, elections and governance is a notable example. But many others have yet to be applied. Even when concrete measures

---

[5] Article 28 states that "Every individual shall have the duty to respect and consider his fellow beings without discrimination and to maintain relations aimed at promoting, safeguarding and reinforcing mutual respect and tolerance."

have already been applied, a *contra legem* practice often contradicts the good intentions and undermines the value of the adopted principles. This was the case with the mode of constitutional change of government in Côte d'Ivoire under General Gueï's government, and in Togo with regard to the succession of General Eyadema. The transition in Madagascar, although carried out according to form, raised many questions; and the risk of a new secession by the island of Anjouan in the Comoros is also cause for concern. Further questions are raised by the Organization's current management of conflicts in Africa, for example in the Great Lakes region or the Horn of Africa where the Union has played a relatively limited role, but also in Côte d'Ivoire and Darfur, where its powerlessness was obvious.

Should we re-examine the established institutional framework to enable the organization to function? It might be tempting to think considering the apparent gap between the affirmation of objectives and principles that are indispensable to our era and their actual, legally authorized application, as well as the obvious mismatch with the current institutional framework. In this regard, the plethora of uncompleted projects is equalled only by the lack of resources and capacities with which the organs and authorities of the Union are sometimes forced to promote the new phase of the pan-African project.

Clearly, uncertainty prevails. The progress is tangible; all that is needed is to give it concrete expression. There is no pessimism here; rather, there is hope for a radiant future.

PART II. STRUCTURE AND ORGANS OF THE AFRICAN UNION

CHAPTER 4.
THE ASSEMBLY, EXECUTIVE COUNCIL AND COMMISSION

Joram Mukama Biswaro

1. Introduction

The establishment of the African Union ushered in an unprecedented level of hopes and expectations inside and outside Africa. The success of this important institution will, however, largely depend on the performance of its key organs, notably: the Assembly, the Executive Council and the Commission. The three Organs are responsible for initiating and translating the objectives, vision and mission of the Organization.

They are the engines and institutional memory of the Organization. This Chapter therefore seeks to explore the vital role of the abovementioned organs in realizing the stated objectives, vision and mission of the new Organization and make some recommendations.

2. Background

At its 37th Ordinary Session, held in Lusaka, Zambia from 9 to 11 July 2001, the Assembly of Heads of State and Government of the OAU mandated the Secretary-General to work with Member States through the then Committee of Ambassadors (now Permanent Representatives) and experts on the implementation of the Sirte Summit declaration on the establishment of the African Union. The results of that exercise were first to be examined by a selected team of Ministers representing the five regions of the OAU and later by the Council and ultimately the Assembly.[1]

The Assembly also mandated the Secretary-General to undertake the necessary consultations with Member States and other International Organizations with a view to working out the modalities and guidelines for the launching of the organs of the African Union including the preparation of the draft rules of procedure of these organs and ensuring the effective exercise of their authority and the discharge of their responsibilities. In undertaking this task, priority was to be given to the launching of the key organs notably: the Assembly, the Executive Council, the Commission and the Permanent Representatives' Committee. With regard to the Commission, the Assembly further mandated the Secretary-General, in consultation with Member States, to submit proposals regarding its structure, functions and powers.[2]

The decision was faithfully implemented giving priority to the launching of the above key organs. Brainstorming sessions were held within and outside the General Secretariat of the OAU, generating healthy and constructive ideas on the implementation of the Lusaka Summit decision.

To elaborate these documentations, the General Secretariat was guided by the relevant provisions of the Constitutive Act and the various decisions of the Assembly of the Heads of State and Government, particularly the Lusaka Decision which suggested a gradual approach in the establishment of the organs of the union. It was inspired by the same gradual approach when suggesting that the Union should be provided with initial powers exercised by its organs. The results of these consultations were presented to the Committee of Ambassadors and experts, the Ministerial Committee of fifteen and the 75th ordinary session of the Council of Ministers in Addis Ababa on 21 January, 12 and 13 March 2002 respectively.

---

[1] OAU Doc. AHG/Dec. 160 (XXXVII).
[2] Report of the Secretary General of the OAU on the Implementation of the Lusaka Summit, Addis Ababa, December 2001.

3. The dynamics of the Union and its policy organs

The Sirte Declaration provides for a profound articulation of the institutional organs of the African Union. It is stated in paragraph 6 that:

> "in order to cope with these challenges and to effectively address the new social, political and economic realities in Africa and in the world, we are determined to fulfil our peoples' aspirations for greater unity in conformity with the objectives of the OAU Charter and the Treaty Establishing the African Economic Community."[3]

This spirit is further reinforced by the objectives that the African Union aspires to achieve to broaden the scope of the collective endeavour of its Member States. The Constitutive Act gives the Union new responsibilities that the OAU Charter did not originally address. The tasks that the organs of the African Union have to undertake not only incorporate a wider range of sectors but also involve a more complex set of activities such as: the acceleration of political and socio-economic integration of the continent; the promotion of peace, security and stability of the continent; the promotion of democratic principles and institutions; the popular participation; and the good governance.

To some degree, these are not necessarily novel tasks. The OAU, despite its limited objectives, was obliged to undertake some of these responsibilities in view of the realities on the grounds. However, by stipulating these objectives in the Constitutive Act of the African Union, it can be assumed that the leaders of the continent were determined to provide a basis for the creation of the appropriate structures and capacities to meet the challenges facing the peoples of Africa and their Governments.

The necessity of empowering the organs of the African Union, particularly as compared to those of the OAU, is also underscored by the fact that the Constitutive Act has taken the process of integration a step beyond the Abuja Treaty. It reflects the conviction and dire need

---

[3] Sirte Declaration of the OAU Extraordinary Summit, 9th September 1999, OAU Doc. EAHG/Decl. (IV) Rev. 1.

to accelerate the process of implementation of the Treaty to achieve greater unity and solidarity among African countries. More specifically, Articles 13, 14, 15, 19, 22 of the Act provide details on economic integration.[4] Besides, the involvement of the African people and the introduction of the social and cultural aspects make the Act even more comprehensive than the Abuja Treaty.

There is an additional dynamic that also rendered necessary the establishment of organs that are more robust and proactive than what existed in the OAU Charter. The fundamental essence of the principles enunciated by the Constitutive Act reaffirmed, in very explicit terms, that the Union was formed among independent nation-States which retain their distinct nationhood. These sovereign States which also share a common vision about their destiny and some fundamental values pertaining to a number of spheres committed themselves to enhancing the areas of cooperation and integration among them. In this regard, the main challenge remains the harmonization of Article 3 which calls for stronger unity and solidarity with Article 4 which emphasizes sovereignty and nationhood.

The establishment of new organs and bodies such as the Peace and Security Council and the financial institutions under the Constitutive Act shows a determination to increase and deepen the space for collective action among the Member States. Equally, the promotion of democratic principles and institutions, popular participation and good governance and the right of the Union to intervene in a Member State in respect of grave circumstances such as war crimes, genocide and crime against humanity[5] are meant to provide the organs of the Union with the legitimacy to pursue collective action on behalf of the peoples of the continent and not only on behalf of governments.

Both in political and operational terms, the realization of this ideal entails the identification of certain areas of authority presently exercised by Member States to be pooled together for collective initiative and cooperation under the auspices of the Africa Union. The spirit of the Abuja Treaty which is embedded into the Sirte

---

[4] Constitutive Act of the African Union.
[5] Article 4(h) and (j) of the Constitutive Act of the African Union.

Declaration and the Constitutive Act points towards the direction of the elaboration of a common vision, mission, policies and action which in turn, necessitates the need to put in place the important structures that can advance the implementation of such a common agenda. Indeed, there are number of such areas in which African countries have already developed common positions and coherent plans of action. Likewise, some of the cross-cutting challenges, such as the HIV/AIDS pandemics, environmental degradation, disaster management, terrorism, money laundering; external trade, migration and food security provide a strong legitimacy for a continental approach in solving them.

As the supreme organ of the Union, the Assembly is also the ultimate custodian and repository of collective authority shared by Member States. Article 9 of the Act, outlines the powers and functions of the Assembly and how this authority should be exercised on behalf of the Union's members, namely, through decision-making, monitoring and implementation, approving and adopting the budget, giving directives, and confirming or dismissing the high officials of some institutions. The Assembly may delegate some of its powers and functions to other organs. Articles 13 and 15 of the AU Constitutive Act also outline how the Executive Council and the Specialized Committees can facilitate the works of the Assembly in exercising its authority.

The Executive Council coordinates and takes decisions on policies in areas of common interest to the Member States. It is responsible to the Assembly and it shall consider issues referred to it and monitor the implementation of policies adopted by the Assembly. It also prepares the sessions of the Assembly and determines the issues to be submitted to the Assembly for decision. It is equally tasked to consider the structure, functions and statutes of the Commission and make recommendations thereon to the Assembly; as it also elects the Commissioners to be appointed by the Assembly.

The Commission, as one of the main organs of the Union, was envisaged to acquire its essential features from the nature of the Union to be established. Similarly, the Commission would carry out its tasks in relation to other organs of the Union in accordance with the Sirte Declaration.

As specifically stipulated in Article 20 of the Act, the Commission is also the Secretariat of the Union. It is, therefore, the only body that is expected to deal with the operational matters of the African Union on daily basis servicing all the other organs. To some degree this is similar to Article 155 of the Rome Treaty in terms of responsibilities of the European Union Commission.[6] Of course, this should not preclude the fact that certain specialized organs such as the Pan-African Parliament, financial institutions, and the African Court of Justice need to have their own support structures to serve them.

The relationship between the Commission and the other organs will be evolving over time as the Union and its structures gain momentum and become more consolidated. For instance, it is expected that, in the long run, members of the Commission will have to be confirmed by the Pan-African Parliament. Based on this understanding of the Constitutive Act, at an operational level, it can be said that the Commission remains the driving force in initiating, executing and following up on various decisions of other organs. In practical terms, for the Commission to be able to assume these functions and perform them efficiently and affectively, it has to be endowed with the requisite capacities, particularly in terms of human and material resources, and it has also to be provided with a commensurate authority.

The legitimacy of delegating this authority to the Commission emanates from the fact that it is an organ that should function and operate through the principle of consistent coalescence of the interest of the Union which should always transcend the separate individual interests of the Member States. In this connection, the Commission assumes the status of embodiment of the personality of the Union and it upholds its general interests.

This legitimacy is further enhanced by the appointment of the members of the Commission by the Assembly on the basis of proven eligibility criteria that underscore competence as well as Pan-Africanism orientation. An arrangement of regular consultations with the Pan-African Parliament, the PRC, the ECOSOCC, Member

---

[6] See Leonard D., *Guide to the European Community,* London: The Economist Publications, 1988, pp. 45-49.

States in general as well as closer collaboration with the Specialized Technical Committees should further enhance the legitimacy of its functioning. Equally important, the monitoring authority of the Executive Council as provided for in Article 13, paragraph 2, is supposed to enhance the accountability of the Commission.

The Constitutive Act provides for a broad general area of competence for the Union. As stated above, the objectives and principles cover a number of activities in the political, economic and social spheres. As laid down in the provisions of the Constitutive Act, the Commission's functions include: representing the Union and defending its interests, acting as a custodian of the Constitutive Act and implementing various decisions. The functions of the Commission remain however intergovernmental rather that supranational.[7]

In the execution of its mission, the Commission has to deploy its conferred authority and perform at a higher level than a mere secretariat. In this regard, it has to assume its active role more rigorously. It has to serve as a driving force of the Union in sustaining its momentum by submitting proposals and initiatives. Once these are considered and agreed upon and the broad policy and procedural parameters are defined, the Commission should proceed in working towards their implementation. Similarly, the Commission should consistently engage itself in assisting Member States in overcoming bottlenecks, obstacles and inefficiencies through the collective endeavour.

This calls for a lean but efficient Commission. The determination of the size of the Commission is dictated by the scope of its functions and affordability by Member States. Since, the African Union involves more operational tasks than the OAU, the accomplishment of these tasks will entail expanding the institutional structures and deploying additional staff and expertise. The increase needs to be gradual and incremental. Ultimately, any increase will have to balance the necessity for effective and efficient operation and its sustainability. The challenge in this respect is to have highly qualified personnel, who are well motivated, and who can constitute the core Commission

---

[7] Amate C.O.C., *Inside the OAU, Pan-Africanism in Practice*, Macmillan Publishers, Hong Kong, 1986, pp. 83-126.

staff. Other experts can be hired on a contract basis, and when the need arises. This approach reduces cost and burden to Member States whose economies are mostly in intensive care unit.

On the issue of the staff, the Commission needed to be supported by experts recruited among nationals of member states on the basis of proven expertise and competition. The conducting of services would have to be so designed as comparable with other international organizations. This would help to attract the best brains and expertise available on the continent. The OAU staff found to possess the requisite qualifications for assuming important functions in the Commission would need to be re-oriented and undergo a programme of capacity enhancement. It was against this background that the Durban Summit postponed the exercise of appointment for the Commission till the following year at the Maputo Summit. This was a judicious decision.

4. Critical Evaluation

The inception of AU brought higher but genuine expectations within and outside the continent. The Constitutive Act is with no doubt a relatively good document. This has contributed to the generation of the expectations. It, however, needs to be translated into concrete actions so as to live to its expectations. The actualization of the AU principles resides within the Member States. By extension, the Member States expect the AU principal organs notably: the Assembly, the Executive Council and the Commission to implement this. Of the three organs, the main engine is the Commission.

As stated before, it is the Commission which in most cases, is supposed to propose and initiate various activities deemed relevant to the organization on the basis of the Constitutive Act. Furthermore, the Commission is responsible for operationalizing various decisions and directives of the Assembly as well as of the Executive Council. In a nutshell, the success of the Union depends significantly on the efficiency, competency and quality of the Commission. The Commission is the institutional memory of the Union. It is the organ which translates the decisions of the Assembly or the Executive Council into concrete actions. A capable Commission can also initiate ideas, strategies and present them to the higher policy organs for consideration and approval.

In the past however, the OAU General Secretariat had the reputation rightly or wrongly, for being a poorly performing institution. The responsibility for this resided not only with the OAU Secretariat but also in the Member State's failure to pay their assessed contributions. In the same vein, some countries have engaged in micro-politics with positions rather than insisting on professionalism. The questions that come immediately to our mind include: What takes one to render the Commission perform? What leadership qualities and competence are essential for the performance of the AU? In the past, there has not been serious discussion on these issues except to either lament or blame staff. At times, this has been unfair to the staff as there is a cluster of diligent workers within the Organization who have been tarnished by these blanket condemnations.[8] In this context, it is advisable that the performance of the AU should be everybody's business.

Immediately after the Member States of the AU had created the new Organization in Durban, they looked into the structure, functions, rules of procedure and the kind of Commission which could rise to the occasion. For a period of one year there was an interim Commission. This was in line with Articles 33 (4) of the Constitutive Act. At the 2nd Summit held in Maputo, Mozambique, the commissioners were elected. This included the Chairperson of the Commission Prof. Alpha Omar Konare, an ex-President from the Republic of Mali, and Deputy-Chairperson, Patrick Mazimhaka, plus eight commissioners in different fields of competence. The gender balance of 50% male and 50% female was taken on board. Hence, presently, there are five male and five female commissioners.

A quick assessment of the performance of the AU since it was established gives mixed results. On the one hand, undoubtedly, the Commission has tried to rise to the occasion.

It is true that having Prof. Alpha Oumar Konare, at the helm of the organization, as the First Chairperson of the Commission, has given

---

[8] Biswaro J., *Perspectives on Africa's Integration and Cooperation from OAU to AU, Old Wine in A New Bottle?* Tanzania Publishing House: Dar es Salaam, 2005, pp. 170-171.

an unprecedented visibility and international credibility. In the recent past, Addis Ababa has been a true diplomatic hub of Africa. Partners (Europe, America and Asia) have all expressed, in one way or another, the need for a strategic partnership with the African Union Commission. Furthermore, the current team of the Commission came up in its own right with vision, mission and above all impeccable credentials. In doing so, the AU through the Commission has opened up to the African civil society to a larger extent than the OAU. The Commission has also tried to set its activities through a strategic plan contributed by resource persons from all over Africa. On the other hand, it is a fact that the current Commission (2007) has a very weak absorptive capacity due to insufficient staffing and very debatable records of recruitment.

This has had a negative impact on the organization. Besides, the Commission is renown to have flouted its own rules of procedure particularly in so far as financial management is concerned. Collegiality is said to be weak. It is further claimed that the difference of vision and personality between the Chairperson (2007) and the rest is quite vivid. This raises the issue of whether or not the organization should be led by a former president. Some would argue that the ex-president comes with the presidential terms and therefore expects everybody to respect him/her with the accompanying protocols. Others contend that an ex-president is good because he can make things move fast by a direct access to the incumbent presidents. He/she solves matters without much bureaucracy.

The PRC has tried its best to accompany the current team whilst ensuring that they enforce the rules and regulations of the Organization. This has not always been easy and successful due to the fact that sometimes the Commission pointedly ignores them and communicates directly with their Heads of State and Government or Ministers. In addition, within the African setting, an ex-Head of State is too much used to control everything and to make policies and decisions, on his/her own. In a nutshell, much as the Commission has tried to live up to its expectations, it has a long way to go. Some of the notable areas of weakness that need to be addressed in those are discussed below.

5. Finance

Financing the activities of the AU Commission has always presented a major obstacle to the Commission's performance both under the AU and the OAU. Ironically, the Commission has inherited this problem from the OAU General Secretariat. The question of financing the AU needs to be realistically addressed. Short of that, African detractors and sceptics will be proved right and consequently conclude that nothing has changed except the name and therefore no qualitative change. For example, as at December 2006 over 30 countries were in arrears. Under these circumstances, the Organization cannot easily realize its objectives. Most of its projects and programs depend on Member States' contributions. In view of this, it is our considered submission that Member States should make a commitment to pay their assessed contributions as regularly and timely as possible. The contributions are the main source of the AU Commission's Fund. Keeping the organization on short financial leash is invariably counter-productive. In the same context, the sanctions for defaulting on the payment of assessed contributions should be strictly observed and enforced. Certainly, the provisions of the Resolution of the Council of Ministers 1279 (LII), paragraph 2(d), needs to be revisited.[9] According to this resolution any Member State of the Organization, in accordance with its obligations as enacted in the Charter, shall not participate in either the vote on AU decisions if the amount of its arrears is equal to or in excess of the contribution due by such state for the two complete financial years. Defaulting Member States shall be deprived of:
- The right to speak at AU meetings;
- The right to present candidates for AU post (political appointees and other officials); and
- The right to present candidates for AU decision making bodies (officers, commissions, committees, etc.).

---

[9] See OAU Doc. CM/Res. 1279 (LII), para. 2(d).

Furthermore, there should be judicious utilization and management of the scarce financial resources of the Organization in order to enhance accountability. There have been situations whereby some members of staff have violated financial rules and regulations of the Organization and do away with it unpunished. Punitive measures need to be taken against such employees.

Besides the resources from Member States' contributions, it is recommended that extra-budgetary sources of funding the various activities of the AU be explored. These could include: external mobilization of resources such as sensitizing of the Africans in Diaspora and the introduction of value added tax (VAT) levy on insurance and airline.

6. Nature and timeliness of reports

In the past, the reports submitted by the Secretary-General played an important part of the deliberations of the various OAU meetings. However, more often than not, and due to political sensitivities, the reports were drafted in such a way that they did not capture the realities of the situation on the ground to be dealt with. In particular, the reports avoided stating bitter facts in order to be politically correct and in turn reduced the ability of the Organization to take informed and objective decisions.

Even whereby the reports prepared by the Secretary-General met the desired comprehensiveness and quality the fact that they were not circulated in time to Member States to facilitate consultations reduced the prospects of discussions. This tendency has to some extent continued with the AU Commission. This is partly due to the fact that both Member States and, to a large extent, the staff of the Commission have remained the same and therefore business as usual. Furthermore, given the human nature, attitudes and perception take time to change and adapt to new circumstances.

To redress these weaknesses, the Commission should, *inter alia*, prepare reports that rise above political sensitivities so long as the reports are factual and objective. In turn, Member States should accept to swallow the bitter pill. The fulfilment of the objectives of the Organization requires such comprehensive factual and accurate reports. In addition, the Commission must be endowed with the necessary and competent human resources to cope with the workload.

7. The deliberations

Alongside with this, the deliberations of various issues at different levels over the past years were constrained by the prevailing diplomatic pleasantries and political culture. As a result, debates within the organization lacked the necessary in-depth, frankness and punch. This made it more difficult for them to take crucial decisions required by the situation. A case in point is the Darfur crisis. The AU should as much as possible avoid this. It should reverse the prevailing culture of niceties and discuss issues in depth based on the rules of procedure.

During the time under review, the AU has tried to depart from this culture. The debates on UN reforms and the creation of the African Union Government were cases in point. The deliberations on these issues were characterized by frank and realistic debates. However, more needs to be done. The rules of procedure of the relevant Organs should only be guided by the objectives of the Organization and should therefore be as candid as possible and adhered to.

8. The agenda

While the OAU draft agenda was prepared by the General Secretariat in consultation with the Chairperson of the Organization, the AU Commission continues to do the same. In practice however, the consent of the State or States concerned is crucially necessary in order to have any item inscribed on the agenda of the organization. At times, this requirement obstructs preventive action of the state or group of States opposing the inclusion of such an item on the agenda. This state of affairs seems not to have changed much.[10] It is recommended that the agendas of the organization should include general review of a

---

[10] Biswaro J., "Africa's Search for Peace," Addis Ababa 2002, p.97.

selected region in order to facilitate broad discussions of the overall situation in various regions. Such approach would provide a good entry point.

9. Recruitment

In the past, the recruitment process has been the centre of controversy. Apart from the appointments of the Secretary-General and the assistant Secretaries-General which were avowedly political, the appointments of the OAU staff members that were supposed to be strictly on merit had, in number of cases, also tended to be influenced largely by political considerations, with the result that many of the appointees found themselves in positions for which they were not qualified either by education or experience. This situation which started in the 1960s continued throughout the existence of the OAU. It was to the detriment of both efficiency and competence in the General Secretariat. Frankly speaking, and in practical terms, almost all of the Secretaries-General as well as many OAU Member States tended to indulge. This practice was worst under Edem Kodjo, who made no secret of using appointments to certain key position in the General Secretariat and the Executive secretariat as a means of trading for support for himself from the OAU Member States.[11] This was self-aggrandizement.

The AU vowed to avoid this malpractice. To realize this goal, it engaged consultants to carry out this exercise. It dutifully did a commendable job and submitted its report to the Commission for implementation.

Unfortunately, the implementation process of this exercise has not been transparent enough to warrant engaging the most qualified personnel on the continent. There have been allegations that some of the appointees did not undergo rigorous interviews. This has been a source of concern to both members of staff of the Commission as well as the general public. The Member States as the main employer need to rectify this anomaly. The quota system needs to be encouraged. Indeed, as C.O.C. Amate rightly observed, it will be

---

[11] Amate C.O.C., *Inside the OAU, Pan-Africanism in Practice,* Macmillan Publishers, Hong Kong 1986, p. 124.

unrealistic to expect that politics will ever cease to be an important consideration in the appointment and operations of the Commission and the rest of its staff.[12]

But if the Commission is to be built into an efficient and effective international civil service, which should be the aim of all the Member States, they will first have to purge themselves of the tendency to allow themselves to be unduly influenced by ideological and nationalistic consideration in their choice of the Chairperson of the Commission and in their relations with the commission as a whole. Having done that, they will also have to be as ready to speak out against undue interference by certain member state in the affairs of the Commission.

In view of the foregoing, it is our considered opinion that members of the Commission including the Chairperson, should be competent men and women with proper experience, commensurable leadership qualities and an impressive track-record in government, parliament, international organizations or other relevant sectors of the society. Above all, they need to be Pan-Africanists capable of articulating the AU agenda in the 21st century.

10. Concluding Remarks

From the above, it can be summed up that since the founding of the African Union and its Constitutive Act entering into force, there have been high expectations from the people within and outside Africa. All the three important Organs of the Union responsible to actualize its objectives namely the Assembly, the Executive Council and the Commission have been in place.

Under the Lusaka decision XXXVII of 2001, the structure of the Commission should be lean and incremental. The new Commission has more than 760 personnel as opposed to the OAU General Secretariat which had about 350 staff. Before the new recruitment a transparent evaluation was carried out. Unfortunately the recruitment has not been transparent enough leading to dubious

---

[12] Amate C.O.C., *Inside the OAU, Pan-Africanism in Practice,* Macmillan Publishers, Hong Kong 1986, p. 125.

results. At times, there have been questionable transfers aimed at concealing this weakness. This situation has resulted into acrimony and demoralizing of the staff who felt that justice was not done. It also meant additional costs to the Organization and by extension to Member States.

Be this as it may, the three policy Organs of the AU namely the Assembly, the Executive Council and the Commission have tried as much as possible to translate the objectives of the Constitutive Act into reality. Surely, they have performed better than during the OAU era, particularly, in matters concerning unconstitutional change of governments and African integration in general. However, they could have performed much better than they have done so far had it not been due to a number of constraints.

Some of those bottlenecks are: flouting of rules of procedure and regulations; lack of enough funds to finance the projects and programs of the Organization due to defaulting Member States who do not pay their assessed contributions; lack of competent personnel, and mismanagement of funds. The defaulting Member States need to live up to their promises by meeting their continental obligations in time. This is a Pan-African Organization. By not paying the annual assessed contributions, its membership's ownership and control is questionable. Depending mainly on donors, the AU's agenda is likely to be hijacked. This will not augur well to Africa. All of us being stakeholders, we should meet our obligations timely in the interest of the present and future generations. It can be done, play your part.

CHAPTER 5.
THE PAN-AFRICAN PARLIAMENT

Sani L. Mohamed

1. Introduction

In all democratic systems, parliaments, as the directly elected bodies, are the institutions through which the people express their will and exercise their sovereignty. They are the primary constituencies that link the people to the government, represent and act on behalf of the citizenry. The Pan-African Parliament (PAP) is established for the same purpose, although it is not fashioned in the same form as those in the member countries of the Union. It is established

> "to give concrete expression to the common vision of a united, integrated and strong Africa and to act as a common platform for African peoples and their grass-root organizations to be more involved with discussions and decision-making on the problems and challenges facing the continent."[1]

The idea of establishing a Pan-African Parliament could be traced to the dreams of the founding fathers of the African Nations, who contended that only a United Africa can achieve true democracy and meaningful development. The legal basis of the Pan-African Parliament is to be found in the Treaty establishing the African Economic Community (AEC),[2] which enumerated it as one of the organs of the Community (Article 7). It further stipulated that its

---
[1] Preamble of the Protocol to the Treaty Establishing the African Economic Community Relating to the Pan-African Parliament.
[2] Treaty Establishing the African Economic Community, 3 June 1991, Abuja (Nigeria).

A.A. Yusuf & F. Ouguergouz (eds.), *The African Union: Legal and Institutional Framework. A Manual on the Pan-African Organization*, 95-117.

composition, functions and powers and organization should be defined in a related protocol (Article 14). The Treaty also introduced the continental universal suffrage of the membership of the PAP (Article 6).[3] The AEC Treaty, which was signed in Abuja, on 3 June 1991 and came into force in May 1994, was intended "to promote economic, social, and cultural development and the integration of the African economies." It envisaged that the PAP would be established by the year 2000, but this did not materialize. In the meantime, the African States' determination to move the continent forward towards integration resulted in the adoption of the Sirte Declaration in September 1999, at the Fourth Extraordinary Session of the Assembly of the Organization of the African Unity (OAU) held in Sirte, Libya. The Declaration provided for the establishment of an African Union (AU) and the speedy establishment of all institutions provided in the Abuja Treaty, including the Pan-African Parliament.[4]

The Constitutive Act of the African Union was adopted at the 36th Ordinary Session of the Assembly of the OAU, held in July 2000, in Lomé, Togo. The Act provided that the Union is established

> "to promote and protect human and people's rights, consolidate democratic institutions and culture, ensure good governance and rule of law, and achieve greater unity and solidarity between African countries and peoples."

The PAP is enumerated as one of the organs of the AU in Article 5 of the Constitutive Act which provided that its composition, powers and functions, and its organization shall be defined in a protocol relating thereto (Article 17).

In furtherance of the objective of establishing the PAP, a historic meeting of African Parliamentarians was held in Pretoria, South Africa, in November 2000, which was attended by about 200 delegates from 41 OAU Member States. The delegates comprising Speakers, Deputy Speakers, Clerks and Parliamentary staff and other

---

[3] The principle of popular participation had its foundation laid in The Arusha and Khartoum Declaration, as well as in the African Charter on Human and Peoples' Rights.

[4] See the Sirte Declaration of 9.9.1999 of the OAU Summit, OAU Doc. EAHG/Decl. (IV) Rev. 1.

representatives expressed support for the establishment of the PAP. They declared that its establishment was one of the ways of involving the African peoples in the on-going process of political and socio-economic integration in the continent. Subsequently, the Fifth Extraordinary Session of the Assembly of the OAU held in March 2001 in Sirte, Libya, took the milestone decision of adopting the Protocol to the Treaty Establishing the African Economic Community relating to the Pan African Parliament (Protocol). This decision provided for the first time for the establishment of a supranational parliament for the African continent. The *raison d'être* for its establishment as contained in the Protocol is

> "to give concrete expression to the common vision of a united, integrated and strong Africa; and to further consolidate the aspirations of the African peoples for greater unity, solidarity and cohesion in a larger community transcending cultural, ideological, ethnic, religious and national differences; and to ensure full participation of the African peoples in the economic development and integration of the continent."[5]

In order to hasten the process of the PAP's establishment, the AU Assembly, held in Durban, South Africa in July 2002, set up a Steering Committee to mobilize support for early signature and ratifications of its Protocol. Additionally, a meeting of African Parliaments was held in June 2003 in Cape Town, South Africa to obtain further support for the establishment of the PAP. Soon after, the Protocol obtained the mandatory number of ratifications and came into force on 14 December 2003, thus formally establishing the PAP. Its inaugural session was held in March 2004 in Addis Ababa, Ethiopia. Thereafter, its subsequent Sessions were held at its seat in South Africa.

There is no doubt that the establishment of the PAP represents a significant step towards achieving the ideals and commitments

---

[5] Protocol to the Treaty Establishing the African Economic Community Relating to the Pan-African Parliament done at Sirte (Libya), 2 March 2001 and the Status List of Treaty Protocol to the Treaty Establishing the African Economic Community Relating to the Pan-African Parliament Code 0021 (53 countries, 47 signatures, 46 ratifications and 46 deposits). The Protocol entered into force on 14 December 2003.

articulated in the principles, objectives and values enshrined in the Constitutive Act of the AU, the Treaty Establishing the African Economic Community and that of the Organization of the African Unity. This chapter will examine the salient features of the PAP, particularly its composition, functions, powers, organization and operation. It would also consider and evaluate the challenges that this vital organ of the AU, would encounter in its effort to empower the African peoples to reap the dividends of a United Africa, in terms of peace, security, development, integration and cooperation. Finally, it will make some conclusions and recommendations.

2. Composition and Membership of the Parliament

The composition of the PAP is provided for in Article 4 of the Protocol, which states that, "'during the interim period' (before the introduction of direct elections to the Parliament) Member States shall be represented in the Parliament by equal number of Parliamentarians." It further provides that each Member State shall be represented by five (5) members at least one of whom must be a woman. In addition, the representation must reflect the diverse political opinions within the Member States and that the members should be drawn from the national Parliaments or other deliberative organs of the Member States.

It is worth noting that the equal representation principle of five members for each Member State is not in consonance with the practice of some supranational parliaments. Both the European Union (EU) and the Economic Community of West African States (ECOWAS) take cognisance of the size of member countries in allocating seats. Conversely, the East African Legislative Assembly (EALA), like the PAP, has 27 elected members, nine from each Member State. However, the EALA has five ex-officio members, the three Ministers responsible for regional co-operation, the Secretary-General and the Counsel to the Community.

As regards the European Parliament, with a membership of 732, it allocated to Germany 99 seats, while France, Italy, and the United Kingdom have 78 seats each respectively. The smaller countries like Cyprus, Estonia and Luxembourg have six each, while Malta the smallest country has five seats. Similarly, the ECOWAS Parliament has 115 seats and it allocated each of its 15 Member States a minimum of five seats each. The remaining seats are shared based on the population of each Member State. Based on this formula, Nigeria has 35 seats, Ghana 8, Côte d'Ivoire 7, and the other Member States have six or five seats respectively. It is submitted here that the equal number of representation irrespective of population size should not be a permanent feature for the PAP. This provision needs to be reviewed in due course especially when the principle of direct elections to the parliament will be introduced.

The stipulation on gender representation requiring the inclusion of one woman among the five (5) members from each country is both innovative and a good step in the right direction. Hitherto, the representation of women in the Parliaments of Member States was negligible and this deliberate effort to enhance the participation of women in governance and participatory democracy would ultimately enhance their contributions in the development of the continent. However, what needs to be seen is how the women would use this number (20%) to assert their collective influence on the activities of the PAP. In contrast, the representation of women in the European Union Parliament has grown over time.

Regarding the qualification for membership, the requirement to reflect the diverse political opinions within the Member States would appear to be the most difficult aspect to fulfil. This is because in Africa, the national political groups do not follow conventional alignment of political parties based on ideologies, such as the socialists, the liberals, the social democrats, and the conservatives. Therefore, it would be a daunting task to have parliamentarians classified on the basis of diverse political ideologies and opinions. This is more so because in many African countries the role of religion, clan and ethnicity in the formation of political parties, although officially outlawed, still continues to be very important. Perhaps in the future political parties in Africa will be formed, according to political programmes or ideologies. It is only at that time that representation in the PAP will reflect the diverse political opinions within Member States and voting along lines of political programmes and ideologies rather than national or ethnic lines will occur.

An equally controversial provision in the Protocol is the one on recall contained in Article 5(f), which states that "a seat of a member of the Pan-African Parliament shall become vacant if the National Parliament or any deliberative organ recalls him or her." This threat of the recall might impinge on the member's ability to be vocal in matters regarding his or her country in order to avoid the consequences of a recall. The intention of the provision is by no means similar to the recall process of members by their constituencies in national assemblies. There is therefore the need to review this provision to prevent its being used by the authorities of Member States as a form of pressure on the PAP members.

Ideally citizens should directly elect their representatives to all law making bodies. This mandatory requirement is contained in Article 6 of the Abuja Treaty. However, it is evident that the continental universal suffrage of the membership of the PAP, which provides that the people of Africa shall directly elect their representatives has for now been put in abeyance. Although, direct popular participation ensures more legitimacy, even the European Parliament established in 1952, had its first directly elected members only in 1979 after 27 years of existence. The European Parliament despite the high level of the development of its Member States developed incrementally over time increasing its influence and reputation, which should also be the case with the PAP. However, it is only when such a parliament is directly elected by the people that it can be said to achieve the objective of its establishment "to give a strong representational mandate from the people they serve and to widen the democratic process in Africa."

3. Objectives of the Parliament

The process of African integration presupposes the transfer of some responsibilities from the national to the continental bodies. It is for this reason that the provisions regarding the objectives of the parliament are very extensive. The objectives of the Parliament, as enshrined in Article 3 of the Protocol, are to:
1. Facilitate the effective implementation of the policies and objectives of the AU/AEC and, ultimately, of the African Union;
2. Promote the principles of human rights and democracy in Africa;

3. Encourage good governance, transparency and accountability in Member States;
4. Familiarize the peoples of Africa with the objectives and policies aimed at integrating the African Continent within the framework of the establishment of the African Union;
5. Promote peace, security and stability;
6. Contribute to more prosperous future for the peoples of Africa by promoting collective self-reliance and economic recovery;
7. Facilitate cooperation and development in Africa;
8. Strengthen Continental solidarity and build a sense of common destiny among the peoples of Africa;
9. Facilitate cooperation among regional economic communities and their parliamentary fora.

These objectives of the PAP are very wide-ranging and can even be described as contradictory, if its powers are limited only to consultative and advisory role. The purpose of these wide-ranging objectives is understandable in so far as they are meant to enable the new parliament to be an equal partner with other organs of the African Union in the process of African integration. Nevertheless, the objective of the PAP to oversee the AU Executive constitutes an enormous challenge. In a sense it is the one measure that would ultimately be seen as the yardstick by which the realisation of the rationale of establishing the parliament could be assessed. However, this can only be achieved if there is a strong commitment to the promotion of democratic principles and good governance, and the promotion and protection of human and people's rights, transparency and accountability in Africa.

At the moment, the PAP's functions are limited only to consultative and advisory. However, according to Article 2(3) of the Protocol the ultimate aim of the Parliament is to evolve into an institution with full legislative powers, after an amendment is made to the Protocol. Even after the PAP acquires a legislative role, it will not be easy for it to deal with the amalgam of different legal cultures and parliamentary systems. This is because in the Member States, the legal systems are based on civil law, common law and Islamic traditions as well as Roman-Dutch and customary law.

In the case of the European Parliament, which was established in 1957, it has to date only a limited legislative mandate, but has the power to reject or amend the EU Budget. As regards the ECOWAS Parliament, the Protocol pertaining to its creation was signed in 1994 but only entered into force on 14 March 2000. The ECOWAS Parliament has to date not addressed any resolution to other organs of the Community even though as far back as on 13 September 2002 a resolution Relating to Enhancement of the Community Parliament gave it wide powers. This situation is not restricted to supranational parliaments, even though with respect to the PAP some commentators have asked the question as to whether the PAP is not just creating an unrealisable sense of hope and optimism for ordinary Africans. Nevertheless, despite these criticisms one principal objective, which the PAP should not lose sight of is its role in ensuring that it serves as the bastion for the struggle to institutionalise effective democracy in Africa.

4. Functions and Powers of the Parliament

The provisions regarding the powers and functions of the parliament are contained in Article 11 of the Protocol, which states that in addition to the powers that may be conferred to the Parliament by the Assembly (Heads of State and Government of the AU), the Parliament shall have the following functions, namely to:

(a) Examine, discuss or express an opinion on any matter, either on its own initiative or at the request of the Assembly or other policy organs and make any recommendations it may deem fit relating to human rights, consolidation of democratic institutions and the culture of democracy as well as the promotion of good governance and the rule of law;

(b) Discuss its budget and the budget of the community and make recommendations thereon prior to its approval by the Assembly;

(c) Work towards the harmonization or coordination of the laws of Member States;

(d) Make recommendations aimed at contribution to the attainment of the objective of AU/AEC and draw attention to the challenges facing the integration process in Africa as well the strategies for dealing with them;

(e) Request officials of the AU/AEC to attend its sessions produce documents or assist in the discharge of its duties;

(f) Promote the programmes and objectives of the AU/AEC, in the constituencies of the Member States;

(g) Promote the coordination and harmonization of policies, measures, programmes and activities of the Regional Economic Communities and the parliamentary fora of Africa;

(h) Adopt its rules of procedure, elect its own President and propose to the Council and the Assembly the size and nature of the support staff of the Parliament;

(i) Perform such other functions, as it deems appropriate to achieve the objectives set out in Article 3 of the Protocol.

Additionally, Rule 4(1) of the Rules of Procedure of the PAP, provides that in its consultative and advisory role and in accordance with the provisions of Articles 3, 11 and 18 of the Protocol (which deal with objectives; functions and powers and relations with regional, national and other deliberative organs) the Parliament shall:

(a) Facilitate the implementation of the policies, objectives and programmes of the Union and oversee their effective implementation by the various organs of the Union;

(b) Promote human and peoples' rights, consolidate democratic institutions and the democratic culture, good governance, transparency and the rule of the law by all Organs of the Union, Regional Economic Communities and Member States;

(c) Participate in creating awareness among the peoples of Africa on:
  i) Objectives, policies, aims and programmes of the African Union;
  ii) The strengthening of continental solidarity, cooperation and development;
  iii) The promotion of peace, security and stability on the African Continent, and
  iv) The necessity for the pursuit of a common economic recovery strategy;

(d) Contribute to the harmonization and coordination of the legislative texts of Member States in accordance with Article 11(3) of the Protocol;

(e) Promote the coordination of the policies, measures, programmes and activities of Regional Economic Communities and their respective Legislative Bodies;

(f) Draft, examine and adopt its budget, its Rules of Procedure, elect its members of the Bureau, employ and manage its staff, in conformity with Article 11 (2) and (8) of the Protocol;

(g) Examine and debate the Budget of the African Union and make recommendations thereon prior to its approval by the Assembly;

(h) Exercise legislative and other functions as shall be defined by the Assembly in conformity with Article 11 of the Protocol;

(i) Perform all other functions as are incidental to or likely to enhance the carrying out of the above functions;

Whereas, according to Rule 5 of the Rules of Procedure the Parliament in the discharge of its functions as provided in Rule 4 of the Rules of Procedure (above) shall have powers to:

(a) Oversee the development and implementation of policies and programmes of the Union;

(b) Organise debate on the objectives, policies, aims, programmes and activities of Regional Economic Communities, on all matters relating to the proper functioning of organs and the life of the African Union;

(c) Examine, discuss or express an opinion or give advice on its own initiative or at the request of any of the Organs of the African Union, a Regional Economic Community or the Legislative Body of any Member State;

(d) Make recommendations and take resolutions on any matter relating to the African Union and its organs, Regional Economic Communities and their respective organs, Member States and their organs and institutions;

(e) Issue invitations to the representatives of the organs of the African Union, Regional Economic Communities and their organs, Member States and their organs and institutions to furnish explanations in plenary on issues affecting or likely to affect the life of the African Union;

(f) Exercise all other powers as are incidental or auxiliary to the discharge of its functions.

The foregoing provisions (Articles 3 and 11 of the Protocol as well as Rules 4 and 5 of the Rules of Procedure) provide very wide and extensive powers and functions for the parliament. The rationale of having wide powers is understandable, since it is to enable the parliament to enhance the process of African integration, but in practice, it is very difficult for these powers to be exercised at this initial stage of the Parliament's life. In interpreting its role through the rules of procedure, the parliament should try to anticipate what ideally should be its functions and powers, which could be achieved overtime. This is more so because the PAP has now no legislative or supervisory powers and does not participate in important decision-making in the AU, despite a clear mandate for it to do so, even as it relates to the budget. The budgetary power of the PAP to discuss the budget and make recommendations to the Assembly thereon prior to its approval by the Assembly is yet to be put in practice. It is pertinent to note that even in the case of the EU, the budgetary power that the Parliament acquired was obtained over time as it also started as a classical consultative body. It is as such important for the PAP to strive to acquire budgetary power, which is a crucial instrument to any parliament, national or regional.[6]

On the supervisory powers, both the Protocol and Rules of Procedure provide that the PAP may examine, discuss or express an opinion on any matter, pertaining to human rights and consolidation of democratic institutions and make recommendations thereon. It is absolutely essential for the Parliament to have powers to oversee the development and implementation of policies and programmes of the Union. Akin to the exercise of supervisory power, is the mandate to establish committees of enquiry, which is not yet granted to the Parliament. However, the power to issue invitations to the representatives of the organs of the AU and others as contained in Rule 5(e) of the Rules of Procedure if utilized would enable the Parliament to make more persuasive recommendations. In this

---

[6] Resolutions and Recommendations: Res. 1-6 (II) and Res. 001-008/05 adopted at the 2nd and 3rd sessions dated 1st October 2004 and 11th April 2005.

regard, the PAP should use this power wisely and concentrate on the political and economic matters that bedevil the continent. If the Parliament opens itself to too many issues, it will lose focus.

The power of litigation, which is now accorded, to the EU Parliament to institute proceedings against institutions and respond if proceedings are brought against it before the European Court of Justice is an innovative development. The PAP must look forward to exercising this power, especially after the establishment of the African Court of Justice and Human Rights. The access to the Court would enhance the ability of the parliament to have its views more respected on important issues that affect the continent, particularly if given a legal backing. The EU Parliament has the power to institute a legal challenge to acts of the Council and Commission on the grounds of lack of competence, infringement of an essential procedural requirement, or that of the Treaty establishing the European Commission or any rule of law relating to its application, or misuse of powers.

The policy-making function of the PAP needs to be enhanced to enable it to exert more influence on the organs of the AU. It would also be essential to enable the Parliament to participate in the preparation, making, implementation and control of decisions produced by the Council and the Assembly of the AU. The PAP although presently consultative, must strive to make itself relevant to the advancement of the continent just like the EU Parliament did in many respects. For instance, the EU Parliament has now acquired an elective function with regard to the investiture of the members of the Commission.

5. Organization and operation of the Parliament

The organization and operation of the Parliament could be loosely interpreted as the means by which the powers, function and roles of the Parliament are to be exercised. On the organization and operation of the Parliament, Article 12 of the Protocol provides that:
(a) The Parliament shall adopt its own Rules of Procedure on the basis of a two-thirds majority of all its members;

(b) The Parliament shall elect, at its first sitting following its election, by secret ballot, from among its members a President and four (4) Vice-Presidents representing the regions of Africa as determined by the AU. The election shall, in each case, be simple majority of the members present and voting;

(c) The terms of office of the President and the Vice-Presidents shall run with the National Parliament or the deliberative organ, which elects or designates them;

(d) The Vice-Presidents shall be ranked in the order of first, second, third and fourth initially, in accordance with the result of the vote and subsequently by rotation;

(e) The President and the Vice-Presidents shall be the officers of the Parliament. The officers, under the control and direction of the President and subject to such directives as may be issued by the Parliament, shall be responsible for the management and administration of the affairs and the facilities of the Parliament and its organs. In the discharge of their duties, the clerk and the two Deputy Clerks shall assist the officers;

(f) The Parliament shall appoint a clerk, two Deputy Clerks and such other staff and functionaries as it may deem necessary for the proper discharge of its functions and may by regulations provide for their terms and conditions of office in accordance with the relevant AU practice;

(g) The President shall preside over all Parliamentary proceedings except those held in committee and, in his or her absence the Vice-President shall act in rotation in accordance with the Rules of Procedure, which shall also deal with the powers of the person presiding over Parliamentary proceedings.

Article 12 further provides that the Office of the President or the Vice-President shall become vacant if he or she:
(a) Dies;
(b) Resigns in writing;
(c) Is unable to perform his or her functions for reasons of physical or mental incapacity;
(d) Is removed on grounds of misconduct;

(e) Ceases to be a member of the National parliament or other deliberative organ;
(f) Is recalled by the National Parliament or other deliberative organ;
(g) Ceases to be a Parliamentarian in accordance with Article 19 of the Protocol.

The article also provides that removal on grounds stipulated in (c) or (d) above, shall be on a motion to be decided on by secret ballot and supported at the end of the debate by two-thirds majority of all the Parliamentarians. In the case of removal on the ground stipulated in (c) above, the motion shall in addition be supported by a medical report. A vacancy in the Office of the President or Vice-President shall be filled at the sitting of the Parliament immediately following its occurrence.

The quorum for a meeting of the Parliament shall be by a simple majority. Each Parliamentarian shall have one vote. Decisions shall be made by consensus or, failing which, by a two-thirds majority of all the Members present and voting. However, on procedural matters, (including the question of whether a matter is one of procedure or not), decisions shall be taken by a simple majority of those present and voting, unless otherwise stipulated in the Rules of Procedure. In the event of an equal number of votes, the person presiding shall have a casting vote. The Parliament may establish such committees, as it deems fit, for the proper discharge of its functions and in accordance with its Rules of Procedure.

According to Article 12(5) of the Protocol, the President and the Vice-Presidents shall be the officers of the Pan-African Parliament. During its inaugural ceremony, Mrs Mongella Gertrude Ibengwe of Tanzania was elected as the President. Also elected were the four Vice-Presidents from regions that did not produce the President. Collectively, the President and four Vice Presidents constitute the Bureau of the PAP. The officers under the control and direction of the President and subject to such directives as may be issued by the Pan-African Parliament shall be responsible for the management and administration of the affairs and facilities of the Pan-African Parliament and its organs. According to Rule 17 of the Rules of Procedure, the functions of the Bureau shall be:

i) The management and administration of the affairs and facilities of Parliament and its organs;

ii) Regulating the procedures relating to the financial, organizational and administrative needs in accordance with Financial Rules of the AU and matters concerning Members and the internal organization of Parliament and its organs;

iii) To determine the draft agenda and the programmes of the sessions of Parliament;

iv) To determine the establishment, plan and structure of the Secretariat and lay down regulations for the staff, including their terms and conditions of service; and

v) To propose to Parliament for adoption the establishment and job descriptions of its support staff;

vi) To propose, to the Pan African Parliament, the appointment of the Clerk and Deputy Clerks to Parliament;

vii) The preparation of the draft budget and its presentation to the responsible committee;

viii) Coordinating and harmonizing the functions of Permanent Committees;

ix) Any other matters in accordance with the directives issued by Parliament; and

x) To carry out any other functions as may be prescribed by Parliament or incidental to these functions.

The provisions of Article 12 of the Protocol and Article 17 of the Rules of Procedure encapsulate the standard operational procedures and organization of most supranational parliaments. The management bodies, committees and the independent operation of the work of the Parliament as provided in Article 12 of the Protocol conforms with the procedures and management standards of existing supranational parliaments derived mostly from the practices of the national parliaments. The only known exception is that of the South African Development Community (SADC) Parliamentary Forum where it is established only as a forum not as a parliament. However, the SADC Parliamentary Forum was created for similar purpose as the PAP "to promote dialogue and popular participation at the grass roots level." The forum seeks to act as a sub-regional resource centre on issues of strong and effective integration, democratisation, parliamentary practices, governance and human rights. Its main objective is to facilitate the attainment of bringing SADC closer to the people.

Although members of the Pan-African Parliament are not elected directly and do not bear political lineage like its European counterpart, efforts to establish informal political groups whereby members would belong to some form of loose political association or affinities would be very useful. Nevertheless, on a positive note, the PAP has been able to acquire a permanent seat in South Africa, unlike the European Parliament where the Member States have failed to agree on a single place, as its seat, so that the sessions of the institution are still rotated between Brussels, Luxembourg and Strasbourg.

The PAP, since its establishment, has started operating and adopted resolutions and made recommendations on issues affecting the continent. It adopted more importantly, its Rules of Procedure, under which it established ten (10) Permanent committees intended to address the objectives of the PAP. They are as follows:

i) Rural Economy, Agriculture, Natural Resources and Environment; Monetary and Financial Affairs;
ii) Cooperation on Trade, Customs and Immigration Matters;
iii) Cooperation, International Relations and Conflict Resolutions;
iv) Transport, Industry, Communications, Energy, Science and Technology;
v) Health, Labour and Social Affairs;
vi) Education, Culture, Tourism and Human Resources;
vii) Gender, Family, Youth and People with Disability;
viii) Justice and Human Rights; and
ix) Rules, Privileges and Discipline.

The sessions of the PAP are held twice a year for a period of ten working days each, which may be inadequate. This is more so because it was initially envisaged that the parliament was to have two sessions of one month each every year. However, in view of the Parliament's finances as well as limited responsibilities at the moment, the two sessions have been maintained but not for a period of one month.

In the course of its sessions thus far, the Parliament took several pertinent decisions such as:

(a) that the Assembly should review the Protocol and establish a clear term limit of five years for its first term;

(b) that the President of the PAP be a member of the five-person panel of the wise, (an Independent, Objective Advisory body to the Peace and Security Council); and

(c) that the reports of the Peace Security Council (PSC) on conflict resolution efforts of the AU be presented to the PAP for consideration, observation and recommendations.

The Parliament also requested regular reports on NEPAD and that all the reports of the African Peer Review Mechanism be submitted to the PAP for debate, observations and recommendations. Additionally, the Parliamentarians from national parliaments set up an African Parliamentarian Network against Corruption (APNAC) committee.

6. Factors that could militate against the success of the PAP

In the foregoing sections, we have seen the history of the PAP's establishment, its composition, powers and functions, as well as its organization and its operations. We would now consider some of the factors that could impede the effective implementation of its important objectives. In no particular order of importance and without being an exhaustive list, the ones that standout more clearly are the legal mandate; relations with national Parliaments; the need for sufficient and experience staff; and adequate finances. These factors are capable of preventing the PAP from achieving its objectives. However, more importantly there is the need to sustain the political will and commitment of Member States to continue to support the ideals that necessitated the establishment of the Parliament.

6.1. Legal Mandate of the Parliament

The first possible impediment to the success of the PAP is its current mandate, which characterizes it as an advisory and consultative body. This situation is serious because it is doubtful whether under such circumstances it can fulfil the responsibility invested in the Parliament to "facilitate the effective implementation of the policies and objectives of the AU/AEC and, ultimately, of the establishment of an African Union." Similarly, the PAP is bestowed with the responsibility of "familiarizing the people of Africa with the objectives and policies aimed at integrating the African continent within the framework of the establishment of the African Union," which cannot also be achieved through its current legal mandate of "advice or consultation." There is no doubt that to discharge its responsibilities, the PAP requires a stronger legal mandate to be able to better promote the integration of policies and programmes of African integration and translate them into legislation that could be implemented.

The PAP with its current legal mandate would not equally be able "to promote the principles of human rights and democracy in Africa; and encourage good governance, transparency and accountability in Member States," since the power to advice or be consulted only is a serious limitation and would prevent it from harmonizing and coordinating any legislation. At the moment it can only pass non-binding recommendations and resolutions, and it does not possess any enforcement provisions that could facilitate their effective implementation. In the foreseeable future, therefore, the PAP's decisions, recommendations and opinions are not likely to receive the attention that they deserve from the African Heads of State and Government.

6.2. Relations with national parliaments

The PAP's relations with national parliaments constitute a second factor that is capable of impeding its success or undermining its role. In fact there is at the moment no consensus as to what the legal competences would be at each level of jurisdiction from the PAP, down to the Regional and National Assemblies.[7] The principle of "subsidiarity", which is utilized to determine the authority that should perform particular tasks that cannot be performed effectively at a more

---

[7] Pan-African Parliament, "Strategic Plan 2006-2010. One Africa, One Voice", November 2005.

immediate or lower level, has not yet taken root in the operations of the parliament or any of the established supranational parliaments in Africa. Therefore, there is the immediate need to establish a legal framework that would clearly spell out the role of the PAP and the National/Regional Parliaments of Member States regarding its recommendations and resolutions. Otherwise the recommendations and resolutions would have the same value as the paper on which they are printed.

Similarly, there is a total absence of standardized parliamentary mechanisms for coordinating the PAP or the PAP-related Parliamentary activities. Ideally, national parliaments should establish parliamentary committees on foreign affairs; regional cooperation; AU and NEPAD matters to create a direct network with the PAP. Even in countries where this has been done, there is no evidence that this has been put to any practical use. Additionally, sectoral ministries should be able to report or have access to the PAP on matters of common interest to both. What is required is for the PAP's deliberations to be able to dovetail into national parliamentary debates and vice versa. One possibility suggested by the PAP in its Strategic Report is "to set up special committees that would formulate and initiate an agenda for regional issues to be debated in the national parliaments."[8] In their view

> "these committees would also serve as contact points for the PAP and be structurally linked to the PAP Bureau, thereby ensuring smooth and efficient information flow and access to the support services of the PAP."

However, for this to succeed, the PAP must first create awareness of its activities to the national parliaments. This situation is in fact not limited to the PAP, since there is dearth of information and knowledge on continental development issues at both national and regional level parliaments. Therefore unless this is resolved even national parliaments cannot effectively exercise their influence and perform legislative roles, for the sustainable socio-economic integration and development of the continent.

---

[8] *Communiqué* of the Conference of African Parliamentarians on the New Partnership for Africa's Development held in Abuja (Nigeria), 20-23 June 2005.

It is imperative for both the PAP and National Parliaments to have access to value-added information on various policy and development issues to support the work of their Committees. At the moment the PAP should be preoccupied with building of its capacity to interact with the national parliaments, civil society, private actors and the public. This has been recognised by the parliament as stated in its report that

> "there is also the need to create partnerships and synergies with all other relevant sectors such as universities and research institutes to facilitate access to knowledge, in the areas of Pan African and regional economic issues."[9]

More importantly, the PAP should encourage collaboration with all stakeholders to promote regional integration laws, policies and processes in Africa.

6.3. Availability of funds and human resources

A factor that could easily have an effect on the success of the PAP to function effectively is the availability of experienced staff and funds. The PAP must establish a dynamic and functional human resource management policy to attract good staff to enable it to discharge its onerous mandate. According to Article 12(5), the Bureau of the PAP is responsible for the management and administration of the affairs and facilities of the Parliament and its organs. It performs functions that are of key importance for the efficient and effective functioning of the PAP, such as the preparation of the budget, the management of staff and the coordination and harmonization of the functions of Permanent committees. The PAP Bureau and Secretariat, which are expected to be the engine of the PAP and of the integration process, must have the necessary capacities to assist the parliament to discharge its mandate.

It is also anticipated that as the mandate of the PAP moves from advisory to a legislative role, the PAP will require substantive increase in staff numbers and the reinforcement of specific skills and capabilities. It is the view of the parliament that the

---

[9] *Ibid.*

"current skeletal staff has done relatively well to maintain the momentum of the PAP's activities, although its ability to bring the PAP to the next level of full-time engagement with the issues of regional integration is clearly compromised by its smallness."[10]

There is at present lack of adequate resources allocated to the PAP. According to Article 15(2) of the Protocol, the annual budget of the PAP shall constitute an integral part of the regular budget of the AU. Furthermore, Article 15 states that the budget shall be drawn up by the PAP in accordance with the Financial Rules and Regulations of the AU and shall be approved by the Assembly until such a time when the PAP shall start to exercise legislative powers. Annual contributions by Member States underpin the budget, which is also grossly inadequate and comes in a piece-meal manner to the Organization.

Moreover, some national parliaments are unable to support or pay for their PAP representatives' participation at meetings, thus causing some committees not to execute their work plans or severely constraining the Bureau's work and reducing sessions of the PAP's meetings. In short, the PAP's inadequate funding seriously hampers its effectiveness; thus creating an urgent need to identify alternative sources of financing to reinforce the available resources, in order to enable the PAP to successfully implement its agenda. The concept of a trust fund has been identified as one alternative source of funding.

7. Conclusion and Recommendations

In most African countries, the structure of the Government is centralized and the possession of political power can be extremely lucrative. The law-making bodies are often unclear as to their mandate, do not function effectively, and reflect little more than theoretical tolerance for opposition, perform cursory or no oversight function over the executive and often do not have the means to do so, even if they had the will. Against these characteristics of the African Parliaments, there was high expectation and hope to believe that the Pan-African Parliament would be different. Despite its perceived

---

[10] Report of the PAP, AU Doc. EX.CL/237 (VIII), 16-21 January 2006.

weaknesses of being only consultative and advisory in nature, Africans looked upon the PAP to ensure good governance, respect for human rights and guarantee sustainable development. This view was echoed during the launching ceremony of the PAP, where several speeches were made highlighting the hopes and aspirations of the African peoples on the role of the PAP to strive for the rapid growth and development of the continent.

Notwithstanding the establishment of the PAP, Heads of State and Government, who form the supreme organ of the AU, continue to dictate the tune of the continental policies. The PAP must set its agenda since it has no draft law to debate and must make its work visible to the public. There are reasons to assume that the institutionalisation of a direct role of national parliaments in the activities of the PAP, would improve its democratic and social legitimacy and act as a check to the "predominance of the executives." A serious problem that must be addressed by the PAP is the need for its tasks to be clearly understood, and its structure and powers to be harnessed to advance the conditions of the African peoples. It therefore must generate sufficient and meaningful debate on its agenda.

Many sub-regional organizations have established parliaments in order to give them strong representational mandate from the people they serve. These include that of Southern Africa Development Commission (SADC) Parliamentary Forum established in 1996, ECOWAS Parliament in 2000, and East African Legislative Council (EALC) in 2001, all before PAP, which was established in 2004. The performance of all these supranational parliaments could not be expressed as satisfactory at the moment, because of serious deficit of human and financial resources and the apparent lack of political powers in some cases. However, there is a glimpse of hope that the situation would change for the better, especially with the PAP if it is given legislative powers.

Finally, it should be recognized that the process of integration involves transferring some responsibilities that used to be exercised by national governments to joint institutions thus diminishing the role of the national parliaments as legislative, budgetary and controlling authorities. In the case of the European Union the transfer of responsibilities from national level to the European level has largely been to the Council, and the European Parliament has not acquired the powers that would have enabled it to play a full parliamentary role in the Community, thus creating a "democratic deficit." It has also been observed in the case of the European Union that national parliaments have been concerned with loss of influence and try to control more their government's involvement with European affairs and the European parliamentarians try to forge better relations with national parliaments.

In order to remedy these situations, which would also arise with the PAP, the latter must utilize the experience from the European Union by adopting another Protocol on the Role of the National Parliaments and Regional Parliaments, especially after the de-linking that would arise out of the direct relations envisaged in the not too distant future. The Protocol should specify the need for consultation and examination of proposals jointly. Additionally, a Conference of Presidents of the Parliamentary Assemblies of the African Union should be established to discuss precise questions of cooperation between the Pan-African Parliament and the national parliaments. This would gradually develop into a synergy between the PAP parliamentary committees and the national parliaments and eventually foster political and administrative cooperation.

CHAPTER 6.
THE AFRICAN COURT OF JUSTICE AND HUMAN RIGHTS

Fatsah Ouguergouz

1. Introduction

The creation of the African Court of Justice and Human Rights (hereinafter the "Court" or the "African Court") is provided for by the Protocol on the Statute of the African Court of Justice and Human Rights (hereinafter the "Protocol"), adopted on 1st July 2008 by the 11th Ordinary Assembly of the African Union held at Sharm El-Sheikh (Egypt). The decision to create this new Court was taken by the African Union Assembly of Heads of State and Government at its Third Ordinary Session held in Addis Ababa (Ethiopia) in July 2004. Indeed, the Assembly then decided that "the African Court of Human and Peoples' Rights and the Court of Justice should be integrated into one Court."[1] The African Court of Human and Peoples' Rights was created by the Protocol to the African Charter on Human and Peoples' Rights on the Establishment of an African Court of Human and Peoples' Rights, adopted in Ouagadougou (Burkina Faso) on 10 June 1998,[2] the Court of Justice, the establishment of which is provided for by Article 18 of the Constitutive Act of the African Union, was for its part created by the Protocol of the Court of Justice of the African Union adopted in Maputo (Mozambique) on

---

[1] Decision on the Seats of the African Union, AU Doc. Assembly/AU/Dec.45 (III), para. 4.
[2] This Protocol entered into force on 24 January 2004, after its ratification by 15 States. See the website of the African Union.

11 July 2003.[3] The decision to merge the two Courts was proposed by the bureau of the Assembly and was based "on the need to rationalize the two Courts and to make them efficient and cost effective."[4]

The Protocol on the Statute of the African Court of Justice and Human Rights is still not in force,[5] it will enter into force after its ratification by 15 States. Under the terms of Article 7 of the Protocol, the Protocol on the Establishment of the African Court of Human and Peoples' Rights will however remain in force for a certain period of time, to enable the African Court of Human and Peoples' Rights to take the necessary measures for the transfer of its prerogatives, assets, rights and obligations to the new Court. Once the Court is established, references made to the Court of Justice in the Constitutive Act of the African Union will then have to be read as references to the African Court of Justice and Human Rights (Art. 3 of the Protocol). Article 2 of the Statute annexed to the Protocol is entitled "Functions of the Court" but is rather vague in this regard; it simply provides that "the African Court of Justice and Human Rights shall be the main judicial organ of the African Union." Since the new Court is intended to replace the African Court of Human and Peoples' Rights and the Court of Justice of the African Union, it is however clear that it will take up the main functions of these two latter judicial bodies, that is the contentious and advisory ones. We will examine below the organization, the operation, the contentious and advisory functions of this Court, as provided for by its Statute.

2. Organization of the Court

For a better understanding of the organization of the Court, it is important to look into its composition, the provisions on its seat and the material and human resources at its disposal.

---

[3] This Protocol entered into force on 11 February 2009, after its ratification by 15 States, see the website of the African Union.

[4] Report on the Decision of the Assembly of the Union to merge the African Court on Human and Peoples' Rights and the Court of Justice of the African Union, AU Doc. EX.CL/162 (VI).

[5] As of 31 December 2010, it has been ratified by three States: Burkina Faso, Libya and Mali; for the current status of ratification, see the website of the African Union.

2.1. The Bench

Article 3 of the Statute lays down that the Court shall be composed of sixteen judges[6] and that in no case may it include more than one national from the same State. Article 16 further provides that the Court "shall have two (2) Sections: a General Affairs Section composed of eight (8) Judges and a Human Rights Section composed of eight (8) Judges." To be eligible, candidates must meet certain conditions and, once they are elected, the exercise of their office must comply with certain rules.

The first condition here is laid down by Article 3 of the Statute, which requires candidates to have the nationality of a State party to the Protocol. The second condition is provided for by Article 4 of the Statute, according to which

> "the Court shall be composed of impartial and independent Judges elected from among persons of high moral character, who possess the qualifications required in their respective countries for appointment to the highest judicial offices, or are jurisconsults of recognized competence and experience in international law and/or human rights law."

Judges are elected by secret ballot by the Executive Council of the African Union, and appointed by the Assembly of Heads of State and Government on a proposal from the States Parties to the Protocol (Arts. 5 and 7). Upon entry into force of the Protocol, the Chairperson of the Commission shall request the States Parties to the Protocol to present, within ninety (90) days of such a request, their nominees for the office of judge; the Chairperson of the Commission then draws up two alphabetical lists of candidates: a list A containing the names of candidates having recognized competence and experience in

---

[6] This restricted composition should be contrasted with that of the European Court of Human Rights for example, which includes one member for each State party (Art. 20 of the European Convention), in other words, 46 judges. The unwieldiness which would have resulted from every State party being represented (the African Union has 53 Member States), most certainly justified this solution; the number of judges in the Inter-American Court (7) is also much smaller than the number of States Parties to the American Convention (Art. 55). See also Article 3 of the Statute of the International Court of Justice; the latter consists of 15 judges.

international law, and a list B containing the names of candidates possessing recognized competence and experience in human rights law. Each State party may present up to a maximum of two candidates and shall choose the list on which the candidates may be placed. Article 5 also stipulates that in this process of nomination due consideration shall be given to equitable gender representation.

The balance in gender representation needs also to be ensured in the election of judges as such (Art. 7(5)). Article 7(4) of the Statute also lays down that, in the elections of the judges "the Assembly shall ensure that in the Court as a whole there is equitable representation of the regions of Africa and the principal legal traditions of the Continent." Article 3(3) specifies that "each geographical region of the Continent [...] shall, where possible, be represented by three (3) Judges except the Western Region which shall have four (4) Judges."

Judges are elected for a term of six years and may be re-elected only once. To ensure the gradual renewal of the composition of the Court, the term of office of eight of the Judges, four from each section, elected in the first election ends after four years (Art. 8); the names of the Judges concerned are chosen by lot by the Chairperson of the Assembly or the Executive Council immediately after the first election.

Once elected and before beginning their duties, Judges must make a solemn declaration to discharge their duties faithfully (Art. 11). Under the terms of Article 8 (4), all Judges with the exception of the President and the Vice-President, shall perform their functions on a part-time basis.

The Court shall act "impartially, fairly and justly" (Art. 12(1)). Judges may not perform any other activity incompatible with their status as judge (Art. 13(1)). According to Article 13(2), Judges "shall not exercise the function of agent, or counsel, or lawyer in any case before the Court." This is a very strange provision since it seems obvious that such functions would necessarily undermine the impartiality of the concerned Judges. It would have been more relevant to forbid the exercise of such functions before other international courts or tribunals.

Also with a view to ensuring the independence of the Judges, the Statute provides that "Judges shall be immune from legal proceedings for any act or omission committed in the discharge of their judicial functions" (Art. 15(2)) and that a "Judge shall not be suspended or removed from office save, where, on the recommendation of two-thirds majority of the other members, he/she no longer meets the requisite conditions to be a Judge." As far as the members of the African Court of Human and Peoples' Rights are concerned, the unanimous decision of the other judges of the Court is required (Art. 19(1) of the Protocol establishing the Court). Article 8(4) further provides that any recommendation of the Court in this respect "shall become final upon its adoption by the Assembly." This provision, which clearly gives the Heads of State and Government the right to intervene, is not found in the statutes of the two other regional courts or in the Statute of the International Court of Justice for instance.

The independence of the Judges is reinforced by the enjoyment of the diplomatic privileges and immunities laid down by the OAU Convention of the same name,[7] as implicitly indicated by Article 12(1). It will also be noted that, under the terms of Article 14(1), no judge may hear a case in which he has previously taken part as agent, counsel or lawyer of one of the parties or as a member of a national or international court or a commission of enquiry or in any other capacity.

The Statute provides, moreover, that "a Judge of the nationality of a State Party to a case before the full Court or one of its Sections shall not have the right to sit on the case" (Art. 14(3)). In the case of the International Court of Justice and the Inter-American Court, the national judge concerned retains his/her right to sit and the other State has the right to appoint an *ad hoc* judge. In the European system this question does not arise, since the European Court consists of a number of judges equal to that of the States Parties to the Convention.

2.2. Bureau

Under the terms of Article 22 of the Statute, the Court shall elect its President and one Vice-President from the two different

---

[7] General Convention on the Privileges and Immunities of the Organization of African Unity, adopted at Accra (Ghana) on 25 October 1965.

lists of judges. They are elected for a period of three years and may be re-elected once. The President shall preside over the sessions of the full Court and those of the Section to which he or she belongs; the Vice-President shall preside over the sessions of the Section to which he or she belongs. Both the President and the Vice-President shall reside at the seat of the Court.

2.3. Seat

Article 25 of the Statute provides that the seat of the Court shall be the same as the current seat of the African Court of Human and Peoples' Rights, that is in Arusha (Tanzania).

2.4. Registry

Article 22(4) of the Statute provides for the appointment by the Court of a Registrar and other staff of the registry. Article 6 of the Protocol on the Statute of the African Court however lays down that "the Registrar of the African Court on Human and Peoples' Rights shall remain in office until the appointment of a new Registrar for the African Court of Justice and Human Rights." The staff of the current African Court of Human and Peoples' Rights consists of 46 civil servants. This staff would have to be expanded to meet the requirements of the wide jurisdiction of the African Court of Justice and Human Rights.

3. Operation of the Court

The Statute is relatively discreet on the operation of the Court, and it will therefore be for the Court to lay down the precise details of this in its Rules of procedure. In this context, it might be useful to examine three aspects of the operation of the Court regulated by the Statute, namely its Rules of procedure, its budget and its annual reports.

3.1. Rules of Procedure

Article 27 of the Statute provides that the Court shall draw up its own Rules, bearing in mind "the complementarity it maintains with the African Commission and the African Committee of Experts." In this connection, it should be recalled that the Court is designed to "supplement and strengthen the mission of the African Commission on Human and Peoples' Rights as well as the African Committee of Experts on the Rights and Welfare of the Child" (Preamble of the Protocol on the Statute of the African Court, paragraph 5). Article 38 entitled "Procedure before the Court," also provides that "the procedures before the Court shall be laid out in the Rules of Court, taking into account the complementarity between the Court and other treaty bodies of the Union." One would hope that when elaborating its own Rules, the Court will not "reinvent the wheel" and will draw inspiration from the existing Rules of Procedure of the African Court of Human and Peoples' Rights.[8]

3.2. Budget

Article 26 lays down that "the budget of the Court shall be borne by the African Union." As a judicial body entrusted with a very wide jurisdiction, the African Court will need to have an adequate budget with a view to both its effectiveness and its credibility. The Registry of the Court (the legal and linguistic departments among others) will in particular need to be strengthened. In 2010, the African Court of Human and Peoples' Rights was allocated a total budget of 7,939,375 US$ (6,169,591 US$ of Regular budget and 1,769,784 US$ of Programme budget). This budget will have to be increased in view of the wide jurisdiction of the African Court of Justice and Human Rights.

---

[8] For the text of these Rules, see the website of the African Court.

3.3. Reports

Article 57 of the Statute provides that "the Court shall submit to the Assembly, an annual report on its work during the previous year. The report shall specify, in particular, the cases in which a party has not complied with the judgment of the Court." The presentation of an annual report is not laid down by the European Convention[9] but is by the American Convention (Art. 65). The presentation of a report of this kind is important, for it helps to tighten the links between the African Court and the African Union. The presentation of the annual report, as well as the discussion it generally gives rise to, can, indeed, provide an excellent opportunity for raising the awareness of Member States – whether or not they are parties to the Protocol – to the Court's activities and to the problems it encounters in performing the tasks entrusted to it.

4. The Contentious Function of the Court

Although the Court has not yet been established, it is worthwhile to examine its jurisdiction, the procedure it will follow during the consideration of the cases brought before it, and the decisions it has the power to take under its Statute.

4.1. Jurisdiction of the Court

As the Statute does not clearly delimit the jurisdiction of the Court, we will endeavour to sketch its main features with regard to the material and personal aspects thereof. Regarding the material jurisdiction (jurisdiction *ratione materiae*), Article 28 of the Statute states that:

> "The Court shall have jurisdiction over all cases and all legal disputes submitted to it in accordance with the present Statute which relates to:

---

[9] The Statute of the International Court of Justice also does not require the submission of an annual report by the Court (however, see Art. 15(2) of the United Nations Charter), yet in practice the Court prepares a report in August each year, which is then transmitted to the General Assembly and presented to it orally by the President of the Court.

(a) The interpretation and application of the Constitutive Act;

(b) The interpretation, application or validity of other Union Treaties and all subsidiary legal instruments adopted within the framework of the Union or the Organization of African Unity;

(c) The interpretation and the application of the African Charter, the Charter on the Rights and Welfare of the Child, the Protocol to the African Charter on Human and Peoples' Rights on the Rights of Women in Africa, or any other legal instrument relating to human rights, ratified by the States Parties concerned;

(d) Any question of international law;

(e) All acts, decisions, regulations and directives of the organs of the Union;

(f) All matters specifically provided for in any other agreements that States Parties may conclude among themselves, or with the Union and which confer jurisdiction on the Court;

(g) The existence of any fact which, if established, would constitute a breach of an obligation owed to a State Party or to the Union;

(h) The nature or extent of the reparation to be made for the breach of an international obligation."

Article 28 of the Statute thus provides the Court with a very broad jurisdiction. To begin with, it allows the Court to deal with any constitutional issue that may be raised within the framework of the African Union (paragraphs (a), (b) and (e)). This is for example the kind of jurisdiction that is entrusted to the Court of Justice of Luxembourg in the framework of the European Union. Article 28 makes also possible for the Court to entertain disputes relating to any question of international law (paragraphs (d), (g) and (h)), as it is for example the case of the International Court of Justice, which is the main judicial organ of the United Nations. *Last but not least,* Article 28 entrusts the Court with a jurisdiction in the field of human rights (paragraph (c)), as it is the case for the current African Court of Human and Peoples' Rights. The originality of this provision resides in the fact that the Court can deal with cases relating to the interpretation and application not only of the African Charter itself and its protocols or the 1990 African Charter on the Rights and Welfare of the Child, but also of any other human rights treaty "ratified by the States Parties concerned." By way of comparison, the jurisdiction *ratione materiae* of the European Court of Human Rights extends only to matters concerning the interpretation and application of the European Convention and its Protocols;[10] the jurisdiction *ratione materiae* of the Inter-American Court of Human Rights is also limited to the interpretation and application of the American Convention alone.[11] The jurisdiction *ratione materiae* of the African Court is ultimately not "linked" to that of the African Commission, which can only deal with the interpretation and application of the rights guaranteed by the African Charter (see Arts. 45(2 & 3) of the Charter).

Regarding personal jurisdiction (jurisdiction *ratione personae*), Article 29 of the Statute provides that cases may be brought before the Court by:

"(a) States Parties to the Protocol;

(b) The Assembly, the Parliament and other organs of the Union authorized by the Assembly;

(c) A staff member of the African Union, on appeal, in a dispute and within the limits and under the terms and conditions laid down in the Staff Rules and Regulations of the Union."

As defined by this provision, access to the African Court is thus relatively liberal when compared to access to the International Court of Justice before which only States can appear in contentious cases.

Article 30 allows other entities to seize the Court with cases relating to violations of rights guaranteed by one of the legal instruments referred to in Article 28(c). Those entities are:

"(a) States Parties to the Protocol;

(b) The African Commission on Human and Peoples' Rights;

(c) The African Committee of Experts on the Rights and Welfare of the Child;

(d) African Intergovernmental Organizations accredited to the Union or its organs;

(e) African National Human Rights Institutions;

---

[10] Articles 32, 33 and 34 of the European Convention.
[11] Article 62 (1) of the American Convention.

(f) Individuals or relevant Non-Governmental Organizations accredited to the African Union or to its organs, subject to provisions of Article 8 of the Protocol."

As defined by Article 30, access to the Court in human rights matters is also very liberal when compared to access to the Inter-American Court of Human Rights before which only the Inter-American Commission and States Parties to the American Convention are entitled to bring a case before the Court.[12] It should also be pointed out that, in the latter case, the Respondent State must have accepted the jurisdiction of the Court either unconditionally or on condition of reciprocity.[13]

The only entities that have a limited access to the African Court are the individuals and Non-Governmental Organizations, since the latter can bring human rights cases before the Court only if the State concerned has made a declaration accepting the jurisdiction of the Court to receive such cases; this is what is provided for in rather unclear manner by Article 8(3) of the Protocol.[14] This provision has the same purpose as Article 34(6) of the Protocol establishing the African Court of Human and Peoples' Rights. This "contracting-in" clause has ultimately been preferred to the "contracting-out" one that had initially been proposed. In the very first Draft of the Protocol, which was discussed in Algiers in November 2005, it was indeed provided that individuals and Non-Governmental Organizations would have an automatic access to the Court, unless the State concerned has made a declaration to the contrary when ratifying the Protocol.[15]

---

[12] Article 61(1) of the American Convention.
[13] Article 62 of the American Convention.
[14] "Any Member State may, at the time of signature or when depositing its instrument of ratification or accession, or at any time thereafter, make a declaration accepting the competence of the Court to receive cases under Article 30(f) involving a State which has not made such a declaration"; this latter part of the provision is rather ambiguous.
[15] See Article 32(2) of the Preliminary Draft Statute, Draft of the Single Legal Instrument (African Court of Justice and Human Rights), Meeting of Legal Experts on the Draft Legal Instrument relating to the Merger of the African Court on Human and Peoples' Rights and the Court of Justice of the African Union, 21-25 November 2005, Algiers (Algeria), AU Doc. UA/EXP/Fusion.cours. 3 (I); see also Article 8 (4) of the Draft Protocol and

The Statute therefore lays down the compulsory jurisdiction of the African Court for all cases brought before it by the entities listed in Articles 29 and 30, with the exception of individuals and Non-Governmental Organizations for human rights cases. By way of comparison, States Parties to the Statute of the International Court of Justice can only be brought before the Court if they have accepted its jurisdiction by filing an optional declaration, by concluding a special agreement or by any other means,[16] as mentioned above; while States Parties to the American Convention can be brought before the Inter-American Court only if they have accepted its jurisdiction.[17]

As far as the limitation relating to access by individuals or Non-Governmental Organizations is concerned, the question arises whether a State may nevertheless agree to be brought before the Court by expressing its consent on a case-by-case basis, other than by the prior deposit of its declaration as laid down in Article 8(3). The American Convention,[18] like the European Convention before it was amended by Protocol No. 11,[19] allowed for this possibility. The African Court of Human and Peoples' Rights has not provided for such a possibility in its Rules of Procedure with respect to a case brought by an individual or non-governmental organization, thus creating the possibility of a *forum prorogatum*. Nonetheless, such possibility was implicitly contemplated in the first case brought before the Court.[20]

To sum up, the jurisdiction of the Court is extremely broad: the Court has indeed the combined jurisdictions of four different kinds of judicial bodies. It has a jurisdiction in the field of human rights, like the European Court of Human Rights (Strasbourg), a jurisdiction in constitutional issues relating to the African Union, like the Court of Justice (Luxembourg) in the framework of the European Union, a

---

Article 31 of the Draft Statute, Draft Protocol on the Statute of the African Court of Justice and Human Rights, Meeting of the Permanent Representatives Committee and Legal Experts on Legal Matters, 16-19 May 2006, Addis Ababa (Ethiopia), AU Doc. EX.CL/211 (VIII) Rev. 1, Annex II.

[16] See Article 36 of the ICJ Statute.
[17] See text under footnote 13.
[18] Article 62 (3) of the American Convention.
[19] Article 48 of the European Convention before the latter was amended by Protocol No. 11.
[20] See my Separate Opinion appended to the *Michelot Yogogombaye v. Senegal* Judgment of 15 December 2009.

jurisdiction to deal with any issues of international law, like the International Court of Justice (The Hague) in the framework of the United Nations and a jurisdiction in the field of staff appeal, like the United Nations Dispute Tribunal within the UN Internal Justice System.

4.2. Procedure before the Court

The Statute devotes a whole chapter (Chapter IV) to the procedure before the Court but is silent on some important issues such as the one of admissibility of applications relating to human rights issues, the main procedural steps or the amicable settlement for example. Article 38, entitled "Procedure before the Court," however, provides that "the procedures before the Court shall be laid out in the Rules of Court, taking into account the complementarity between the Court and other treaty bodies of the Union."

Articles 33 and 34 of the Statute, relating to institution of proceedings before the two Sections of the Court, indicate that cases shall be submitted to the Court by written application addressed to the Registrar. They do not provide for conditions of admissibility of applications relating to appeals from staff members of the African Union or to human rights issues.

As far the latter issues are concerned, it is however to be hoped that the Human Rights Section of the Court will draw inspiration from the Protocol establishing the African Court of Human and Peoples' Rights and follow the practice of the latter body. There are seven such conditions for communications from individuals or non-governmental organizations; these communications shall indeed be considered only if they:

1. Indicate their authors even if the latter request anonymity;

2. Are compatible with the Constitutive Act of the African Union or with the African Charter;

3. Are not written in disparaging or insulting language directed against the State concerned and its institutions or the African Union;

4. Are not based exclusively on news disseminated through the mass media;

5. Are sent after exhausting local remedies, if any, unless it is obvious that this procedure is unduly prolonged;
6. Are submitted within a reasonable period from the time local remedies are exhausted or from the date the Commission is seized of the matter; and
7. Do not deal with cases which have been settled by these States involved in accordance with the principles of the Charter of the United Nations, or the Constitutive Act of the African Union or the provisions of the African Charter.[21]

Where the admissibility of applications from States is concerned, it should normally be governed by a single condition, which is the exhaustion of local remedies by the victim of the human rights violation on behalf of whom the State party brings the case before the Court.

Unlike the Statute of the International Court of Justice, the Statute of the African Court gives few details regarding the procedure for the consideration of applications on the merits. However, it seeks to regulate certain specific matters such as the Court's hearings in a case, laying down the exclusion of a judge if he is a national of a State Party to a case submitted to the Court,[22] or the option given to the Court to make on-site visits.[23] It also regulates other equally specific and important matters such as the applicable law, representation of the parties, hearings, interim measures, intervention, judgments, interpretation and revision. Unlike the Protocol establishing the African Court of Human and Peoples' Rights,[24] the Statute does not deal with the issues of evidence or amicable settlement. The space

---

[21] On this question of admissibility, see Ouguergouz F., "The Establishment of an African Court of Human and Peoples' Rights: a Judicial Premiere for the African Union," *African Yearbook of International Law* 11 (2003), pp. 118-122.

[22] Its Article 14(3) lays down that "a Judge of the nationality of a State Party before the full Court or one of its Sections shall not have the right to sit on the case."

[23] Its Article 25(1) states that the Court "may sit in any other Member State, if circumstances warrant, and with the consent of the Member State concerned"; the language of this provision is similar to that of Article 58(1) of the American Convention; however, it is Rule 44(4) of the Rules of Procedure of the Inter-American Court that provides explicitly for the possibility of *in situ* investigations.

[24] Articles 9 and 26.

does not allow us to embark on the examination of each and every of these aspects of the procedure before the Court; we will therefore focus on the most important of them.

4.2.1. Applicable Law

In its consideration of the merits of applications, the Court enjoys great latitude as regards the applicable law. Indeed, Article 31 of the Statute is drafted along the lines of Article 38 of the Statute of the International Court of Justice. It provides that

"in carrying out its functions, the Court shall have regard to:

(a) The Constitutive Act [of the African Union];

(b) International treaties, whether general or particular, ratified by the contesting States;

(c) International custom, as evidence of a general practice accepted as law;

(d) The general principles of law recognized universally or by African States;

(e) Subject to the provisions of paragraph 1, of Article 46 of the present Statute, judicial decisions and writings of the most highly qualified publicists of various nations as well as the regulations, directives and decisions of the Union, as subsidiary means for the determination of the rules of law;

(f) Any other law relevant to the determination of the case."

The large variety of the law applicable by the Court is thus commensurate to the wide material jurisdiction of the latter.

Like Article 38(2) of the Statute of the International Court of Justice, Article 31 also allows the Court "to decide a case *ex aequo et bono*, if the parties agree thereto," i.e. to decide the case on the sole basis of equity.

4.2.2. Interim Measures

Article 35(1) of the Statute provides that

"the Court shall have the power, on its motion or on application by the parties, to indicate, if it considers that circumstances so require any provisional measures which ought to be taken to preserve the respective rights of the parties."

This provision, drafted along the lines of Article 41 of the Statute of the International Court of Justice, does not specify what could be the circumstances contemplated, thus giving a wide margin of appreciation to the Court. Article 27(2) of the Protocol establishing the African Court of Human and Peoples' Rights is more specific in this regard since it provides that "in cases of extreme gravity and urgency, and when necessary to avoid irreparable harm to persons, the Court shall adopt such provisional measures as it deems necessary." This latter Court has considered that such conditions were met in the situation prevailing in Libya in February and March 2011. Indeed, on 25 March 2011, it has, on its own motion, adopted an order requesting the Government of Libya to

> "immediately refrain from any action that would result in loss of life or violation of physical integrity of persons, which could be in breach of the provisions of the Charter or of other international human rights instruments to which it is a party."[25]

Article 35 of the Statute does not specify whether the provisional measures are binding or not on the States Parties concerned.[26]

4.3. Decisions and Judgments of the Court

Article 43 of the Statute is entitled "Judgments and Decisions" but does not explain the difference it makes between these two concepts.[27] According to the Statute, decisions of the Court shall be taken "by a majority of the Judges present" (Art. 42); judgments of the Court shall be reasoned (Art. 43(2)), shall be binding on the parties

---

[25] See *In the Matter of African Commission on Human and Peoples' Rights v. Great Socialist People's Libyan Arab Jamahiriya*, Application No. 004/2011, Order for Provisional Measures.

[26] In its Judgment of 27 June 2001 *LaGrand (Germany v. United States of America), Judgment, I.C.J. Reports 2001*, p. 466, para. 109, the International Court of Justice found that orders indicating provisional measures are legally binding.

[27] The concept of "decisions" is generally broader than the one of "judgments", and encompasses other rulings of a Court such as its "orders."

and shall be final (Art. 46). They may nevertheless be the subject of a request for interpretation (Art. 47) or revision (Art. 48).[28]

According to Article 45 of the Statute, "the Court may, if it considers that there was a violation of a human or peoples' rights, order any appropriate measures in order to remedy the situation, including granting fair compensation."

It is interesting to note that Article 43 lays down that the judgment of the Court shall be notified not only to the parties to the case, the Member States of the African Union and the Commission of the Union, but also to the Executive Council which "shall monitor its execution on behalf of the Assembly" of Heads of State and Government.[29] This is an important provision, the purpose of which is to ensure that the Court's decision is made public and implemented. The concern of the authors of the Statute to guarantee as far as possible that the decisions of the Court are respected by the State or States concerned is also clearly apparent in Article 46 entitled "Binding Force and Execution of Judgments." Paragraph 3 of this provision reads as follows: "The parties shall comply with the judgment made by the Court in any dispute to which they are parties within the time stipulated by the Court and shall guarantee its execution."[30] Paragraphs 4 and 5 of Article 46 are even more explicit. Paragraph 4 indeed provides that "where a party has failed to comply with a judgment, the Court shall refer the matter to the Assembly, which shall decide upon measures to be taken to give effect to that judgment". Paragraph 5, for its part, provides that "the Assembly may impose sanctions by virtue of paragraph 2 of Article 23 of the Constitutive Act." It should indeed be recalled that the Constitutive Act of the African Union makes provision for

---

[28] The Court may indeed "review its decision in the light of new evidence under conditions to be set out in the Rules of Procedure."
[29] The wording of Article 43(6) should be likened to that of Article 46(2) of the European Convention, which lays down that "the final judgment of the Court shall be transmitted to the Committee of Ministers, which shall supervise its execution."
[30] This provision thus goes a little bit further than Article 94(1) of the United Nations Charter, according to which: "Each Member of the United Nations undertakes to comply with the decision of the International Court of Justice in any case to which it is a party."

sanctions with respect to States Parties that fail to comply with the decisions and policies of the Union.

5. The Advisory Function of the Court

Chapter V of the Statute[31] confers an advisory function on the Court, like the International Court of Justice, or the Inter-American and European Human Rights Courts, whose powers in this matter are governed respectively by Articles 65 to 68 of the ICJ Statute, Article 64 of the American Convention and Articles 47 to 49 of the European Convention.

Article 53(1) of the Statute provides that:

> "The Court may give an advisory opinion on any legal question at the request of the Assembly, the Parliament, the Executive Council, the Peace and Security Council, the Economic, Social and Cultural Council (ECOSOCC), the Financial institutions or any other organ of the Union as may be authorized by the Assembly."

Article 53(2) further provides that the "request for an advisory opinion must not be related to a pending application before the African Commission or the African Committee of Experts."

We will examine below how a request for an advisory opinion is to be initiated and by whom, the material scope of the jurisdiction of the Court in this domain and the action the Court can take on receipt of such a request.

5.1. Request for an advisory opinion

Regarding the entities that may request an advisory opinion from the Court, the Statute differs somewhat from the Protocol establishing the African Court of Human and Peoples' Rights. Indeed, unlike Article 4(1) of the latter instrument, Article 53(1) of the Statute does

---

[31] Chapter V of the Statute is drafted along the lines of Chapter IV of the Statute of the International Court of Justice.

not authorize requests for advisory opinions by States[32] or by "African organizations recognized by the African Union."[33]

The solution enshrined in Article 53 of the Statute is thus similar to the one adopted in the United Nations system to the extent that only the General Assembly, the Security Council and other United Nations organs or specialized agencies duly authorized, may request an advisory opinion from the International Court of Justice (Art. 96 of the UN Charter and Art. 65(1) of the ICJ Statute).[34]

5.2. Material scope of the Court's advisory jurisdiction

There are only two limitations on the material jurisdiction of the Court: the opinion may only concern a "legal question" and it "must not be related to a pending application before the African Commission or the African Committee of Experts."

The purpose of the latter limitation is probably to prevent the Court, in the exercise of its advisory function, from prejudicing the integrity of the quasi-judicial function of the African Commission and the African Committee of Experts as regards the protection of human and peoples' rights, and to safeguard the full freedom of decision of these two bodies. It would, moreover, be most regrettable if these bodies and the Court were to give divergent interpretations of the same legal issue. In this connection, it should be noted that, under Article 45(3) of the African Charter, the African Commission is vested with the power to interpret any provision of the Charter outside any consideration of a case pending before it; in other words, independently of its function of protection properly speaking. However, Article 53 of the Statute does not envisage such a potential

---

[32] Article 64 of the American Convention authorizes Member States of the Organization of American States and some of its organs to request an advisory opinion from the Inter-American Court.

[33] This expression most likely targets the Regional Economic Communities such as the Union of Arab Maghreb, the Economic Community of West African States or the East African Community for example.

[34] Article 47 of the European Convention, for its part, entitles the sole Committee of Ministers of the Council of Europe to request advisory opinions.

conflict between the respective powers of the Court and the Commission in this area.

It should also be observed that the power of specialized organs such as the ECOSOCC or the financial institutions to request advisory opinions of the Court is not limited. In the context of the American Convention,[35] the Inter-American Court may only deal with requests for opinions from specified international organizations if they relate to legal matters falling "within their spheres of competence"; the same applies to the United Nations Charter,[36] which only authorizes certain organs of the Organization and certain specialized agencies to request an advisory opinion of the International Court of Justice in relation to legal matters "arising within the scope of their activities."[37] In the Statute, the power of certain organs of the African Union to request an advisory opinion from the Court is not hedged round by any such form of words. It would nevertheless seem desirable and logical for this power to be governed by the speciality principle as, ultimately, such a power will probably have been conferred on them solely to enable them to effectively perform the task entrusted to them by their Statutes. The Court should therefore lay down such a condition in its Rules of Procedure.

Since the material scope of the Court's advisory jurisdiction is very broad, the Court will itself have to establish limits on a case by case basis. Such discretionary power is strongly suggested by the verb "may" (and not "shall") used in Article 54.

---

[35] See Article 64(1).
[36] See Article 96(2); see also Article 65 of the Statute of the Court.
[37] *Application for Review of Judgement No. 273 of the United Nations Administrative Tribunal, Advisory Opinion, I.C.J. Reports 1982*, pp. 333-334, para. 21. In its advisory opinion of 8 July 1996 concerning the *Legality of the Use by a State of Nuclear Weapons in Armed Conflict, Advisory Opinion, I.C.J Reports 1996*, p. 66, para. 31 (p. 84), the Court had for example concluded that the request for an advisory opinion submitted by the World Health Organization did not relate to a question which arises within the scope of the activities of this organization.

5.3. Action following a request for an advisory opinion

It should indeed be noted that the language of Article 53 (1) is permissive ("the Court may give an advisory opinion"); in other words, the Court's power to issue advisory opinions is purely discretionary, like that of the other regional courts[38] or the International Court of Justice.[39] Indeed, the Court could decline to issue an opinion on grounds of judicial expediency, even if the conditions for submitting a request to it laid down by Article 53 are met. Yet this discretionary power is not infinite, for, as the Inter-American Court has stated:

> "This broad power of appreciation [of the Inter-American Court] should not be confused, however, with unfettered discretion to grant or deny a request for an advisory opinion. The Court must have compelling reasons founded in the conviction that the request exceeds the limits of its advisory jurisdiction under the Convention before it may refrain from complying with a request for an opinion. Moreover, any decision by the Court declining to render an advisory opinion must conform to the provisions of Article 66 of the Convention, which require that reasons be given for the decision."[40]

The African Court should not therefore decline to act on a request for an advisory opinion unless there are compelling reasons for doing so. Be this as it may, it must in the reasoning of its opinion explain why it has declined. Unlike the Protocol establishing the African Court of Human and Peoples' Rights (Art. 4(2)), the Statute does not place an obligation on the Court to give reasons for its opinions. It does not either offer every judge the chance to append his separate or dissenting opinion to the opinion of the Court. However, Article 56 provides that in the exercise of its advisory function, the

---

[38] Inter-American Court of Human Rights, Advisory Opinion OC-3/83 of September 8, 1983, Restrictions to the Death Penalty (Arts. 4 (2) and 4 (4) of the American Convention on Human Rights), para. 36.

[39] *Interpretation of Peace Treaties, Advisory Opinion: I.C.J. Reports* 1950, p. 65, esp. p. 72.

[40] Inter-American Court of Human Rights, Advisory Opinion OC-1/82 of 24 September 1982, "Other Treaties" Subject to the Consultative Jurisdiction of the Court, Art. 64 American Convention on Human Rights, para. 30.

Court should apply *mutatis mutandis* the provisions of the Statute applicable in contentious matters.[41] Another characteristic element of the contentious procedure that the Statute has expressly provided for is the delivery of the advisory opinions in open court (Art. 55).

Lastly, it should be noted that although the question of the legal force of the Court's advisory opinions is not dealt with by the Statute, it is nevertheless clear that, as their name suggests, they are solely advisory.[42] Yet while not binding, the advisory opinions delivered by international judicial bodies are not bereft of all legal value and generally possess great moral authority. The same authority ought therefore also to characterize the advisory opinions of the African Court of Justice and Human Rights; yet that authority will largely depend on the nature of the questions they relate to and the quality of the legal reasoning which underpins them.

6. Conclusion

The task of the drafters of the Protocol on the Statute of the African Court of Justice and Human Rights was not an easy one inasmuch as it consisted in creating a new Court, using the provisions of the constitutive agreements of two different courts, and in securing the smooth replacement of the African Court of Human and Peoples' Rights, already established, by the one to be established. One could say that they have satisfactorily met this difficult challenge. The 2008 Protocol is indeed a rather innovative and comprehensive legal instrument. It displays a certain generosity, such as with respect to the material and personal jurisdiction of the Court. The Protocol however suffers from a number of weaknesses and shortcomings, such as the fact

---

[41] Article 56 is identical to Article 68 of the Statute of the International Court of Justice, which provides that "In the exercise of its advisory functions the Court shall further be guided by the provisions of the present Statute which apply in contentious cases to the extent to which it recognizes them to be applicable."

[42] In its advisory opinion on the *Interpretation of Peace Treaties with Bulgaria, Hungary and Romania*, the International Court of Justice said, in connection with its own advisory opinions, that: "The Court's reply is only of an advisory character: as such, it has no binding force", *I.C.J. Reports 1950*, p. 71.

that access to the Court by individuals and non-governmental organizations, as far as violations of human rights are concerned, is still subject to an optional declaration by States Parties. Another matter of concern relates to the fate of the cases pending before the African Court of Human and Peoples' Rights. According to Article 5 of the Protocol,

> "cases pending before the African Court of Human and Peoples' Rights, that have not been concluded before the entry into force of the present Protocol, shall be transferred to the Human Rights Section of the African Court of Justice and Human Rights on the understanding that such case shall be dealt with in accordance with the Protocol on the establishment of the African Court on Human and Peoples' Rights."

Problems will arise when in an inter-State case, one or both of the States Parties to the case are not yet parties to the 2008 Protocol establishing the African Court of Justice and Human Rights. The same problems will also arise when in a case brought by individuals or NGOs, the respondent State is not party to the new Protocol or has not made the optional declaration. The operationalization phase of the new Court will also necessarily take some time, thus delaying the examination of the pending human rights cases and the new cases. This is all the more true, given the problem of institutional memory that the new Court might face since the Protocol provides for the resigning of the judges of the African Court of Human and Peoples' Rights and the election of a new bench; the same goes with the replacement of the Registrar. The efficacy of the Court and the attainment of the objectives assigned to it will ultimately depend not only on endogenous factors but also on exogenous ones such as the provision by the African Union of sufficient financial means enabling the Court to cope with its broad jurisdiction or the readiness of African States to bring cases to the Court rather than to the International Court of Justice for example.[43]

---

[43] Since 1978, no less than 23 cases were brought before the International Court Justice by or against an African State. As of 31 December 2010, out of 14 pending cases before the Court, four were brought by or against an African State; as of the same date, out of 66 declarations of acceptance of the compulsory

The establishment in July 2006 of the African Court of Human and Peoples' Rights definitely marked a great turning point in the history of the protection of human rights in the African continent; it is now to be hoped that the creation of the African Court of Justice and Human Rights will not ultimately be detrimental to the human rights protection in Africa and that this new judicial organ will successfully take up the challenge of its broad jurisdiction.

---

jurisdiction of the International Court of Justice made under Article 36(2) of the Statute, 22 originated from African States.

CHAPTER 7.
THE PEACE AND SECURITY COUNCIL

Roland Adjovi

1. Introduction

In establishing the Commission on Mediation, Conciliation and Arbitration,[1] the Founding Member States of the Organization of African Unity (OAU) were trying to develop their own peaceful disputes settlement mechanism, not unlike other regional organizations adhering to this principle. Unfortunately, this organ never came into being due to political differences among States, especially the prevailing ideologies during the Cold War. In 1993, in an ebullient international environment characterised by a sort of democratic "New Deal," the Heads of State and Government, meeting in Cairo in Egypt, adopted the Declaration on the Mechanism for Conflict Prevention, Management and Resolution.[2] The Mechanism thus established operated around a Central Organ which might in retrospect be viewed as the forerunner of the Peace and Security Council. In 2001 in Lusaka, while the Lomé treaty was already one year old though yet to come into force, the Heads of State and Government decided to integrate the Central Organ into the African Union.[3] On 9 July 2002 in Durban in South Africa, the limitations of this organ and the need to review its legal framework prompted the elaboration of the Protocol establishing the Peace and Security

---

[1] Articles 7 and 19 of the Charter of the Organization of African Unity, 1963.
[2] OAU Document AHG/Decl. 3 (XXIX).
[3] Decision on the Implementation of the Sirte Summit Decision on the African Union, OAU Document AHG/Dec. 160 (XXXVII).

Council.[4] This Protocol is intended to take a more forward-looking approach to security on the continent, emphasising increased efficiency and taking into account the new legal framework established by the Lomé treaty. The Protocol affords the supreme and plenary organ of the African Union a more inclusive and better-structured overview of the regional security system. Article 22(5) of the Protocol provides for its entry into force after ratification by a simple majority of Member States, that is, 27 States. Given the urgency of implementing this new instrument, the Conference of Heads of States and Governments called on Member States to accelerate ratification in order to allow the Protocol to come into force quickly.[5] Accordingly, on 26 December 2003, a year and a half after it was adopted, Nigeria became the 27th member state to ratify the Protocol, which thus entered into force. This ratification, welcomed by the Executive Council[6] and the Assembly,[7] rendered the new organ effective.

However, the legal framework of the newly established organ is not limited to the Protocol, but extends to other instruments, not least the

---

[4] Decision on the Establishment of the Peace and Security Council of the African Union, AU Document Assembly/AU/Dec. 2 (I).

[5] In its Decision on the Operationalisation of the Protocol relating to the Establishment of the Peace and Security Council [AU Document Assembly/AU/Dec. 16 (II)] to urge all those countries that have not yet done so to ratify the Protocol so that it could come into force as soon as possible, while authorising the Executive Council and the Commission to take the necessary measures that would, once the Protocol came into force, ensure its institutional effectiveness. The Assembly adopted another Decision [AU Document Assembly/AU/Dec. 34 (III)] to welcome the entry into force of the Protocol (para. 1) and approve all measures by the Executive Council geared towards the Operationalisation of the new organ (para. 2), the adoption of its rules of procedure and the election of its members (para. 3).

[6] Decision on the establishment of the Peace and Security Council [AU Document Ex.CL/Dec. 79 (IV)], March 2004. By this same decision (para. 5), acting on behalf of the Assembly, the Executive Council adopted the Council's rules of procedure to increase the effectiveness of the Operationalisation.

[7] Decision on the Operationalisation of the Protocol relating to the Establishment of the Peace and Security Council of the African Union [AU Document Assembly/AU/Dec. 34 (III)], July 2004. By this Decision, the Assembly approved the measures adopted by the Council (para. 2) and urged the chairperson of the Commission to take all the other measures as soon as practicable for the complete Operationalisation of the Protocol (para. 5).

Constitutive Act of the Union itself, all previous decisions pertaining to peace and security and, in particular, the central organ which can assist in interpreting the Protocol, in the light of African Union law, and universal international law centred on the United Nations Charter and the specific powers that States have vested in the United Nations Security Council.

This Chapter focuses on the Peace and Security Council, in order to shed light on the mandate and activities of this important pan-African institution. The Chapter therefore mainly entails an institutional presentation of the new organ based on an analysis of the Protocol, while including a more general study of the legal framework in which the organ exercises its powers. In addition to the Peace and Security Council, the Protocol establishes a series of mechanisms around the Council to guarantee peace and security in Africa. Our aim in this Chapter is to examine this system as a whole by presenting the Council and the mechanisms and then by contextualising the system within the broader context of the collective security system and the African regional system in general.

2. The Organ

Pursuant to Article 2 (1) of the Protocol, the Peace and Security Council is a standing organ of the African Union, established by the Assembly pursuant to Article 5 (2) of the AU Constitutive Act. It has its own mandate, and its composition is more limited than that of the Assembly, which is the supreme, plenary organ of the African Union. It also has different procedures, which are, however, subject to consensus.

2.1. Mandate

Article 2(1) of the Protocol defines the organ as part of "a collective security and early-warning arrangement to facilitate timely and efficient response to conflict and crisis situations in Africa" whose objective is to prevent conflicts and manage them if they occur (Article 3). The wording of Article 3 of the Protocol encompasses the functions set out in Article 6 of the same instrument as well as the powers laid down in Article 7. The activities of the Council since its inception have reflected this dual mandate. On the one hand, the Council acted promptly in taking a stand on events leading up to open conflict, for example in Togo, with the communiqué of 7 February 2005.[8] In this communiqué, the Council condemned the unconstitutional transfer of power, invited the authorities to comply with the instruments in force in order to avoid any major crisis, and demanded that the armed forces refrain from becoming involved in politics. On the other hand, the Council is actively involved in managing several ongoing conflicts, in particular those in Côte d'Ivoire and the Sudan.[9] In Côte d'Ivoire, the Council played a key role alongside the Economic Community of West African States (ECOWAS), and the Security Council, to extend the scope of the measures adopted.[10] In the case of the Sudan, the role of the Council is much more complex with the deployment of a peacekeeping mission, the African Union Mission in Sudan (AMIS) and, later on, the establishment of the first ever hybrid peacekeeping mission.[11]

---

[8] AU Document PSC/PR/Comm. (XXIV).

[9] So far, the Peace and Security Council has issued opinions on the following crises: Angola (peacebuilding), Burundi (internal armed conflict and peacebuilding), the Central African Republic (peacebuilding), Comoros (peacebuilding), the Democratic Republic of the Congo (internal armed conflict), between the Democratic Republic of the Congo and Rwanda, in Côte d'Ivoire (internal armed conflict), between Eritrea and Ethiopia, between Eritrea and the Sudan, Liberia (peacebuilding), Mauritania (*coup d'état* of 3 August 2005, and the reestablishment of constitutional order), Sierra Leone (peacebuilding), Somalia (persistent armed conflict), the Sudan (internal armed conflict, the death of John Garang, and the Darfur crisis), between the Sudan and Chad, and Togo (unconstitutional transfer of power after the death of President Gnassingbe Eyadema).

[10] The Council has instituted close cooperation with ECOWAS which, in September 2005, led it to evaluate the implementation of the Pretoria Agreement and propose measures for a successful transition. Following a report submitted by ECOWAS, the Council issued a communiqué adopting the recommendations and referred the case to the United Nations Security Council in order to request stronger support. This was granted.

[11] In the current crisis in Darfur (Sudan), the Council took a more significant initiative by instituting in April 2004, under the authority of the Assembly, an observation force (AMIS) with the mandate to monitor the ceasefire agreement. AMIS benefited from the United Nations support including with the deployment of a reduced force. Since then, there have been discussions regarding the substitution of a UN force for the African force. The initiative came from the UN

Beyond these two explicit aspects of the Council's mandate, it is also necessary to consider the concept of conflict management as involving peacebuilding – hence the extension of the Peace and Security Council's mandate. Article 3(c) bears out this view, in that it includes "promot[ing] and implement[ing] peacebuilding and post-conflict reconstruction activities to consolidate peace and prevent the resurgence of violence."

Article 6 (1) (e) also States, in the same vein, that one of the functions of the Council is peacebuilding and post-conflict reconstruction. The communiqué of 25 May 2004[12] can be seen in this light. The Council, meeting at Heads of State and Government level, welcomed the developments in Angola and Sierra Leone, amongst other situations, while emphasising the need for the union to work on peace (paras. 1 and 2). In other decisions, the Council is similarly interested in resolving conflicts in sustainable manner.[13]

Furthermore, and this should be considered as part of prevention, the Protocol gives the Council a general mandate to foster the rule of law. Accordingly, Article 3(f) requires the Council to

"promote and encourage democratic practices, good governance and the rule of law, and to protect human rights and fundamental freedoms, respect for the sanctity of human life and international humanitarian law, as part of efforts for preventing conflicts."

This provision can be applied extensively, in that the Council can intervene in a very wide range of situations. The decision taken regarding Togo on 7 February 2005 clearly falls within this mandate, since the Council backed an option that was in keeping with the laws of Togo, in other words, the rule of law.

Lastly, while this is still at a very early planning stage, the Council has a mandate to develop a common defence policy (Article 3 (e)). The Conference's adoption of a Non-Aggression and Common

---

Security Council itself, with the agreement of the African Union. This led to the United Nations Security Council Resolution 1769 creating the hybrid United Nations – African Union Mission in Darfur (UNAMID), on 31 July 2007.

[12] AU Document PSC/AHG/Comm. (IX).

[13] See for instance PSC/PR/Comm. 1 (CCXLVI) on Côte d'Ivoire where the Council "[noted] with satisfaction" all steps leading to the elections that aim at bringing the conflict to a definitive and sustainable end.

Defence Pact on 31 January 2005 in Abuja, Nigeria, is noteworthy in this context.[14] This pact develops and extends the Council's competence by giving the Council the mandate to activate its implementation (Article 9). Pursuant to the provisions of articles 9 and 11 of the pact, the Council may, under the authority of the Assembly, request the provision of mutual military assistance if the need arises. The Council may approach not only States, but also any organ of the Union, and in particular the African Peace Academy, the African Centre for Study and Research on Terrorism, and the African Union Commission on International Law, which were either established by the pact or by other instruments of the African Union. The Council may also establish any mechanism it deems necessary to fulfil its mandate.

To support the exercise of this mandate, Article 4 of the Protocol sets out principles, which are for the most part conventional. It is worth noting that while these principles are innovative they are rather ambiguous in their enunciation of the African Union's right to intervene, and in their recapitulation of the international legal framework which is binding on Member States, particularly the United Nations Charter and the specific powers accorded to the Security Council in this regard. Clearly, the Protocol does not seek to establish a framework that could be inconsistent with collective security as legally enshrined in the United Nations system. Rather, it seeks cooperation. To the Protocol's provisions should be added the acts of the African Union that are part of the legal framework within which the Council operates, in particular decisions and declarations on unconstitutional changes of Government,[15] on the Conference on Security, Stability, Development and Cooperation in Africa (CSSDCA),[16] on NEPAD,[17] on the Code of Conduct for Inter-African

---

[14] This Pact entered into force on 18 December 2009. Current Member States are: Algeria, Burkina Faso, Chad, Congo (Brazzaville), Gabon, Gambia, Ghana, Guinea, Libya, Mali, Mauritania, Mozambique, Niger, Rwanda, Sahrawi Arab Democratic Republic, Senegal and Togo.

[15] See for instance: AU Documents AHG/Dec. 141 and 142 (XXXV), AHG/Decl. 5 (XXXVI).

[16] AU Document AHG/Decl. 4 (XXXVI).

[17] AU Document AHG/Decl. 1 (XXXVII).

Relations,[18] and on arms (nuclear weapons, mines, light and small calibre arms, etc.).[19] Some of these decisions have already served as a basis for decisions taken by the Council, particularly with respect to unconstitutional change of Governments.[20]

This broad and complex mandate is supported by an equally original composition of the Council, intended to guarantee its effectiveness.

2.2. Composition

Article 5 of the Protocol provides for fifteen members divided into two categories according to the duration of their term of office. While a majority of the members of the Council (ten) hold office for two years, one-third (that is, five) hold office for three years "in order to ensure continuity." However, it is clearly stated that the members have equal rights, which explicitly rules out any possibility of veto power.

Article 5(2) sets out the criteria for the election of Council members. The first is equitable regional representation, which implies a balanced distribution of seats on the Council: each of the 5 regions of Africa has 3 seats (two seats for two years and one for three years), except for North Africa, which has only one seat in each category, and West Africa, which has three seats for two years and one seat for three years. Though West Africa has at least one two-year seat more than the other regions, it also has more States than the other regions, particularly North Africa, which comprises only five Member States.

The second criterion is rotation. Within regions, States must sit on the Council in turn, although the frequency of rotation is not fixed. However, the Protocol allows for the re-election of an outgoing

---

[18] AU Document AHG/Decl. 2 (XXX).
[19] See for instance the African Nuclear Weapon-Free Zone Treaty (Pelindaba Treaty), adopted on 11 April 1996 and entered into force on 15 July 2009. The current Member States are: Algeria, Benin, Botswana, Burkina Faso, Burundi, Cameroon, Cote d'Ivoire, Ethiopia, Gabon, Gambia, Ghana, Guinea, Guinea (Equatorial), Kenya, Libya, Lesotho, Madagascar, Mali, Malawi, Mozambique, Mauritania, Mauritius, Nigeria, Rwanda, South Africa, Senegal, Swaziland, Tanzania, Togo, Tunisia, Zambia and Zimbabwe.
[20] See for instance AU Document PSC/PR/BR. (CCLXXXIII) on Madagascar.

member (Article 5(3)), and makes it possible in theory for a State to sit permanently or, at least, for a substantial period in the Council. Lastly – and this is in our view a key criterion – election to the Council – must take account of democratic practice within the State, its commitment and willingness to defend the principles of the African Union, and its contribution to peacekeeping efforts on the continent (Article 5(2)). This is an important criterion which could affect the principle of rotation, and even equality between regions. But it is not impossible that class solidarity, which prevailed in the days of the Organization of African Unity, could continue to play an important role in undermining the real effect of this paragraph.

2.3. Procedure

Article 8(14) of the Protocol provides that the Council shall submit its own rules of procedure for approval by the Assembly. Rules of procedure were drafted and submitted to the Assembly for approval on the Council's establishment. In March 2004, the Executive Council adopted these rules of procedure on behalf of the Assembly and they effectively have the weight of a negotiated inter-State instrument since they were adopted by the States Parties as part of the Constitutive Act of the African Union.[21] The rules of procedure came into force on their adoption by the Assembly. Any amendment will be adopted by the Assembly on the recommendation of the Council, and on the same conditions.

The Council holds meetings on three levels: a meeting of permanent representatives of member States based at the headquarters of the African Union; the meeting of ministers; and the meeting of Heads of State and Government. While the permanent representatives meet at least twice a month and the ministers at least once a year, there is no fixed frequency for the highest level, the meeting of Heads of

---

[21] Decision on the establishment of the Peace and Security Council, AU Document Ex.CL/Dec. 79 (IV), para. 5. The Assembly endorsed this decision during its July 2004 summit. See AU Document Assembly/AU/Dec. 34 (III), para. 2.

State and Government.[22] All meetings are held at the headquarters of the African Union in Addis Ababa. The holding of a meeting away from the headquarters must be approved by two-thirds of the fifteen members, and the State making the proposal must bear the additional costs. While the frequency of meetings is determined by default, the chair of the Council or any of its members, the chair of the Union, and the chair of the Commission may convene meetings. Furthermore, a quorum of two-thirds is required for each meeting.

The provisional agenda of each meeting is fixed by the chair of the Council on the basis of proposals from any of the fifteen Member States, the chair of the Commission or the chair of the Union. It is further provided that no State may oppose the inclusion of any item on the agenda. The agenda is then submitted to a vote of the Council. In addition, any item included on the agenda on which the Council has not completed its discussion is automatically carried over into the agenda of the next meeting. It should be noted that decisions are made by consensus, or in the absence of consensus, a qualified majority of two-thirds with the exception of procedural decisions, for which only a simple majority is required.

Meetings of the Council are held in camera. However, the Council may also hold public meetings with the provision that Member States whose interests are at stake may be invited, as well as regional and civil society organizations with observer status at the Union.

Lastly, the chair of the Council is held on a rotating basis; the fifteen Member States take turns by alphabetical order.

In our view, these procedural provisions raise two issues. Firstly, the confidential nature of the meetings and meeting transcripts is problematic because it is essential for the Council to have access to all available information at all times. Thus, a State which was not a member of the Council at a particular time would not have access to confidential information pertaining to that time. However, this information may be necessary for the State to participate effectively in the decision-making process. Moreover, if this State can only access the information when the issue is raised again, it seems to us that it

---

[22] For example, in September 2005, the Heads of State and Government held a meeting on Côte d'Ivoire while they were in New York for a United Nations Summit.

would not be in a position to understand all the ramifications of the issue. Consequently, it would seem necessary for all Member States to have access at all times to all the information generated by meetings of the Council, and it would then be incumbent upon each State to respect the confidentiality of the proceedings.

Secondly, the conditions for the participation of the chair of the Commission in the Council's activities are established by the rules of procedure, and Article 7(1) sets out the powers shared between the Council and the Chair of the Commission. However, this does not rule out an initiative originating from the Chair of the Commission and addressed directly to the Assembly. Nonetheless, the relationship between the Council and the Assembly is not exactly clear, for example, in exercising the right of intervention. Can the Council undertake an operation at its discretion or must it make a proposal to this effect to the Assembly, which has the exclusive right to do so? Article 7(1)(a)-(c) seems to establish a certain degree of autonomy on the part of the Council, while article 7(1)(e) provides that the Council "recommend to the Assembly [...] intervention [...] on behalf of the Union."

In addition, the Council has various other mechanisms that, all together, form the new security mechanism of the African Union. But the lack of precision with respect to the sharing of powers with the chair of the Council does not affect these mechanisms as their role is clearly defined as being to *serve* the Council in fulfilling its mandate.

3. The mechanisms of the Peace and Security Council

Article 2(2) of the Protocol provides for four mechanisms to support the Council: a Panel of the Wise, a Continental Early Warning System, an African Standby Force, and a Special Fund.

Pursuant to Article 11, the Panel of the Wise shall be composed of "five highly respected African personalities from various segments of society who have made outstanding contribution to the cause of peace, security and development on the continent" selected by the Chairperson of the Commission in consultation with the Member States concerned, on the basis of regional representation, and appointed by the Assembly to serve for a period of three years. The Panel of the Wise advises the Council, particularly on issues pertaining to conflict prevention.

Article 12 of the Protocol states that the Continental Early Warning System shall be composed of an observation and monitoring centre or "Situation Room," based at the Conflict Management Directorate at the Union's headquarters, and observation and monitoring units of the Regional Mechanisms, linked to the Situation Room. This system is intended to ensure the timely provision of information to the Union and the Council to allow for better security and conflict management. This system is by its nature interconnected with all the other established mechanisms, in particular the United Nations system and research centres, especially in universities, which have useful information.

The proposed African Standby Force (Article 13) is an adaptation of an earlier proposal within the United Nations by its former Secretary-General, Boutros Boutros-Ghali, for the creation of a standby force. This involves the creation by Member States of units within their armed forces which would always be ready for deployment to missions of the Union. Since the 1990s, many military partnerships have enabled African soldiers to receive training in peacekeeping and to prepare them for the eventual creation of the standby force.

As in the case of the United Nations, provision is made for a military staff committee. This differs from the global framework in that the mechanism comes into operation to a greater or lesser extent depending on events, and it has already proved its mettle in part in deploying observation and buffer forces in the Sudan. While it does not appear to be an established, permanent military staff committee, an *ad hoc* committee was able to meet to provide operational management of the deployment in the Sudan.[23]

It is impossible as yet to be entirely certain where the operationalisation of the three mechanisms of the African Union

---

[23] On 25 April 2005, for example, the Military Staff Committee submitted a report on the prevailing situation in Darfur, Sudan.

stands. Nonetheless, in a decision at the Banjul summit in July 2006,[24] the Assembly requested the Peace and Security Council to

> "particularly ensure completion of the implementation of the Continental Peace and Security Framework, in particular, the establishment and the effective functioning of the Panel of the Wise as well as the establishment of the Continental Early-Warning System and the African Defense Force."

It is now for the Peace and Security Council to implement this decision and render the three mechanisms operational.

Lastly, Article 21 establishes a Peace Fund to finance the Union's activities for peace. This Fund is to be financed by voluntary contributions from Member States and other sources in Africa and elsewhere. In July 2003, the Assembly invited the European Union to establish an operational peace facility.[25] The European Union responded favourably to this request in a decision of 11 December 2003.[26] Strangely enough, however, it is unclear whether this European facility is to be integrated into the Fund, although such integration would appear to be a matter of course. Similarly, the Union has already received peace donations from other States, for example Japan in 2002.[27]

4. The Peace and Security Council within the African security system

As regionalisation was structured at the beginning of the 1990s by the Agenda for Peace of the then United Nations Secretary-General, the different security systems were arranged in a pyramid whose base was formed by collective security and the central role played by the

---

[24] AU Document Assembly/AU/Dec. 120 (VII).

[25] Decision on the Establishment by the European Union of a Peace Facility for Africa, AU Document Assembly/AU/Dec.16 (II).

[26] Decision No 3/2003 of the ACP-EC Council of Ministers of 11 December 2003 on the use of resources from the long-term development envelope of the ninth European Development Fund for the creation of a Peace Facility for Africa, *Official Journal of the European Union*, L345/108, 31 December 2003, pp. 0108-0111.

[27] Press Release No. 45/2002 of 1 November 2002. It should be noted that the press release mentions several contributions from Japan, which are funding ongoing operations.

United Nations Security Council. Within this regionalisation structure, regional organizations were vested with greater responsibility and received support from the United Nations while acting as the armed presence of the United Nations on the ground. In the specific case of the African Union, civil society is also included in the system for advice and information.

4.1. The Peace and Security Council and the United Nations Security Council

It is very tempting to compare these two organs, drawing on conventional categorisation to highlight their similarities and differences,[28] but it would be more interesting to examine the relationship between the two. In this regard, it should be noted that the African Union has clearly given greater pre-eminence to the primary responsibility of the Security Council,[29] although this does not supplant the Union's responsibility as a regional interstate organ for guaranteeing the peace and security of its Member States. In practical terms this means that the African Union informs the Security Council of its peace and security activities and requests its support for the deployment of armed forces. Thus, there is close cooperation between the United Nations and the African Union as demonstrated by the establishment by the Secretary-General of a liaison office at the Union's headquarters, and by the briefing sessions on conflicts that the Security Council has organised with representatives of the Union, as well as by situations in which the Security Council has vested the Union with specific mandates. In the Sudan, at the express request of the African Union, the Security Council has decided to deploy a United Nations operation to support an African Union one which was losing momentum on the ground.[30] For the African forces already

---

[28] The dual nature of membership status, even in the absence of veto power within the Peace and Security Council, and the number of members on both sides, as well as the specific powers of each organ, are cases in point.

[29] See the Preamble of the Protocol, which recalls the principal responsibility of the United Nations Security Council in peacekeeping and international security.

[30] See the Communiqués of the Peace and Security Council of 10 March 2006 [AU Document PSC/MIN/Comm.(XLVI), para. 2] and 15 May 2006 [AU Document PSC/MIN/Comm/1(LI), para. 15], instruments adopted by the

involved, this will be mainly a matter of changing berets and an increase in the number of persons deployed, with contingents from non-African States, while maintaining the current assistance of the North Atlantic Treaty Organization (NATO).

At a more restricted geographical level, the Peace and Security Council also maintains relations with the various African regions, as well as with other bodies within the Union itself which extend its powers.

4.2. The Peace and Security Council and regional African mechanisms

This close cooperation at a global level is supplemented by the internal mechanisms of the African Union and similar cooperation with sub-regional mechanisms.

First, within the African Union itself, the Peace and Security Council appears to be the central organ of the security system. Thus, any new peace and security initiative within the Union is to be referred to the Council. Accordingly, a proposal for a collective defence policy, mainly supported by Libya and centred on the Council, was referred to it for action. The proposal was designed around the Council as a way of buttressing its powers. Similarly, a Non-Aggression and Common Defence Pact was signed in January 2005 in Abuja, Nigeria, with the objective of promoting a policy of non-aggression amongst African States by providing a detailed definition of aggression and by organising a mutual defence mechanism between these States and prioritising relationships based on geographical proximity over all relations with non-African States. Naturally, the right to intervene is at the heart of this conventional mechanism. The Peace and Security Council is responsible for bringing this project to fruition.

Security Council, in particular the resolution of 24 March 2006 [UN Doc. S/RES/1663 (2006)] and the statement by it president of 3 February 2006 [UN Doc. S/PRST/2006/5] in addition to discussions within the Security Council: see, for example, the report of 15 June 2006 [UN Doc. S/PV.5462]. From 4 to 10 June 2006, the Security Council conducted a mission to the Sudan and Chad, of which a report of the Secretary-General [UN Doc. S/2006/433] was discussed on 29 June 2006 [UN Doc. S/PV.5478].

At a sub-regional level, the Union could not ignore the advanced mechanisms established by some of the sub-regions, in particular ECOWAS, which even has common armed forces, and the Southern African Development Committee (SADC). The Union organises consultation with sub-regional mechanisms on a continuing basis, encouraging their representation in Addis Ababa and opening its own sub-regional office to improve its monitoring of the activities of these organizations. Regrettably, however, the sub-regional mechanisms are not well positioned within the structure of the Council: they can only be invited to selected Council meetings, and apparently only public meetings.

4.3. The Peace and Security Council and non-African organizations

In a continually changing approach to regionalisation, the partnerships of the African Union and its Peace and Security Council are not limited to intra-African organizations and the United Nations to provide security on the continent. The Peace and Security Council also tries to forge partnerships with other regional organizations such as the European Union and NATO. As mentioned above, the European Union has offered funding to the African Union Peace Fund through the peacebuilding facility. However, the EU has provided more extensive financial support, of which part is dedicated to ongoing peace operations and part to the establishment of the Panel of the Wise.[31] In this context, the partnership with NATO is even more innovative, in that NATO has agreed to provide military assistance for the deployment of African troops in the Sudan. This is innovative in two respects: first, NATO is working outside the confines of its role as a military alliance which only acts when the security of one of its members is at risk; and second, it means that the African Union has bilateral military relations in its own right, neither through the United Nations nor its Member States.

---

[31] European Union Press Releases, European Commission, Memo/04/71, "Q&A – EU / African Union Strategic Partnership," 24 March 2004.

5. Conclusion

This extension of the partnership for peace to non-African organizations is not the only innovative approach of the African Union, as the instruments also, for example, provide for relations with civil society organizations (Article 8(10)(c)). However, in the absence of information on this aspect, a discussion does not seem worthwhile. In conclusion we should rather attempt an evaluation of the first few years of the Peace and Security Council.

There is no doubt that the establishment of the African Union itself is intended to set off a certain progressive dynamic which has led to Africa organising itself better and assuming its responsibilities. The Peace and Security Council is part of this progress. By its very existence, and the provisions that govern its operation, it represents a great amount of progress. In practice, its actions also demonstrate the assumption of more responsibilities by African States, in that dialogue is increasingly open and solutions are being sought. And yet conflicts persist in different places, in the north, south, east, west and centre of the continent.

At the same time, there are signs of unprecedented activism with African peacekeeping forces deployed in various parts of the continent. Civil society also plays a role in these developments by reporting what goes wrong. In this respect, therefore, the assessment is positive, and all that remains is to make conflict resolution effective. This effectiveness can be attained as soon as States assume all their responsibilities and the instruments are implemented more stringently. First, it is essential for all the States of the Union to be party to the Protocol establishing the Peace and Security Council, and for the election of the fifteen Member States of the Council to be carried out with due regard for the internal situation of the Member States. These are future challenges for Africa that will reveal the extent of its commitment to basic human rights.

CHAPTER 8.
THE ECONOMIC, SOCIAL, AND CULTURAL COUNCIL OF THE AFRICAN UNION

Mohamed Sameh Amr

1. Introduction

The Constitutive Act of the AU specifies that, among many objectives, the AU seeks to achieve the following: (i) accelerate the political and socio-economic integration of the continent; (ii) encourage international cooperation, taking due account of the Charter of the United Nations and the Universal Declaration of Human Rights; (iii) establish the necessary conditions which enable the continent to play its rightful role in the global economy and in international negotiations; (iv) promote sustainable development at the economic, social, and cultural levels as well as the integration of African economies; (v) promote co-operation in all fields of human activity to raise the living standards of African peoples; (vi) coordinate and harmonize the policies between the existing and future Regional Economic Communities for the gradual attainment of the objectives of the Union; and (vii) work with relevant international partners in the eradication of preventable diseases and the promotion of good health on the continent.

In order to realize and implement the AU objectives, the AU created several organs,[1] among them is the Economic, Social and

---

[1] The 10 organs are: the Assembly; The Executive Council; the Pan-African Parliament (PAP); the African Court of Justice; the Commission; the ECOSOC, the Permanent Representatives' Committee; the Specialised Technical Committees; the Peace and Security Council; and the financial institutions

Cultural Council (ECOSOCC), which is an advisory organ composed of different social and professional groups of the Member States of the Union.

This chapter shall focus on the ECOSOCC as one of the AU organs, created in order to help the AU to realize human and peoples' social, economic, civil, cultural, and political rights, including, but not limited to, the rights to peace, security, development, and to participate in processes affecting their lives. The ECOSOCC was also created to achieve the AU's common vision of a united and strong Africa and on the need to build a partnership among governments and all segments of civil society, in particular women, youth, and the private sector, in order to strengthen solidarity and cohesion amongst the peoples of Africa.

2. Establishment of The ECOSOCC

The ECOSOCC, like the Pan-African Parliament (PAP), the Peace and Security Council (PSC), and the Court of Justice, is a new organ of the AU that did not exist within the OAU.[2] In its first ordinary meeting in 2002, the AU's Assembly decided that:

(financial institutions: the Central African Bank, the African Monetary Fund, and the African Investment Bank.).

[2] It is important to note that even before transition to the AU; the OAU had a working relationship with civil society organizations, albeit in an *ad hoc* manner. CSOs were granted observer status. Article 90 of the AEC Treaty also supported the participation of CSOs in the Union: "The community, in the context of mobilising the human and natural resources in Africa, shall establish relations of cooperation with African NGOs with a view to encouraging the involvement of the African people in the process of integrating and mobilising their technical, material, and financial support" (AEC: 1991). The Constitutive Act of the AU and the AEC (1991), also make provisions for CSOs to take part in the activities of the AU and its structures. The Act, for example, refers to: "A common vision of a united and strong Africa and the need to build a partnership between governments and all segments of civil society, in particular women, youth, and the private sector" (Constitutive Act, 2002). In 1997, the Secretary-General of the OAU, made a plea for a formal and effective collaboration between the OAU and CSOs before the Council of Ministers and the Assembly of Heads of State and Government. This resulted in three conferences. The first took place on the 11th-15th of June 2001 in Addis Ababa under the theme, "Building Partnerships for Promoting Peace and Development in Africa." Its objective was to "assist in promoting a home-grown African civil society and enhancing its contribution to

"In order to ensure the involvement of our peoples and their civil society organizations in the activities of the Union, we recommit ourselves to the early establishment of the Pan African Parliament and the Economic, Social and Cultural Council (ECOSOCC) as envisaged in the Constitutive Act of our Union."[3]

The first draft of the ECOSOCC statutes were drawn up and submitted to the AU Commission by the Conference on Security, Stability, Development and Cooperation in African Union (CSSDCA),

---

the fulfilment of the Union's mission." The second was held in Addis Ababa between the 11th-14th of June 2002 under the theme, "Developing Partnerships between the OAU and African Civil Society Organizations." The aim was to "Consolidate the progress made from the first as well as develop modalities and mechanisms for collaboration between the OAU and CSOs." The conference elected a consultative working committee (Provisional Working Group to draw up statutes and modalities to institutionalise the ECOSOCC). The CSSDCA (the current CIDO at the AU Commission) has since appointed civil society officers who act as the focal point for civil society activities at the AU Commission. The third meeting took place in 2004, also in Addis Ababa, where CSOs were presented with the Strategic Plan of the AU. See: Establishing a Civil Society Support Mechanism with the Pan-African Parliament (PAP), the New Partnership for Africa's Development (NEPAD) and the African Peer Review Mechanism (APRM), Final Research Report, (published by Southern Africa Trust 2007), July 2007, p. 23.

It should also be noted that in its decision, OAU Doc. AHG Dec. 160 (XXXII) of July 2001 in Lusaka, the Assembly of Heads of State and Government, who considered the transition from the OAU to the African Union, requested the Secretary General to submit to the 76th Ordinary Session of Council (i.e. July 2002), a report on the ECOSOCC with recommendations on structure, areas of competence, criteria for selecting members of the ECOSOCC, relationship between the ECOSOCC and African regional NGOs and professional groups, the ECOSOCC Rules of Procedure and its work programme. The Lusaka Summit decision on the ECOSOCC directs that member states will have to decide on the structure, functioning, areas of competence, selection criteria, Rules of Procedure, and work programme of the ECOSOCC. In that same Decision, the Assembly requested the Interim Chairperson of the AU, in consultation with a group of experts and CSOs working as Group Representatives, submit a comprehensive report during its 2003 Maputo Summit on the ECOSOCC with recommendations on these issues that member states will have to decide on. See: Report issued by the Department of International Relations and Cooperation, Republic of South Africa, May 2002.

[3] See: Decisions and Declarations of the Assembly of the African Union, First Ordinary Session, 9-10 July 2002, Durban, South Africa, AU Doc. ASS/AU/Dec. 1-8 (I).

which was held in Accra (Ghana) in October 2002. They were adopted the African Union at its Third Summit Conference in Addis Ababa, Ethiopia in July 2004 and the Interim ECOSOCC was launched on the 29th of March 2005 in Addis Abba, Ethiopia. The establishment of this important organ is to enable the African people and institutions not only to contribute to the programmes and decisions of the AU, but also to assume ownership of these programmes and be responsible for their implementation. This has now been extended to participation in various other institutions and committees such as the Pan-African Parliament, the African Court of Justice, the Conference on Security, Stability, Development and Cooperation (CSSDCA), and Specialized Technical Committees, all of which are required to involve CSOs in their work.

The ECOSOCC finds its legal basis in Articles 5 and 22 of the Constitutive Act of the AU.[4] It was launched through an Interim Assembly whose mandate was to lay the groundwork for setting up of the Permanent Assembly of the ECOSOCC. The Interim Assembly played a role in facilitating the holding of national, regional and continental elections and was assigned the mission to prepare for the full operationalization of the ECOSOCC. The Permanent ECOSOCC Assembly was launched in September 2008. The membership of the Permanent General Assembly in 2008 was: Angola, Djibouti,

---

[4] Article 5(1) states: "The organs of the Union shall be:
a. The Assembly of the Union;
b. The Executive Council;
c. The Pan-African Parliament;
d. The Court of Justice;
e. The Commission;
f. The Permanent Representatives Committee;
g. The Specialized Technical Committees;
h. The Economic, Social and Cultural Council;
i. The Financial Institutions."
Article (22) states:
"1. The Economic, Social and Cultural Council shall be an advisory organ composed of different social and professional groups of the Member States of the Union.
2. The functions, powers, composition and organization of the Economic, Social and Cultural council shall be determined by the Assembly."

Rwanda, Lesotho, Libya, Mozambique, Senegal, Seychelles, Swaziland, Togo, and the Central and North Africa regions.[5]

The Rules of Procedures of the ECOSOCC was adopted by the ECOSOCC Assembly in Abuja, December 2008.

3. Composition and Membership of ECOSOCC

The ECOSOCC, as an advisory organ, is composed of different social and professional civil society groups from AU Member States, particularly youth and women's organizations.[6] According to Article 4 of the ECOSOCC Statutes, the Council is composed of 150 Civil Society Organizations (CSOs) representing various social groups, such as those representing women, children, young people, the elderly, and people with disabilities and special needs; professional groups such as associations of artists, engineers, health practitioners, social workers, media representatives, teachers, sport associations, legal professionals, social scientists, academics, business organizations, national chambers of commerce, industry, and agriculture, as well as other private sector interest groups; non-governmental organizations (NGOs), community-based organizations (CBOs), and voluntary organizations; and cultural organizations and associations. The ECOSOCC shall also include social and professional groups in the non-governmental organizations of the African Diaspora in accordance with the definition approved by the Executive Council of the AU.

The term of office of each CSOs is 4 years and a member may be re-elected only once. These CSOs are elected as follows: (i) two CSOs from each AU Member State following election by civil society in a Member State; (ii) ten CSOs operating at the regional level of the continent (two from each of five regions); (iii) eight CSOs at the continental level also following election; (iv) twenty CSOs elected

---

[5] See: Report of the President of the Permanent General Assembly of the Economic, Social and Cultural Council of the African Union, July 2009, p. 2.

[6] It should be noted that it is not clear whether these CSOs are African CSOs or CSOs in Africa.

from the African Diaspora as defined by the Executive Council,[7] covering the various continents of the world following an appropriate process for determining modalities;[8] (v) six CSOs in *ex-officio* capacity, nominated by the Commission based on special considerations and appropriate criteria, in consultation with Member States.

With the exception of the CSOs nominated by the Commission, representation must ensure fifty percent (50%) gender equality and fifty percent (50%) of the representatives must be between the ages of 18-35. It is to be noted that such a requirement is a novelty that ensures the representation of one of the groups often politically marginalized in Africa.

Article 5 of the Statute clarifies the election of members, as follows:

(i) Competent CSO authorities in each Member State shall establish a consultation process, in accordance with the provisions of Article 6 of these Statutes, for the purpose of determining modalities for election, of two CSOs to the ECOSOCC General Assembly;

(ii) Regional and continental CSOs shall establish an appropriate consultative process to determine modalities for election, and elect eighteen CSOs to the ECOSOCC General Assembly; and

---

[7] In accordance with the definition approved by the Executive Council Meeting in Sirte, Libya in June 2005, African Diaspora means: "The African Diaspora consists of peoples of African origin living outside the continent, irrespective of their citizenship and nationality and who are willing to contribute to the development of the continent and the building of the African Union."

[8] It should be noted that during the Kampala meeting of the Standing Committee (December 2009), the President of the Permanent General Assembly of the ECOSOCC observed that while the Statute of the ECOSOCC allocate 20 seats to the Diaspora, the practical organization of proper elections that will permit their membership into the ECOSOCC remains a challenge. The increase in interest and the mobilization of the Diaspora as regard the ECOSOCC, while constituting a cause for excitement, might well make the ECOSOCC a victim of its own success, if not harnessed in rational manner. The President of the General Assembly hoped that 2010 will see, at the very least, the adoption of an adequate formula for Diaspora participation on an elected basis. See: Report of the President of the Permanent General Assembly of the Economic, Social and Cultural Council of the African Union (ECOSOCC), January 2010, pp. 4-5.

(iii) African Diaspora organizations shall establish an appropriate process for determining modalities for elections and elect twenty CSOs to the ECOSOCC General Assembly.

Not all CSOs can be members of the ECOSOCC. Membership is based on the eligibility criteria provided under Article 6 of the ECOSOCC Statutes. The requirements to be fulfilled by CSOs seeking membership are as follows:

- Be a national, regional, continental, or African Diaspora CSO, without (legal) restriction to undertake regional or international activities;
- Have objectives and principles that are consistent with the principles and objectives of the AU as set out in Articles 3 and 4 of the Constitutive Act;
- Be registered as follows: (i) in a Member State of the AU; and/or (ii) meet the general conditions of eligibility for the granting of observer status to non-governmental organizations; and/or (iii) show a minimum of three years' proof of registration as either an African or an African Diaspora CSO prior to the date of submission of application, including proof of operations for those years;
- Provide annual audit statements prepared by an independent auditing company;
- Show proof that the ownership and management of the CSO is made up of not less than fifty percent (50%) Africans or members of the African Diaspora;
- The basic resources of such an organization shall substantially, at least fifty percent (50 %), be derived from contributions by the members of the organization. Where external voluntary contributions have been received, their amounts and donors shall be faithfully revealed in the application for membership. Any financial or other support or contribution, direct or indirect, from a government to the Organization shall be declared and fully recorded in the financial records of the Organization;
- Provide information on funding sources for the preceding three years.
- For regional and continental CSOs, show proof of activities in which they are engaged or are operative in at least three Member States of the AU.

In addition to the above, Article 6 provides that CSOs that discriminate on the basis of religion, gender, tribe, ethnicity, race, or political opinion shall be barred from representation to the ECOSOCC. Finally, members must adhere to a code of ethics and conduct for civil society organizations affiliated to or working with the AU. The members of the ECOSOCC shall have a mandate of four years and may be re-elected only once.

Members of the ECOSOCC may resign in writing and the resignations shall be addressed to the Presiding Officer who shall declare the seat vacant. Where a member of the ECOSOCC fails to maintain the eligibility requirements stipulated in the Statute, the Presiding Officer, after consultation with the Bureau, shall call upon the ECOSOCC to remove that member from office and the seat shall be declared vacant. The Presiding Officer shall notify the other members of the ECOSOCC after verifying the vacancy created by the operations of this Rule and the vacancy so created shall be filled at the next election of the ECOSOCC.[9]

A member of the ECOSOCC who has not been represented at three consecutive meetings of the General Assembly or whose representative, without a valid reason, has not attended three consecutive meetings to which he or she has been duly invited shall not be eligible for re-election. A representative of a member of the ECOSOCC who is unable to attend a meeting to which he or she has been duly invited shall give notice of his or her absence in writing to the Presiding Officer or the Chairperson of the Committee of which the representative is a member. A representative who is unable to attend a meeting other than a meeting of the General Assembly, may, after giving notice to the Presiding Officer or Chairperson of the Committee that called the meeting, appoint another representative of a member of the ECOSOCC to act as his proxy at the meeting. The form of proxy shall be determined by the Standing Committee. A proxy so appointed shall attend only the meeting in respect of which the proxy was issued.[10]

---

[9] Rule 65 of the ECOSOCC Rules of Procedures.
[10] Rule 66 of the ECOSOCC Rules of Procedures.

A member of the ECOSOCC may remove its representative by giving written notice of the removal to the Presiding Officer. The member may immediately replace the representative by another person who shall be duly accredited by the Credentials Committee. Where a representative serving on either the Standing Committee or Sectoral Cluster Committee fails to attend three consecutive Committee meetings to which he or she has been duly invited and he or she has not appointed a proxy, the Chairperson of the Committee shall call upon the representative to vacate the seat. The representative of a member of the ECOSOCC may tender his or her resignation in writing addressed to the Presiding Officer who shall declare the seat vacant. When a vacancy is declared in accordance with this rule and if the term of office of the member has more than six months to run from the date of the declaration of the vacancy, the Standing Committee shall immediately notify the member concerned and the member shall within one month of the notification replace the representative. The credentials of such representative shall immediately be forwarded to the Credentials Committee for accreditation. If duly accredited, a representative appointed to fill a vacancy under these rules shall hold office for the remainder of the term of the member he or she is representing.[11]

4. Institutional Structure of the ECOSOCC

According to Article 8 of the ECOSOCC Statutes, the organ has some key entities, headed by a bureau of five regional representatives.[12] The structure of the ECOSOCC includes: (a) General Assembly; (b) Standing Committee; (c) Credentials Committee; (d) Sectoral Cluster Committees; and (e) a Secretariat.

---

[11] Rule 67 of the ECOSOCC Rules of Procedures.
[12] Current members of the bureau are: Interim Presiding Officer Prof. Wangari Mathaai, and the Interim Deputy Presiding Officers: (1) M. Maurice Tadajeu (Central), (2) Mrs. Fatima Zohra Karadja (North), (3) M. Charles Mutasa (South), and (4) M. Ayo Aderinwale (West). (In line with the distinction between the Interim ECOSOCC Assembly and the Permanent Assembly, the information on the Bureau needs to be updated to reflect the composition of the current Bureau.

4.1. General Assembly

The General Assembly is the final authority and the highest decision, and policy-making body within the ECOSOCC. It is composed of all ECOSOCC members (150 members). The term of office of the General Assembly is four years and members can be re-elected only once.[13]

During its meeting held in Sharm el-Sheikh (Egypt) on 24-28 June 2008, the AU's Executive Council requested the Chairperson of the Commission, in consultation with the Chairperson of the Union, to set an early date for launching the Permanent Assembly of the ECOSOCC and to take all necessary measures to facilitate the process. The Council also requested all Member States to provide adequate support for this process and to the Permanent Assembly of the ECOSOCC as soon as it is established. Finally, the Council requested the Permanent Assembly of the ECOSOCC, when established, to take urgent and necessary steps to ensure that elections are organized in the remaining Member States where elections have not yet taken place.[14]

In October 2008, the Permanent General Assembly was elected as a result of thorough consultation and development of the elections process, replacing the ECOSOCC initial interim structure.[15]

---

[13] Article 9(4) of the Statute.

[14] Decision on the report of the Commission on the Economic, Social and Cultural Council (ECOSOCC), AU Doc. EX.CL/412 (XIII)). Executive Council 13th Ordinary Council 24-28 June 2008, Sharm el-Sheikh, Egypt, AU Doc. EX.CL/Dec.422 (XIII).

[15] Although its Interim General Assembly was first convened in March 2005, the ECOSOCC was not officially launched and its Credentials Committee was not elected until September 2008.
The ECOSOCC interim assembly was considered to be a transitional arrangement to ensure the speedy launch of the ECOSOCC. Therefore, the Commission convened a General Civil Society Conference in Addis Ababa on 24 March 2005, which was constituted and launched as an interim General Assembly of the ECOSOCC. This Assembly elected an AU-civil society provisional working group, which was to serve as the interim standing committee (ISC) of the ECOSOCC. The mandate of the ISC was to facilitate the organization of elections for CSO representatives from national, regional, continental, and Diaspora constituencies, in preparation for the launch of a permanent assembly of the ECOSOCC. ISC was given a 2-year mandate to put into place a permanent assembly. The election of CSO representatives into the

The launch of the Permanent General Assembly allowed the ECOSOCC to start functioning on a permanent basis.

The ECOSOCC constituencies are the CSOs that elect the representatives and give them the mandate to sit in the ECOSOCC General Assembly. The membership of the ECOSOCC General Assembly lies with CSOs, and not with individuals. Individuals are only representatives of elected CSOs.[16]

According to Article 9 of the ECOSOCC's Statute, the functions of the General Assembly are as follows:
- Elect members of the Standing Committee for a term of 2 years and oversee its work;
- Prepare and submit advisory opinions and reports as appropriate;
- Submit proposals on the budget and activities of the ECOSOCC;
- Approve and amend the code of ethics and conduct for CSOs affiliated to, or working with, the Union;
- Review the activities of the ECOSOCC and propose appropriate actions and recommendations.

The General Assembly is headed by a presiding officer and five deputy presiding officers who make up the bureau of the Assembly,[17]

---

permanent the ECOSOCC General Assembly began on 31 October 2007 at the headquarters of the AU in Addis Ababa with the election of the continental CSO representatives. This was followed by election of national CSO representatives for 25 countries as well as representatives for the East, West and Southern African regions.

[16] Rule (2) of the ECOSOCC Rules of Procedures states that: "The General Assembly of ECOSOCC shall comprise the representative of CSOs elected at the national, regional, continental and the African Diaspora levels in accordance with Article 4 of the Statute of ECOSOCC and accredited by the Credentials Committee in accordance with Article 12 (2) of the Statute of ECOSOCC."

[17] Article 9/4 of the Statute provides: "The General Assembly shall:
a) Elect a Bureau composed of a Presiding Officer and five (5) Deputy Presiding Officers on the basis of equitable geographical distribution and rotation, including one (1) from the Diaspora.
b) The term of office of the Presiding Officer and the Bureau shall be two (2) years."
There was a specific Rule (Rule 5) in the draft Rules of Procedures of ECOSOCC titled "Election Tribunal." This Rule was deleted from the adopted ECOSOCC Rules of Procedures. Rule (5) of the draft Rules of Procedures stated that: Regarding "election of the Presiding Officer and the Deputy Presiding

each of whom serves a term of 2 years. The Bureau is eligible for re-election only once. The General Assembly ordinary sessions are to be held once every 2 years.[18]

The General Assembly may also convene extraordinary sessions under conditions specified in the Rules of Procedures of the ECOSOCC. According to Rule 21 of the Rules of Procedures, extraordinary sessions shall be held if requested by: (i) a simple majority of the members of the General Assembly, or (ii) the Standing Committee in consultation with the Bureau; or (iii) the Commission. A request for an extraordinary meeting may also be made by a member state of the Union or the Pan-African Parliament. In the event of such a request, the Presiding Officer shall communicate the request to all the members of the ECOSOCC.

The Presiding Officer shall circulate the Notice of the opening date and venue of an Ordinary Session at least 28 days before the commencement of the Ordinary Session and at least seven (7) days

---

Officers the General Assembly, the election tribunal set up under Rule 5 shall have regard to the following considerations:
(a) The equitable geographical rotation of the office of Presiding Officer among the five regions of Africa.
(b) The four Deputy Presiding Officers shall be elected on the basis of equitable geographical distribution from regions other than the one to which the Presiding Officer belongs."
According to Rule (6) of the Rules of Procedures of the ECOSOCC, (titled "Methods of Elections") states that:
"1. Candidates for any election shall be nominated by a duly accredited representative and seconded by another.
2. Except where the General Assembly otherwise decides, voting shall be by secret ballot.
3. The candidate with the highest number of valid votes cast shall be declared duly elected.
4. Where only one elective post is to be filled by the election, and no candidate emerges as winner after the first ballot:
(a) A second ballot shall be held and shall be restricted to the two candidates with the largest number of votes in the first ballot.
(b) If the second ballot results in a tie, the process shall be recommenced till a victor emerges.
5. Where the first ballot produces a tie of three or more candidates, a special ballot shall be held to reduce their number to two and if the special ballot still results in a tie, the rule outlines in 5 (b) will apply."

[18] Article 9(3) of the Statute.

before an Extraordinary Session.[19] The Presiding Officer, in consultation with the Standing Committee, may, in special cases, alter the date and place of a meeting. At the request of a simple majority of the members of the ECOSOCC, the Presiding Officer may also alter the date and place of a meeting.

4.2. Standing Committee

The Standing Committee runs the ECOSOCC in between sessions of the General Assembly. The Standing Committee is composed of 18 members to be elected by the General Assembly, with a 2-year term of office. The Chairperson of each Sectoral Committee serves as *ex-officio* member of the Standing Committee together with two representatives of the AU Commission. The Standing Committee meets as often as circumstances require.

The Standing Committee coordinates the ECOSOCC's work, prepares the General Assembly's meetings and submits the ECOSOCC's annual report to the Assembly.

It also plays a role in the meetings of the General Assembly of the ECOSOCC, where it approves the provisional agenda for each meeting,[20] as well as performing the role assigned to the ECOSOCC itself. For example, when a matter requiring an opinion or advisory report is referred to the ECOSOCC by the Commission, the Pan-African Parliament, one of the Specialised Technical Committees of the African Union (STCs), or any other authorised organ of the Union, the Presiding Officer, in consultation with the other members of the Standing Committee, shall identify a Committee with the relevant expertise from among the Sectoral Committees to consider the matter.

---

[19] Rule (23) of the Rules of Procedures of the ECOSOCC. It should be noted that the draft Rules of Procedures (Rule 31) stated that the notice of an Ordinary Session shall be circulated at least six (6) weeks before the commencement of the Ordinary Session.

[20] Rule 25 of the Rules of Procedures of the ECOSOCC. It should be noted that as per Rule 34 of the draft Rules of Procedures, the Standing Committee was entrusted to draw up the agenda of the meeting, while according to Rule 25 the role of the Standing Committee is limited to the approval of the agenda of the meeting.

The Presiding Officer shall immediately notify the Chairperson of the Committee of the matter and the time limit, if any, for dealing with it.

The Sectoral Committee to which a matter has been referred shall forthwith, or within the time limit prescribed, if any, prepare and submit draft opinions and/or advisory reports on the questions referred to it in accordance with these rules. Subject to the approval of the Standing Committee, the Sectoral Committee, may consult with and hold joint meetings with any other Sectoral Committee or organ of the Commission of the Union.[21]

4.3. Credentials Committee

The Credentials Committee, established under the ECOSOCC Statutes,[22] consists of nine members, to serve for a term of two years, as follows:
- One CSO representative from each of Africa's five regions;
- One CSO representative from the African Diaspora;
- One nominated representative for special interest groups such as vulnerable groups, the aged, the physically challenged, and people living with HIV/AIDS; and
- Two representatives of the Commission.

The Credential Committee is responsible for reviewing the list of nominations for membership in the General Assembly to ensure nominees comply with the criteria set out in the ECOSOCC Statutes. It is responsible for examining the credentials of CSO members of the ECOSOCC and of their representative.[23]

---

[21] Rule 14 of the Rule of Procedures of the ECOSOCC.
[22] Article 12/1 of the Statute.
[23] Article 12 of the Statute. It should be noted that the draft Rules of Procedures contained a specific rule (Rule 18) titled "functions and powers of the credential committee." The adopted ECOSOCC Rules of Procedures contain no similar rule. Rule 18 of the draft Rules of Procedures of the ECOSOCC provided that:
"1. The Credentials Committee shall be responsible for examining the qualifications and credentials of the representatives of members of ECOSOCC.
2. The Credentials Committee shall carry out such other functions as the General Assembly may assign to it."

Rule 30 of the Rules of Procedures of the ECOSOCC stated that all questions regarding the validity of the credentials of any representative shall be submitted in writing to the Secretariat. The Secretariat shall immediately forward all credentials and questions submitted to it to the Credentials Committee.[24]

4.4. Sectoral Cluster Committees

The Sectoral Committees were established as the key operational mechanisms of the ECOSOCC and are entrusted with principal tasks to formulate opinions and provide inputs to policies and programmes for the AU,[25] along with the preparation and submission of advisory opinions and reports for the ECOSOCC. The Sectoral Committees create space for ample input from gender advocates. These committees can also perform any other functions as may be assigned to them.[26]

There are 10 Sectoral Cluster Committees that are the key operational mechanisms of the ECOSOCC to the AU.[27] The current Sectoral Cluster committees are as follows:[28]

---

[24] This rule is based on Rule 42 of the draft Rules of Procedures. We believe that Rule (42) was much better if we compare it to Rule (30). Rule (42) stated clearly that: "the Credentials Committee has sole authority to decide all questions concerning credentials and accredited representatives must display approved credentials at all times during meetings."

[25] Article (11/1) of the Statutes and Rule (10/1) of the ECOSOCC Rules of Procedures. It should be noted that Rules (15/1) of the draft Rules of Procedures stated that: "The General Assembly shall establish at least 12 Sectoral Committee as its key operational mechanism."

[26] Article (11/3) of the Statute.

[27] Rule (10/1) of the Rules of Procedures of ECOSOCC states that: "The General Assembly shall establish at least 10 Sectoral Cluster Committees as its key operational mechanism." It should be noted that the corresponding rule (Rule 15/1) of the ECOSOCC draft Rules of Procedures stated that: "The General Assembly shall establish at least 12 Sectoral Committees as its key operational mechanism."
In this regards, it should be noted that during the three-days meeting of the AU summit in Sirte, Libya (2009), the ECOSOCC was offered the opportunity to constitute cluster committees that would set ECOSOCC on the path to fulfilling the mandate given it by the AU. See the website of the Affiliated Networks on Social Accountability in Africa (ANSA-Africa).

(i) Peace and Security Committee: created to deal with conflict anticipation, prevention, management, and resolution, post-conflict reconstruction and peace building, prevention and combating of terrorism, use of child soldiers, drug trafficking, illicit proliferation of small arms and light weapons, and security reforms.

(ii) Political Affairs Committee: created to deal with human rights, rule of law, democracy, good governance, power sharing, electoral institutions, humanitarian affairs, and assistance.

(iii) Infrastructure and Energy Committee: created to deal with energy, transport, communications, infrastructure, and tourism.

(iv) Social Affairs and Health Committee: created to deal with health, children, drug control, population, migration, labour and employment, family, the aged, the physically challenged, sports, youth, and protection of social integration.[29]

(v) Human Resources, Sciences and Technology Committee: created to deal with: education, illiteracy, information technology, communications, human resources, and technology.

(vi) Trade and Industry Committee: created to deal with trade, industry, handcrafts, customs, and immigration matters.

(vii) Rural Economy and Agriculture Committee: created to deal with rural economies, agriculture and food security, livestock, the environment, natural resources, and desertification.

(viii) Economic Affairs Committee: created to deal with financial matters within Africa, as, economic integration, monetary and financial affairs, and private sector development, including the informal sector and resource mobilization.

(ix) Women and Gender Committee: created to deal with the women, gender, and development as cross-cutting issues. This committee can advise the AU regarding gender mainstreaming in all its activities in accordance with its principle of gender equality.[30]

---

[28] According to Article (11) of the ECOSOCC Statute, these committees may be amended by the General Assembly as it may be deemed necessary from time to time.

[29] Currently chaired by Mr. Muzwakhe Sighudla.

[30] It has been noted that this Committee should collaborate with the Women, Gender and Development Directorate of the Commission as well as the Executive Council of the AU. Accordingly, it has been noted that the ECOSOCC is well placed as a platform for women's voices due to its advisory mandate. See:

(x) Cross-Cutting Programs Committee: created to deal with issues not explicitly dealt with by other committees, such as HIV/AIDS and International cooperation.

It has been noted by the President of the Permanent General Assembly of ECOSOCC that: "the activation of Cluster Committees has set the pace for the full operationalization of the ECOSOCC. The Committees will work with the various departments of the Commission and organs and units or instruments of the Union in order to achieve their objectives. In particular the Peace and Security Cluster Committee will start to coordinate CSO interaction with the Peace and Security Council of the Union in accordance with the Livingstone formula adopted by the Peace and Security Council in December 2008.[31]

Rule (10/2) of the ECOSOCC Rules of Procedures provides that the General Assembly shall establish ten Sectoral Cluster Committees. The number of members who shall constitute each Committee shall be determined by the General Assembly. Every representative of a member of the ECOSOCC shall belong to at least one Committee except the Presiding Officer. No member may belong to more than two Committees except where there is a justifiable need to ensure fair representation of the Member States of the Union and the African Diaspora. Each Committee shall be headed by a Chairperson assisted by a Secretary, both of whom shall be chosen from among its members. Each Cluster Committee shall include *ex-officio* members drawn from CSO networks and organizations with pointed expertise in the relevant sectors.[32] The Rules of Procedures, unlike the draft Rules of Procedures, do not refer to the terms of the members of each Committee.[33]

Each Sectoral Cluster Committee shall submit to the ECOSOCC a report on their activities as well as those of their subsidiary bodies.

Stefiszyn, K., "The African Union: Challenges and Opportunities for Women," *African Human Rights Law Journal*, 5 (2005) pp. 370, 378.

[31] Report of the President of the Permanent General Assembly of the Economic, Social and Cultural Council of the African Union (ECOSOCC), July 2009, p. 2.

[32] Rule (10) of the Rules of Procedures of the ECOSOCC.

[33] It should be noted that the draft Rules of Procedures contained a rule (Rule 16) that stated: "… members of each Committee shall serve for a term of four years."

The Secretariat shall draw up the Guidelines for the contents of the reports to be submitted to the ECOSOCC. Such Reports shall be circulated at least four weeks before the opening session of the General Assembly. If, in the opinion of the General Assembly, the report does not contain sufficient information, it shall require additional information, indicating the manner as well as the time limit within which the additional information shall be submitted.[34]

4.5. *The Secretariat*

The ECOSOCC has a secretariat that is hosted by the African Citizens Directorate Organization (CIDO) within the office of the Chairperson of the AU. Article (14) of the ECOSOCC Statute provides that: "the competent unit of the Commission shall serve as the Secretariat of ECOSOCC within the Commission."[35]

The Secretariat is charged with managing the day-to-day activities of the ECOSOCC, ensuring, among other things, that the CSOs' inputs that come through the ECOSOCC are fed into the broader AU processes, and that feedback is appropriately channelled to the relevant the ECOSOCC organs and role players.[36]

The ECOSOCC, through its Secretariat in CIDO, has set in motion the process of mapping African civil society organizations. The objective of the mapping exercise is to identify CSOs in the various thematic areas and use the strength they represent and their participation, to foster partnership globally and within the AU framework. In this regard, it was noted by the President of the Permanent General Assembly of the ECOSOCC that:

---

[34] Rule (69) of the ECOSOCC Rules of Procedures.
[35] The ECOSOCC Rules of Procedures, unlike the draft Rules of Procedures, contain no provision regarding the Secretariat. The draft Rules of Procedures contained two rules on this matter. Rule (20) provided that: "the Commission shall establish a Secretariat for ECOSOCC. The Secretariat shall co-ordinate the ECOSOCC activities with CIDO and shall serve as the focal point for the ECOSOCC activities." Rule (21) provided that: "In addition to its duties under Rule 20, the Secretariat also performs other duties as the Commission may assign to it."
[36] Article (14) of the Statute.

"the exercise will allow for a better interface between AU, Member States and Civil Society and provide effective support for electoral processes of ECOSOCC and its contribution to the wider family of the African Union. The mapping of civil society organizations would also help the AU to identify the required technical support from the larger civil society community."[37]

The CIDO is also helping in the consideration by the ECOSOC of the rather complex issue of organizing the participation of the Diaspora in the ECOSOCC processes.

5. Conduct of Business of the ECOSOCC

The quorum for holding the meetings of the ECOSOCC is at least 51 percent of the members of the ECOSOCC. Representatives may request quorum verification through a motion and if the motion is carried the Presiding Officer shall proceed with quorum verification by initiating a Roll Call. The Presiding Officer may rule the motion dilatory and the ruling shall not be subject to appeal. If no quorum is formed, the Presiding Officer shall adjourn the meeting to a time he or she considers appropriate. The numbers of accredited representatives present at an adjourned meeting shall form a quorum.[38]

The Presiding Officer shall declare open and close the plenary meetings of the General Assembly, preside over the discussion and generally ensure the observance of these rules. In this regard, the Presiding Officer shall: (i) maintain order; and (ii) rule on points of order and procedure.

The Presiding Officer may, on his or her own initiative or at the request of a duly accredited representative, propose the following to the General Assembly:

---

[37] It should be noted that the idea of mapping African civil society organizations was one of the key recommendations of the Audit Panel of the Union that was endorsed by the Council and the Assembly. See: Report of the President of the Permanent General Assembly of the Economic, Social and Cultural Council of the African Union (ECOSOCC), July 2009, p. 3.
[38] Rule (31) of the Rules of Procedures of ECOSOCC.

(a) The closure of the list of speakers after announcing the names on the list;
(b) Limit the time each speaker may speak;
(c) Determine the number of times an accredited representative may speak on an item under discussion;
(d) Adjourn or close a debate with the consent of the General Assembly;
(e) Suspend or adjourn a meeting.[39]

Any member may submit a motion or a draft proposal on a subject or item on the provisional agenda. A draft proposal shall contain at least one preamble and one operative clause and must be sponsored by at least 10 duly accredited representatives. It shall be submitted to the Secretariat not later than the opening of the meeting at which that subject or item will be debated. The procedure for the submission of draft proposals or motions for a subject or item on the provisional agenda as well as the supplementary items shall be determined by the Standing Committee.[40]

Each member of the ECOSOCC shall have one vote and decision-making shall be by consensus,[41] failing which it shall be by a simple majority of those present and voting.[42]

---

[39] The decision, in this event, shall be taken only by two accredited representatives shall be allowed to speak on the motion in favour of each proposal and two against. The motion shall thereafter immediately be put to the vote. (Rule 32/3) of the ECOSOCC Rules of Procedures.

[40] Rule (33) of the ECOSOCC Rules of Procedures.

[41] Rule (64) provides that: "An accredited representative may request the adoption of an amendment, draft proposal, or texts of opinion or advisory report by consensus at any time after closure of a debate. The Presiding Officer shall encourage the adoption of amendments and draft proposals, texts of opinions and advisory reports by consensus.
The Presiding Officer shall ask whether there is any objection to a consensus. If there is no objection, the proposal shall be deemed to have been approved by consensus, but if there is any objection, a vote shall be taken in accordance with these rules."

[42] Rule (56/2) of the ECOSOCC Rules of Procedures. The draft Rules of Procedures (Rule 69) stated that: "the method of voting, stating that no decision shall be taken on any matter or issue unless a two-thirds majority or a figure nearest a two-thirds majority of the accredited representatives of the members of ECOSOCC is present and voting."

The texts of the proposals or resolutions and other formal decisions adopted by the ECOSOCC shall be distributed to all its members and other participants at the session. Such texts shall also be communicated to the Commission, Pan African Parliament, Member States of the AU and other organs of the AU.[43]

Representatives of Intergovernmental Organizations or Civil Society Organizations, which have been granted Observer Status, may participate in the deliberations of the ECOSOCC without the right to vote.[44]

6. Role and Function of the ECOSOCC

The aim of the ECOSOCC is to create a people-driven and community-based partnership between governments and all segments of civil society, particularly women, young people, and the private sector in order to strengthen cohesion and solidarity among African peoples. ECOSOCC provides a forum for African civil society to influence the policies and evaluate the implementation of AU programmes. This organ is meant to give effect to the principle of participation of the African peoples in the activities of the Union and recognition of the need to build a partnership between governments and all segments of civil society. In this regard, the ECOSOCC is to provide a solid foundation for democracy; guaranteeing observance of the rule of law, human rights, democratic transformation, and good governance.

According to Article (7) of its Statute, the ECOSOCC has wide-ranging functions, including those of undertaking studies recommended or deemed necessary by any other organ of the Union and submitting recommendations, contributing to the popularization of, popular participation in, and sharing of best practices and expertise

---

Rule (57) provides that: "Voting may be by a show of hands, open ballot, or by secret ballot if so demanded by the rules or by a simple majority of the representatives. If the vote is a tie, the Presiding Officer shall have a casting vote."

[43] Rule (70) of the ECOSOCC Rules of Procedures.
[44] Rule (69) of ECOSOCC Rules of Procedures.

regarding human rights, the rule of law, good governance, democratic principles, gender equality and child rights.

- The ECOSOCC operates mainly through ten Sectoral Cluster Committees, which formulate opinions and provide inputs into the policies and programmes of the AU. According to Article (11/2), these Sectoral Cluster Committees are required to prepare and submit advisory opinions and reports which take effect as "advisory opinions and reports of ECOSOCC."

In light of the above, it may be noted that the ECOSOCC has three roles: advisory, representative, and monitoring. As a representative organ, it is expected to connect African peoples in all their diversity to the AU, and by so doing, enhance the democratic foundations and legitimacy of the AU and its Member States. This will also lead to broadening of the space for people's participation at all levels of governance in Africa. In this context, the ECOSOCC serves as a network of expertise and as a catalyst to inject the values, knowledge, and ideas of African civil society into AU policy process. The ECOSOCC is also expected to monitor and evaluate the feedback on results achieved by the AU.

As for its advisory role, Article (22) of the AU's Constitutive Act, which states: "[t]he Economic, Social and Cultural Council shall be an advisory organ," while Article (3/1) of the ECOSOCC's Statute, states that: "ECOSOCC shall be an advisory organ of the African Union." Accordingly, all of the AU components and organs may request advisory opinions from ECOSOCC. Therefore, it is safe to conclude that the ECOSOCC can give advice to the AU Commission in relation to NEPAD and other relevant organs and institutions.[45] Moreover,

---

[45] In order to justify this view, the following brief example is given to clarify this point: an NGO with standing before the ECOSOCC wants to channel the views of children about a dam project in rural Ethiopia to NEPAD. It can choose to organize a children's forum where the children's views about the project and how it affects their lives can be profiled. Apart from blocking their passage to the only primary school in the area (making access to primary education difficult), it might transpire from the views of the children that the dam has increased the incidence of malaria among children living around it, thereby affecting their right to health. The children might also underscore that their right to life, survival and development is affected as the dam makes it significantly more difficult to catch fish. Accordingly, this NGO can carry out this study and submit recommendations as appropriate to the ECOSOCC which in turn can

some commentators also raised the possibility of the ECOSOCC to undertake studies and issues of its own initiative and recommending actions to the relevant AU organs. In these and other ways, the ECOSOCC would be in an advantaged position to secure strategic relevance within the AU.

It remains however to be seen how an advisory institution can influence an organization like the AU that has historically avoided consultation with civil society and policy debates involving the public.

7. Conclusion and Recommendation

The ECOSOCC is in a position to demonstrate two particular strengths: It is the vehicle through which the voice of the African people can make itself heard, and if it is able to partner with the necessarily wide range of civil society organizations required for effective action, it will be able to provide the AU with the capacity to monitor Member States' actions and ensure their compliance with the commitments undertaken.

Launching the ECOSOCC as the official platform for civil society in the AU opened up the space for civil society organizations to demand more effective inclusion in the decision-making processes at the continental level. It presents opportunities for civil society to contribute to the regional and continental debates and discourses around democracy and development.

The ECOSOCC represents a real effort on the part of politicians to explicitly engage African civil society – including organizations representing the African Diaspora – in the continent's development, as a departure from widely held policies that view civil society with hostility. The ECOSOCC will enable African people to contribute to the programs and decisions of the AU, and to assume ownership of these programs and play a role in their implementation.

---

communicate the findings and recommendations to NEPAD, HSGIC or even the General Assembly of the Heads of States and Governments of the AU. It can submit the same to the Political Affairs Sectoral Cluster Committee which is in charge of human rights under the ECOSOCC. See: Advocating for Child Participation in NEPAD, The African Child Policy Forum, Addis Ababa, Ethiopia, March 2008, pp. 41-42.

Uncertainty exists, however, about the status, powers, and functions of the ECOSOCC, and its advisory role in the AU's decision-making processes. Relationships between the ECOSOCC and other organs of the Union have not been clarified, hampering the ability of 8 CSOs to have a greater voice in the activities of emerging processes and institutions.

It is important for the AU to strengthen people's participation and ownership of programs and initiatives and to ensure that the priorities and aspirations of the African people are fully reflected. However, much of Africa's civil society still has weak institutional capacity and may fail the ECOSOCC's current accountability test for membership. The organization must either delay enforcement of some areas of these membership tests or assist CSOs to meet its criteria if it wishes to be truly inclusive. The ECOSOCC should also be encouraging CSOs to organize themselves at the sub-regional level, since unity within sub-regions is a necessary condition for continental unity. Many African Governments are still uneasy about empowered African civil society and continue to treat it with disdain. In some Member States, CSOs face, at worst, threats, and at best, continuing operational concerns simply to keep their doors open. However, there are some specific ways in which the ECOSOCC could positively influence relations between national CSOs and their governments:

First, the ECOSOC could encourage ministries of foreign affairs to broaden the set of institutions that contribute to the development of national positions on AU policy proposals. This should include relevant parliamentary committees, constitutional bodies such as national human rights institutions, the ECOSOCC national chapters, the media, and other fora organised by civil society organizations. "Best practices" in this regard should be encouraged in all Member States.

Secondly, Member States should be encouraged to create civil society/ECOSOCC focal points in their departments of foreign affairs and provide guidance to embassies in Addis Ababa to respond to requests for information from civil society organizations.

To conclude, if the primary goal of the ECOSOCC is to bring civil society into the AU, the ECOSOCC must provide a two-way process. First, it should become more active in facilitating the participation of civil society organizations in the AU's work. This should be complemented by efforts at national level to encourage a closer relationship between governments and civil society organizations. Secondly, it should serve as a network of expertise and be a catalyst for the inclusion of values, knowledge, and ideas of African civil society into AU policy processes. This can also add value through the implementation and monitoring process within the AU structures, as the ECOSOCC is intended to provide policy advice and play an advocacy role.

PART III. ECONOMIC INTEGRATION, DEVELOPMENT AND GOOD GOVERNANCE

CHAPTER 9.
THE AFRICAN ECONOMIC COMMUNITY

Makane Moïse Mbenge and Ousseni Illy

1. Introduction

Africa was the first continent to create, in 1991, an economic community (hereinafter AEC) bringing all its States together. According to A. Mahiou,

"Although it was the last to emerge on the international scene, it is through a remarkable paradox that the young States of a 'new' continent defied a challenge that the older nations of other continents did not take up."[1]

The AEC was born out of the pan-Africanist ideal, first shared by the national liberation movements during the colonial era, then by the young independent African States. However, the tenor of this ideal varies from one State to another or from one era to another. For some, pan-Africanism connotes the need for immediate political unity of Africa, while for others it simply denotes solidarity among sovereign States, while for yet others, it is a long-term and phased project for uniting African States.[2]

---

[1] Mahiou A., « La Communauté économique africaine », *Annuaire Africain de Droit International* 1 (1993) p. 798. In this regard, the African venture differs, for example from the European experience. Europe adopted an approach which relied on a nucleus, extending gradually to include new States. It started in 1957 with Europe of the six countries, and has grown today into Europe of the 27. Such a project does not exist in Asia and America either, apart from the Free Trade Area of the Americas idea floated by the United States since 1990, which seems to be stalling since 2003.

[2] *Ibid.*, p. 799.

A.A. Yusuf & F. Ouguergouz (eds.), *The African Union: Legal and Institutional Framework. A Manual on the Pan-African Organization*, 187-202.

The most fervent proponent of immediate "pan-Africanist federation" was the first Ghanaian Head of State, Dr. Kwame Nkrumah, who at the time of the creation of the Organisation of African Unity (OAU) in 1963, made a case for a United States of Africa. Based on the realisation of the economic, political and diplomatic weakness of the newly-independent States, he felt the urgent need to achieve political unity, as this was a necessary precondition to advancement on the continent. He therefore rejected the stage by stage and sector by sector approach, by immediately proposing a federal form of organisation, with a common African government, parliament, defence, diplomacy, citizenship, bank and currency.[3]

This maximalist venture, supported by very few African States at the Addis Ababa Conference which saw the birth of the OAU, was considered not only too ambitious but also dangerous by others who preferred limiting themselves to a conventional intergovernmental organisation for cooperation. The latter group thus had no difficulty in defeating it and creating an *OAU for cooperation* rather than an *OAU for integration* as envisioned by Kwame Nkrumah.[4]

However, thirty years on, the tables seem to have turned somewhat in favour of the proponents of federalism. Faced with a continent whose economic situation is not improving since its political liberation, and in a global political context marked by dwindling public aid to development and the failure of a more just and balanced "New International Economic Order," African States decided in Abuja, Nigeria to create the Africa Economic Community on 3 June 1991. This was admittedly an over-ambitious project intended to merge all economic dimensions of the continent into an Economic Union, in the hope of finally ensuring an improvement in Africa's situation in the world.[5]

---

[3] Nkrumah K., *Africa Must Unite*, Panaf, 1963.
[4] Mahiou A., « La Communauté économique africaine », *op. cit.*, p. 799.
[5] Articles 4 and 6 of the Treaty establishing the AEC; also Bedjaoui M., « Le projet de création d'une communauté économique africaine : problèmes institutionnels et juridiques », *Revue Algérienne des relations internationales*, 3ème trimestre, 1986, pp. 35 et ss.

The AEC was born out of a long process which began with the Monrovia Symposium of 1979. This Symposium which was held in Liberia in February 1979 was the outcome of several meetings of African leaders on the issue of the economic independence of Africa. During those various meetings, there was the painful realisation that if Africa wanted to lift itself out of underdevelopment, it could only count on itself. One of the meetings was the Eleventh Extraordinary Session of the OAU Council of Ministers, held in Kinshasa, in the Democratic Republic of Congo (ex Zaire) in December 1976. This session resulted in the adoption of the "Kinshasa Declaration" which proclaimed the permanent sovereignty of African States over African natural resources and called for the establishment of an African Common Market, an African Energy Commission and an African Economic Community. In the same vein, the Fourth Conference of Ministers of the Economic Commission for Africa, held in Kinshasa in February 1977, adopted The Revised Master Plan for a New International Economic Order in Africa.[6] This fourth Conference further elaborated on the concept of individual and collective autonomy of Africa. Finally, the OAU Summit Meeting held in Libreville Gabon in July 1977 approved the recommendations in the "Kinshasa Declaration" and The Revised Master Plan.

In anticipation of disengaging from the old order and taking control of the development of Africa, African leaders, at the request of the Secretary General of the OAU, met in Monrovia in February 1979 in a symposium whose purpose was to outline the foundation for the growth and development of Africa by the year 2000. The conclusions of the Monrovia Symposium were reviewed by the Fifth Economic Commission for Africa Conference of Ministers, in Rabat, from 20–28 March 1979, which also adopted a document on "The Economic Development Strategy for Africa."[7] This document was then submitted for adoption to the Summit Meeting of OAU Heads of State and Government which convened an extraordinary session to discuss African economic issues, in April 1980.

---

[6] Ikome F., *From the Lagos Plan of Action to the New Partnership for Africa's Development. The Political Economy of African Regional Initiatives*, Institute for Global Dialogue, Midrand, South Africa, 2007, p. 72.
[7] *Ibid.*, p. 73.

This summit meeting took place on 28 and 29 April 1980 in Lagos, Nigeria. In their final declaration, the Heads of State adopted the Lagos plan of action for the economic development of Africa and the Final Act of Lagos (Annex I to the Plan of Action) with a view to implementing "The Economic Development Strategy for Africa" outlined in Monrovia and reviewed in Rabat a year earlier.[8]

In the Final Act of Lagos the African Heads of State and Government reaffirmed their "commitment to set up, by the year 2000, on the basis of a treaty to be concluded, an African Economic Community, so as to ensure the economic, social and cultural integration of our continent."[9]

The Conference of Heads of State and Government resolved to initiate the process leading to the creation of that Community. It urged the Secretary General of the OAU to implement the decision in collaboration with the United Nations Economic Commission for Africa. The Secretary General held consultations in this regard, and the preparatory works culminated in the signing by 51 out of the 52 OAU States of the Treaty establishing the AEC on 3 June 1991. This Treaty entered into force on 12 May 1994. It was reaffirmed and endorsed by the African Union (AU), which succeeded the OAU on 26 May 2001.[10]

It is this Treaty whose genesis has just been retraced which will be the subject of this Chapter. Emphasis will be placed on the objectives of the Treaty as well as the strategies it deploys in order to attain continental African economic integration. Regarding the bodies, there is no more autonomous institutional framework for the AEC since the creation of the African Union[11] as shown in Part II of this *Manual* which addresses the structure and organs of the AU.

---

[8] The Plan of Action and the Final Act are available on the website of the Economic Commission for Africa.
[9] Section II.A of the Lagos Final Act.
[10] Preamble of the Constitutive Act of the AU.
[11] Article 33 of the Constitutive Act of the AU.

2. Objectives of the AEC

In concluding the Abuja Treaty, African States set themselves an ambitious objective from the onset: the creation of an integrated community which emphasises, but does not limit itself to economic issues. Two types of objectives can be inferred from the AEC Treaty: the general or long-term objectives and the specific or immediate objectives.

2.1. General or Long-Term Objectives

These are: (a) the traditional issue of economic development in Africa; and (b) the other equally long-standing one of a better integration in international trade.

2.1.1. African Economic Development

Regional integration as a strategy for African economic development is not new. In order to fill the void on economic cooperation created by the OAU Charter,[12] African States had to establish the AEC in the hope that this new institution would assist them to achieve integration and overcome their economic underdevelopment. In its Preamble, the Treaty establishing the AEC notes the "various factors which hinder the development of the Continent and seriously jeopardise the future of its peoples" and recalls the responsibility of African Heads of State to "develop and utilise the human and natural resources of the Continent for the general well-being of our peoples in all fields of human endeavour."[13]

The AEC was specifically conceived as a framework that would enable Africa:

> "(a) To promote economic, social and cultural development and the integration of African economies in order to increase economic self-reliance and promote an endogenous and self-sustained development;

---

[12] The OAU was essentially a political organisation and development issues were not really accorded a prominent position. Its Constitutive Charter remains evasive on this matter (Article II).
[13] Preamble of Treaty establishing the AEC, paragraphs 4 and 3.

(b) To establish, on a continental scale, a framework for the development, mobilisation and utilisation of the human and material resources of Africa in order to achieve a self-reliant development;

(c) To promote co-operation in all fields of human endeavour in order to raise the standard of living of African peoples, and maintain and enhance economic stability, foster close and peaceful relations among Member States and contribute to the progress, development and the economic integration of the Continent; and

(d) To coordinate and harmonize policies among existing and future economic communities in order to foster the gradual establishment of the Community."[14]

2.1.2. A Better Integration of Africa in Global Trade

Since independence, African States have experimented with several strategies in an attempt to move their peoples out of economic stagnation and underdevelopment and to actively participate in global trade. The first strategies were the autarchic type, marked by national development plans and protectionist measures that translated into high trade (customs) barriers. The first attempts of economic integration were based on this strategy of import substitution. They were also meant to challenge the post Second World War neo-liberal global economic order through the quest for a new, more balanced and just economic order. The result yielded by this policy by the end of the 1980's was however disappointing; the total revenue of Africa remained insignificant (lower than that of Spain for example). The average GDP per country was equal to that of a city of 60,000 inhabitants in an industrialised country, and the entire continent accounted for less than 3% of world trade.[15]

Given this situation, new strategies had to be developed. African States realised that international trade is one of the instruments of development and instead of excluding themselves,

---

[14] Article 4.1 of the AEC Treaty.
[15] Tenier J., *Intégrations régionales et mondialisation, op. cit.,* p. 86. These figures have not really changed today. Some, like world trade, where Africa's share has fallen from 4 to 2% between 1970 and 2000. Hugon P. (dir.), *Les économies en développement à l'heure de la régionalisation,* Paris, Karthala, 2003, p. 16.

they needed to deploy strategies that would ensure them a prominent position. This new orientation emerged and crystallised in the new economic integration accords of the early 1990's. There, African countries freely opted for liberal policies, and the regional liberalisation of trade was henceforth seen as a means of meeting global competition and a vehicle for more active participation in international trade.

The AEC is more or less within this scheme. Article 42.1 (c) of its Treaty is on "North-South Trade" and provides that Member States pledge to undertake measures intended to "Promote better terms of trade for African commodities and improve market access for Community products" and further pledge to participate, "as a group" in international trade negotiations under the ambit of GATT (WTO) and UNCTAD, or any other forum dealing with these issues. The option of competing in world markets is therefore clear and the AEC is designed as an instrument to enhance African competitiveness and not only to protect Africa. For the architects of the AEC, such an approach requires the precondition of a stronger integration of African economies. Hence the proposal for the creation of a single African market.

2.2. Specific Objectives or "Immediate Goals": The Creation of a Pan-African Economic and Monetary Union (PEMU)

The immediate goals of the AEC Treaty do not necessarily translate into the instant creation of PEMU – far from that, and this is evidenced in the projected schedule – but they rather signify that this Union is a priority objective and a necessary condition to the realisation of the objectives mentioned earlier i.e. economic development and a better integration into world trade.

Article 6 (f) (iii) of the AEC Treaty provides that the process of continental integration should culminate in the establishment of an African Central Bank, an African Monetary Fund as well as a single African Currency. These institutions depend on an economic and monetary union whose creation is expressly referred to in Article 6.[16]

---

[16] Article 6 (f) (ii) of the AEC Treaty.

Economic union is a form of economic integration which extends beyond the limits of a customs union or a common market. It is a kind of merger of the economies of the states concerned. Beyond economic and monetary union we are entering the realm of federated states.

By opting for this course, African states have thus set the standard of continental integration very high. Can they honour this commitment? That is the big question. In any event, the midterm achievements raise some doubts.

3. The AEC Integration Strategy: Continental Integration in Successive Stages

The AEC will be established progressively over a transitional period, not exceeding forty years, from the entry into force of the Abuja Treaty.[17] In this regard, six stages have been carefully defined, with specific deadlines and a number of specific actions for each one of them. Here, one cannot miss the extensive voluntarism of the signatories of the document.

3.1. Stage One: Strengthening Existing Regional Economic Communities (RECs) and the Establishment of New RECs

The AEC was established in a particular context characterized by the prior existence of various regional economic communities on the African continent. The question then was whether to build on the foundations of these communities or whether to simply set them aside and create the new pan African institution that was the AEC.

At the constituent meeting of the OAU, the same issue arose between the federalists and the anti-federalists. For the former, regional organisations were a reproduction of the colonial and post-colonial divisions of the continent, in accordance with the interests of the former colonialists. According to them, not only should African countries abstain from creating new ones, but they should also dissolve the existing ones, which were impediments to

---

[17] Article 6.5 of the AEC Treaty. Normally, the Community should be created within 34 years (Art. 6.1 of the Treaty). Given that the Abuja Treaty entered into force in 1994, the AEC integration process should end in 2034 at the latest.

African unity. For anti-federalists, however, regional organizations constituted the launching pad of the process of cooperation, followed by integration of the continent and as such, their replication and consolidation ought to be promoted, while emphasising the economic or technical dimensions and with due regard to the specific solidarity of each entity.[18]

We know that the outcome played in favour of the latter group. Thus, the architects of the AEC did not have to reopen this debate. Right from the outset, they opted for continental integration, using the RECs as pillars. However on account of their multiplicity at the time, it was necessary to select. Ideally, this would have meant one economic community per region of the continent, artificially divided into five regions for the purpose: North Africa, East Africa, West Africa, Central and Southern Africa.[19] At the time of the creation of the AEC, two of these regions did not have (or no longer had) RECs. These were East Africa, where the East African Community (EAC) had had been dissolved in 1977 and Southern Africa, where the Southern African Customs Union (SACU) was not suitable, bringing together only the five States situated in the southernmost end of Africa, to the exclusion of the other States of Southern Africa.

The communities were then identified in the other regions, pending the creation of regional communities in these two regions of the continent. Thus, in North Africa the Arab Maghreb Union was selected, while the Economic Community of Central African States (ECCAS) was chosen for Central Africa and the Economic Community of West African States (ECOWAS) for West Africa. Later on, the Southern African Development Community (SADC), then the Intergovernmental Authority on Development (IGAD) were added to these organisations. More recently, COMESA (Common Market for Eastern and Southern Africa), the EAC (re-established in 1999), and the Community of Sahel-Saharan States (CEN-SAD) were recognised as RECs of the AEC. Today, eight RECs make up the AEC, or at least are considered its pillars in its

---

[18] Mahiou A., « La Communauté économique africaine », *op. cit.*, p. 799.
[19] Resolution CM/RES.464 (XXVI) of the OAU Council of Ministers of 1 March 1976.

quest for pan-African economic integration towards which they should work to reinforce the process.

This stage of the continental African integration should not have lasted more than five years from the entry into force of the Abuja Treaty.[20] In principle therefore, it is now closed and there should be no further recognition of RECs by the AEC. One may however ponder over the place of smaller ("sub-regional") RECs which exist in all parts of the continent, such as the West African Economic and Monetary Union (UEMOA), the Monetary and Economic Community of Central Africa (CEMAC), or the Southern African Customs Union (SACU).

The AEC does not directly take them into account, but it does not overlook them either. It urges them to merge with the regional communities that it has already selected. But as we shall see, this task is not an easy one.

3.2. Second Stage: Freezing Trade Barrier Within Each REC

This stage, which is supposed to run at most for eight years from the end of the first stage,[21] is crucial for the integration process. By proscribing the introduction of new trade restrictions from the entry into force of the AEC Treaty, it leads the way to the next stage, i.e. the establishment of free trade areas (FTA). Article 6.2 (b) of the Treaty on the establishment of the AEC, provides that during this period, each REC must take measures to stabilize tariff barriers and non-tariff barriers, customs duties and internal taxes existing within it, as of the date of entry into force of the Abuja Treaty. At the same time, studies should be carried out with the object of drawing up a schedule for their phased elimination. Projections indicate that this phase should have been concluded in 2007. But this does not appear to be the case.

---

[20] Article 6.2(a) of the AEC Treaty. The Treaty entered into force in 1994. Thus, this stage's programme should have ended in 1999.
[21] Article 6.2(b)(*i*) of the AEC Treaty

3.3. Third Stage: Transformation of all RECs into FTAs then into Customs Unions

During this phase which should cover a period of at most ten years, beginning from the end of the second stage (2017), each REC should remove all barriers within its area, by establishing a FTA.[22] Further, during this same phase the Treaty requires each community to establish of full customs unions, by adopting a common external tariff *vis-à-vis* third States.[23]

This phase is one of the most important ones, but also one of the most difficult to achieve. How is the AEC to ensure that all the communities attain this level at the same time when each one is known to have its own schedule for liberalisation, depending on the political and economic realities of their constituent States? Herein lies one of the weaknesses of the AEC; setting deadlines for RECs without being in control of their programmes. It is therefore not surprising that the deadlines are often not effectively met.

3.4. Fourth Stage: Coordination and Harmonisation of the Regional Customs Unions and Creation of the African Customs Union

This is the shortest phase, lasting two years,[24] and understandably so. If indeed all the regional communities have evolved into customs unions, the continental customs union stage is then easily attainable. However, the architects of the Abuja Treaty may have been too optimistic. The coordination and harmonization of the various common external tariffs (CET) of the various RECs and the establishment of a single African CET are not such easy tasks as they may seem. Coordination entails ensuring that the activities of the communities concerned are channelled into continental integration, while harmonisation requires a more prescriptive action, involving the attainment of well-defined objectives and the restriction of the freedom of action of each partner. From the technical legal standpoint, coordination and harmonisation can sometimes

---

[22] Article 6.2(c) of the AEC Treaty.
[23] *Ibid.*
[24] Article 6.2(d) of the AEC Treaty. It should become effective in 2019.

involve the same procedures, the distinction being only in the outcome. Chronologically, however, coordination generally precedes harmonisation.

The AEC Member States intend to accomplish the coordination and harmonisation of the CET in a maximum period of two years. Although this indicates a resolve to move ahead more quickly with African integration, it may in practice turn out to be unrealistic.

3.5. Fifth Stage: Establishment of A Common Market

The African Common Market was to be established in the four years following the creation of the African Customs Union (2023).[25] In this regard, four major activities would be carried out during this phase:

1) The adoption of a common policy in several areas such as agriculture, transport and communications, industry, energy and scientific research;
2) The harmonisation of monetary, financial and fiscal policies;
3) The implementation of free movement of persons as well as the rights of residence and establishment; and
4) The creation of the common resources of the Community.[26]

When completed, these activities should open the way to the sixth and final stage of the AEC, with the creation of the Pan African Economic and Monetary Union.

3.6. Sixth Stage: Establishment of the Pan-African Economic and Monetary Union.

This is the final stage of the continental African integration process. Article 6.2 (f) of the Abuja Treaty provides that during the five years following the establishment of the African Common Market, the African economic integration would be completed with the establishment of the African Economic and

---

[25] Article 6.2(e) of the Abuja Treaty.
[26] Ibid.

Monetary Union (2028). This Union will be supported by the creation of an African Monetary Fund as well as an African Central Bank with a single currency.[27]

4. Conclusion

It is difficult today to make an overall evaluation of the AEC for the simple fact that the process is still ongoing. However, twenty years after its creation, it does not seem to be achieving its mission of channelling integration efforts in the continent towards the much-expected African common market. The first phase of the process is already fraught with problems, since instead of the five regional communities initially proposed, it has to deal with eight RECs, besides the six other smaller integration schemes that it is obliged to take into account. Consequently, the harmonisation process has also become complicated. Regarding the other phases of the process, particularly the second (i.e. freezing of barrier levels within the RECs planned to end in 2007), there is no clear indication that it has been achieved. It is therefore difficult today to know exactly where we are in the AEC schedule. Lately, the issue of the creation of the Central Bank and the African Monetary Fund has been raised, but if it were to come into being at this stage, it would be completely outside the AEC process, since as per the AEC Treaty these two institutions were listed for the end of the process, after the establishment of the common market, which for now is illusory.

Further, the AEC is suffering from several flaws, including the legal confusion surrounding its relationship with the AU and with the RECs. The position of the AEC in the institutional AU set-up remains ambiguous. The AEC was set-up by the OAU, and its treaty considered it as an integral part of that organisation. Legally however, these were two separate and distinct organisations, obviously with common organs, such as the Assembly of Heads of State, the Council of Ministers, the Secretariat, but also separate organs, like the Court of Justice, the Specialised Technical Committees, etc.

---

[27] Article 6.2(f)(iii) of the Abuja Treaty.

The concrete relationships of the two organisations had never been clarified.

The AU, which succeeded the OAU, did not significantly improve the situation. The Constitutive Act of the AU which was adopted on 11 July 2000 in Lomé, Togo, provides that it shall "take precedence over and supersede any inconsistent or contrary provision" of the Abuja Treaty.

Apart from the legal ambiguity and lack of clarity regarding the relationship between the two entities, this situation is awkward for the AEC, since in practice, it is steered by the AU (specifically the AU Commission) which is more preoccupied with political issues. All the Union's resources (already meagre) are channelled into those efforts, thus placing the AEC on the back burner.

It is therefore not surprising that the AEC currently lacks visibility and is virtually relegated to the bottom of the continental priority list. Besides the circle of African integration specialists and a few well-informed politicians, very few people, within and without Africa, are aware of the very existence of this pan-African economic integration project. At the current stage of the history of Africa, dominated by all sorts of political and military conflicts, the AEC ought to be an independent body within the African Union, or even outside it with its own secretariat, within which the continent's economic and trade issues are discussed.

Regarding AEC's relationship with the RECs, Article 10 of the Abuja Treaty provides that all decisions taken by the Assembly of Heads of State and Government of the AEC are mandatory for Member States and the Community's organs, excluding the Court of Justice, as well as for the RECs.[28] This provision could be considered a step forward in the implementation of the decision of African leaders to promote a real African integration. Placing the RECs under the AEC should have favoured integration at the continental level over sub-regional groupings. However, the conclusion of the Protocol on relationships between the AEC and the RECs in 1998, seems to have obscured this hierarchy defined in the Abuja Treaty. Adopted on 28 February 1998, pursuant to Article 88 of the AEC Treaty, this

---

[28] Article 10.2 of the AEC Treaty.

Protocol was signed among six regional communities (COMESA, CEN-SAD, ECCSA, ECOWAS, IGAD, SADC) and the AEC with the objective, *inter alia,* of strengthening the existing RECs, enhancing the coordination and harmonisation of policies, measures and programmes of RECs in light of the AEC treaty, promoting a closer cooperation among the RECs and providing an institutional framework to manage relationships between the RECs and the AEC.[29]

In order to attain this objective, the Protocol provides for a coordination framework, with well-defined coordination bodies, i.e. the Coordinating Committee and the Committee of Secretariat Officials which meets at least once a year (for the Coordinating Committee) and at least twice a year (for the Committee of Secretariat Officials).[30]

This Protocol never operated as it should. The overly cautious and exhortative nature of its wording is evidence of some distrust, particularly on the part of the RECs which do not appear to appreciate an "interference" by the AEC in their activities. Some excerpts from Article 4 reveal the spirit of the Protocol: "The Parties *undertake, ... to coordinate* their policies, measures, programmes and activities..."; "To this end, they agree to ensure that the policies, measures, programmes and activities which they adopt are not overlapping or do not impede the achievement of the objectives of the community." Everything is presented as if the AEC is an extraneous creation being imposed on the regional communities. Seen against this background, one can understand why the AEC is encountering problems coordinating their activities.

The Protocol does not stipulate the exact relationships between the AEC and the various RECs either. Are they members of the AEC? In other words, are the RECs organs or institutions of the AEC? Or conversely are they totally independent and equal organisations? In failing to answer these questions clearly, the Protocol contributed to the ineffectiveness of the AEC. Since the RECs are not statutory bodies of the AEC, they do not owe any obligation towards it.

---

[29] Article 3 of the Protocol.
[30] Articles 6, 8, and 10 of the Protocol. Articles 7 and 8 for the composition of these two organs.

Hence, the AEC's inability to coordinate and harmonise their activities. On 24 June 2004, the Coordinating Committee adopted a new protocol on the relationships between the AU and the RECs which will enter into force once the AU, (acting as the AEC's Secretariat), and chiefs of Secretariat of at least three regional communities would have signed it. This protocol, intended to replace the former protocol on relationships between the AEC and RECs, has two major innovations: firstly, the AU will be vested with the authority to sanction the RECs or member countries who do not comply with its directives, and secondly, it contemplates a mechanism for the resolution of disputes. Hopefully, this Protocol will help to bring a little more order to the efforts of harmonising the activities of the RECs.[31]

---

[31] UNECA/AU, *Assessing Regional Integration in Africa II: Rationalizing Regional Economic Communities*, Addis Ababa, Ethiopia, 2006, p. 110.

CHAPTER 10.
THE NEW PARTNERSHIP FOR AFRICA'S DEVELOPMENT (NEPAD)

Edward Kannyo

1. Introduction

The creation of the New Partnership for Africa's Development (NEPAD) and the transformation of the Organization of African Unity (OAU) into the African Union (AU) at the beginning of the 21st century reflected major changes in the political and ideological forces that had marked the continent's first 40 years of post-colonial history. They were both inaugurated in 2002.

After almost eight years of an ambiguous relationship, the AU decided in January 2010 to fully merge NEPAD into the parent body. The 14th Ordinary Summit Meeting held in Addis Ababa, Ethiopia in January 2010 decided that the NEPAD Secretariat will be replaced by the "NEPAD Planning and Coordinating Agency" (NPCA) that will be run from the office of the Chairperson of the Union.

This Chapter discusses the background, goals and structures of the NEPAD, including its affiliated African Peer Review Mechanism (APRM). It concludes with a preliminary assessment of the project since its inauguration in 2002.

2. Historical and Political Background

The first 40 years of African independence, beginning in the early 1960s for most countries, had witnessed both positive and negative economic and political developments. On the positive side, the process of decolonization had been completed with the independence of Namibia in 1990. A few years later, the racist regime of *apartheid* in South Africa came to an end.

During the 1960s, there were some notable achievements in many African countries in the realms of education, expansion of the physical infrastructure and some import-substitution industrialization. However, by the 1980s, the continent was marked by authoritarianism, State failure and venality and the deterioration of the economic and social conditions of the majority of the people.

Since the 1980s, African leaders had gradually come to accept the fact that in the emerging global economic and political system, they were in a weak position to put up or maintain barriers against external political pressures. Mismanagement and egregious violations of basic human rights were not going to be ignored by other States. The first major demonstration of this change was the drafting and approval of the African Charter on Human and Peoples' Rights in 1981. For the first time, the principle that other African States could investigate and pass judgment on the internal political affairs of a Member State was accepted.

Another major indicator of the political and social developments that would be reflected in NEPAD is the *African Charter for Popular Participation in Development and Transformation*. It was issued by a meeting of some 500 participants from a wide range of peasant, women, youth, trade union organizations, African governmental officials, UN agencies, non-African NGOs, donor governments and others who met in Arusha, Tanzania in 1990. The document emphasized the need to open up political processes and accommodate freedom of opinion and unfettered political participation by all citizens as well as the promotion of the status of women. It recommended the creation of a mechanism to monitor government performance in the areas of freedom of association, representative government, rule of law, freedom of the media and political accountability at all levels through checks and balances.[1]

---

[1] "*African Charter for Popular Participation in Development and Transformation*", Arusha, Tanzania, 16 February 1990.

Another major landmark in the evolving attitudes towards human rights was the declaration that came out of the First OAU Ministerial Conference on Human Rights in Africa that was held in April 1999 in Grand Bay, Mauritius. It stated, *inter alia*, that the promotion and protection of human rights "is a matter of priority for Africa," the observance of human rights "is a key tool for promoting collective security, durable peace and sustainable development," and affirmed the "interdependence" of the principles of good governance, the rule of law, democracy and development. Among the causes of human rights violations identified were: mismanagement, bad governance and corruption; lack of accountability in the management of public affairs; monopoly in the exercise of power; lack of independence of the judiciary; lack of independent human rights institutions and freedom of the press and association.[2]

Another major background factor that is relevant for the assessment of NEPAD is the end of the Cold War during the last decade of the 20th century. The dissolution of the Soviet Union and the continued evolution of China away from state socialism and towards a capitalist economic system all marked the practical and symbolic defeat of any serious alternative model to the capitalist system – at least for the foreseeable future. This factor was bound to have a profound impact on efforts of African leaders to promote alternative economic developmental models and protect state sovereignty and autonomy in an increasingly globalizing world.

At the institutional level, the formulation of NEPAD is traceable to the Organization of African Unity's (OAU) Extraordinary Summit Meeting held in Sirte, Libya in September 1999. It gave a mandate to Presidents Abdelaziz Bouteflika of Algeria and Thabo Mbeki of South Africa to undertake discussions with Africa's creditors with the view to the cancellation of their international debts. Subsequently, the South Summit of the Nonaligned Movement and the G77 meeting in Havana, Cuba, in April 2000 mandated Presidents Mbeki and Olusegun Obasanjo of Nigeria to engage in discussions with the G8 and the Bretton Woods Institutions on the economic and financial problems of the South.

---

[2] Grand Bay (Mauritius): Declaration and Plan of Action (1999).

The OAU Summit held in Togo in July 2000 authorized the three presidents to discuss Africa's economic problems with the Western Powers. Their work resulted in the publication of a document that came to be called the "Millennium Partnership for the African Recovery Programme" (MAP). In the meantime, President Abdoulaye Wade of Senegal drafted another document reflecting his ideas about the development of the continent's physical and social infrastructure named the "Omega Plan." It was presented to the Franco-African Summit in Yaoundé, Cameroon in January 2001.

At the time when the beginnings of what later became NEPAD were being formulated, three of the four presidents who played leading roles in the formulation of the project occupied top positions in important international organizations. Mbeki was head of the Non-Aligned Movement (NAM) as well as the Southern African Development Community (SADC); Obasanjo was head of the G-77; and Bouteflika was Chairman of the Organization of African Unity (OAU). President Mubarak of Egypt was also an important supporter of the project.

President Wade's *Omega Plan* highlighted the negative impacts of the reduction of official development assistance, the burden of foreign debt and the need for regional economic integration in Africa. It particularly focused on the needs of the continent in the areas of education, health, agriculture and physical infrastructure and the ways in which funds could be raised to address them. It proposed a regional and sub-regional strategy for identifying projects and mobilizing the necessary funds. The sources were to be domestic as well as international, official and private.[3]

The core ideas of the MAP were influenced by the vision of the "African Renaissance" expounded by Thabo Mbeki before he became President of South Africa.[4] It was a diagnosis, a critique and a set of prescriptions for putting Africa on the road to modernity, liberal

---

[3] Republic of Senegal, "One People-One Goal-One Faith, Omega Plan for Africa", Prepared by H.E. Mr. Abdoulaye Wade, President of the Republic of Senegal.

[4] "The African Renaissance, South Africa and the World" South African Deputy President Thabo Mbeki Speaks at the United Nations University, 9 April 1998.

democracy, economic prosperity and independence. The means of effecting the "Renaissance" included good governance, privatization and encouragement of the private sector, regional economic cooperation, the empowerment of women, the provision of basic services to the people and strong partnerships with external economic institutions and governments.

The MAP was described as "anchored" in the determination of Africans to "extricate themselves and the continent from the malaise of underdevelopment and exclusion in a globalizing world."[5] The document described the "mutual" interest of Africans and the rest of the international community in the rapid development of the continent and the consequent need for a partnership to resolve the pressing developmental problems. A key aspect of NEPAD that is foreshadowed in the MAP is the linkage between democracy and development:

> "The MAP has, as one of its foundations, the expansion of democratic frontiers and the deepening of the culture of human rights. A democratic Africa will become one of the pillars of world democracy, human rights and tolerance."[6]

President Mbeki presented the MAP to the World Economic Forum at Davos, Switzerland in January 2001.

During the 5th Extraordinary Summit of the OAU at Sirte in March 2001, a decision was made to merge the work of the four presidents, i.e. Bouteflika, Obasanjo, Mbeki and Wade into one continental program. The same meeting decided to replace the Organization of African Unity with the "African Union."

Earlier in November 2000, during a meeting of African Ministers of Finance held in Addis Ababa, Ethiopia, the Executive Secretary of the United Nations Economic Commission for Africa (ECA) had called for a "Compact with Africa" engaging the developed countries and African countries in the resolution of the continent's economic and social problems. The former would provide aid, debt relief and

---

[5] "Millennium Partnership for the African Recovery Programme" (MAP), (March 2001), Paragraph 1.
[6] *Ibid.*, para. 49.

market access while the latter would carry out political reforms in order to facilitate economic recovery and development. The ministers endorsed the idea and requested the ECA to develop it for further consideration at their next meeting.

The ECA eventually came up with the "Compact for African Recovery" published in April 2001 and described as a source of technical and analytical support for the MAP. The document emphasized the need for "Good Governance", peace and security; investment in economic and social spheres; a "new international partnership" between Africa and the international community; and enhancing the role of the private sector.[7] The African Ministers of Finance and Economic Development and Planning who met in May 2001 in Algiers, Algeria endorsed it.

As the process of formulating the initiative proceeded, steps were taken to involve officials and experts from a broader range of African States. They came from Egypt, Gabon, Mali, Tanzania and Mozambique, Uganda and Libya. Discussions were held between June and July 2001 in Abuja, Nigeria; Dakar, Senegal; Cairo; Egypt; and Pretoria, South Africa. The meetings led to the adoption of a new document synthesizing the principles and goals of the MAP and Omega. It was entitled *A New African Initiative: Merger of the Millennium Partnership for the African Recovery Programme and the Omega Plan* (NAI).

In July 2001, the NAI was presented to and approved by the 37th Summit Meeting of the OAU (the last before the creation of the African Union) that was held in Lusaka, Zambia. The first meeting of the Heads of State and Government Implementation Committee (HSGIC) (comprising representatives of Nigeria, South Africa, Algeria, Senegal, Egypt, Mozambique, Botswana, Tunisia, Mali, Ethiopia, Mauritius, Rwanda, São Tomé and Príncipe, Gabon and Cameroon) met in Abuja, Nigeria in October 2001 and decided on the final name: the "New Partnership for Africa's Development."

---

[7] United Nations Economic Commission for Africa, "Compact for Africa Recovery, Operationalising the Millennium Partnership for the African Recovery Programme."

The first Summit Meeting of the new African Union (AU) held in Durban, South Africa in July 2002 endorsed NEPAD and adopted the "Declaration on Democracy, Political, Economic and Corporate Governance." The document asserted that the Heads of State and Government had agreed to work together in pursuit of the following objectives:
- Democracy and Good Political Governance;
- Economic and Corporate Governance;
- Socio-Economic Development;
- African Peer Review Mechanism.

The leaders declared that they were determined to enforce the rule of law, equality of all citizens and individual liberty; individual and collective freedoms, "including the right to form and join political parties and trade unions in conformity with the constitution", equality of opportunity for all, the right of political participation through free, credible and democratic processes involving periodic election of leaders for fixed terms of office; and adherence to the principles of the separation of powers, the independence of the judiciary and effective legislative organs. The Meeting formally endorsed the Peer Review Mechanism as one of the means to achieve the economic, social and political goals to which they committed themselves.[8]

3. Economic and Social Background

At the beginning of the new millennium, African economic indicators painted a bleak picture, particularly when juxtaposed against the much brighter economic and social conditions in other parts of the developing world. While the continent's 832 million people represented 13% of the global total, the region received only 1% of direct foreign investment and contributed only 2% of global trade. Of the world's least developed countries, over 30 were in Africa.

---

[8] African Union, "The New Partnership for Africa's Development (NEPAD), Declaration on Democracy, Political, Economic and Corporate Governance," OAU Doc. AHG/235 (XXXVIII), Annex 1.

The economic problems of African States – particularly the large external debt – had compelled large numbers of States to submit to the economic and financial tutelage of the International Monetary Fund (IMF) and the World Bank. A number of them had large portions of their annual operating budgets covered by foreign governments and other external agencies. The result was diminished capacity to independently determine domestic economic and social policy. The effort to preserve sovereign autonomy in domestic and international affairs was clearly compromised to a degree that could not have been anticipated in the halcyon early years of independence.

NEPAD reflects the results of several decades of theoretical reflections and debates as well as the practical experience of the African region with economic and political development strategies. By the end of the 1990s, there was a growing consensus among African and foreign academic, political and civic leaders concerning the roots of economic and political failure and prescriptions for the future.

The International Monetary Fund, the World Bank and Western governments began to move away from previous policies of conditionality and almost exclusive focus on economic indicators towards "partnership" and a broader view of the goals of development that included sustainability, equity and democracy. African leaders too came to the conclusion that they could not continue to receive economic aid without genuine commitment to improved governance and making serious efforts to create more liberal and democratic societies.

A final major background factor was the history of efforts to create regional economic and political integration schemes. The three oldest and most comprehensive such efforts are the East African Community (EAC); the Economic Community of West African States (ECOWAS) and the Southern African Development Community (SADC). Others include the Economic Community of Central African States (ECCAS); the Community of Sahelo-Saharan States (CEN-SAD); and the Common Market of Eastern and Southern Africa (COMESA).

In 1991, 51 African Heads of States meeting in Abuja, Nigeria signed a treaty establishing the modalities for creating the "African Economic Community" at the end of a long process of economic integration within a period of 30-40 years. The organizational framework was set up as an integral program of the OAU. It is noteworthy that two of the principles laid out in the treaty included: (Article 3) (g) "Recognition, promotion and protection of human and peoples' rights"; and (h) "accountability, economic justice and popular participation in development."

The objectives (Article 4) included: (a) promotion of the economic, social and cultural development and integration of the African economies; (b) establishment, on a continental scale, of a framework for the development, mobilization and utilization of the human and material resources of the continent and (d) coordination and harmonization of policies among existing and future economic communities "in order to foster the gradual establishment of the Community."[9] The goals and structures stipulated in the treaty presaged major aspects of the ambitions and structures of the African Union. It came into force in 1994.

In addition to efforts to create economic integration schemes, African leaders and international development agencies have endeavoured over the years to come up with developmental strategies defining the appropriate policies regarding the roles of the state, the market and foreign corporate agents. The most prominent have been:
- Revised Framework for Principles for the Implementation of the New International Order in Africa (1976)
- Monrovia Strategy (1979)
- Lagos Plan of Action for the Economic Development of Africa, 1980-2000 (LPA) and the Final Act of Lagos (1980)
- World Bank's Accelerated Development in Sub-Saharan Africa (1981)
- UN Program for Africa's Economic Recovery and Development (1986)
- African Alternative Framework to Structural Adjustment Programmes for Socio-Economic Recovery and Transformation (AAF-SAP, 1989)
- African Charter for Popular Participation for Development (1990)

---

[9] Treaty Establishing the African Economic Community, 3 June 1991, Abuja, Nigeria.

- United Nations New Agenda for the Development of Africa in the 1990s (UN-NADAF, 1991).

These developmental projects did not have much impact on the processes of regional socio-economic decline that continued apace in the 1980s and 1990s. A number of factors explain their failure, including political crises that distracted African leaders; autocratic, arbitrary and patrimonial political practices; limited and incipient indigenous private capital and the absence of serious commitment to the implementation of the political measures that these plans demanded. These failures led to major shifts in the theoretical and normative paradigms that had dominated the developmental discourse and practice during the first two decades of independence.

The African Alternative Framework to Structural Adjustment Programmes, published by the Economic Commission for Africa in 1989, reflected on the efforts to deal with the continued socio-economic decline of the 1980s. The document highlighted eight factors that were either causes or characteristics of underdevelopment, i.e.: (a) predominance of subsistence and commercial activities; (b) narrow production base with deficient technology; (c) unsupported informal sector; (d) a degraded environment; (e) the urban bias of development policies; (f) continental economic fragmentation; (g) external dependence; and (h) weak institutions. It criticized the "Structural Adjustment Policies" (SAP) that the IMF and the World Bank had been imposing on African and other countries as part of the effort to deal with their ballooning public debts.

The alternative suggested approach accepted some of the SAP perspectives, such as giving a greater role to the market and greater fiscal discipline but generally argued for a less doctrinaire approach ("adjustment with transformation"). The document advocated the goal of ending economic dependence, integration of economic activities within the region and stipulated the need to work towards full democracy and citizen participation in the implementation of the economic reforms.[10]

The United Nations also highlighted the nexus between participatory governance and economic transformation. *The UN New Agenda for the Development of Africa*, issued in 1991, stated that the international community "accepts the principle of shared responsibility and full partnership with Africa." The document asserted that African leaders were convinced that growth and development on a sustained and sustainable basis "can come about only as a result of the full participation of the people in the development process, and to this end continued to be committed to pursuing the process of democratization."[11]

A document issued in 1999 by the World Bank, *the Comprehensive Development Framework* (CDF) advocated a comprehensive and long-term approach to African development involving "a participatory national consultation process" that was not imposed on the country but was freely adopted. CDF emphasized partnership between government, civil society, the private sector and external assistance agencies.[12]

NEPAD was formulated and issued in the wake of the United Nations Millennium Summit that met in New York in September 2000. Described as the largest gathering of world leaders in history, it was attended by up to 150 world leaders and issued a Declaration reflecting their views and prescriptions for the global community at the start of the New Millennium. It stated, *inter alia*, that the central challenge the world faced was to ensure that globalization became a positive force for all the world's people: "...We recognize that developing countries with economies in

---

[10] United Nations, Economic Commission for Africa, "African Alternative Framework to Structural Adjustment Programmes for Socio-Economic Recovery and Transformation (AAF-SAP)", OAU Doc. E/ECA/CM.15/6/Rev.3.

[11] United Nations "New Agenda for the Development of Africa in the 1990s", UNGA Resolution 46/151, paras. 1 and 13.

[12] *"The International Monetary Fund, The Comprehensive Development Framework (CDF) and Poverty Reduction Strategy Papers (PRSP)"*, Joint Note by James D. Wolfensohn and Stanley Fischer (5 April 2000).

transition face special difficulties in responding to this central challenge."[13]

A special chapter on Africa pledged support for the consolidation of democracy and promised to assist the continent in the struggle for lasting peace, poverty eradication and sustainable development, "thereby bringing Africa into the mainstream of the world economy"[14] and full support for the political and institutional structures of emerging democracies on the continent. The leaders pledged to take "special measures" to address the challenge of poverty eradication and sustainable development, including debt cancellation, improved market access, enhanced development assistance, increased foreign direct investment and transfers of technology.[15]

The Declaration was the basis for the formulation of the eight Millennium Development Goals to be achieved by the year 2015 that have constantly featured in global development discourse, particularly with regard to Africa. They are: (1) the eradication of poverty and hunger; (2) achievement of universal primary education; (3) promotion of gender equality and the empowerment of women; (4) reduction of child mortality; (5) improvement of maternal health; (6) combating HIV/AIDS, malaria and other diseases; (7) ensuring environmental sustainability; and (8) developing a global partnership for development.

The Declaration reflected the optimism and goodwill that prevailed in the international community at the dawn of the 21st century. These conditions partly explain the positive reception that NEPAD was accorded by the major Western governments and international developmental organizations.

NEPAD merges economic, social and political visions generated by the negative as well as positive experiences of the last half century of African independence. They are reflected in the Objectives (Article 3) stipulated by the Constitutive Act of the African Union i.e., (Article 3) (c) accelerating the political and socio-economic

---

[13] United Nations, General Assembly, "United Nations Millennium Declaration" (UN Doc. A/RES/55/2), para. 5.
[14] *Ibid.*, para. 27.
[15] *Ibid.*, para. 28.

integration of the continent; (g) promoting democratic principles and institutions, popular participation and good governance; (k) promoting co-operation to raise the living standards of African peoples and (l) coordinating and harmonizing the policies between existing and future Regional Economic Communities. Key Principles (Article 4) include: (m) respect for democratic principles, human rights, the rule of law and good governance.[16]

4. Principles and Goals

The principles and goals of NEPAD reflect several different facets of the challenges that Africa faces at the beginning of the 21st century and the analysis and prescriptions that the leaders propose. In the first place, it provides a diagnosis of the causes of continued poverty and socio-economic stagnation in the continent. They are primarily resource outflows and unfavourable terms of trade as well as failures of political and economic leadership that "impede the effective mobilization and utilization of scarce resources into productive areas of activity in order to attract and facilitate domestic and foreign investment."[17]

NEPAD is a manifesto reflecting commitment to the goals of the eradication of poverty through positive engagement with the current processes of globalization. Africa's economic and social potential remains untapped "because of its limited integration into the global economy."[18] In the same vein, the document states that: "While globalisation has increased the cost of Africa's ability to compete, we hold that the advantages of an effectively managed integration present the best prospects for future economic prosperity and poverty reduction."[19]

Through NEPAD, African leaders reaffirm the proposition that peace, security, democracy, good governance, human rights and sound economic management are interrelated conditions for development.

---

[16] The Constitutive Act of the African Union.
[17] The New Partnership for Africa's Development (NEPAD), para. 34.
[18] *Ibid.*, para. 16.
[19] *Ibid.*, para. 28.

They thus pledge to "work, both individually and collectively, to promote these principles in their countries and sub-regions and on the continent."[20]

NEPAD seeks to re-orient the policies of the African governments and external governmental and non-governmental agencies in a way that would eliminate the kind of dependency that has been inherent to the previous patterns of aid-dependent efforts at economic development. This would be achieved by giving greater weight to international trade rather than foreign "aid". The document proclaims that development "is a process of empowerment and self-reliance. Accordingly, Africans must not be wards of benevolent guardians; rather they must be the architects of their own sustained upliftment."[21]

Another significant aspect of NEPAD relates to the position it takes with regard to the ideological framework of economic development. In contrast with the earlier resistance to the capitalist thrust of the globalization process as pushed and guided by the international financial and trade institutions and Western governments, NEPAD explicitly accepts the capitalist model as the path to the future. One of the major goals and objectives is the promotion of the private sector through the creation of "a sound and conducive environment for private sector activities, with particular emphasis on domestic entrepreneurs" and the encouragement of foreign direct investment "with special emphasis on exports."[22]

NEPAD proposes a number of developmental benchmarks and targets to be achieved over the next 15 years (by the year 2017), i.e. a continental GDP growth rate of 7% per annum for the following 15 years; reduction of the proportion of people living in extreme poverty by half between 1990 and 2015; enrolment of all primary school age children by 2015; elimination of gender disparities in primary and secondary enrolment by 2005; reduction of infant and child mortality ratios by two thirds between 1990 and 2015 and maternal mortality ratios by three quarters between 1990 and 2015.[23]

---

[20] *Ibid.*, para. 71.
[21] *Ibid.*, para. 27.
[22] *Ibid.*, para. 163.
[23] *Ibid.*, para. 68.

The major goal is to seek a balanced relationship between African States, donor States – particularly the G8 countries – and the Bretton Woods institutions. African States would be partners-in-development rather than supplicants and dependents subject to the imperious dictates of the powerful. They would undertake democratic and economic liberalization reforms in return for increased aid in various forms. Aid would include assistance in conflict resolution on the continent; debt reduction for heavily indebted countries; reversing decline in aid levels; facilitating African exports; encouraging private investment; providing technical support for planning and development management; and supporting the call for reform of multilateral financial institutions to meet the needs of African States.

The NEPAD foundational document puts the multifaceted problems of Africa's development into the global perspective of economic, social and ecological interdependence. It argues that the continent's material, aesthetic and cultural resources are global assets.[24] The global expansion of industrial production and the growth in poverty contribute to environmental degradation of the oceans, atmosphere and natural vegetation. If not addressed, these will set in motion processes that will increasingly slip beyond the control of governments, both in developed and developing countries.[25] This paragraph evokes the 1986 United Nations *Programme of Action for African Economic Recovery and Development*, (1986-1990) that stated, *inter alia*, that:

> "Without durable and sustained economic development in the world's poor regions, of which Africa is a notable example, there is a real danger to international peace and security and an impediment to world economic growth and development."[26]

---

[24] NEPAD, paras. 9-17.
[25] *Ibid.,* para. 37.
[26] United Nations, General Assembly: "United Nations Programme of Action for African Economic Recovery and Development", UN Doc. A/RES/S-13/2, 1986-1990, (1 June 1986).

5. Institutions and Organs

Until the 2010 decision to merge NEPAD into the AU, the highest authority of the partnership was the Heads of State and Government Implementation Committee (HSGIC) comprised of representatives of three States from each of the five regions used by the AU for political purposes.[27] The Chair of HSGIC reported to the AU Summit on an annual basis. The HSGIC was assisted by a Steering Committee comprised of the Personal Representatives of the Heads of State and Government. Its role was to oversee projects and programs. The Secretariat was based in South Africa.

From the beginning, there was a certain ambiguity in the relationship between the African Union and NEPAD. Gradually, steps were taken to bring the latter within the political and administrative umbrella of the Union. In July 2003, the Second Summit Meeting (Assembly) of the AU in Maputo, Mozambique authorized the Chair of the AU Commission to appoint the Executive Head of the NEPAD Secretariat following consultations with the Chair of HSGIC.

The rotating Chair of the African Union (Head of State/Government) and the Chair of the Commission have been *ex-officio* members of the HSGIC. In addition, AU Commissioners have been ex officio members of the NEPAD Steering Committee.

The NEPAD Secretariat was designed as a framework for promoting, co-coordinating and harmonizing regionally focused developmental projects and encouraging mobilization of funding and investments for them. Its other activities include communication and interaction with civil society groups in the Member States as well as international NGOs that address issues of concern to Africa. A Chief Executive Officer led it from its headquarters in Midrand, South Africa.

---

[27] The Implementation Committee is comprised of the following 15 states: Algeria, Egypt and Tunisia (North Africa); Nigeria, Senegal and Mali (West Africa); Cameroon, Gabon, and São Tomé and Principé (Central Africa); Ethiopia, Mauritius and Rwanda (East Africa); and South Africa, Botswana and Mozambique (Southern Africa).

6. Programs and Activities

NEPAD is envisaged "as a long-term vision of an African-owned and African-led development programme."[28] The immediate goal is to promote investments in the development of the continent's physical infrastructure, capital accumulation, human capital, institutions, structural diversification, competitiveness, health, and good stewardship of the environment."[29] The basic approach involves

> "rationalising the institutional framework for economic integration, by identifying common projects compatible with integrated country and regional development programmes, and on the harmonisation of economic and investment policies and practices."[30]

As a developmental initiative, NEPAD seeks to promote better economic and corporate governance. The immediate goals in this realm include improvement of public financial management, creation of assessment mechanisms, and mobilization of resources for capacity building in these areas.[31]

The project uses the following eight Regional Economic Communities: Arab Maghreb Union (AMU/UMA); Common Market for Eastern and Southern Africa (COMESA); Community of Sahelo-Saharan States (CEN-SAD); East African Community (EAC); Economic Community of Central African States (ECCAS); Economic Community of West African States (ECOWAS); Intergovernmental Authority on Development (IGAD); and Southern African Development Community (SADC).

The "priority initiatives" that NEPAD is currently promoting fall into nine sectors, i.e.: (1) infrastructure; (2) agriculture and food security; (3) human resource development; (4) science and technology; (5) trade, industry, market access and private sector development; (6) environment and climate change;

---

[28] NEPAD, para. 60.
[29] *Ibid*, para. 64.
[30] *Ibid.*, para. 92.
[31] *Ibid.*, paras. 86-89.

(7) governance and public administration; (8) capacity development; and (9) gender development.

Specifically, NEPAD seeks to attain these goals by "mobilizing political will", facilitating resource mobilization, developing a "strategic framework" to monitor and update programs for regional infrastructure and facilitating "knowledge sharing" among countries, Regional Economic Communities and technical agencies.[32] The AU/NEPAD African Action Plan (AAP) was drawn up in 2005-2006 as a continental policy guide to the realization of these objectives.[33]

NEPAD recognizes that economic growth and development is dependent on a supportive political and social environment. The foundational document states that development "is impossible" in the absence of true democracy, respect for human rights, peace and good governance. The democratic standards that NEPAD adopts include political pluralism, and fair and open elections "periodically organized to enable people to choose their leaders freely."[34]

As the name implies, a major focus of the NEPAD process is partnership between African States and the richer States and corporations that are expected to provide resources for the continent's economic development. It expects developed countries and international development agencies to contribute to the achievements of its goals by politically and practically supporting processes of conflict prevention and resolution; accelerating debt reduction; reversing the decline of foreign aid; encouraging foreign investment; and setting up coordinated mechanisms for combating corruption, including the return of monies acquired by corrupt means.[35]

International support for NEPAD is coordinated through the "African Partnership Forum" (APF) established in 2003. It brings together African Heads of State and Government who are participants in NEPAD, the Chair of the African Union, Heads of the regional

---

[32] New Partnership for Africa's Development (NEPAD), "Preparation of a Medium to Long Term Plan of Action/Strategic Framework (MLTSF)," *Briefing Note* (2003).
[33] African Union, "AU/NEPAD African Action Plan 2010-2015: Advancing Regional and Continental Integration in Africa Strategic Overview, (2009)."
[34] NEPAD, para. 79.
[35] *Ibid.*, para. 185.

communities, the African Development Bank, Leaders of the industrialized countries that support the project, the European Commission, the Organization for Cooperation and Development (OECD) and the United Nations and affiliated developmental organizations such as the United Nations Development Program (UNDP), the International Monetary Fund (IMF), the World Bank and the World Trade Organization (WTO).

In 2003, the United Nations Secretary-General created the Office of the Special Adviser on Africa (OSAA). Its mission includes facilitating inter-governmental deliberations on African issues with special reference to NEPAD. Other UN and UN-affiliated agencies that have supported NEPAD include the Economic Commission for Africa (ECA); the UN Department of Economic and Social Affairs; the International Atomic Agency; the United Nations Industrial Development Organization (UNIDO); the United Nations Education, Science and Cultural Organization (UNESCO), the International Civil Aviation Organization (ICAO); the World Trade Organization (WTO); the World Health Organization (WHO) and the United Nations Development Program (UNDP).[36] World Bank support for NEPAD has included financial support for regional projects, technical support for regional bodies, and advocacy in efforts to mobilize resources from donors for the development of regional infrastructure.[37]

China, Africa's growing economic and developmental partner, has also expressed an interest in working with NEPAD. In 2006, China donated funds to support a program to train African nurses and midwives. In 2007, the Chinese Academy of Fisheries Sciences, the World Fish Centre and NEPAD signed an agreement to assist African fisheries scientists increase their expertise and work with them in fisheries and aquaculture research and technology development under the auspices of "NEPAD FISH". In January 2010, the "Africa-Britain-China Conference on Agriculture and Fisheries" was held in Beijing.

---

[36] United Nations, Economic and Social Council, "United Nations System Support for the New Partnership for Africa's Development," UN Doc. E/AC.51/2009/7, 27 March 2009.

[37] World Bank, "Support to NEPAD," *Period of Report: July 2008 to June 2009.*

The meeting was organized by the Chinese Ministry of Agriculture and the British Department of International Development (DFID). Delegates included representatives of the UK, China, Sierra Leone, and the NEPAD Secretariat. They agreed to cooperate on issues of food security, engage in personnel exchange and other activities involving NEPAD's agricultural programs.[38]

7. The African Peer Review Mechanism (APRM)

The First Summit Meeting of the African Union held in Durban, South Africa in July 2002 decided to establish the Africa Peer Review Mechanism. The decision was incorporated in the Declaration on Democracy, Political, Economic and Corporate Governance. It affirmed, *inter alia*, the leaders' commitment to the basic principles of liberal democracy, i.e. rule of law, equality before the law, individual liberty, the freedom of association, the right to participate in government and separation of powers and the independence of the judiciary.[39]

The APRM seeks to encourage signatory States to promote the principles laid out in the Declaration on Democracy.[40] Signatory States are expected to invite an examination of their performance in the areas of: (a) "Democracy and Political Governance"; (b) "Economic Governance"; (c) "Corporate Governance"; and "Socio-Economic Development."

Performance criteria have been broken down into over 90 indicators, of which 41 relate to Democracy and Political Governance. They include: the existence of an "effectively independent judicial services commission to ensure professionalism and integrity with responsibility for the appointment of judges"; the adequacy of a legal framework for "free" association and formation of non-governmental

---

[38] United Kingdom, Department for International Development (DfID), "Minutes for the Africa-Britain-China Conference on Agriculture and Fisheries," 12-14 January 2010, Beijing.

[39] The New Partnership for Africa's Development (NEPAD), "Declaration on Democracy, Political, Economic and Corporate Governance."

[40] The New Partnership for Africa's Development (NEPAD), "The African Peer Review Mechanism (APRM)," (2003).

organizations and unions; ensuring the effectiveness of human rights institutions; the existence of inter-party committees in parliament that exercise "effective" oversight and freedom of independent media; independence and effectiveness of Electoral Commissions to ensure free and fair elections; and constitutional provisions to fight corruption and steps to ensure full and meaningful participation of women in all aspects of national life.

The Committee of Participating Heads of State and Governments that have acceded to the process (the APR Forum) overseas the review process.

A panel of 5-7 "Eminent Persons" composed of Africans of "high moral stature", who are qualified and have demonstrated a commitment to the ideals of Pan-Africanism, guides the process. They are nominated by the participating States, short-listed by a Committee of Ministers and appointed by the Heads of States and Government that have signed on to the process. The members serve four-year terms except for the Chair who serves five years.

The system of review involves: (a) a "base" review carried out within 18-months of adherence to the mechanism; (b) subsequent periodic reviews every two to four years; (c) reviews that may be requested by the state and (d) reviews that may be initiated by the Heads of States of participating countries in another signatory state when an "impending" political or economic crisis is deemed to require the exercise.

The process starts with the preparation of background documents by the APRM Secretariat and the country under review ("Self Assessment" Report) and a "Draft National Plan of Action" drawn up by the country under review. The APRM Guidelines stipulate that the final National Program of Action is the "key input" that the country contributes to the peer review. It serves to lay out and clarify the "responsibilities of various stakeholders in government, civil society and the private sector in implementing the Programme"; describe the national consultations that take place during the self-assessment and drafting of the program and; outline the "feedback mechanism" established to keep local stakeholders involved in the process.[41]

The next stage involves a Country Review Mission led by a member of the Panel of Experts. The team conducts consultations with all "stakeholders" including the government, political parties, members of the legislature and civil society organizations.

The third stage involves the drafting of the Country Report based on material prepared by the APRM Secretariat as well as information gathered within the country from official and non-official sources.

The government is given an opportunity to respond to any issues raised in the draft report that it wishes to challenge or comment on before the publication of the final document. It is then presented to the APR Panel for eventual submission to the APR Forum.

The fourth stage involves submission of the report to the Heads of State and Government of the participating countries (HSGIC) that reviews it and takes a decision about the outcome of the process. The APRM Basic document contains an intriguing stipulation that suggests the possibility of some unspecified measures in cases where a country review pinpoints problems that the government refuses to correct or address. Paragraph 24 states:

> "If the Government of the country in question shows a demonstrable will to rectify the identified shortcomings, then it will be incumbent upon participating Governments to provide what assistance they can, as well as to urge donor governments and agencies also to come to the assistance of the country reviewed. However, if the necessary political will is not forthcoming from the Government, the participating states should first do everything practicable to engage it in constructive dialogue, offering in the process technical and other appropriate assistance. If dialogue proves unavailing, the participating Heads of State and Government may wish to put the Government on notice of their collective intention to proceed with appropriate measures by a given date. The interval should concentrate the mind of the Government and provide a further opportunity for addressing the

---

[41] NEPAD, "Guidelines for Countries to Prepare for and Participate in the African Peer Review Mechanism (APRM)," paras. 32 & 33.

identified shortcomings under a process of constructive dialogue. All considered, such measures should always be utilized as a last resort."[42]

The exact nature of the potential "punitive" response is left unclear. Six months after consideration by the HSGIC, the report is publicly tabled in "key" regional and sub-regional forums such as the Pan-African Parliament, the African Commission on Human and Peoples' Rights, the Peace and Security Council and the Economic, Social and Cultural Council of the African Union.

By July 2009, 30 States had acceded to the APRM, namely Algeria, Angola, Benin, Burkina Faso, Cameroon, Cape Verde, (Republic of) Congo, Djibouti, Egypt, Ethiopia, Gabon, Ghana, Kenya, Lesotho, Malawi, Mali, Mauritania, Mauritius, Mozambique, Nigeria, Rwanda, São Tomé and Principé, Senegal, Sierra Leone, South Africa, Sudan, Tanzania, Togo, Uganda and Zambia. Twelve of them had been through one review: Algeria, Benin, Burkina Faso, Ghana, Mali, Mozambique, Nigeria, Kenya, Lesotho, Rwanda, South Africa and Uganda.

8. Preliminary Evaluation of NEPAD

An assessment of the nearly 10 years of NEPAD's experience must start with some basic assumptions about contemporary African and international political and legal facts. It is worth emphasizing that African integration schemes have never involved surrender of national sovereignty. Although it takes a more assertive stance with regard to violations of the rules of law and constitutional government, the African Union has not found a way to implement Article 4(h) of the Constitutive Act that stipulates the "right of the Union" to intervene in Member States in which war crimes, genocide and crimes against humanity occur.

NEPAD's success is best judged in terms of the extent to which it serves to promote and consolidate greater intra-regional economic cooperation and act as a catalyst to induce more inflow of productive financial resources. However, even in this sphere, the reality of 53

---

[42] African Peer Review Mechanism Basic Document.

separate States with different geographical, ecological and economic conditions and histories must limit the ambitions of NEPAD as a coordinating agency.

The inherited colonial pattern of external orientation of economic, infrastructural and social relations exacerbates territorial and economic fragmentation. The impact of the separate legacies is reflected in the limited scale of legitimate trade and economic integration between States even when they share common borders and cultural patterns. President Wade pointed out in his *Omega Plan* that in spite of several integration schemes and projects, intra-community trade barely accounted for 10 percent of total volume of trade "mainly because of national economies that are compartmentalized."[43]

Within these limits, NEPAD has come to be accepted by the major governments and inter-governmental institutions involved in African development as the main regional coordinating framework. At the symbolic and rhetorical level, it has also contributed to the beginning of a shift away from a paternalist to a more respectful discourse concerning Western assistance for African developmental efforts.

Over the past decade, African governments have demonstrated greater interest in integrated approaches to regional developmental issues. Working in close collaboration with Western and other extra-continental governments and inter-governmental organizations, NEPAD has focused on the mobilization of resources and coordination of physical infrastructure, energy generation, Information Technology, agriculture, health, education and the protection of the environment.[44]

In the period 2008-2009, the UN Secretary-General's report on the African project pointed to continued progress in the implantation of NEPAD projects. These included the plans for the Dakar-Ndjamena-Djibouti Transport Corridor; the development of the

---

[43] Omega Plan, para. 44.
[44] United Nations, General Assembly, "The New Partnership for Africa's Development: Fourth Consolidated Report on Progress in Implementation and International Support," *Report of the Secretary-General*, UN Doc. A/61/212, (28 September 2006).

ICT broadband infrastructure network and the Comprehensive African Agriculture Development Programme (CAADP).[45]

As far as improved governance and democracy are concerned, it is tempting but unrealistic to expect more than a limited role for NEPAD or the APRM. No external mechanism can prevent the emergence or persistence of authoritarian or neo-patrimonial regimes in Africa or elsewhere. What NEPAD can do through the APRM process is to play the role of a catalyst for the evolution of stronger civil society and the emergence of a participatory and liberal democratic political culture on the continent. It can accomplish this through the opportunity it provides civil society organizations to participate in the evaluation process. As the APRM Guidelines document states, guaranteeing public participation in the review process is a central aspect of enhancing the state of governance and socioeconomic development in the participating country. "Such interactions can build trust, establish and clarify mechanisms for ongoing engagement and empowerment of stakeholders.[46]

The record of the first group of countries to be reviewed demonstrates different degrees of receptivity to criticism by governments. In some cases, such as Rwanda and South Africa, they tried to downplay reports of weaknesses. By contrast, Ghana, the first state to undergo a review, the government received generally positive evaluations. There is also evidence of positive government response to the recommendations of the APR Panel in some of the countries that have been reviewed.[47]

Considering the novelty of the experience and the unprecedented willingness of participant States' governments to allow the kind of intrusion into domestic matters that has not been observed anywhere else in the world, the initial modest achievements of the APRM to date, are remarkable.

---

[45] United Nations, General Assembly, "New Partnership for Africa's Development: Seventh Consolidate Progress Report on Implementation and International Support," *Report of the Secretary-General*, UN Doc. A/64/204, (31 July 2009).
[46] APRM Guidelines, para. 36.
[47] Herbert R., & Gruzd S., *The African Peer Review Mechanism, Lessons From the Pioneers*, The South African Institute of International Affairs, Jan Smuts House, Johannesburg, 2008.

From the perspective of liberalization and democratization, the most important effect is the enhanced legitimization of the role of the citizen, directly and through civil society organizations, to expose misgovernment and demand redress. The APRM process is an affirmation of the right to transparent and accountable governance. Beyond periodic electoral exercises, this is the ultimate test of democracy.

9. Conclusions

The creation of NEPAD is part of a long history of attempts to formulate a collective African economic and political strategy designed to deal with the intractable problems of poverty and political instability on the continent. It reflects three principal developments of the last two decades of the 20th century: (1) the economic and political failure of most developmental projects on the continent; (2) the increased dependency of African States; and (3) collapse of the Soviet Bloc and State socialism, ensuring the triumph of global capitalism and the liberal democratic paradigm.

In contrast to earlier perspectives on development, NEPAD reflects the view that in the 21st century, socio-economic development cannot be divorced from the creation of political and social systems that are accountable and respect the human dignity of their citizens. Liberation and democratization are ends in themselves. However, insofar as they facilitate public accountability, they are also regarded as catalysts for the efficient governance and the effective mobilization of natural and human resources for rapid socio-economic development.

From the point of view of the promotion of democratic governance, the African Peer Review Mechanism is the most important development in the evolution of African regional institutions. It is a unique experiment that provides some openings into the traditional legal and political walls of national sovereignty and domestic jurisdiction. This development is consistent with the evolution of international law and politics since the end of the Second World War.

It is significant to note that some States that do not have good human rights records have nonetheless subscribed to this intrusive process. This provides the fledgling civil society and democratic forces of these as well as better performing States with an invaluable platform to use to push forward the processes of liberalization and democratization.

Ultimately, the success of NEPAD will depend on the uncertain concatenation of domestic and international economic, political, social and cultural forces whose evolution will take a long time. The long road towards progress will undoubtedly be marked by advance as well as reversals. Observers are likely to oscillate between optimism and pessimism – as they have always done when looking at developments on the African scene.

CHAPTER 11.
THE REGIONAL ECONOMIC COMMUNITIES

Stephen Karangizi

1. Background

The efforts by African States to bring about the economic and political integration of the continent date back to the period preceding the adoption of the OAU Charter in May 1963. At the time of concluding the OAU Charter, emphasis was placed on attaining political integration. The African leaders agreed on uniting Africa through initially the political liberation of the territories under foreign colonial rule. The expectation was that after the political liberation of the whole continent was attained, it would be easier to integrate the continent economically.

However from 1968 onwards, African leaders started taking concrete steps to launch continental economic integration. Several OAU Sessions of Assembly of Heads of State made declarations that culminated in the adoption of the Lagos Plan of Action and the Final Act of Lagos in 1980 which called for the creation of an African Economic Community. The Treaty establishing the African Economic Community[1] was signed in 1991 and came into force in 1994, by which time many Regional Economic Communities (also referred to as RECs) had already been established under their own treaties.

---

[1] The AEC Treaty is also known as the Abuja Treaty as it was signed in Abuja (Nigeria), on 3rd June 1991.

There are eight major Regional Economic Communities (RECs) in Africa which are recognised by the African Union namely:

(a) Economic Community for West African States (ECOWAS) established in 1975;

(b) Common Market for Eastern and Southern Africa (COMESA) established initially as the Preferential Trade Area of Eastern and Southern States in 1981 and transformed into COMESA in 1994;

(c) Southern African Development Community (SADC) established in the current form in 1992 initially established in 1980 as a Development Coordination Conference (SADCC);

(d) Economic Community for Central African States (ECCAS) established in 1983;

(e) Arab Maghreb Union (UMA) established in 1989;

(f) East African Community (EAC) established in 1999;

(g) Intergovernmental Authority on Development (IGAD) established in 1996 initially established in 1986 as an Authority for dealing with Drought and Desertification (IGADD); and

(h) Community of Sahel-Saharan States (CEN-SAD) established in 1999.

Each of the RECs (apart from UMA) has signed the Protocol on Relations between the RECs and the African Union. However each of the RECs in Africa has a different historical background that influences its current role in the integration of Africa.

Six other groupings have an integration agenda that can contribute towards the African Economic Community. These are: Mano River Union (MRU), Indian Ocean Commission (IOC), West African Monetary Union (UEMOA), Central African Economic and Monetary Community (CEMAC), Economic Community of the Great Lakes (CEPGL) and the Southern African Customs Union (SACU). However all these other institutions have not set as their principal objective to contribute as building blocs to the attainment of the African Economic Community and are considered more or less as subsets of the eight recognised communities.

There are many other institutions in Africa that can also contribute to the integration of Africa but which do not have as their principal mission to be building blocs of the AEC.

2. The OAU declarations that led to the Abuja Treaty

Several OAU declarations were passed between 1973 and 1984 which tended to remain as plans without actualisation of a concrete agenda for the integration of Africa. A 1997 report of the OAU[2] outlines the evolution of the decisions to establish an African Economic Community as reflected in the declarations and resolutions of the OAU Summit discussed below.

Firstly, the "African Declaration on Cooperation, Development and Industry" adopted by the Tenth Ordinary Session of the OAU Assembly of Heads of State and Government in 1973, set out the basic principles for collective or individual actions by African Countries in the areas of transport and communications, infrastructure, industrialisation, monetary, financial and trade cooperation.

Secondly, under the 1976 Kinshasa Declaration, adopted by the Fifteenth Extraordinary Session of the Council of Ministers of the OAU held in Kinshasa, Democratic Republic Congo (then Zaire), Member States undertook to promote sub-regional and regional economic and technical cooperation in various ways.

To that end, they called for the establishment of an African Economic Community within a period of 15 to 25 years in successive stages. The Strategy adopted to attain that objective was through sub-regional and regional integration based on sectoral integration, leading to the establishment of an African Economic Community.

Thirdly, the Monrovia Strategy adopted by the Assembly of Heads of State and Government of the OAU held in the Liberian capital in July 1979 provided for the promotion of economic integration in Africa.

Fourthly, the Lagos Plan of Action and Final Act of 1980 were adopted at the Lagos Session of the OAU Assembly of Heads of State and Government of that year. The final framework provided for under

---

[2] OAU: "Strategy and Approach to the Implementation of the Treaty Establishing the African Economic Community"; OAU Doc. AEC/ECOSOC/3(1); published in 1997 at pp. 2-4. The past decisions can also be found on the AU website.

the Plan of Action was to set up by the Year 2000, on the basis of a Treaty to be concluded, an African Economic Community so as to ensure the economic, social and cultural integration of the Continent. The Heads of State defined the broad guidelines of the actions to be taken and mapped out the stages to give concrete effort to their commitment by strengthening the existing regional economic communities and establishing new ones where they did not exist in the 1980s with a common goal of establishing an African Common Market. The Lagos Plan of Action also undertook to deepen in the 1990's sectoral integration through harmonisation of strategies, policies and economic development plans.

Fifthly, the Twentieth Ordinary Session of the Assembly of Heads of State and Government of the OAU, held in Addis Ababa, Ethiopia, in November 1984, established a Steering Committee on economic matters charged mainly with designing an economic recovery programme of Africa which was later made permanent by the Assembly of Heads of State and Government meeting at its Twenty-first Ordinary Session held in 1985.

Furthermore, at its Twenty-third Ordinary Session held in 1987, the Assembly of Heads of State and Government requested the Permanent Steering Committee to prepare the Draft Treaty for Establishing the Community which was eventually completed and adopted in 1991 at Abuja, Nigeria.

From the process outlined above, it is quite apparent that the period of eleven years it took to convert the Lagos Plan of Action into the Abuja Treaty was too long and may have negatively dampened the initial enthusiasm to establish an African Economic Community. Moreover, as will be explained later, by the time the Abuja Treaty was signed, new RECs had been established, thereby thwarting the original desire to work with only five RECs.

3. Relationship between the Regional Economic Communities and the African Economic Community

The Treaty establishing the African Economic Community was the first legal text that provided for a link between the Continental integration aspirations on the one hand and the regional economic communities on the other. The Treaty provided as one of its objectives in Article 4 (paragraph 1 (a)) to "coordinate and harmonise policies among existing and future economic communities in order to foster the gradual establishment of the Community."

The relationship between the Regional Economic Communities and the African Union is now governed by three legal texts: The Abuja Treaty, the Constitutive Act of the African Union and the Protocol on relations between the Regional Economic Communities and the African Economic Community.

The relationship between the African Union and the regional economic communities can be viewed as a paradox in itself from a conceptual point as each institution is meant to exist as a separate legal entity with supranational powers. It is therefore implied that the regional economic communities would be expected eventually to give way to the larger supranational body, the AU. This was aptly reflected in the spirit and provisions of the Treaty Establishing the African Economic Community which envisaged six stages of gradual integration of the RECs into the African Economic Community over a period of forty years. In addition, the first stage of five years was intended to be the period during which the Regional Economic Communities were to be strengthened. This process was intended to end in 1999. However, the same provision created more confusion by providing that new Regional Economic Communities were to be established where they did not exist.

Although the OAU continued to work at various sectoral, institutional, functional and operational levels within the existing Regional Economic Communities (RECs) not much progress seems to have been made in implementing the provisions of the Abuja Treaty. The expectation was that through the RECs, simultaneous efforts would be made to implement the second stage of the Community which calls for the stabilisation and gradual removal of the Tariffs and Non-Tariff Barriers to intra-Community trade. The second stage also calls for strengthening of sectoral integration at the regional and continental levels in the fields of trade, agriculture, money and finance, transport and communication, industry and energy.

The main reason for lack of progress in implementing the Abuja Treaty could have been due to the fact that the OAU seemed to be unable to devise a strategic way in dealing with the regional economic communities. For instance, at its Assembly of Heads of States and Government held in Harare Zimbabwe on 3rd June, 1997, the Assembly constituted itself into the First Ordinary Assembly of Heads of States and Government of the African Economic Community. However, this initiative was never repeated even after the transformation of the OAU into the AU, hence its intended effect never materialised. Nonetheless, the main achievement of the Harare Assembly of Heads of States and Government was to adopt the Protocol on Relations between the African Economic Community and the Regional Economic Communities. The Assembly also authorized the Secretary General of the OAU-African Economic Community to sign, on behalf of all Member States, the "Protocol on relations between the African Economic Community and the Regional Economic Communities."

The final key decision taken by the same Assembly was to request the Member States concerned to identify the Regional Economic Community which would serve as a pillar of the African Economic Community in each region, since there were, in some instances, more than one in the same region. The rationale for this was that the original OAU Lagos Plan of Action envisaged that there would be only five RECs each covering the five designated regions of Africa (North, East, West, Central and South). The same principle had been reflected in the Abuja Treaty. It was now a matter of concern that most States belonged to more than one REC and this was ostensibly slowing the growth of the RECs as it was a burden on the States ability to meet their commitments to them.

While the Abuja Treaty provided for the establishment of REC's in the five regions of Africa, no indication was given of the exact geographical configuration of the regions or the number of countries which would constitute a viable regional economic community. There was an assumption that the geographical configuration would follow the alignment established for political purposes in the determination of the Bureau for the OAU organs as contained in Resolution CM/Res.464 (XXVI) of the OAU Council of Ministers.

The choice by the African countries to pursue integration through the existing regional blocs was indeed a unique approach to integration. Some of the RECs also provided in their Treaties as a key objective "to contribute towards the establishment, progress and the realisation of the objectives of the African Economic Community."[3]

This approach, though unique, lends itself to many questions and issues. There are also various assumptions underlying this option that still needs to be addressed. One of the major assumptions was that the different regional blocs would attain integration at the same pace. Secondly, there was an assumption that the blocs would maintain as their ultimate objective the pursuit of continental integration. Thirdly, there also was the assumption that Africa would become more homogeneous without much influence from global changes. As will be seen later in this Chapter, those assumptions have been continuously put into question.

It should be noted that the RECs were formed without the direct involvement of the OAU. As they evolved and expanded, many of the RECS expanded beyond the designated five regions of Africa. The "geographical" regions covered by the eight RECs identified under the AEC in 1999 are not consistent with those adopted by the OAU Council of Ministers. This has resulted in countries belonging to RECs outside the OAU designated geographical areas and also to dual membership.

Various reports have therefore argued that the overlap among regional economic communities adds to the burdens of Member States and that such overlap tends to dissipate collective efforts towards the common goal of the African Union.[4] The regional and sub-regional economic communities are said not to be in line with the basic idea in the AEC Treaty of a co-ordinated and progressive process that systematically evolves into the AEC. The proposal to rationalise these institutions in the sense of geographical configuration has been difficult due to political sensitivities involved, particularly as co-operation between States are sovereign acts normally taken on

---

[3] COMESA Treaty paragraph (f) of Article 3 and the ECOWAS Revised Treaty (1993), Articles 78 and 79.

[4] See United Nations Economic Commission for Africa, *Assessing Regional Integration in Africa*, Addis Ababa, Ethiopia, 2004, at pp. 40-41.

the basis of national interests as determined by the individual States themselves.

In view of the difficulty in attaining a perfect situation where there are no overlapping mandates of the RECs, the need for coordination and harmonisation of regional economic groups can be said to be the major challenge to the attainment of African integration. There has been a far-reaching debate as to whether the strategy for the AU should be to seek to achieve continental integration through the regional blocs as was envisaged under the Abuja Treaty. On the other hand, the AU could consider changing the strategy by setting out a comprehensive integration agenda which would be followed by all African States and regional economic communities irrespective of the membership issues.

However, it is also obvious that there are many reasons that have driven States to forming many regional communities, the major one being strategic alliances, thus making it inevitable that the previous strategy of relying on five blocs to attain continental integration is now difficult to implement. Indeed one Report[5] argues that

> "Regional Integration is good politics: it meets political needs, such as security or enhanced bargaining power, and it satisfies influential lobbies. Indeed the purpose of integration is often political, and the economic consequences, good or bad, are side effects of the political payoff."

The drive for meeting strategic political objectives within RECs by individual States lends support to the problem of addressing the issue of the multiplicity of regional economic communities in Africa. States will be less keen to abandon an economic community for the sake of geographical alignment if their strategic reasons for joining that grouping are still relevant irrespective of the cost or non-performance of such a group.

There is no doubt that one of the major contributions to the advancement of economic integration in Africa will be the deepening of coordination and harmonisation of programmes between the RECs.

---

[5] See World Bank, *Trade Blocs, Volume 763, World Bank Policy Research Report*, Oxford University Press, USA, 1994, p. 11.

Several reports[6] on some of the main efforts made by the RECs to coordinate their programmes in the context of the Protocol on Relations between the AEC and RECs on coordination highlight the measures adopted which include the following:

a) The joint SADC/COMESA initiative of establishing a joint COMESA/SADC Task Force[7] to coordinate the process of rationalizing and harmonizing the programmes of both institutions due to overlapping membership of some countries;

b) The Memoranda of Understanding (MOUs) between COMESA and IGAD, COMESA and IOC, COMESA and EAC, COMESA and CEN-SAD all intended to foster harmonisation of their policies and programmes;

c) In East and Southern Africa IGAD and IOC are applying most of the integration instruments adopted by COMESA;

d) In Central Africa, ECCAS is adopting a trade regime that takes into account the dispensations in CEMAC;

e) The establishment of Joint Committee between ECOWAS and UEMOA to harmonize their programmes has already led to a joint agreement to establish a Single Monetary Zone for West Africa by year 2004;

f) The growing rapport between ECOWAS and UEMOA has borne fruit in a common programme of action on trade liberalisation and macroeconomic policy convergence. Both have agreed to adopt new common rules of origin to enhance the flow of trade. Other important aspects for harmonisation are customs declaration forms (to be a single document) and compensation mechanisms (ECOWAS has already agreed to adopt the system applied by UEMOA);

g) There are also ongoing adoptions by RECs of each other's projects and programmes, e.g. the emulation of the ECOWAS sectoral programmes and projects established under the private sector leadership forum by other RECs so as to encourage private sector participation in share capital; and

---

[6] See, for example, UNECA, *Assessing Regional Integration in Africa*, (2004), p. 42.

[7] The task force was set up in Cairo, Egypt by the Chairperson of COMESA and that of SADC in 2001.

h) There is also an ongoing attendance and participation by RECs of each other's policy organs meetings.

4. Coordination Framework between the African Economic Community and the Regional Economic Communities

The AEC and the RECs formalised their relations and coordination operations through the Protocol on Relations between the African Economic Community and the Regional economic Communities signed on 25th February 1998 in accordance with Article 95 of the AEC Treaty.

The Protocol was intended to provide the coordination framework between the African Economic Community and the RECs. The Protocol applies to the relations between the parties and measures that the parties shall implement in order to fulfil the responsibilities placed on them by the Abuja Treaty.

The main objective of the Protocol was to strengthen the existing regional economic communities and promote the co-ordination and harmonisation of the policies, measures, programmes and activities of regional economic communities to ensure that the regional economic communities would at a later stage be infused into the African Common Market.

The Protocol also provided an institutional structure for the co-ordination of relations between the Community and the regional economic communities on the implementation of the various stages set out in Article 6 of the Treaty.

The Protocol established two organs for co-ordinating polices, measure, programmes and activities of regional economic communities and ensuring the implementation of activities arising from the provisions of the Protocol. The two organs are a Committee on Co-ordination and a Committee of Secretariat Officials.

The Committee on Co-ordination consists of the Executive Head of the African Union (Chairperson of the Commission); the Chief Executives of the regional economic communities; the Executive Secretary of the Economic Commission for Africa (ECA); and the President of the African Development Bank (ADB). The Committee is tasked with providing the policy orientation pertaining to implementation of the Protocol as well as coordinating and monitoring the progress made by the RECs towards attainment of the stages set out in Article 6 of the Abuja Treaty.

The Committee of Secretariat Officials is composed of senior officials of the African Union responsible for Community Affairs; designated senior officials of the regional economic communities; and designated senior officials of the ECA and ADB. The Committee of Secretariat Officials was set up to prepare the necessary technical reports for consideration by the Committee on Co-ordination.

Article 88 of the AEC Treaty provides that the Community shall be established mainly through the coordination and harmonization of the activities of the RECs and their eventual integration into the African Common Market, a process meant to lead towards the establishment of the Community. It should however been observed that, in spite of the 1998 Protocol on Relations between the AEC and RECs, the latter's involvement in the formulation and implementation of programmes of each other has been marginal. In addition, the sharing of experiences and exchange of information on sectoral programmes among RECs and with RECs and the AEC has also been at best minimal.

While the legal provisions in the treaties of the AU/AEC and RECs do provide some linkages, the operational mechanisms are totally inadequate. It is not enough for staff of the AU to attend meetings of the RECs as observers. They should be able to take active part in the reviews of the activities of RECs in their supervisory and monitoring role assuming that the AU would have set a vision and strategy for continental integration which the RECs would be expected to pursue.

The Committee on Co-ordination has made several recommendations on the operations of the RECs.[8] The recommendations include a proposal that the RECs should harmonise policies and legislation on the development of infrastructure with a view to creating an environment conducive to

---

[8] OAU/African Economic Community, "Committee on Co-ordination, Second Meeting, Addis Ababa", OAU Doc. OAU-AEC/COMCOR/Rpt (II), 5-6 June 2001 and "Meeting of the OAU and Regional Economic Communities on Relations between the African Union and RECs", Addis Ababa, OAU Doc. AU/RECs.1 Rpt, 10-12 June 2002.

investment in the private sector; a proposal to harmonise macroeconomic policies as well as sectoral policies in the areas of services, production and infrastructure; the strengthening of co-operation ties and promotion of exchange of experiences and programmes among RECs; the proposal that the RECs should be mandated to meet once a year where the Chief Executives host the meetings on a rotational basis. These meetings should be attended by AU Commissioners and the heads of the Directorates of the Commission.

However, the Committee on Coordination has not been able to meet on a regular basis and there is no coherent agenda and timeframe set for the RECs to work together. In addition the meetings have tended to be informal without making any significant lasting recommendations. It may be argued that this could happen because, prior to the adoption of the Constitutive Act, it was not clear if the decisions of the OAU/EAC were binding on the RECs which have a distinct different legal status. However, since the Constitutive Act provides in paragraph 3 of Article 33 that its provisions "... shall take precedence over and supersede any inconsistent or contrary provisions of the Treaty establishing the African Economic Community", the African Union has a unique opportunity to advance its coordination role of the RECs.

5. Legal Status of the AEC and RECs under the AU Constitutive Act

The Constitutive Act of the African Union provides in paragraph 1 of Article 33 that: "The provisions of this Act (Constitutive Act) shall take precedence over and supersede any inconsistent or contrary provisions of the Treaty establishing the African Economic Community."

Since the Abuja Treaty is not repealed by the AU Constitutive Act as was done with the OAU Charter, it follows that the Abuja Treaty continued in force except for provisions which are inconsistent with the AU Constitutive Act. Article 3 (l) of the AU Constitutive Act states, as one of its objectives to "coordinate and harmonize the policies between the existing and future Regional Economic

Communities for the gradual attainment of the objectives of the Union."

Two of the preambles of the Act also provide for taking account of the principles and objectives stated in the Abuja Treaty as well as of the need to accelerate the process of implementing the Abuja Treaty in order to promote the socio-economic development of Africa and to face more effectively the challenges posed by globalisation.

It is quite clear that the Protocol on Relations between the African Economic Community and the Regional Economic Communities is also a binding document. This is because there is nothing to show that the Protocol is inconsistent or contrary to the Constitutive Act, recalling that paragraph 3 of Article 33 of the Constitutive Act provides that the provisions of that Act shall take precedence over and supersede any inconsistent or contrary provisions of the Treaty establishing the African Economic Community. Although the Protocol is in the process of being revised to take into account the new realities following the conclusion of the Constitutive Act establishing the African Union, the main tenets of the Protocol are still valid. It would also follow that some of the institutions of the AEC have been overtaken by similar institutions of the AU under the Constitutive Act. These include the Pan-African Parliament, the Court of Justice, the Economic and Social Council, the Specialised Technical Committees, African Monetary Union, and the Solidarity, Development and Compensation Fund (Article 80).

This linkage between the AEC institutions with those of the AU constitutes further indication of the fact that the AEC Treaty is preserved and the devolution of its assets to the Union became possible because the same organs are charged with the attainment of the objectives of the Union and the AEC. There is also an understanding that under the prevailing circumstances, "... the AEC, if it ever did before, now has no separate legal personality."[9] The problem, however, is that it is unlikely that the parties ever intended that the AEC as a major and specialized institution with its

---

[9] Eze O., "Institution Building and Consolidation of The African Union" in *The African Union and The Challenges of Cooperation and Integration*, Abuja, Spectrum Books, 2002, p. 51 quoted by Ndlela, *ibid*, p. 8.

own elaborate programme of work should simply melt into the Constitutive Act, which is itself and for all practical purposes, mainly an instrument for political integration. It might, therefore, be instructive for the African Union to take a hard look at the experience of Europe, where specialized agencies were for a long period kept out of the mainstream of the European Union. These observations are pertinent when relations between the AU and the RECs are brought into play with the latter becoming effective building blocs of the African Union.

The African Union Summit held in Banjul, the Gambia in July 2006, endorsed the decision of the AU Ministers responsible for Integration, on the Rationalization of Regional Economic Communities (RECs). The AU Summit[10] decided that a moratorium be imposed on the recognition of any new RECs. Accordingly, the eight RECs already recognised would continue to be recognised as the building blocs for the AU.

The AU Summit also agreed to revisit the Abuja Treaty to rearrange the timetable of its implementation taking into account the provisions of the Sirte Declaration of 9th September 1999, and finalize the new Protocol on Relations between the AUC and the RECs for signature in the shortest time possible.

The AU Summit further directed the AUC and the RECs to:
- Harmonize and coordinate policies and programmes of RECs as important strategies for rationalization;
- Put in place mechanisms to facilitate the process of harmonization and coordination within and among the RECs;
- Carry out an institutional audit of the RECs to assess the challenges and efficiency constraints in implementing the Abuja Treaty. The AUC in collaboration with the ECA should, in consultation with the RECs provide a clear timetable and benchmarks for the implementation of the Treaty, taking into account the Sirte Declaration of 9th September 1999;

In addition, the AU Assembly agreed to institutionalise the meeting of African Ministers responsible for economic integration to follow up

---

[10] AU Commission: Press Release on the AU website.

on the continental integration process. The decision of the AU Assembly would seem not to be time-bound which could make it difficult to be implemented within a reasonable period. Moreover no correlation seems to have been made by the AU between that decision and the existing provisions of the Abuja Treaty which are still in force.

6. Regional Integration in Africa and the World Trade Organization

While it is clear that there is continuing political support of regional integration by all African States, the future of regional integration in Africa would appear to be heavily reliant on global developments.

The integration process in Africa and in other regions of the world is increasingly being affected by the on-going multilateral negotiations in the context of the World Trade Organization (WTO). The WTO offers both opportunities and challenges for regional integration in Africa. Through stronger RECs, the African countries are able to consolidate their negotiating capacity in the multilateral trading arrangement.

The fundamental principle underlying the multilateral trading system embodied in the World Trade Organization (WTO) is the obligation to conduct international trade in a non-discriminatory manner. The General Agreement on Tariffs and Trade 1994 (GATT) provides in Article 1 that all WTO members are obliged to extend most-favoured-nation (MFN) treatment to one another. However, Article 1 is subject to two exceptions under Article XXIV, which allows for the establishment of regional trade agreements (RTAs), subject to compliance with a number of specified conditions, and the Enabling Clause,[11] which allows WTO members (categorised as developing countries) to derogate from the provisions of Article I for the purpose of extending differential and more

---

[11] GATT, "The Decision on Differential and More Favourable Treatment, Reciprocity and Fuller Participation of Developing Countries," GATT BISD, 26th Supp, GATT Doc. L/4903 (1979) (Decision adopted on 28 November 1979).

favourable treatment to other developing countries. As compared to Article XXIV, the Enabling Clause has limited obligations on developing countries wishing to extend preferential treatment to one another through the establishment of Regional Trade Agreements.[12]

All African countries were party to the trade and development agreement – the Lomé Convention between the ACP-EU, which lasted a quarter of a century from 1975 to 2000. The greatest impetus for the evolution and expansion of trade from ACP to EU countries was the non-reciprocal and preferential market access accorded to ACP countries over all other suppliers to the EU. The non-reciprocal arrangements of the Lomé Convention was replaced with the Cotonou Agreement (The new ACP-EU agreements were signed on 23 June 2000 in Cotonou, Benin),[13] which foresees the establishment of Economic Partnership Agreements (EPAs) between the EU and African, Caribbean and Pacific (ACP) countries, in preparation for free trade arrangements in the longer term.

The possible benefits of entering into an Economic Partnership Agreement (with provision for a Free Trade Area) with the EU would include the following: to protect ACP access to EU markets from further deterioration; to help Africa to lock its gains made in trade liberalization; to be used as a vehicle for assistance from the EU regional integration; and to act as a platform for negotiations with the EU and under the WTO. The African States still needs to agree with the EU on a number of issues, including the development dimension of the EPAs and market access particularly of agricultural products.

One of the major challenges facing the African States under the EPA negotiations is to ensure that the final EPA is WTO compatible. Art XXIV of the GATT deals with FTA and Customs Unions and allows the members of Regional Trade Agreements to offer one another more favourable terms of trade than they extend to non-members provided the RTA fulfil certain conditions.

---

[12] The term Regional Trade Agreements used under the WTO refers to Groupings or economic communities that have set out to establish a Free Trade Area or Customs Union which applies to the eight recognised RECs of Africa.

[13] ACP-EU: Partnership Agreement (Also known as the Cotonou Agreement) signed in Cotonou on 23 June 2000. See the website of the European Union.

Those conditions include the removal of tariffs and non-tariff barriers on substantially all trade among members within a ten-year period and the requirement that the RTA should not result in higher barriers to trade with other WTO members than those applying before the RTA is adopted. However, Article XXIV does not cover Regional Trade Agreements between developed and developing countries as is the case with the proposed EPAs between the EU and the ACP States. As such in the case of a proposed RTA between the EU and ACP countries, what is substantially all trade and reasonable transitional periods, remain outstanding issues. The negotiations within Doha Development Agenda have not progressed to offer any guidance in this area. Another major concern is limited progress on key WTO issues such as agricultural support, market access and trade facilitation in the Doha Development Agenda. The extent to which African countries will benefit from the proposed EPAs with the EU will therefore be influenced by ongoing negotiations at the WTO level.

The debate on negotiations with the EU have also been juxtaposed with the configuration of RECs that will be relied upon in view of existing overlapping membership in various regional economic integration initiatives. This is because it would be expected that for a region to conclude an Agreement with the EU, such a region should be a Customs Union in order for such Agreement to be WTO compatible as outlined above.

It should be noted that the Cotonou Agreement provided in paragraph 5 Article 37 that

"Negotiations of the economic partnership agreements will be undertaken with ACP countries which consider themselves in a position to do so, at the level they consider appropriate and in accordance with the procedures agreed by the ACP Group, taking into account regional integration process within the ACP".

The negotiations between the European Union and the African States have been led by different regional economic communities. ECOWAS and UEMOA have led the negotiations for the West African States; SADC has led the negotiations for some of the Southern African States (seven States); COMESA has led the negotiations for the Eastern and many of the other Southern African

States in consultation with EAC and IOC under an informal arrangement called the Eastern and Southern African Group (ESA Group); CEMAC has led the negotiations for the Central African States. It is important to note that the configuration of the RECs leading the EPA negotiations do not necessarily follow the configuration designated by the AU for continental integration. On the other hand many African States have also entered into long-term bilateral agreements with the EU providing for the establishment of Free Trade Areas between the respective parties. These include the EU-Tunisia Euro-Mediterranean Agreement, the EU-Egypt Euro-Mediterranean Agreement and the 1999 EU-South Africa Free Trade Agreement.[14]

In many ways therefore the integration process in Africa is being increasingly influenced by the multilateral negotiations mentioned above.

7. Conclusion

The future of African economic integration lies in the full implementation of the commitments enshrined in the Constitutive Act of the AU, the Sirte Declaration and the Abuja Treaty. In light of the ongoing regional and global developments, and in order to realize the ultimate goal for Africa to attain continental integration, it would be necessary for the AU to provide a comprehensive strategy in working towards achieving the third and fourth stages envisaged under the Abuja Treaty.

Considering that the strategy for economic integration in Africa is based on the performance of the Regional Economic Communities (RECs) as building blocs there will be a need to address the challenges faced by those building blocs. The building blocs have progressed with integration at varying levels. While some of them have made rapid progress, others have remained rather stagnant. Some of the challenges identified include the institutional set up of the RECs; inadequate capacity and resources among countries and RECs to

---

[14] WTO, "Regional Trade Agreements Notified to the WTO," WTO Doc. WT/REG91/1 and WT/REG69/1.

spearhead the integration process; inability to make integration objectives, plans and programmes part of national development frameworks; divergent and unstable national macroeconomic policies; lack of coherence and links among sectoral cooperation programmes and macroeconomic policies pursued by regional economic communities; and weak national coordination institutions.[15]

The AU should be in a position to work out a detailed programme on the modalities for phasing the current RECs into the AEC, as a way of working towards an African Customs Union and eventually an African Common Market within a specific timeframe.

---

[15] UNECA, "Assessing Regional Integration n Africa", *op. cit.*, p. 33. See also: Global Coalition for Africa, "Regional Integration in Sub-Saharan Africa: Towards Rationalisation and Greater Effectiveness", Document No. GCA/EC/02/4/2001, Published on the website of the Global Coalition for Africa. This document outlines the various challenges similar to these ones to regional integration in Africa.

CHAPTER 12.
THE PROHIBITION OF UNCONSTITUTIONAL CHANGE OF GOVERNMENT

Muna Ndulo

1. Introduction

The most common form of unconstitutional change of government is a military coup that overthrows the civilian government and replaces it with a military regime. The term, however, encompasses other forms of unconstitutional change of government. The African Union (AU) Committee on Unconstitutional Changes defined unconstitutional change of government as any of the following situations: (a) intervention by mercenaries to replace a democratically elected government; (b) replacement of a democratically elected government by armed dissident groups and rebel movements; and (c) refusal by an incumbent government to relinquish power to the winning party after free and fair elections.[1] All three situations involve the use of military force to gain or retain power. At the heart of unconstitutional rule is the fact that power is sustained through the use of or threat of force rather than by popular consensus. With unconstitutional change of government, the constitution is typically abrogated, suspended, or significantly amended and the normal democratic process terminated. Rule by decree is established by those who have usurped power.

---

[1] This definition was first adopted by the Lomé Declaration of July 2000 on "the Framework for an OAU Response to Unconstitutional Change of Government," AU Doc. AHG/Decl. 5 (XXXVI).

A.A. Yusuf & F. Ouguergouz (eds.), *The African Union: Legal and Institutional Framework. A Manual on the Pan-African Organization*, 251-274.

When eventually there is a handover of power, the military oversees the replacement of the old constitution with a brand new document that provides the military rulers with immunity from prosecution. Worse still, the military leader may also seek election as the new "civilian" president, thus perpetuating the undue influence of the military in national life. This Chapter examines the African Union's response to unconstitutional change of government. The first section of the Chapter examines the incidence of unconstitutional changes of government in Africa in the last few years and the Organization of African Unity (OAU)/African Union (AU) response to those unconstitutional changes of government. The section that follows looks at applying AU norms to unconstitutional change of government. The survey of unconstitutional takeovers in this chapter is restricted to the period of democratic revival (1996-2006). In the period before 1996, military regimes were routinely accepted by both the OAU and the international community. The Chapter finally examines the question of what measures can be adopted to deter would-be perpetrators of coups and the issue of immunity for perpetrators of unconstitutional changes of government.

2. A Survey of Unconstitutional Takeovers of Government (1996-2006)

Independent African States have experienced over 100 military coups. In the period before 1996, although routinely deplored, most military regimes were after an interval able to count on recognition and reception back into the OAU and international community fold. Since the democratic revival of the 1990s, however, coups have encountered growing intolerance. Increasingly, African leaders have recognized the linkage between democracy, peace, and development.[2] They have come to realize that democracy, good governance, respect

---

[2] The AU Constitutive Act in its preamble categorically states that "conscious of the fact that the scourge of conflicts in Africa constitutes a major impediment to the socio-economic development of the continent and of the need to promote peace, security and stability as a prerequisite for the implementation of our development and integration agenda", Constitutive Act of the African Union, Lomé (Togo), 11 July 2000.

for human rights, and the rule of law are prerequisites for the security, stability, and development of the continent. This has translated into a growing search for means and ways of discouraging unconstitutional changes of government. Although much progress has been made, this has been a slow process and one in which norms are still evolving.[3] In Burundi in July 1996, the military deposed the President. The coup was widely condemned by African States. In response to this coup, a regional summit resolved to exert maximum pressure including economic sanctions on the illegal regime. This action was fully endorsed by the OAU. In Sierra Leone on 25 May 1997, the democratically elected government of President Ahmed Tejan Kabbah was toppled by a group of soldiers from the SLA (Sierra Leone Army) calling themselves the Armed Forces Revolutionary Council (AFRC). They were led by Johnny Paul Koroma, previously part of a group of nine soldiers that had attempted to overthrow the government in 1996. Joining the AFRC in the rebellion was a rebel group called the Revolutionary United Front (RUF) and together these two groups became known as the People's Army.

The Sierra Leone coup happened very close to the thirty-third summit held on the 2nd of June in Harare, Zimbabwe. The OAU summit condemned the May coup and called on the international community at large to refrain from recognizing the military regime.[4] The OAU gave a mandate to Economic Community for West African States (ECOWAS) to facilitate the restoration of constitutional order and made a general call on other African countries as well as members of the international community to assist ECOWAS in this regard. While constitutional order was eventually restored to Sierra Leone, this development had little to do with the OAU. The Economic Community of West African States Cease-fire Monitoring Group (ECOMOG) forces, as well as reinforcement troops from Nigeria, Guinea, and Ghana, were ultimately responsible for ousting the People's Army regime and the restoration of the constitutional

---

[3] A Charter on Democracy, Elections and Governance is being elaborated. Africa Union Draft/Charter/II/Rev.2.
[4] Meldrum A., "Coups no longer acceptable: OAU, Summit extols democracy; African Economic Community is inaugurated," *Africa Recovery* 11 (1997) 1, p. 5.

Kabbah government into power. The Sierra Leone coup was one of the developments that prompted the OAU to pass a resolution at the Algiers summit of 1999, in which they decided to bar the future attendance of all governments that came to power in an undemocratic and unconstitutional way. The resolution unanimously rejected any unconstitutional change of government as unacceptable and an anachronistic act that contradicted the OAU's commitment to promote democratic principles and conditions. The meeting further mandated the central organ of the OAU Mechanism for Conflict Prevention, Management, and Resolution to reactivate as a matter of urgency the subcommittee on unconstitutional change of governments, in order to finalize its work as regards the mechanisms to apply where a *coup d'état* has occurred in a Member State.

On 30 April 1997, the Comoros army took power after an unsuccessful attempt to reintegrate the breakaway island of Anjouan led to violent demonstrations. The OAU condemned the coup and called on the leaders to return to constitutional order.[5] The Comoro coup was quickly followed by a coup in Guinea-Bissau on 19 May 1999. The coup in Guinea-Bissau was followed by fighting resulting in the deaths of over a hundred people when the military leader sent forces to attack the presidential guards of President Joao Bernardo Vieira and to remove him from office. ECOWAS, the OAU, and UN Secretary-General Kofi Annan condemned the coup.[6] A bloodless military coup on 25 December 1999 ousted President Bedie of Côte d'Ivoire who subsequently fled to France. The coup was led by General Guei, who quickly moved to form a new government, promising to hold elections in less than a year. The OAU condemned the coup and banned Ivory Coast from attending the 2000 Togo Summit. OAU Secretary-General, Salim Ahmed Salim, said that there would be no exceptions made for Ivory Coast and its military regime would not be recognized. He stated that "all those who come to power by force will not have their place in Africa." During the Togo summit, the OAU established a 'Group of 10' mandated to ensure that any

---

[5] BBC World Africa, "UN Condemns Comoros Coup," 30 April 1999.
[6] Johnson T., "New military coup in Guinea-Bissau leaves one hundred dead," 19 May 1999, World Socialist Website.

transition of government resulting from forthcoming elections in the Côte d'Ivoire be peaceful. This group of 10 held a meeting with Côte d'Ivoire's political leaders in September to assess the situation in that country and to ensure that forthcoming elections (set to take place in October) were free and fair. At the meeting, OAU member representatives stressed that the elections should be transparent and that the OAU would not accept any form of manipulation in the elections. The OAU requested Guei and the opposition party leaders to form a National Transitional Council and to postpone the presidential elections until after legislative elections had taken place.

The OAU meeting proved pointless and ineffective as the organizations' requests were ignored. Prior to the elections, the Supreme Court (the judges of which had all been handpicked by General Guei) established a criteria that both parents of presidential aspirants must be Ivorian and that presidential candidates must not at any time have held citizenship in another country. This new law effectively disqualified the candidates from the two major opposing political parties, leaving the presidential race to be between Guei and Laurent Gbagbo, the leader of the Front Populaire Ivoirien (FPI) party only. The elections proceeded (despite low voter turnout because of widespread boycotting) and when early results indicated that Gbagbo was convincingly in the lead, Guei disrupted the process, disbanded the electoral commission, and declared himself winner. This intervention sparked protests and a heavily violent uprising saw Guei relinquish power and Gbagbo, the likely winner of the elections, sworn in as president.

In Madagascar, initial results in the December 2001 elections between the incumbent Didier Ratsiraka and presidential hopeful Mark Ravalomanana indicated that a second round of voting would be required to declare a winner. Several sources indicated that the latter had been the winner of the first round. Ravalomanana proceeded to declare himself president amidst widespread support. The OAU vehemently denounced Ravalomanana's declaration and tried to mediate between the parties without much success. The OAU argued that the election had not resulted in a "constitutional and legally constituted government." It refused to recognize the Ravalomanana regime and Madagascar was banned from participating in the organization's activities. When the AU was inaugurated at the Durban Summit in 2002, Madagascar's seat remained vacant. To justify this stance, the AU invoked the OAU's principle adopted at the Algiers summit and elaborated in the Lomé Declaration of not recognizing governments that came to power in an undemocratic and unconstitutional way. The impasse was finally broken when the AU (at a session held on 10-12 July 2003 in Maputo) agreed that Madagascar should be allowed to join the Union.[7] By this time, the former incumbent had fled the country and the challenger had won a convincing majority in National Assembly elections. The AU's recognition of the Ravalomanana regime came after USA, French, and German recognition. The Madagascar crisis undermined confidence in the AU's ability to enforce its norms on unconstitutional change of government.

In the Central Africa Republic (CAR), on 15 March 2003, the army chief-of-staff Francois Bozize overthrew President Patasse, took over the capital, and declared himself president. He also suspended the Constitution and dissolved the National Assembly. On 17 March 2003, the AU, through their Central Organ of the Mechanism for Conflict Prevention, Management, and Resolution, held a session to review the situation in the CAR following the 15 March military coup.[8] Ambassador Baso Sangu (South Africa's permanent representative to the AU) chaired the meeting and the session was briefed by the representative of the AU-appointed commission tasked with monitoring and analyzing the situation in the CAR. At this session, the Central Organ of the AU issued a strong condemnation of the coup, recalling their Lome Summit commitment to the total rejection of all unconstitutional changes of government.[9] The AU also lamented that the coup had taken place while national dialogue (overseen by CEMAC and CENSAD) was underway to find a solution to the political crisis unfolding in the CAR at the time.

---

[7] See: AU Document Assembly/AU/Dec. 4 (II), Decision on Madagascar, p. 4.
[8] See: OAU Document Central Organ/MEC/AMB/Comm. (XC), 17 March 2003, Addis Ababa, Ethiopia.
[9] *Ibid.*

It called upon Bozize and his supporters to relinquish their hold and reinstate the democratically elected government of Patasse. In accordance with the Lomé Declaration requirement, the Central Organ recommended the suspension of CAR from the AU and all its activities until such time that constitutional order was restored. In efforts to return the country to constitutional rule, the AU requested the interim chairperson of the commission to establish contacts with all the relevant parties in the CAR, and to dispatch a special envoy to the CAR to review the situation and hold consultations with the stakeholders in the region. It issued a warning to the military regime in the CAR in which it cautioned them to ensure the safety of the civilian populace, failing which they would be collectively and individually accountable for any human rights or other violations. However, despite these decisions, the AU failed to take any decisive action towards the perpetrators of the 2003 coup d'état. The Central Organ's demands for the restoration of constitutional order and the reinstatement of the democratically elected government were ignored and no consequences or sanctions followed. Further, the AU failed to suspend CAR from the AU in accordance with the Lomé declaration. A new constitution was passed by referendum in December 2004. In March 2005, the country held its first elections since the 2003 coup in which Bozize defeated his opponent, former Prime Minister Martin Ziguele, and legitimized his constitutional position.

In São Tomé and Principe on 16 July 2003, army rebels seized power from the government of President Fradigue de Menzes while he was in Abuja attending the Sixth Leone Sullivan Summit of Influential African and African-American Leaders and Business People. The rebels issued a statement in which they claimed to have dissolved all national institutions in the hope of forming a transition government. The coup perpetrators seized several key government officials including Prime Minister Maria das Neves, Head of the National Assembly Dionisio Dias, Defense Minister Fernando Daqua, and Natural Resources Minister Rafael Branco. In their statement, the rebels promised that these officials would not be harmed. The rebels cited corruption and the fact that expected oil revenues would be inequitably divided as the reason for the coup.

The AU condemned the coup d'état and swiftly began efforts to restore Menzes' regime.[10] An International Mediation committee was set up comprising representatives of the Economic Community of Central African States (ECCAS), the AU, the DRC, Nigeria, and the Community of Portuguese Speaking People. During the mediation, the committee urged the rebels to hand over power to the democratically elected government while the rebels demanded that proceeds from the forthcoming oil sales be distributed transparently and equitably.[11] The mediation was effective and successful and an agreement was reached between the rebels and President Menezes' government within one week of the coup. An accord was subsequently signed by the factions.[12] Power was handed back to President Menezes and the seized officials were released. Critics have argued that the speed and intensity with which the AU and the international community (the US in the forefront) responded to the coup had more to do with São Tomé's windfall of off-shore oil producing fields (of particular strategic importance to the US) than with their desire to see constitutional order restored or the implementation of AU norms on the unconstitutional change of government.

On 14 September 2003, there was yet another coup in Guinea-Bissau. President Yala's government was toppled by the army led by Chief of Defense General Verrisimo Correia Seabra. Soon thereafter, he announced his voluntary resignation and was placed under house arrest. His overthrow was widely celebrated by civilians as Yala had for a long time run an incompetent, corrupt, and repressive government that refused to undertake the much sought-after constitutional and legislative reform that would facilitate democratization in the country. Even though the National Assembly had approved a new constitution in April 2001, Yala sat on it, neglecting to either veto or promulgate it. In November 2002, he proceeded to dismiss the government of Prime Minister Alamara Nhasse, dissolve the National Assembly, and subsequently appoint a

---

[10] See: Central Organ/MEC/AMB/COMM. (XCIII), 24 July 2003, Addis Ababa, Ethiopia.
[11] Ibid.
[12] IRIN, Humanitarian News and Analysis, "São Tomé and Principe: Coup leaders hand power back to civilian president," 23 July 2003. See the IRIN Website.

caretaker government pending legislative elections which he originally scheduled for April 2003 but later postponed to June and then October. The last straw came when on 12 September 2003, the President of the National Elections Commission announced that October elections would not be possible. The Army intervened two days later, and toppled Yala's regime, dissolved the government, and set up a Committee for the Restoration of Democracy and Constitutional Order.

The AU Commission, in tandem with ECOWAS, dispatched a delegation to Guinea-Bissau and other countries in the region to analyze and devise ways in which constitutional order could be restored. On 18 September, the Central Organ of the AU held a session in which it condemned the coup d'état and proclaimed it to be in violation of AU principles and the Lome declaration on Unconstitutional Changes of Government.[13] It declared its support to ECOWAS (already seized of the matter) and welcomed ECOWAS' decision to send an investigative delegation to Guinea-Bissau.

Soon after the coup, a truce was agreed upon and a transitional government set up. The truce and transitional arrangements were largely the result of the mediation by ECOWAS and CPS with the AU merely playing a supportive role. While the coup in Guinea-Bissau was condemned both by the AU and the UN Security Council, there seems to have been an implicit understanding that the pervasive political conditions in the country mitigated the illegality of the unconstitutional takeover of government.[14] Indeed, UN Security Council members expressed an understanding that the coup occurred as a result of deteriorating political and economic conditions. On 28 September 2003, businessman Henrique Rosa was sworn in as president amidst support by most political parties and civil society. On 28 and 30 March 2004, Guinea-Bissau held legislative elections deemed free and fair by international observers. The following year on 10 August 2005, presidential elections were held. These were again deemed free and fair and Joao Bernardo Vieira emerged victorious.

---

[13] *Ibid.*
[14] *Ibid.*

In Mauritania, on 3 August 2005, Maaouya Ould Sid'Ahmed Taya's 21-year reign was ended by a military coup led by Colonel Ely Ould Mohamed Vall. The coup was perpetrated while President Taya was away attending King Fahd's funeral in Saudi Arabia. Colonel Vall was subsequently installed as president. The AU Peace and Security Council suspended Mauritania from participating in all AU organs shortly after the coup and said that the suspension would remain in place until there was restoration of constitutional order in the country.[15] The AU also sent an investigative delegation to Mauritania to assess the situation. The military regime allowed the AU free access and after conducting interviews with Mauritanians on the ground, the delegation concluded that the coup enjoyed popular support.[16]

The results of the delegation's enquiry weakened the AU's condemnatory stance on Mauritania. The AU promised support and assistance to the new government in its preparation for elections. The AU stance weakened the evolving norms in its failure to reject a government formed as a result of an unconstitutional change of government. The military regime promised to hold elections within two years. A referendum held on 26 June 2006 showed that 97% of Mauritanians approved a new constitution which would limit the president's term of office to two terms. Colonel Vall issued a statement promising to abide by the referendum and transfer power in a peaceful fashion to an elected Government. He did so.

In Togo, shortly after the death of President Gnassingbe Eyadema, the Togolese army suspended the Constitution and declared Eyadema's son Faure Gnassingbe Eyadema as the new leader. This was in violation of the Togolese Constitution which stipulated that upon the death of the Head of State, the Speaker of Parliament must assume the presidency pending elections which are to be held within 60 days of the death of the President. The AU denounced the installation of Eyadema's son in the strongest of terms and labelled it

---

[15] See: AU Doc. PSC/PR/Stat. (XXXVI)-(ii), 4 August 2005.
[16] BBC News Africa, "Mauritania officers 'seize power'," 4 August 2005. See the BBC News Website.

a coup d'état.[17] The Togolese parliament tried to regularize the son's appointment by amending the Constitution, but this sparked even more condemnation and protests. The Peace and Security Council of the AU threatened unspecified sanctions if constitutional order was not restored.

Enormous pressure from the AU and the greater international community resulted in the stepping down of the newly appointed President and agreeing to hold elections within the 60-day period. In a statement on national radio, Gnassingbe said

> "In order to guarantee the transparency and fairness of [the forthcoming] election and to give the same chance to all the different candidates, I have decided to resign from the post of President of the National Assembly, through which I provisionally exercised the role of President of the Republic."

Gnassingbe also announced his presidential candidacy and subsequently won the elections amidst opposition party scepticism and widespread claims that the votes were rigged. The AU deemed the elections to be 'reasonably fair' and AU President Obasanjo sought to negotiate between the Gnassingbe regime and disgruntled opposition leaders in the hopes of establishing a coalition government. These efforts seem to have born some fruit as a few months later, Gnassingbe named opposition leader Edem Kodjo as Prime Minister.

3. The Emerging AU Norms on Unconstitutional Change of Government

Under international customary law, government recognition is an acknowledgement by other States that the government is in effective control of the State. It is a matter that is left to individual countries to decide. Recognition is often not dependent upon a particular government's legitimacy or constitutionality. Government recognition is often followed by the establishment of diplomatic relations. In the post-Cold War era, governments and intergovernmental organizations increasingly consider the legitimacy and democratic nature of a

---

[17] BBC News Africa, "Togo succession 'coup' denounced," 6 February 2005.

government before recognizing it or granting it membership in an organization.

Governments increasingly recognize that their legitimacy depends on meeting a normative expectation of the international community. Intergovernmental and regional organizations often prescribe criteria relating to admission or membership which requires Member States to meet certain conditions before being admitted or allowed to enjoy the attributes of membership. These often include the need for Member States to respect principles of good governance, constitutional order, and human rights. In its objectives, the AU commits Member States to the promotion of democratic principles and institutions, popular participation, and good governance.[18] The attitude of most intergovernmental organizations towards unconstitutional change of government is typically informed by the organization's fundamental principles and the fact that an unconstitutional change of government is a violation of citizens' rights. It is a violation of the right to take part in government, the right to vote, and the right to be elected. The Universal Declaration of Human Rights states that the will of the people shall be the basis for the authority of government.[19] In its preamble, the AU pledges to promote and protect human and peoples' rights, consolidate democratic institutions and culture, and to ensure good governance and the rule of law.[20] Clearly, an unconstitutional change of government is a violation of this preamble. The AU, recognizing the prevalence of unconstitutional changes of government in Africa and the instability and the damage to the continent's reputation that results from such changes, has sought to develop norms to deter would-be perpetrators of unconstitutional changes in government. The OAU did not begin to address the continued prevalence of coup d'état in the African continent until the Burundi coup of July 1996. Previous to the coup in Burundi, fearing a repetition of Rwanda, the OAU, led by Julius Nyerere as facilitator,

---

[18] African Union Constitutive Act, *supra* article 3 (2).
[19] Universal Declaration of Human Rights, G.A. Res 217A (III), U.N. GAOR, 3rd sess., pmbl., UN Doc. A/810 (1948); Article 21 (3) "The will of the people shall be the basis of the authority of government: this shall be expressed in periodic and genuine elections."
[20] AU Constitutive Act.

had sought to mediate between the Tutsi-led army and the majority Hutu population. However, pressed by Nigeria and South Africa to defuse the extremely dangerous situation, the OAU Central Organ warned the Tutsis led army in no uncertain terms against any attempt to take power through illegal means as this would not be accepted by Africa and will be strongly condemned by the OAU. Should a coup occur, it called on Africa and the international community to isolate completely and impose sanctions on those responsible. Despite the warning, the army in Burundi took power. In response, a regional summit resolved to exert maximum pressure including economic sanctions on the illegal regime. The OAU fully endorsed this position. The emerging norm was further developed after the 1997 Sierra Leone coup which took place while an OAU summit was underway in Harare, Zimbabwe. The OAU deliberations on the Sierra Leone coup culminated in the adoption of the Harare Declaration that strongly and unequivocally condemned the Sierra Leonean coup. The summit this time went further and appealed to the regional organization, ECOWAS, to intervene militarily to restore constitutional order to the country. Nevertheless, little action was taken to follow up the Harare Declaration. The OAU Central Organ did appoint a Committee on Unconstitutional Changes but it failed to pursue the matter. In 1999, there were four coups within a month - Niger, Ivory Coast, Guinea-Bissau, and Comoros. As a result, the OAU members led by South Africa and Nigeria expressed grave concern at the resurgence of coups d'état and called on the OAU Central Organ to reactivate as matter of urgency its Committee on Unconstitutional Changes. In 1999, the OAU's thirty-fifth ordinary session of the Assembly of Heads of States and Governments in Algiers adopted the Algiers Declaration.[21] In this declaration, the OUA Assembly went beyond denunciation. In spelling out measures to be taken against unconstitutional governments, it represented a tougher stance and a strengthening of OAU norms on unconstitutional changes. The declaration prohibited unconstitutional change of government and denied recognition to any government that comes to power

---

[21] Heads of State and Government of the organization of African Unity, Thirty-fifth Session July 1999, Algiers: OAU Doc. AHG/Dec.141 (XXXV).

through such means. It gave an ultimatum to all member governments that carried out unconstitutional changes after the 1997 Harare summit to return to constitutional rule by the following summit or face sanctions.[22]

At the Lomé summit in 1999, the OAU considered the problem of unconstitutional change of government and adopted a comprehensive statement on the matter. They adopted a framework that contained the following elements: (a) a set of common values and principles for democratic governance; (b) a definition of what constitutes an unconstitutional change of government; (c) measures and actions that the OAU would take to respond to unconstitutional change of government; and (d) an implementation mechanism. The Lomé Declaration[23] expressed grave concern about the resurgence of coups d'état in Africa. It recognized that unconstitutional changes of government were a threat to the peace and security of the continent and noted that they constituted a very disturbing trend and a serious setback to the ongoing process of democratization in the continent.[24] Part of the framework of the Lomé Declaration called for immediate and public condemnation of any unconstitutional change while urging for speedy return to constitutional order. Under the Lomé framework, whenever an unconstitutional change of government occurred, the Chairman of the AOU and the Secretary-General should convey a clear and unequivocal warning to the perpetrators of the unconstitutional change that under no circumstances will their illegal action be tolerated or recognized by the OAU. The perpetrators were to be given a period of six months to return to constitutional order. During that six-month period, the country was to be suspended from participating in OAU policy organs. The Declaration provided for limited and targeted sanctions against the regime that stubbornly refuses to restore constitutional order, including suspension from

---

[22] OAU, "Heads of States and Government, Thirty-fifth Ordinary Session," Algiers, July 1999: OAU Doc. AHG/Dec. 142(XXXV).
[23] Lomé Declaration of July 2000 on the "Framework for an OAU Response to Unconstitutional Change of Government, adopted by Heads of State and Governments of the OAU meeting at the Thirty-sixth Ordinary Session", Lomé, Togo from 10-12 July 2000: OAU Doc. AHG/Decl. 5(XXXVI).
[24] *Ibid.*

OAU policy organs, visa denials for perpetrators of unconstitutional change, restrictions on government to government contacts, and trade restrictions.[25] In addition, the Lomé Declaration called for the elaboration of principles of democratic governance. The Heads of State and Government believed that enumeration of these principles in a coherent manner would encourage Member States to adhere to a common concept of democracy and contribute to the reduction of factors that lead to unconstitutional changes of government. The following principles were adopted: (a) States were encouraged to adopt democratic constitutions whose preparation, content, and method of revision should be in conformity with generally acceptable principles of democracy;(b) respect for the constitution and adherence to the provisions of the law and other legislative enactments adopted by parliament; (c) separation of powers and independence of the judiciary; (d) promoting political pluralism or any other form of participatory democracy and the role of the African civil society, including enhancing gender balance in the political process; (e) acceptance of the principle of democratic change and recognition of a role for the opposition; (f) organization of free and regular elections, in conformity with existing texts; (g) guaranteeing freedom of expression and freedom of the press, including guaranteeing access to the media to all political stake-holders; (h) constitutional recognition of fundamental rights and freedoms in conformity with the Universal Declaration of Human Rights and the African Charter on Human and Peoples' Rights; and (i) guaranteeing and promoting human rights. The Lomé Declaration was not only concerned with reaction to unconstitutional changes of government but also with ensuring that conditions that increased the risks of unconstitutional changes of government were addressed. The Lomé democratic principles were later developed through the African Charter on Democracy, Elections and Governance.[26] The norms adopted by the Lomé Declaration were also further strengthened and clarified by the

---

[25] OAU, "Declaration on the Framework for an OAU Response to Unconstitutional Changes of Government," July 10-12, 2000, Lomé, Togo: OAU Doc. AHG/Decl. 5 (XXXVI).

[26] See African Charter on Democracy, Elections and Governance, African Union, Addis Ababa.

AU Constitutive Act. With the adoption of the Act in July 2002,[27] the norms with respect to unconstitutional change of government adopted at Lomé were firmly enshrined in the AU fundamental law. Article 4 (p) firmly condemns and rejects unconstitutional changes of government. Article 30 of the Act provides that governments which shall come into power through unconstitutional means shall not be allowed to participate in the activities of the Union. In the event of such an occurrence, the approved procedure provides that the AU shall immediately condemn the action, convey a clear and unequivocal warning that such an illegal change shall not be tolerated or recognized, and urge a speedy return to constitutional order. Meanwhile, the AU secretariat shall gather relevant facts and establish appropriate contacts with the perpetrators in order to ascertain their intentions and ensure a return to constitutional order. If the regime refuses to end its illegality, the AU must immediately apply a series of travel, trade, communications, and other sanctions. Insofar as the African Union's Assembly functions include monitoring the implementation of policies and decisions of the Union as well as ensuring compliance by all Member States of AU decisions,[28] the Union has the legal capacity to see to it that its decisions on unconstitutional changes of government are implemented as well as to impose sanctions where a member fails to comply with its decisions. The Constitutive Act recognizes the right of the AU to intervene within a Member State pursuant to a decision of the Assembly[29] in respect of grave circumstances, namely genocide and crimes against humanity, as well as serious threats to legitimate orders to restore peace and stability to a member state of the Union upon the recommendation of the Peace and Security Council.[30] The latter

---

[27] Constitutive Act of the African Union, Lomé, Togo, 11 July 2000.
[28] *Ibid*, article 9 (e).
[29] *Ibid*, article 23 (2).
[30] Article 4, "Heads of States and Government of the African Union Meeting in Their First Extraordinary Session on February 2003, paragraph 23," Report of the Assembly as amended by the Protocol on Amendments to the Constitutive Act of the African Union, adopted by the 1st Extraordinary Session of the Assembly of the Union in Addis Ababa, Ethiopia, on 3 February 2003 and by the 2nd Ordinary Session of the Assembly of the Union in Maputo, Mozambique on 11 July 2003.

provision, which has not yet come into force, could be used where the unconstitutional change of government leads to a breakdown of a law and order in an AU Member State. It could also be used as a basis to restore a legitimate government whenever an unconstitutional change of government occurs, as it can be argued that an unconstitutional change of government is the ultimate threat to legitimate order. The adoption of the African Charter on Democracy, Election and Governance, which is discussed in another Chapter of this work, further clarifies the norms on democracy, governance, and unconstitutional changes of government. Its importance is the recognition by African States that the major contributing factor to unconstitutional changes of governments is the prevalence of undemocratic governance on the continent, and the establishment of a framework for democratic governance and the holding of free and fair elections. Additionally, the Charter introduces new norms that require States to prosecute perpetrators of unconstitutional change of government and States to which they might run to escape prosecution to extradite them.

4. Immunity or Prosecution of Perpetrators of Unconstitutional Change of Government

In the event of an unconstitutional change of government, the AU norms call for speedy negotiations to restore the legitimate government and democracy. One of the issues that often arises is whether or not to grant immunity to individuals who have participated in the unconstitutional change of government. The current AU norms do not include provisions designed to ensure that those that perpetrate unconstitutional change of government should be indicted or extradited to their countries to face prosecution. The need to develop norms that would apply strict juridical measures against those who disrupt or try illegally to overthrow a legitimate government is recognized in the Charter on Democracy, Elections and Governance. Putting military usurpers on trial would send out an important and clear message that the illegal overthrow of governments will not be tolerated. But, is that an appropriate solution or should a peaceful solution incorporate legitimized immunity from prosecution in exchange for peacefully relinquishing power?

Political actors frequently use amnesty grants to induce dictators to relinquish power and to promote a peaceful transition from military to civilian governments. For example, the OAS, the United States, and the United Nations brokered an amnesty grant in Haiti where President Raoul Cedras agreed to relinquish power to the democratically elected President Jean-Bertrand Aristide in exchange for immunity from prosecution. Although the unlimited number of potential amnesty variations makes categorization difficult, it may be noted that there are at least three broad categories of amnesty legislation: (a) self-amnesty; (b) locally legitimized partial immunity; and (c) internationally legitimized partial immunity.

4.1. Self-Amnesties

Self-amnesties are frequently enacted by dictators seeking immunity from prosecution when their tenure in office is nearing its end. These amnesties are often conferred without domestic or international approval and cover a wide array of criminal acts. The Chilean self-amnesties granted during the reign of General Augusto Pinochet provide a typical example of self-amnesty packages and are the least likely to gain either international or domestic legitimacy. In 1996, the Inter-American Commission on Human Rights held that Chile's self-amnesty laws violated Articles 1, 8 and 25 of the American Convention, and thus, were illegitimate and not worthy of international recognition. (Hermosilla et al., Inter-American Commission on Human Rights Report No. 36/96, Case 10.843, Chile, 15 October 1996).

Generally, self-amnesties and blanket amnesties do not establish alternate means of redress for victims, lack provisions for an investigatory body to consider the amnestied acts in a non-criminal context, and serve only the goal of delivering a general amnesty for the crimes of the past. For these reasons, human rights advocates and institutions are generally wary of self-amnesties. Moreover, the frustration and resentment accompanying the complete denial of justice can produce a destabilizing effect on new governments.

Thus, the scope of the amnesty, the identities of the participants in the amnesty proceedings, and the process by which amnesty is granted play key roles in the success of the amnesty legislation and the success of the new government. For these reasons, it is recommended that amnesties, if they are to be granted, be combined with an investigatory process designed to produce an accurate and comprehensive description of atrocities suffered under the previous regime.

4.2. *Locally Legitimized Conditional Amnesties*

Locally legitimized conditional amnesties provide a stark contrast to self-amnesties. Generally, this category of immunity confers partial prosecutorial immunity in exchange for testimony regarding human rights violations and criminal activities. Locally legitimized partial immunity, as opposed to self-amnesty, is characterized by a significant increase in the legitimacy of the amnesty and a significant reduction in the scope of immunity. In order to gain domestic and international legitimacy, the amnesty's procedural framework provides a meaningful adjudication of the issues within the amnesty's ambit. A common form of adjudication is amnesty in exchange for participation in a nationally sponsored or internationally supported truth and reconciliation commission.

Truth commissions present States emerging from authoritarian rule with a unique opportunity to acknowledge state crime through a formalized mechanism of truth telling. Nations seeking a middle-ground between retributive justice and blanket amnesty use truth commissions to institute restorative justice during transitional periods. The commission's principle function is to record the extent and the scale of serious violence during a particular historical period through the use of eyewitness testimony. Most commissions compile a narration of individual stories and acknowledge abuses within "a jurisprudence of forgiveness and reconciliation"[31] that abstracts discrete local events into universally

---

[31] Lin O., "Demythologizing Restorative Justice: South Africa's Truth and Reconciliation Commission and Rwanda's Gacaca Courts in context," *International Law Students Association Journal of International & Comparative*

applicable themes. Thus, because "truth commissions eschew both criminal prosecution and blanket amnesty, they may be considered as a 'middle path' or 'third course.'"[32]

Although the South African TRC was the first truth commission to derive its authority from a democratically elected legislature rather than from an executive act, it was widely recognized as the final product of a compromise between the various South African political forces rather than a clear mandate of popular will. The *quid pro quo* nature of the amnesty package was two-fold: (1) amnesty was given in exchange for an agreement by the National Party (NP) to peacefully relinquish power; and (2) amnesty was granted on an individual basis in exchange for telling the truth in front of the TRC. The TRC was not a judicial body, and thus, was not authorized to determine liability or to punish, but was granted discretionary authority to confer amnesty onto those who confessed their involvement in politically related violations of human rights.

4.3. Internationally Legitimized Immunity

An example of internationally legitimized partial immunity is the restoration of democratically elected Haitian President Jean-Bertrand Aristide to power in 1994. In December 1990, Aristide became Haiti's first democratically elected president.[33] In August 1991, however, a military coup led by General Roul Cedras forced Aristide into exile. Massive human rights violations, including the murder of at least 3,000 civilians, ensued as Cedras' military seized control of the government. The international community responded by applying

---

Law 12 (2005), p. 42 quoting Teitel R., "Transitional Justice Genealogy," *Harvard Human Rights Journal* 16 (2003), p. 81

[32] Daly E., "Transformative Justice: Charting a Path to Reconciliation," *International Legal Perspective* 12 (2002), pp. 76-77.

[33] The significance of Aristide's popularity among the Haitian people should not be overlooked. Following the declaration of his candidacy for president, voter enrollment increased from 25% to 90 %. Moreover, Aristide won the election with 67.5% of the popular vote. Pastor R., "A Popular Democratic Revolution in a Predemocratic Society: The Case of Haiti", in Rotberg R. (ed.), *Haiti Renewed: Political and Economic Prospects*, Washington, D.C., Brookings Institution Press, 1997, pp. 118, 121.

significant pressure on the de facto Haitian government, including a freeze on all assets and an embargo on oil and arms. After nearly two years in exile, Aristide, with the assistance of the United Nations and the United States, attempted to force Cedras to negotiate a power transfer in exchange for general amnesty.[34] In addition to receiving United States support, the amnesty clause was also endorsed by the United Nations Security Council.[35]

Cedras, however, refused to allow Aristide's return to power and refused to allow peacekeeping forces into Haiti. On 31 July 1994, the U.N. Security Council authorized a multilateral invasion of Haiti.[36] On 18 September 1994, the day before the planned invasion, a delegation led by former United States President Jimmy Carter and authorized by President William Clinton, met with Cedras' officials. The negotiations culminated in the Carter-Jonassaint Agreement, which confirmed the plans for a general amnesty and averted an invasion of Haiti.

Although the text of the Haitian amnesty was broad in scope, it did not provide absolute immunity to Cedras and his junta. The amnesty grant applied only to certain political crimes and associated acts, limiting any amnesty to "crimes and misdemeanours against the state, internal and external security, crimes and misdemeanors affecting public order and accessory crimes and misdemeanours."[37] The first three clauses limited the grant of immunity to political crimes "against the State," such as treason. The fourth clause grants amnesty to "accessory crimes and misdemeanors," which arguably includes criminal acts with private party victims if committed as part of an

---

[34] The Situation of Democracy and Human Rights in Haiti: *Report of the Secretary General*, U.N. GAOR, 47th Sess., Agenda Item 22, U.N. Doc. A/47/975-S/26063 (1993); Malone D., *Decision-Making in the UN Security Council: The Case of Haiti, 1990-1997*, Oxford University Press, England, 1998, pp. 86-97.

[35] UN Security Council Resolution 861 (1993), UN SCOR, U.N. Doc S/RES/861 (1993); Malone D., *Decision-Making in the UN Security Council: The Case of Haiti, 1990-1997*, Oxford University Press, England, 1998, pp. 89-92.

[36] UN Security Council Resolution 940, U.N. SCOR, 49th Sess., 3413th meeting, U.N. Doc. S/RES/861 (1993).

[37] "Law Relative to Amnesty," *The Monitor, Official Journal of the Republic of Haiti*, 10 October 1994.

ongoing crime against the State.[38] Thus, the Haitian amnesty strikes a diplomatic balance, and shifts the amnesty debate from the political arena into the courtroom. On one side of the scale are three clauses expressly limiting amnesty to crimes against the amnesty's grantor; while on the other side is the immediate need for transition codified by a vague and potentially all-encompassing conferral of immunity left to interpretation by the courts.

Thus, if peaceful transition to democratic rule and the absence of bloodshed are the measures of an amnesty's success, then the Haitian amnesty is worthy of accolade. On the other hand, justice in Haiti was never served. Cedras left Haiti for Panama and was never forced to answer for his crimes. Therefore, if success is measured by retributive justice or truth and reconciliation, then the Haitian amnesty should be considered a failure or an act of impunity.

Regardless of whether one views the Haitian amnesty as a success or as a failure, it is virtually indisputable that the involvement of the United States and the United Nations legitimized the Haitian amnesty in the eyes of the international community. Moreover, international participation in the creation of any amnesty package is increasingly critical to its viability in light of the international community's recent efforts to stem transitional impunity by providing alternative venues for prosecution when States are unwilling to pursue human rights abusers.[39] Therefore, international authorities, by virtue

---

[38] Burke-White W., "Reframing Impunity: Applying Liberal International Law Theory to an Analysis of Amnesty Legislation", *Harvard International Law Journal* 42 (2001), p. 503.

[39] An example of international legal action where the state is unwilling to carry-out prosecution is currently unfolding with Charles Taylor, the former President of Liberia. In 2003, Taylor agreed to relinquish the Liberian Presidency in exchange for amnesty and asylum in Nigeria. In order to end a civil conflict, rebel leaders agreed to the amnesty on the condition that Taylor refrains from actively participating in Liberian politics. The United States played a significant role in amnesty negotiations. Taylor was granted asylum in Nigeria, but failed to uphold his end of the bargain. In March 2006, the warrant of arrest issued by the Special Court for Sierra Leone was enforced and Taylor arrested on allegations of war crimes perpetrated during the Sierra Leone civil war. Currently, Taylor is in prison awaiting a UN trial. Regardless of the outcome, Taylor's recent troubles are noteworthy because they demonstrate that an amnesty is easily set aside by the international community and foreign states. Comparing Taylor's

of the threat of universal jurisdiction, are rapidly becoming the final arbiter of amnesty packages, and it makes sense to involve these authorities from the onset of amnesty negotiations, rather than run the risk of having an agreement overruled by international authorities.

5. Conclusion

The AU has clearly stated its opposition to unconstitutional changes of government and has, through a process of consensus-building, developed norms which are designed to deal with governments that accede to power through unconstitutional changes as well as discourage would-be perpetrators of the unconstitutional change of governments. For the norms to be effective, the AU must act resolutely and consistently when faced with an unconstitutional change of government. It has, after all, pledged in its preamble to promote and protect human rights and peoples' rights, consolidate democratic institutions and culture, and ensure good governance and the rule of law in Africa. The application of the norms must convince the potential usurpers of power that the risk of failure is high and the gains from success low. It has to be realized however that this problem cannot be solved by legislative measures only. Coups occur where there is a lack of regime legitimacy, absence of adequate dialogue between rulers and the ruled, economic crisis, allegations of corruption within the constitutional government, and exclusion of groups from participation in the governance of the country. The challenge that remains therefore is to promote the development of inclusive and democratic governments and mechanisms and institutions that promote and protect good governance and the

---

tribulations and his pending prosecution to the success of the Haitian amnesty underscores the importance of involving as many international groups and foreign States as possible. In the case of Cedras and Haiti, the United Nations, the United States, and the Organization of American States were intricately involved in drafting the amnesty accord, thus, adding legitimacy to the amnesty and creating a situation where these organizations would appear hypocritical if they were to revoke or alter the amnesty deal they helped draft. On the other hand, Taylor's amnesty and asylum agreement did not rise to the same level of international participation as did the Haitian deal.

rule of law. This includes addressing issues of bad governance such as corruption and economic stagnation, lack of delivery of services and maladministration, perversion of the constitutional system and an unacceptable accumulation of political power and national wealth in a ruling elite to the exclusion of the great majority of the people. This approach would strengthen the norms on unconstitutional change of government developed by the AU and make the incidence of unconstitutional change of government in Africa a rarity.

CHAPTER 13.
THE AFRICAN CHARTER ON DEMOCRACY, ELECTIONS AND GOVERNANCE

Hélène Tigroudja

1. Introduction

The African Charter on Democracy, Elections and Governance (the Charter), adopted on 30 January 2007 by African States, meeting within the ambit of the AU proffers, at least, some partial answers to the democratic challenge currently facing the continent. It is clear right from the initial versions of the Charter that the authors resolutely opted for a universal definition of democracy. This definition could obviously be influenced by the specificities of the factual operational framework, while still remaining the expression of "the universal values and principles of democracy and respect for human rights."[1]

Among the post Second World War regional structures, only the African Union, together with the sub-regional organisation, the Economic Community of West African States (ECOWAS),[2] adopted such a binding text. Though democratic requirements were at the core

---

[1] Article 2(1) of the Charter in its final as well as the draft version of 22 November 2005.
[2] This organisation, set up in 1975, is today made up 15 States (Benin, Burkina Faso, Cape Verde, Côte d'Ivoire, The Gambia, Guinea, Guinea Bissau, Liberia, Mali, Niger, Nigeria, Senegal, Sierra Leone,) adopted a Protocol on Democracy and Good Governance Supplementary to the Protocol relating to the Mechanism For Conflict Prevention, Management, Resolution, Peacekeeping and Security (21 December 2001). The document is available on the ECOWAS website.

A.A. Yusuf & F. Ouguergouz (eds.), *The African Union: Legal and Institutional Framework. A Manual on the Pan-African Organization*, 275-290.

of the Council of Europe law,³ and the Organisation of American States (OAS), none of these two organisations adopted a specific treaty in that regard. The OAS did adopt an Inter-American Democratic Charter in 2001, which we shall examine later, but unlike the African document, it is in the form of a non-binding Resolution of the OAS General Assembly.⁴

Conversely, the African Charter of 2007 is a treaty divided into eleven chapters,⁵ respectively on (1) the definition of the terms used in the treaty; (II) the objectives and (III) principles of the Charter; (IV) democratic requirements, the rule of law and human rights; (V) the culture of democracy and peace; (VI) the institutions that underpin a democratic regime; (VII) the important issue of elections; (VIII) the equally important subject of sanctions in cases of unconstitutional changes of government; (IX) political, economic and social governance; as well as (X) the mechanisms for the implementation of the Charter; (XI) the final clauses. With about 50 articles,⁶ this Charter

---

[3] The Preamble of the Statute of the Council of Europe of 5 May 1949 does make reference to "individual freedom, political liberty and the rule of law, principles which form the basis of all genuine democracy." However, its Articles 1 and 3 do not the cover democratic requirements, highlighting the rule of law and the protection of human rights. It will require an examination of the jurisprudence of the European Court of Human Rights, a monitoring and application organ of the European Convention of Human Rights of 4 November 1950, to find references to democracy and the obligations that such a regime imposes on States Parties to the Convention.

[4] The non-binding nature of the Inter-American Democratic Charter does not prevent the Inter-American Court of Human Rights, tasked with ensuring compliance with the American Convention of Human Rights of 1969, to use it as a source of interpretation of the rights of the Convention. Ref. Judgement of the Inter-American Court of Human Rights in the matter of Claude *Reyes v. Chile* (2006), (freedom of speech and democracy), Judgment of 19 September 2006, Series C N°. 151.

[5] Compared to the versions before 2007, the structure of the Charter has changed slightly; it has not been amended in relation to the March 2007 version. However, it differs somewhat from the November 2005 one which also has eleven Chapters, but sometimes different headings. Thus Chapter V is on "Democracy, Sustainable Development and Human Security", Chapter VIII on "Democratic Culture" and Chapter IX on "Democratic Governance".

[6] More specifically, the Charter has 53 Articles, as against 62 in the earlier versions of November 2005 and March 2006.

intends to establish, strengthen and ensure the sustainability of democracy on the African continent.

The treaty has not yet come into force. Article 48 provides that it will enter into force "thirty (30) days after the deposit of fifteen (15) Instruments of Ratification". But as of 1 March 2010, of the 53 Member States of the AU, only three, Ethiopia, Mauritania and Sierra Leone,[7] have ratified it while 27 others, have only signed it. Regarding the mechanisms for the implementation of the Charter as set forth in its Chapter X (Articles 44 and 45), the AU Commission[8] is entrusted with a central role of a "coordinating structure for the implementation of this Charter,"[9] for example, by assisting States in their democratisation efforts. It is, however obvious that such mechanisms that rely basically on dialogue with States, are never binding and *a priori* do not result in the adjudication of disputes that may arise from an erroneous application or non-application of the instrument. Having said that, it may however be of interest to see how the African Court of Human and Peoples' Rights would use the Charter in setting its standards of reference with regard to the interpretation of the provisions of the African Charter of Human and Peoples' Rights of 1981.

Whatever Member States of the AU make of this Charter, a major achievement has already been made in the adoption of a mandatory instrument with innovative provisions on building democracy, even if

---

[7] Mauritania ratified it on 7 July 2008 and Ethiopia, a few months later, i.e. on December 2008. Sierra Leone followed on 17 February 2009. This information as well as the table of signatory States, are available on the AU website.

[8] For the structure and the role of the Commission within the Union, see the chapter treating it in the present work.

[9] Article 45 of the 2007 Charter provides as follows: "The Commission shall:
(a) Act as the central coordinating structure for the implementation of this Charter;
(b) Assist States Parties in implementing the Charter;
(c) Coordinate evaluation on implementation of the Charter with other key organs of the Union including the Pan-African Parliament, the Peace and Security Council, the African Human Rights Commission, the African Court of Justice and Human Rights, the Economic, Social and Cultural Council, the Regional Economic Communities and appropriate national- level structures."

it is less ambitious than the ECOWAS Protocol of 2001 that we referred to earlier and which we shall revisit.

In substance, the instrument raises several questions, such as whether the vision of the ideal democratic regime that it proffers is of European or Western origin, in general, or based on a purely African approach? What is the exact nature of this regime? How can it be attained and what are the safeguards to protect it? In order to answer these questions and without undertaking an exhaustive study of the 2007 instrument, we intend, through a critical and comparative analysis with the instrument adopted by ECOWAS and the non-binding one by the OAS, to focus on the following four parameters: (1) democracy: source of individual and collective rights; (2) the promotion of internal measures to safeguard democracy; (3) the structure of the ideal democratic African regime; and finally, (4) the sanctions in the event of the overthrow of a democratic regime.

2. Democracy: Source of Subjective Individual and Collective Rights

The Charter clearly and explicitly recognizes the intimate link between human rights and democracy, thus underlining the fact that without the guarantee and respect of the former, the latter would be meaningless (Article 1 of the Charter).

But beyond this basic principle which underpins the Charter, the text of the Charter provides for specific rights whose content and right holders may vary, according to circumstances[10]. Thus, Article 6, for example, refers to "fundamental freedoms and human rights" of "citizens", while Article 4(2) enjoins States Parties to recognise "popular participation through universal suffrage as the inalienable

---

[10] It should be noted that the States readily yielded to the temptation of including what was in vogue then, which is to integrate in a text on democracy and good governance an "environmental clause" with very little link with the main subject of the treaty. Article 42 of the Charter provides as follows "States Parties shall implement policies and strategies to protect the environment to achieve sustainable development for the benefit of the present and future generations. In this regard, States Parties are encouraged to accede to the relevant treaties and other international legal instruments."

right of the people"; and Article 10(3) refers to, without indicating a specific beneficiary, "the right to equality before the law and equal protection by the law as a fundamental precondition for a just and democratic society". As a result, one cannot fail to note the affirmation of an individual right here, a collective right or a right without a predetermined beneficiary there. However, the Charter does not go as far as replicating the formal wording in the Inter-American instrument which provides that "[t]he peoples of the Americas have a right to democracy and their governments have an obligation to promote and defend it."[11] In this regard, the development of the Charter itself over time should be emphasised. The previous versions, including the 2006 one, were bolder and more ambitious, since the draft Article 4 held up democracy as "a fundamental right".[12]

A closer examination indicates that the provisions cited above are the only ones in the Charter to guarantee a fundamental individual right, while the other articles may come under programmatic obligations and soft law, through which the States "commit themselves" or "ensure" the implementation or promotion of one ideal or the other.[13] This wording may be somewhat misleading, for it would not have been futile to recall or assert certain individual or collective rights which are inherent in a democracy, such as those relating to the freedom of expression, freedom of association, the status of political parties which have been aptly interpreted by the European Court and the Inter-American Court of Human Rights.[14]

---

[11] Article 1 of the Inter-American Democratic Charter. The non-binding nature of this Charter, obviously explains this assertion *"The peoples'... right to democracy"*, which is more symbolic than legally significant.

[12] See the wording in the 22 November 2005 version.

[13] See for example how articles 39 and 40 are couched, providing respectively that: "State Parties shall promote a culture of respect, compromise, consensus and tolerance as a means to mitigate conflicts, promote political stability and security, and to harness the creative energies of the African peoples"; "State Parties shall adopt and implement policies, strategies and programmes required to generate productive employment, mitigate the impact of diseases and alleviate poverty and eradicate extreme poverty and illiteracy."

[14] Regarding the status of political parties, see for example the landmark judgement of the European Court of Human Rights in the matter of the *United Communist Party of Turkey et al v. Turkey* (30 January 1998).

Without a free and pluralist press that enables journalists to freely express themselves and for the public to have unfettered access to reliable information on issues of general interest, there cannot be democracy[15]. Similarly, it would have been desirable to spell out the conditions of free elections at regular intervals[16], in the same way as formulated in Article 3 of Protocol N°. 1 to the European Convention of Human Rights[17] and the guarantees relating to the establishment of political parties and access to elected positions without discrimination. Finally, on account of the pivotal role played by the armed forces in coup d'états and the overthrow of constitutional regimes, it would have been useful to reproduce the substance of the relevant provisions of the ECOWAS protocol which seek to subject the army to civilian authority and the respect of the rule of law and the constitution[18]. In this regard, the wording of the Charter is disappointing because in trying to guarantee the various aspects of democratic regimes, it only

---

[15] As emphasised by the settled jurisprudence of the European Court of Human Rights in regard of freedom of expression (Article 10 of the Convention). Similarly, Article 37 of the ECOWAS Protocol raises this principle of pluralism in the media:
"1. Each Member State shall work towards ensuring pluralism of the information sector and the development of the media.
2. Each Member State may give financial assistance to privately-owned media. The distribution and allocation of such assistance shall be done by an independent national body or by a body freely instituted by the journalists themselves."

[16] From this standpoint, again the ECOWAS Protocol of 2001 is more specific (Articles 2 et seq.). It sets forth the framework within which free and transparent elections should be held. Article 4, for example, requests States Parties to "ensure the establishment of a reliable registry of births and deaths. A central registry shall be established in each Member State." Article 7 states that "Adequate arrangements shall be made to hear and dispose of all petitions relating to the conduct of elections and announcement of results."

[17] According to this provision, "The High Contracting Parties undertake to hold free elections at reasonable intervals by secret ballot, under conditions which will ensure the free expression of the opinion of the people in the choice of the legislature."

[18] See Articles 19 to 24 of the 2001 text. Its Article 20 provides that "1. The armed forces, the police and other security agencies shall be under the authority of legally constituted civilian authorities; 2. The civilian authorities shall respect the apolitical nature of the armed forces and police. All political or trade union activities and propaganda shall be forbidden in the barracks and within the armed forces."

calls upon States Parties to undertake "to develop the necessary legislative and policy frameworks to establish and strengthen a culture of democracy and peace" (Article 11); and also to "undertake to implement programmes and carry out activities designed to promote democratic principles and practices as well as consolidate a culture of democracy and peace" (Article 12) or yet still to "re-affirm their commitment to regularly holding transparent, free and fair elections" (Article 17), while recognising "the crucial role of women in development and strengthening of democracy" (Article 29).[19]

In this regard, it should be said that the method adopted by the ECOWAS Protocol of 2001 is more ambitious, being within the context of an organisation which is more integrated than the African Union. In its Article 1, the Protocol sets out the following "constitutional principles shared by all Member States" of the sub-regional Organisation:

"(a) Separation of powers – the Executive, Legislative and Judiciary

Empowerment and strengthening of parliaments and guarantee of parliamentary immunity;

Independence of the Judiciary: Judges shall be independent in the discharge of their duties;

The freedom of the members of the Bar shall be guaranteed; without prejudice to their penal or disciplinary responsibility in the event of contempt of court or breaches of the common law.

(b) Every accession to power must be made through free, fair and transparent elections;

(c) Zero tolerance for power obtained or maintained by unconstitutional means;

(d) Popular participation in decision-making, strict adherence to democratic principles and decentralisation of power at all levels of governance;

(e) The armed forces must be apolitical and must be under the command of a legally constituted political authority; no serving member of the armed forces may seek to run for elective political office;

---

[19] To this list may also be added Article 43 on education. It should be emphasised that even if the provisions detail out more the measures that States Parties should take to attain their objectives, that does not further clarify the obligations nor confirm the existence of well defined individual laws.

(f) Secularism and neutrality of the State in all matters relating to religion; freedom for each individual to practice, within the limits of existing laws, the religion of his/her choice everywhere on the national territory. The secularism shall extend to all parts of the State, but shall not deprive the State of the right to regulate, with due respect to human rights, the different religions practised on the national territory or to intervene when law and order break down as a result of any religious activity;

(g) The State and all its institutions belong to all the citizens; therefore none of their decisions and actions shall involve any form of discrimination, be it on an ethnic, racial, religion or regional basis;

(h) The rights set out in the African Charter on Human and Peoples' Rights and other international instruments shall be guaranteed in each of the ECOWAS Member States; each individual or organisation shall be free to have recourse to the common or civil law courts, a court of special jurisdiction, or any other national institution established within the framework of an international instrument on Human Rights, to ensure the protection of his/her rights. In the absence of a court of special jurisdiction, the present Supplementary Protocol shall be regarded as giving the necessary powers to common or civil law judicial bodies;

(i) Political parties shall be formed and shall have the right to carry out their activities freely, within the limits of the law. Their formation and activities shall not be based on ethnic, religious, regional or racial considerations. They shall participate freely and without hindrance or discrimination in any electoral process. The freedom of the opposition shall be guaranteed. Each Member State may adopt a system for financing political parties, in accordance with criteria set under the law;

(j) The freedom of association and the right to meet and organise peaceful demonstrations shall also be guaranteed;

(k) The freedom of the press shall be guaranteed;

(l) All former Heads of State shall enjoy a special status including freedom of movement. They shall enjoy special benefits compatible to their status as former Heads of State."

The ECOWAS Protocol thus lays the constitutional basis of the African democratic regime based on a set of principles, rules and individual rights; while the 2007 Charter adopted by the African Union is more of an instrument with a less ambitious, and less specific normative content which nonetheless establishes a framework for democracy. The approach here is clearly more procedural than substantive and prescriptive.

3. The Promotion of Internal Measures to Safeguard Democracy

The history of the overthrow of democratic regimes in Africa and elsewhere is often marked by the amendment or suspension of the constitution, by those who take over power in a non-democratic manner. It is therefore not surprising that after recalling the principle of the supremacy of the constitution (Article 10 (1)), the Charter then focuses on its revision. Article 10(2) requests States Parties "to ensure that the process of amendment or revision of their constitution is based on national consensus, obtained if need be, through referendum".

It is unfortunate, however, to note that the Charter does not urge States Parties to set material limits to this revision, as can be found in several constitutions.[20] Article 23, which we shall revisit later, however indicates that a State may be sanctioned by the Union in the event of "Any amendment or revision of the constitution or legal instruments, which is an infringement on the principles of democratic change of government." Further, the Charter could have been more ambitious regarding the very process required to amend the constitution, for example in terms of the majority required, which would be higher than that of an ordinary legislation or for example, in terms of a more direct designation of the holder of constitutional power, i.e. the people or their representatives.

These reservations do not, however, detract from the need to recall the importance of safeguarding the revision process of constitutional texts. These are also covered by the Charter from a normative standpoint, since some of the provisions indicate the minimum content of certain constitutional provisions. Thus, Article 15 of the Charter requires States Parties to "ensure that the independence or autonomy of public institutions is guaranteed by the constitution". Here again, it

---

[20] See for example, Article 79(3) the Fundamental Law of Germany (1949.)

is disappointing that these minimum provisions are so inadequate. Of course, it would have been desirable to include in such minimum requirements the principle of the independence of the judiciary, or of political parties, including minority parties, individual rights and liberties, and the principle of political responsibility of the rulers.

A democratic regime is one that organises access to power, on a non-discriminatory basis, through universal suffrage exercised as part of free, transparent elections held at regular intervals. Such are the rules that the Charter evokes from Articles 17 to 22, relating to "democratic elections."[21] As per these rules, the State shall, among other things, ensure that candidates who lose elections would accept the results (Article 17 (4)), that elections will be organised "regularly" (Article 17) and "ensure fair and equitable access by contesting parties and candidates to State-controlled media during elections." (Article 17(3)).[22]

The African Union is also involved in the regulation of access to power, since States Parties can benefit from the assistance of the Organisation's organs in the form of *"observer missions"* whose roles are outlined in Articles 18 to 21 of the Charter. The Charter is, however, silent on the crucial issue of funding of political parties which, as we know, is critical to equitable access to elections and power, as recalled in Article 5 of the Inter-American Democratic Charter[23] and Article 1 of the ECOWAS Protocol.

4. Structures of the Ideal Democratic African Regime

One of the objectives of the Charter is to promote good governance without which democracy cannot exist. Thus, Article 2(6) requires

---

[21] See Articles 2 to 10 of the ECOWAS Protocol.
[22] In some States like France, equitable access to the media is not limited to state media, but also relates to the private media, so as to obviate a discrimination based on candidates' wealth. We believe that these provisions should not have been limited to a single category of media, for the same reasons.
[23] According to this provision "The strengthening of political parties and other political organizations is a priority for democracy. Special attention will be paid to the problems associated with the high cost of election campaigns and the establishment of a balanced and transparent system for their financing."

States Parties to "nurture, support and consolidate good governance by promoting democratic culture and practice, building and strengthening governance institutions and inculcating political pluralism and tolerance". Further on, reference is made to the need to combat corruption and the assertion of the principle of transparency in the management of public affairs.

Articles 27 *et seq.* spell out the implementation of this good governance and the means to attain it by combating corruption, promoting civil society, improving management of the public sector, promoting press freedom, establishing an efficient and responsible administration, which are all measures likely to ensure "good political governance."[24] Other aspects of good governance are underscored in the Charter,[25] such as "good economic governance" and "good social governance". The former is addressed in a sufficiently clear manner in Article 33 of the Charter[26] while the latter is more diffuse and vague. Article 31(1) of the Charter does not go beyond urging

---

[24] Article 12(1) further provides that States Parties shall "Promote good governance by ensuring transparent and accountable administration."

[25] The Inter-American Democratic Charter also asserts the principle which states that "Democracy and social and economic development are interdependent and are mutually reinforcing." Similarly, the ECOWAS Protocol also dedicates a number of articles to issues relating to poverty, education and "social dialogue". (Articles 25 *et seq.*)

[26] According to this provision, "States Parties shall institutionalize good economic and corporate governance through, *inter alia*:
1. Effective and efficient public sector management;
2. Promoting transparency in public finance management;
3. Preventing and combating corruption and related offences;
4. Efficient management of public debt;
5. Prudent and sustainable utilization of public resources;
6. Equitable allocation of the nation's wealth and natural resources;
7. Poverty alleviation;
8. Enabling legislative and regulatory framework for private sector development;
9. Providing a conducive environment for foreign capital inflows;
10. Developing tax policies that encourage investment;
11. Preventing and combating crime;
12. Elaborating and implementing economic development strategies including private-public sector partnerships;
13. An efficient and effective tax system premised upon transparency and accountability."

States Parties to "promote participation of social groups with special needs, including the Youth and people with disabilities, in the governance process".[27]

It is important to note that the Charter[28] deals with one of the issues which affects the life of many people in Africa and elsewhere in the world: the recognition of minority rights and those of politically vulnerable and marginalized groups. Here, two categories of such groups are specifically targeted: women and "traditional communities."[29] Article 29 of the Charter thus focuses on "the crucial role of women in development and strengthening of democracy" and accordingly urges States Parties to "create the necessary conditions for (their) full and active participation" in political life (Article 29(2)), and to particularly promote parity between men and women during elections and in governing and legislative bodies (Article 29(3)). Though not directly cited, the Maputo Protocol to the African Charter on Human and Peoples' Right adopted in 2003, urged States Parties to promote the political rights of women. The provisions of this Charter are a reminder of the need to give women a place in political and democratic life.[30]

The provisions of the Charter, regarding indigenous communities[31] are vague. The explanation for this could relate to the fact that on the

---

[27] Article 31(2) is not any more enlightening: "States Parties shall ensure systematic and comprehensive civic education in order to encourage full participation of social groups with special needs in democracy and development processes."

[28] Like the ECOWAS Protocol, at least in its Article 40 which recalls the importance of the role of women as an "essential factor(s) for development, progress and peace in the society".

[29] In a broad manner, Article 8(2) of the Charter enjoins States Parties to take measures to improve the conditions of any person belonging to a "marginalized and vulnerable social groups".

[30] In this regard, the lot of women in the African Charter is more satisfactory than in the Inter-American Democratic Charter, where curiously, their situation is dealt with in the last article of the text, with no link with the previous articles nor the chapter in which it is inserted. It is also couched in very vague terms: "States shall promote the full and equal participation of women in the political structures of their countries as a fundamental element in the promotion and exercise of a democratic culture.".

[31] They are not specifically distinguished in the 2001 ECOWAS Protocol.

African continent, the problem of reconciling the construction of a unitary and majority State[32] and the need to take into account community issues is an acute one, as is the case on the American continent for example.[33] Article 35 provides as follows: "Given the enduring and vital role of traditional authorities, particularly in rural communities, the States Parties shall strive to find appropriate ways and means to increase their integration and effectiveness within the larger democratic system."[34]

Finally, the democratic organisation of power and its institutions must make room for decentralisation as stated concisely in Article 34 of the Charter, which provides that "States Parties shall decentralize power to democratically elected local authorities as provided in national laws." However, it does not seem that the principle of subsidiarity, well known in Europe, is considered in the Charter as one the foremost guarantees of democracy. In fact, it is not mentioned among the measures required "to institutionalize good political governance" as defined in Article 32, nor in Article 2 of the Charter.

5. Sanctions in Case of the Overthrow of a Democratic Regime

Beyond reaffirming the principles and structures that underpin a democratic regime, the Charter aims particularly, at establishing safeguards and mechanisms that will trigger a reaction at the regional level, in the event of a change or a disruption of the constitutional order. Thus, Chapter VIII of the Charter focuses on "Sanctions in

---

[32] The construction of this state certainly does not obviate the federalist or decentralised structure.

[33] In this regard, see particularly, the jurisprudence of the Inter-American Court of Human Rights on the rights of indigenous communities, such as *Yatama v. Nicaragua*, 23 June 2005, series C No. 127.

[34] As on the role of women, the Inter-American Democratic Charter is not very compelling on the political situation of indigenous peoples, even though as was indicated, that constitutes a problem in several American countries. The sole provision which mentions their political status, only indirectly, is Article 9 which prohibits discrimination and promotes "human rights of indigenous peoples and migrants, and respect for ethnic, cultural and religious diversity in the Americas" as factors that contribute "to strengthening democracy and citizen participation."

Cases of Unconstitutional Changes of Government", these being sanctions to be applied by the African Union itself.[35]

Article 23 commences with a list of "illegal" means of accession to power, the use of which may draw a reaction from the Union. They include the following: putsch or coup d'état, intervention by mercenaries or the refusal of an incumbent government to recognise the winner in free elections.[36] The Peace and Security Council, which is covered by a separate Protocol,[37] may where appropriate, sanction a State Party by suspending its right to participate in the Organisation's activities (Article 25 (1)). However, where a State Party assists in the illegal accession to power in another State Party, it shall no longer lie with the Peace and Security Council to impose sanctions, but rather with the Assembly of Heads of State and Governments, as stated in Article 25 of the Charter. These measures shall be lifted "once the situation that led to the suspension is resolved."[38]

Here, the Charter's silence should be pointed out, just as in the 2001 ECOWAS Protocol,[39] on other possible and more serious

---

[35] For the Inter-American Charter, see articles 17 *et seq*.
[36] Article 23 of the African Charter.
[37] Regarding the operation and missions of this Council, see the chapter on it in this work.
[38] Article 26 of the African Charter.
[39] Article 45 of this Protocol provides that:
"1. In the event that democracy is abruptly brought to an end by any means or where there is massive violation of Human Rights in a Member State, ECOWAS may impose sanctions on the State concerned.
2. The sanctions which shall be decided by the Authority may take the following forms, in increasing order of severity:
- Refusal to support the candidates presented by the Member State concerned for elective posts in international organisations;
- Refusal to organise ECOWAS meetings in the Member State concerned;
- Suspension of the Member State concerned from all ECOWAS decision-making bodies. During the period of the suspension the Member State concerned shall be obliged to pay its dues for the period.
3. During the period of suspension, ECOWAS shall continue to monitor, encourage and support the efforts being made by the suspended Member State to return to normalcy and constitutional order;
4. On the recommendation of the Mediation and Security Council, a decision may be taken at the appropriate time to proceed as stipulated in Article 45 of the Protocol."

sanctions, than the suspension of State Parties' right of participation in the activities of the Organisation, which may lead to their outright suspension. This eventuality is provided for in the Statute of the Council of Europe.[40] Further, we note that there is no provision, at least not in the text, though the practice may differ, for a preliminary phase of consultations and exhaustion of diplomatic avenues, prior to the imposition of sanctions, as is the case in the Inter-American Democratic Charter. Article 21 of this Charter provides that the General Assembly of the OAS may suspend a member state, whose organs acceded to power illegally, once it is determined that "diplomatic initiatives have failed". It is therefore established as a rule, to exhaust diplomatic avenues to resolve the crisis before applying sanctions against the state. Such is not the case in the African text, as per the Peace and Security Council's reaction to the recent crisis in Niger, and it is very likely that in practice, the sanction of States will be immediate.[41] Finally, it should be indicated that the final version of the provisions on sanctions is the result of the extensively amended earlier versions of November 2005[42] and March 2006.[43] These earlier versions gave the various organs of the Union wide

---

[40] Pursuant to Article 8 of the Statute of the Council of Europe (1949) "Any member of the Council of Europe which has seriously violated Article 3 may be suspended from its rights of representation and requested by the Committee of Ministers to withdraw under Article 7. If such member does not comply with this request, the Committee may decide that it has ceased to be a member of the Council as from such date as the Committee may determine." Its Article 3 provides as follows: "Every member of the Council of Europe must accept the principles of the rule of law and of the enjoyment by all persons within its jurisdiction of human rights and fundamental freedoms, and collaborate sincerely and effectively in the realisation of the aim of the Council as specified in Chapter I." The democratic requirement is certainly not mentioned in Article 3, but the development of the practice within the Council of Europe, such as the exclusion of Greece in 1974, attests to the fact that an undemocratic State may be excluded from the organisation. Similarly, the jurisprudence of the European Court has often evoked the notion of "democratic society" as being part of the essential values of that form the bedrock of the Council.

[41] On 19 February, the suspension of Niger's right of participation in the activities of the African Union was announced.

[42] Article 25 *et seq.* of the draft Charter.

[43] Article 30 *et seq.* of the draft Charter.

powers to intervene in re-establishing the constitutional regime in a State in crisis, without any mention of the prior consent of the State in question. The risk of interfering in the internal affairs of States may have been considered too high and led to the adoption of a much weaker intervention of the organs of the African Union.

6. Conclusion

In spite of the universal democratic ideal that the African Charter on Democracy, Elections and Governance aims at projecting, it must be admitted that, more than three years after its adoption, the instrument has not met with great success among Member States. It has been ratified by only three Members of the African Union which has fifty-three Members States. Besides, current political events on the continent continue to demonstrate that even if there were a consensus making it possible to adopt a final version of the Charter, the principles embodied therein have not yet acquired a real and daily application in the region. Is that sufficient to challenge the effectiveness and therefore the interest of such an instrument? Definitely not. The Charter, just like its predecessor, the ECOWAS Protocol adopted in 2001, lays the foundation of the constitutional principles shared by African States, which in turn, are just an expression of the "universal values and principles" referred to in Article 2 of the Charter. The document is imperfect, it is incomplete and sometimes too soft, but placed in the more general context of the African Union law, it constitutes a cornerstone of the integrated edifice that the African States are striving to build and which holds out hopes of realizing in the continent of a better protection of human rights, the rule of law and democracy.

CHAPTER 14.
THE AFRICAN CONVENTION ON THE PREVENTION AND COMBATING OF CORRUPTION

Mpazi Sinjela

1. Introduction

The African Union (AU) has taken a strong position against corruption due to the fact that corruption has a negative impact on the national development of African countries. Although the term "corruption" is defined variously, its general meaning is well understood. It generally refers to acts from which insiders in public institutions profit at the expense of the general public which is the intended beneficiary.

Corruption also refers to the giving of something usually of a monetary value, or a bribe as consideration, to a public official in order to secure their influence or to have them perform something in an arbitrary manner or outside the rules or established procedures. The World Bank has defined corruption as the abuse of public office for private gain. Public office is abused for private gain when an official accepts, solicits, or extorts a bribe. The Bank has also noted that public office is abused when private agents actively offer bribes to circumvent public policies and processes for competitive advantage and profit. It is true also that public office is abused for personal benefit even if no bribery occurs, through patronage and nepotism, the theft of State assets or the diversion of state resources.[1]

---

[1] World Bank, "Helping Combat Corruption: The Role of the World Bank", 1997. The Asian Development Bank, on the other hand defines corruption to mean "the behavior on the part of officials in the public and private sectors, in which they

The concern of the AU over corruption centres around the fact that funds usually intended for public benefit never reach the intended beneficiaries due to bribery and corruption. Corruption enriches few people at the expense of the majority, mostly the vulnerable groups, in a society[2] and blocks development, as limited scarce resources end up in the pockets of a few individuals.

Corruption has large social and economic consequences on countries and impedes economic and social development through diversion of funds from public expenditure into private pockets. Corruption is also associated with high levels of tax evasion. In a corrupt society, public officials may be bribed in order to evade payment of taxes. In such cases, government revenues are lost and without taxes, it is difficult for a government to meet its responsibilities of providing for the well being of its people. In addition, corruption pushes up the cost of social services offered by the state.

As the AU Member States know all too well, corruption has a negative effect on promoting private and foreign investment in a country. A high level of corruption in a country is a recipe for discouraging direct foreign investment. Furthermore, corruption and bribery are often associated with organized crime, which has a negative impact on national as well as international security.

Therefore, corruption is no longer viewed as a private matter between the person corrupting and the person being corrupted. Its consequences are far wider than the individuals involved in its commission and may affect the entire country. Therefore, corruption is a matter of great concern to all countries of the world, and particularly for the developing countries of Africa. For this reason, corruption has been viewed to be a major impediment to development in developing countries and countries in transition to a market economy.

---

improperly and unlawfully enrich themselves and/or those closely related to them, or induce others to do so, by misusing the position in which they are placed." See Osita Agbu, "Corruption and Human Trafficking: The Nigerian Case", *West African Review* 4 (2003), p. 1.

[2] Oxfam Briefing Paper: "Africa at the Crossroads: Time to deliver", p. 2.

2. International Efforts Aimed at Fighting Corruption

Efforts to eradicate corruption have been on the international and regional agenda for a long time. A number of international and regional treaties have been adopted aimed at eradicating or reducing the phenomenon of corruption. Notable among such conventions are the following: the Organization of Economic Cooperation and Development (OECD) Convention on Combating Bribery of Foreign Public Officials in International Business Transactions;[3] the Council of Europe Criminal Law Convention on Corruption;[4] the European Convention on the same subject of May 1997;[5] the Inter-American Convention Against Corruption;[6] and the United Nations Convention against Corruption[7] adopted on 9 December 2003.

3. African Union: Efforts to Prevent and Combat Corruption

Since corruption has much wider consequences on weak developing and least developed nations, most of which are in Africa, the AU has expressed great concern on the negative effects of corruption and its impunity on the political, economic, social and cultural stability of the countries of Africa. It has also recognized corruption's devastating effects on the economic and social development of the people of Africa.[8] This expression of concern therefore led the AU to adopt the Convention on the Prevention and Combating of Corruption. This fact has entailed not only recognition of corruption as a heinous crime, but the need to adopt common penal policy aimed at protecting the African people against its negative effects.[9]

---

[3] Adopted in December 1997 and came into force on 15 February 1999.
[4] Adopted on 27 January 1999. See E.T.S. 173 (came into force in 2002), on the Website of the European Union.
[5] *Idem.*
[6] Entered into force on 6 March 1997.
[7] See the Website of the United Nations Office on Drug and Crime (UNODC).
[8] See: Preamble, African Convention against Corruption, In Transparency International (TI), global, regional and country Reports, p. 117.
[9] *Ibid.*

The basis of this Convention is to be found in various African instruments, such as the African Charter on Human and Peoples Rights; the 1990 Declaration on the Fundamental Changes Taking Place in the World and their Implications for Africa; the 1994 Cairo Agenda for Action Re-launching Africa's Socio-economic Transformation; and the Plan of Action Against Impunity. These instruments underlined the need to observe principles of good governance, the rule of law, human rights, and democratization and popular participation by the African States in the process of continental integration.[10] The declaration concerning the New Partnership for Africa (NEPAD), adopted by the AU Assembly of Heads of States and Government in Lusaka, Zambia in July 2001 and in Durban, South Africa in July 2002, also called for the establishment of a coordinated mechanism for effectively combating corruption.[11]

The adoption of this Convention has been hailed as a promising sign of serious commitment by the governments of the AU Member States to stamp out corruption and recognized to introduce "innovative and new concepts which are at the cutting-edge of jurisprudence and practical strategies for preventing and combating corruption".

4. Objectives of the Convention

The aim of the Convention is to promote and develop mechanisms to prevent, detect, punish and eradicate corruption both in public as well as private sectors. It also aims to facilitate and regulate cooperation among the States Parties in order to ensure that measures and actions are adopted for the effective detection, punishment and eradication of corruption. The Convention sets out as one of its main objectives, the coordination and harmonization of policies and legislation among the States Parties, with a view to promoting socio-economic development by ensuring that public funds are used for the purpose they are intended for. The Convention is also designed at

---

[10] See "The New Partnership for Africa's Development (NEPAD), AU Doc. ASSG, p. 35 (XXXVIII), Annex 1.
[11] See Transparency International Press Release, on the Website of the Organization.

establishing the necessary conditions for fostering transparency and accountability in the management of public affairs.

The Convention provides broad scope for offences constituting acts of corruption. Such offences do not only include those committed by public officials but may also involve acts committed by private persons. Offences may include solicitation or acceptance by, or the offering or granting to a public official or any other person, goods of monetary value in exchange for the illegal commission of acts. Offences may also involve illicit acts intended to obtain benefits for an individual or third party or a diversion of state property. They also encompass the offering and promising or accepting an undue advantage from a person who works for a private sector in breach as public official of his duties. Illicit enrichment is also considered to be an act of corruption.

5. Legislation and other Measures

The Convention imposes an obligation on State Parties to adopt legislative measures that establish as offences acts identified as corruption. It also requires State Parties to strengthen control mechanisms to ensure that foreign companies investing in their countries respect national legislation. State Parties are equally called upon to establish independent anti-corruption authorities and to create, maintain and strengthen internal accounting, auditing and follow-up systems in order to make it easier to detect acts of corruption and ill gotten wealth and thus subject the individuals concerned to prosecution.

Protection of informants has been identified as an important principle if information is to be freely obtained to enable prosecution and conviction of persons involved in corrupt acts. The Convention therefore calls upon States Parties to adopt measures that would ensure the protection of informants and witnesses, including their identity, in corruption cases. This is an important provision given the secrecy under which corruption-related offences take place. It is also important since many corruption-related offences, particularly those involving large amounts of funds, may also be linked to organized crime.

6. Money Laundering

The Convention contains wide-ranging provisions against money laundering. As bribery and corruption involve illegal activities sometimes associated with organized crime, perpetrators of such crimes hide their proceeds by money laundering. States Parties are therefore required to adopt legislation making it a criminal offence for any person to convert, transfer or dispose of property knowing that it was derived from corrupt or related offences and has the intention of concealing or disguising the illicit origin of that property. The offence of money laundering is also committed when a person knowingly helps the person involved in committing such an offence to evade prosecution.

The Convention makes it an offence when one conceals or disguises the true nature, source, location, disposition, movement or ownership of or rights regarding the property that is the subject of corruption. States Parties are thus required to make a criminal offence the acquisition, possession or use of property which is known to have been acquired through corrupt or related means.

In order to combat corruption, the Convention places an obligation on public officials to show how they acquired wealth that is more than what their income would command. States Parties are requested to adopt measure obliging public officials to declare their assets before taking up office as well as at the end of their public service.

The Convention makes illicit enrichment an offence to be considered as corruption. States Parties are requested to establish such an offence in their national legislation. Such an inclusion could be criticized by some, in the sense that stating that it might undermine the well-established principle of presumption of innocence. Indeed, in the present situation, the prosecution would only need to show, not beyond reasonable doubt that the public official in question has acquired wealth that exceeds his income. A presumption therefore arises that such unjustified income was derived from corruption.

As noted above, efforts aimed at combating corruption are not only directed at the public officials, but private individuals as well. State Parties are therefore required to adopt legislation to prevent and combat acts of corruption committed by private individuals in the private sector. The Convention also calls on member states to establish mechanisms directed at encouraging the participation of the private sector in the fight against unfair competition, respect of the tender procedures and property rights. The measures to be adopted should be directed at preventing companies from paying bribes in order to win tenders.

7. Jurisdiction

A very wide jurisdiction is established by the convention for corruption offences. State Parties are given jurisdiction for such offences when the breach takes place in the territory of the State Party whether in part or wholly; when the offence is committed by one of its nationals outside its territory or by a resident of its territory; or when the person alleged to have committed the offence is actually in that territory and the State Party does not extradite him to the State where the offence is said to have been committed. Jurisdiction is also assumed when a State Party feels such acts impact on its vital interests even when the offence took place outside its territory. In order to safeguard the interest of an offender from being prosecuted twice, guarantees are provided against such an eventuality.[12]

The Convention also provides for fair trial in a criminal proceeding in accordance with the minimum guarantees contained in the African Charter of Human and Peoples' Rights and any other international human rights instruments recognized by the Party concerned.[13]

8. Extradition

There are several possibilities provided for extradition of alleged offenders. Offences established in accordance with the Convention may trigger a request for extradition. An innovative system for extradition of offenders has been introduced. Offences under the Convention are automatically deemed to have been included in the internal laws of State Parties as extraditable offences. Therefore,

---

[12] See Article 13 of the Convention.
[13] See Article 14 of the Convention.

members are required to include such offences as extraditable offences in extradition treaties existing between them.

Another innovative provision included in the Convention is the requirement that where a State Party makes extradition conditional upon the existence of a treaty and that State receives a request for extradition from another Party with which it does not have an extradition treaty, the present Convention could be considered as a legal basis for extradition. The Convention requests member states to extradite alleged offenders. If any party refuses to extradite, in such a case, the alleged offender is to be handed over to the competent authorities for prosecution.[14]

The Convention also calls on member states to adopt legislation giving power to competent authorities to "search, identify, trace, administer and freeze or seize the instrumentalities and proceeds of corruption pending final judgment". The authorities may also confiscate the proceeds or property whose value is equal to the proceeds of the corrupt act and may repatriate the proceeds to the affected country.[15] Similarly, banks may be ordered to seize any banking, financial or commercial documents relating to the offence for the purpose of implementing the Convention. In such a case, Member States are called upon not to invoke banking secrecy to justify their refusal to cooperate.[16]

The Convention addresses the question of cooperation and mutual legal assistance at both the national, regional and international levels. The inclusion of this requirement was felt necessary due to the fact that the fight against corruption, which has an international dimension, can only be won through cooperation and mutual assistance by all States. The Convention therefore requires State Parties to accord each other "the greatest possible technical cooperation and assistance in dealing immediately with requests ... to prevent, detect, investigate and punish acts of corruption and related offences".[17] State Parties are also called upon to collaborate with the countries of origin of multinationals and to criminalize and punish the practice of offering secret

---

[14] See Article 15 of the Convention.
[15] See Article 16 of the Convention.
[16] See Article 17 of the Convention.
[17] See Article 18, paragraph 1 of the Convention.

commissions during international trade transactions. While calling on State Parties to foster cooperation at all levels to prevent corrupt practices in international trade, the Convention also encourages them to take legislative measures to prevent corrupt officials from enjoying ill-acquired assets. The bank accounts of such officials should therefore be frozen and State Parties should facilitate repatriation of such assets to countries of origin. State Parties are also encouraged to work closely with financial institutions in order to eradicate corruption in development aid and cooperation programs. The way this is to be achieved includes strictly defining the regulations to be followed by persons working in the development policy area of the government.[18]

9. Implementation and Monitoring Mechanism

The question of the implementation of any convention is crucial in order to attain its objectives. A weak mechanism for implementation is likely to frustrate the attainment of such objectives. This point appears to have been fully appraised by the drafters of the Convention. In the implementation and monitoring of the Convention therefore, an eleven member Advisory Board was established. The members of the Board, who are to be elected by State Parties, should be persons who possess the requisite expertise and highest personal integrity, impartiality, and recognized competence in the field of preventing and combating corruption. The Board should take into account gender balance and equitable geographical representation.

The functions of the Board include promotion and encouragement of the adoption and application of anti-corruption measures in Africa; collection of documents and information; advising governments on how to deal with the scourge of corruption in their domestic jurisdiction and developing methodologies for the analysis of the nature and extent of corruption in Africa.

The other functions of the Board are to collect information regarding the behavior of multinational corporations operating in Africa. Such information is to be analyzed and offered to national authorities for combating corruption. The Board is also mandated to

---

[18] See Article 19 of the Convention.

develop and promote adoption of harmonized codes of conduct of public officials. Other functions of equal importance include building partnerships with the African Commission on Human and Peoples Rights and civil society, governmental and non-governmental organizations. Such partnerships are intended to facilitate dialogue among all stakeholders in the fight against corruption.

The Advisory Board submits its reports to the African Union on a regular basis concerning the progress made by each State Party in the implementation of the Convention. State Parties are also requested to communicate information to the Advisory Board within a year following the entry into force of the Convention. Such information should relate to the progress made by them in the implementation of the Convention.

As the term suggests, the Board is advisory in nature and does not have any investigative authority or the power to prosecute any alleged offender. It submits its findings to the Executive Council of the AU for its decision and action.

10. Conclusion

The AU's efforts in tackling corruption through the adoption of this Convention which is the first continent-wide legal framework in the fight against corruption among the member States of the African Union are laudable. While the responsibility for ensuring compliance with the letter and spirit of the Convention lies with the State Parties, it is all too well known however that most such States may not have sufficient material and human resources to carry this through. It is therefore suggested that in addition to the efforts of State Parties, the civil society and other non-governmental groups should actively get involved and become the watch dog of the implementation of the provisions of the Convention and the fight against corruption. This partnership between the governmental agencies and the civil society is more likely to bring about a successful implementation of the Convention and thus avoid it becoming a dead letter even before the ink dries up. Adoption of the Convention is indeed just a first step, and reflects a strong resolution by the State Parties to fight against this heinous crime and ensure its eradication. Once public officials and private ones alike know the serious consequences of engaging in corrupt practices, they are likely to refrain from becoming involved or tempted in such activities. The peoples of the African continent will be much better off without the scourge of corruption in their societies. For having started the process, the AU will have earned itself a major victory.

PART IV. PEACE AND SECURITY

CHAPTER 15.
THE ROLE OF THE UNION IN CONFLICT PREVENTION AND RESOLUTION

Mesmer L. Gueuyou

1. Introduction

The collective security of States is a primary objective of international political organizations and an essential aspect of international cooperation. In Africa more than anywhere else, it highlights the problems raised by the phenomenon of global interdependence, which would be addressed by the action of African organizations – the OAU, followed by the AU, and sub-regional bodies – and by non-African organizations such as the United Nations. The phenomenon of international organizations springs from the awareness of increasing interdependence between States in their search for ways and means of improving the lot of their peoples. In addition, regionalism comes from the desire of all regions of the international community to benefit from peace, security and universal prosperity. This pre-supposes the existence of effective mechanisms for managing disputes and collective security. With the system established by the United Nations Charter, there has been an attempt to organise international law and to forge a concept of centralised collective security of all its Member States. This would seem to be the only area where the creation of a universal super-State has been attempted. However, this system allows regions the possibility of creating their own security system while strongly emphasising the primary responsibility of the Security Council in this regard.

The African Union follows this trend, as Africa has, for more than four decades now, been the region in the world most prone to armed struggles and political crises that engender conflict. Since 1970, there have been more than thirty wars, together accounting for more than half of all conflict-related deaths, and generating more than eight million refugees and displaced persons.[1] In addition, unlike the wars of independence, current armed conflicts are characterised by an endemic nature and distinguished by the scale of harm they cause among populations, in particular women and children, who are the most vulnerable. It has been observed that these conflicts have a tendency to grow incrementally rather than to succeed each other,[2] and that they sometimes have strong regional interconnections. In fact, from strictly intrastate or inter-state origins, conflicts have been aggravated by a strong cross-border dimension, resulting in the destabilisation of entire regions. During the past decade alone, the conflicts in the DRC, Liberia, the Sudan, Somalia and Angola have all had regional overtones, and have together enmeshed fourteen African countries in a web of violence.

Sadly, the continent seems to be an excellent laboratory for applied and envisaged security mechanisms at the global, regional and sub-regional levels. The now defunct OAU Charter already included in its principles the peaceful resolution of conflict through negotiation, mediation, reconciliation and arbitration (Article 3(4)). To this end, Article 19 provided for the establishment of a commission, although this remained a dead letter. The replacement of the OAU by the AU was intended to have enabled African leaders to bring about a revolution in the principles governing peace and security in Africa. Well before the Union was established, discussions by Heads of State and Government during their 26th Summit in Addis Ababa in July 1990 on fostering a climate of peace on the continent led to the Cairo Declaration of 30 July 1993 and instituted a mechanism for

---

[1] *Report of the United Nations Secretary General on the causes of conflict and the promotion of durable peace and sustainable development in Africa*, UN Doc. A/52/871 – S/1998/318.

[2] See: Press Release of the African Social Forum in Lusaka (Zambia), "Paix et Conflits en Afrique. Les sentiers à explorer pour la paix", December 2004, on the website of the Panos Institute West Africa.

conflict prevention and management. By this means, the organization created more flexible and operational structures through the constitution of a central organ inspired by the United Nations Security Council. That said, this mechanism was most successful in the area of conflict prevention, as the institution lacked the significant resources required to bring about lasting peace in conflict areas. Among the achievements of this mechanism, which outlived the OAU by several months, was the institution of implementation missions on the ground, for example in Rwanda, Burundi and the Comoros.[3] Under the aegis of the Union, this organ also initiated and deployed an inter-African force of more than 2000 soldiers to manage the Burundi conflict in 2003. Commissions of inquiry and diplomatic activity also served as a tool for conflict prevention in Africa.

This activism on the part of the OAU was limited by the provisions of its Charter and the principles governing inter-African relations. The sacrosanct principle of sovereignty, and its corollary, non-interference in the internal affairs of other States, are now viewed as having hampered the effective involvement of the OAU and African leaders in conflict management and prevention on the continent. The establishment of the Union and its Constitutive Act undeniably signalled the abandonment of this wait-and-see philosophy, and the transformation of the regional system of collective security. The adaptation of the institution to the new international environment, and new conflict situations in Africa based more on factional fighting within States, and sometimes without designated adversaries of the government in power, became a categorical imperative that would allow the failings of the OAU to be avoided. All in all, it was not the fact of changing an organization which could have provided the cure-all in the search for lasting collective peace and security in Africa, but rather the real political will and the pooling of adequate means to achieve it. The Union was to act as the forum in which means were sought to influence the conduct of various stakeholders and interests, thus allowing this common objective to be achieved. One of the concerns of the initiators was indeed

---

[3] See Chapter 17 in this *Manual* authored by Mutoy Mubiala.

the "concern not to reduce the Union merely to the OAU under another name."[4]

Generally speaking, the powers of the AU are considerably wider than those of its predecessor, covering issues such as democracy, the rule of law, good governance and fundamental human rights, which are essential to conflict prevention and to fostering an atmosphere of peace and security.[5] The quantitative and qualitative transformation in 2002 thus offer unprecedented opportunities for an efficient and legitimate approach to the security problems that have sapped African countries since independence, especially as African countries have no choice but to manage the continent's problems themselves. The United Nations no longer has the capacity to respond to repeated conflicts in Africa, and the former colonial powers had up till then responded only inadequately to the expectations of victims.[6] Aware of this situation, the Heads of State on several occasions expressed their intention to provide stronger conflict prevention mechanisms, encouraged in this by Chapter VII of the United Nations Charter, which requires members of regional arrangements to make every effort to achieve pacific settlement of local disputes through such arrangements. In his report of 13 April 1998 on the causes of conflict and the promotion of durable peace and sustainable development in Africa, the former United Nations Secretary General highlighted the need for Africa to take charge of its affairs, with external support, by stating the following:

> "Within the context of the United Nations primary responsibility which is to ensure international peace and security, it is necessary and desirable to provide support for regional and sub-regional initiatives in Africa. Such support is necessary because the United Nations lacks the capacity, resources and expertise to address all problems that may arise in Africa. It is desirable because wherever possible the international community should strive to

---

[4] Bourgi A., "L'Union Africaine: entre les textes et la réalité", *Annuaire Français de Relations Internationales* 5 (2004), p. 328.
[5] *Ibid.*, p. 329.
[6] Nevertheless, the United Kingdom intervened in Sierra Leone in 2000, and France has been active in Côte d'Ivoire since 2002.

complement rather than supplant African efforts to resolve Africa's problems."[7]

The establishment of the Union was accompanied by the establishment of an African peace and security framework more ambitious than the OAU's conflict prevention mechanism, which was constrained by lack of resources and political will, as any accusation against a State was considered a breach of its sovereignty. The basis of the system is the Peace and Security Council, established by protocol on 9 July 2002. It embodies one of the key objectives of the Union, which is to promote peace, security and stability on the continent according to the principles of the peaceful settlement of disputes by the means deemed appropriate by the Assembly of the Union, and of respect for the sovereignty and territorial integrity of Member States, while affirming the Union's right to intervene in a Member State following a decision of the Assembly in certain grave circumstances (war crimes, genocide and crimes against humanity). The Union also intends to set up a standby force in each of the five regions of the continent, in liaison with sub-regional organizations, in order to intervene directly in countries in times of crisis. The Union also assumes a dominant role on the continent in the area of conflict prevention and management, and has moved into a new phase, centred on intervention, in terms of peacekeeping and regional security. As a result, in his annual follow-up report on conflicts in Africa for 2004, Mr. Kofi Annan highlighted the increased effectiveness of the African Union and sub-regional organizations in conflict prevention and management, considering that they have stood out as key partners on the continent, where they are increasingly showing the way forward and in some cases even directing peace-keeping operations, hence the interest and support of some donors, whose attention was attracted by these aspects of the AU's actions in favour of peace and security. The incorporation of this cornerstone of conflict prevention in its activities and the central role it plays on the continent reflects the Union's intention of strengthening the capacities of regional economic communities which are part and parcel of the African system of

---

[7] UN Doc. A/52/871 – S/1998/318.

conflict prevention and management. The AU has also adopted a proactive approach through, on the one hand, the institutional mechanism established to prevent and manage conflicts, and on the other hand, a strategy in light of the operational framework provided for in the Constitutive Act and basic documents of the Union. But of what value is a document or a mechanism if it cannot be applied on the ground?

2. A Proactive Approach in Light of Institutional Mechanisms

The profound change noted in the vision and practice of peacekeeping and collective security in Africa is accompanied by the mobilisation of the main organs of the Union to attain the key objective of peacebuilding. Far from stunting the system, this proliferation of structures that are more or less involved in conflict prevention and management is proof of a firmer political will and of the proactive stance of the Union and its Constitutive Act. This is true for the Union's special programmes, whose initial objectives of economic development have been extended to peace and security issues.

2.1. The proliferation of organs dealing with conflict prevention and management

Apart from the Peace and Security Council, whose purpose is unambiguous, other organs of the African Union support its primary mission to a varying degree. One might think that this concerns only the key organs considered as priorities by the Lusaka summit of 2003. These are the Assembly, the Executive Council, the Committee of Permanent Representatives, and the Commission. However, the Protocol relating to the establishment of a Peace and Security Council reveals the central role played by the Commission, the Panel of the Wise, the Pan-African Parliament and the Conflict Management Division, which are responsible for setting up the continental early warning system.

2.1.1. The role of the political organs of the AU as set out in the Constitutive Act

In the OAU, the Assembly of Heads of State and Government and the Council of Ministers played a primary role in conflict resolution in Africa. Article 8 of the Charter, confirmed by Article 3 of the Rules of Procedure of the Assembly, vested it with overall powers to discuss any matter of interest to African countries.[8] The Assembly of the Union and the Executive Council operate within the same register. With regard to the Assembly, the Constitutive Act stipulates that it is the supreme organ of the Union. In addition to determining the Union's common policies, its other powers include the establishment of any organ of the Union, as is the case with the Peace and Security Council.

With regard to peacekeeping specifically, Article 9(g) provides that the Assembly shall "give directives to the Executive Council on the management of conflicts, war and other emergency situations and the restoration of peace". As the supreme political organ, the Assembly may exercise all necessary prerogatives with a view to preventing or managing an African conflict. On 6 July 2004, the third summit in Addis Ababa decided to send a protection force of some 300 soldiers to Darfur, where thousands of Darfur people were being persecuted and killed in attacks by government-supported militias. In addition, while the Peace and Security Council accepted the principle of deploying a peace support mission to Somalia during its meeting of 5 January 2005, it is the Heads of State and Government, meeting at the Abuja summit of 24 to 31 January 2005, who requested the Council to assign the organization of this force without delay to the Inter-governmental Authority on Development (IGAD), which is composed of countries of the sub-region.

As the linchpin of the institution, by the frequency of its meetings in ordinary and extraordinary session, its range of powers and its varied composition, the Executive Council best reflects the political

---

[8] See: Gueuyou M., *Les rapports entre l'ONU et l'OUA/UA au regard du chapitre VIII de la Charte des Nations Unies*, Doctoral Thesis, Université de Paris X-Nanterre, 2002, p. 195.

aspects of the Union. Its wide range of powers includes the examination of all matters pertaining to peace and security on the continent, as indicated in the Assembly's powers. During the OAU era, its ability to meet – which it has retained – enabled it to be apprised of almost all inter-African conflicts. However, in light of the system of centralisation of power in Africa, the range of its action was somewhat limited by the fact that ministers of foreign affairs, not being vested with supreme power in their respective States, could not take definite positions on a conflict pitting two or more Member States against one another.[9] This situation has not improved with the change of institution, as the nature of political regimes has not changed. The comparison with the OAU is all the more striking, as it was the Assembly's delegation to the Council of Ministers of the power to make binding and executive decisions that enabled the OAU to find a means of solving any conflict more easily. The Assembly then contented itself with taking the actions and decisions recommended by the Council of Ministers, and encouraged it to continue its work of pacification.[10] Article 9(2) of the Constitutive Act under which "[t]he Assembly may delegate any of its powers and functions to any organ of the Union" can be read in this context.

The Permanent Representatives' Committee, which provides the daily link between the Council and the Commission, is tasked with preparing the proceedings of the Commission and acting upon its instructions. Thus, as a result of the organization's hierarchical structure, it can be asked to study any issue relating to conflict prevention and management. It should be noted that, as with the central body in the OAU's Cairo Mechanism, the Peace and Security Council can meet both at the level of permanent representatives at least twice a year and at the level of Ministers or Heads of State at least once a year. The protocol establishing the Council defines the institutional architecture of peace and security in Africa more clearly.

---

[9] Djiena-Wembou M.-C., *L'OUA à l'aube du 21ème siècle: bilan, diagnostic et perspectives*, LGDJ, Paris, 1995, p. 238.

[10] Gueuyou M., *op. cit.*, p. 198.

2.1.2. The powers conferred by the Protocol on the Establishment of the Peace and Security Council

The Heads of State and Government of the African Union wanted their institution to be at the centre of peace and security mechanisms in Africa, and strongly affirmed this in the preamble of the Protocol on the establishment of the Peace and Security Council. They are resolved to increase their capacity to deal with the plague of conflicts on the continent, and to ensure that, through the African Union, the continent can play a key role in restoring its peace, stability and security. Thus the Commission, particularly its Chairperson, the Panel of the Wise established by Article 11 of the Protocol, and the Pan-African Parliament have powers of varying levels of significance. The operational framework is supplemented by the Staff Committee and the African Standby Force, as discussed later.

The Protocol gives the Chairperson a greater role, similar to that played by the UN Secretary-General, particularly through his or her power of initiative. There are a number of avenues for the Chairperson's dispute settlement activities: the power of initiative vested in him or her by Article 99 of the United Nations Charter; the functions arising from the implementation of resolutions to vest multilateral organs with powers and prerogatives; and the will of the Member States. In the Union, the Chairperson of the Commission may include on the agenda of the Peace and Security Council any issue that he or she deems necessary for the peace and security of the continent. This power is vested in him or her, together with Member States by Article 8(7) of the Protocol. This is similar to the third option available to the UN Secretary-General. The Chairperson of the Commission may also bring to the attention of and initiate action by the Council, particularly with regard to potential or actual conflicts, concomitantly with the Panel of the Wise, regional mechanisms, and with the Council itself, where the Council decides to seize itself of an issue.

In addition to the Chairperson, as an organ of the Union, the Commission is also a stakeholder in activities to seek peace and security on the continent. The Chairperson is assisted in the performance of his duties by the Commissioner in charge of Peace and Security, while the Commission has a Continental Early Warning System composed of a Situation Room and the observation and monitoring units of the regional mechanisms. Furthermore, the Secretariat of the Peace and Security Council is also located in the Directorate in charge of conflict prevention, management and resolution.

The role of the Commission in the institutional framework for peace, security and stability in Africa is often recalled by the Assembly of Heads of State and Government in its annual resolutions and decisions. After the 8th Summit in Addis Ababa from 29-30 January 2007, the Assembly took note

"of the efforts deployed by the Commission to implement the Policy on Post-Conflict Reconstruction and Development and encourage[d] it to intensify these efforts, including through the fielding of multi-disciplinary missions of experts to evaluate the situation on the ground and make recommendations on the assistance that could be provided by Member States and the Commission."[11]

The Assembly concluded by encouraging the Commission to pursue its efforts towards the structural prevention of conflicts.

The Protocol adds a new organ to the institutional framework. This is the Panel of the Wise, whose goal is to foster conflict prevention. This is an idea drawn from the Cairo Mechanism, which allowed the Secretary General of the OAU, to seek ways and means of increasing the ability of the Secretary General to accomplish his new mission. As part of his efforts in this area, the Secretary General could request the services of distinguished African personalities, in consultation with their countries.[12]

The most important point to bear in mind with regard to the Panel of the Wise is undoubtedly its power of initiative, which enables it to undertake actions deemed appropriate to support efforts of the Peace and Security Council and those of the Chairperson of the Commission for the prevention of conflicts, and to pronounce itself on issues

---

[11] AU Doc. AU/Dec. 145 (VIII), para. 5.
[12] Gueuyou M., *op. cit.*, p. 208.

relating to the promotion and maintenance of peace, security and stability in Africa. It may also act at the request of the Peace and Security Council or the Chairperson of the Commission. The Protocol stipulates that the personalities of the Panel of the Wise must be highly respected and have made an outstanding contribution to the cause of peace, security and development in Africa. It seems clear that this rather curious provision is aimed at some of the former Heads of State. The recent decision by the Assembly endorsing the appointment of members of this group is in similar vein. Of the five personalities, two are former Heads of State, the third is the former Secretary General of the OAU, and the remaining two are women.[13]

Article 18 of the Protocol Relating to the Establishment of the Peace and Security Council stipulates the relations between it and the Pan-African Parliament in furtherance of peace, security and stability in Africa.[14] In order to facilitate the discharge of its responsibilities, the Peace and Security Council is required to submit reports, through the Chairperson of the Commission, and to present an annual report on the state of peace and security in the continent to the Pan-African Parliament. During its fourth session in December 2005, the Parliament adopted its strategic plan for 2006-2010, drafted by a working group composed of seven countries, dealing with the organization of its resources and activities, including in particular its observation missions to Darfur and Mauritania, and various elections. Although modest, the contribution of the Parliament is necessary to make the continent safe and peaceful. Hence, Article 20 of the Protocol invites the contribution of civil society organizations and in particular women's organizations, which may, when required, be invited to address the Peace and Security Council, and may also participate in promoting peace and security in Africa. Unsurprisingly, in light of the difficulties posed to Africa's development by the

---

[13] They are Ahmed Ben Bella (former President of Algeria), Miguel Trovoada (former President of Sao Tomé and Principe), Salim Ahmed Salim (former Secretary General of the OAU), Brigalia Bam (Chairperson of South Africa's independent electoral commission), and Elizabeth Pognon (President of the Constitutional Court of Benin).

[14] Article 3(5) of the Protocol to the Treaty establishing the African Economic Community relating to the Pan-African Parliament.

various conflicts raging on the continent, a link is established between economic development and peacekeeping and security.

2.2. The extension of special development programmes to peace and security issues: NEPAD and CSSDCA

Effective conflict prevention and resolution in case of breaches of the peace requires knowledge of their signs and symptoms as well as their causes. Unequal access to natural resources, opportunities and political power, the proliferation of small arms and bad governance all contribute to long-lasting conflicts in Africa. Such issues often underpin real and imagined injustices and grievances between groups with distinct identities, sometimes degenerating into ethnic violence. Economic, political and social crises blend into an explosive cocktail whose solution can only be devised upstream, before chaos reigns. This is why conflict prevention is understood to be a long-term activity whose goal is to reduce structural tensions and prevent the ignition, escalation or recurrence of violence. This is also one of the major objectives of the New Partnership for Africa's Development, NEPAD, and the Conference on Security, Stability, Development and Cooperation in Africa, CSSDCA.

2.2.1. The function of NEPAD in conflict prevention in Africa: the initiative for peace and security

The New Partnership for Africa's Development (NEPAD is a development initiative which seeks to contribute to Africa's revival through an integrated and holistic approach. Its priorities include establishing the conditions for sustainable development by ensuring peace and security, democracy, good governance and capacity building. To this end, African leaders adopted certain standards and codes of behaviour through the institutionalisation of commitments to the key values of initiative, conflict management methods and increasing their capacity to prevent, manage and resolve conflicts. They also initiated a long-term consideration of development conditions and security. The NEPAD reference document enjoins African leaders to take on a number of joint responsibilities for, among other things, strengthening mechanisms for conflict prevention, management and resolution at the sub-regional and continental levels, and ensuring that these mechanisms are used to restore and maintain peace. The purposes include promoting and protecting democracy and human rights in their respective countries and regions by developing clear standards of accountability, transparency and participatory governance at the national and sub-national levels.[15]

By emphasising conflict prevention, management and resolution, African leaders are giving concrete expression to the exhortations contained in the NEPAD initiative. The variety of organs established to promote peace and security in the wake of the Union's establishment are proof of an ideological New Deal that needs to be transformed into reality. In designing the African Post-Conflict Reconstruction Policy Framework, the NEPAD Secretariat observed that the key challenge for the continent is to operationalise these institutions and develop the necessary policy mechanisms that will ensure that the institutions in the peace and security cluster are interconnected with other the programmes of the AU/NEPAD and the Regional Economic Communities, so that together they will have a system-wide impact on the prevention, management and resolution of conflicts in Africa.[16]

While NEPAD is an initiative of African leaders subsequently integrated into the African Union, the Conference on Security, Stability, Development and Cooperation in Africa (CSSDCA) is the result of an initiative of African civil society, which has realised that the search for an enabling environment for African peace, security and development is not the sole preserve of politicians, but involves all civil society stakeholders of the continent that can contribute to conflict prevention and peace-building.

---

[15] *New Partnership for Africa's Development*, 2001, p. 11.
[16] NEPAD (Secretariat), *The African Post-Conflict Reconstruction Policy Framework, Governance*, Peace and Security Programme, June 2005.

2.2.2. The contribution of the Conference on Security, Stability, Development and Cooperation in Africa (CSSDCA)

This is a control mechanism whose objective is to vest African leaders with responsibility and increase the transparency of their action. It also appears to represent a new paradigm for collective security in Africa.[17] This programme, which was adopted by the Union after the fact, signals a new approach to the problem of security by taking into account the political, economic, internal and external aspects of security. The first aspect addresses development, stability and freedom. The second deals with cooperation and partnership, and the last with human security.

The idea of a conference on this issue was first raised in 1990 following a meeting organised by an African NGO, the African Leadership Forum, then under the chairmanship of the former Nigerian president, Olusegun Obasanjo. It took ten years for the OAU to endorse the idea, which it did in June 2000 in the form of an *ad hoc* organ with the mandate of defining a new vision of development based on democratic reform and civil society involvement. The Heads of State and Government discussed the content of the programme in Abuja in 1991, in Dakar in 1992, and Cairo in 1993.[18] The African Union then adopted a Memorandum of Understanding in 2002, integrating it into its institutional framework.

Inspired by the Conference for Security and Cooperation in Europe, which later became a permanent organization (OSCE), the CSSDCA includes a number of undertakings covering a broad range of issues relating to human rights, democracy and the rule of law. In theory, this initiative reflects "the objective interrelation of peace, security, stability and development".[19] It is not by chance that this idea sprang up in the wake of the global political upheavals triggered by the fall of the Berlin wall and the democratisation of the former Eastern Bloc

---

[17] Chouala Y.A., "Puissance, résolution des conflits et sécurité collective à l'ère de l'Union africaine, théorie et pratique", *Annuaire Français de Relations Internationales* 6 (2005), p. 301.
[18] Bourgi, *op. cit.*, p. 330.
[19] Chouala, *op. cit.*, p. 301.

countries. Africa has ceased to be a pawn in the Cold War and can build its collective security without the influence of military alliances that offer their protection in exchange for ideological submission. Security thus ceased to be merely the absence of military and non-military threat, also encompassing sustainable development, cooperation and environmental issues. The conceptual framework of security was overhauled to take into account transnational and multilateral aspects, rather than individual States to the extent that such States, the international organizations they form and international civil society have to face the new security challenges collectively.

Economic development is one of the major objectives of the Union and is enshrined in its Constitutive Act. The purpose is to promote cooperation and development in all areas of human activity, and to help raise the living standards of Africans while maintaining and promoting economic stability. Economic development is thus a key tool for conflict prevention, according to Kofi Annan, the former United Nations Secretary-General, for whom "Unless there is reconstruction and development in the aftermath of conflict, there can be little expectation of progress or durable peace."[20] He goes on to say that, poor economic performance or inequitable development have resulted in a severe economic crisis for some States, encouraging internal tensions and greatly diminishing their capacity to respond to those tensions. Both the CSSDCA and NEPAD are part of the search for an enabling environment for peace, security and stability.

Having realised that the frontiers inherited from the colonial era are a recurrent source of conflict, African leaders have taken a stand on this issue first by adopting a decision solemnly reaffirming that all Member States pledge themselves to respect the borders existing on their achievement of national independence.[21] They also included this principle in the Memorandum of Understanding on Security, Stability, Development and Cooperation in Africa.[22] This document, which also establishes the CSSDCA, further stipulates that, pursuant to the Cairo decision on borders, the delimitation and demarcation of borders between African States must be completed before 2012 at the latest,

---

[20] UN Doc. A/52/871 – S/1998/318.
[21] Resolution AHG/Res. 16 (II).
[22] Decision AHG/Dec. 175 (XXXVIII).

where this has not yet been done, if necessary with the assistance of the United Nations Cartographic Section, in order to strengthen peaceful relations between States. A conference of African ministers in charge of border issues in Addis Ababa from 4 to 7 June 2007 agreed that the conclusions of this operation should be submitted to the AU and the UN and that there should be an evaluation of the progress of this exercise every two years until the deadline.

In theory, the application of the values espoused by NEPAD and the CSSDCA would appear to contribute to peacekeeping in Africa. This confluence of the visions of national leaders and of civil society should engender synergy, which should be fuelled by the peer review mechanism – the only real bridge over the inevitable gulf between talk and action. In light of the operational framework of the institutional structure for peace and security in Africa, one may thus take heart from the Union's strategy and approach to power.

3. An Ambitious Strategy in Light of the Operational Mechanism

The African Union's role in conflict prevention and resolution is provided for in the Constitutive Act and the Protocol relating to the Establishment of the Peace and Security Council and in the powers conferred upon this organ. Unlike the OAU, the AU has equipped itself with the normative, institutional and operational means to offer an effective response to crisis situations. This ambitious strategy is manifest in the optimal deployment capacity, although the efficiency of the system as a whole is questionable.

3.1. Optimal deployment capacity

Besides being at the centre of the collective security and early warning system intended to allow a rapid and efficient response to conflict situations in Africa, the Peace and Security Council covers also a broad range of areas from conflict prevention to the implementation of military operations in situations provided for in the Constitutive Act. Also of note is its role in promoting a common defence policy. In the former case, Article 12 of the Protocol establishing the Council provides for the establishment of a

Continental Early Warning System. This system includes an observation and monitoring centre located at the Conflict Management Division, responsible for data collection and analysis on the basis of appropriate early warning indicators. In addition to this central mechanism within the Commission, there is provision for observation and monitoring units in the Regional Mechanisms linked to a Situation Room. Contributions to the functioning of the system are sought from competent structures such as the United Nations, NGOs, research centres and academic institutions. In the second case, the Protocol provides for the establishment of an African Standby Force and a Military Staff Committee. In fact, the functioning of this system within the power framework adopted can only be achieved and operationalised with the support of African sub-regional organizations, and based on a clear African security and defence policy, as enshrined in the Non-Aggression and Common Defence Pact of 31 January 2005.

3.1.1. The African Standby Force and the Military Staff Committee

As the military arm of the Peace and Security Council, the African Standby Force was created by Article 13 of the Protocol of 9 July 2002. This military arm is intended to enable the Union to fulfil its responsibilities in deploying support missions for peace and intervention, in accordance with Article 4(h) and 4(j) of the Constitutive Act. The force is to be composed of multidisciplinary contingents stationed in their countries of origin, the aim being to minimise costs and rationalise the deployment of forces into African theatres in different sub-regions.

The force's mandate is the operational cornerstone of conflict prevention, peacemaking, peacebuilding and intervention. It can be deployed for observation and monitoring missions and for other missions to support peace efforts. It is intended to implement decisions taken on the basis of Articles 4(h) and 4(j) of the Constitutive Act, but also for any preventive deployment to avoid the aggravation, spread, or resurgence of a conflict, and for disarmament and demobilisation. Its mandate also includes humanitarian intervention in both conflict zones and natural disaster zones.

The creation of this force is a clear indication of the qualitative change made by African leaders in designing the new Union's role in peace, security and stability on the continent. Although it does not yet exist in a physical sense, one can easily imagine the support that such a force could provide in light of the Union's decision to send a protection force to Darfur in August 2004. This is a clear manifestation of power, especially given the Sudanese government's opposition. Thus "demobilisation by force is already integrated in the Union's methods of action", in that the intervention mission set up by the Council had a mandate and the required personnel, with a particular focus on the disarmament and neutralisation of Janjaweed militias and the protection of the civilian population within the limits of the force's capacity.[23] This also provides an arresting insight into the concept of responsibility for protection enshrined in the African Union's Constitutive Act. The non-indifference principle is emphasised in the Union's project, and the Declaration of Commitment of member Heads of State and Government unequivocally refers to this new paradigm. They have resolved to manage every conflict efficiently and establish objectives as soon as it begins by using all the means at their disposal, and no conflict on the continent will be considered beyond the jurisdiction of the Union. "Where grave abuses of human rights, crimes against humanity and genocide occur, the Peace and Security Council must be the first to condemn, and take swift action". Hence the need to have at its disposal an operational military tool that can be mobilised for emergencies.

The Peace and Security Council and its operational mechanisms are clearly different from those of the defunct OAU. The first difference is found in its broader mandate. The mechanism for the prevention, management and resolution of conflicts was previously subject to the principles of the OAU Charter, and in particular to the principle of non-interference in the internal affairs of Member States, sometimes even when there were widespread violations of human rights and civil disturbance. But the Peace and Security Council opens a legal avenue

---

[23] Communiqué of the 13th meeting of the Peace and Security Council, 27 July 2004, PSC/PR/Comm. (XIII) and Chouala, *op. cit.*, p. 299.

into this inter-State neutrality, thus meeting the aspirations of Africans to peace, while marking a radical break with the past. Another difference with regard to the Cairo Mechanism is found in the substantially reinforced role and powers of the Council.[24] The African Standby Force and the Continental Early Warning System are a clear reflection of the strengthening of the role and powers of the Union's peace and security institutions. However, the Protocol stipulates that, in performing its duties, this force will cooperate as necessary with the United Nations and its agencies, as well as with other relevant regional and international organizations, and with national authorities and NGOs.

With regard to the functional aspects of this Force, the Union has drawn on the model of collective security, organised around peacekeeping or peacebuilding, as practised by the United Nations. In terms of command of the standby force, the Chairperson of the Commission appoints a Special Representative and a Force Commander for each operation undertaken by the Union. The bottom of the hierarchy is filled by the Contingent Commanders who report to the Force Commander, who in turn reports to the Special Representative, who then reports to the Chairperson of the Commission through the appropriate official channels. Although the Protocol does not state this clearly, the final recipient of the information in this chain of command is the Assembly of Heads of State and Government which, in the final analysis, adopts the deployment activities decided upon by the Peace and Security Council.

To assist and advise the Peace and Security Council in military and security issues for peacekeeping, there is a Military Staff Committee composed of senior military officers of the Members of the Peace and Security Council, which meets as often as necessary. In fact, there is nothing to prevent the chiefs of staff from meeting in this capacity, and they may submit recommendations to the Chairperson of the Commission on the best means of strengthening Africa's capacity in supporting peace operations. Since the issue of the force's

---

[24] *Statement by the interim Chairperson of the African Union, H. E. Amara Essy*, at the 22nd Africa – France summit on the sub-theme of partnership for peace and security in Africa, particularly on crisis resolution, Paris, 6 February 2003.

composition is still at the project phase, the senior officers of the Peace and Security Council met in Addis Ababa on 21 February 2007, together with their colleagues of the European Union and some diplomats, to evaluate the military and political ramifications of the programme to strengthen African peacekeeping capacity. At the end of the proceedings, the AU Commissioner for Peace and Security declared that, with the assistance of African partners, the AU had made progress on the establishment of the standby force. In order to improve African policy in this area, the superior officers analysed documents relating to the force's logistics, the chain of command, the concept of communication and the information system, with the objective of harmonising them prior to their submission for approval to African security and defence ministers and the Staff Committee.

3.1.2. The implementation of the Non-Aggression and Common Defence Pact and its mechanisms

Article 7(h) of the Protocol on the Establishment the Peace and Security Council charges the Council with implementing the common defence policy of the Union. The Assembly of Heads of State and Government made a commitment in the Solemn Declaration on this policy, adopted in Sirte in 2004, to conclude and ratify non-aggression pacts between African countries and harmonise them subsequently. These recommendations allowed the adoption of the Union's Non-Aggression Pact during the fourth ordinary session of the 31 January 2005 Abuja Assembly. The pact's mechanisms provide the basis for the complex and prolific African collective security system.

Inspired by the tragedies of Rwanda, Somalia, Côte-d'Ivoire, Liberia and his own country, President Sassou Nguesso of Congo proposed the Pact as a theoretical framework that analysts were quick to describe as the "Sassou Doctrine". First submitted to the scientific community in the journal *African Geopolitics* in April 2003, this idea was further explained by its promoter to his peers during their second Assembly in Maputo three months later. In his view, the draft Pact should be built around three complementary areas. In the first, entitled "Commitment of African States against aggression", the States Parties to the Pact should strengthen Africa's security by uniting their forces.

Thus, they should define aggression and seek African economic integration as a means of fostering durable peace. The second area concerns "African principles of conflict prevention", including all measures to be implemented for maintaining, re-establishing or imposing peace. The last area deals with "Instruments of conflict prevention and resolution", and sets out the means provided for in the Pact to prevent any conflict situations from reaching a critical level.

At President Sassou Nguesso's request, his proposal was synthesized by a committee of experts charged with drafting a Pact for submission to the AU Commission. However, the current text is a summary of two other documents, one initiated by the Chairperson of the Commission and the other by Libya, which advocated the forming of a single African army. In spite of the difficult negotiations, the Congolese text was adopted with amendments, particularly concerning common defence. The Pact is based on the right to intervention, and its scope is designed to provide a framework for humanitarian action that guarantees respect for international humanitarian law in inter-State conflicts and conflicts between African countries.

The Pact defines aggression following the wording of UN General Assembly resolution 3314, adopted in 1974. It describes situations of aggression in eleven instances, while the threat of aggression is understood to be "any harmful conduct or statement by a State, group of States, organization of States, or non-State actor(s) which though falling short of a declaration of war, might lead to an act of aggression". The Pact also extends the Union's security agenda by redefining and extending the frontiers of collective peace and security to the concept of human security, and by taking account of political, economic and social dimensions. Human security means the security of the individual in terms of satisfaction of his/her basic needs. It also includes the creation of the social, economic, political, environmental and cultural conditions necessary for the survival and dignity of the individual, the protection of and respect for human rights, good governance, and the guarantee to each individual of opportunities and choices for his/her full development. This is in line with the desire for coherence with the CSSDCA, discussed in detail above.

There are many common points between the Pact and the Protocol establishing the Peace and Security Council. Article 9 of the Pact states that under the authority of the Assembly, the Peace and Security Council is responsible for the implementation of the Pact. States Parties undertake to provide all possible assistance towards the military operations approved by the Peace and Security Council, including the use of the African Standby Force. States Parties also undertake to develop and strengthen their collaboration with the Command Headquarters and Military Staff Committee of the Standby Force. Three institutions are established to make a significant contribution to conflict prevention and management. The African Peace Academy is to serve as a framework for the promotion of peace and stability in Africa, and as a centre of excellence for research and development of an African peace doctrine. The African Centre for Study and Research on Terrorism is to centralise, collect and disseminate information, studies and analysis on terrorism and terrorist groups, develop training programs in order to prevent and combat terrorist acts in Africa. The Centre is also to assist Member States to develop the expertise and strategies for the prevention and combating of terrorism. Lastly, the objectives of the African Union Commission on International Law include studying all legal matters related to the promotion of peace and security in Africa, including the demarcation and delineation of African borders.

Finally, Article 15 of the Pact provides that States Parties involved in any dispute shall first seek a solution by negotiation, inquiry, mediation, conciliation, arbitration, judicial settlement, or resort to regional and continental mechanisms or arrangements, or by other peaceful means. This is a stipulation of Chapter VIII of the UN Charter dealing with the relations between the UN and regional peace and security organizations and agreements. Assuming that the principal functions of regionalism are to replace a failing universalism and to act as its natural complement, and interpreting Chapter VIII of the UN Charter as establishing cooperation by distributing powers between the UN and regional organizations in the peaceful settlement of disputes and the maintenance of international peace and security, this should result in better management of crises in Africa in particular. However, the plethora of new collective security institutions and mechanisms, the limited means at the disposal of the

Union and the militarised sub-regional institutions, raises questions about the efficiency of the system as a whole.

3.2. The efficiency of the African conflict prevention and resolution system

The construction of the African collective security system remains incomplete because of the non-ratification by the required number of Member States of the Non-Aggression and Common Defence Pact. However, many States have signed the instrument and the legislative process for ratification has been set in motion in other countries. Undoubtedly, the Pact will come into force before the end of this decade. While the Pact is not binding in nature, it should be assumed that it is workable so that it can serve as a basis for a more accurate evaluation of the system. Here, three questions come to mind: that of the effectiveness of standards currently in force in the African judicial framework, especially as concerns the rules governing peace, stability and security in Africa, in conjunction with the question of the operationalisation of the mechanisms arising from these standards, and the crucial question of the resources committed to this end.

3.2.1. Effectiveness of standards and operationality of mechanisms

The legal framework for conflict prevention and resolution in the African Union is growing by virtue of the many legal instruments adopted and the institutions established. This regulatory activism does not necessarily signal greater participation and should not overshadow the central issue of effective action on the part of the organization to preserve peace and security. The most important legal instrument is the Constitutive Act. Other instruments, of varying legal importance, range from the Protocol relating to the Establishment of the Peace and Security Council, the two Solemn Declarations on the CSSDCA and the Common African Defence and Security Policy, pending the entry into force of the Non-Aggression Pact. Some provisions in the NEPAD framework could also inform the Union's action for peace, security and stability for economic development. In addition, there are many instruments governing the action of sub-regional economic communities whose role in support of the Union is indispensable for the attainment of the stated objectives. The first obvious consequence is the non-invocability of these texts with regard to Member States that have not ratified them. This is particularly true of the Protocol, and will soon be so for the Pact. This web of instruments makes the issue of the relative effect of treaties particularly relevant. Another consequence of the plethora of instruments is the institutional overload of instruments because "the African Union does not err on the side of caution with regard to the institutions to bring it into being, but on the side of excess".[25]

The OAU was often criticised for its passivity when it came to translating its decisions, often taken with great pomp and circumstance, into concrete action. But the Union is monitored at every Summit to ensure that its commitments are followed by action. This has not always been the case, especially during its early years. Between 2002 and 2004, the continent experienced many crises and conflicts, and the organization often did no more than condemn them and protest, with some Heads of State taking solitary action, often in the guise of mediators. For example, the 19 September 2002 coup d'état in Côte d'Ivoire should have offered an opportunity to apply Article 4(p) of the Constitutive Act on the condemnation and rejection of unconstitutional changes of government, which is a source of many African conflicts. After the usual condemnations and failure to take alternative action, however, the Union merely referred the matter to the central institution of the Cairo Mechanism and appointed a special envoy of the Chairperson of the Commission to monitor the proceedings of the Assembly of Heads of State and Government of the Economic Community of West African States[26]. The application of the provisions on the unconstitutional changes has substantially improved since then, resulting often in the imposition of sanctions on recalcitrant governments.

---

[25] Kodjo E., "L'Union africaine entre la peur et l'espoir", *Géopolitique africaine* 15-16 (Summer – Autumn 2004).
[26] Bourgi, *op. cit.*, p. 342.

The issue of military intervention provided for in the Constitutive Act, which seems to receive the enthusiastic support of many observers, cannot be applied concretely without defining the exact terms of reference – as evidenced by the Darfur situation, where there have been divergent views. The UN Security Council has the primary responsibility for maintaining international peace and security, pursuant to Article 24 of the UN Charter. In Article 103, the Charter codifies a universal supra-legality which the African legal framework cannot disregard.[27]

An overview of the Union's peace and security framework shows a multiplicity of institutions, organs and mechanisms involved in seeking the same objective. Furthermore, the overlap between the provisions of the Protocol and those of the Pact is not negligible, especially if not all the Member States are parties to these instruments. This proliferation raises problems of synergy and coordination as well as redundancy and waste of means and effort. A few examples serve to highlight the risk of poor management as a result of having taken on too much. The objectives of the CSSDCA and NEPAD do not necessarily differ significantly, rather including a series of undertakings on a broad range of issues linked to democracy, good governance, human rights, development, etc. And yet an identical guarantee mechanism has been provided for: the peer review mechanism, whose membership is not obligatory. Obviously, these two initiatives overlap, and it would be appropriate to coordinate them so as to harmonise the applicable regulations and share out responsibilities between the two review systems. There is some argument for increasing efficiency by simply merging both initiatives and integrating them into the Commission.

The operational viability of the mechanisms established to contribute to the achievement of peace is by no means certain, due to the growing competition among organs pursuing the same objective. In responding to cases of crisis or conflict, should the Chairpersons of the Union and of the Commission, and even the Parliament, remain

---

[27] Gueuyou M., "Articulation normative des systèmes africains de maintien de la paix et de la sécurité", in Bangoura D. (ed.), *l'Union africaine face aux enjeux de paix, de sécurité et de défense*, l'Harmattan, 2003, pp. 133-144.

inactive while the Panel of the Wise takes action, or should they act in accordance with their mandates at the risk of seeing several competing and consequently counterproductive initiatives? What role should the Peace and Security Council play in such circumstances? It should be noted that this Council is in and of itself a collective security and early warning system as well as a decision-making organ. If the issue of its exact role is not resolved in the Pact, it might well become an instrument to serve the interests of its signatory States. Similarly, there is the question of how to coordinate the action of sub-regional organizations in light of the emergence of poles of power that enable the more influential countries to blur the boundaries between local hegemony and the common policy of the Union for the common good of Africa. Nigeria and South Africa, for example, project themselves as the policemen of their respective regions. It is difficult to reconcile this attitude with the Union's intention of subsuming these regional bodies under continental mechanisms. Furthermore,

> "the plethora of integrative institutions covering the same geographical area is a problem and a risk. State membership in several organizations and institutions for economic cooperation hampers rather than favours the march towards regional integration and African unity. The AU, which must necessarily coordinate the activities of these communities and organizations, should not itself suffer from the institutional redundancy that the current situation seems to indicate."[28]

Lastly, the AU's action is hampered by its chronic financial difficulties.

3.2.2. Meagre resources

Budgetary constraints have constantly hampered the action of African organizations in many areas, including peacekeeping. The OAU limited itself to small-scale peace support operations for lack of funds, and the African Union appears to be experiencing the same structural financial difficulties. Arrears in contributions are equal to the Union's yearly budget. The multiplicity of economic and

---

[28] Kodjo, *op. cit.*

political groupings that African States belong to requires them to pay various amounts as contributions. Given that some fragile States are unable to meet even the basic needs of their populations, should they be held to account? It is unrealistic, for example, to expect a country such as Somalia, beset by successive profound crises, to fulfil its financial obligations. Neither do wealthier States seem any more inclined to provide the Union with the means to pursue its new ambitions for peace and security. Thus, there is always the risk that the Peace and Security Council may be reduced to issuing hollow pronouncements and declarations.

The international community's mobilisation for Africa and its organizations appears also to be on a par with Africa's inability to look after itself. In a realistic assessment of Africa's situation, the Security Council reaffirmed

> "the need to adopt a broad strategy of conflict prevention, which addresses the root causes of armed conflict and political and social crises in a comprehensive manner, including by promoting sustainable development, poverty eradication, national reconciliation, good governance, democracy, gender equality, the rule of law and respect for and protection of human rights."[29]

On the basis of this affirmation, the Chair of the Security Council, Ms. Nkosazana Dlamini-Zuma of South Africa, stressed in a statement on 28 March 2007 the importance of supporting and improving in a sustained way the resource base and capacity of the African Union.[30]

External contributions make up the bulk of the African Union's resources. In 2004, in response to a request by the AU during the Maputo Summit, the European Union established a mechanism with funding of 250 million Euros. This "Peace Support Facility" is intended to assist peace support operations in Africa and to build capacity in the areas of peace and security. It is accompanied by a "Plan to Enhance African Capabilities to Undertake Peace Support Operations" adopted by the G8 Heads of State and Government meeting in Sea Island in the United States on 10 June 2004.

---

[29] Resolution 1625 (2005) of 14 September 2005.
[30] UN Doc. SC/8984.

They made a commitment to organise and fund training for up to 75 000 soldiers until 2010, and to provide some of them with equipment, in order to accelerate the implementation of peacekeeping operations in countries that require them, particularly operations carried out in Sub-Saharan African countries under the direction of the United Nations.

Although the African Union is the institution under whose aegis regional peace and security programmes can be coordinated, particularly as regards the management of financial resources obtained from partners, the principle of subsidiarity increases the involvement of RECs in conflict prevention and resolution. The RECs therefore also hope to receive financial assistance that might otherwise only go to the African Union. This situation can cause tensions between these organizations, which are pursuing the same objective, especially as donors do not necessarily fulfil their commitments. A G8 report on the implementation of the plan of action for Africa shows that while much has been done, in practice words outweigh action and financial support. The promised plan on enhancing African capacity for peace support operations freely admits that considerable time and resources are needed to create and establish the conditions for supporting the full range of capacities needed for peace support and related activities.

For the time being, the euphoria experienced in the wake of the transformation of the OAU into an African Union seems unabated. The new philosophy adopted by the Union with respect to conflicts is in contrast with the over-cautiousness of the OAU. This guarantees that it is paid special attention by the international community. In fact, as early as 15 and 16 December 2005, the European Council adopted a European Union strategy for Africa and decided to strengthen the peace support facility through substantial, flexible and sustainable long-term funding. The viability of the AU's standby force project is linked to the disbursement of these funds, particularly for preparatory workshops, policy and standardisation of modes of operation, for which the European Union is the key partner. In spite of such external funding, the shortcomings will remain until the Union itself achieves autonomy through the contributions of its members. Providing the Union with a budget that can enable the range of institutions and mechanisms provided for in the Protocol and Non-Aggression and

Common Defence Pact to function as hoped would be a strong signal. The Union can only lay claim to its key role as the principal promoter of peace and security in Africa on the basis of its efforts to acquire the means to implement its policies.

CHAPTER 16.
THE RIGHT OF FORCIBLE INTERVENTION IN CERTAIN CONFLICTS

Abdulqawi A. Yusuf

1. Introduction

The Constitutive Act of the African Union (AU) – which has replaced the Organization of African Unity (OAU) – provides as one of the basic principles of the new Pan-African intergovernmental Organization under Article 4(h): "The right of the Union to intervene in a Member State pursuant to a decision of the Assembly in respect of grave circumstances, namely: war crimes, genocide and crimes against humanity". This constitutes a fundamental departure from the conservative stance of the OAU whose Charter – adopted soon after the independence of most African States in 1963 – established as one of its guiding principles "Non-interference in the internal affairs of States".[1] It also represents an innovative legal proposition since it establishes for the first time in the history of regional arrangements or organizations the right to intervene in a Member State on grounds of violation of human rights or humanitarian law. A protocol on Amendments to The Constitutive Act Of the AU adopted on 3 February 2003 adds a new sub-paragraph to Article 4(h) which extends the scope of the right of intervention to situations where there is "a serious threat to legitimate order" in a Member State "to restore

---

[1] Article 3(2), Charter of the Organization of African Unity. For an analysis, See Cervenka Z., *The organization of African Unity*, New York, 1969, pp. 30-68.

A.A. Yusuf & F. Ouguergouz (eds.), *The African Union: Legal and Institutional Framework. A Manual on the Pan-African Organization*, 335-353.

peace and stability to the Member State upon the recommendation of the Peace and Security Council".[2]

This Chapter examines the background to the right of intervention under the AU Constitutive Act, its scope and the possible implications of its application, as well as its relation to the UN Charter, and to the role of the Security Council as the organ on which all UN Member States, including African States, have conferred "primary responsibility for the maintenance of international peace and security".[3] Finally, the paper addresses the question whether this legal principle represents a paradigm shift in regional enforcement action under the Charter system.

2. Background

When the first Pan-African intergovernmental organization (the OAU) was established on 25 May 1963, article XIX of its Charter entitled "Commission of Mediation, Conciliation, and Arbitration" provided that:

"Member States pledge to settle all disputes among themselves by peaceful means and, to this end decide to establish a Commission of Mediation, Conciliation, and Arbitration, the composition of which and conditions of service shall be defined by a separate protocol to be approved by the Assembly of Heads of State and Government. Said Protocol shall be regarded as forming an integral part of the present Charter".

The protocol of Mediation, Conciliation, and Arbitration was adopted on 21 July 1964 in Cairo, Egypt. As evidenced by this important provision in the OAU Charter, for which there is no corresponding provision in the Constitutive Act of the AU, the main concern of the African States at the time was the prevention and settlement of interstate disputes rather than intrastate conflicts. The main emphasis of the OAU Charter, and its protocol, were

---

[2] Protocol on Amendments to the Constitutive Act of the African Union adopted by the 1st Extraordinary Session of the Assembly of the African Union, Addis-Ababa, Ethiopia, 3 February 2003 (Article 4). The protocol has not yet entered into force.
[3] Article 24 of the UN Charter.

therefore on the manner in which conflicts between Member States of the Organization would be settled.[4] As no disputes had ever been referred to the Commission, it died of institutional irrelevance following the abolition of its Permanent Bureau by the OAU. As pointed out by S. Tiewul "in view of its history, the bureau's abolition perhaps entailed no great loss".[5] Neither did the subsequent disappearance of the Commission itself.

Forty years later, the principal emphasis of the Constitutive Act of the African Union as well as its Protocol Relating to the Establishment of the Peace and Security Council of the African Union (hereinafter the Peace and Security Protocol) is explicitly on internal conflicts. This shift has come about in a gradual manner as civil wars, and government and institutional collapse have become widespread phenomena in the continent from the late 1980's to the present. In a Declaration adopted in Cairo, Egypt, in 1993 (hereinafter the Cairo Declaration) the OAU established a Mechanism for Conflict Prevention, Management and Resolution[6] which, in keeping with the overarching concern regarding internal conflicts, omitted any reference to the Mediation, Conciliation and Arbitration protocol. Nonetheless, the Cairo Declaration mentions both internal and inter-State conflicts. Thus, it is stated in Paragraph 9 of the Declaration that:

> "No single internal factor has contributed more to the present socio-economic problems in the continent than the scourge of conflicts in and among our countries. They have brought about death and human suffering, engendered hate and divided nations and families. Conflicts have forced millions of our people into a drifting life as refugees and displaced persons, deprived of their means of livelihood, human dignity and hope. Conflicts have gobbled up scarce resources, and undermined the ability of our countries to address the many compelling needs of our people".

---

[4] Tiewul S.A., "Relations between the United Nations Organization and the Organization of African Unity" *Harvard International Law Journal* 16 (1975), p. 278, where he observes in respect of the Commission that "the strict limitation of its competence to interstate disputes under article XIX of the OAU Charter rendered it irrelevant for the settlement of internal conflicts".

[5] *Ibid.*

[6] OAU Doc. AHG/DECL.3 (XXIX), 1993.

The Declaration also acknowledges that the establishment of the Conflict Prevention Mechanism was motivated by the need to bring a new institutional dynamism to the process of dealing with conflicts in the continent, thus implicitly recognizing the failure of the procedures laid down under the Mediation, Conciliation and Arbitration Protocol which had never been fully implemented or utilised. A major characteristic, and perhaps the principal weakness, of the Mechanism established under the Cairo Declaration was that it was based on, and was explicitly to be guided by, the principles and objectives of the OAU Charter which strictly limited the capacity of the Organization to interfere in the internal affairs of Member States. These principles and objectives (including non-interference in the internal affairs of States, respect of the sovereignty and territorial integrity of Member States and inviolability of borders inherited from colonialism) are recalled in Paragraph 14 of the Declaration which further provides that the Mechanism will "function on the basis of the consent and the cooperation of the parties to a conflict". The requirement that the consent of the parties to a conflict had to be obtained before any action could be undertaken in the context of the Mechanism substantially weakened its effectiveness and undermined its utility, particularly in internal conflicts.

A primary objective of the Mechanism was to be the anticipation and prevention of conflicts. It was built on the assumption that

"emphasis on anticipatory and preventive measures, and concerted action in peace-making and peace-building will obviate the need to resort to the complex and resource-demanding peace-keeping operations, which (our) countries will find difficult to finance".

Although this might have been, in theory, a reasonable and logical approach to deal with conflicts for a resource-strapped Organization such as the OAU, it did not work in practice since the Secretariat of the OAU, which was designated as the "operational arm" of the Mechanism neither had the institutional capacity nor the wherewithal to perform the functions entrusted to it. Thus, the Mechanism failed to have any impact whatsoever on the most murderous and destructive conflicts in the continent during the 1990's namely Rwanda, Somalia, Sierra Leone, Liberia and DRC. Nonetheless, it deployed some observer missions in Burundi, Central African Republic and Côte d'Ivoire. Faced with the lack of effectiveness of its own Mechanism, the OAU had to resort, with regard to the majority of the African conflicts in the 1990s, to the fallback position it had already provided for in the Cairo Declaration which was to seek the assistance or where appropriate the services of the United Nations under the general terms of the Charter, particularly in cases where such conflicts required collective international intervention and policing.[7]

3. The Right of the Union to Intervene in a Member State

It was against this background of failed attempts at devising appropriate mechanisms for the solution of the chronic conflicts in the continent under the OAU Charter that African leaders decided to insert a right of intervention in the Constitutive Act of their new Organization, the African Union. The inclusion of a right of intervention in the AU Constitution might also be attributed to a determination to overcome the state of paralysis caused by strict adherence under the OAU to the principle of non-interference in the internal Affairs of Member States.[8] In the AU, the principle of non-interference has been reformulated so that it does not apply anymore to the actions of the Member States of the Union acting collectively, but solely to interference in the internal affairs of a Member State by another Member State (unilateral intervention).[9]

The grounds for the exercise of the right to intervene, as currently envisaged in Article 4(h) of the Constitutive Act, are restricted to "grave circumstances" defined as the occurrence of war crimes,

---

[7] Paragraph 16 of the Cairo Declaration.
[8] See: Kioko B., "The Right of Intervention Under the African Union's Constitutive Act: From Non-Interference to Non-Intervention", *International Review of the Red Cross* 85 (December 2003), pp. 807-825. The author argues that the decision "to incorporate the right of intervention ... stemmed from concern about the OAU's failure to intervene in order to stop the gross and massive human rights violations witnessed in Africa in the past, such as the excesses of Idi Amin in Uganda and Bokassa in the Central African Republic in the 1970's and the genocide in Rwanda in 1994" (p. 812).
[9] Article 4(g).

genocide and crimes against humanity in a Member State. An additional ground for intervention is contemplated in a protocol of amendments to the Constitutive Act that has not yet come into force, in respect of serious threats to legitimate order in a Member State. The scope of this amendment, which according to some commentators was accepted by the African Union to keep Libya "inside the AU tent",[10] is less clear and could prove much more controversial than the original provision of Article 4(h). It might also take a long time before it is fully integrated into the law of the African Union. The concept of "legitimate order" is not easy to define in a continent plagued since independence by military coup d'états, civil wars and murderous dictatorships. There is no doubt that many African governments are now working their way towards the establishment of viable democratic institutions, while others have gained a measure of legitimacy in their countries through peaceful handover of power and multi-party elections. "Legitimate order" remains, however, in many instances a fragile and elusive concept and may need to be further developed before it can crystallize into a commonly-shared governance value for the protection of which the AU can legitimately exercise the right to intervene. Otherwise, the continental organization may find itself in the embarrassing situation of trying to prop up unpopular or repressive regimes desperately holding on to power against the will of their own people.

It is much easier to delimit the scope of the right to intervene in respect of grave circumstances arising from war crimes, genocide and crimes against humanity. These are well-known concepts in international law. The Peace and Security Protocol acknowledges as much under Article 7(e) which provides among the powers of the Peace and Security Council to

"recommend to the Assembly, pursuant to Article 4(h) of the Constitutive Act, intervention on behalf of the Union, in a Member State in respect of grave circumstances, namely war crimes, genocide and crimes against humanity, *as defined in relevant international conventions and instruments*" (italics added).

---

[10] Baimu E. & Sturman K., "Amendment to the African Union's Right to Intervene: A Shift from Human Security to Regime Security?", *African Security Review* 12 (2003) 2, p. 2.

These conventions and instruments include the international conventions on the laws of war (Hague and Geneva Conventions) as well as the additional Geneva Protocols, the UN Convention on the Prevention and Punishment of the Crime of Genocide, the Statutes of the UN International Criminal Tribunals for Former Yugoslavia and Rwanda, and of the International Criminal Court. Thus, the existence of grave circumstances will be determined by the Peace and Security Council based on a finding that war crimes, genocide or crimes against humanity, as defined in international legal instruments, have occurred or are about to occur in a Member State. The Council may then recommend intervention by the Union to the Assembly of Heads of State and Government which will take final decision on the matter. The wording of Article 4(h) clearly limits the grave circumstances that may justify intervention in a Member State by the Union to the three situations specified in this provision. If those three situations did not exist or were not considered to be in the process of arising, in the opinion of the Peace and Security Council and the Assembly, then the Union would not have the right to intervene in a Member States, unless the latter requested such intervention under Article 4(j) of the Constitutive Act.

Equally relevant to the scope of Article 4(h) is the definition of intervention for the above-described purposes. It is stated in Article 13 of the Peace and Security Protocol that:

> "In order to enable the Peace and Security Council to perform its responsibilities with respect to the deployment of peace support missions and intervention pursuant to Article 4(h) and (j) of the Constitutive Act, an African standby force shall be established."

This implies that intervention is used in the context of the AU in the sense of coercive action involving armed force in a Member State without the consent of the government of that State. According to the Report of the International Commission on Intervention and State Sovereignty (ICISS), intervention may take three forms: political, economic or other sanctions; international criminal prosecution; and military intervention for humanitarian ends.[11] The AU Constitutive Act, particularly when read together with the Peace and Security Protocol, appears, however, to exclude the first two forms identified by the ICISS and to focus exclusively on military intervention for humanitarian ends, at least insofar as Article 4(h) is concerned, to help a population in distress following grave and massive violations of human rights and humanitarian law.

What are the implications of this right to intervene for the law of the UN Charter? Would the African Union undertake enforcement action in a Member State without prior authorization by the UN Security Council? With standby forces at its disposal to effect military intervention in situations involving massive violations of human rights and humanitarian law, would the AU continue to sit on the sidelines if the Security Council failed to act? These issues are addressed below.

4. Relation to the UN Charter and to the Role of the Security Council

The UN Charter prohibits the threat or use of force by States individually or collectively against the territorial integrity or political independence of other States.[12] Two exceptions to this rule are contemplated in the Charter. The first relates to the right of individual or collective self-defence in case of an armed attack against a Member of the United Nations.[13] The second pertains to the system of collective security under which the Security Council may, if necessary, take military enforcement action to maintain or restore international peace and security, after having determined that a threat to the peace, breach of the peace, or act of aggression has occurred. In the exercise of this prerogative the Security Council may utilize regional organizations for enforcement action under its authority.[14] However, the Charter prohibits such regional organization from

---

[11] *The Responsibility to Protect: Report of the International Commission on Intervention and State Sovereignty"*, International Development Research Center, Ottawa, 2001, p. 16.
[12] Article 2(4) of the UN Charter.
[13] Article 51 of the UN Charter.
[14] Article 53(1) of the UN Charter.

undertaking enforcement action at their own initiative and without the authorization of the Security Council, the only exception being measures against so-called "enemy States" or in the case of "regional arrangements directed against the renewal of aggressive policy on the part of such State" both of which are considered obsolete today. The scope of this prohibition must be assessed, in our view, in the light of the other Charter provisions, particularly Articles 52 and 54, relating to regional arrangements and their activities with regard to the maintenance of international peace and security.

The authority and competence of regional arrangements for dealing with matters relating to the maintenance of international peace and security is clearly recognized in article 52(1), but is subject to two conditions. First, the matters dealt with by the regional arrangements with regard to the maintenance of peace and security must be "appropriate for regional action". Secondly, such arrangements themselves as well as well as their activities must be "consistent with the purposes and principles of the United Nations". The importance of this provision for the implementation of the AU Charter principles on intervention in Member States for humanitarian purposes is manifold. In the first instance, the maintenance of peace and security among nations has evolved in recent years in the practice of the United Nations to encompass the protection of human security within nations. Massive human rights violations, genocide, war crimes and crimes against humanity within the borders of nation States are increasingly considered by the United Nations as matters affecting international peace and security among nations. Secondly, the UN has frequently resorted, in its recent practice, to the use of coalitions of States or regional organizations for the implementation of Chapter VII enforcement measures, thus liberalizing and expanding the system of authorization for military action to restore peace and security within Member States to the extent that this approach has been assimilated by some commentators to a "franchising system".[15] It could therefore be argued that this practice constitutes evidence of a growing recognition by the UN of the "appropriateness" of regional action, including those

---

[15] Simma B., "NATO, The UN and the Use of Force: Legal Aspects", *European Journal of International Law* 10 (1999), p. 3.

undertaken by the AU (or its predecessor the OAU), for dealing with internal upheavals affecting international peace and security. Thirdly, in view of the close interaction and cooperation between the UN and the AU (and its predecessor the OAU), the Pan-African regional organization and its activities in the continent appear to have so far been viewed as being consistent with the purposes and principles of the United Nations Charter.[16]

Article 54 of the UN Charter is equally important for the determination and circumscription of the scope of the authority of regional arrangements to take action for the maintenance of peace and security within their own region. It prescribes that the Security Council be kept fully informed of the activities undertaken or in contemplation under regional arrangements for the maintenance of international peace and security. The word "activities" is rather vague, but does not necessarily exclude military action, although it definitely includes other measures that may be adopted by regional arrangements for the maintenance of peace and security in their area of jurisdiction. In the case of such other measures, the reference to "activities undertaken or in contemplation" does not appear to imply any possible conflict with the prohibition prescribed under Article 53. The matter becomes a little bit more complicated with regard to enforcement action. In the latter case, the relationship between the requirement for notification of the Security Council with regard to "activities in contemplation" (Article 54) and the process of obtaining the necessary "authorization "from it in respect of enforcement action (Article 53) seems to be clear in so far as regional arrangements would presumably be expected to submit such notification to the Council and wait for its decision before embarking on an enforcement action. Much less clear is, however, the relationship between the requirement of authorization in Article 53 and the notification to the Council

---

[16] Cervenka made the following observation in 1969 with respect to the relationship between the UN and the OAU: "A very strong argument supporting the view that the OAU is, after all, a regional organization within the meaning of Chapter VIII of the UN Charter, emerged from the two major cases dealt with by both the United Nations and the OAU. The first was the situation in the Congo (Kinshasa) in 1964 and the second was the Rhodesia crisis in 1965. In both cases the Security Council invited the OAU to undertake action complementing that of the United Nations itself". Cervenka Z., *op. cit.*, p. 112.

regarding activities already "undertaken" by a regional arrangement in Article 54. Could the activities "undertaken" include enforcement action? If so, the reference to authorization in article 53 would have to be interpreted to include not only "prior authorization" but also "*ex post facto* endorsement". In the case of the AU, an *ex post facto* endorsement could perhaps become relevant for the implementation of the right to intervene under certain circumstances, as discussed below, although it does not transpire from a reading of the Peace and Security Protocol that such a possibility was contemplated by the Union.

Article 17 of the Peace and Security Protocol deals with the "Relationship with the United Nations and Other International Organizations". The first three paragraphs of the Article read as follows:

"1. In the fulfilment of its mandate in the promotion and maintenance of peace, security and stability in Africa, the Peace and Security Council shall cooperate and work closely with the United Nations Security Council, which has the primary responsibility for the maintenance of international Peace and Security. The peace and Security Council shall also cooperate with other relevant UN agencies in the promotion of peace, security and stability in Africa.

2. Where necessary, recourse will be made to the United Nations to provide the necessary financial, logistical and military support for the African Union's activities in the promotion and maintenance of peace, security and stability in Africa, in keeping with the provisions of Chapter VIII of the UN Charter on the role of Regional Organizations in the maintenance of international peace and security.

3. The peace and Security Council and the Chairperson of the Commission shall maintain close and continued interaction with the United Nations Security Council, its African members, as well as with the Secretary-General, including holding periodic meetings and regular consultations on questions of peace, security and stability in Africa."

Under these provisions, the AU clearly recognizes that the primary responsibility for the maintenance of international peace and security in Africa and elsewhere in the world lies squarely with the Security Council of the United Nations. While fulfilling its mandate, which includes the power to recommend to the Assembly intervention in a

Member State, the AU Peace and Security Council shall cooperate and work closely with the UN Security Council. It follows from this recognition that the Pan-African organization is determined to act within the parameters of the UN Charter, including its provisions on the need for authorization by the Security Council, in implementing its right to intervene for humanitarian reasons in Member States. This determination is further reinforced by the clear reference in Article 17, paragraph 2, to the provisions of Chapter VIII of the UN Charter on the role of regional organizations as well as by the obligation imposed on the Peace and Security Council and the Chairperson of the AU Commission to maintain close and continued interaction with the UN Security Council, its African members, as well as with the Secretary-General on questions of peace, security and stability in Africa.

In the elaboration of the general principles earlier enunciated in the AU Constitutive Act through the Peace and Security Protocol, the Member States of the Union appear to have decided to spell out not only the respective roles of their regional organization and of the UN in the maintenance of international peace and security in Africa, in a manner compatible with the UN Charter, but also their renewed commitment to act in consonance with the Security Council in undertaking enforcement action in a Member State. It may therefore be concluded that the actual exercise of the African Union's right to intervene in Member States would involve close consultation, cooperation and coordination with the United Nations as well as respect for the primary responsibility of the Security Council for the maintenance of international peace and security.

The question, however, arises whether the AU would require express and prior authorization of the Security Council in all cases before being able to exercise the right of intervention in Member States for humanitarian purposes? What happens if the UN fails to act or to give the necessary authorization in time? The AU has committed itself through its own Peace and Security Protocol to cooperate and work closely with UN Security Council. Its organs are also mandated to maintain close and continued interaction with the Secretary-General of the UN and the Security Council. It is therefore very unlikely that it would embark on an enforcement action without the blessing or the support of the UN organs. Nevertheless, should the UN Security Council fail to act, the grave circumstances in respect of which the African Organization is empowered to take military action, namely genocide, war crimes and crimes against humanity, may sometimes require the adoption of emergency measures, including military action, aimed at saving human lives. Even in such a situation, the AU may still not be considered in breach of its international law obligations, so long as its action meets the conditions and criteria laid down in Articles 52 and 54 of the Charter, as discussed above, and thus becomes eligible for an *ex post facto* endorsement or subsequent acquiescence by the Security Council.

It was with regard to such circumstances that the UN Secretary-General raised the following question in a report to the General Assembly:

> "To those for whom the greatest threat to the future of international order is the use of force in the absence of Security Council mandate, one might ask – not in the context of Kosovo- but in the context of Rwanda: If in those dark days and hours leading up to the genocide, a coalition of States had been prepared to act in defence of the Tutsi population, but did not receive prompt Council authorization, should such a coalition have stood aside and allowed the horror to unfold".[17]

It could perhaps be argued that a regional organization, such as the AU, would have greater legitimacy than an *ad hoc* coalition to undertake such intervention on the basis of the Charter provisions on the activities of regional arrangements.

Yet, it appears very doubtful that, in case of hesitation, delay or failure by the UN Security Council to act on its own or to authorize the AU to do so, the Organs of the African Organization, particularly its Assembly of Heads of State and Government, which has the ultimate decision on intervention, would muster the requisite political will to undertake on its own prompt and targeted military intervention in a Member State. Equally important is the issue of financial and logistical requirements for an effective military intervention where at

---

[17] Secretary-General Presents his Annual Report to General Assembly, UN Press Release SG/SM/7136, GA/9596 (20 September 1999).

present the capacities of the Pan-African organization appear to be rather limited.

Article 17, paragraph 2, of the Peace and Security Protocol acknowledges as much in stipulating that, where necessary, recourse will be made to the United Nations to provide the necessary financial, logistical and military support for the African Union's activities in the promotion and maintenance of peace and stability in Africa "in keeping with the provisions of Chapter VIII of the UN Charter". Thus, it is most likely that, for the foreseeable future, the AU will most often act either in conjunction with the UN or as a surrogate regional organization under Chapter VIII of the Charter in matters requiring enforcement action in a Member State. It is not however a mean achievement that, in contrast to its predecessor (the OAU), this new Pan-African Organization has at least equipped itself with the power to intervene in Member States to safeguard African populations against wholesale slaughter or massive violations of human rights. The pioneering role in international law of this innovative AU principle deserves to be equally acknowledged.

5. A New Paradigm in Regional Enforcement Action?

Until very recently, military intervention on "humanitarian grounds" was viewed by most States, particularly in the third world, with utmost suspicion and apprehension. It was considered an instrument for seeking political advantage or promoting national interest by powerful nations at the expense of weak States on the pretext of assisting them or their populations.

Legally, unless undertaken by the United Nations itself acting under Chapter VII or with its authorization, military intervention, however justified, would run afoul of the Charter prohibition of the use or threat of use of force (Article 2(4)) and of the principle of non-interference in the internal affairs of States (Article 2(7)). A British government position paper on the subject states that:

> "the overwhelming majority of contemporary legal opinion comes down against the existence of a right of humanitarian intervention, for three main reasons: first, the UN Charter and the corpus of modern international law do not seem to specifically incorporate such a right; secondly, State practice in

the past two centuries, and especially since 1945, at best provides only a handful of genuine cases of humanitarian intervention, and on most assessments, none at all; and finally, on prudential grounds, that the scope for abusing such a right argues strongly against its creation... In essence, therefore, the case against making humanitarian intervention an exception to the principle of non-intervention is that its doubtful benefits would be heavily outweighed by its costs in terms of respect for international law".[18]

Thus, although it is largely settled today that the UN Security Council has the right to authorize intervention on humanitarian grounds by characterizing it as a threat to the peace or a breach to the peace under Chapter VII of the Charter, this has come about more as subsequent practice (and a very recent one at that) rather than as a Charter principle empowering it to do so. Moreover, despite having authorized or undertaken interventions on humanitarian grounds on several instances in the early nineties (e.g. Somalia, Iraq, Haiti), after determining that gross violations of human rights in those countries constituted a threat to international peace and security, the UN Security Council has on many other occasions failed to take a decision or shown a disinclination to act in the face of grave human rights violations (e.g. Rwanda). Consequently, even within the United Nations itself, the tension between the normative constraints on military intervention and the need to act against mass slaughter does not appear to have yet been fully resolved. This was summarized by the then UN Secretary-General, Kofi Annan, in a statement to the General Assembly in 1999, as follows:

"Just as we have learned that the world can not stand aside when gross and systematic violations of human rights are taking place, so we have also learned that intervention must be based on legitimate and universal principles if it is to enjoy the sustained support of the world's peoples. This developing international norm in favour of intervention to protect civilians from wholesale slaughter will no doubt continue to pose profound challenges to the international community."[19]

---

[18] UK Foreign Office Policy document No. 148 reprinted in *British Yearbook of International Law* 57 (1986), p. 614.

[19] Statement of the Secretary-General to the UN General Assembly on 20 September 1999.

At the regional level, the right to intervene, be it for humanitarian or other reasons, had traditionally been resisted in much stronger terms and an obligation of non- intervention clearly laid down in multilateral treaties establishing regional organizations. As discussed above, the OAU provisions on non-interference in the internal affairs of Member States had long stymied any action by the now-defunct African Organization for humanitarian purposes. In Latin America, the OAS (Organization of American States) Charter provides in Article 18 that "[n]o State or group of States has the right to intervene, directly or indirectly, for any reason whatever, in the internal or external affairs of any other State".[20] It is interesting to note that in the case of the OAS the duty not to intervene applies not only to unilateral intervention but also to collective intervention. It would perhaps be safe to assume that the prohibition of collective intervention would not apply to enforcement action authorized by the UN Security Council, taking into account Article 103 of the UN Charter, but rather to actions undertaken by a coalition of States outside the UN Charter. Nevertheless, one major effect of the stringent principles of non-intervention at the regional level was to make it more difficult for the UN to utilize such regional arrangements for enforcement action in accordance with Article 53 of the Charter. A regional arrangement prohibited by its own Charter to intervene in Member States would not necessarily offer its services to the United Nations to undertake enforcement action on its behalf, but would most likely prefer that such intervention be carried out directly by the United Nations itself.

It is against this background that the right to intervene enshrined in the AU's Constitutive Act is to be assessed as to whether or not it constitutes a paradigm shift particularly as regards regional enforcement action under the Charter. No other regional organization has ever before incorporated such a right in its Constitutive instrument. Nor does the UN Charter itself explicitly recognize the right of the world body to undertake military intervention in Member States in situations of massive violation of human rights, although in recent years the UN has authorized forcible intervention on several

---

[20] 119 *UNTS* 3 (30 April 1948).

occasions by portraying the situations concerned as a threat to international peace and security under Chapter VII of the Charter.[21] Thus, with the introduction into the AU Constitutive Act of the new principle regarding intervention in Member States a shift appears to have occurred at the regional level – at least in Africa – in favour of collective intervention for humanitarian purposes.

A number of legal consequences flow from this paradigm shift. First, having subscribed to the principle of intervention to safeguard human rights, African States seem to have finally resolved the tension between sovereignty-based values and human-rights values in favour of the latter. Thus, State sovereignty may no longer be used in the African continent as a cloak for human rights abuse and repressive policies within the territory of a Member State. Secondly, to intervene in a Member State, the African Union no longer needs a UN Security Council determination of threat to the peace or a breach of the peace under Chapter VII of the Charter. It is the AU itself that determines the grounds for intervention and the sole action it requires from the UN is under Chapter VIII of the Charter, besides of course, in view of the economic circumstances currently prevailing in the African Continent, financial and logistical support for military operations. As the initiative moves to the AU, it will become more difficult, both legally and politically, for outside powers to block in the Security Council an African solution to African problems. Thirdly, the AU principle imparts a new meaning to the concept of enforcement in the Charter in respect of the maintenance of international peace and security and establishes a new relationship between the world body and the Pan-African organization in the field of humanitarian intervention. Finally, with the explicit recognition of the right to intervene on humanitarian grounds by all African States, at least when undertaken by their regional organization, a pioneering step has been accomplished in international law where, in the absence of specific and clear provisions on humanitarian intervention, scholars had hitherto resorted to moral and ethical justifications to argue the

---

[21] Le Mon C.J. and Taylor R.S., "Security Council Action in the Name of Human Rights", *African Yearbook of International Law* 11 (2003), pp. 263-300.

existence of such a right.[22] In the case of Africa, the right to intervene to stop the brutalisation of civilian populations by their own governments, home-grown militias or warlords has now become part and parcel of the emerging public law of Africa.

6. Concluding Remarks

It is a basic principle of international law that States may limit their sovereignty by treaty. African States have done so in the Constitutive Act of the African Union. They have decided that sovereignty would no longer trump human rights should the latter be abused by the governments whose basic obligation it is to protect them.[23] They have consequently conferred a right of intervention on their regional organization in respect of grave circumstances specified in the AU Constitutive Act. The possible occurrence or actual existence of these circumstances is to be determined by the AU Peace and Security Council. Intervention may then be authorized by the Assembly of the Union. Will the Assembly ever do it? It is too soon to say.

Nonetheless, it must be recognized that the incorporation of the principle in the basic law of the African Union constitutes a pioneering act in international law. A right to intervene in cases of grave circumstances regarding human rights violations now exists in Africa. This right also represents a paradigm shift in enforcement action by regional organizations under the UN Charter. The African Union no longer needs to seek a determination by the UN Security Council that a humanitarian crisis in an African State constitutes a threat to the peace or a breach of the peace. It still requires however a formal endorsement and support from the Security Council under Chapter VIII of the Charter. The AU itself recognizes the need for such endorsement not only to respect the law of the Charter, which is important for avoiding chaos and insecurity in international relations;

---

[22] Cassese A., "*Ex iniuria ius Oritur:* Are we Moving Towards International Legitimation of Forcible Humanitarian Countermeasures in the World Community," *European Journal of International Law* 10 (1999) 1, pp. 23-30.

[23] According to the then UN Secretary-General "State sovereignty, in its most basic sense, is being redefined... States, are now widely understood to be instruments at the service of their peoples, and not vice versa". Kofi A. Annan: "Two Concepts of Sovereignty", *The Economist*, 18 September 1999, p. 49.

but also to obtain financial and logistical assistance for costly military operations. In a continent where internal conflicts have acquired epidemic proportions, the welfare of the peoples of Africa may depend in the future to a large extent on the manner in which this right is implemented by their newly-created organization.

CHAPTER 17.
PEACEKEEPING OPERATIONS: THE EXAMPLES OF BURUNDI AND SUDAN

Mutoy Mubiala

1. Introduction

Since independence, Africa has seen many peacekeeping operations (PKOs) as a result of the persistent conflicts that have plagued it. United Nations operations, which have been the most numerous in the past 50 years, have gone through several phases, ranging from several phases of exceptional intervention (1956-1988), through robust intervention (1989-1994) and withdrawal (1994-1995), to shared responsibility between the UN and African regional and sub-regional organizations (1995 to date). During the first and last phases, these were local initiatives, generally taken over by the UN (particularly during the last phase). Desirous of improving Africa's peacekeeping record, within the context of the current approach of shared responsibility between the UN and regional organizations, African States amended the institutional framework of their Conflict Prevention, Management and Resolution Mechanism as part of the replacement of the OAU by the African Union. Specifically, this entailed replacing the central institution of the Mechanism with a Peace and Security Council organised along the same lines as the UN Security Council. One of the major consequences of this reform is that the African Union is increasingly active in peacekeeping.

In ten years of existence, the African Union has deployed three peacekeeping operations: in Burundi in 2003, in the Sudan in 2004, and in Somalia in 2007. This chapter analyses the first two

A.A. Yusuf & F. Ouguergouz (eds.), *The African Union: Legal and Institutional Framework. A Manual on the Pan-African Organization*, 355-374.

peacekeeping forces, the Inter-African Mission in Burundi (AMIB) and the African Union Mission in Sudan (AMIS). Its purpose is to evaluate the progress made and the obstacles encountered by the African Union in this area, with a view to proposing solutions for more effective peacekeeping in Africa. Before analysing these two missions, however, we examine African regional and sub-regional precedents in this area.

2. African Regional and Sub-Regional Peacekeeping Precedents

While the OAU was the first African organization to deploy a peacekeeping operation in Africa, sub-regional economic cooperation organizations have since done so more frequently, off-setting its shortcomings in this area.

2.1. The OAU

In its 38 years of existence (1963-2001), the OAU deployed over twenty military observer missions on the continent as part of is overall mission to establish and maintain the conditions of peace necessary for human progress (paragraph 6 of the OAU Charter, 25 May 1963). However, only the Inter-African Force in Chad ("the Force") can be appropriately classified as a peacekeeping operation due to is structure and size.

The Force was created within the OAU to help stabilise and resolve the internal conflict that tore Chad apart in the late 1970s, which saw the intervention of other countries within and outside the region. The deployment of the Force was itself made possible by these external interventions: some powers, particularly France, saw it as an opportunity to make the withdrawal of their troops conditional upon the withdrawal of those deployed by Libya on behalf of the Chadian National Union Government (GUNT) led by Goukouni Weddeye.

2.1.1. The Inter-African Force in Chad (1981-1982)

The force was first envisaged in the Lagos Agreement of 21 August 1979, which provided that it should be composed of contingents from countries not sharing a border with Chad. However, it was formally established only in June 1981 by a decision of the Assembly of States and Government of the OAU in Nairobi. The force included contingents totalling 4,500 soldiers provided by Nigeria (50%), Senegal and Zaïre, deployed respectively in the three operational zones of the East, the Centre and the North (excluding the Aouzou Strip). Under the authority of the Secretary-General of the OAU, the general operational command of Nigeria, and the political oversight of the Standing Committee under the authority of the incumbent chairperson of the OAU, President Daniel Arap Moi (Kenya), the Force's mission was to provide security pending a political resolution of the conflict and the formation of an integrated Chadian army. However, its delayed and chaotic deployment in November 1981 did not end the fighting between government troops and the National Armed Forces (FAN) until the latter entered N'Djaména in June 1982. Despite the Inter-African Force's failure to contain the resumption of hostilities and prevent the fall of GUNT, it did have some positive effects.

The Inter-African Force also sets an interesting precedent with regard to the funding of African regional PKOs, which has become a recurrent problem since then.

The failure of the Inter-African Force in Chad led the OAU to scale down its peacekeeping ambitions, subsequently confining itself to deploying military observer missions of limited scope.

2.1.2. The OAU's Military Observer Missions

OAU deployments of military observer missions in situations of internal, regional and international crisis or armed conflict included, in particular:
- The Group of Neutral Military Observers (GOMN I, 1991-July 1993 and GOMN II, August-October 1993);
- The Inter-African Observer Mission in Burundi (MIOB), December 1993-July 1996;
- The Observer Mission to the Comoros (OMIC I, October 1997-May 1998; OMIC II, December 2001-February 2002 and OMIC III, March-May 2002);

- The Joint Verification Commission in the Democratic Republic of the Congo (November 1999-November 2000);
- The OAU Ethiopia-Eritrea Liaison Mission (OLMEE, from 2000).

The OAU experience in Chad and its limited operational capacity contributed substantially both to the high level of involvement of the United Nations in peacekeeping Africa, and also to the involvement of sub-regional economic communities in peacekeeping, in the realisation that their Member States could not rely on the OAU in this area, and that their own action was indispensable for increased integration and sustainable development.

2.2. Sub-regional Precedents

Notable among the regional economic communities which became involved in peacekeeping and acted effectively from an operational standpoint were the Economic Community of West African States (ECOWAS), the Southern African Development Community (SADC), CEN-SAD and the Economic and Monetary Community of Central Africa (CEMAC).

2.2.1. ECOWAS

In 1990, ECOWAS created a military observer group (ECOWAS Ceasefire Monitoring Group or ECOMOG) to deal with the conflict in Liberia. This force, which was largely dominated and funded by Nigeria, has since intervened in several conflicts in West Africa, including in Sierra Leone (1998), in Guinea Bissau (2000), again in Liberia (2003) and, more recently, in Côte d'Ivoire (2002-2003). In 1999, following the adoption of the Protocol establishing the West Africa Conflict Prevention, Management and Resolution Mechanism, ECOMOG was transformed into a standing peacekeeping force and became the operational arm of ECOWAS for military and humanitarian matters. In several of the conflicts mentioned above, ECOMOG helped to stabilise the situation, in some cases in cooperation with forces deployed by the UN. While its efficiency and the discipline of its troops were called into question in a few cases,

ECOMOG is generally considered to be a model force[1] which greatly influenced other sub-regional economic communities such as SADC and CEMAC.

2.2.2. SADC

SADC created an Organ on Politics, Security and Defence at its Gaborone meeting in 1996. Through this Organ, SADC deployed a peace force in Lesotho in 1998. The force was composed of troops from South Africa and Botswana. Its purpose was to countermand the decision by the King and army of Lesotho to dissolve a democratically elected parliament. Subsequently, in 1998 – in controversial circumstances and despite South African opposition – the Organ decided to send troops provided by Angola, Namibia and Zimbabwe to support the legal government of the DRC, in its conflict with the neighbouring countries of Uganda and Rwanda. While they would have preferred a diplomatic solution, SADC Member States subsequently approved the Force's intervention, which allowed the signing of several agreements between the countries involved, including the Lusaka Ceasefire Agreement of July 1999, and the subsequent withdrawal of the foreign troops involved in this "African World War" in Congo, including those from SADC countries.[2]

2.2.3. Operations deployed in the Central African Republic by CEN-SAD and CEMAC

From 1996, the Central African Republic was caught up in a spiral of political and military instability characterised by armed conflict between various factions against a backdrop of African interventions. In response, first the Francophone African countries deployed the Inter-African Force to Monitor the Implementation of the Bangui Agreements (MISAB) in 1997 with French support, and then the UN took over from this force with the deployment of the United Nations

---

[1] Rowe S.E., "ECOMOG: A Model for African Peacekeeping", *African Law Today*, 16 October 1998, pp. 1-4.
[2] See esp. Sundi Mbambi P., "La politique sécuritaire et de défense de la SADC et la crise congolaise", *Congo-Afrique* 45 (2005), pp. 357-365.

Mission in the CAR (MINURCA) in April 1998. This allowed the organization of democratic elections, which were won by Mr. Ange-Félix Patassé. Dissident officers then began to launch attacks on government positions, particularly from Chadian territory. In response, the Central African government provided similar support to the rebellion of Moïse Kété in Southern Chad, bringing the two countries to the brink of armed conflict. In order to end this tension, CEN-SAD, of which both countries were members, deployed a contingent composed of Libyan, Djiboutian and Sudanese troops in 2001 to observe the situation and offer protection to the Central African President. CEMAC, of which both countries were also members, subsequently took over the Chad-Central African question, and decided in a meeting of Heads of State of Member States on 2 October 2002 that Chad and the CAR should deploy their regular armies along their common border to carry out mixed security patrols. They also decided to deploy a contingent of 300 to 350 soldiers provided by Gabon, Congo and Equatorial Guinea, with French logistical support, to observe these security operations and support the restructuring of the Central African armed forces (FACA). On 25 October 2002, when negotiations on the composition and deployment of this force had barely begun, the rebel troops of General François Bozizé attacked Bangui and were repulsed. Despite the withdrawal of CEN-SAD troops and their replacement by those of CEMAC, fighting continued between government and rebel forces until Bangui was taken by the rebels on 15 March 2003. Faced with this *fait accompli*, the Heads of State of CEMAC, meeting in Libreville a week later, decided not only to maintain the military contingent, but also to increase its size through Chadian participation, and to transform it into a peacekeeping force. Composed of a battalion of Congolese, Gabonese and Chadian contingents, the mission of the CEMAC multinational force (FOMUC), pursuant to article 3 of the Libreville Protocol of 3 June 2003, is:

> "to contribute to security in Central African Republic (RCA); aid the restructuring of the Central African Armed Forces (FACA); and support the transition process for national reconciliation, the rapid return of constitutional order and lasting peace."

also recognised by the Security Council Mission to the Great Lakes region in November 2005.[5]

3.2. The African Union Mission in Sudan (AMIS)

The deployment of the African Union Mission in Sudan (AMIS) took place in a complex context, representing the first real test of the African Union's peacekeeping capacity.

3.2.1. Background

The Darfur crisis, which escalated militarily in 2003, added another layer to an inter-Sudanese conflict of almost two decades that was in the process of resolution through mediation initiated by the Inter-Governmental Authority for Development (IGAD), with support from the international community. This conflict was initially based in Southern Sudan and pitted the Government of Sudan against the late John Garang's Sudan Peoples' Liberation Movement/Army (SPLM/A), subsequently spreading to the Upper Nile region. The two largest rebel movements and some smaller ones signed up to a common platform as part of the peace process leading to the Comprehensive Peace Agreement signed in Nairobi on 9 January 2005. This included many protocols, especially those related to the power and wealth sharing regime. While generally portrayed as a clash between the Muslim North and the Christian/Animist South, the conflict is fuelled primarily by political and economic factors (marginalisation), exacerbated by religious factors (particularly the application of Sharia Law to non-Muslims).

In Darfur, the same causes produced the same effects. The economic and political marginalisation of the people of Darfur (a region of Western Sudan that covers 20% of the country), exacerbated by the increasing scarcity of pastoral and agricultural resources and the consequent conflicts between animal breeders and farmers, led to the continuing rebellion in the region.

---

[5] UN Doc. S/2005/716.

Whatever its roots, the Darfur conflict has become Africa's first human tragedy of the 21st Century. The brutality of the government-supported militias, which have committed massacres, torched villages, stolen livestock and forced the displacement of the inhabitants, appears to have caused the death of more than 200 000 people, the internal displacement of 2 million, and the exile of nearly 300 000 more to Eastern Chad. Due to a high level of media interest in the conflict as from March 2003, the international community became interested in the Darfur situation. The US Secretary of State Colin Powell, the UN Secretary-General, and the UN High Commissioner for Human Rights visited the area in 2004.[6] The UN High Commissioner for Refugees travelled to Eastern Chad in October of the same year to visit the Darfur refugee camps. African States did not hold back from involvement in the Darfur crisis, especially as the Sudanese government, motivated by international geopolitical considerations, expressed a preference for an African solution to the conflict. In light of this, several regional heads of State offered to mediate, including the Chadian president, Idriss Déby Itno.

As a result of his mediation, conducted with the support of the African Union, the parties to the conflict signed a Humanitarian Ceasefire Agreement and a Protocol on the delivery of humanitarian assistance to Darfur on 8 April 2004, providing for an end to hostilities and the proclamation of a ceasefire, joint verification of the ceasefire, the facilitation of the delivery of humanitarian assistance and the establishment of a comprehensive and definitive peace in Darfur.[7] Several other agreements on the practical modalities for the implementation of the Agreement and its Protocol were signed

---

[6] Several commissions of enquiry set up by the High Commission for Human Rights visited Darfur in 2004. The report of the commission deployed in May 2004, which the Secretary-General transmitted to the Security Council and which mentions the preparation of crimes against humanity and ethnic cleansing, led the Security Council to adopt resolution 1593 (on 15 March 2005) referring the situation in Darfur to the International Criminal Court. Regarding the human rights situation in Darfur, see the United Nations "Report of the Representative of the Secretary-General on Internally Displaced Persons", Francis M. Deng, on His Mission to the Sudan (25 July-1 August 2004), UN Doc. E/CN.4/2005/8.

[7] African Union (Peace and Security Council): "Briefing Note on the renewal of the Mandate of the AU Mission in the Sudan (AMIS)", AU Doc. PSC/PR/2 (XLII), 20 October 2005, p. 1.

subsequently. It should also be noted that the African Union and the parties to the conflict signed an agreement in Addis Ababa on 28 May 2004,[8] setting out the modalities for the deployment of observers to Darfur and for monitoring and verification of the ceasefire.

3.2.2. From AMIS to the Joint UN-African Union Mission in Darfur (UNAMID)

A Ceasefire Commission was established pursuant to articles 3 and 4 of the Humanitarian Ceasefire Agreement of 8 April 2004. It reports to the Joint Commission composed of the parties to the conflict, the African Union, the European Union and the United States of America (operating at ambassadorial level). Article III of the agreement with the parties to the Darfur conflict on the Ceasefire Commission provides as follows:

"I. The mandate of the CFC shall consist of:

- Planning, verifying and ensuring the implementation of the rules and provisions of the ceasefire;

- Defining the routes for the movement of forces in order to reduce the risks of incidents; the administrative movements shall be notified to the CFC;

- Requesting appropriate assistance with demining operations;

- Receiving, verifying, analyzing and judging complaints related to possible violations of the ceasefire;

- Developing adequate measures to guard against such incidents in the future;

- Determining clearly the sites occupied by the combatants of the armed opposition and verifying the neutralization of the armed militias."

The Ceasefire Commission is composed of representatives of the above-mentioned organizations and countries, and is chaired by the African Union. Article 4 of the Agreement on the Modalities for the Establishment of the Ceasefire Commission and the Deployment of Observers in the Darfur provides that "the operational arm of the Ceasefire Commission shall be the African Union Mission". Under the

---

[8] *Ibid.*, "Agreement With the Sudanese Parties on the Modalities for the Establishment of the Ceasefire Commission and the Deployment of Observers in the Darfur", Addis Ababa, 28 May 2004 (mimeo).

terms of the Agreement, the military observers, who act under the authority of the African Union and report to the Ceasefire Commission, should be lightly armed. However, these observers, of whom 60 were initially provided for, were to be protected in their monitoring activities by 300 soldiers of an African Union force. Since the limited size of this mission (AMIS I) did not allow it to perform the huge task it faced, the Africa Union decided to deploy an actual peacekeeping force (AMIS II).

As stated in an official document of the African Union:

"[…]

6. The effectiveness of the initial AMIS deployment was constrained by its small size and by logistical challenges. The small number of MILOBs, regardless of their efficiency and dedication, were unable to provide meaningful monitoring coverage for an area roughly the size of France, and particularly in a situation where the parties have not complied with the provisions of the HCFA they had signed. The Government of the Sudan (GoS), the armed Movements and the international community had indicated that AMIS I was not always able to carry out its tasks in a timely and efficient manner, due to its limited capacity. Due to these factors, the general consensus was that AMIS I should be strengthened.

7. It is in recognition of this situation that the 13th meeting of the Peace and Security Council (PSC), held on 27 July 2004, requested the Chairperson of the Commission to submit, for consideration, a comprehensive plan on how best to enhance the effectiveness of the AU Mission on the ground, including the possibility of transforming it into a full-fledged peacekeeping mission, with the requisite mandate and strengthen, in order to ensure the effective implementation of the Ceasefire Agreement, with particular emphasis on the disarmament and the neutralization of the Janjaweed militia, the protection of the civilian population, and the facilitation of the delivery of humanitarian assistance.

8. The plan was subsequently formulated by the Commission with the assistance of the UN and other partners. This plan, AMIS II, which proposed the transformation of the nature, scope and composition of the Mission and called for the enhancement of both the mandate and the strength of the military observers and the protection force, was approved by the PSC, at its 17th meeting held on 20 October 2004. The PSC decided "that AMIS shall consist of 3,320 personnel, including 2,341 military personnel, among them

450 observers, up to 815 civilian police personnel, as well as the appropriate civilian personnel. The enhanced Mission should be headed by a Special Representative of the Chairperson of the Commission (SRCC), who shall ensure the overall direction and coordination of the activities of the Mission and shall maintain close contact with the Sudanese parties, as well as the UN and all other concerned actors".

9. AMIS II was deployed for a period of one year and was mandated to:
- Monitor and observe compliance with the HCFA of 8 April 2004 and all such agreements in the future;
- Assist in the process of building confidence;
- Contribute to a secure environment for the delivery of humanitarian relief and, beyond that, the return of IDPs and refugees to their homes, in order to assist in increasing the level of compliance of all parties with the HCFA and to contribute to the improvement of the security situation throughout Darfur."[9]

This deployment of a stronger force was programmed in two phases. The first, scheduled for late May 2005, aimed to deploy 3320 men (including 2341 military personnel, 450 military observers and 815 civilian police); and the second, scheduled for late September 2005, was to increase the force to 6171 men (including 1560 police). As of 20 October 2005, the force was composed of troops provided by Nigeria (2040 soldiers), Rwanda (1756), Senegal (538), Gambia (196), Chad (40), Kenya (35) and South Africa (285).[10]

While the African Union received financial assistance from the European Union to strengthen AMIS, the force's limited operational capacity led it to turn to NATO.[11] Approaching these two competing partners led to a power play and contributed to the delay in attaining its stated objectives.[12] The reluctance of some African leaders, including the Sudanese, to involve NATO was also a significant obstacle to the effective reinforcement of AMIS. However, faced with

---

[9] See above, footnote 7, p. 2.
[10] *Id.*, pp. 3-4.
[11] International Crisis Group, *The AU's Mission in Darfur: Bridging the Gaps*, Brussels/Nairobi, Africa Briefing No. 28, 6 July 2005.
[12] "Compromis entre Paris et Washington sur le Darfour", *Le Monde*, 11 June 2005, p. 6.

the force's inability to carry out the tasks defined in its mandate, the United Nations Mission in Sudan (UNMIS), which was deployed to implement the Global Peace Agreement for Southern Sudan, established a bridge with AMIS in order to strengthen its capacity. Nonetheless, the operational limitations of AMIS led the African Union to request its replacement with a UN peacekeeping force. The UN Security Council approved this in resolution 1706 (2006) of 31 August 2006, extending the mandate of UNMIS in Darfur and authorising the force to be increased to 20 000 soldiers.[13] Faced with the Sudanese government's refusal to allow UN troops into Darfur, the African Union and the UN organised a High-Level Consultation on 16 November 2006 with a view to proposing a global solution to the Darfur conflict. This included reinforcing AMIS in three phases, culminating in its transformation into a hybrid AU-UN force. While this approach was approved by the UN,[14] and by the AU Peace and Security Council during its 66th meeting in Abuja on 30 November 2006, it proved difficult to implement due to the Sudanese government's reluctance to authorize deployment of UN forces in Darfur. Thus, it was only on 31 July 2007 that the UN Security Council adopted resolution 1763 which authorized the deployment of a joint UN-AU peacekeeping mission in Darfur (UNAMID). However, due to the insistence of the Sudanese Government in the African composition of the forces, the resources of the operation continued to be inadequate both in terms of troops and of logistical support. The situation was further complicated by the indictment of President Omar Al Bashir of Sudan by the International Criminal Court on 4 March 2009.

---

[13] In paragraph 9 of the resolution, the Security Council requested that the Secretary-General evaluate the possibility of deploying a multipurpose peacekeeping force to address the regional security problems experienced in Eastern Chad and the North-Eastern Central African Republic as a result of the Darfur conflict.

[14] Statement by the Chairperson of the Security Council, 19 December 2006, UN Doc. S/PRST/2006/55.

4. Tentative Evaluation of African Union Peacekeeping Operations and Prospects

While it is agreed that AMIB's performance produced results, this is not the case for AMIS which later became UNAMID, especially as regards the protection of civilians and displaced persons. In both cases, however, it was imperative for the UN to take over in order to overcome the financial and logistical difficulties of the African Union. The major lesson for the African Union is the importance of increasing its cooperation with the EU and the UN in order to strengthen its financial and operational capacity for peacekeeping.

4.1. Financial and logistical problems of the African Union's PKOs

Faced with already huge challenges, compounded by the size of Darfur (equal in size to France or the state of Texas in the United States), AMIS (later UNAMID) experienced financial and logistical difficulties beyond those which could be resolved by support from the European Union and cooperation with UNMIS.[15] In its communiqué of 12 January 2006, the AU's Peace and Security Council called on the UN:

"The Peace and Security Council (PSC) of the African Union (AU), at its 45th meeting, held on 12 January 2006, adopted the following decision on the situation in Darfur:

The *Council*,

1. *Takes note* of the Report of the Chairperson of the Commission on the situation in Darfur [PSC/PR/2 (XLV)] and the pertinent observations contained therein;

2. *Expresses satisfaction* at the very significant progress made in the deployment of the African Mission in the Sudan (AMIS), as well as at the fact that, in spite of serious financial, logistical and other constraints facing the Mission, AMIS has contributed significantly to the protection of the

---

[15] See esp. International Crisis Group, "The EU/AU Partnership in Darfur: Not Yet a Winning Combination", *Africa Report* No. 99, Brussels/Nairobi, 25 October 2005; and United Nations, Monthly report of the Secretary General on Darfur, UN Doc. S/2005/650, 14 October 2005, p. 7.

civilian population and the improvement of the security and humanitarian situation in Darfur; [...].

3. *Expresses its support*, in principle, to a transition from AMIS to a UN operation, within the framework of the partnership between the AU and the United Nations in the promotion of peace, security and stability in Africa, and decides to convene a meeting of the Peace and Security Council at ministerial level, in Addis Ababa, before the end of March 2006, to review the situation and make a final decision on the issue of the transition towards a UN operation in Darfur and its modalities. In this respect, Council *requests* the Chairperson of the Commission to initiate appropriate consultations with the United Nations and other stakeholders, with a view to providing the proposed meeting of the Peace and Security Council at ministerial level with all relevant additional information, including on the modalities for a transition towards a UN operation and the financial aspects of the ongoing operation in Darfur."[16]

The final decision to deploy a hybrid AU-UN force should represent an effective response to the operational weaknesses of AMIS. Its implementation in other situations should contribute to the strengthening of the African Union's peacekeeping capacity and the respective roles of regional UN organizations in peacekeeping.[17]

4.2. Strengthening the African Union's Peacekeeping Capacity

The issue of strengthening the capacity of Africa in general, and of the African Union in particular, has been amply addressed by peace research institutions.[18] At the operational level, external powers,

---

[16] Peace and Security Council, Communiqué, 12 January 2006, AU Doc. PSC/PR/Comm. (XLV).

[17] "The UN and Regional Organisations", Security Council Report No. 3, 23 March 2007. Regarding the potential contribution of joint operations to strengthening the capacities of the African Union, see Mubiala M., "Towards United Nations-African Union Joint-Ventures for Peace and Security in Africa", A Policy Paper Proposal for the 2007 ACUNS/ASIL Summer Workshop on International Organizations Studies, Ghent, Belgium, 24 July – 4 August 2007.

[18] See esp. Berman E.G. and Sams K.E., *Peacekeeping in Africa: Capabilities and Culpabilities*, Geneva, UNIDIR/Institute for Security Studies, 2000; Juma C. & Mengistu A., *The Infrastructure of Peace in Africa. Assessing the Peacebuilding Capacity of African Institutions*, report submitted by the African Program of the

desirous of divesting themselves of the burden of peacekeeping in Africa, have adopted initiatives aimed at strengthening African peacekeeping capacity. These include, in particular, the Reinforcement of African Peacekeeping Capabilities (RECAMP) (France); the Peace Support Operation Facility (European Union); the African Conflict Prevention Pool (ACPP) (United Kingdom); Training for Peace (Norway); the African Contingency Operations Training Assistance (ACOTA), the African Regional Peacekeeping Program, the International Military Education and Training Program (IMET) and Enhanced International Peacekeeping Capabilities (EIPC) (United States). In a new international environment characterised by a more prominent role of regional organizations in peacekeeping and their cooperation with the United Nations,[19] the African Union is moving towards increased cooperation with the European Union[20] and the United Nations.[21] In particular, there have been interesting developments in the framework for cooperation between the African Union and the UN, through the adoption on 16 November 2006 of the Declaration entitled "Enhancing UN-AU Cooperation Framework for the 10-year Capacity-Building Programme for the African Union" by the former Chairperson of the African Union Commission, Alpha Oumar Konaré, and the then United Nations Secretary-General, Kofi Annan.[22]

International Peace Academy to the Ford Foundation, New York, International Peace Academy, September 2002.

[19] Graham K., "Regionalisation and Responses to Armed Conflict, with Special Focus on Conflict Prevention and Peacekeeping", *Occasional Paper* No. 0-2005/21, United Nations University-Comparative Regional Integration Studies (UNU-CRIS), October 2005, pp. 18-26.

[20] Council of the European Union, "The EU and Africa: Towards a Strategic Partnership", Brussels, 19 December 2005, EU Doc. 15961/05 (press 367), p. 2.

[21] African Union, "Memorandum on Prospects of Effective Cooperation between the African Union and the United Nations: World Summit Outcome and 10-Year Capacity Building Plan for the African Union", Addis Ababa, 24 November 2005, pp. 3-4 (mimeo).

[22] UN Doc. A/61/630, 12 December 2006. Regarding cooperation between the UN and African regional organizations in peacekeeping, see the Chapter in this *Manual* by Djacoba Liva Tehindrazanarivelo on the relations between the African Union and the United Nations in peacekeeping.

5. Conclusion

African Union operations follow the principles governing the UN's peacekeeping operations, including the consent of the parties to the conflict to their deployment, the non-use of offensive force and the impartiality of regional troops. As in the UN, they are under the authority of the Chairperson of the African Union Commission through his Special Representative. In the relationship between the African Union and the UN, the primary role of the Security Council in peacekeeping is recognised and established through the African Union's reports to the Security Council through the UN Secretary-General. Similarly, a study of the Burundi and Sudan cases confirms the close cooperation of the African Union and the UN in peacekeeping, whose modalities range from logistical and technical support to the joint deployment of operations (for example, the AU-UN hybrid force in Darfur – UNAMID), including taking over African Union operations by UN operations (Burundi and project planned for Somalia). This practice consolidates that of the OAU era with respect to operations deployed by African sub-regional organizations, notably ECOMOG. This is a significant contribution to the implementation of Chapter VIII of the United Nations Charter. Finally, developments in peacekeeping have also influenced the early experience of the African Union. They are reflected in the design of these operations and the extension of the mandate of African Union operations to activities that are not strictly military, such as monitoring respect for human rights, humanitarian assistance, support for democratic electoral processes, etc.

However, like the African Union itself, its operations are characterised by limited operational capacity. This has led to recourse to external support forces, which are not free of power politics, leading in turn to power play. As has been observed in the analysis of the Sudan situation, such power play can adversely affect the effectiveness and credibility of operations. The future of African Union operations therefore depends on strengthening its capacities, first by creating the regional brigades provided for as part of the Standby Force, and second by providing them with appropriate training, equipment and funding.

CHAPTER 18.
THE AFRICAN UNION'S RELATIONSHIP WITH THE UNITED NATIONS IN THE MAINTENANCE OF PEACE AND SECURITY

Djacoba Liva Tehindrazanarivelo

1. Introduction

The relationship between the United Nations (UN) and regional arrangements or organizations was not part of the Dumbarton Oaks proposals, which served as the basis for discussions at the 1945 San Francisco Conference on the creation of the UN. This was due to scepticism about the system of alliances and the balance of power, whose polarisation had led to the two world wars.

But the impetus of the Latin American countries – accounting for 20 of the 50 States participating in the San Francisco Conference – who had developed the Inter-American system as far back as the 19th Century, supported by the six Arab countries which had just formed the League of Arab States in February 1945, led to a distinction being made between regional arrangements, whose purpose was to regulate and strengthen relations between their members, and outward-looking alliances directed against a common enemy. Regional arrangements could thus serve as sub-systems or adjuncts of the UN, and to some extent divest it of responsibility for its primary objective of maintaining international peace and security.

The result was Chapter VIII of the United Nations Charter, entitled "Regional Arrangements". This vests the UN – an organization whose members are exclusively States – with the principal responsibility for maintaining international peace and security, while recognising the existence of regional arrangements or agencies and according them some powers in dispute settlement and peacekeeping. Chapter VIII defines the scope of the powers exercised by regional organizations in these areas, and thus provides the legal framework for the relationship between the UN and the African Union. This will be addressed in Section 2 below.

Over time, practice showed the potentially decisive contribution regional organizations could make to maintaining and consolidating peace and stability in their respective regions. Cooperation between the UN and regional organizations has now become a key element of the UN's collective security strategy – "an imperative need imposed by new global realities."[1] How is this cooperation manifested in the case of African regional organizations? And what role do the African Union and other regional organizations expect the UN to play in their various peace activities? We will try to answer these questions in Section 3 below.

2. The Legal Framework of Relations Between the UN and the African Union

This framework is defined by Chapter VIII of the United Nations Charter, and has subsequently evolved through the development of relations between the UN and the Organization of African Unity (OAU), the AU's predecessor, and other African sub-regional organizations.[2] We therefore analyse first the principles of cooperation inherited from the OAU, which have been adopted in current relations with the UN, and then the new cooperation mechanisms established since the creation of the African Union in light of the new role it seeks to play in resolving conflicts in Africa.

---

[1] Statement by the representative of Algeria, Mr. Baali, to the Security Council, UN Doc. S/PV.5282, 17 October 2005, p. 14.

[2] In this study, as in UN texts, the term world organization refer to the UN, regional organization to the OAU-AU, and sub-regional organization for all other organizations of countries in the various regions of Africa. Within the African Union, regional organizations will be referred to as "regional mechanism" or "regional economic communities" (RECs).

2.1. The constitutional framework: Chapter VIII of the United Nations Charter

Chapter VIII of the Charter, composed of three Articles (Articles 52 to 54), provides first for a non-exclusive preference for regional organizations in the peaceful settlement of regional disputes, so as to divest the UN of some of its responsibilities. Next, it provides for the pre-eminence of the UN over regional organizations for coercive action.

Article 52 recognises the legitimacy of regional arrangements or agencies, provided their activities are consistent with the goals and principles of the United Nations, and urges Member States of these agencies to refer the settlement of local or regional disputes to them in the first instance. This confirms the provisions of Article 33 of the Charter, which calls on States to settle any disputes by peaceful means of their own choice, including referral to regional agencies and arrangements. However, this primacy of regional organizations is not exclusive, in that the Security Council or the UN General Assembly may intervene or seize themselves of a local or regional dispute, even if it has already been referred to a regional organization.

Article 53 provides that, where appropriate, the Security Council may *have recourse to* regional arrangements or agencies *to enforce any measures it adopts*. It establishes the primacy of the UN over regional organizations by subjecting enforcement by regional organizations to prior authorisation by the Security Council. The 1990s provided us with examples of enforcement by regional organizations without prior authorisation by the Security Council some of which received approval from the Security Council after the fact.[3]

The primacy of the UN and its continued monitoring of regional action are further established in Article 54, which sets forth the obligation of regional organizations to keep the Security Council fully informed of their "activities undertaken or in contemplation" to maintain peace and security in their regions.

---

[3] These include in particular the activities of ECOWAS in Liberia and Sierra Leone in the 1990s.

2.2. Past relations between the UN, the OAU and African sub-regional organizations

Institutional relations between the UN and a regional organization generally begin with an invitation from the UN Secretary-General to the regional organization to participate as an observer in the proceedings of the General Assembly, and the participation of the UN Secretary-General in a conference or meeting of the regional organization.[4] This is a form of recognition by the UN of the regional organization and the compatibility of its constitutive act with the United Nations Charter.

Pursuant to the principles set forth in Chapter VIII of the Charter, the OAU affirmed early on its preference for seeking solutions to any conflict between its Member States within an exclusively African framework. It should be noted that neither the OAU Charter creating the Mediation, Conciliation and Arbitration Commission nor its organising protocol make reference to a UN role in the peaceful settlement of disputes between OAU members. This position was subsequently clarified through various instances of disapproval by the OAU of direct referrals to the Security Council for the peaceful settlement of some disputes between African States.[5] For their part, UN organs often recommended that African countries settle their disputes within the framework of the OAU.[6]

The OAU's position changed slightly during the 1990s. The Cairo Declaration of 1993 establishing the Mechanism for Conflict Prevention, Management and Resolution provides that

---

[4] The UN Secretary-General extended this invitation to the OAU on the basis of General Assembly resolution 2011 (XX) of 11 October 1965, entitled "Cooperation between the UN and the OAU". The UN Secretary-General attended an OAU session for the first time at the Assembly of Heads of State and Government in Kinshasa in September 1967.

[5] Andemicael B., *Peaceful settlement among African States: Roles of the United Nations and the Organization of African Unity*, New York, UNITAR, 1973, p. 57.

[6] In the Congo crisis, for example, the Security Council considered that the OAU "should be able, in the context of Article 52 of the Charter of the United Nations, to help find a peaceful solution to all the problems and disputes affecting peace and security in the continent of Africa". UN Doc. S/RES/199 (1964), 30 December 1964.

"The OAU shall also cooperate and work closely with the United Nations not only with regard to issues relating to peace-making but, and especially, also those relating to peacekeeping."[7]

Nonetheless, African States continued to maintain that the OAU bore the primary responsibility for peace in Africa and should act first, while the UN should act only in extreme cases to provide material, human and financial assistance to OAU action.

As regards areas of cooperation, the OAU was very active in situations concerning decolonisation, but often limited itself merely to condemnation and exhortation when other conflict situations arose, primarily due to a restrictive interpretation of the principles of non-intervention in the internal affairs of States. Enforcement was mostly carried out by the UN, to which the OAU applied through the Africa Group formed in New York. The first case of United Nations sanctions against Rhodesia in the 1960s fell within this ambit.

Before the creation of the African Union, African enforcement in conflict situations on the continent was sometimes carried out by regional organizations acting without the prior authorisation of the Security Council. This was initially the case, for example, of ECOWAS activities in Liberia and Sierra Leone, which were later endorsed by the UN Security Council.

In current relations between the UN and the African Union, the legal bases for cooperation are more precise and the areas of cooperation are broader, although previous mechanisms existing with the OAU are also maintained.

2.3. The current framework for relations between the UN and the African Union

2.3.1. The applicable legal texts

In the United Nations, the continuity of relations with the African continental organization was affirmed in General Assembly resolution 57/48 adopted a few months after the inaugural session of

---

[7] AU Doc. AHG/Decl. 3 (XXIX), June 1993, para. 25.

the African Union.[8] The resolution called on "the United Nations system to continue to support the African Union […] in strengthening the institutional and operational capacity of the Peace and Security Council of the African Union",[9] and set out the areas where, in the General Assembly's view, such cooperation was particularly important. These were conflict prevention,[10] peacekeeping operations,[11] peacebuilding[12] and the fight against terrorism.[13]

For its part, the Security Council, through its Chairperson, affirmed after its Nairobi meeting of November 2004 that cooperation with regional and sub-regional organizations, including the institutional relations between the United Nations and the African Union, is an important aspect of the collective security system instituted by the UN Charter. It then went on to welcome the creation of the African Union's Peace and Security Council, the African Standby Force and the early warning system in Africa (para. 1). It also

"… particularly welcome[d] the leading role of the African Union in efforts to settle crises in the African Continent and expresse[d] its full support for the peace initiatives conducted by the African Union, and through sub-regional organizations such as the Economic Community of West African States (ECOWAS), Southern African Development Community (SADC), Economic and Monetary Community of Central Africa (CEMAC), Intergovernmental Authority on Development (IGAD) and other regional

---

[8] UN Doc. A/RES/57/48, 21 November 2002, entitled "Cooperation between the United Nations and the African Union".
[9] Ibid., para. 7.
[10] Establishment of the early warning system already provided for in Article 12 of the Protocol on the Establishment of a Peace and Security (PSC Protocol); regular exchange and follow-up of information, information coordination, particularly between the early warning systems of the two organizations.
[11] Technical assistance and training of civilian and military personnel, assistance in establishing an African standby force, support for African Union field missions in the different Member States, and support to the PSC for humanitarian operations on the continent in accordance with the PSC Protocol.
[12] Strengthening peace-building capacity before and after the end of hostilities on the continent, implementation of concrete programmes to combat the proliferation of small arms and antipersonnel mines within the framework of the relevant declarations and resolutions of both organizations.
[13] Strengthening cooperation by implementing treaties, protocols and other relevant regional and international instruments designed to fight terrorism, in particular the Algiers Plan of Action of 14 September 2002. UN Doc. A/RES/57/48, paras. 7, 8, 13 and 16).

Sub-regional African organizations are also invited to take part in examining any issue submitted to the Peace and Security Council that is also being examined by the Council or that is of special interest to them. Conversely, the Chairperson of the Commission is to be invited to participate in meetings and deliberations of sub-regional organizations on a particular situation.

Lastly, provision is made for the Union and sub-regional organizations to establish liaison offices within their respective Secretariats,[28] and for "periodic meetings, but at least once a year, with the Chief Executives and/or the officials in charge of peace and security within the Regional Mechanisms".[29] This last point is reminiscent of the periodic meetings the UN holds with regional organizations that it recognizes around the world, through which it acts as coordinator and leader of their various peace initiatives.

This role of a continental organization acting as a conduit between the UN and sub-regional organizations for conflict resolution has been seen as limiting the risks of partiality and tension between neighbouring States in the activities of sub-regional organizations, including suspicions of ambitions towards hegemony. The major advantage of this role

> "is that the organization is neither too far from, nor too near to the theatre of conflicts. In its direct involvement, the OAU [now the AU] is also in a position to coordinate all the activities relating to conflict as performed by the various sub-regional entities."[30]

3. Relations Within the Framework of Activities of Common Interest

There are many activities of common interest to the African Union and the United Nations. General Assembly resolution 57/48, adopted in 2002, refers to strengthening the institutional and operational capacity of the Union's peace mechanism, combating the proliferation

---

[28] *Ibid.*, Articles 16(5), 16(6), 16(7) and 16(8).
[29] *Ibid.*, Article 16(4).
[30] Salim A.S., "The OAU Role in Conflict Management", in Otunnu O. and Doyle M. (eds.), *Peacemaking and Peacekeeping for the New Century*, Lanham, M.D., Rowman & Littlefield, 1996, p. 245.

of small arms and anti-personnel mines, fighting terrorism, supporting the Peace and Security Council in carrying out humanitarian operations on the continent, sustainable economic development, combating the spread of infectious diseases (HIV/AIDS, tuberculosis, malaria, etc.), defending human rights, and protecting refugees. In his 2000 report on cooperation between the UN and the OAU, the United Nations Secretary-General set out seven priority areas for cooperation between the two organizations, additionally including debt reduction and cancellation, information-sharing on and joint management of conflict, education, and democracy and good governance.[31]

The Security Council's follow-up to the Secretary-General's report on "The causes of conflict [...] in Africa"[32] suggests that its interest in peace and security in Africa focuses on the effectiveness of arms embargos, strengthening African capacity for peacekeeping, regional cooperation, the establishment of an international mechanism for the security and neutrality of refugee camps, the circulation of weapons, and strengthening capacity for monitoring activities authorised by the Security Council.

While all these issues remain part of the common concerns of the African Union and the UN, this Chapter deals primarily with international peace and security, as provided for in Chapter VIII of the United Nations Charter. It also examines the relations between the African Union and the UN in conflict prevention, conflict management, and particularly the establishment of peacekeeping or peace-building operations in Africa, and responses to widespread human rights violations on the continent. The analysis therefore focuses on the respective roles of the two organizations and efforts to coordinate their activities in each of these areas.

3.1. Conflict prevention

On conflict prevention, the Security Council advocates the establishment of an effective partnership with regional organizations, as a means of strengthening the UN's own prevention capacity. As a general policy, it emphasises

---

[31] UN Doc. A/55/498, 19 October 2000, Section III, paras. 9 *et seq.*
[32] UN Doc. A/52/871 – S/19998/318, 13 April 1998.

"the need to adopt a broad strategy of conflict prevention, which addresses the root causes of armed conflict and political and social crises in a comprehensive manner, including by promoting sustainable development, poverty eradication, national reconciliation, good governance, democracy, gender equality, the rule of law and respect for and protection of human rights."[33]

In relation to Africa in particular, the Security Council seeks to establish an effective partnership with "the African Union and *its* subregional organizations, in order to enable early responses to disputes and emerging crises".[34] It also encourages African States to adhere to the African Union Non-Aggression and Common Defence Pact adopted in Abuja on 31 January 2005, and where appropriate to sign sub-regional pacts on peace, security, democracy, good governance and development. It goes on to call on the United Nations system and the international community to support the implementation of such Pacts.[35]

These calls to adhere to the various security and defence pacts are part of the efforts to promote confidence-building measures between African States that can help prevent conflict and foster peace on the continent. The 2005 Pact referred to by the Security Council aims precisely to promote cooperation and peaceful coexistence between African States, to prevent conflict between and within these States, and to ensure the peaceful settlement of disputes.[36]

Of the eight measures provided for by the Security Council to strengthen the UN's conflict prevention capacity, four are of interest to Africa and its regional organizations. These are assessing regularly the developments in regions at risk of armed conflict; supporting regional mediation initiatives; supporting regional and sub-regional

---

[33] "Declaration on strengthening the effectiveness of the Security Council's role in conflict prevention, particularly in Africa", UN Doc. S/RES/1625 (2005), 14 September 2005, Annex, para. 2.
[34] *Ibid.*, para. 7; italics added.
[35] *Ibid.*, para. 8. Also worth mentioning here is the Security Council's support for the Pact on Security, Stability and Development signed between the Great Lakes countries in December 2006. UN Doc. S/PRST/2006/57, 20 December 2006.
[36] African Union Non-Aggression and Common Defence Pact, 31 January 2005, Article 2(a).

capacities for early warning; enabling prompt action in response to early warning indicators; and supporting African States' efforts to build independent and reliable national judicial institutions.[37]

In accordance with these principles, the United Nations created mechanisms for consultation and for promotion of preventive diplomacy initiatives with the African Union and African sub-regional organizations. These mechanisms for consultation include the appointment of special representatives for regions experiencing conflict situations, some of whom are even appointed jointly by both organizations – as for example in the Great Lakes region. Also noteworthy is the UN's creation in 1992 of the United Nations Standing Advisory Committee on Security Questions in Central Africa, whose periodic meetings at Head of State and ministerial level played a significant role in formulating a "new architecture for peace and security" in Central Africa.[38]

One example of the strengthening of African conflict prevention capacity is the United Nations' technical and financial support for the establishment of African early warning systems. As said before, the African Union provided for the setting up of a continental early warning system,[39] the intention being to link this to sub-regional early warning systems, particularly those of ECOWAS in West Africa (ECOWATCH), SADC in Southern Africa,[40] ECCAS in Central Africa (MARAC) and IGAD in East Africa (CEWARN).

But, where preventive measures have failed to prevent the outbreak of conflict, what have the UN and the AU done to manage such conflicts, including, where applicable, through use of force?

3.2. Conflict management

As its 2006 Annual report[41] shows, the Security Council examined the conflict situations in Burundi, Côte d'Ivoire, Guinea-Bissau,

---

[37] UN Doc. S/RES/1625 (2005), Annex, paras. 2 (a), (c), (d), and (h).
[38] Mubiala M., *Coopérer pour la paix en Afrique centrale*, United Nations, UNIDIR, 2003, pp. 5-14 and 25.
[39] PSC Protocol, Article 12.
[40] In addition to its early warning system for food security (article 3 (b), see SADC Protocol on Politics, Defence, and Security, 2001)).
[41] UN Doc. A/61/2, covering the period from 1 August 2005 to 31 July 2006.

Liberia, the Democratic Republic of the Congo (DRC), Western Sahara, Sierra Leone, Somalia, Sudan, and the border conflict between Eritrea and Ethiopia. In its 2004 communiqué on the formal launching of its proceedings, the AU Peace and Security Council also examined many of these situations,[42] as well as others which are no longer on the Security Council's agenda or which it has not discussed for some years.[43] This indicates that some conflict situations in Africa appear simultaneously on the agendas of the UN Security Council and the AU Peace and Security Council, while others are monitored chiefly through the African peace framework. It is therefore interesting to consider how the UN and the African Union interact according to whether or not they are jointly involved in the management of a particular conflict.

3.2.1. Relations in management of conflicts appearing simultaneously on the agendas of the UN and the African Union

It should be noted at the outset that there is no legal text prohibiting the African Union from dealing with, or restricting its ability to take decisions on, a conflict of which the Security Council has already been seized. Given the Security Council's principal responsibility for maintaining peace around the world, the reverse is also true. However, as members of the United Nations, the Member States of the African Union must ensure that the Union's decisions are not inconsistent with those of the Security Council.[44]

Due to limited space, we shall not examine the management of all the conflicts both organizations have recently dealt with simultaneously. Rather, we propose to examine a few salient facts illustrating an unprecedented form of cooperation between the two organizations in the past decade. Other conflict situations will be examined in subsequent sections.

Given the exceptional nature of the decisions taken by the UN, the AU and ECOWAS, the interaction between these organizations in managing the situation in Côte d'Ivoire merits closer examination.

---

[42] AU Doc. PSC/AHG/Comm. (IX), 25 May 2004.
[43] The situation in Angola and the Comoros.
[44] Article 48(2) of the UN Charter.

The UN considered this situation to be "a threat to international peace and security in the region",[45] and accordingly imposed an arms embargo on the entire country, after which it threatened those hampering the implementation of the peace agreements with restrictions on international travel and freezes on financial assets,[46] as well as deploying peacekeeping operations as discussed later. While the African Union now has extended powers to sanction its Member States,[47] it was the Security Council which took the necessary enforcement measures, the Union merely affirming its support for the targeted sanctions envisaged.[48]

Conversely, in the mediation to re-establish peace and security in the country, one sees the Security Council taking a back seat and allowing the African Union and ECOWAS to initiate discussions with the parties in the conflict and take the appropriate measures. In so doing, the Council has repeatedly expressed its full support for the facilitation mission undertaken by the South African President on behalf of the African Union and in cooperation with ECOWAS, and for the decisions of the Peace and Security Council on efforts to re-establish peace and ensure stability in Côte d'Ivoire.[49]

This support subsequently extended to substantive decisions of the Peace and Security Council. Faced with the impossibility, recognised by all the Ivorian parties, of organising elections before the end of the term of office of President Laurent Gbagbo on 30 October 2005, the Peace and Security Council decided to establish a transitional period of up to one year, starting on 31 October 2005. During this

---

[45] UN Doc. S/RES/1464 (2003), 4 February 2003, last paragraph.
[46] UN Doc. S/RES/1572 (2004), 15 November 2004, paras. 7, 9 and 11.
[47] Regarding this power to impose sanctions and the changes since the OAU era, see Tehindrazanarivelo D.L., "Les sanctions dans le cadre de l'Union africaine: réflexions préliminaires" in Ayissi A. and Tehindrazanarivelo D.L. (eds.), *Les défis de l'Afrique au XXIe siècle, Actes du 1er colloque international sur l'Afrique*, Geneva, IUHEI, 2005, pp. 89-120.
[48] AU Doc. PSC/AHG/Comm.(XL), 6 October 2005, para. 12.
[49] UN Doc. S/RES/1584 (2005), paras. 6 and 7; UN Doc. S/RES/1594 (2005), para. 4; UN Doc. S/RES/1600 (2005), para. 1, welcoming the signature on 6 April 2005 of the Pretoria Agreement as a result of mediation by the African Union; and UN Doc. S/RES/1603 (2005), para. 2, which emphasises that should the Ivorian parties fail to respect the commitments made in Pretoria before President Thabo Mbeki, this could lead to the imposition of the targeted sanction provided for in resolution 1572 (2004).

period, Mr. Laurent Gbagbo was to remain Head of State, but the transitional government was under the full authority of a Prime Minister accepted by all the signatories of the Linas-Marcoussis Agreement – Mr. Charles Konnan Banny – who would not be eligible for the elections to be organised during the transitional period. The Peace and Security Council also decided to establish an International Working Group (IWG) to assist the Ivorian government in completing the country's reconciliation and to monitor the parties' compliance with their undertakings under the peace agreements.[50] The composition of this group itself indicates the close cooperation that exists between African organizations, the United Nations system, and other external partners.[51]

These Peace and Security Council decisions were taken in consultation with ECOWAS, on the basis of discussions at its extraordinary summit of 30 September 2005. This was called at the request of the African Union,[52] and saw the participation of three United Nations representatives in the region.[53]

The Peace and Security Council's decision of 6 October 2005 was submitted to the Security Council to "obtain its support,"[54] and received its full backing. Security Council decisions on the transitional period in Côte d'Ivoire, taken pursuant to Chapter VII of the Charter, essentially reflect the decisions of the Peace and Security Council. Thus, the Security Council endorsed the opinion of ECOWAS and the Peace and Security Council on the end of the mandate of the Ivorian President, indicated its support for the International Working Group, fully supported the decision of the Peace and Security Council relating to the powers of the Ivorian Prime Minister, and accordingly

---

[50] AU Doc. PSC/AHG/Comm. (XL), 6 October 2005, para. 10.
[51] The IWG was composed of six African States, three permanent members of the United Nations Security Council, and representatives from the UN, AU, ECOWAS, the EU, the Francophonie, the World Bank and the International Monetary Fund. Its secretariat was placed under the authority of UN Special Representatives, the Secretary-General of ECOWAS, and the Chairperson of the AU Commission, under UN coordination; *ibid.,* paras. 10(vi) and 10(vii).
[52] AU Doc. PSC/AHG/Comm. (XXXVIII), 14 September 2005, para. 4.
[53] The Special Representative of the Secretary-General in Côte d'Ivoire, the United Nations High Representative for Elections in Côte d'Ivoire, and the Secretary-General's Special Representative for West Africa.
[54] AU Doc. PSC/AHG/Comm. (XL), para. 14.

requested the IWG to verify that the Prime Minister had all the necessary powers and resources to carry out his role.[55] The Security Council further took several measures intended to give effect to the transitional measures adopted by the Peace and Security Council.[56]

On 1 November 2006, the Security Council was obliged once again to take note of the impossibility of organising presidential and legislative elections on the intended date, and of the expiry on 31 October 2006 of the transitional period and the mandates of the President and the Prime Minister. As before, the Security Council endorsed the prior decision of the Peace and Security Council to establish a "new and final transitional period", to expire on 30 October 2007, and to extend the constitutional mandate of President Gbagbo and the international mandate of the Prime Minister, Mr. Konnan Banny.[57]

This is an unprecedented case where the UN fully and expressly supported the decisions taken by an African organization to re-establish peace by repeatedly referring to these decisions and taking additional measures to ensure their implementation. The measures provided for in Security Council resolutions 1633 (2005) and 1721 (2006) can only be fully understood in the context of the communiqués of the Peace and Security Council. Moreover, the Security Council's reference to African Union decisions makes them universal, thus rendering the transitional arrangements in Côte d'Ivoire enforceable on all Member States of the United Nations.

This support for a regional solution is all the more remarkable as the extension of a presidential mandate, for two consecutive years, appears to be a break with United Nations previous practice with regard to democratic transition and consolidation of the State. UN practice in this context was rather to establish an international

---

[55] UN Doc. S/RES/1633 (2005), 21 October 2005, paras. 3, 4, 5, 6, 10, 12, 18, 22 and 23.
[56] See, in particular, paras. 5, 8 and 13 of resolution 1633 (2005).
[57] UN Doc. S/RES/1721 (2006), paras. 3, 4 and 5. It should be noted, however, that this international arrangement was superseded by a "political agreement" signed in Ouagadougou on 4 March 2007 between Messrs. Laurent Gbagbo and Guillaume K. Soro, Secretary General of the *Forces Nouvelles*. Under this agreement, Mr. Gbagbo remained President of the Republic and M. Soro became Prime Minister of a new government.

transitional administration which it managed directly, and which included the various parties to the conflict, for the purpose of restoring and consolidating state institutions.

It is also noteworthy that the Security Council linked the application of individual sanctions which it announced to the failure to respect the commitments made during the African Union's mediation, and that the Security Council approved the Peace and Security Council decision to have only one mediator in the Ivorian conflict (the incumbent Chairperson of the African Union), "to avoid multiple and conflicting mediation efforts".[58] In general, mediation and efforts to find a political solution in this situation have been led by the African Union, while enforcement measures have been taken by the United Nations, with the full approval of the African Union.

In the transitional situation in Liberia, however, the views of the UN and the African Union differed with respect to United Nations sanctions on Liberian diamonds and timber. For the United Nations, these sanctions had to remain in place as long as the Liberian government could not exercise effective control over timber-producing regions, and the sanctions would ensure that public revenue from the Liberian forestry sector was used for legitimate ends in the interest of the people of Liberia. The same applied to the boycott of Liberian diamonds, which was contingent upon the establishment of an effective, transparent and verifiable diamond certification system.[59] Observing the continued failure of the Liberian government to meet these conditions, the Security Council renewed the sanctions in 2004, 2005, and 2006.[60] In the view of the African Union, these "strict ... sanctions" deprived Liberia of the resources necessary for the country's rehabilitation and development. It therefore recommended that the Africa Group in New York explore the possibility of a review of the sanctions to enable Liberia to procure the resources to "rebuild

---

[58] UN Doc. S/RES/1721 (2006), para. 20.
[59] UN Doc. S/RES/1521 (2003), 22 December 2003, paras. 6 and 8; 10 and 12.
[60] UN Doc. S/RES/1579 (2004), 21 December 2004, paras. 1 and 2; UN Doc. S/RES/1609 (2005), 21 June 2005, para. 1; and UN Doc. S/RES/1647, 20 December 2005, para. 1.

its structures of governance and be in a position to provide basic services and ensure the human security of its people".[61]

During her address to the Security Council on 17 March 2006, the President of Liberia, Ellen Johnson-Sirleaf, requested the lifting of these sanctions, though admitting that Liberia had not yet fulfilled all the criteria for their removal.[62]

Nonetheless, it should be noted that African States are under an obligation to ensure the application of these United Nations sanctions by the African Union and other sub-regional organizations of which they are members, in addition to their individual obligation to apply them.[63]

3.2.2. UN assistance for conflict management where the African Union is primarily active

Practice has shown that the African Union is active primarily in situations concerning unconstitutional changes of government. The Union condemns and rejects such changes, which are interpreted as threats to the order and stability of the African continent as a whole. It also provides for the exclusion from its activities of governments that come to power in this way.[64] Pursuant to these principles, the Union has thus condemned attempted coups d'états, coups d'états and other means of gaining power inconsistent with the Constitution in force at the time of the events. It has also suspended some States from participating in the organization's meetings, and threatened others with enforcement measures if constitutional order was not re-established.[65]

---

[61] AU Doc. PSC/PR/2(XXXV), Report of the Chairperson of the Commission on the Situation in Liberia, 25 July 2005, para. 33(vi). Previously, the OAU had asked the United Nations to lift sanctions imposed on an African State, in the case of Libya, and then decided not to comply with the sanctions after a three-month moratorium (AU Doc. AHG/Dec.(XXXIV), 10 June 1998).
[62] UN news centre, communiqué of 17 March 2006.
[63] In accordance with Article 48(1)-(2) of the United Nations Charter.
[64] Constitutive Act of the African Union, Articles 4(m), 4(p) and 30.
[65] On this practice and the legal basis for these reactivities, see Tehindrazanarivelo D.L., "Les sanctions de l'Union africaine contre les coups d'Etats et autres changements anticonstitutionnels de gouvernement: potentialités et mesures de

In such situations, the African Union often requests support from the UN to apply the measures it has adopted, in the form of a call on the international community as a whole to respect its position on the crises of which it is seized. The UN generally supports the positions subsequently taken by the African Union in this context. This occurred in the case of Togo, where the Secretary-General voiced his support for regional activities on several occasions.[66] In a message to the summit of African Heads of State on Togo, he expressed his profound gratitude for the constructive role that ECOWAS had played in the situation, in consultation with the African Union, in contributing to the re-establishment of constitutional order in Togo.[67]

In the case of Mauritania, the United Nations Secretary-General condemned the coup d'état of 3 August 2005 and called for a return to constitutional order and the respect for human rights and the rule of law.[68] However, he did not make reference to the condemnation of the coup by the African Union, nor was there a Security Council resolution or a formal statement on the situation by its Chairperson. For its part, the African Union approved a call to the UN by Mauritania's transitional government for assistance in the supervision of elections intended to lead to a restoration of constitutional order, and specifically in the organization of a constitutional referendum "on July 2006, at the latest, to be followed by presidential and legislative elections before 3 August 2007."[69] In fact, rather than a restoration of the overthrown government, this involved accepting a transitional period of one year during which the country would be run by those who carried out the coup d'état. In return, the perpetrators of the coup made an undertaking to organise free and democratic elections under international supervision, and not to stand in any of the elections to be organised. International recognition of the transitional government led by the perpetrators of the coup was based on these unilateral undertakings.

---

renforcement", *African Yearbook of International Law* 12 (2004), pp. 255-308; and the contribution by M. Ndulo to this *Manual*.

[66] UN Doc. SG/SM/9728, 19 February. 2005, and UN Doc. SG/SM/9841 – AFR/1146.
[67] UN Doc. SG/SM/9882 – AFR/1164, Communiqué of 19 May 2005.
[68] UN Doc. SG/SM/10030, Communiqué of 4 August 2005.
[69] AU Doc. PSC/PR/Comm.1 (XXXVII), para. 3, 8 September 2005.

Except where the situation has deteriorated into armed clashes following an unconstitutional seizure of power, as in Côte d'Ivoire, the Central African Republic and Guinea-Bissau, the United Nations appears to leave the management of unconstitutional changes of government to regional organizations. However, the UN, through its Secretary-General, takes part in mediation efforts to resolve such crises of accession to power in cooperation with the African Union and the relevant sub-regional organization, and generally in consonance with their position.

It should, however, be noted that the suspension of a State by the African Union does not automatically entail its non-participation in the proceedings of the UN and other partner organizations. In the view of the UN, a suspension of one of its Member States is subject to its own rules, particularly where the State has been subject to prevention and enforcement measures adopted by the Security Council (Article 5 of the Charter). A State suspended by the African Union would also be suspended by the UN only if the situation deteriorated and, in the eyes of the Security Council, constituted a threat to peace, in which case the Security Council would impose sanctions on the State in question. But these would be United Nations sanctions.

If the African Union's response to unconstitutional seizures of power, which are among the sources of instability on the continent, is to be effective, the international community must adopt a unanimous and unambiguous position in each case.

3.3. Peacekeeping and peace-building operations

United Nations bodies have often stressed the need for close coordination between the UN and regional organizations in cases of peacebuilding, with particular emphasis on the specific needs of Africa, especially in relation to financial, material and logistical support.[70]

---

[70] See in particular the statement of the Chairperson of the Security Council on 22 February 1995, UN Doc. S/PRST/1995/9; the report of the Special Committee on Peacekeeping Operations of 22 June 1995, UN Doc. A/50/230, para. 83; and the Secretary-General's report, UN Doc. A/50/711 – S/1995/911, of

Such financial, material and logistical support is an important aspect of the current relations between the UN and the African Union in relation to keeping and re-establishing peace. This raises the issue of the primary responsibility of the United Nations for peacekeeping in Africa, even where the continent's own organizations become involved. The development of regional peace initiatives should not lead the UN to abandon its responsibility in this regard to the relevant regional organization.

At present, the organization contributing most to the funding of African peacekeeping operations is the European Union through the Peace Facility for Africa.[71] Created in 2003 in response to a request by the African Union during the Maputo Summit (2003), this Facility has most notably contributed to funding peace efforts in Darfur and the Central African Republic.

Eight United Nations operations are currently under way in Africa, and four have been deployed since the African Union was created.[72] In general, these United Nations operations take over from African operations. It is therefore worth considering the degree of interaction between the two organizations in these operations and, in cases of double deployment, whether there is a clear delimitation of roles and responsibilities for each of the operations deployed. First, however, we consider briefly a special case of deployment of an African operation in response to the end of a UN operation more than a decade earlier.

---

1 November 1995 on "Improving preparedness for conflict prevention and peacekeeping in Africa".

[71] European Union, Decision No. 3/2003 of the ACP-EC Council of Ministers of 11 December 2003 on the Use of Resources from the Long-Term Development Envelope of the Ninth EDF for the Creation of a Peace Facility for Africa, *Official Journal of the European Union*, 31 December 2003, L 345/108.

[72] They are UNMIL in Liberia, created on 19 September 2003 by UN Doc. S/RES/1509(2003); UNOCI in Côte d'Ivoire, created on 27 February 2004 by UN Doc. S/RES/1528(2004); UNOB in Burundi, created on 21 May 2004 by UN Doc. S/RES/1545(2004); and UNMIS in Sudan, created on 24 March 2005 by UN Doc. S/RES/1590(2005). The other four operations are MINURSO in Western Sahara, created in 1992; UNAMSIL in Sierra Leone, MONUC in the Democratic Republic of the Congo, created in 1999; and UNMEE, which is an interposition force between Ethiopia and Eritrea, created in 2000.

3.3.1. UN support for purely African operations

Examples of these are the IGAD Peace Support Mission to Somalia (IGASOM), and the African Union's operation in Somalia (AMISOM).

With the full support of the African Union, IGASOM was established to support the reconciliation process in Somalia and the security and ceasefire monitoring activities of the transitional federal authorities. It was also intended that it should be replaced by an AU peace support mission.[73] The deployment of Phase I of IGASOM, pursuant to the decision of the 24th ordinary session of the IGAD council of ministers, was authorised by the Peace and Security Council in May 2005.[74] Its authorisation by the Union can be explained by the absence from the relevant legal texts of IGAD of provisions for the deployment of a peacekeeping operation or the use of force.[75] Jurisdiction was therefore provided by a decision of the Peace and Security Council; and, as members of the African Union, the IGAD States are bound by decisions of the Peace and Security Council, pursuant to Article 7(3) of the Protocol establishing it.[76]

United Nations support for such an operation, decided at regional level, came in the form of express authorisation for the deployment and the lifting of an arms embargo which was imposed on the whole of Somalia since 1992 (through resolution 733).

Thus, after the Peace and Security Council had requested an exemption to enable the envisaged operation to fulfil its mandate

---

[73] AU Doc. PSC/Min/Comm. (XXXIV)-(i), 3 July 2005, Communiqué on the Situation in Somalia.

[74] AU Doc. PSC/PR/Comm. (XXIX), 12 May 2005, Communiqué of the 29th meeting.

[75] Levitt J.I., "The Peace and Security Council of the African Union and the United Nations Security Council: The Case of Darfur, Sudan", in Blokker N.M. & Schrijver N.J. (eds.), *The Security Council and the Use of Force. Theory and Reality – A Need for Change?*, Leiden/Boston, Martinus Nijhoff, 2005, p. 219, note 40.

[76] "The Member States agree to accept and implement the decisions of the Peace and Security Council, in accordance with the Constitutive Act." Article 1(i) of the PSC Protocol states: "'Member States' shall mean Member States of the African Union".

effectively,[77] the Security Council initially took note of this measure and stated that it "[stood] ready to consider this matter [...] in due course", on the basis of a detailed mission plan in line with the national security and stabilisation plan prepared by the transitional government of Somalia.[78] In a resolution adopted on 6 December 2006, the Security Council "[d]ecide[d] to authorize IGAD and Member States of the African Union to establish a protection and training mission in Somalia" (IGASOM) for an initial period of six months. It also granted an exemption from the embargo on the delivery of arms and technical assistance intended solely for the support of the authorised African forces.[79] This authorisation by the Council followed a statement by its Chairperson, who "welcomed" the decision by the African Union concerning the deployment of IGASOM and the AU mission which followed it.[80]

In this resolution, the Security Council also approved an important principle established by IGAD that "those States that border Somalia would not deploy troops to Somalia."[81]

In the spirit of these provisions, and particularly in light of the new circumstances following Ethiopia's military intervention in December 2006, which enabled the transitional government to take control of the capital, an African Union mission in Somalia (AMISOM) with Ugandan troops was deployed on 6 March 2007.[82] This deployment was decided by the Peace and Security Council on 19 January 2007, taking into account what it saw as the unique and unprecedented opportunity to re-establish government institutions and peace in Somalia as a result of the recent events. The operation was then authorised by Security Council on 20 February 2007, for a six-month period, pursuant to the decision of the Peace and Security

---

[77] AU Doc. PSC/Min/Comm.(XXXIV)-(i), 3 July 2005, para. 6, repeating a similar request in its communiqué of 12 May 2005.
[78] UN Doc. S/PRST/2005/32, 14 July 2005, p. 2, and UN Doc. S/PRST/2006/11, 15 March 2006, p. 2.
[79] UN Doc. S/RES/1725 (2006), 6 December 2006, respectively paras. 3 and 5.
[80] UN Doc. S/PRST/2006/11, 15 March 2006, p. 2.
[81] UN Doc. S/RES/1725 (2006), para. 4.
[82] AU Press Release, 6 March 2007, on the website of the Organization.

Council.[83] For the African Union, the deployment of AMISOM represented an initial phase of the stabilisation of Somalia, in support of the political process. It was to contribute to creating the conditions for the deployment of a United Nations operation for long-term stabilisation and post-conflict reconstruction of Somalia.[84]

Responding to this wish, the Security Council invited the Secretary-General to send a Technical Assessment Mission to the African Union headquarters and Somalia as soon as possible to report on the possibility of a UN Peacekeeping Operation following the AU's deployment.[85] The Security Council also decided to set aside its previous decisions regarding the establishment of AMISOM, while granting it the same exemptions from the arms embargo.[86] The Council also saw the deployment of AMISOM as potentially "creat[ing] the conditions for the withdrawal of all other foreign forces from Somalia."[87]

More than a decade after the withdrawal of UNOSOM in March 1995, these successive (and future) deployments herald a new phase in the commitment of the international community to re-establishing peace in Somalia. The initiative was largely that of the sub-regional organization concerned (IGAD), supported by the African Union and ultimately endorsed by the United Nations. During this process, the composition and mandate, as well as the deployment, were decided by regional organizations and subsequently adopted by the Security Council, accompanied, on each occasion, by express authorisation of the deployment decided at the regional level.

---

[83] UN Doc. S/RES/1744 (2007), para. 4. The PSC decision was published as United Nations Document S/2007/34. We shall only examine the relationship between AMISOM and the UN. For the mandates and other information, see the two referenced documents and, more generally, the chapter authored by Mubiala M. in this *Manual*.
[84] Communiqué of the 69th PSC meeting, UN Doc. S/2007/34, Annex, para. 9.
[85] UN Doc. S/RES/1744 (2006), para. 9.
[86] *Ibid.*, paras. 6 and 12.
[87] *Ibid.*, para. 5.

3.3.2. Replacement of an African operation by a UN operation

In recent practice, the UN has taken over from an African operation in the situations in Burundi, in Côte d'Ivoire and the Central African Republic (CAR).

The inter-African mission in Burundi (MIAB) was the first African Union peacekeeping mission, deployed in Burundi from April 2003 to June 2004. It was transformed into a United Nations peacekeeping operation at the request of the African Union. Following this request, the Security Council decided to establish the United Nations Operation in Burundi (ONUB), on 1 June 2004, in order to support and accompany Burundi's efforts to establish lasting peace and national reconciliation in the country, as provided for in the Arusha Peace Accord. ONUB was initially formed of existing MIAB forces, composed of South African, Ethiopian and Mozambican contingents.[88] In its press release of 8 September 2004 on the end of the reconciliation process in Burundi, the Peace and Security Council commended all international actors involved in Burundi for their activities.[89]

This incorporation of the forces of the African peace mission into those of the United Nations which followed it appears to be an established practice, as we shall see in the cases discussed below. The same transfer of forces was initially considered as part of the transformation of the African Union mission in Darfur into a United Nations mission.[90] This practice enables a rapid deployment of the UN mission that is taking over.

In the Ivorian crisis, French forces and an ECOWAS peace force in Côte d'Ivoire (ECOFORCE) were deployed initially. The Security Council welcomed the deployment of ECOFORCE, in January 2003, authorising it, and the French troops, to use force ("to take the necessary steps") to protect its personnel and perform its mandate,

---

[88] UN Doc. S/RES/1545 (2004), 21 May 2004, paras. 2 and 3.
[89] AU Doc. PSC/PR/Comm.2 (XXXVII), Communiqué of the 37th PSC meeting, 8 September 2004.
[90] This mission was finally transformed into a UN-AU "hybrid force" after the Sudanese government refused to allow a purely UN operation; for more information, see the chapter authored by Mubiala M. in this *Manual*.

particularly monitoring the ceasefire and disarming rebel groups.[91] These forces were initially supported by a United Nations mission in Côte d'Ivoire (MINUCI), whose mandate was to facilitate the implementation by the Ivorian parties of the Linas-Marcoussis agreement and to liaise between the French forces and ECOFORCE.[92] Subsequently, ECOFORCE and MINUCI were replaced by the United Nations Operation in Côte d'Ivoire (ONUCI), created by resolution 1528 of 27 February 2004.

Cooperation between the UN and ECOWAS continued after this transition. Thus, as part of the fulfilment of ONUCI's mandate,[93] the Security Council requested the support of the African Union and ECOWAS in three areas: first, support for redeployment of the administration, to help the national reconciliation government to re-establish the authority of the State throughout Ivorian territory and the institutions responsible for the socio-economic revival of the country; second, support for the organization of elections, the Security Council requesting both African organizations to provide the necessary technical assistance for the organization of presidential and legislative elections that would be open to all, free, fair and transparent, and within the time limit provided for by the Constitution of Côte d'Ivoire,[94] and finally, public order, the African Union and ECOWAS being called upon to support ONUCI in assisting the government to re-establish a civilian police presence, judicial authority and the rule of law throughout the country. The three organizations were also to advise the government on the reorganization of internal security services, and to help Ivorian parties to implement temporary measures in the north of the country.[95] In this situation, the African Union and ECOWAS were placed on an equal footing by the Security Council, without any hierarchical distinction between them.

---

[91] UN Doc. S/RES/1464 (2003), 4 February 2003, paras. 8 and 9.
[92] UN Doc. S/RES/1479 (2003), 13 May 2003.
[93] UN Doc. S/RES/1528 (2004), 27 February 2004, para. 6.
[94] We do know now that afterwards, these elections did not take place within the specified time limit and that two successive transitional periods were agreed by the African Union and ECOWAS in 2005 and 2006, with the support of the United Nations.
[95] UN Doc. S/RES/1609 (2005), 24 June 2005, para. 2.

A United Nations Mission in the Central African Republic (MINURCAT) was deployed from April 1998 to February 2000. As in Liberia and Sierra Leone, this deployment was part of a legitimisation operation to vest the peacekeeping forces already established by the countries of the region with wider international authority.[96] It followed an Inter-African Mission to Monitor the Implementation of the Bangui Agreements (MISAB), a Francophone inter-African force deployed in the Central African capital in February 1997 with strong logistical support from France. MISAB's deployment was the subject of a request for Security Council authorisation from the presidents of the Central African Republic and Gabon.[97] This request sought to draw greater attention to the situation in the Central African Republic and to establish more clearly the legitimacy of the international force in light of the continued tensions between the parties to the conflict.[98] The Security Council gave its authorisation in resolution 1125 of 6 August 1997, describing the situation in the CAR as a threat to international peace and security, and making its authorisation subject to periodic activity reports by MISAB to the Security Council.

Following the weakening of MISAB by France's decision to withdraw its troops from the CAR, and a subsequent request from the Central African president for a UN presence, the Security Council created MINURCAT to replace MISAB in March 1998.[99] MINURCAT was deployed on the ground only a month after its creation, due to the agreement by the African States providing the MISAB contingents to reassign them to the new United Nations operation. The operation's mission was to provide security in the capital and its environs, to supervise the process of disarming former dissident troops, and, in the long term, to provide administrative support for the electoral process. The mission ended in February 2000, following elections in the CAR in late 1999.

---

[96] MacQueen N., *United Nations Peacekeeping in Africa since 1960*, London, Longman, 2002, p. 96.
[97] UN Doc. S/1997/561, 4 July 1997 and S/1997/543, 7 July 1997 respectively.
[98] MacQueen N., *op. cit.*, p. 100.
[99] UN Doc. S/RES/1159 (1998), 27 March 1998.

At the end of MINURCAT's mandate, the UN also established a political mission, United Nations Peace-building Office in the Central African Republic (BONUCA). BONUCA, which was charged with supporting and supervising the electoral process in the country, later received the support of a sub-regional operation, the CEMAC multinational force (FOMUC). FOMUC was charged with improving the security and military situation in the Central African Republic during the transitional period and following the presidential and legislative elections of March and May 2005. This mission was supported by the African Union, which also backed CEMAC's request for EU assistance under the Peace Support Facility, to fund the extension of FOMUC's mandate.[100] Recognising the work of FOMUC and the countries of the region, the Peace and Security Council asked these countries to maintain FOMUC until security and stability (including transborder security) were restored in the CAR.[101]

In this situation, the taking over of an African peacekeeping operation (MISAB) by a UN operation (MINURCAT) was followed by the joint presence of a political operation of the UN (BONUCA) and a sub-regional operation (FOMUC). BONUCA was active in the political arena through mediation and fostering dialogue between political actors, support for the Central African government in the promotion of national unity and reconciliation, and promotion of a culture of peace and social justice to ensure the stability of the State. For its part, FOMUC was active in security, particularly in strengthening the capacity of the Central African security and defence forces, with technical support from BONUCA.[102] The Security Council thus recognised and expressed its appreciation for the key role played by FOMUC in ensuring the security of the electoral process. It also supported FOMUC's continued efforts to consolidate constitutional order and re-establish the rule of law after the entry into service of the new institutions created following the legislative and

---

[100] See PSC, Briefing note on the Situation in the Central African Republic, 33rd meeting, Addis Ababa, 24 June 2005, para. 5.
[101] AU Doc. PSC/PR/Comm.(XLIV), 29 December 2005, paras. 4 and 5.
[102] UN Doc. S/2005/679, 27 October 2005, paras. 7 *et seq*.

presidential elections of May 2005, and welcomed the decision of the Heads of State of CEMAC to extend FOMUC's mandate.[103]

3.2.3. Sharing responsibilities in case of double deployment of UN and African operations

With the deployment of UNMIL in 1993, the Liberian civil war became the first case of a United Nations operation being deployed at the same time as an African one. The African force was ECOMOG, set up by ECOWAS. This co-deployment was subsequently repeated in Rwanda and Sierra Leone.[104]

The first deployment of an African Union force in parallel with a United Nations operation occurred in Sudan. Such co-deployment was also planned in the Democratic Republic of the Congo (DRC).

In the DRC, the co-deployment was requested by the Security Council in light of the African Union's constant support for peace efforts in Eastern DRC. In March 2005, the Council asked the African Union to define what role it might play in the region, in close cooperation with MONUC,[105] which had been deployed in the DRC since 1999. In its communiqué of 24 June 2005, the Peace and Security Council expressed the African Union's readiness to define this role and reaffirmed its determination to contribute to the disarmament and neutralisation of the former FAR/*Interahamwe* and other armed groups in the Eastern DRC in accordance with PSC/AHG/Comm.(XXIII).[106] This decision provided for the deployment of an African force in the DRC. The modalities for implementation, such as the calendar and the size of the force, were discussed with representatives of the DRC and concerned neighbouring States, and with the relevant United Nations bodies. An evaluation mission was initiated to study the conditions for involvement of a Union force in the context of a forced disarmament of the FDLR and other armed groups in the DRC, in close cooperation

---

[103] UN Doc. S/PRST/2005/35, 22 July 2005, p. 1, para. 4.
[104] Francis D.J. et al., *Dangers of Co-deployment. UN Cooperative Peacekeeping in Africa*, Aldershot, Ashgate, 2005, pp. 3-4; 119 *et seq*.
[105] UN Doc. S/RES/1592 (2005), 30 March 2005, para. 4.
[106] AU Doc. PSC/PR/Comm. (XXXIII), 24 June 2005, paras. 4 and 7.

with MONUC and the armed forces of the DRC. This mission was also to consider the modalities for cooperation with neighbouring States as armed groups being hunted in the DRC fell back into their respective territories.[107]

In Sudan, the African Union Mission in Sudan[108] was joined by a United Nations Mission in Sudan (UNMIS). In the resolution creating UNMIS, the Security Council requested that the new mission closely and continuously liaise and coordinate its action with AMIS at all levels.[109] In this context, AMIS intervenes more specifically in the situation in Darfur, while UNMIS is concerned with the implementation of the overall peace agreement signed between Southern and Northern Sudan on 9 January 2005. AMIS was subsequently replaced with a hybrid UN-AU force, as discussed later.

AMIS was established by the African Union in June 2004 as the operational arm of the Ceasefire Commission provided for in the 28 May 2004 Addis Ababa Peace Accord. As soon as the mission was deployed, the Union replaced Chad in leading the mediation between the parties to the Darfur conflict, and conducted the Abuja peace talks. On 20 October 2004, the Peace and Security Council increased the AMIS contingent from 464 to 3320 for an extended mandate of patrols around settlements, establishing trust between the parties, and protecting "civilians...under imminent threat and in the immediate vicinity".[110] The objective of AMIS as a whole was to help the parties to reach a political agreement in Darfur for a stable, peaceful and united Sudan, the strategic end-state being the restoration of a secure situation in the region, thereby providing a safe environment for the return of internally-displaced persons and refugees.[111]

UNMIS, which was created in March 2005, supports the overall peace agreement of 9 January 2005 ending more than 30 years of

---

[107] AU Doc. PSC/PR/2 (XXXIII), 24 June 2005, Report of the Chairperson of the Commission on the Follow-up on the Decision of the 23rd meeting of the PSC on the situation in Eastern DRC and Rwanda, esp. paras. 10, 11 and 17.

[108] MUAS in the French version of the United Nations documents, while, in the African Union documents, AMIS is invariably used, including in documents issued in French.

[109] UN Doc. S/RES/1590 (2005), 24 March 2005, para. 2.

[110] AU Doc. PSC/PR/Comm. (XVII).

[111] AU Doc. PSC/PR/2 (XLII), 20 October 2005, para. 11.

conflict between Northern and Southern Sudan. At the institutional level, UNMIS works in close liaison with AMIS through regular contact with the Special Representative of the Chairperson of the AU Commission in Sudan, and through the United Nations Support Section in Addis Ababa, which assists the Union in planning its offers of technical advice to AMIS.[112]

It should be noted, however, that some tension arose at one point between the African Union and the UN when the latter signed an Action Plan for Darfur with the Sudanese government, in order to secure concrete advances from the government in the implementation of Security Council resolution 1556 (2004). This Plan's provision for security zones protected by the Sudanese government was at odds with a provision of the N'Djamena Peace Accord, whose implementation on the ground was supervised by the African Union. This prohibited the Sudanese parties from undertaking any military action or deployment which would result in an increase in the territory under their control, the AU establishing the authors of violations. The deletion of "security zones" in subsequent Security Council resolutions thus marked the beginning of close cooperation between the African Union and the UN.

Relations between UNMIS and AMIS are maintained through regular contact between the head of UNMIS in Khartoum and AMIS personnel in Darfur, and by periodic meetings between the United Nations Support Section and the African Union Commission in Addis Ababa.

Faced with persistent violence against civilians in Darfur, and the inadequacy of African Union resources in the face of a Herculean task, the UN and the African Union agreed on the principle of moving from AMIS to a United Nations operation in Darfur. A joint technical evaluation mission was sent to Darfur in late March 2006.[113] Pending final agreement on a plan and a transfer calendar, the Security Council decided on 31 August 2006 to expand the mandate of UNMIS to support the implementation of the peace accord of 5 May 2006 between the parties in the Darfur conflict. It therefore "invited" the

---

[112] UN Doc. S/2005/579, 12 September 2005, para. 21.

[113] UN Doc. S/RES/1663 (2006) of 24 March 2006, and the Secretary-General's report of 5 April 2006, UN Doc. S/2006/218, paras. 38-48.

Sudanese government to agree to this deployment of UNMIS to Darfur.[114] Faced with the Sudanese government's refusal to allow this deployment, an intermediate solution was found: a "hybrid force" composed of UN and African Union personnel. The Sudanese government gave its agreement in principle for deployment of this hybrid force in three phases. However, its effective deployment has been obstructed by Sudanese government reservations with regard to command of the force, its size, and other factors beyond the scope of this study.

Meanwhile, on the ground, violence and attacks on civilians continue, raising question as about AU and UN responses to such activities on the continent.

3.4. Response to widespread human rights violations

The measures to be taken by the United Nations in response to widespread human rights violations are based on Chapter VII of the United Nations Charter, through the characterisation of these violations as a threat to international peace and security, which may be followed by enforcement, militarily or otherwise, deployment of a force to impose peace, or a call for armed intervention by a regional organization. The implementation of the famous 'responsibility to protect" must also follow the same decision-making process.

The African Union, under Article 4(h) of its Constitutive Act, is vested with the right to "intervene in a Member State pursuant to a decision of the Assembly in respect of grave circumstances, namely: war crimes, genocide and crimes against humanity". Since this is discussed elsewhere,[115] we focus here on the intended role of the United Nations in relation to the actions provided for in Article 4(h).

The Constitutive Act of the African Union and the Protocol relating to the establishment of the Peace and Security Council do not expressly mention the requirement of prior authorisation from the Security Council for the Union to initiate action pursuant to Article 4(h) of the Constitutive Act, as stipulated in Article 53 of the

---

[114] UN Doc. S/RES/1706 (2006), para. 1.
[115] See the chapter authored by Yusuf A. in this *Manual*.

United Nations Charter. How should this silence be interpreted with regard to the Union's compliance with the provisions of the Charter?

A first indication might be found in the common position on the reform of the United Nations, adopted by the Executive Council of the African Union[116] following a report of the United Nations High-level Panel.[117] In the common position, the Executive Council concedes that the Security Council must authorise an armed intervention by a regional organization, but it emphasises that the need for timely action in some circumstances may require it to request such approval after the fact. According to the Executive Council:

"Since the General Assembly and the Security Council are often far from the scenes of conflicts and may not be in a position to undertake effectively a proper appreciation of the nature and development of conflict situations, it is imperative that Regional Organizations, in areas of proximity to conflicts, are empowered to take actions in this regard. The African Union agrees with the Panel that the intervention of Regional Organizations should be with the approval of the Security Council; although in certain situations, such approval could be granted "after the fact" in circumstances requiring urgent action. In such cases, the UN should assume responsibility for financing such operations."[118]

The Executive Council then goes on to present Article 4(h) of the Constitutive Act of the African Union in parallel with Article 51 of the United Nations Charter. Requiring scrupulous compliance with the terms of the Charter, while recalling the provisions of Article 4(h), it concludes that "[A]ny recourse to force outside the framework of Article 51 of the UN Charter and Article 4 (h) of the AU Constitutive Act should be prohibited."[119]

This passage seems to imply that intervention by the African Union is on the same footing as legitimate individual or collective self-defence, as exceptions to the principle of prohibition of the use of

---

[116] Common position known as "the Ezulwini Consensus", adopted at the 7th extraordinary session of the Executive Council, 7-8 March 2005, AU Doc. Ext./EX.CL/2(VII).
[117] UN Doc. A/59/565, 2 December 2004.
[118] "The Ezulwini Consensus", op. cit., p. 8.
[119] Ibid.

force in international relations provided for in Article 2(4) of the United Nations Charter. However, this is an erroneous interpretation of this principle. If we pursue the Executive Council's reasoning further, like legitimate self-defence provided in Article 51 of the Charter, such intervention would therefore not require prior authorisation by the Security Council.

Was this the intended interpretation of this passage? This is completely out of the question. In any event, it is a policy statement of sorts, of dubious legality, but expressing a position of the AU Executive Council.

Fortunately, practice offers us another interpretation of the African Union's position on the requirement of prior authorisation by the Security Council. As we have seen, African Union peace operations involving the use of force have received the express authorisation of the Security Council following applications by the African Union. Such an application may be implicit where the Union submits its decision to the Security Council for its support. Moreover, the texts currently being discussed regarding the establishment of African Standby Forces explicitly provide for required authorisation from the Security Council, referring to Chapter VIII of the Charter.[120]

The African Union's intervention in Darfur provides an example of Security Council support for African action to protect victims of widespread human rights violations. While it was initially a conventional ceasefire observation mission, AMIS was subsequently requested to protect civilians under threat of physical violence, without prejudice to the responsibility of the Sudanese Government in this regard.[121] This new function received the express support of the Security Council in resolution 1574 (2004) of 19 November 2004, which requested Member States to provide AMIS with material, logistical and financial support and other necessary resources (para. 13).

While both the UN and the African Union acknowledge the need for prosecution of the perpetrators of international crimes – an extension of the protection of the victims of such crimes – this has

---

[120] AU, "Roadmap for the Operationalization of the African Standby Force", AU Doc. EXP/AU-RECs/ASF/4(I), 23 March 2005.
[121] AU Doc. PSC/PR/Comm. (XVII), Communiqué of the 17th meeting, para. 6.

given rise to certain differences in approach between the two. The Security Council's decision to refer the Darfur situation to the International Criminal Court (ICC)[122] was not the Union's preferred solution. The AU wished rather to conduct these criminal proceedings within an African mechanism, in a spirit of national reconciliation of the Sudanese peoples.[123] Voting against the resolution, Algeria deplored the failure to take the African position into account, stating that the African Union, as the only organization that had dared to send soldiers to monitor the ceasefire and protect the civilian population, was best placed to take on the sensitive and delicate mission of fighting impunity in Darfur, and that in so doing, it could "satisfy the requirements for peace without sacrificing the requirement of justice". In Algeria's view,

> "one cannot claim to support the African Union and leave to it the task of proposing African solutions suited to the various types of crises the continent has experienced, only to brush aside its proposals to the Council without even deigning to consider them."[124]

4. Final Observations

Should the relationship between the UN and regional organizations exceed the ambit of Chapter VIII of the Charter, as suggested in the statements of some States when the Security Council adopts resolutions on this relationship? Without going as far as to endorse this conclusion, it has rightly been said that this chapter was "crafted at a time when regionalism was anything but the driving force it certainly represents today". It has not kept up with the changes that have occurred over the past six decades. Consequently, the time has come to "determine how to make the most of Chapter VIII, and

---

[122] In resolution 1593 (2005) of 31 March 2005.
[123] The same position was adopted in the discussions on the trial of Hissène Habré, where the African Union, repeating its commitment to fighting against impunity, requested that the Committee of Eminent African Jurists it had just established examine the aspects of this trial to give "[p]riority [to] an African mechanism", AU Doc. Assembly/AU/Dec.103 (VI), "Decision on the Hissène Habré case and the African Union", 6th Ordinary Session of the Assembly, Khartoum (Sudan), 23-24 January 2006, para. 3(f).
[124] UN Doc. S/PV.5158, pp. 4-5.

enhance global, regional and sub-regional national synergies in the areas of conflict prevention and management…"[125]

Based on our analysis of the relationship between the African Union and the UN, what conclusions can we draw from the course these relations have taken in light of Chapter VIII of the United Nations Charter, which, in accordance with Security Council resolution 1631 (2005), should govern all relations between the UN and regional organizations?

Firstly, the scepticism about regional organizations and arrangements that prevailed when the UN was created has now given way to recognition of the importance of the activities of regional organizations in attaining the primary objective of the United Nations, that of maintaining international peace and security. This is particularly true for Africa, with its numerous organizations, formed mainly for economic purposes, which are now involved in the search for peace, security and stability in their respective regions. This development accords with the African Union's stated objective of coordinating and harmonising the various sub-regional activities and those of external partners for peace in Africa.

Secondly, the African Union appears to emphasise complementarity in its relationship with the United Nations. It seeks to be actively involved in the search for peace and security in Africa, highlighting its proximity to the conflict zones, its better knowledge of the realities on the ground, and its members' greater interest in resolving conflicts on their borders. While aware of these comparative advantages, however, the African Union does not propose to deal with conflicts on its own. Rather, it asks the United Nations to fulfil its primary responsibility for maintaining international peace and security, which, in the view of the African Union, can be achieved though institutional, material and financial support for its efforts for peace. Moreover, as this study has shown, both organizations are keen to work together and coordinate their activities, although financial assistance from the United Nations must be provided in compliance

---

[125] Statement by the representative of Romania, then Chairperson of the Security Council, during the adoption of resolution 1631(2005), UN Doc. S/PV.5282, p. 3.

with its strict rules, and may also raise the issue of command of the operation to be funded.

Thirdly, despite the omissions in some texts, made more out of prudence than defiance, the African Union has largely recognised the formal primacy of the role of the United Nations in the maintenance of peace and security in the world, and therefore in Africa. This acknowledgment of the primacy of the role of the UN applies both to the duty to keep it informed of the Union's activities in the area of peace and to the need for Security Council authorisation for measures that may entail the use of force. This last point is demonstrated by the peacekeeping operations deployed by the African Union and the draft statute of the African Standby Force.

However, above and beyond this formal primacy, there is a genuine complementarity between the UN, the African Union and sub-regional African organizations. Several important decisions of the Security Council on conflict situations in Africa have been based on, or at least referred extensively to, previous decisions of the African Union's Peace and Security Council, which are themselves generally taken in consultation with the relevant sub-regional organization.

In future, this good practice of coordinated and complementary activities between the three levels of organizations should be extended to partners for peace in Africa, whether States, groups of States, non-African international organizations, NGOs or other representatives of civil society. Only good harmonisation of these activities will enable these various actors to attain their immediate objectives, including the provision of humanitarian assistance, prosecution of the perpetrators of international crimes, the establishment of fact through international investigations, successful peace talks, etc, while reducing the risk of mutual exclusion. This aspect of cooperation for peace and security merits in-depth study.

PART V. HUMAN RIGHTS

CHAPTER 19.
THE AFRICAN CHARTER ON HUMAN AND PEOPLES' RIGHTS

Michelo Hansungule

1. Introduction

The African Charter on Human and Peoples' Rights (hereinafter the Charter) was adopted by the Assembly of Heads of State and Government (AHSG) of the Organization of African Unity (OAU) held at Nairobi, Kenya, in June 1981.[1] It came with force on 21 October 1986, three months after the Secretary-General of the OAU confirmed receipt of the instrument marking "a simple majority of the members" of the OAU as provided for in Article 63(3).

The African Charter is a creature of the OAU. The AHSG of the OAU, at its Summit meeting held at Monrovia, Liberia, in July 1979, "realising that the political regime which protects basic human rights and democratic freedoms is essential for mobilizing the creative initiative of our people for rapid economic development including scientific and technological innovation"[2] unanimously decided to call on the Secretary-General to *inter alia*,

---

[1] Resolution Adopting the Draft African Charter on Human and Peoples' Rights, 24-27 June 1981. OAU Doc. AHG/Dft.Res.55.
[2] OAU Doc. AHG/ST.3 (XV1) Rev. 1, 17-20 July 1978.

"organise as soon as possible, in an African capital, a restricted meeting of highly qualified experts to prepare a preliminary draft on an 'African Charter on Human and Peoples' Rights'...".[3]

In keeping with this instruction, the Secretary-General quickly brought together twenty African legal experts whom he tasked with the responsibility to draw up the instrument. Chosen on the basis of their expertise and knowledge of human rights problems in Africa, the experts met for the first time from 28 November to 8 December 1979 in Dakar, Senegal.[4] This led to the first Draft of the Charter. The Draft was submitted to three ministerial meetings the first already in January 1980 where, however, only a few articles were considered and agreed upon. The rest of the articles were considered at the second meeting.

Besides the States, it is important to recognize the keen interest international NGOs took towards the development of the framework. For example, it was the International Commission of Jurists (ICJ)[5] which organized the Conference of African Jurists that adopted in 1961 the Lagos Act which, among other things, called on newly independent African States to introduce a regional convention to promote and protect human rights. But it would appear that this was rather too early to be taken seriously. Newly independent States on the

---

[3] OAU Doc. AHG/Dec.115 (XV1) Rev. 1, Secretary General's Report on the Preliminary Draft African Charter on Human and Peoples' Rights, CAB/LEG/67/6.

[4] The two neighbouring countries, Senegal and the Gambia, were so closely associated with the development of the Charter that it can be said that without their efforts, there would probably be no Charter. The Charter is due to the original efforts of both Presidents Senghor and Sir Dawda Jawara of Senegal and The Gambia respectively. In 1988, after the coming into force of the Charter, Zambian President Kenneth Kaunda was singled out by the Organization of African Unity (OAU) together with the Secretary General for special mention for their steering work towards the operationalisation of the Charter and appointment of the commissioners. Ironically, Sir Dawada Jawara and President Kaunda became two of the earliest victims of human rights abuses to approach the Commission: the former directly, the latter through a complainant (see below, notes 20 and 22).

[5] See *Report on the Proceedings of the Conference*, ICJ, Geneva, 1961. This aspect of the Charter is a striking feature of its origin. The role of the ICJ together with African countries like Senegal, Gambia and Zambia means the Charter was a joint product of both non-governmental organizations (NGOs) and the handful of the progressive African States at the time.

continent were still mostly concerned with state consolidation and therefore had their attention on safeguarding their sovereignty. Consequently, even the barbarism orchestrated, for example, by Idi Amin in Uganda, was never formally condemned by the OAU.

In the two decades following independence, African countries appear to have moved systematically within the framework of the OAU, concentrating at first on the liberation of the rest of the continent from colonialism and racism, and then, at the special Session in Lagos, focusing attention on economic integration and development; and later, at the 1979 Monrovia Summit, dealing with yet another vital area in the achievement of the aspirations of African peoples, the promotion and protection of Human and Peoples' Rights.[6]

2. Normative Character of the African Charter

The African Charter encapsulates all the three different types of human and collective rights in one document and provides for their enforcement by means of a single method. The drafters of the Charter were guided by African traditions and culture which, in the words of the Gambian President were to serve as the bedrock on which the Charter rested:

> "We should not, however, strive to prepare an African Charter merely because we want a Charter concluded by African States. A truly African Charter should reflect those of our traditions that are worth preserving, our values and the legitimate aspirations of our peoples to complement the global international approach to strengthen the application of Human Rights'."[7]

Some of the main characteristics of the Charter include the following:
a) Providing the principle of non-discrimination as a fundamental right of a people;
b) Emphasizing the rules relating to the objectives of the African Union as stated in Articles 3 & 4 of the AU Constitutive Act;
c) Stating the rights of peoples in addition to individual rights;

---

[6] 17-20 July 1978, OAU Doc. AHG/ST.3 (XVI), Rev. 1.
[7] *Ibid.*, p. 5.

d) Determining the duties of each person towards the communities in which he/she lives and more particularly towards the family and State;
e) Attaching great importance to African values and morals;
f) Giving economic, social and cultural rights the place they deserve in human rights' legislation.

While the Charter in a number of ways mirrors conventions that predated it, there are several areas in which it is quite distinct from other instruments, particularly the following:
a) Laying special emphasis on peoples' rights;
b) Establishing certain duties for individuals in the exercise of their human rights;
c) Providing safeguards in the implementation of the rights' jurisdiction by the Charter through: (a) the guarantee of the rights by the State Parties to the Charter; (b) the institution of an African Commission on Human and Peoples' Rights with the role of promoting and protecting human rights by gathering information, establishing facts, considering them and making recommendations to the Assembly of Heads of State and Governments.

2.1. Obligations of States Parties

Article 1 of the Charter imposes a duty on States Parties to adopt the necessary measures (legislative and others) to give effect to the rights, duties and freedoms enshrined in the Charter. This is of crucial importance.[8] The African Commission on Human and Peoples' Rights

---

[8] See: *International Pen v. Chad*, Communication No. 55/91, 7th Annual Activity Report: 1993-1994; *Legal Resources Foundation v. Zambia*, African Human Rights Law Reports 2001, Centre for Human Rights, p. 56. In the Chadian communication, the Commission decided as to the meaning of article 1 "… if a State neglects to ensure the rights in the African Charter, this can constitute a violation, even if the State or its agent are not the immediate cause of the violation." Therefore, Article 1 obligations are two-fold in nature. In the first instance, States Parties are obliged under the article to "undertake to give effect to the measures specified in the Charter" and based on that to refrain from defeating the Charter guaranteed rights. Second, to positively go out into the field to prevent others including private parties from doing anything that would violate the guaranteed rights which by becoming a party, the State has undertaken to abide by."

(ACHPR), the monitoring body of the Charter, has defined the nature and scope of Article 1 as imposing a positive obligation, which is added to the implicit duty of respecting what is stipulated in the Charter. The Commission held that "if a State fails to ensure respect of the rights contained in the African Charter, this constitutes violation of the Charter even if its agents were not the perpetrators of the violation" complained of.[9] More importantly, the Commission also held in respect of the practice of suspending the national Bill of Rights or certain parts of it, for example, as a result of a military coup or an emergency that

"The suspension of a Bill of Rights and consequently the application of the Charter was not only a violation of the Charter but also a restriction on the enjoyment of the rights and freedoms enshrined in the Charter".[10]

Therefore, Article 1 has a dual role in the sense that the domestic legislative action vested in each State Party affects and is affected by all the rights and freedoms consecrated in the first Part of the Charter.

The thrust of Article 1 is that when implemented, it turns such rights into a practical shield for individual protection not only at the domestic level, but also at the Inter-American level; while non-implementation leaves such rights squarely at the domestic level. Unfortunately, Article 1 has not yet been implemented by most States Parties to the Charter through their domestic legislation. In terms of conferring explicit recognition of the Charter in domestic law, Nigeria is the only State in common law jurisdictions to have directly done so, i.e. legislated the Charter into its domestic law. This was achieved by means of an ordinary enactment of the African Charter on Human and Peoples' Rights (Ratification and Enforcement) as Act Chapter 10 of the Laws of the Federation of Nigeria, 1990. Subsequently, this was reinforced by the historic decision of the Nigerian Supreme Court in the seminal case of *Abacha v. Fawehinmi*[11] in which, based on the spirit of Article 1, the Supreme Court declared the Charter to be

---

[9] *Mouvement Burkinabe des Droits de l'Homme et des peuples v. Burkina Faso*, Communication No. 207/1997, para. 42.
[10] *Sir Dawada Jawara v. The Gambia*, Communication Nos. 147/95 and 149/96, para. 50.
[11] *Abacha v. Fawehnmi* (2006) 6 *NWLR* (Pt 660) 228; *SCZJ* 400.

justiciable and enforceable in Nigeria. Of course, it is an open question what this really means i.e. whether it means that from incorporation the Charter is at par with the Constitution or stands on the same footing as ordinary statutes of which it is one.

2.2. Non-discrimination

Article 2 has a wording similar to that of other international instruments which deal with the right to non-discrimination, since it does not recognize this right *per se*, but rather binds it necessarily to the enjoyment of rights and freedoms enshrined in the Charter. Nonetheless, it is significantly completed by Article 18 (3) – concerning the elimination of every form of discrimination against women – and Article 28 – related to every individual's duty to respect and consider human fellow beings without discrimination. The three articles should be read conjunctively as the anti-discrimination regime in the Charter. Disjunctive reading could deprive them of the full scope of the principle of non-discrimination in the Charter. In fact, the principle of non-discrimination quite evidently permeates the Charter as a whole as the touchstone of the African concept of human rights. In a communication concerning Mauritania, the Commission, in an *obiter dicta*, made the following observation:

> "From the foregoing, it is apparent that international human rights law and the community of States accord a certain importance to the eradication of discrimination of all its guises. Various texts adopted at the global and regional levels have indeed affirmed this repeatedly. Consequently, for a country to subject its own indigenes to discriminatory treatment only because of the colour of their skins is an unacceptable discriminatory attitude and a violation of the very spirit of the African Charter and the letter of its article 2."[12]

In fact, the Commission maintains a very narrow distinction between non-discrimination and equality even though the Charter

---

[12] *Malawi African Association & 6 others v. Mauritania*, Communication Nos. 54/91, 61/91, 98/93, 164/97, 196/76, and 210/98, para. 131.

provides for them separately. Thus, in a communication concerning Sudan, the Commission observed:

> "These issues should be considered in relation to article 2 of the Charter, which provides for equal protection under the laws, and Article 8, on religious freedom, which will be treated below. While fully respecting the religious freedoms of Muslims in Sudan, the Commission cannot countenance the application of law in such a way as to cause discrimination and distress to others."[13]

A noticeable feature of this is that the ban on discrimination which comes without the necessary nexus with the enjoyment of rights and freedoms spelt out in the Charter, makes it quite advanced and novel. It is neither similar to the European nor the American Conventions. The particularity of Article 2 in including among the grounds of non-discrimination the "ethnic distinction" factor is also worth noting, both because it is not found in other international instruments, and because it complements the equally notable peoples' rights provisions of the Charter. With the African society in mind, it is not surprising the drafters opted for this formulation.

Based on the communications before it, the Commission has used the opportunity to state that "Article 2 obligates States to ensure that all persons living on their territory whether national or non-national enjoy the rights guaranteed in the Charter".[14] In this communication, the Commission found that the government of Angola had discriminated against those national of other African countries who were expelled from its territory on the basis of local law, in so far as they were not allowed equal protection of the law. Hence, by seeking to remove them from its jurisdiction without ensuring their right to be heard by a Court of Law constituted discrimination which is explicitly forbidden under the Charter.

---

[13] *Amnesty International & 3 others v. Sudan*, Communication Nos. 48/90, 50/91, 52/91 and 89/93, para. 73.

[14] *Union Inter Africaine des Droits de l'Homme & 4 others v. Angola*, Communication No. 159/96, para. 18.

2.3. Claw-back Clauses

Based on the approach adopted in the Universal Declaration of Human Rights before it, Articles 2-14 of the African Charter enshrine the individual civil and political rights while Articles 15-18 guarantee the economic, social and cultural rights. States Parties have committed themselves to observe, respect, promote and fulfil both categories of rights. However, not borrowed from the Declaration is the fact that many of the civil and political rights carry limitations otherwise known as claw-back clauses i.e. clauses that allow suspension or violation of enunciated rights based on *ordre public* in accordance with domestic legislation.

Civil and political rights in particular are protected by the Charter in an insufficiently narrow way. Most of them are subject to restrictions, which are so expansive as to leave nothing but a mere skeleton of the right to be protected. Why did the drafters qualify the rights or impose such expansive limitations on their enjoyment? They probably had to do it in view of the fact that the prevailing constitutional arrangements in most of the African countries at the time would not allow for a more robust protection mechanism. The Terms of Reference of the Experts that drew up the Charter included the following: "Not to exceed that which the African States were ready to accept in the field of the protection of human rights".[15] With this, the dilemma they faced was how to have universal rights (though what constitutes universal is hotly disputed) but at the same time rights which would specifically relate to the African paradigm. The result was to have a Charter that stipulated a set of generally acknowledged universal rights but ceded as little territory as possible to the body entrusted with its implementation so that its hands are so effectively tied that it can hardly function.

---

[15] Address by the Secretary-General of the OAU, Meeting of the Experts Preparing Draft African Charter on Human and Peoples' Rights, Dakar, 28 November – 8 December 1979. Also, see: Hansungule M., "African Charter on Human and Peoples' Rights, A Critical Review", *African Yearbook of International Law* 8 (2000), pp. 273-274.

Nevertheless, in its actual operations the Commission has not been as disappointing as predicted on the basis of these limitations. In fact, the Commission has shamed those that thought the claw-back clauses in the Charter will prove to be its graveyard. Its pioneering decision on this matter concerned the 1995/96 Communication submitted to it by the same man who was principally behind the formulation of the Charter – ex-president Sir Dawda K. Jawara of the Gambia. In his communication,[16] the ex-president, following the overthrow of his government in a military coup, complained of massive violations of human rights perpetrated by the new regime against former officials of his government including former cabinet ministers some of whom he alleged were tortured or killed.

It was in the course of responding to this particular aspect of the complaint alleging violation of Article 6 guaranteeing personal liberty that the respondent State sought to justify its action based on the claw-back enshrined along with the basic liberty guarantee in Article 6 of the Charter. The government denied effecting arrests arbitrarily in violation of Article 6 but sought to justify this by stating that it acted "in conformity with laws previously laid down by domestic legislation". Strict wording of part of Article 6 provides that "no one may be deprived of his freedom except for reasons and conditions previously laid down by law. In particular, no one may be arbitrarily arrested or detained". After considering the allegation, the response by the State as well as its own previous jurisprudence on the matter, the Commission concluded: "The competent authorities shall not override constitutional provisions or undermine fundamental rights guaranteed in the Constitution or in international human rights standards". It went on: "For a State to avail itself of this plea, it must show that such a law is consistent with the obligations of the Charter". As a result, the Commission rejected out of hand the respondent State's bid to justify the arrests and detentions on the basis of previous law.

A similar ruling was made in a subsequent communication brought by the *Legal Resources Foundation v. Zambia*.[17] Zambia had enacted a new Constitution which effectively restricted the right of many third

---

[16] See footnote 10 above.
[17] *Legal Resources Foundation v. Zambia*, Communication No. 211/98 (2001).

generation Zambians to contest political office i.e. the so-called 'parentage clause'. Only Zambians by birth, both of whose parents were Zambians by birth or descent retained eligibility to contest the country's presidency. It was alleged by the complainant that among other things the respondent had acted in violation of Article 13. Article 13 guarantees the civic right of participation. However, Zambia, relying on the limitation clause argued that participation was not absolutely guaranteed. Further, Zambia argued that even its own Constitution did not accord absolute guarantee to the principle of non-discrimination. However, the Commission did not agree. It held:

> "The Commission has argued forcefully that no State Party to the Charter should avoid its responsibilities by recourse to the limitations and 'claw-back' clauses in the Charter ... the Charter cannot be used to justify violations of sections of it. The Charter must be interpreted holistically and all clauses must reinforce each other. The purpose or effect of any limitation must also be examined, as the limitation or the right cannot be used to subvert rights already enjoyed. Justification, therefore, cannot be derived solely from popular will, as such cannot be used to limit the responsibilities of States Parties in terms of the Charter ...".[18]

2.4. Derogation from the Charter

It is particularly interesting to note that the Charter does not make use of the derogation clauses[19] which are present in many other international instruments. Derogations meticulously define the limits of State action towards its nationals during situations of emergency, i.e. when States are most apt to violate human rights. Contrary to popular opinion, derogations are not meant to subtract from but in fact to add to the individual subject the means with which to defend her

---

[18] *Ibid.*, para. 70.
[19] Decision to the effect that the Charter does not yield to derogations was reinforced by the Commission in the *International Pen v. Chad*, Communication No. 55/91, 7th Annual Activity Report: 1993-1994. In this case, the Commission decided: "The African Charter, unlike other human rights instruments, does not allow for States Parties to derogate from their treaty obligations during emergency situations. Thus, even a civil war in Chad cannot be used as an excuse by the State which violates or permits violations of the guaranteed rights in the African Charter."

rights particularly in such an unpredictable situation. Thus, the derogation clauses have a *ratione temporis* and *ratione situationis* application determined by the instrument of protection itself, besides enabling the external control as to the pertinence of the violation or suspension of the rights enshrined in the instrument concerned, which is normally carried out by the implementation body – in this case, the African Commission. Without these safeguards, a derogation is *ultra vires* and would be so pronounced in constitutional States.

Despite existence of opinion to the effect that derogation clauses constitute a type of claw-back clause, it seems that the best construction is the one that distinguishes them from such clauses. Thus, on the one hand, derogation clauses permit, as already mentioned, suspension or violation of certain obligations in circumstances of war or public emergency. On the other hand, claw-back clauses allow, in normal circumstances, the breach of an obligation for specific number of public reasons. Derogations are associated with public disorders while claw-backs are concerned with manifestly normal times. At the time the Charter was adopted, several commentators suggested that this characteristic of the claw-back clauses would significantly jeopardize the effective application of the Charter's provisions, specifically with regard to the civil and political rights which are often the ones most amenable to suffer the effects of such State action. The fear was that if the grounds for suspension or violation of the Charter due to circumstances beyond normal are not stipulated on paper as in this case and therefore are made subject solely to the political convenience of the governments concerned – which naturally make them – the whole protection system would be difficult to predict. Luckily, most of these fears have been proved to be unjustified.

This writer does not adhere to the argument by some scholars to the effect that where a derogation is manifestly missing from a treaty text, it can be read from a claw-back clause. In fact, a derogation clause, regardless of the existence of a claw-back clause, must be secured in all international instruments of human rights protection, so as to make them more predictable and less vulnerable to political and other temptations. Of course such a clause must be to the extent and time strictly required by the exigencies of the situation, non-discriminatory in nature, and it should not violate the State's other obligations under international law. As enshrined in Article 4 of the International Covenant on Civil and Political Rights (ICCPR), the Charter should provide for situations of "public emergences which threaten the life of the nation". The "collective security" and "common interest" limitation in Article 27 (2) of the Charter which are imposed on the exercise of individual rights do not suggest them only during an emergency threatening the life of the nation.

In the case of the emergence of a doubt regarding the legitimacy of the violation or suspension of a determined right foreseen in the Charter, by the domestic legislation of one of the States Parties, the African Commission is the organ responsible for putting meaning to letters of the suspending legislation and equally the fate of the impugned right. In the first communication to come before the Commission in which Chad pleaded extraordinary circumstances for the failure to apply the Charter, the Commission observed:

> "The African Charter, unlike other human rights instruments, does not allow for State parties to derogate from their treaty obligations during emergency situations. Thus, even a civil war in Chad cannot be used as an excuse by the State violating or permitting violations of rights in the African Charter."[20]

2.5. The Search for Persuasive Authority

Given the nature of the African system, reliance on persuasive authority is an absolute necessity. In fact, it was widely anticipated already from its legislative development that the Commission in discharging its mandate will inevitably pay homage to Article 60 of the Charter. In the few communications to reach the Commission in which this subject was at issue, the Commission ended up with its own interpretation. According to Article 60:

> "The Commission must draw inspiration from international law on human and peoples' rights, particularly from the provisions of the various African instruments on human and peoples' rights, the Charter of the United Nations, the Charter of the Organization of African Unity, the Universal Declaration

---

[20] *Commission Nationale des Droits de l'Homme et des Libertés v. Chad*, Communication No. 74/94, 9th Annual Activity Report: 1995-1996.

of Human Rights, other instruments adopted by the United Nations and by African countries in the field of human rights and peoples' rights as well as from the provisions of various instruments adopted within the Specialized Agencies of the United Nations of which the parties to the present Charter are members".[21]

This clause has not been easy to assign a meaning to. In one sense, it could be said to be advocating for multilateralism in human rights, which is a very good sign. It is good because not only does it add flavour to the Charter, but it also makes the instrument much more flexible. Besides, as a regional treaty, the African Charter does not necessarily have international status of a universal nature but acquires some sort of universality through the application of Articles 60 and 61. The two articles seek to legitimize the Charter's multilateral scope.

Therefore, instead of questioning Article 60, as others have done, it should be welcomed because through it, the Charter achieves extra territorial scope which is important in view of the fact that matters involving certain basic rights and obligations in international law, such as those pertaining to torture raise simultaneously issues of domestic as well as universal jurisdiction.

Therefore, it is not only reasonable but also legally correct to have recourse to the practice established by the United Nations[22] when the provisions of the Banjul Charter do not fulfil the expectations regarding their clarity and precision. Thus, the African Commission,

---

[21] The motivation behind Articles 60 and 61 derive from a United Nations' sponsored workshop convened in August 1979, soon after the OAU decision directing the Secretary-General to appoint a committee of high qualified experts with the mandate to write the Charter. During that meeting, the possibility that OAU Member States may take too long to ratify or even not ratify the Charter was seriously entertained. In anticipation of this, the two articles were included in the draft so that the Commission would have a basis to act on if the Charter ended up being still born. More interesting is the July 2003 Protocol on Women's Rights in Africa which devotes a large part of its preamble to refer to international instruments including the Conventions on Discrimination against Women and the child of 1979 and 1989 respectively leaving no doubt they constitute the sources of the protocol's normative standards.

[22] See *Legal Resources Foundation v. Zambia*. In this Communication, the Commission, among other things, cited General Comments by the Committee on Economic, Social and Cultural Rights as well as the comments of the UN Committee on Human Rights

in seeking to determine to what extent the domestic law of a State Party may have violated or suspended a right protected by the Charter, it has had recourse to the provisions of other instruments as well as the case-law of other jurisdictions. Consequently, the Commission in a number of cases has tried to interpret norms consistently with international practice while keeping in mind the African specificity.

2.6. The Notion of "Peoples" in the Charter

The African Charter, in recognizing the human and peoples' rights in their dialectic relationship, enshrines the latter in Articles 19 through to 24. This is deliberate. Basically, the dialectic approach was meant to underline the philosophical thoughts and underpinnings current on the continent at the time about the concept of human rights. So that conceptually, human rights in Africa were conceived as not only limited to the civil and political rights or economic, social and cultural rights but extended also to group or collective rights.

Although the African Charter is the only international instrument in force, both at regional and at global level, to provide for the peoples' rights in a legally-binding form, and more especially the right to development, there is nevertheless a plethora of United Nations documents that have already referred or alluded to them. Among these is the UN Charter itself, which in Article 1 (2) recognizes the right of all peoples to self-determination; the UN General Assembly Resolution 32/130, of 16 December 1977, which in its paragraph 1(c) asserts that "All human rights and fundamental liberties of the human being and of the peoples are inalienable"; and, of course, the UN Declaration on the right to Development adopted in 1986. On the African scene, we should include the 1986 Algiers Declaration on Peoples' Rights set out by a group of progressive and independent African intellectuals.[23] In fact, the Charter Articles 19 to 24 were based or at least inspired by the Algiers Declaration. Nevertheless, in spite of the significant role played by the United Nations in establishing the concept of human rights and promoting that of the

---

[23] See: Shivji I., *The Concept of Human Rights in Africa*, CODESRIA Book Series, 1989, pp. 111-115.

peoples' rights, there has not been significant progress towards their concrete application.

The Banjul Charter has wisely refrained from engaging in unnecessary controversies that an attempt to define what ought to be understood by "peoples" would provoke.[24] It was feared that to engage in this would most certainly have slowed down the drafting of the Charter and that given the notoriety of this subject in Africa, discussion would be infinite and in any case unprofitable. Some of the provisions of the Charter are of extreme importance in terms of understanding what exactly the Banjul Charter intended or meant by "peoples" – and of course to what is deemed to be "peoples' rights". In its preamble's fourth clause the African Charter affirms as follows:

> "Recognizing on the one hand, that fundamental human rights stem from the attributes of human beings, which justifies their national and international protection and on the other hand that the reality and respect of peoples rights should necessarily guarantee human rights".

This provision has at least two significant elements: firstly, it asserts that human rights are the attributes of human beings, i.e. that human rights are inalienable and intrinsic to the human person; secondly, it states that peoples' rights and human rights are not in conflict or in competition with each other, but rather are complimentary concepts that are mutually exclusive. Despite this exegetic effort, the truth is that the African Charter's provisions on peoples' rights are too vague and too sweeping in their formulation. If not carefully articulated, provisions on peoples' rights are bound to bring about confusion and distract attention rather than promote enlightened interpretation. The use in the Charter of the word "peoples" without defining it may have been wise as regards the immediate political need of getting the instrument agreed upon and subsequently endorsed but has given rise to other issues. It has indeed

---

[24] See the statement by Judge Keba Mbaye, one of the drafters of the Charter in the Rapporteur's Report, in which it is reported that the drafters "deliberately refused to indulge in the definition of such notions as 'peoples' so as not to end up in difficult discussions". Rapporteurs' Report, Council of Ministers, Thirty-Seventh Ordinary Session, 15-21 June 1981, Nairobi, Kenya, M/1149 (XXXVII), Annex 1, p. 4.

led to "fishing expeditions" in State Party reports as to who is and is not included in the term "peoples" or whether it simply meant the whole population in a given country.

An opportunity presented itself for the Commission to deal with this matter in the *Katangese Peoples' Congress v. Zaire*[25] and later in *Social and Economic Rights Action Centre & another v. Nigeria*,[26] in both communications in an indirect way. However, the Commission refused to be dragged into the controversy and successfully dodged the subject. Recently, the Commission has appointed[27] a "Working Group of Experts on Indigenous Populations/Communities" in the hope of addressing the issue. Yet again, the Commission, in the report of its Working Group, ducked the issue of a definition of peoples, referring instead to the more generic and vague terms of "populations" and communities.[28]

Perhaps instead of trying to define "peoples" one can probably concentrate on drawing basic or general characteristics with which to identify the "peoples referred to in the Charter". The African society is far too complicated to fit in any predetermined "box" and the drafters of the Charter could not have been wiser in leaving it open. Besides, this is not the aim of the present Chapter. Without jeopardizing the principle of universality of human rights, it

---

[25] *Katangese Peoples' Congress v. Zaire*, Communication No. 75/92, 8th Annual Activity Report: 1994-1995.
[26] *Social and Economic Rights Action Centre & another v. Nigeria*, 2001.
[27] See Resolutions on the Rights of Indigenous Populations/Communities, 28th Ordinary Session of the African Commission on Human and Peoples' Rights, October 2000; Report of the African Commission's Working Group of Experts on Indigenous Populations/Communities, African Commission on Human and Peoples' Rights, November 2003.
[28] Although not yet universally accepted, Aureliu Critescu, UN Special Rapporteur of the Special Sub-Commission on Prevention of Discrimination and Protection of Minorities, proposes useful elements that could broadly capture at least the essence of the notion of "peoples", as follows:
a) The term "people" denotes a social entity that possesses a clear identity and own characteristics;
b) There is a relationship with the territory, even if the people in question have been wrongfully expelled from it, and artificially substituted by another population;
c) A people cannot be mistaken for ethnic, religious or linguistic minorities, whose existence and rights are recognized in Article 27 of the International Covenant on Civil and Political Rights.

can be said without any fear or doubt that the African concept of "peoples" is very likely to be far away from the postulates of natural rights theory – which focus upon human rights under an exceedingly individualist viewpoint.

Although there has been a number of writings on the lack of a definition of what is meant by "peoples" in the Banjul Charter, it seems the main problem faced by the African Commission is not connected to this very topic, or to the definition of collective rights *per se*, but rather to the balancing of collective rights against individual ones in specific cases. Furthermore, there was at the time of the drafting of the Charter a certain difficulty in conceptualizing, in legal terms, how the peoples' rights of the African Charter were to form the basis of claims before the African Commission, in contrast with individual rights. This is somewhat resolved or at least played down by the Commission in both the Katangese Peoples' Congress[29] and the SERAC[30] communications referred to above.

Therefore, based on the foregoing, it can be said that "individual" rights do not exist in the human rights sphere any more than do "collective" rights; i.e. all rights are individual because, in the final analysis, they are held by individuals, and at the same time, "collective" due to the process of recognition, mode of exercise and means of protection. Nevertheless, both concepts ought to be differentiated, so as to achieve a better protection – which does not exclude the artificial character of this division.

When stating *inter alia* that all peoples shall have the right to existence and to self-determination, Article 20 of the Banjul Charter puts forward one of the main goals of this instrument. The right to self-determination had already been foreseen in the 1963 OAU Charter. This by the way is the only provision of the OAU Charter save for the preamble that referred to the Universal Declaration of Human Rights and in this sense extended recognition to the notion of human rights in the Charter. Due to the practice of this Organization, as well as to inferences that can be drawn from this Charter, it is very unlikely that the right of self-determination, therein

---

[29] See footnote 25 above.
[30] See footnote 26 above.

enshrined, may be considered an encouragement to the claim of secessionist movements in independent African States.[31]

If one divides self-determination into two components, i.e. political and economic, one may say that the former has already been successfully exercised by the majority of the African sovereign States, while the latter remains yet to be realized. This is certainly the reason for the unnecessarily long wording of provisions regarding *inter alia*:

(i) the free disposal that the peoples from the African States have, of their wealth and natural resources;
(ii) an adequate compensation in case of spoliation;
(iii) the elimination of all forms of foreign economic exploitation;
(iv) the right to economic, social and cultural development;
(v) the equal enjoyment of the common heritage of mankind;
(vi) the right to national and international peace and security;
(vi) the principles of solidarity and friendly relations; as well as
(vii) the right to generally satisfactory environment favourable to their development.

The enjoyment by the African States of their right to economic self-determination is thus dependant upon the progressive implementation and enjoyment of their economic, social and cultural rights.

It was also targeting this right to an economic self-determination that the right to development[32] was included in the Banjul Charter. Having or not its conceptual source in the standard-setting practice of the United Nations, the point is that the Right to Development in the African context – as well as in the developing countries' – has the goal to serve as an instrument of change, which seeks a more just and humane society, the developed countries' on the contrary, see in the right to development – and generally in the human rights as a whole –

---

[31] The cases of Eritrea and South Sudan are probably the closest one could go in State practice in Africa in trying to identify claims to the right of political self-determination within existing States. But, they are both consensual secessions.

[32] See Article 22. However, the development paradigm in this provision ominously skips "political" development a feature of the 1986 UN Declaration already alluded to above. At that time (1981), none of the African States would stomach guaranteeing "political development" given the political systems in their countries.

2.7. The Right to Life & Respect of Dignity

The Charter protects the right to life in Article 4, not as an unqualified right. In *Forum of Conscious v. Sierra Leone*, the Commission, after listening to dreadful stories of execution of victims by firing squad tersely stated:

> "The right to life is a fulcrum of all rights. It is the fountain through which other rights flow, and any violation of this right without due process amounts to arbitrary violation of life."[33]

However, the majority of African countries still keep the death penalty on their statute books but do not practice it subject to few exceptions.[34] Consequently, what Article 4 forbids is arbitrary deprivation of life. However, the Commission has given this clause such a progressive interpretation that it may now be construed to cover situations not anticipated in the original text. For example, the Commission has interpreted the clause to extend to a situation where an individual goes into hiding for fear of his life;[35] where authorities deny prisoners food and medical attention and where forced disappearances occur.[36] All these constitute violations of the right to life in Article 4.

Just like non-discrimination and equality, the Commission treats life and dignity more or less on the same wavelength. For example, in the Rwanda Communication,[37] similar to the set of facts in the Mauritanian case, it found conditions of "detention in which children, women and the aged are held" to violate their physical and psychological integrity and therefore constitute violation of Article 5. Similarly, "denial of medical attention under health threatening

---

[33] *Forum of Conscious v. Sierra Leone*, Communication No. 223/98, para. 20.
[34] See footnote 13 above, para. 120.
[35] *Kazeem Aminu v. Nigeria*, Communication No. 223/98, para. 20.
[36] *Mouvement Burkinabe des Droits de l'Homme et des peuples v. Burkina Faso*, para. 44.
[37] *Organisation Mondiale contre la torture and 3 others v. Rwanda*, Communication Nos. 27/89, 46/91, 49/91 and 99/93, para. 27.

conditions" and "denial of access to the outside world" was said to fall outside the province of "respect of the dignity inherent in a human being and to the recognition of his legal status,"[38] again a violation of Article 5.

2.8. The Duties of the Individual in the Charter

Chapter 11 of Part 1 of the African Charter comprises Articles 27-29, which deal with individual duties. In the traditional African setting, this implies that in their natural setting, rights cannot be isolated from the idea of duty. Thus, the African approach is that there is a rights-duties nexus, and that both concepts merge towards an integrated whole. Instead of rights in isolation, the traditional African philosophy of law emphasises the "duty-right reciprocity" principle by which when extremely interpreted, one may understand that your rights depend on your respect and observance of other peoples' rights as well as on your service to your community.

Besides the Banjul Charter, the only other international human rights instrument that enshrines duties that should be observed by individuals is the 1948 American Declaration of the Rights and Duties of Man. The American Declaration spells out several duties including duties towards the family, the community, and to humanity. There is a similar wording, however, in the Universal Declaration, Article 29 provides that "everyone has duties towards the community in which alone the free and full development of his personality is possible."

Not all the specific duties enumerated in the African Charter appear capable of implementation in law; this causes them to be in some instances merely of moral value, guide or code of conduct to be respected by the African citizens. When analyzing the real purposes of the duties proclaimed by the Banjul Charter, one may come to the conclusion that they fall into two broad categories, namely, one that encompasses the duties which can be characterized as correlatives of rights; and another one that restricts the enjoyment of some rights, i.e. limiting provisions that are guised as duties. This second category suffers from the same problem related to the claw-back clauses, since

---

[38] *Huri-Laws v. Nigeria*, Communication No. 225/98, para. 41.

the extension of the duties is not established, being thus at the free disposal and discretion of the State Parties. It can, therefore, be concluded that though the concept of duties proclaimed by the Banjul Charter was predicted as likely to be abused by some governments, this has not so far happened in practice.

3. African Commission: Composition, Organization, and Competence

Like other regional instruments on human rights, the Banjul Charter created the African Commission on Human and Peoples' Rights, which, as the body competent to implement the Charter, is to promote and secure the protection of human and peoples' rights in Africa, besides also having an advisory mandate.

It must be mentioned, however, that the possibility of establishing a Court in addition to the Commission was entertained by the drafters of the Charter from the very beginning. Already in the first Draft which as indicated was drawn towards the end of 1979, it was reported that

"the establishment of a Human Rights Court to redress violations of human rights is not included in the Draft Charter. It is premature to do so at this stage. The idea is, no doubt, a good and useful one which could be introduced in future by means of an additional protocol to the Charter."[39]

Later, in the same report, it was stated that:

"It should be mentioned that a delegation proposed an amendment according to which the meeting was to draft a text establishing an African Court to judge crimes against mankind and violations of human rights. The participants took note of this amendment but were of the opinion that it was untimely to discuss it."[40]

After these failed attempts at establishing the Court, it was decided to settle for the Commission in the meantime. Years later, in 1998, the Court was established.[41]

---

[39] See footnote 25 above.
[40] *Ibid*, p. 26.
[41] See the chapter authored by Ouguergouz F. on the African Court, in this *Manual*.

3.1. Elections to the Commission

The first Commissioners were elected on 29 July 1987.[42] This took place during the Twenty-third Session of the Assembly of Heads of state and Government of the OAU held in Addis Ababa, Ethiopia. Formally, the Commission commenced its work in November 1987.

Following a request by the Government of The Gambia to host the Commission, the Assembly of Heads of State and Government of the OAU accepted in 1988 to have the seat of the Commission in Banjul. As indicated before, The Gambia did a lot through then President Jawara to promote the development of the Charter so that it was natural that OAU States would agree to have this country host the Commission. Nevertheless, a pattern has emerged of alternating the meetings of the Commission between Banjul and other African capitals.

The Commission comprises 11 members, who are not necessarily jurists, but who ought to have competence in matters of human and peoples' rights. By establishing that the members shall serve in their personal capacity, the Charter intended to ensure their independence, particularly with respect to their countries of origin. Members of the Commission, which cannot include more than one national of the same State are elected by secret ballot by the Assembly of Heads of State and Government, from a list of persons nominated by the States Parties to the Charter. It is interesting to note that the candidates must have the nationality of the State that submits their nomination. This provision aims at enabling the participation in the work of the Commission – which actually transcends national boundaries – of renowned experts, whose countries' of origin may, for political or other reasons, not nominate for election. The election of the Commission by the AU Assembly has been criticized by many

---

[42] These were Dr. Ibrahim Ali Badawi El Sheikh (Egypt), Mr. Sourahata Baboucar Sernega Janneh (The Gambia), Mr. Beye Alioune Bloudin (Cote D'Ivoire), Mr. Buhedma Ali Mahmoud (Libya), Mr. Gabou Alexis Congo Brazzaville), Justice Robert Kisanga (Tanzania), Mr. Moleleki D. Mokama (Botswana), Mr. Ndiaye Youssoupha (Senegal), Mr. Isaac Nguema (Gabon), Prof. U. Oji Umozirike (Nigeria), and Mubanga Chipoya (Zambia).

commentators, mainly because of the unavoidable and intrinsic political considerations which unfortunately infiltrate the process.

3.2. Commission's Competences Generally

Article 45 of the Charter deals with the competences of the Commission.[43] Its first paragraph enshrines the promotional competences, which, in the initial phase of the Commission, were the ones that were stressed. Amongst them special attention was given to the following: collecting of documents, disseminating information, promoting co-operation between institutions, as well as formulating and drafting principles and rules aimed at solving legal problems and serving as a basis for drafting legislation in the concerned countries. By and large, the promotional mandate is yet to be completed.

Article 45(2) asserts that the Commission shall ensure the protection of human and peoples' rights under the conditions lay down by the African Charter, declaring thus the jurisdictional competence of the Commission. The advisory competence of the Commission is foreseen in Article 45(3), which provides that one of the functions of the Commission is to interpret all the provisions of the Charter at the request of a State Party, an institution of the OAU/AU or an African Organization recognized by the OAU/AU. The advisory opinions are not exempted from the confidentiality rule of the Commission that certainly attenuates the impact of its work vis-à-vis the promotion and protection of human and peoples' rights. During the final draft of the Charter, in January 1981, in Banjul, The Gambia, some States like Burundi, Ghana, Kenya, Mali, Tanzania and Zambia – made reservations to this very competence, and except for the Malian reservation,[44] were all quietly persuaded to withdraw them for the

---

[43] These are now expanding, in fact, rapidly. The latest competences being a series of Working Groups on: (a) the death penalty; (b) economic, social and cultural rights; (c) indigenous populations/communities; (d) on specific issues; and (e) on implementation of the Robben Island Guidelines on the prohibition against torture.

[44] Reservation of Mali, CAB/LEG/67/1/53. In part, it reads: "… Meanwhile, the Government of the Republic of Mali has expressed reservations on the mission entrusted to the commission on Human and Peoples' Rights to interpret the OAU Charter".

sake of the so-called African tradition of reaching decisions unanimously by consensus. Nevertheless, it is possible that the reluctance of some African States to be bound by the Banjul Charter was precisely due to the fact that they did not agree with the granting of the advisory competence to the Commission, since they reckoned that the Assembly of Heads of State and Government was the only body more appropriate to discharge the function, which is consistent with the political ideology at the time.

Similarly, according to Article 45(4), the Commission has the function to perform "any other tasks which may be entrusted to it by the Assembly of Heads of State and Government". This happened for the first time when the Assembly of Heads of State authorized the Commission, according to a request addressed by the latter, to receive from the States Parties biannual reports which are due in conformity with Article 62 of the Charter.

There are two kinds of communications that may be addressed to the Commission, namely, the ones coming from a State Party,[45] and the "other" communications. The former may be lodged by means of two distinct procedures. The first is set up by bilateral contacts between the parties in dispute, when the State Party, that has good reasons to believe that another State Party has violated the provisions of the Banjul Charter, must draw, by written communication, the attention of the latter as well as address this communication to the AU Commission Chairperson and to the Chairman of the African Human Rights Commission. This formal contact between the States, before the Commission's intervention, is a singularly distinctive feature of the African Charter. The States in dispute have a time limit of three months to negotiate, with a view to settling the matter in a peaceful way.

State Party communications can be used for settling Charter-based disputes under the African Peer Review Mechanism (APRM).[46] Introduced in 2003, the APRM seeks to provide a unique mechanism for sitting African Heads of State to open themselves to both internal and external scrutiny in regard to their democracy, human rights and

---

[45] The first inter-State communication was brought by the Democratic Republic of the Congo (DRC) against Burundi, Rwanda and Uganda, ACHPR, 2004.
[46] See the website of the APRM.

governance records. The "peer pressure" that they committed themselves to, is very similar to the process in Articles 47 to 49 of the African Charter. Perhaps the African Commission and the APRM may need to sit down together to reconcile their processes and consider joint mechanisms of achieving their objectives.

In case the issue is not settled to the satisfaction of the States involved either through bilateral negotiations or by other peaceful procedure, either State may submit the matter to the Commission, notifying at the same time the other State(s) involved. The only admissibility condition is the previous exhaustion of all local remedies. This can only be demanded of if the object of the communication is to complain of the violation of an individual right by the State. The Commission, after having obtained all the information it deems necessary and after having tried an amicable solution, shall prepare, within a reasonable period of time, a report stating the facts and its findings – which shall be sent to the States concerned and to the Assembly of Heads of State and Government. The measures that the Assembly of Heads of State and Government may take highlight once more the importance of the procedure on "peer pressure".

The second type of communications is the one that does not originate from States. These communications,[47] dubbed "other communications". Article 55 of the Charter makes no restriction as to who may address them to the Commission so that individuals, groups of individuals, or non-governmental organizations, being the victims or not of violations, are entitled to send this type of communications to the Commission. After having decided that the communications will be considered, the Commission considers as to whether they fulfil the admissibility conditions prescribed in Article 56. Its structure is similar to the one existing in the Inter-American system, though there are some slight differences. One of them is the non-establishment of a determined time-limit,[48] after the exhaustion of local remedies,[49]

---

[47] Procedure for this has been elaborated in Information Sheet No. 3 on Communication Procedure.
[48] Article 56(6) states: "are submitted within 'reasonable period' from the time local remedies are exhausted or from the date the Commission is seized of the matter…"

pertinent to the addressing of the communication before the Commission – it is only laid down that this period must be reasonable. The other is that in the African Commission, deciding the *prima facie* status of the communication, is a quasi-judicial function of the Commission itself whereas it is often dealt with in the American system as a secretarial function by the legal officer, though the Commission may later overturn the decision.

Though criticized as unreal in the African context, the Commission has had no problem insisting on it in the majority of cases and only dispensing with it in few cases where deficits of democracy, rule of law and human rights make it impossible to insist on it. For example, in *Civil Liberties Organization v. Nigeria*,[50] the Commission laid down the important "remedy exception rule" which stipulated that "it is reasonable to assume that domestic remedies will not only be prolonged but are certain to yield no results". In this case, the military Government of Nigeria, then in power, had issued a series of Decrees in which it suspended the Constitution, dissolved political parties, and ousted the jurisdiction of regular courts from entertaining legal challenges against them. Given this, the Commission invoked Article 56 (5) and admitted the communication as an exception without the requirement to exhaust local remedies. Several other communications subsequent to this were treated the same way.[51]

After the admissibility phase, the next step for the Commission is to draw the attention of the Assembly of Heads of State and Government to the "special cases" which reveal the existence of a series of serious or massive violations of human and peoples' rights. When this happens, the Assembly of Heads of State and Government may then request the Commission to undertake an in-depth study of these cases and make a factual report, accompanied by its findings and

---

[49] Article 56(5). There is plenty of case law on this matter. An interesting one on the negative side involves *Kenya Human Rights Commission v. Kenya* (Communication No. 135/94, 9th Annual Activity Report: 1995-1996).

[50] *Civil Liberties Organization v. Nigeria*, Communication No. 129/94, 19th Annual Activity Report: 1995-1996.

[51] *Media Rights Agenda & 2 others v. Nigeria*, Communication No. 105/93, 12th Annual Activity Report: 1998-1999; *Constitutional Rights Project and another v. Nigeria*, Communication No. 145/95, 13th Annual Activity Report: 1999-2000.

recommendations. This procedure is exceedingly similar to the system created by ECOSOC Resolution 1503, which lays down that the UN Commission on Human Rights should consider all communications that appear to reveal a consistent pattern of gross violations of human rights. This concept of "a series of serious violations" was no doubt introduced to ensure that the Commission would not deal with isolated violations of the Charter. If a State Party regularly commits or tolerates serious individual violations, whether related or not, the matter could be brought within the jurisdiction of the Commission.

Furthermore, with regard to the "other" communications, there is no such provision built in the Charter itself – as there is in relation to State communications – providing for the Commission's initiative with a view to reaching an amicable solution based on respect for human and peoples' rights. Instead, the Commission has developed a set of procedures in its Rules of Procedure.[52]

An interesting innovation in the rules of procedure is the rule on "standing" known by its more popular term *locus standi*. Based on the African Commission's interpretation of Article 56(1) read with Article 55, virtually anyone can complain on behalf of another who claims to be victims of violation of the African Charter standards. In the "Mauritanian case,"[53] the Commission on this particular point decided that Article 56(1), the article on identity of the complainant, required only that the complainant revealed his/her identity that is even if she/he wanted to request to remain anonymous. Significantly, the complainant did not have to be the victim of the violation or member of his or her family. It concluded:

> "This characteristic of the African Charter reflected the sensitivity to the practical difficulties that individuals can face in countries where human rights are violated. The national or international channels of remedy may not be accessible to the victims themselves or may be dangerous to pursue…"

Consequently, a number of communications that should otherwise have been dismissed for lack of *locus standi* on the part of the

---

[52] The current Rules of Procedure were adopted by the African Commission on 6 October 1995.
[53] See footnote 12 above, paras. 78-79.

complainant nevertheless have been saved. Thus, not only complainants need not be the victims but can be complete strangers to the one whose right is the subject of the complaint. Without this saver, only a handful of communications would have been triggered by the Charter to the Commission. It is notorious that majority of African people are illiterate. It would be cruel to expect them to use the mechanism on their own and by themselves. Instead, most of the Commission jurisprudence has been triggered by communications engineered by NGOs which is not surprising.

It is also worth noting that the African Charter does not make any mention of remedies, which is difficult to understand given its basic concerns with gross violations with human rights. Nevertheless, provisions on remedies and redress have since been incorporated in the Protocol[54] to the Charter on the Establishment of the Court of Human and Peoples' Rights, a subject of a different Chapter in this book.

3.3. Specific Functions of the Commission

The Charter empowers the Commission to undertake studies and research on African problems in the field of human and peoples' rights, and to formulate and lay down principles and rules aimed at solving legal problems relating to human and peoples' rights and fundamental freedoms upon which African Governments may base their legislation. The Working Group is an excellent example of this.[55] Article 45(b) read with Rule 66, Chapter VI, of the Commission's Rules of Procedure, provides a framework within which the Commission is enabled to appoint thematic Rapporteurs[56] on

---

[54] Article 30 of the Protocol provides that: "The States parties to the present Protocol undertake to comply with the judgment in any case to which they are parties within the time stipulated by the Court and to guarantee its execution".
[55] *Ibid.*
[56] The Commission has since appointed several of its commissioners as Rapporteurs as follows: (a) Rapporteur on Extra-Judicial, Summary or Arbitrary Executions; (b) Rapporteur on Rights of Women in Africa; (c) Rapporteur on Prisons and Prison Conditions in Africa; (d) Rapporteur on Freedom of Expression in Africa; (e) Rapporteur on Human Rights Defenders in Africa, and Rapporteur on Refugees, Asylum and Internally Displaced Persons in Africa.

identified human rights issues and problems under the African Charter and to formulate relevant standards on the basis of the reports of the Rapporteurs. There are not yet country Rapporteurs, as such, although Commissioners have divided States among themselves more or less based on their language competences for the purposes of conducting promotional work. There is no doubt that the work of the Rapporteurs contributes to the promotion of the Charter given the African context is a natural first priority in seeking to secure the effective implementation of human and, of course, peoples' rights. Besides promotions, and based on Article 58, the Charter anticipates at least two types of missions. The first one is "massive or series of violations" related missions. The other is based on the mandate of the Commission to watch out for "emergency cases duly noticed". Both situations can in theory trigger a mission. In both cases, however, permission is needed. Either the AHSG or the Chairman of the AHSG respectively must authorize the visit prior to undertaking it. In practice, a Commissioner must obtain a visa from authorities of the State Party before the visit can take place. These have not been forthcoming in the majority of cases. This has made Article 58 practically redundant.

It is instructive that the Rule 118(3) of the Rules of Procedure states that

"The Assembly of its Chairman may request the Commission to conduct an in-depth study on these cases and to submit a factual report accompanied by its findings and recommendations, in accordance with the provisions of Article 58 sub-paragraph 2 of the Charter".

The logical interpretation of this is that the Assembly had intended that Article 58 procedure of how to go about investigating cases of massive or systematic violation of human and peoples' rights belongs to them not only to sanction but to receive the recommendations arising thereof and based on that to decide what should be done. Though these rules have since been replaced, there is no doubt this is what might have been behind Zimbabwe government position when confronted with the bashing report prepared by the Commission on its human rights record. The entire Article 58 wording does not leave room for the Commission's independent exercise of its powers.

Besides ordinary visits, Special Procedures exist which mechanism also provides for visits to selected countries. Thus far, the Commission has developed mechanisms in the form of Rapporteurs and Working Groups, including on:

a) Extrajudicial Executions;
b) Prison Conditions in Africa;
c) Women's Rights in Africa;
d) Refugees, Asylum Seekers and Displaced Persons;
e) Human Rights Defenders
f) Press Freedom;
g) Indigenous Communities/Populations

Again, Commissioners responsible for these particular mechanisms have produced reports[57] on their work covering particular periods. The essence behind this is to feed into the work of the Commission and make it more competent but in the process promote and protect human rights.

Promotion has also taken particularly the form of Resolutions. During a session, the Commission deliberates on a number of issues such as communications brought to their attention by the victims or others on their behalf but also on current issues with potential to impact on the Commission's mandate. The subject matter of resolutions concerns *inter alia*:

- Human rights situation in Africa;
- The right to fair trial and legal assistance in Africa;
- States to envisage a moratorium on the death penalty;
- The observance of the 30th Anniversary of the OAU Convention Governing Specific Aspects of Refugee Problems in Africa;
- The Western Sahara;
- The human rights situation in Eritrea, Sudan, Zimbabwe, etc.

Obviously, this has embarrassed States to whom these resolutions were directed resulting in frosty relations between the Commission and the AU. As a result, it has been decided by the AU that all

---

[57] See: "Report on Extrajudicial, Summary or Arbitrary Executions", by Dr. Hatem Ben Salem, Special Rapporteur, OAU Doc. AHG/210 (XXXIII), Annex VI, adopted during the 16th Ordinary Session (October 1994).

resolutions of the Commission would be embargoed and not released to the public nor submitted to the Assembly till after clearing with the States concerned. In other words, harangued States have won a right to comment or authorize the release of resolutions. Thus, no State may agree in future to publication of a resolution critical of its human rights situation.

3.4. Admissibility & Related Issues

In practice, the greatest nightmare to most victims is how to exhaust local remedies in order to reach the Commission. Local remedies in most jurisdictions are notoriously laborious and even murderous of complaints that may be well-founded. Previously, the Commission would insist that the author of the complaint should indicate measures taken at local level with a view to exhaust locally available remedies. Revised Rule 104(1)(f) allows the complainant to approach the Commission merely by indicating why local remedies may be futile, as in most cases. The Commission has power to consider the communication where local remedies may be unreasonably prolonged.

Another aspect of the reform in the Commission Rules of Procedure is that the Commission is bound to decide a matter on the admissibility stage within three months after requesting the State for information on this aspect. In spite of these changes, however, admissibility remains the single most challenging hurdle to most complainants to overcome. As a result, the following principles have been developed to act as a guide in the application of the rule.

First, unless the local remedies are, as a practical matter unavailable or unduly prolonged, the Commission insists that they be pursued and exhausted.[58] In one of the communications, the Commission explained the purpose of the remedy rule in a series of communications as including the requirement that government should have notice of a human right violation in order to have the opportunity to remedy such violations before being called to account for the same

---

[58] *Organisation mondiale contre la Torture & 2 others v. Rwanda*, Communication Nos. 48/90, 50/91, 52/91, 89/93, para. 17, etc.

before an international tribunal;[59] and to avoid contradictory judgments of law at national and international levels.[60] Thus, the rule ensures that the Commission does not become a tribunal of first instance for cases for which an effective domestic remedy exists,[61] to provide it with an opportunity to save its reputation which would be inevitably tarnished if it were brought before an international jurisdiction and, to enable to reiterate that it has "to avoid playing the role of a court of first instance, a role it cannot under any circumstances arrogate itself."[62] Consequently, the Commission developed three major criteria for use in determining this rule, namely, that the domestic remedy must be available, effective and sufficient. In *Sir Dawda K. Jawara v. The Gambia*,[63] already cited, the Commission decided that

> "A remedy is considered available if the petitioner can pursue it without impediment, it is deemed effective if it offers a prospect of success, and it is found sufficient if it is capable of redressing the complaint".

Conversely, the rule does not apply if local remedies "are not available or accessible to the complainant,"[64] and there is no need to exhaust remedies that are unduly prolonged;[65] or if the complaint involves instances of massive human rights violations.[66] However, Government has the duty to demonstrate the existence of such remedies.[67]

3.5. The 1995 Rules of Procedure

The present Rules of Procedure of the Commission were adopted at its Ordinary Session held at Praia, Cape Verde, in October 1995, the

---

[59] *Ibid.*
[60] See footnote 26 above, para. 37.
[61] *Ibid.*, para. 39.
[62] See footnote 25 above, para. 80.
[63] See footnote 10 above, para. 32.
[64] See footnote 15 above, para. 12.
[65] *John K. Modise v. Botswana*, Communication No. 97/93, para. 20.
[66] See footnote 38 above, para. 18; and footnote 13 above, para. 85.
[67] *Rencontre Africaine pour la Défense des Droits de l'Homme v. Zambia*, Communication No. 71/92, para. 12.

first Rules having been adopted in 1988, soon after the Commission started its work.

In several ways, the 1995 Rules[68] represent a fundamental departure from, and improvement over the 1988 Rules. For example, Rule 32 of the 1988 Rules provided that the sittings of the Commission and its subsidiary bodies "shall be held in private and shall be held in camera". This, of course, was very excessive. There were numerous complaints that the Commission was hiding its work from the public domain. Due to internal and external pressure, this was revised. The new Rules 106 and 107 provide for both private and public sessions. Private sessions are essentially meant for consideration of communications, though administrative and financial matters are also catered for under this Rule. While the public are excluded from private sessions, the Parties more especially the victim is entitled to attend. On the other hand, public sessions cater for general issues. Normally, examination of a State Party report is a general issue and hence it is open to the public. In practice, this follows the opening ceremony and the first few days thereafter.

Often, victims would like to know whether the African Commission has time-limits for considering communications. This is because prolonged hearings in domestic systems are 'normal' driving most people away from Courts. Rule 117 directed that the Commission will have to decide the issue of admissibility of a Communication within three months from seizure if the State Party has not cooperated in its attempts to get information from it as regards to the admissibility of the matter. This is a fundamental improvement because in the past, the Commission would decide only after the State had responded which in most cases took a long time much to the chagrin of the victim. Also on the issue of information, Rule 74(1) now requires that the Commission Secretary informs NGOs four weeks before the date and agenda of a forthcoming session. This is substantially being complied with by the Commission since the Rule was adopted. Previously, NGOs even with observer status had no right to attend public sessions unless only when issues touching on their areas of competence were being discussed. This is the procedure

---

[68] See: OAU Doc. ACHPR/RP/X1X.

observed in the United Nations system. However, the African system in Rule 75 has revised Rule 76 and now NGOs can attend all public sessions regardless of whether or not the matters on the agenda bear on their competence. This has substantially improved communications between NGOs and the Commission.

However, there are carry-overs from the previous Rules. For instance, it was not very clear to the Commission under the old Rules how to remind defaulting States that they had breached their State reporting cycle under the State Party reporting mechanism. The previous rule provided that the Commission shall send a "report" to the State concerned informing it of the overdue report and it was not quite clear what report the Rules required the Commission to send. Revised Rule 8 unfortunately states that the Commission may send a "Report or Reminder" thereby repeating the word "Report" but at the same time making it easier for the Commission to simply send reminders to defaulting States.

One of the controversial issues is the status of "provisional measures" in the Charter system. Rule 111 states that provisional measures are measures issued to a State Party before the Commission makes known its "final views" to the Assembly on a communication to prevent or avoid irreparable harm. In the cases of urgent matters or matters that by their nature cannot wait, Rule 111(2) mandates the Commission or its Bureau to issue "interim measures". The Bureau comprises the Chairperson, Vice-Chairperson and the Commission Secretary. The trio acts as "full-time" officers of the Commission in the absence of the Commission. The problem though is not addressed. How the Commission issues and more especially serves these measures is controversial. States have previously claimed that they have not received the measures in time and therefore went ahead to implement the decision whose implementation the Commission was seeking to stay pending its decision on the merits in order to prevent rendering the Commission procedure academic.

An equally popular question is whether the Commission after declaring a communication inadmissible can turn round and admit it. Sometimes, decisions are based on insufficient evidence. Rule 118(2) empowers the Commission to reconsider its decision declaring a communication inadmissible so that it is perfectly sound for the

Commission to admit what it had previously rejected as long as there are plausible reasons to do so.

4. Conclusion

From what has been exposed, one may conclude that the African Charter on Human and Peoples' Rights, just like any other instrument pertaining to human rights, brings with it a combination and a variety of legal, political and institutional considerations and trajectories which, depending on the context, may serve different purposes. In any case, the Charter, with this range of architecture, aims to achieve an effective system for the protection and promotion of human and peoples' rights. But to this end a series of obstacles needs to be overcome.[69]

Amongst them, one may mention the crisis of legitimacy that the Commission suffers. It is not clear whether Commissioners want to be Commissioners as defined by the Charter or Governmental Representatives. While the letter and spirit of the Charter would seem to be to place the Commission out of reach of Governments or politicians who appoint them to office, individual Commissioners on the other hand seem to want to be as close to Government as possible. In this connection, even if they did not come originally from Government to the Commission, they usually go straight to Government immediately after their tenure on the Commission. This has a serious negative effect on the Commission.

The second obstacle appears through the restrictive provisions pertaining to the Commission's competence, which it needs to carry out its functions within a very limited margin of flexibility, besides having to observe and comply with many provisions distinguished by its flourished rhetoric. Even though seemingly cured by the African Court's Protocol particularly Article 30, it is nevertheless a problem that obstructs the Commission's effective implementation of

---

[69] Compare the elucidations of the African Commission problems immediately after its establishment and now, more than twenty years down the line. The situation is the same. See: Badawi El-Sheikh I., "The African Charter on Human and Peoples' Rights: Prospects and Problems", *Netherlands Quarterly of Human Rights* 7 (1989) 3, 272-283.

its mandate. It is not clear as the Charter stands what is the exact status of the outcome of its deliberations whether it is a decision, recommendation or resolution; and what is the effect of this outcome on States Parties.

Third, the failure by most States Parties to domesticate the Charter, as discussed on page 11, renders the Charter foreign within the domestic arena of African countries. Most African countries are either too slow or not interested at all to domesticate the Charter as well as international law in general so as to give it legal backing in local jurisdiction. Besides domestication, there are proper mechanisms and machineries in most of these countries to implement decisions and recommendations by the Commission. This is a major problem to victims. Victims do not only expect a pronouncement in their favour or that they have "won" a decision but would like to see such decision translate into tangible redresses to repair the damage caused by the violation. Implementation of the Commission recommendations is a major problem hindering the effectiveness of the Charter.

However, when deciding to grant the Commission the appropriate means necessary to the carrying out of its tasks, attention ought to be given to the peculiarities of the African culture. A good example of evolution in this field is the conclusion of the African Charter on children's rights. This instrument sets up a Committee that, contrary to the African Commission, is empowered to, on its own motion and by an appropriate method of investigation, to seek from States Parties any relevant information regarding implementation of the Charter provisions and the nature and scope of any implementing measures adopted. It is mandated to submit a Report on its activities biennially to the ordinary session of the Assembly of Heads of State and Government, and has the power to publish its Report after consideration by the Assembly and Members can circulate it widely to the public in their own countries. The fact that some African countries have recently agreed upon binding their States to this practice may offer the possibility that, in a non-distant future, the African Commission will also be endowed with the freedom of publishing its own reports – which would, doubtlessly, have a significantly positive repercussion in regard to its protective and promotional competences.

Yet, despite the problems that beset it, the Banjul Charter and its protocols must be seen as a timely motion, a major step on the right direction, towards a democratic future for Africa, where both human and peoples' rights are recognized, promoted and protected on the basis of the sacred principles of equality and non-discrimination.

CHAPTER 20.
THE PROTOCOL ON THE RIGHTS OF WOMEN IN AFRICA

Rachel Mayanja

1. Introduction

The Preamble to the Charter of the Organization of African Unity (OAU) sets out a conceptual framework for the rights of the African peoples, which is founded in the conviction that it is the "inalienable right of all peoples to control their own destiny; that freedom, equality, justice and dignity are essential objectives for the achievement of the legitimate aspirations of the African peoples". Through the Charter, the Member States of the OAU acknowledged their responsibility of harnessing the natural and human resources of the African continent for the total advancement of their peoples.

The African (Banjul) Charter on Human and Peoples' Rights built on and expanded these ideas. It articulated the vision that individual human rights and peoples' rights are mutually reinforcing. It is stated in its sixth preambular paragraph "recognizing on the one hand, that fundamental human rights stem from the attributes of human beings which justifies their national and international protection and on the other hand that the reality and respect of peoples rights should necessarily guarantee human rights". Article 2 confers on every individual the right to the enjoyment of the rights and freedoms recognized and guaranteed in the Charter without distinction of any kind such as race, ethnic group, color, sex, language, political or any other opinion, national and social origin, fortune, birth or other status. Article 18(3) specifically prohibits discrimination against women and imposes on the States Parties the responsibility of ensuring the protection of the rights of the woman and the child as stipulated in international declarations and conventions. Article 19 goes further by declaring that "All peoples shall be equal; they shall enjoy the same respect and shall have the same rights. Nothing shall justify the domination of a people by another."

Despite these powerful undertakings and guarantees, women in Africa suffer from both *de jure* and *de facto* discrimination on a daily basis, which ranges from denial of equality in marriage and family life, discrimination in the enjoyment of civil, political, economic, social and cultural rights, in particular equal rights with respect to land and other resources, and violence, including harmful traditional practices, and in particular in the context of armed conflict. Denial of rights has contributed to the fact that African women, especially the young, are disproportionately victims of HIV/AIDS. Negative traditional and customary practices justify and perpetuate violations of the human rights of women in Africa while the impunity of perpetrators of these violations denies them justice. Furthermore, weak and ineffectual governance affords them neither support nor protection.

This Chapter focuses on the contribution of the Protocol to the African Charter on Human and People's Rights on the Rights of Women in Africa (hereinafter "the Protocol") to the creation of a culture of respect for women's human rights in Africa. It is composed of four sections in addition to the introduction and conclusion. Section 2 reviews developments leading up to the adoption of the Protocol. Section 3 examines the innovative aspects of the Protocol and their implications for the creation of "rights specific to African women" or an African approach dictated by the realities of the lives of African women, and the particular challenges they face in enjoying their human rights and freedoms. Section 4 examines the obligations of States Parties created by the Protocol, while Section 5 reviews the remedies provided, its implementation and monitoring. The conclusion (Section 6) considers the potential of the Protocol towards achievement of equality for African women.

2. Background

Despite the absence in its Charter of principles or rules dealing specifically with gender equality, the OAU can be credited with engaging in concrete actions to advance African women's rights. These were driven to a large extent by the role that African women played in the liberation struggle that prompted the OAU to focus more concretely on the rights of women, in particular on the need to increase participation of women in decision-making. In addition, the participation of African States in the global dialogue on women's equality, development and peace – the theme of the first women's decade following the first world conference for women held in Mexico in 1975 – coupled with concerted action by African women activists as well as civil society organizations, seen most clearly in their strong participation at the end of the decade conference held in Nairobi, Kenya in 1985, underscored the critical need to address African women's rights.

From a normative perspective, the first concrete action came through the adoption on 27 June 1981 of the African Charter on Human and Peoples' Rights, under which the OAU turned its attention, for the first time, to the establishment of an African legal framework on individual and peoples' rights. The OAU sought to encapsulate within the Banjul Charter what it considered to be the African concept of 'human' rights: the intimate interconnectedness between individual human rights and peoples'/(collective) rights. With regard to the rights of women, the Banjul Charter contains one sub-paragraph only, Article 18(3), which is under the article dealing with the family. It states: "The State shall ensure the elimination of every discrimination against women and also ensure the protection of the rights of the woman and the child as stipulated in international declarations and conventions." This paragraph is preceded by the following two paragraphs which emphasize the importance of the family as a microcosm of society:

"(1) The family shall be the natural unit and basis of society. It shall be protected by the State which shall take care of its physical and moral health.
(2) The State shall have the duty to assist the family which is the custodian of morals and traditional values recognized by the community."

By placing the sole non-discrimination clause against women under the umbrella of the family, along with others considered vulnerable, such as the aged and disabled, Article 18 of the Banjul Charter signals the OAU's main concern over the vulnerability of the family and certain of its members in respect of which it imposes a duty on the State to assist and protect the family. This unfortunate placement undermined from the outset the importance and effectiveness of the clause purporting to establish a framework of human rights for African women. It is not surprising therefore, that the Banjul Charter has not been considered by women's groups as an adequate instrument for the promotion and protection of women's rights and freedoms.

Conscious of the absence of a legally binding African instrument addressing the rights of women, the Inter-African Committee on Traditional Practices Affecting the Health of Women and Children decided to draft a legal instrument on the elimination of harmful traditional practices affecting the fundamental rights of women and girls. This idea emerged before the question of a Protocol on women's rights was advanced, although the OAU secretariat, women's organizations, civil society organizations and jurists were also simultaneously focusing on an instrument dealing with the rights of women.

In March 1995, the African Commission on Human and Peoples' Rights convened a seminar in Togo to address the promotion and protection of women's rights. Deliberations focused on:
- Measures to promote and protect women's rights in Africa.
- Results of the Dakar Preparatory Conference on Women's Rights prior to the Beijing Conference.
- The Banjul Charter as an instrument to protect women's rights in Africa.
- The need for a Protocol on women's rights in Africa to be annexed to the Charter.

- The need for the Commission and States Parties to take measures for the protection of women's rights.

With regard to a protocol on women's rights, participants were of the view that such a protocol could contain two parts – a general part on sexual equality and another on rights specific to women. This was considered to be justified on the basis of the Charter's silence on gender issues and gender equality. In addition, it was proposed that a Special Rapporteur responsible for women's rights should be nominated by the OAU. Participants further proposed an amendment to the electoral process for membership of the African Commission to increase the number of female commissioners. The African Commission was urged to interpret the Banjul Charter provisions in a manner that would improve the protection of women's rights and to focus and speak out on women's rights.

At its 17th session, the African Commission on Human and Peoples' Rights adopted the following recommendations emanating from a seminar on women's rights held in Lomé, Togo:
(a) An additional protocol on the rights of women should be prepared;
(b) Pending the adoption of the additional protocol some interim measures should be taken by States Parties in order to allow women to fully enjoy their rights; and
(c) The Commission should recommend to the OAU the nomination of a Special Rapporteur to the Commission who would be responsible for the protection of women's rights.

The Commission entrusted to two of its members the task of to initiating work on an additional protocol on the rights of women.[1]

The Protocol on the Rights of Women in Africa was adopted in July 2003 and came into force on 25 November 2005, one month after its fifteenth ratification. This constituted an important milestone in the recognition of the rights of women in Africa, although daily violations of such rights still continue and cause immense suffering. Shortly, before the adoption of the Protocol, the OAU was also replaced by the

---

[1] African Commission on Human and Peoples' Rights, Report of the 17th session, 1995, pp. 25-26. The Commissioners Dr. Duarte Martin and Prof. Dankwa were designated by the Commission.

African Union. Unlike the OAU Charter, the Constitutive Act of the African Union recognizes in its seventh preambular paragraph "the need to build a partnership between governments and all segments of civil society, in particular women ..." Importantly, among the principles of the African Union set out in Article 4 are the promotion of gender equality (para. *l*); respect for democratic principles, human rights, the rule of law and good governance (para. *m*); and respect for the sanctity of human life, condemnation and rejection of impunity (para. *o*); all of which are essential to the promotion and protection of women's rights. These two instruments have therefore created a new hope for the effective observance of women's rights in the African continent.

3. Rights Specific to African Women/or Simply an African Approach?

The Protocol, in the spirit of other African instruments, sets out the rights of African women in an African context. It consists of a preamble and 32 articles, with the preamble recalling instruments and agreements designed to eliminate all forms of discrimination and promote equality between women and men, but expressing concern that despite these commitments, women in Africa still continue to be victims of discrimination and harmful practices.

The Protocol begins with a definitional provision in which discrimination against women is defined as

"any distinction, exclusion or restriction or any differential treatment based on sex and whose objectives or effects compromise or destroy the recognition, enjoyment or the exercise by women, regardless of their marital status, of human rights and fundamental freedoms in all spheres of life."

This definition is consistent with Article 1 of Part I of the Convention on the Elimination of All Forms of Discrimination against Women (CEDAW), which defines discrimination against women as any distinction, exclusion or restriction made on the basis of sex which has the effect or purpose of impairing or nullifying the recognition, enjoyment or exercise by women, irrespective of their marital status, on a basis of equality of men and women, of human rights and fundamental freedoms in the political, economic, social, cultural, civil or other field. However, the Protocol's definition is much broader as it includes "differential treatment". Importantly, the Protocol unlike CEDAW does not include the phrase "on a basis of equality of men and women," suggesting a conscious and deliberate decision on the part of its drafters to recognize women's *rights* on their own *merits and* distinctly from those of men. Thus, the central focus of the Protocol is to secure women's empowerment and their status as rights-holders and to ensure that those rights are central to the African human rights regime. Through the Protocol, African women can authoritatively demand elimination of laws, practices, conduct, actions, attitudes, etc., that have hitherto discriminated against them directly or indirectly, kept them under subordination and denied them the full enjoyment of their rights and freedoms.

The Protocol contains general provisions derived from the Banjul Charter covering civil, political, economic, social and cultural rights. It also specifically addresses access to justice and equal protection before the law; the right to participation in the political and decision-making process; the right to education and training; economic and welfare rights; the right to adequate housing; the right to a positive cultural context and rights to a healthy and sustainable environment and sustainable development, which are formulated in gender-sensitive terms and take account of the particular requirements which women have to access those rights. Thus, for example, Article 8 relating to access to justice and equal protection before the law, requires the establishment of adequate educational and other appropriate structures with particular attention to women and to sensitize everyone to the rights of women. It also requires that women be represented equally in the judiciary and law enforcement organs. Under Article 13 concerning economic and social welfare, the Protocol requires States Parties to adopt and enforce legislative and other measures to guarantee women equal opportunities in work and career advancement and other economic opportunities, *inter alia* ensuring transparency in recruitment, promotion and dismissal of women and through combating and punishing sexual harassment in the workplace.

The Protocol also contains innovative provisions of specific relevance to African women covering aspects of marriage, security, health and harmful practices. In addition, the Protocol identifies groups of women whose enjoyment of rights has been subject to particular challenges: widows, elderly women, women with disabilities and women in distress.[2] These provisions both recognize the reality of the lives of African women and in some respects establish for them new rights and standards.

Underpinning the Protocol is the recognition of the right of every African woman to dignity and respect, denied through persistent discrimination, stereotypical classification and negative traditions and customs. Article 3 specifically addresses this right. It recognises the right to dignity inherent in a human being and the right to respect as a person and to the free development of her personality. The lack of respect and dignity for women is the essence of the perpetuation of discrimination. Traditions and customs that place limited worth on women are key instruments for discriminatory treatment and violence against women. The following sub-sections examine a number of areas in which African women have been denied their rights and how the Protocol redresses the situation.

3.1. Security

Article 4 establishes for every woman the right to respect for life, integrity and security of person. All forms of exploitation, cruel, inhuman or degrading punishment and treatment are prohibited. States Parties have an obligation to act to end impunity, punish perpetrators of violence against women and implement programmes for the rehabilitation of women victims.[3]

The Protocol's approach to the right to security is three-fold. First, it reaffirms the right to life as a fundamental human right of every woman. Second, the security and integrity of the person of every woman is a human right. The inviolability of the woman's life precludes any form of violence, exploitation, cruel and inhuman or

---

[2] Articles 20-21(m) widows; 22, elderly women; 23, women with disabilities; 24, women in distress.
[3] Article 4(2)(e).

degrading punishment. It requires that every woman has access to basic necessities. Third, the security of every woman invokes State responsibility to intervene to guarantee protection of women's rights.

Violence against women is defined to include

> "all acts perpetrated against women which cause or could cause them physical, sexual, psychological and economic harm, including the threat to take such acts; or to undertake the imposition of arbitrary restrictions on or deprivation of fundamental freedoms in private or public life, in peace time and during situations of armed conflicts or of war."[4]

This deliberately broad definition aims to eliminate all forms of violence, wherever it occurs, including in the private domain. States Parties have a responsibility to protect women. Respect for privacy does not exonerate them from taking the necessary action to protect women from violence.

Article 11 on the protection of women in armed conflict, in acknowledgement of the vulnerability of women refugees, returnees and internally displaced, recognizes the legitimate rights of States Parties to classify rape and other forms of sexual exploitation as war crimes, genocide and/or crimes against humanity. States Parties must act to end impunity, to restore respect for the rule of law and confidence in the justice system. While this article does not articulate specific rights for women, it recalls the rules of international humanitarian law applicable to armed conflict, focusing on the responsibility of the States Parties to protect. This responsibility is invoked in the cases of civilians, including women, asylum seekers, refugees, returnees, internally displaced persons and children, especially girls under the age of 18. The responsibility extends from protection against all forms of violence to preventing children from participating directly in hostilities including as child soldiers, to enacting legislation classifying all forms of violence, rape and other forms of sexual exploitation, as war crimes, genocide and/or crimes against humanity. States Parties are also obliged to end impunity. They must take action to prosecute all perpetrators of such crimes without exception.

---

[4] Article 1(j).

The widespread armed conflicts in Africa have left not only women and girls irreparably damaged, in situation of war, but they have also sown distrust, hatred and divisions within and among communities. Increasingly, community reconciliation, through mechanisms such as the Truth and Reconciliation Commission or the Gacaca Courts or similar processes, takes priority over individual redress. Inadequate attention has been paid to the women emerging out of these conflict situations. Priority must be equally accorded to the redress of the irreparable damage suffered by women survivors of violence, by providing them with effective remedies. It remains to be seen whether through the interpretative authority of the African Court or the monitoring role of the African Commission, this would be addressed.

Linked to women's right to security is their right to peace. Article 10 states that women have the right to a peaceful existence and the right to participate in the promotion and maintenance of peace. States Parties are to take appropriate measures to ensure the increased participation in conflict prevention, peacemaking and peacebuilding and to take the necessary measures to reduce military expenditure significantly in favour of spending on social development in general, and the promotion of women in particular.

3.2. Harmful Practices

Harmful practices against African women have attracted attention in almost every forum where the rights of African women are discussed, be it at the global, regional or national level. In accordance with Article 1, harmful practices include "all behaviour, attitudes and/or practices which negatively affect the fundamental rights of women and girls, such as their right to life, health, dignity, education and physical identity".[5] They are recognized as a form of violence against girls and women. This definition is viewed as an expansion of the ordinary understanding of "harmful practices" to include "negative mindsets". It is clear, however, that by including negative mindsets, the Commission intended to include "the position" adopted by those closely associated with both the victims and the protagonists of the

---

[5] Article 1(g).

harmful practices. The perpetuation of practices that are harmful to girls and women is the direct consequence of an "attitude" of non-intervention, even where evidence clearly demonstrates the serious adverse consequences of such practices. The result is a culture of "indifference". The Protocol seeks to end this culture of "indifference" by holding all with such attitude accountable. States Parties' responsibility and accountability underlies the Protocol and accounts for the detailed provisions on the States Parties' obligations.

Article 5 on the elimination of harmful practices does not create any rights for women *per se*, but imposes an obligation on States Parties to act with due diligence to eliminate harmful practices which negatively affect the human rights of women. Many African States in explaining the inadequate implementation of CEDAW cite traditions and customs as responsible for the perpetuation of harmful practices.[6] The Protocol removes any of these grounds as justification for inaction on the part of the States Parties.

Although Article 5 addresses all forms of harmful practices which negatively affect the human rights of women, such as scarification, it singles out female genital mutilation (FGM), including its medicalization and para-medicalization. FGM is one of the most severe harmful traditional practices against women. It violates the right to dignity and respect[7] and the fundamental right to life in cases where the procedure leads to death. Within the African Commission the elimination of FGM is considered vital to the full enjoyment by women of their human rights.

---

[6] Country reports to CEDAW, e.g. Kenya, South Africa (48th session of the CEDAW Committee) and Ethiopia, Zambia (49th session of the CEDAW Committee). See on the website of the Office of the High Commissioner for Human Rights.

[7] For detailed discussion of FGM and its consequences, see: Orubuloye I.O., "When Culture Harms The Girls: The Globalization of Female Genital Mutilation", Article featured on the website of the Africa Regional Sexuality Resource Centre, 2005.

3.3. Marriage

Article 6 of the Protocol on marriage confirms that the regulation of marital relations falls within the domestic jurisdiction of States Parties. In exercise of that authority, States Parties must ensure that women and men enjoy equal rights and are regarded as equal partners in marriage. However, the validity of a marriage in terms of this article requires the following:
- Free and full consent of both parties;
- Proof that the woman is at a minimum 18 years old; and
- Proof that the marriage has been duly recorded in writing and has been registered.

It follows that States Parties should enact legislative provisions to ensure that child and arranged marriages without the consent of the woman are null and void. Customary and common law marriages must satisfy these provisions in order to be valid. The Protocol recognizes both monogamous and polygamous marriages and expresses a preference for monogamous marriages. This falls short of CEDAW's general recommendation 21 which considers polygamous marriages as a form of discrimination against women as it places women in such a marriage at unequal status, and as such may entrench the unequal situation of women in polygamous marriages.

The article bestows on a married woman the right to choose to retain her maiden name or take that of her husband; to retain her nationality or acquire that of her husband; to acquire, administer and manage her own property during the marriage. With respect to the nationality of their children, however, the equal rights of women and men are subject to national legislation and security interests. Notably, this is the only article in the Protocol containing a claw-back clause. This provision is also inconsistent with Article 9 of CEDAW which grants women equal rights with men with respect to the nationality of their children.

Responsibility for the safeguard of the interests of the family, protection and education of the children is to be shared jointly by both spouses. This article seeks to address the widespread practice of placement of responsibility solely on the woman despite her subordinate status in the family. Significantly, the Protocol creates a legal obligation for the husband *vis-à-vis* responsibility for the support of the family thereby codifying the principle of shared responsibility. Paragraph 1 of Article 13 on Economic and Social Welfare rights reinforces the concept of shared responsibility of parents for the upbringing and development of children but goes further to extend such responsibility, albeit in a secondary capacity only, to the State and the private sector.[8]

In accordance with Article 7, a marriage may only be dissolved through a judicial order at the initiation of either party. Both spouses are guaranteed reciprocal rights and responsibilities towards their children and an equitable sharing of the joint property deriving from the marriage.

3.4. Health and Reproductive Rights

Article 14 of the Protocol on Health and Reproductive Rights, makes clear that the right to health of women, including sexual and reproductive health includes:

(a) The right to control their fertility;

(b) The right to decide whether to have children, the number of children and the spacing of children;

(c) The right to choose any method of contraception;

(d) The right to self-protection and to be protected against sexually transmitted infections, including HIV/AIDS;

(e) The right to be informed of one's health status and of the status of one's partner, particularly if affected with sexually transmitted infections, including HIV/AIDS, in accordance with internationally recognized standards and best practices;

(f) The right to have family planning education.

---

[8] Article 13(e).

States Parties shall take all appropriate measures to:
(a) Provide adequate, affordable and accessible health services, including information, education and communication programmes to women especially those in rural areas;
(b) Establish and strengthen existing pre-natal, delivery and post-natal health and nutritional services for women during pregnancy and while they are breast-feeding;
(c) Protect the reproductive rights of women by authorizing medical abortion in cases of sexual assault, rape, incest, and where the continued pregnancy endangers the mental and physical health of the mother or the life of the mother or the foetus.

Article 14 underscores the futility of the existence of a right that is neither known nor understood by the rights holders. It, therefore, underlines the importance of the dissemination of this right, the provision of guidance and means for its exercise and the support by the States Parties to ensure its enjoyment. Thus, the article provides that States Parties shall take all appropriate measures to provide adequate, affordable and accessible health services, including information, education and communication programmes to women, especially those in rural areas; and establish and strengthen existing pre-natal, delivery and post-natal health and nutritional services for women during pregnancy and while they are breastfeeding.

Article 14 has been hailed as a landmark treaty provision as it "affirms reproductive choice and autonomy as a key human right ... it represents the first time that an international human rights instrument has explicitly articulated a woman's right to abortion ..."[9] This achievement is considered a global victory that extends beyond Africa. It represents a right that applies to women worldwide but a right that is often curtailed or totally denied. It has been suggested that

> "Sub-Saharan Africa has the worst indicators of women's health – particularly of reproductive health – of any world region. These indicators include the highest number of HIV-positive women and the highest

---

[9] See on the website of the Centre for Reproductive Rights, the Protocol on the Rights of Women in Africa: An Instrument for Advancing Reproductive and Sexual Rights.

infant, maternal and HIV-related death rates worldwide. The ability of a woman to make her own decisions regarding her body and her reproductive life is key to improving these indicators."[10]

When women are empowered to take charge and control of their bodies they are better placed to embrace all other rights. For African women whose unequal status has been characterized by limited freedom of expression and decision-making in this realm, article 14 represents a great victory.

3.5. Status of Particular Groups of Women

Several of the Protocol's articles acknowledge the vulnerability of particular groups of women to denial of rights.

The gross injustice experienced by African *widows* in many of the African States is entrenched in negative customs and traditions which leave widows and their children destitute, plunge them deep into poverty and render them vulnerable. Article 20 provides that States Parties shall take appropriate legal measures to ensure that widows enjoy all human rights through ensuring that they are not subjected to inhuman, humiliating or degrading treatment, that they shall automatically become the guardian and custodian of their children after the death of their husbands, unless this is contrary to the interests and welfare of the children and that they shall have the right to remarry and in that event, to marry the person of their choice. Article 21 seeks to address the frequent denial of the rights of widows with respect to property, in particular through the 'grabbing' of the matrimonial home by the husband's relatives. It provides that a widow

> "has the right to an equitable share in the inheritance of the property of her husband. A widow shall have the right to continue to live in the matrimonial house. In case of remarriage, she shall retain this right if the house belongs to her or she has inherited it."[11]
>
> "Women and men shall have the right to inherit, in equitable shares, their parents' properties."[12]

---

[10] *Ibid.*
[11] Article 21(1).
[12] Article 21(2).

Under article 22, States Parties undertake to provide special protection to elderly women, ensuring their rights to freedom from violence, including sexual abuse, discrimination based on age and the right to be treated with dignity. In anticipation of the protection offered by the United Nations Convention on the Rights of Persons with Disabilities adopted by the General Assembly on 13 December 2006, the Protocol in Article 23 calls on States Parties to ensure protection of women with disabilities. Recognizing the multiple discriminations that women and girls with disabilities are subject to, States Parties undertake to ensure their full and equal enjoyment of all their human rights and fundamental freedoms.

The Protocol also recognizes a category of women described as *women in distress* and provides that States Parties undertake to ensure the protection of poor women and women heads of families including women from marginalized population groups and provide them an environment suitable to their condition and their special physical, economic and social needs. It also requires States Parties to ensure the rights of pregnant or nursing women or women in detention by providing them with an environment which is suitable to their condition and the right to be treated with dignity.

The Protocol clearly contains a number of innovative provisions. Yet its main achievements are three-fold. First, it translates the common-standard of achievement enshrined in the Universal Declaration of Human Rights into a legally binding African instrument. Second, it develops many of these standards taking into account the situation of African women. To that end, it might be viewed as creating new rights. Third, it adopts an approach to States Parties' responsibilities and obligations which reflects the economic, social and cultural status of African women. It seeks to achieve a balance between, on the one hand, the preservation of the African value system in the context of the African traditions and customs, and on the other hand avoiding the perpetuation of the negative aspects. It demonstrates the African Union's readiness to chart into new grounds and impose broad obligations on States Parties.

4. Obligations of States Parties

The Protocol obliges States Parties to undertake measures including legislation, training, information dissemination and awareness-raising, and provision of resources to ensure the protection of the rights of women. Although obligations specific to particular rights are contained in Articles 4 to 24 of the Protocol, Article 2 is the core provision which elaborates States' obligations as parties to the Protocol. This article makes clear that States Parties have two essential obligations, first, to combat all forms of discrimination against women; and second, to modify the social and cultural patterns of conduct of women and men, with a view to achieving the elimination of harmful cultural and traditional practices and all other practices which are based on the idea of the inferiority or the superiority of either of the sexes, or on stereotyped roles for women and men. A list of actions to be undertaken by States Parties to meet those obligations are provided in paragraph 1 as follows:

(a) Include in their national constitutions and other legislative instruments, if not already done, the principle of equality between women and men and ensure its effective application;

(b) Enact and effectively implement appropriate legislative and regulatory measures, including those prohibiting and curbing all forms of discrimination, particularly those harmful practices which endanger the health and general well-being of women;

(c) Integrate a gender perspective in their policy decisions, legislation, development plans, programmes and activities and in all other spheres of life;

(d) Take corrective and positive action in those areas where discrimination against women in law and in fact continues to exist;

(e) Support the local, national, regional and continental initiatives directed at eradicating all forms of discrimination against women

The obligations of States Parties are mandatory and extend beyond the public realm into the private sphere.

The obligations elaborated above are consistent with State responsibility under other human rights and humanitarian law to ensure respect of the human rights and freedoms of women, the protection of such rights and the enjoyment of those rights. The States Parties have a duty to take appropriate action to fulfil those rights. By outlining the types of action required, the Protocol seeks to create an environment in which women's human rights and freedoms would be fully respected and enforced. It provides States Parties with benchmarks against which the Commission will review States Parties' periodic reports as well as any claims that might be submitted for its consideration.

The provisions of the Protocol go to the heart of the governance of African States that has historically placed greater importance on the maintenance of cultural and traditional values over women's and girls' human rights and freedoms, and signal a determination to bring an end to that culture.

Under Article 26, States Parties are further obliged to include in their periodic reports to the African Commission under Article 62 of the Banjul Charter, the legislative and other measures undertaken for the full realization of the rights under the Protocol. Finally, States Parties have the obligation to make budgetary and other resources available to ensure the full and effective implementation of the Protocol.

5. Remedies, Implementation and Monitoring

5.1. Remedies

Article 25 provides for remedies to be awarded to any woman whose rights or freedoms under the Protocol are violated. Accordingly, States Parties shall undertake to:
(a) Provide appropriate remedies to any woman whose rights or freedoms, as herein recognized, have been violated;
(b) Ensure that such remedies are determined by competent judicial, administrative or legislative authorities, or by any other competent authority provided for by law.

This article is significant in light of Article 50 of the Banjul Charter setting out conditions precedent to the intervention of the African

Union organs, which include pursuit of remedies through national legal means.

5.2. Implementing and Monitoring

Article 26 of the Protocol calls on States Parties to ensure implementation of its provisions at the national level. It mandates the States Parties to indicate in accordance with Article 62 of the Banjul Charter, in their biennial periodic reports, legislative and other measures undertaken for the full realization of the rights set out in the Protocol. Reporting by States Parties began in 1991, but the weakness of an oversight system that heavily relies on voluntary reporting has unfolded in the case of the Banjul Charter where only about half of the AU Member States have complied. Thus, the role of the two treaty bodies, namely, the African Commission and the African Court assume heightened importance.

The African Court on Human and Peoples' Rights shall be seized with matters of interpretation arising from the application or implementation of the Protocol.[13] However, unlike the Banjul Charter, the Protocol is silent on which body or institution would promote the rights of women and ensure their protection in Africa. In the absence of an express provision, it can be deduced that the enforcement machinery established by the Charter in Part II would apply. Accordingly, the African Commission on Human and Peoples' Rights established in Chapter I of part II of the Banjul Charter would be the enforcement machinery.

The African Commission on Human and Peoples Rights has been granted the responsibility, in accordance with Article 30 of the Banjul Charter, "to promote human and peoples' rights and ensure their protection in Africa". It has both promotional and quasi-judicial functions. Through its promotional function, the Commission has a broad range of options to be undertaken to ensure the observance of human and peoples' rights, including awareness-raising and dissemination of information, organization of seminars, symposia and conferences, undertake studies, issue publications and partner with

---

[13] Article 27.

national institutions. Should the Commission discover in the process of the aforementioned actions any situations that would cause concern or threaten the enjoyment of rights stipulated in the Charter and the Protocol, it has the authority to bring them to the States Parties' attention. The Commission, under this authority has recommended the appointment of thematic or special rapporteurs as well as country rapporteurs, including the Special Rapporteur on the rights of women.

As such the Commission would have a "preventive" role. The provisions of the Charter regarding the role of the Commission, if applied creatively, could very well usher in a new approach to enforcement of human and peoples' rights in Africa, including women's rights.

The quasi-judicial powers of the Commission under Article 45 of the Charter include interpretation of "all the provisions of the present Charter at the request of a State Party, an institution of the OAU or an African Organization recognized by the OAU" (para. 3). However, since the Protocol expressly assigns issues of interpretation to the African Court, the Commission's interpretative function under the Charter would not extend to the Protocol. In the absence of a specific clause in the Protocol governing the formulation of principles and rules aimed at solving legal problems it would be assumed that the provisions of the Charter apply. Accordingly, Article 45, 1(b) which outlines as one of the functions of the Commission "to formulate and lay down, principles and rules aimed at solving legal problems relating to human and people's rights and fundamental freedoms upon which African Governments may base their legislation" applies. Thus, the Commission is empowered to propose both legislation and legal solutions to disputes.

While the Commission's powers for dispute resolution appear to be largely for inter-state complaints, the Commission has, through its individual communications mechanism developed a body of jurisprudence through case law that would be relevant for disputes emanating from the Protocol. Although none of the cases has alleged violation of the provisions of the Protocol, many cases have dealt with the same fundamental civil and political rights stipulated both in the

Banjul Charter and in the Protocol, as well as some which address substantive issues concerning economic, social and cultural rights.[14]

6. Conclusion

The Protocol to the African Charter on Human and Peoples' Rights on the Rights of Women in Africa addresses for the first time, in a comprehensive manner, in a single human rights instrument, the rights and freedoms owed to African women and outlines measures for their promotion and protection. It highlights the need for expeditious action to be taken to end the egregious violation of the human rights and fundamental freedoms of African women.

Yet, the Protocol also exposes the challenges facing African States in discharging their obligation to enforce respect for human and people's rights. It demonstrates the complex relationship between cherished African traditions and culture and human rights. It also shows the weaknesses embedded in the governance structures that are impotent to act decisively against negative traditions and culture that perpetuate the violation of women's rights. The message emanating from the adoption and speedy coming into force of the Protocol is clear. African women are no longer willing to accept the persisting discrimination and violation of their rights and freedoms. They are determined to hold States accountable for the promotion and protection of their human rights.

The Protocol aims not only at achieving equality between men and women through guarantee of women's rights, but also at eliminating the root causes of inequality, including stereotypes, attitudes, as well as negative cultural and traditional values. It seeks to promote improved governance through establishment of standards which, if universally applied throughout Africa, will enhance respect for individual human rights and the rule of law. As of March 2010, only 27 countries had ratified the Protocol.[15] Therefore, efforts must be

---

[14] See *Human Rights Quarterly* 235 (1998).
[15] Angola, Benin, Burkina Faso, Cape Verde, Comoros, Djibouti, Democratic Republic of Congo, Gambia, Ghana, Guinea-Bissau, Libya, Lesotho, Liberia, Mali, Malawi, Mozambique, Mauritania, Namibia, Nigeria, Rwanda, South Africa, Senegal, Seychelles, Tanzania, Togo, Zambia, Zimbabwe.

intensified to obtain the speedy ratification of the Protocol by all African States. Only then would the Protocol truly serve as an African human rights instrument for the benefit of all African women.

Through its rigorous enforcement, the Protocol promises to become the Bill of Rights for African women. In this regard the promotional function of the African Commission on Human and Peoples' Rights is critical. The Protocol would need to be widely disseminated, including to all government and academic institutions. Special attention will need to be paid to rural women.

States Parties must demonstrate their commitment to the Protocol through discharge of the obligations it sets out. The specific actions taken by States Parties must be included in their periodic reports whose timely and regular submission would enable the prompt redress of any human rights violations.

CHAPTER 21.
THE AFRICAN CHARTER ON THE RIGHTS AND WELFARE OF THE CHILD

Chris Maina Peter and Ummy Ally Mwalimu

"It is the duty of parents, caregivers and governments to ensure that all basic rights for children are respected, protected and fulfilled. Care and affection during the first years of life enable a child to thrive. For young infants, holding, cuddling and talking to them stimulates growth."
Sosthenes Paulo Mwita[1]

1. Introduction

When the African Charter on Human and Peoples' Rights was adopted in 1981, the issue of the rights of the child were not addressed seriously. This can be explained by the main focus of this instrument i.e. the violations of human rights by the African dictators of the 1970s. Therefore, one finds a brief sweeping reference to children in the Charter.[2] Therefore, the adoption of the African Charter on the Rights and Welfare of the Child in 1990 was, *inter alia*, an attempt to make up for this relative neglect.

---

[1] Mwita S.P., "Mind That Child: Every Child Must Enjoy Parental Protection," *Daily News* (Tanzania), 12 August 2006, p. 7.
[2] Article 18 of the African Charter on Human and Peoples' Rights, in Ouguergouz F., *The African Charter on Human and Peoples' Rights: A Comprehensive Agenda for Human Dignity and Sustainable Democracy in Africa*, The Hague/ London and New York: Martinus Nijhoff Publishers, 2003.

However, the way to the Charter was not smooth as many would like to believe. The process began back in 1979 during the 16th Ordinary Session of the Assembly of the Heads of State and Government of the then Organization of African Unity (OAU) meeting in Monrovia, Liberia. A Declaration on the Rights and Welfare of the African Child was adopted which, *inter alia*, recognised the need to take all appropriate measures to promote and protect the rights and welfare of the child. However, the process was to take exactly 20 years before a binding Convention was prepared, adopted, ratified and became operational.

As the Draft was being discussed within the OAU, Member States kept on raising various issues which should be taken aboard. Among them were that the Draft should take into account and reflect the economic and social conditions in Africa adequately; and take note that more than 50% of the overall population of the continent were young people and that in some countries 55% of the population were younger than eighteen. Yet others wanted that the rights of children born out of wedlock be specified in the Draft as well as the rights of the parents over their children. There was also a group of member States who wanted an implementation strategy of the Charter be agreed upon before the approval of the Charter. All these and other concerns raised by Members States were seriously addressed and discussed during the preparatory phase of the Charter.

Eventually, the African Charter on the Rights and Welfare of the Child was adopted by the twenty sixth Assembly of Heads of State and Government of the OAU on 11 July 1990 in Addis Ababa, Ethiopia.[3] It came into force on 29 November 1999 and, at the time of writing this Chapter, there were thirty-nine (39) out of fifty-three (53) African States which became parties to the Charter.[4] The latest member to deposit instruments of ratification was the Republic of Congo.[5]

---

[3] OAU Doc. CAB/LEG/24.9/49 (1990).
[4] Status of Ratification of treaties and conventions on the website of the African Union.
[5] Members of the African Union which have not ratified the Charter to date include: Central African Republic, Côte d'Ivoire, Djibouti, Democratic Republic of the Congo, Gabon, Guinea-Bissau, Liberia, Saharawi Arab Democratic

The Charter is the first regional treaty on the human rights of children. A number of reasons have been advanced for the adoption of the Charter less than a year after the adoption of the United Nations Convention on the Rights of the Child (CRC) in 1989.[6] The most obvious reason given for a separate African Charter on the Rights and Welfare of the Child was the belief that Africa was under-represented during the drafting process of United Nations Convention on the Rights of the Child of 1989. Only Algeria, Morocco, Senegal and Egypt participated meaningfully in the drafting process. The CRC was also considered, in the search for consensus between States from diverse backgrounds, to have omitted some important aspects in relation to children in the African context. Some of the peculiarities of the African situation omitted from the CRC were identified as the situation of children living under the then prevailing *Apartheid* regime in South Africa, practices and attitudes having a negative effect on the life of the girl child and widespread practices in African society such as female genital mutilation. Other issues not considered by the CRC were problems of displaced persons arising from internal conflicts, the African conception of the community's responsibilities and duties and the particularly difficult socio-economic conditions of the continent. The CRC was also perceived to negate the role of the family, especially the extended family, in its treatment of the upbringing of the child and in matters of adoption and fostering.[7]

    Republic, Somalia, Sao Tome & Principe, Sudan, Swaziland, Tunisia, and Zambia.

[6] United Nations General Assembly Resolution 44/25 of 20 November 1989. This Convention has been widely accepted by the members of the international community. It came into force in September 1990. At present 192 States are parties to the Convention, with Somalia and the United States of America being the only UN Member States not to have ratified the Convention.

[7] On the Convention on the Right of the Child of 1989 and its implementation see *inter alia*, Hodgkin R. and Newell P., *Implementation Handbook for the Convention on the Rights of the Child*, New York: United Nations Children's Fund, 2002; Kijo-Bisimba H., *Rights of the Child: An Assessment of the United Nations Convention on the Rights of the Child and Its Implementation and Enforceability in Tanzania*, Master of Laws Dissertation, University of Dar es Salaam, 1994; Verhellen E., *Convention on the Rights of the Child: Background, Motivation, Strategies, Main Themes*, Leuven: Garant, 2000; Concepcion N.P., "The Convention on the Rights of the Child after Ten Years: Success or Failure?" *Human Rights Brief* 7 (2000) 2, p. 2; and Detrick S., *A Commentary on*

Accordingly, the African Charter seeks to complement the UN Convention on the Rights of the Child, taking into account social and cultural values of Africa and offering protection against violations of children's rights. It combines African values with international norms by proclaiming collective rights and individual duties. These include the duty of individuals to their family, community and State. The uniqueness of the Charter is to be found in the originality of its normative content. It covers civil and political rights as well as economic, social and cultural rights and some protective rights that are specific to children. Furthermore, the African Charter covers third generation rights, and gives due importance to the assumption that a person has duties as well as rights in the community.

The aim of this Chapter is to examine the African Charter on the Rights and Welfare of the Child of 1990. The main focus is on substantive provisions of the Charter. In this process, we will also examine to what extent the Charter has increased the standard of children's rights already attained under the UN Convention on the Rights of the Child. The African Committee of Experts on the Rights and Welfare of the Child (ACERWC) has already become operational as a tool in implementing the rights of the child in Africa.[8] Therefore, the role of the Committee is given substantial consideration as well.

2. Salient Features of the African Charter on the Rights and Welfare of the Child

2.1. Defining the Child

The definition of the child under the Charter is contained in Article 2. It is one of the most advanced features of the Charter. Every person under the age of eighteen is regarded as a child falling within the scope of the Charter. Unlike the CRC, the Charter is very clear and does not allow for any limitations on the concept of childhood by including phrases such as "unless majority is attained

---

the United Nations Convention on the Rights of the Child, The Hague/ Boston and London: Martinus Nijhoff Publishers, 1999.

[8] Members of the Committee were first appointed by the 37th Assembly of Heads of State and Government of the OAU on 10 July 2001 in Lusaka, Zambia.

earlier." The Charter therefore applies to every person below the age of 18. Traditionally, in many African societies, the termination of childhood has very little to do with the attainment of any predetermined age but with the physical capacity to perform acts which are normally reserved for adults: e.g. initiation ceremonies, or marriage. In this way, the Charter's notion of childhood may be said to clash with the African traditional cultural understanding.

Even though the Charter's provision defining childhood may appear disconnected from African traditional concepts, the wording of Article 2 is clear and therefore provides a comprehensive protection for all persons under the age of 18 years who are deemed to be in need of protection. Therefore it must be said that the Charter is more advanced than the CRC in so far as its definition on childhood is absolute and does not allow for any exceptions.

2.2. Obligations of the State Parties

The general obligations of the States Parties are provided under Article 1 of the Charter. Member States of the OAU parties to this Charter "shall recognize the rights of the child and undertake to take the necessary steps, in accordance with their constitutional processes and with the provisions of the Charter, to adopt such legislative and other measures as may be necessary to give effect to the provisions of the Charter." These obligations entail combination of both negative and positive duties to make sure that the rights are realised.

It must be noted that the Charter does not explicitly distinguish between civil and political rights and economic, social and cultural rights. While the CRC states that socio-economic rights shall be given effect only to the maximum extent of the available resources, Article 1 of the Charter does not contain such a limitation. Nevertheless, in the more specific provisions of the Charter dealing with socio-economic rights, limitations related to the availability of resources seem to be permissible. Article 11(3) on the right to education and Article 13(3) on the rights of handicapped children could illustrate this argument. These illustrative Articles contain rights that could be categorized as socio-economic and speak of progressive realization. It can be assumed, therefore, that even though the distinction between categories of rights is less obvious in the Charter, such a distinction can nonetheless be found underlying certain of the Charter's provisions.

Furthermore, it must be noted that Article 1 of the Charter stipulates that the rights enshrined therein shall be regarded as the minimum standard rights and shall not hinder the effectiveness of rights contained in other instruments which grant a higher level of protection than the Charter itself. This suggests that the Charter recognizes that its level of protection may be complemented by other human rights instruments.

Article 1(3) of the Charter puts an obligation on African States Parties to discourage certain behaviours which are inconsistent with the Charter's provisions. This provision is very important in the African context where potentially harmful religious and cultural practices are widely carried out.

3. The Rights and Freedoms of the Child Under the Charter

3.1. Protection of the Most Vulnerable Children

3.1.1. Handicapped Children

Special provision is made for disabled children under Article 13 of the Charter which states that the disabled child shall have the right to special measures of protection. The wording of the Charter, in comparison with the CRC, is very specific and narrow as CRC provides a broad and unspecific provision by stating that a disabled child should enjoy a full and decent life. This does not necessarily mean that the State has to undertake special measures to provide for such rights. The Charter makes ample provision for the protection of the most vulnerable children and imposes clear obligations on States Parties to respect and ensure respect with regard to the rights and special measures of protection of such vulnerable children.

A disabled child is, therefore, entitled under the Charter to receive the special assistance of the State even if his or her parents live in circumstances that would permit them to care for the needs of the child and without help from the State. This could translate into a higher level of protection for the child because the circle of persons eligible for State's assistance is wider.

Article 13(2) lists facilities and services to which the disabled child should have access. They include access to training, preparation for employment and recreation opportunities in a manner conducive to the child achieving the fullest possible social integration, individual development and cultural and moral development.

With regard to the listed facilities and services to which the disabled child should have access, it should be noted that the Charter left out education, health care services and rehabilitation services as provided by CRC. Even though education is catered for in Article 11 of the Charter, which applies to all children including disabled children, it must be borne in mind that the educational needs of children with disabilities are different from those of non-handicapped children. Omission of the word education in Article 13(2) is therefore regrettable.

Article 13(3) aims at guaranteeing mobility of the disabled child and his or her access to public institutions or facilities. This right, however, is subject to the availability of resources and progressive realisation. This provision should be regarded as being of utmost importance to the realisation of the rights of children with disabilities not only in Africa but also everywhere in the world.

3.1.2. Children in Custody

Administration of juvenile justice is covered under Article 17 of the Charter. This article provides for special treatment of children *accused or found guilty* of having infringed penal law in a manner consistent with the child's sense of dignity and worth and which reinforces the child's respect for human rights and fundamental freedoms of others. This provision of the Charter is vital because it covers children who have already been convicted and those whose fate has not been decided by the relevant judicial institutions. These include those detained on mere suspicion of having committed an offence or a crime. As the general law presumes every accused person innocent until the contrary is proved, children in this category deserve special protection and in such cases Article 17 should be seen as an important fall-back position to rescue them. Due to the vagaries of detention and what can happen to young children in such circumstances, it is important for State authorities to ensure that children accused of having infringed the law are guaranteed the highest level of protection.

Article 17(2) provides for separation of imprisoned or detained children from imprisoned or detained adults. Principles of presumption of innocence, access to legal assistance as well as impartial tribunals are also covered therein.

Furthermore, the Charter contains provisions on how to deal with a child appearing before the judicial organs of the State.[9] In order to protect such a child, the public and the media should be kept out of the trial.[10] It is emphasised that the handling of the child during the arrest, trial and incarceration should be aimed at reforming such a child so as to be able to re-integrate him or her into the family and society and be easily rehabilitated.

3.1.3. Children in Armed Conflict

The Charter provides a progressive development on the protection of a child victim of armed conflict. Article 22(1) vests obligations on African governments to respect and ensure respect for rules of international humanitarian law applicable in armed conflicts which affect the child. The words "which affect" could mean that States Parties should take into account not only children in armed conflicts but other forms of hostilities, tensions and strives. This could spell out an obligation of the State party to use all diplomatic or other internationally lawful means to ensure respect of this law wherever armed conflicts occur. Such measures could consist of the use of economic pressure, humanitarian help or the participation in actions undertaken by the United Nations. In this respect, the obligation set out by the Charter exceeds the one contained in the CRC in protecting children worldwide.

Furthermore, the Charter prohibits recruitment of any child and therefore of any person under the age of 18 years into any military

---

[9] Article 17(3) of the Charter.
[10] Article 17(2)(d) of the Charter.

undertaking.[11] Article 22(3) explicitly states that the rules set out in Article 22 are applicable in situations of internal armed conflict. The armed conflict need therefore not be an international or a cross border incursion. This provision is of particular relevance to African conflicts which are mostly internal armed conflicts and it provides for a comprehensive protection of the child in such situations.

3.1.4. Refugee Children

Article 23 provides for a specific protection and care to refugee children. States Parties, when dealing with refugees, are requested to take care, as a matter of priority, of children seeking refugee status. They shall make sure that refugee children receive appropriate protection and humanitarian assistance in the enjoyment of the rights set out in the Children's Charter. Similar to the CRC, States Parties are obliged to cooperate with existing international organizations which protect and assist refugees in their efforts to protect and assist an unaccompanied refugee child, including tracing their parents or other close relatives for the purpose of family reunifications. Where parents or close relatives cannot be found, then the States Parties take the responsibility to provide special protection and assistance to the unaccompanied refugee child. It is important to stress that under the African children's Charter the protection is extended to internally displaced children whether through natural disaster, internal armed conflict or any other reason. Nothing similar is found in the CRC.

3.1.5. Adopted Children

Article 24 of the Charter covers adoption. It provides for States Parties to recognize the system of adoption and therefore places an obligation on States to establish competent authorities in accordance with applicable law and procedures to determine matters of adoption. The Charter provides that inter-country adoption should be considered as a matter of last resort. This means that if there are no other suitable

---

[11] Article 22(2) of the Charter.

means of caring for a child in his or her own country, the Charter provides that an inter-country adoption should be possible.

This provision of the Charter requires States to take all appropriate measures to ensure that inter-country adoption and placement does not result in trafficking or improper financial gains for those involved. Finally, the Charter obliges States to provide for appropriate monitoring of the well being of the adopted child.

3.1.6. Children Separated From Parents

Article 25 provides safeguards for a child separated permanently or temporarily from his or her parents. Different possibilities for alternative family care are listed under Article 25(2). These include foster placement or placement in suitable institutions for the care of children. Reunification of children with parents and relatives in the case of internal or external displacement caused by armed conflict or natural disasters can also be found in Article 22(2). Article 22(3) focuses on alternative family care of the child and the best interests of the child. Thus, due regard must be paid to the desirability of continuity in a child's upbringing and to the child's ethnic, religious or linguistic background.

4. The Responsibilities of the Parents and Guardians Under the Charter

Article 20 of the Charter spells out the duties of parents or other persons responsible for the child who are vested with primary responsibility for the upbringing and development of the child. Contrary to CRC, the Charter avoids the term "legal guardian" and instead uses the expression "other persons responsible for the child". This is very relevant in the African context where the care of the children particularly in rural areas lies with the extended family or with the tribal or rural community rather than with parents or legal guardians. It may be argued that, under this formulation, it may not be possible to impose real legal duties on people who care only *de facto* for a child without having the legal responsibilities for doing so. Nonetheless, the most important consideration is to ensure the best interest of the child is the basic concern at all times for those responsible, who should secure within their abilities and financial capacities, conditions of living necessary to the child's development and ensure that domestic discipline is administered with humanity and in a manner consistent with the inherent dignity of the child.

5. The Responsibilities of the Child Under the Charter

The Charter's unique feature is the inclusion of the concept of children's responsibilities. These are contained in Article 31. Concerns may be raised with regard to the obligation of the child to respect his parents, superiors and elders at all times. For instance, it could be argued that this responsibility to respect elders at all time is too unquestioning and general and that there is a contradiction in the Charter in so far as children have to respect their parents even in cases where these parents abuse them. It should however be observed that rights and duties in the Charter are meant to complement and balance each other. Thus, the duty of the child to obey, for example, could be said to be balanced by the prohibition of harmful cultural practices. It should therefore be emphasized that the child's duty must be viewed within the context of the whole Charter where duties would have to be given content in this way to be harmonised with the framework of already established rights.

6. Implementation of the African Charter on the Rights and Welfare of the Child

The African Charter on the Rights of the Child establishes the African Committee of Experts on the Rights and Welfare of the Child as a supervisory mechanism for the realisation of Children's rights in Africa.[12] The Committee is composed of 11 members elected by the Assembly of Heads of State and Government of the African Union. Members of the African Committee should be of high moral standing, integrity, impartiality and competence. Members serve in their

---

[12] Article 32 of the Charter.

personal capacities and the Committee is not supposed to include more than one national of the same State.[13]

Article 37 provides for the term of office by stating that the members of the Committee are elected for a term of five years, but unlike the African Commission, may not be re-elected. The Committee shall meet at least once a year. The first ordinary session was held in July 2001. Subsequent sessions have so far been convened once every two years, instead of once a year, perhaps for financial reasons.

The Committee's functions are to promote and protect the rights enshrined in the Charter, monitor their implementation and ensure their respect, interpret the provisions of the Charter at the request of the State Parties, institutions of the OAU/AU or any other institutions, and, finally, to carry out any other duties entrusted to it by the Assembly of Heads of State and Government, the Secretary General of the OAU/AU or any other organ of the Organization.[14]

According to its mandate, the Committee is empowered to receive and examine the reports submitted by State parties on the measures they have adopted in order to give effect to the provisions of the Charter as well as the progress achieved in the exercise of the rights recognized.[15] States Parties undertake to submit reports on measures they have adopted to give effect to the provisions of the Charter within a period of two years after the Committee starts its work, and every three years thereafter.[16]

The Charter also authorises the Committee of Experts to receive and consider complaints against States.[17] Grievances against States Parties may concern any issue covered by the Charter, and may be submitted by any person, group or non-governmental organization (NGO) recognised by the OAU/AU, a Member State or the UN. The individual petition provided by the Children's Charter means that, where a child as a family member suffers a violation, as a result of the violation of the family's socio-economic rights, then the family either

---

[13] Article 33 of the Charter.
[14] Article 42 of the Charter.
[15] Article 43 of the Charter.
[16] Ibid.
[17] Article 44 of the Charter.

as a unit or through individual family members is able to seek a direct remedy before the Committee.

The other protective function of the Committee is relating to the investigations procedure. Under Article 45 of the Charter, the Committee is empowered to resort to any appropriate method of investigation in respect of any issue covered by the Charter. The Committee is supposed to submit before each ordinary session of the Assembly of the Heads of State and Government a report on its activities and on any communication made under Article 46 of the Charter. The Committee may publish its report after it has been considered by the Assembly of the Heads of State.

Furthermore, it should be mentioned that the established African Court on Human and Peoples' Rights has power to enforce the rights under the Children's Charter. According to Article 3(1) of the Protocol establishing the Court,

> "the jurisdiction of the Court shall extend to all cases and disputes submitted to it concerning the interpretation and application of the Charter, this Protocol and any other relevant human rights instrument ratified by the States concerned."[18]

The complaints procedure provided for by the Charter is a significant step forward compared to the UN Convention on the Rights of the Child which has no such procedure. It is too early, at this juncture, to evaluate the effectiveness of the Committee in protecting and promoting rights of African child, but as its work progresses, an assessment of its effectiveness will have to be undertaken.

7. Omissions and Shortcomings of the African Children's Charter

A number of omissions and shortcomings may be noted with respect to the contents of the Charter as a comprehensive instrument for protecting children's rights in Africa. One of the most noticed omissions is in the field of juvenile justice. The Charter does not

---

[18] See the Protocol to the African Charter on Human and Peoples' Rights Establishing the African Court on Human and Peoples' Rights adopted by the 34th Ordinary Session of the Assembly of the Heads of State and Government of the Organization of African Unity in Ouagadougou in 1998.

contain sufficient provisions to guarantee children's liberty. Comparatively, the UN Convention on the Rights of the Child contains extensive safeguards for the child and in particular where the child faces juvenile justice. His or her liberty is secured against arbitrary or unlawful curtailment.[19] The Charter is silent on this and does not repeat the provision or its substantive content in any of its Articles. The omission is unfortunate, as it seems that there is no such guarantee and a child can simply be deprived of his or her liberty. Relating to the field of juvenile justice, the Charter does not include any provisions that would ensure arrest, detention or imprisonment of the child is used only as a last resort and for the shortest period of time. In short, Article 17 is just too limited to be of much help to the child in distress. There is also no provision prescribing that life imprisonment without the possibility of release is prohibited with regard to children.

Equally missing in the Charter is a provision which guarantees legal remedies for children deprived of their liberty. It is widely recognised that this kind of provisions are an essential and integral part of the principle of the rule of law. The omission can nevertheless be traced to the fact that while the Charter guarantees a number of rights to be enjoyed by children, it cannot be assumed that children deprived of their liberty shall have no possibility of appealing against such detention before a competent authority. This would be contrary to all the children's rights guaranteed by the Charter.

Furthermore, as the Charter guarantees the right to life of every child, it does not provide clear guidance as to when the human life that is protected starts. It therefore takes no stance on the issue of abortion and leaves this topic open for individual and different approaches in culturally different States.

The Charter does not contain specific provisions regarding the development of the child. Even though Article 5 appears under the heading survival and development, development is only briefly mentioned in Article 5(2). This type of provision is of utmost relevance in the African context as it would help to guarantee that every child has a right to a standard of living adequate to his or her

---

[19] See Article 40 of the Charter.

development. The primary responsibility for this lies with the parents, but the States Parties also have the obligation to assist them in fulfilling this duty even in the form of material assistance. This however could be explained by the lack of financial resources that most African countries suffer. African States are therefore reluctant to undertake such an obligation that could imply massive financial burden on their part. Such fears however could have been overcome if one takes into account the built in claw-back clauses contained in Article 11 in relation to the rights of the child to education and Article 20 on the duty of the State to assist deserving parents to bring up their children responsibly.

Another important provision missing in the Charter relates to the duty to materially maintain the child. This can be particularly crucial in situations where a child is born out of wedlock and the biological parents of such child are not living together. The UN Convention on the Rights of the Child covers this duty in Article 27(4) which provides for the payment of maintenance by parents or other responsible persons and the enforceability of such monetary claims. It remains unclear as to why the drafters of the African Charter omitted such an important safeguard.

Another omission relates to the protection of the child from all forms of physical or mental injury or abuse, neglect or maltreatment including sexual abuse while in care of a parent, legal guardian or any other person who has the care of the child. Article 16 is too narrow when it comes to taking *social and educational* measures to protect the child against any such abuse and/or torture. The Charter only takes into consideration *legislative and administrative measures* for the purpose of implementation. It is not clear why the Charter ignored the importance of social and educational measures to combat child exploitation which is very common in many African communities. In reality, legislative and administrative measures are not enough to address this problem. Such communities would need to be educated in order for them to appreciate and realize that child exploitation is not good.

In conclusion, it can therefore be said although the Charter does not include some important provisions which are to be found in the CRC, it remains a progressive instrument for protection of children's rights in Africa. As such, it may be safely stated that the Charter does not detract from the CRC but rather complements it.

8. Conclusion

This Chapter has addressed the contribution of the African Charter on the Rights and Welfare of the Child of 1990 to the improvement of the rights of the child in the African continent. There is no doubt that this Charter has contributed to a very large extent to improve the situation of the child in Africa.

There is no doubt that the adoption of the Charter is a positive step towards securing the protection of children's rights in Africa. It has improved on areas where the United Nations Convention adopted a year before could but did not go into, for instance, with regard to the definition of the "child". This decision was monumental because for instance now member States cannot authorise their nationals to marry off young children and hide behind national culture and traditions under municipal law. It thus fully protects the child against the vagaries of national jurisdictions.

The Charter recognises the child's unique and privileged place in African society and the African children's need for protection and special care. It seeks to guarantee a number of civil, political, economic, social and cultural rights comparable to those protected by the UN Convention on the Rights of the Child. It also aims to protect the private life of the child and safeguard the child against all forms of economic exploitation and against work that is hazardous, or otherwise interferes with the child's education, or compromises his or her health, or physical, social, mental, spiritual and moral development.

The best interest of the child is the primary consideration of the Charter. The participation and recruitment of children in armed conflict is prohibited. Harmful social and cultural practices are to be eliminated. These include the widely practiced female genital mutilations which has profound effects on the health of women and girls. Child marriages are expressly prohibited but curiously the age bar is set somewhat high at eighteen years.

In relation to refugee children, the Charter adheres to the broad definition of the refugee status as contained in the OAU Convention on Refugee of 1967. The prohibition of child labour is somewhat equivocal, however, requiring State Parties only to adopt legislation and administrative measures to combat this problem, which may be considered inadequate.

Although critics argued that the protection offered by the Charter is not generally as effective as under the CRC, the Charter yields in those situations where it may be considered not to equal national and international standards. Furthermore, in keeping with the African concept of rights, the Charter imposes responsibilities on the child towards his or her family, the community and the State. On the other hand, the measures required of States Parties are more extensive than those of the CRC.

The Charter makes provision for an implementation mechanism. The mandate of the African Committee of Experts on the Rights and Welfare of the Child is positive, broader and better defined than that of the UN CRC. A potentially significant achievement which is not mirrored in the CRC confers upon the Committee jurisdiction to entertain communications from persons, groups, or NGOs relating to the Charter. One could say plainly that the mandate of the African Committee of Experts compares favourably with that of the UN Committee.

In conclusion, it can therefore be said that the Charter should be viewed as a positive development on the whole. It does not detract from the CRC but rather complements it.

CHAPTER 22.
THE CONVENTION GOVERNING THE SPECIFIC ASPECTS OF REFUGEE PROBLEMS IN AFRICA

Osita C. Eze †

1. Introduction

African Refugees, as refugees from all over the globe, are a very vulnerable group. For several reasons, they have fled from their countries of nationality or habitual residence. Until they are granted asylum, which is not automatic and which for various reasons has lately become more problematic, there is no State to ensure their welfare and security. The United Nations system, particularly through the agency of the High Commissioner for Refugees (UNHCR), supplemented by the African Convention on Refugees, fills some of the gap but it serves better as a compliment to State efforts where asylum has been granted. Typically such States have to contend with social, economic, political and security problems associated with the presence of refugees.[1]

Various agencies work to supervise and ensure the implementation of the various refugee regimes namely:

- The United Nations High Commissioner for Refugees with respect to the United Nations Convention (1951) and Protocol (1971);

---

[1] See the Khartoum Declaration on Africa's refugee Crisis, September 1990, paragraph 2, for the text of the Declaration see Institute for Human Rights and Development, *Compilation of Human Rights Instruments*, Gambia, 2000, pp. 192-194.

A.A. Yusuf & F. Ouguergouz (eds.), *The African Union: Legal and Institutional Framework. A Manual on the Pan-African Organization*, 495-518.

- The United Nations High Commissioner for Refugees in Collaboration with the OAU/AU with respect to the UN regime and the African Convention;
- The African Commission and Court on Human and Peoples' Rights with respect to the regime under the African Charter on Human and People Rights;
- The Regional Economic Communities (RECs) also act in collaboration with the United Nations High Commissioner for Refugees with respect to the implementation of both the UN and OAU Conventions';
- The national institutions work hand-in-hand with both the UN and the OAU to implement the refugee regimes.

Apart, therefore, from the conventions, laws and agreement that regulate asylum in Africa, it is necessary to ascertain how their conditions have been ameliorated. It is also important at this point to indicate that the extensive discussion of the UN Convention and Protocol is motivated by the fact that both the OAU Convention and many national legislations "incorporate" and apply them as norms governing refugees.

The evolution of the international regime for the protection of refugees did not at the initial phase concern itself with Africa. It dealt with the peculiar problems that existed in Europe before 1951 and even when by the 1967 Protocol it extended its reach to Africa, being propelled in part, by the then ongoing African Project on a special Refugee Convention, it still fell short of dealing with the specific problems of Africa. It is true to state, however, that before 1960, when most of Africa was under colonial rule, there were no serious refugee problems as the authoritarian colonial regimes ensured control over their respective territories. With the wars of national liberation there emerged mass movements of people across national boundaries with Africa having from the 60s to the 80s and beyond the largest (over 5 million) refugee flows occasioned by, internal strife (resource, ethnic, communal and religious), border conflicts and other forms of inter-State conflicts. Currently, there has been a shift to intra-State (Non-international armed conflicts) as the main cause of refugees in Africa.

These conflicts have to be situated in the context of underlying casual factors:

- Bad governance (both political and economic) including flagrant denial and violation of rights;
- Inability or unwillingness to ensure social justice within and between groups within the State;
- Deepening and perverse poverty even in oil rich countries;
- Inequality in distribution of resources and access to means of production and public offices;
- Continuing underdevelopment in various sectors – education, health care, shelter, employment, industry and agriculture;[2]
- All compounded by globalization that has not only promoted Africa's underdevelopment but has also made refugee flows from Africa to the industrialized countries, already less favoured, more difficult, as well as reduced the flow of humanitarian aid towards Africa.

It is in the context of these developments that African countries will have to contend with protecting African refugees by:

- Providing them adequate security including protection against attacks from their home States;

---

[2] For the assessment of the problems by the African Heads of State and Government in 1990, see The Khartoum Declaration on the Refugees, *op. cit.*, where it stated: "Africa fully realizes that the major root causes of the refugee problem are situated within Africa, and that the total eradication of these causes is the primary responsibility of the African themselves. However, considering the critical economic situation facing the Continent as reflected and articulated in the Lagos Plan of action and the final Act of Lagos, the African Priority Programme for Economic recovery (APPER), and the United Nations Programme of Action for African Economic Recovery and Development (UNPAAERD), it is clear that Africa's capacity to handle the problem is limited especially considering that the majority of the World's Least Developed Countries are situated in Africa. This glaring fact has been recognized by the international community, particularly in the International Conference on Assistance to Refugees in Africa IGARA 1 and 11, the International conference on the Plight of Refugees, Returnees and Displaced Persons in Southern Africa (SARRED), as well as the United Nations system. Additionally, the African refugee crisis was extensively deliberated by the 26th Summit of the African Heads of State and government as reflected in their Declaration on the political and Socio-Economic Situation in Africa and the Fundamental Changes taking place in the World." (Paragraph 2).

- Ensuring the provision of basic needs – means of livelihood, food, shelter, healthcare, education, which takes due account of the special needs of women, children and the aged, as well as the need for families to be together as a unit, without offending the sensibilities of those who reside in the environment where they are located;
- Protecting them from abuse and exploitation and generally ensuring that their rights are guaranteed.

The legal regime on refugees in part responds to the problems that refugees may encounter and it is to this that we shall now turn.

2. The Meaning of the Term "Refugee"

While the focus of this Chapter is on the African Convention on Refugees it must be placed in the context of the global standard setting UN Convention of 1951 and the Protocol of 1967. Members of the OAU/AU who had not signed these instruments were urged to do so for the African Convention adds and supplements, from an African perspective, these basic and universal instruments relating to the status of refugees. Given the wider and more intensive interpretation and application of the UN instruments, they provide also a guide for understanding the meaning of refugee in Article 1 of the African Convention.

It is mainly those who qualify as refugees that are entitled to protection. Under certain circumstances, non-convention refugees may benefit. The term "refugee" is not defined by customary international law. The meaning of the word would thus have to be gathered from several of the international agreements dealing with refugees. A comprehensive definition is to be found in the Statute of the Office of the United Nations High Commissioner for Refugees (the UNHCR Statute), adopted by the UN General Assembly on 14 December 1950. The UN Convention of 1951 has adopted a similar definition. In both instruments certain categories of refugees are specified as being entitled to the protection and facilities provided therein.

2.1 The UN Instruments

Under the UN Convention the term "refugee" is defined to include any person who

"has been considered a refugee under the arrangements of 12 May 1926 and 30 June 1928 or under the Convention of 28 October 1933 and 10 February 1938, the Protocol of 14 September 1939 or the Constitution of the International Refugee Organisation" (UN Convention, Article 1A(1); UNHCR Statute, Article 6 A(i)).

It is clear from the wording of this provision that for a person to qualify as a refugee he must have been recognized as such under the relevant conventions or instruments. While restrictive and liberal interpretations are possible, it would seem in view of the humanitarian aspect of refugee protection that a more liberal interpretation would be preferred. This is more so if one takes into account the Recommendation of the Final Act of 28 July 1951, in which the Conference of Plenipotentiaries expressed the hope

"that the Convention relating to the Status of Refugees will have value as an example exceeding its contractual scope and that all nations will be guided by it in granting so far as possible to persons in their territory as refugees and who would not be covered by the terms of the convention, the treatment for which it provides."

This line of reasoning is also supported by the fact that the United Nations General Assembly has by its various resolutions authorized the High Commissioner for Refugees to use his good offices for the benefit of refugees who did not come within the competence of the United Nations. That is, those refugees who do not come within the conventional meaning of the term. The manner of interpretation will, in any case, ultimately depend on the authority with the competence to determine refugee status.

A reservation was made, however, in relation to those refugees who had not been considered as qualifying for the purposes of the International Refugee Organization. In such cases, the negative decision of the IRO "shall not prevent the status of refugee being accorded to persons who fulfill the conditions of paragraph 2 of this section" (UN Convention, Article 1 A(1); Statute of UNHCR, Article 6A(ii)).

Paragraph 2 of Article 1(A) of the UN Convention in effect gives a general definition of refugees, and this definition is substantially adopted in the OAU Convention on Refugees. The provisions of this paragraph as formulated in the UN Convention, as will become evident from what follows, were intended to apply only to those who became refugees as a result of events occurring before 1 January 1951. This time limitation has, however, been eliminated in the definition of refugees as embodied in the Protocol relating to the Status of Refugees of 31 January 1967, which came into force on 4 October 1967.

Article 1(A)(2) of the UN Convention defines "refugee" for the purposes of the Convention as a person who

"as a result of events occurring before 1 January 1951 and owing to well-founded fear of being persecuted for reasons of race, religion, nationality or political opinion is outside the country of his nationality and is unable or, owing to such fear, is unwilling to avail himself of the protection of that country, or who not having a nationality and being outside the country of his former habitual residence as a result of such events is unwilling to return to it" (UN Convention, Article 1A(2); Statute of UNHCR, Article 6A(ii); OAU Convention).

2.2 The African Convention

Article 1(1) of the OAU Convention contains the following definition:

"For the purposes of this Convention, the term "refugee" shall mean every person who, owing to well-founded fear of being persecuted for reasons of race, religion, nationality, membership of a particular social group or political opinion, is outside the country of his nationality and is unable or, owing to such fear, is unwilling to avail himself of the protection of that country, or who, not having a nationality and being outside the country of his former habitual residence as a result of such events is unable or owing to such fear is unwilling to return to it."

This provision is clearly based on the UN Convention's Article 1(A)(2) and the manner in which a "refugee" is defined there.

The African Convention contains, however, an additional provision, which is probably intended to cater for the peculiarities of Africa, and which clearly distinguishes it from the UN Convention. Paragraph 2 of Article 1 provides that:

> "the term 'refugee' shall also apply to every person who, owing to external aggression, occupation, foreign domination or events seriously disturbing public order in either part of the whole of his country or origin or nationality, is compelled to leave his place of habitual residence in order to seek refuge in another place outside his country of origin or nationality."

This defining aspect of the African Convention on Refugees requires some comments. The first element of the definition is that a person seeking refugee status must be compelled to leave his/her place of habitual residence. This requirement is more flexible than that of the UN Convention, which stipulates that the person should be outside his country of nationality or of habitual residence. A proper interpretation of the provision of the OAU Convention would, it is submitted, imply that the person "has to leave, shall leave", a meaning which can be ascribed to the UN Convention only by a liberal interpretation of its relevant provision. It is also submitted that a person may also qualify where he/she is compelled to leave his country of nationality, since the place of habitual residence might not always correspond with the country of nationality, and in any case "country of habitual residence" can also apply to a person without a nationality. It may be that this formulation was adopted with refugees from colonial territories in mind, although there is no reason why it should not embrace refugees from independent African States. Furthermore nationality is imported into the second limb of the OAU definition of refugees.

The second requirement is that the person be compelled to leave because of external aggression, occupation, foreign domination or events seriously disturbing public order in either part or the whole of his country of origin or nationality. On the face of it, external aggression would become relevant where foreign countries invade or occupy an independent African State, and foreign domination may occur in relation to independent States and colonies, while events seriously disturbing the public order in the country of origin or nationality might be as a result of external aggression, occupation or foreign domination, or of serious internal upheavals.

If this provision is interpreted, however, in the light of the acceptance of the principle of self-determination, it would have a wider application not only for the colonial period but for afterwards. The recognition of the principle of self-determination as applicable to dependent territories imparts to them some international personality necessary to assert that right. The colony would therefore not be regarded as part of the metropolitan territory, and consequently the relations between the metropolis and the colony will not be regarded as falling within the domestic jurisdiction of the administering power. This interpretation in effect implies that the phrases "foreign aggression, occupation or foreign domination" could qualify acts of the administering power perpetrated against a colony as being illegal. It is probable that the drafters of this convention had this interpretation in mind.

Be that as it may, the requirement that a person seeking refugee status must have been compelled to leave his place of habitual residence in order to seek refuge in another place poses a problem where it is sought to include liberation movements within the meaning of Article 1(2) of the African Convention. The main objective of the liberation movements is not just to seek refuge, but to seek a base from which to seize power from the colonial power. Does this objective override the need to seek refuge or is the desire to seek refuge for no matter what purpose sufficient?

The right of self-determination also remains valid where dictatorships impose themselves on the population. The growing obligation to sanction non-democratic regimes (within the framework of the AU and ECOWAS) and the evolving right to democracy – implying the right of a people to *freely choose* and *participate* in their government without external intervention – grounds the view for external support for liberation and recognition of refugees without subverting popular will.

Whatever the problems of interpretation may be, it is submitted that Article 1(2) of the African Convention must have been intended to cover all manner of refugees, whether they be those from independent or dependent African States, whether they are engaged in a liberation war or in a struggle for democracy. They must, however, satisfy the conditions laid down therein before they can qualify as refugees entitled to the protection which the Convention provides. In the liberal tradition of interpreting humanitarian conventions, it is hoped that the African Convention will apply to those who do not strictly fall within its ambit.

The problem that arises with respect to refugees that flow from theatres of conflict is that it is often difficult to separate combatants from civilians. Even when the former might have laid down arms and therefore have become *hors de combat*. They can readily join the conflict against the States from which they have fled. This situation which has occurred in the Mano River area can lead to conflicts, which expose genuine refugees to danger.

In addition to provisions, which deal with the termination of refugee status, which will be discussed later, the African Convention specifies circumstances under which the respective provisions would not apply. They shall not apply to any person with respect to whom there are serious reasons for considering that:

(a) He has committed a crime against peace, a war crime or a crime against humanity, as defined in the international instruments drawn up to make provisions in respect of such crimes;

(b) He has committed a serious non-political crime outside the country of refuge prior to his admission to that country as a refugee;

(c) He has been guilty of acts contrary to the purposes and principles of the OAU Conventions and of purposes and principles of the United Nations Article 1(5)(a)-(d). The OAU Convention might appear to have narrowed down the definition of refugees by making termination non-applicability dependent on non-conformity with the purposes and principles of the OAU Charter. But by its terms, the purposes and principles of the OAU are subject to those of the UN.

Unlike in the UN Convention, it is expressly stated in the OAU Convention that it is the country of asylum which can determine whether any of the abovementioned acts has been committed. It is submitted that the non-express provision for this in the UN Convention does not make it different from similar provisions of the African Convention since, as will be shown later, under the UN Convention it is the country of asylum that can determine refugee status. There is thus a danger that extraneous considerations may influence decisions on refugee status.

The UN Convention also states that the Convention shall not apply to those who are receiving from organs or agencies of the United Nations, other than the United Nations High Commissioner for Refugees, protection or assistance. Where, however, such protection or assistance has ceased for any reason without the position of such persons being definitely settled in accordance with the relevant resolutions adopted by the General Assembly, these persons shall *ipso facto* be entitled to the benefits of the Convention (Article 1(D)).

The UN Convention also does not apply to a person who is recognized by the competent authorities of the country in which he has taken refuge as having rights and obligations which are attached to the possession of nationality of that country (Article 1(E)). Formal acquisition of the nationality of the country in question is therefore not necessary. It is sufficient if the person who was originally admitted as a refugee acquires rights and obligations akin to those of nationals in the country of residence.

It is clear from our discussion of the UN instruments that the conventional meaning of the term "refugee" is rather restrictive; it could exclude those who might otherwise "qualify" as refugees, and is inadequate in the African context. For instance, the UN definition would not embrace those commonly referred to as de facto refugees or "refugees without official status" or "non-statutory refugees", all of which mean the same thing. They include *inter alia* those whose application for refugee status has been rejected and are unable or unwilling for reasons of race, religion, nationality or membership of a particular social group or political opinion to return to their country of origin as well as Stateless persons not recognized as refugees, but who for the same reasons would also be unable and unwilling to return to their country of origin. It has also been pointed out that the UN Conventions, by laying too much emphasis on nationality as a criterion for classification, particularly in view of relatively free movement across African boundaries did not meet African requirements. And does happen that people from the same ethnic group or even kindred inhabit territories divided by international boundaries.

Article 1(2) of the African Convention, may therefore, be considered a welcome development in that it is broad enough to include those refugee situations that have arisen in Africa which might not have been envisaged by the drafters of the UN Convention who were more concerned with European refugees.

3. How is Refugee Status Determined?

Before a refugee can benefit from the provisions of the Conventions, it is necessary to determine whether he is a person entitled to the benefits provided therein. Thus, as a first step, it must be determined whether he is a "refugee" within the meaning of the relevant instruments.

The UNHCR Statute does not contain a specific provision relating to the determination of refugee status. Subject to requiring conformity with the qualifications for refugee status laid down in the Statute, the UNHCR determines refugee status as it thinks fit. There are no set procedures for determining a person's eligibility, although the High Commissioner generally follows the policy directives given him by the General Assembly or the Economic and Social Council (Chapter 1(3)).

As with the UNHCR Statute, the UN Convention does not establish any procedure for determining refugee status. Each country party to the Convention adopts its own procedure for determining refugee status. The practice in this field has varied from place to place. Some countries have established special bodies to deal with refugee problems,[3] while others have dealt with the matter on an ad hoc basis.

In practice, under the supervisory function of the office of the High Commissioner specified in the Convention, the office participates in

---

[3] For example, for the Nigerian Law and Practice, see National Commission for Refugees Act, Cap. 224, Laws of the Federation.

varying degrees in the determination of refugee status both for the purposes of the convention and of municipal law. The degree of participation will ultimately depend on the authorization of the State in which a refugee seeks asylum.

The African Convention stipulates in Article 1(6) that the Contracting State shall determine whether a person is a refugee. It is submitted that the determination should be made in favour of a person who satisfies the conditions laid down in Article 1 of the Convention.

When the refugee problem arose in Africa, particularly as a result of colonial domination and national liberation wars, refugee status was established on a group basis. The endemic sectoral and often resource-based internal conflicts which now pervade Africa continue to produce mass flows of refugees. But there have been increasing numbers of individual refugees who have been forced to leave their homes as a result of internal political and military upheavals, and this has pointed to the need for a procedure to be adopted to deal with individual asylum-seekers. Certain African countries – Algeria, Botswana, Morocco, Nigeria, Senegal, Tanzania, Uganda and Zambia – have established special procedures for the determination of refugee status.

National determination of refugee status is, however, fraught with the problems of establishing effective institutions for the interpretation and application of the relevant provisions of the refugee conventions at the national level, and of ensuring that officers charged with interpretation and application are conversant with the convention.

The duty of a refugee, like any other alien, to obey the laws of the country of asylum is confirmed, and the refugee is required to conform with the laws and regulations as well as with measures taken for the maintenance of public order (African Convention, Article III(1); UN Convention, Article 2). Municipal laws and regulations may thus be used to ensure that refugees who have been granted asylum in their territories do not carry out subversive activities against independent States including those States from which they have fled.[4]

---

[4] African Charter on Human and Peoples' Rights, Article 3.

The same line of reasoning did not obviously apply to liberation movements fighting against colonial and racist regimes, since if this were so the right of self-determination as we understand it and the dedication of African States to the total emancipation of African territories would be rendered meaningless. With new commitments to human rights, including the right to democracy under Article 12(3) of the African Charter on Human and Peoples' Rights (1984), it is a moot point to what extent the same argument can apply to those who fight to liberate their countries from dictators, as indicated by recent events in various African countries.

Extradition may also be considered under this head. A State is under no obligation, in the absence of an agreement providing for such, to extradite a refugee, whether he be a refugee within the meaning of the refugee Conventions being discussed or a fugitive from justice. Regarding refugees within the meaning of the Refugee Convention, the principle of *non-refoulement* will certainly preclude extradition. The question of whether the acceptance of the principle of non-extradition for political refugees has elevated it to a rule of law independent of treaty law is not settled. Insofar as the principle is contained only in domestic legislation, it may be evidence of a general principle of law recognized by civilized nations. But States can change their domestic laws at will.

4. The Treatment of Refugees

The UN Convention of 1951, unlike the African Convention, contains elaborate provisions dealing with rights accorded to refugees in the territories of States Parties to the Convention. Both Conventions, however, contain stipulations requiring that Member States apply the provisions of the respective Conventions without discrimination. Under the UN Convention the Contracting States undertake to apply the provisions of the Convention without discrimination, as to race, religion or country or origin (Article 3). The non-discrimination clause of the African Convention is more elaborate in that it prohibits, in addition, discrimination in the application of the Convention on grounds of membership of a particular social group or political opinions (Article IV).

The UN Convention establishes four standards of treatment. These are the national treatment, treatment as accorded to nationals of the country of their habitual residence, the most-favoured nation treatment, and treatment as favourable as possible and in any case not less favourable than that accorded to aliens generally in the same circumstances.

The standard of national treatment applies in certain specified situations. First, the national standard is accorded to refugees staying in a Contracting State with respect to, *inter alia*, such rights as the freedom of refugees to practice religion and the religious education of their children; wage-earning employment after the refugee had resided for three years in the country; elementary education; public relief and assistance; labour legislation and social security.

Secondly, treatment as accorded to its nationals by the country of habitual residence forms the basis of treatment in another Contracting State. This is the position in respect of such rights of refugees, as protection of industrial property rights and rights in literary, artistic and scientific works, and access to Courts including legal assistance.

Thirdly, in respect of rights of association in non-political and non-profit-making associations and trade unions, and wage-earning employment for refugees who have not been granted national treatment, it is the "most favoured nation" treatment that is operative.

Finally, regarding treatment as favourable as possible and, in any event, not less favourable than that accorded to aliens generally in the same circumstances, it is to be noted that this standard relates to rights concerning movable and immovable property, self-employment in agriculture, commerce, industry, handcrafts, exercise of liberal professions, housing, secondary and higher education, recognition of foreign diplomas and the award of scholarships.

While the rights granted to refugees under the UN Convention are steps in the right direction, the national treatment standard envisaged in relation to wage-earning employment, after the refugee has resided for three years in the country – elementary education, public relief and assistance as well as labour legislation and social security – could pay, prove to be a great burden on the economies of the African countries who are disposed to admit refugees into their territories. It is clear that in many of these countries there are just not enough places in primary schools for nationals, and a government might find it difficult to justify giving equal opportunity to both its own citizens and to refugees. As far as wage-earning employment is concerned, most African countries, like other developing countries have a hard time providing enough jobs for the pool of unemployed. National interest, given the scarce resources of African countries and their reluctance to allow foreigners to become part of the mainstream of the indigenous labour associations, would also militate against according them national treatment with respect to labour legislation and social security.

Certain solutions to these problems may be proposed. First, one of these is, in fact, envisaged in the Convention which permits reservations to be made to the relevant provisions, thus excluding responsibility for the asylum State (Article 42).

Secondly, a special provision, which takes into account the inability of the African countries to offer these facilities, could be included in the convention. Thus, a provision which is promotional rather than being instantly obligatory could be inserted into the Convention.

Finally, while not ignoring the valuable assistance which is being given by the United Nations and its agencies, as well as several voluntary agencies, more assistance that responds to the new demands should be made available to the asylum States to enable them to grant as many of these rights as possible to the refugees. In effect assistance should not only keep pace with the new dimensions of refugee flows but also with dealing with those caught in the theatre of conflicts.

Certain provisions of the UN Convention are also intended to facilitate and buttress the rights and advantages accorded to refugees thereunder. It is provided in Article 7(1) that except where the Convention contains more favourable provisions, a Contracting State shall accord to refugees the same treatment as is accorded to aliens generally. Refugees are also to be exempted from legislative reciprocity, after a period of three years in the territory of Contracting States (Article 7(2)). The Contracting States have also undertaken to continue to accord to refugees the rights and benefits to which they were entitled in the absence of reciprocity at the date of entry into force of the Convention for that (Article 7(2)) State.

Exemption from reciprocity clearly serves a useful function in relation to refugees. The principle of reciprocity is normally applicable between the grantor State and the State of the person seeking to enjoy the rights in question. It is difficult to see how this principle can apply to a refugee who has in any case broken the link with his country of nationality. It is even more difficult to envisage the principle as applicable in the case of Stateless refugees.

Article 8 of the UN Convention prohibits the Contracting States from applying to refugees exceptional measures which may be taken against the person, property or interests of nationals of a foreign State solely on account of such refugees formally possessing the nationality of such foreign State. It is also provided that "Contracting States which, under their legislation, are prevented from applying the general principles expressed in this Article, shall in appropriate cases, grant exemptions in favour of such refugees". The wording of this sentence is unfortunate, since it may be interpreted as subordinating the international "obligation" to domestic legislation. It could in fact be argued that Article 8(1) does not impose any obligation on a State Party to the Convention. Besides, even if under existing local legislation a State is able to conform with the provision of Article 8, the State may nevertheless avoid compliance by altering its domestic legislation.

As has already been stated, the African Convention does not contain the specific rights discussed above. The rights of refugees like that of other aliens, subject however to the minimum standard or except where a State has become a party to the 1951 Convention and/or 1967 Protocol, will be governed by the laws and policies of the Contracting State.

We have seen above that States Parties to the Refugee Conventions have the competence to determine refugee status. Determination of refugee status is normally effected when the person-seeking refugee status presents herself to the relevant authorities of the country in question. The UN Convention has certain provisions, which deal, to some extent, with the admission and expulsion of refugees. It must be made clear, however, that under customary international law a State has the right to admit or not to admit aliens, including refugees.

Benin has an express provision in its Constitution which permits the grant of asylum to certain categories of refugees.[5]

Article 31 makes provision in relation to refugees unlawfully in the country of asylum. The Contracting States undertake not to impose penalties, on account of their illegal entry or presence

> "on refugees, who coming directly from a territory where their life or freedom was threatened in the sense of Article 1, enter or are present in their territory without authorization, provided they present themselves without delay to the authorities and show good cause for their illegal entry or presence".

The Contracting State in question can either regularize the status of such a refugee by granting him asylum or by allowing him a reasonable period and all the necessary facilities to obtain admission to another country. Article 31 does not thus impose a duty on a Contracting State to grant asylum to refugees.

Article 32 of the UN Convention provides that Contracting States shall not expel a refugee lawfully in their territory save on grounds of national security or public order. It is further provided that expulsion shall only be in pursuance of a decision reached in accordance with due process of law. The refugee is also to be allowed, except where compelling reasons of national security otherwise require, to submit evidence to clear himself, and to appeal and be represented for the purpose before competent authority or a person or persons specifically designated by the competent authority. As with Article 31, Article 32 does not impose on a State the duty to grant asylum. All that is required of a Contracting State is not to expel such refugees, subject of course to requirements of national security or public order, but to allow them a reasonable period within which to seek legal admission into another country.

---

[5] Article 144 of La Loi fondamentale of Benin of 26 August 1977 provides, « La République Populaire du Bénin accorde le droit de résidence à tous les étrangers poursuivis pour avoir défendu la juste cause de la paix et de la démocratie, pour leur participation à un mouvement révolutionnaire ou en raison de leurs activités scientifiques, artistiques ou culturelles ».

While Article 32 deals with expulsion, *simpliciter*, Article 33 introduces the principle of *non-refoulement*, which specifies a limit to the already restricted right of expulsion. Contracting States undertake not to expel or return ("refouler") a refugee in any manner whatsoever to the frontiers of territories where his life or freedom would be threatened on account of his race, religion, nationality, membership of a particular social group, or political opinion. This will preclude expulsion or return to a country from which he had fled or to another country, which may return him to the same.

It is not clear whether Article 33 applies only to refugees within the territory or country of refuge or to those refugees who present themselves at the frontier as well. An interpretation which includes the latter, within the operational scope of Article 33, will seem to be more in accord with the humanitarian protection to the refugee against his *refoulement* to a country where he may be persecuted merely because, after having arrived at the frontiers of the State of refuge, he failed to penetrate its territory.

Article 33 does not apply to a refugee where there are reasonable grounds for regarding him as a danger to the security of the country in which he is, or to a refugee who having been convicted by a final judgment of a particularly serious crime, constitutes a danger to the community of that country (Article 33(2)).

Attempts have made both before and after the adoption of the UN Convention to include in an international instrument the duty to grant asylum. Thus Article 14(1) of the Universal Declaration of Human Rights of 1948 provides that "everyone has the right to seek and enjoy in other countries asylum from persecution". As originally drafted the provision read that "everyone has the right to seek and to be granted asylum in other countries from persecution". This formulation was rejected by States on the ground that it impinged on the sovereign rights of States to grant or not to grant asylum. Even if the original formulation was adopted it would not by itself have created any legal obligation, since the Declaration does not by itself create legal obligations for States who voted for its adoption. The States were thus more concerned with a possible development of an obligation to grant asylum rather than an immediate impact on their sovereignty.

Enforcement of refugee rights would, in the final result, depend on the legal system of the country of refuge as well as the relevant human rights conventions, which in any event in appropriate cases apply to parties to the refugee conventions who have adhered to them. Indeed Article 3 of the Protocol to the African Charter on the Establishment of the African Court extends the jurisdiction of the Court to "any other human rights instruments ratified by the States concerned". While the State of asylum might protect him against the acts of other Contracting States contrary to the provisions of the Convention, he has no effective means of enforcing his rights against the State of asylum. Nor can he rely on the protection of the State from which he has fled. Where the country of origin of a refugee is a party to the UN Convention, he no doubt can ensure conformity with the provisions which are intended to protect the rights of refugees, but he may not have any interest in doing so.

There is clearly a need to provide an international machinery to ensure the enforcement of refugee rights. The refugee himself is helpless in the country of refuge, since his insistence on his rights might earn him the displeasure of the host State, which might be inclined to terminate his refuge status under one of the several escape clauses contained in the Convention.

5. Assistance to Refugees

Apart from identity papers, which the Contracting States have undertaken to issue to refugees in their territory, they have also undertaken to issue travel documents to refugees (UN Convention, Articles 27 and 28). The Contracting States shall issue to refugees lawfully staying in their territory travel documents for the purpose of travel outside their territory unless compelling reasons of national security or public order otherwise require. The schedule annexed to the Convention contains detailed provisions relating to travel documents. A model travel document is also annexed to the schedule.

Contracting States have discretion to issue travel documents to other refugees in their territory, and it is recommended that they should in particular issue such documents to refugees in their territory who are unable to obtain them from the country of their lawful residence. It is submitted, however, that apart from a refusal to issues a travel document on compelling grounds of national security or public order, a State commits a breach of the Convention if it refuses to issue a travel document to a refugee lawfully in its territory. There is some evidence that some African countries have not followed the injunction of this provision.

Travel documents issued to refugees under previous international agreements by parties thereto are to be recognized and treated as if they had been issued pursuant to the Article (UN Convention, Article 28(2)).

Travel documents issued under the Convention are valid for one or two years, depending on the discretion of the issuing authority (Paragraph 5 of Schedule to UN Convention). The Contracting States undertake to recognize the validity of documents issued in accordance with the provisions of Article 28. As far as admission into, transit through or residence or establishment in the territories is concerned, it is the laws of the relevant Contracting State that are operative. Thus, visas and work permits might be required in appropriate circumstances (Paragraph 14 of Schedule to UN Convention).

It is expressly stated that the issue of the document does not in anyway entitle the holder to the protection of the diplomatic or consular authorities of the country of issue and does not confer on these authorities a right of protection (Paragraph 16 of Schedule to UN Convention). It has already been argued that the State of asylum can protect refugees against acts of other States Parties contrary to the Convention. What is thus precluded under this provision is the diplomatic and consular protection, which normally applies to nationals of the protecting State.

The African Convention provides that travel documents shall be issued to refugees lawfully staying in the territories of Member States in accordance with the UN Convention and the Schedule and annex thereto. The African Convention, however, makes the issue of travel documents subject to Article III, which deals *inter alia*, with the prohibition of subversive activities. In addition, a Contracting State shall grant such documents unless compelling reasons of national security or public order otherwise require. It may also issue the same to refugees other than those lawfully in its territory (Article 6).

The UN Convention deals with measures of administrative assistance, which are to be given to refugees in order to enable them to enjoy their rights. It is clear that where such assistance is to be given by the authorities of the country from which he has fled, these authorities might not be willing to cooperate. Hence it is provided that "[t]he Contracting State in whose territory he is residing shall arrange that such assistance be afforded to him by their own authorities or by an international body" (Article 25(1) of the UN Convention). The assistance envisaged to the issue to the refugee of such documents or certifications as would normally be delivered to aliens by or through their national authorities (Article 25(2)). The documents or certifications are to stand in the stead of the official instruments delivered to aliens by or through their national authorities, and are to be given credence in the absence of proof to the contrary (Article 25(3)). The African Convention does not contain provisions on administrative assistance to refugees.

6. Supervision and Enforcement

Since refugee status implies rights for refugees, it is important to examine how these are actualized. The African Union has competent organs charged with the responsibility for refugee matters:
- The Refugee Commission charged with the responsibility of examining issues relative to refugees and making recommendations to the Executive Council of the African Union on measures for relocating them and providing necessary assistance. In this, the Refugee Commission is assisted by the Committee for the Coordination of Assistance to Refugees and the Division of Refugees, Displaced Persons and Humanitarian Affairs;
- The Committee for Coordination of Assistance to Refugees is a consultative organ composed of representatives of the United Nations, Intergovernmental Organizations and NGOs. The Committee is charged with matters and programme that are of benefit to refugees; and

- The Division for Refugees, Displaced Persons and Humanitarian Affairs (formerly known as the Bureau for the Placement and Education of Refugees) has *inter alia* the following functions:
(i) Monitor the refugee situation in Africa;
(ii) Keep Member States of the AU and the international community informed of the causes and consequences of movement of refugees in Africa;
(iii) Give assistance and protection, in collaboration with the Bureau of the High Commission for Refugees, to refugees who are not informed about their rights and intercede on their behalf before their host governments;
(iv) Assist them to get better educated by giving them financial assistance as well as acquire skills that will enable them make a living;
(v) In collaboration with the High Commission for Refugees, ensure settlement of qualified refugees by seeking employment for them in Member States.

Regional organizations, such as ECOWAS, IGAD, SADC and CEEAC, have at the insistence of the AU established mechanism for the prevention, management and resolution of internal conflicts, which remains one of the main causes of African Refugees.

The implementation and "supervision" of the African Refugee Convention is sought to be achieved, by provisions made in other African conventions adopted by the OAU or the AU. Violation of refugee rights in Article 12 of the African Charter on Human and Peoples' Rights, as well as those of Women (Article 11(2) Protocol to the African Charter on Human and Peoples' Rights on the Rights of Women in Africa), and the Child (Article 23) are subject to the mechanisms under the respective conventions.

Furthermore, African Regional Economic Communities such as SADC and ECOWAS, as well as the OAU, have entered into agreement with the United Nations High Commission for Refugees for the purpose of implementing both the UN and OAU/AU refugee regimes.[6]

---

[6] Cooperation Agreement between the Office of the United Nations High Commission for Refugees and the Organisation of African Unity, 9 April 2001; Memorandum of Understanding between the Southern African Development

Finally, the OAU/AU collaborates with national institutions on refugees for the implementation of the Convention and other associated matters.

7. Conclusion

The African Refugee Convention has to be seen as a supplement at least for States Parties to both the African and the UN Conventions. The wider scope of the former is intended to deal with the multiple problems, which Africa faces. It is hoped that a liberal approach will include those (such as persons affected by serious economic conditions) not specifically covered under the UN instruments. It can thus be seen that refugee problem is likely to be a matter of great concern in Africa for the foreseeable future given its underdevelopment, and intense competition for power and scarce resources.

As long as the common good principle remains distant, adequate provisions must be made to take care of the basic needs of refugees, particularly, women, children and the aged. In the first instance, this can be done at the place of refuge. Then at the next place of refuge. But the better options would appear to be integration by naturalization or assimilation in the local communities, where they would be accorded national treatment or better still voluntary repatriation to their country of nationality or habitual residence. In each case, underdevelopment must be tackled and poverty uprooted for they impede the capacity of African States not only to prevent the root causes of refugee problems but also to ensure the welfare of Africans whether nationals or refugees.

Community and the United Nations High Commission for Refugees, 25 July 1996; Protocole d'Accord entre la Communauté économique des Etats de l'Afrique de l'Ouest, ci-après dénommée "CEDEAO" d'une part et le Haut Commissariat de Nations Unies aux Réfugiés, ci-après dénommée "HCR" d'autre part, 19 November 2001; Memorandum of Understanding between the African Commission on Human and Peoples' Rights and the United Nations High Commissioner for Refugees (unrelated).

In the end, the collaborative effort between the UN High Commissioner for Refugees and the African Union, as well as with the Regional Economic Communities and natural institutions need to be backed by better funding. The commitment to eliminating the root causes of refugees, i.e. bad governance, poverty and conflicts, should be pursued with vigour, while repatriation, reintegration and assimilation of refugees would continue.

APPENDICES

APPENDICE A.
SIRTE DECLARATION

1. We, the Heads Of State and Government of the Organization of African Unity (OAU), met at the fourth Extraordinary Session of our Assembly in Sirte, in the Great Socialist People's Libyan Arab Jamahiriya, from 8 – 9 September 1999, at the invitation of the Leader of the Al Fatah Revolution, Colonel Muammar Ghaddafi, and as agreed upon during the Thirty-fifth Ordinary Session of our Summit in Algiers, Algeria from 12 – 14 July 1999.

2. We deliberated extensively on the ways and means of strengthening our continental Organisation to make it more effective so as to keep pace with the political, economic and social developments taking place within and outside our continent.

3. In this endeavour, we were inspired by the ideals which guided the Founding Fathers of our Organization and Generations of Pan-Africanists in their resolve to forge unity, solidarity and cohesion, as well as co-operation between African peoples and among African States.

4. We recall the heroic struggles waged by our peoples and our countries during the last century of this millennium for political independence, human dignity and economic emancipation. We take pride in the achievements made to promote and consolidate African unity and we salute the heroism and the sacrifices of our peoples, particularly during the liberation struggles.

5. As we prepare to enter the 21st century and cognisant of the challenges that will confront our continent and peoples, we emphasise the imperative need and a high sense of urgency to rekindle the aspirations of our peoples for stronger unity, solidarity and cohesion in a larger community of peoples transcending cultural, ideological, ethnic and national differences.

6. In order to cope with those challenges and to effectively address the new social, political and economic realities in Africa and in the world, we are determined to fulfil our peoples' aspirations for greater unity in conformity with the objectives o the OAU Charter and the Treaty establishing the African Economic Community. It is also our conviction that our Continental Organisation needs to be revitalised in order to be able to play a more active role and continue to be relevant to the needs of our peoples and responsive to the demands of the prevailing circumstances. We are also determined to eliminate the scourge of conflicts, which constitutes a major impediment to the implementation of our development and integration agenda.

7. In our deliberations, we have been inspired by the important proposals submitted by Colonel Muammar Ghaddafi, Leader of the Great Al Fatah Libyan Revolution and particularly, by his vision for a strong and united Africa, capable of meeting global challenges and shouldering its responsibility to harness the human and natural resources of the continent in order to improve the living conditions of its peoples.

8. Having discussed frankly and extensively on how to proceed with the strengthening of the unity of our continent and its peoples, in the light of those proposals, and hearing in mind the current situation on the Continent, we decide to:

(i)   Establish an African Union, in conformity with the ultimate objectives of the Charter of our Continental Organisation and the provisions of the Treaty establishing the African Economic Community.

(ii) Accelerate the process of implementing the Treaty establishing the African Economic Community, in particular:

(a) Shorten the implementation periods of the Abuja Treaty;

(b) Ensure the speedy establishment of all the institutions provided for in the Abuja Treaty; such as the African Central Bank, the African Monetary Union, the African Court of Justice and in particular, the Pan-African Parliament. We aim to establish that Parliament by the year 2000, to provide a common platform for our peoples and their grass-root organizations to be more involved in discussions and decision-making on the problems and challenges facing our continent;

(c) Strengthening and consolidating the Regional Economic Communities as the pillars for achieving the objectives of the African Economic Community and realising the envisaged Union.

(iii) Mandate the Council of Ministers to take the necessary measures to ensure the implementation of the above decisions and in particular, to prepare the constitutive legal text of the Union, taking into account the Charter of the OAU and the Treaty establishing the African Economic Community. Member States should encourage the participation of Parliamentarians in that process. The Council should submit its report to the Thirty-sixth Ordinary Session of our Assembly for appropriate action. Member States should work towards finalising the process of ratification, where appropriate, by December 2000, in order for a constitutive Act to be solemnly adopted in the year 2001, at an Extra-Ordinary Summit, to be convened in Sirte.

(iv) Mandate our Current Chairman, President Abdelaziz Bouteflika of Algeria and President Thabo Mbeki of South Africa in consultation with the OAU Contact Group on Africa's External Debt to engage African creditors on our behalf on the EAHG/Draft/Decl. (IV) Rev.1 Sirte Declaration issue of Africa's external indebtedness, with a view to securing the total cancellation of Africa's debt, as a matter of urgency.

(v) Convene an African Ministerial Conference on Security, Stability, Development and Cooperation in the Continent, as soon as possible.

(vi) Request the Secretary General of our Organisation, as a matter of priority, to take all appropriate measures to follow up the implementation of these decisions.

Done at Sirte Great Socialist People's Libyan Arab Jamahiriya, September 9, 1999.

APPENDICE B.
CONSTITUTIVE ACT OF THE AFRICAN UNION

WE, Heads of State and Government of the Member States of the Organization of African Unity (OAU):

1. The President of the People's Democratic Republic of Algeria
2. The President of the Republic of Angola
3. The President of the Republic of Benin
4. The President of the Republic of Botswana
5. The President of Burkina Faso
6. The President of the Republic of Burundi
7. The President of the Republic of Cameroon
8. The President of the Republic of Cape Verde
9. The President of the Central African Republic
10. The President of the Republic of Chad
11. The President of the Islamic Federal Republic of the Comoros
12. The President of the Republic of the Congo
13. The President of the Republic of Cote d'Ivoire
14. The President of the Democratic Republic of Congo
15. The President of the Republic of Djibouti
16. The President of the Arab Republic of Egypt
17. The President of the State of Eritrea
18. The Prime Minister of the Federal Democratic Republic of Ethiopia
19. The President of the Republic of Equatorial Guinea
20. The President of the Gabonese Republic
21. The President of the Republic of The Gambia
22. The President of the Republic of Ghana
23. The President of the Republic of Guinea
24. The President of the Republic of Guinea Bissau

25. The President of the Republic of Kenya
26. The Prime Minister of Lesotho
27. The President of the Republic of Liberia
28. The Leader of the 1st of September Revolution of the Great Socialist People's Libyan Arab Jamahiriya
29. The President of the Republic of Madagascar
30. The President of the Republic of Malawi
31. The President of the Republic of Mali
32. The President of the Islamic Republic of Mauritania
33. The Prime Minister of the Republic of Mauritius
34. The President of the Republic of Mozambique
35. The President of the Republic of Namibia
36. The President of the Republic of Niger
37. The President of the Federal Republic of Nigeria
38. The President of the Republic of Rwanda
39. The President of the Sahrawi Arab Democratic Republic
40. The President of the Republic of Sao Tome and Principe
41. The President of the Republic of Senegal
42. The President of the Republic of Seychelles
43. The President of the Republic of Sierra Leone
44. The President of the Republic of Somalia
45. The President of the Republic of South Africa
46. The President of the Republic of Sudan
47. The King of Swaziland
48. The President of the United Republic of Tanzania
49. The President of the Togolese Republic
50. The President of the Republic of Tunisia
51. The President of the Republic of Uganda
52. The President of the Republic of Zambia
53. The President of the Republic of Zimbabwe

INSPIRED by the noble ideals which guided the founding fathers of our Continental Organization and generations of Pan-Africanists in their determination to promote unity, solidarity, cohesion and cooperation among the peoples of Africa and African States;

CONSIDERING the principles and objectives stated in the Charter of the Organization of African Unity and the Treaty establishing the African Economic Community;

RECALLING the heroic struggles waged by our peoples and our countries for political independence, human dignity and economic emancipation;

CONSIDERING that since its inception, the Organization of African Unity has played a determining and invaluable role in the liberation of the continent, the affirmation of a common identity and the process of attainment of the unity of our Continent and has provided a unique framework for our collective action in Africa and in our relations with the rest of the world;

DETERMINED to take up the multifaceted challenges that confront our continent and peoples in the light of the social, economic and political changes taking place in the world;

CONVINCED of the need to accelerate the process of implementing the Treaty establishing the African Economic Community in order to promote the socio-economic development of Africa and to face more effectively the challenges posed by globalization;

GUIDED by our common vision of a united and strong Africa and by the need to build a partnership between governments and all segments of civil society, in particular women, youth and the private sector in order to strengthen solidarity and cohesion among our peoples;

CONSCIOUS of the fact that the scourge of conflicts in Africa constitutes a major impediment to the socio-economic development of the continent and of the need to promote peace, security and stability as a prerequisite for the implementation of our development and integration agenda;

DETERMINED to promote and protect human and peoples' rights, consolidate democratic institutions and culture, and to ensure good governance and the rule of law;

FURTHER DETERMINED to take all necessary measures to strengthen our common institutions and provide them with the necessary powers and resources to enable them discharge their respective mandates effectively;

RECALLING the Declaration which we adopted at the Fourth Extraordinary Session of our Assembly in Sirte, the Great Socialist People's Libyan Arab Jamahiriya, on 9.9. 99, in which we decided to establish an African Union, in conformity with the ultimate objectives of the Charter of our Continental Organization and the Treaty establishing the African Economic Community;

HAVE AGREED AS FOLLOWS:

Article 1
Definitions

In this Constitutive Act:
"Act" means the present Constitutive Act;
"AEC" means the African Economic Community;
"Assembly" means the Assembly of Heads of State and Government of the Union;
"Charter" means the Charter of the OAU;
"Committee" means a Specialized Technical Committee of the Union;
"Council" means the Economic, Social and Cultural Council of the Union;
"Court" means the Court of Justice of the Union;
"Executive Council" means the Executive Council of Ministers of the Union;
"Member State" means a Member State of the Union;
"OAU" means the Organization of African Unity;
"Parliament" means the Pan-African Parliament of the Union;

"Union" means the African Union established by the present Constitutive Act.

Article 2
Establishment

The African Union is hereby established in accordance with the provisions of this Act.

Article 3
Objectives

The objectives of the Union shall be to:
(a) Achieve greater unity and solidarity between the African counties and the peoples of Africa;
(b) Defend the sovereignty, territorial integrity and independence of its Member States;
(c) Accelerate the political and socio-economic integration of the continent;
(d) Promote and defend African common positions on issues of interest to the continent and its peoples;
(e) Encourage international cooperation, taking due account of the Charter of the United Nations and the Universal Declaration of Human Rights;
(f) Promote peace, security, and stability on the continent;
(g) Promote democratic principles and institutions, popular participation and good governance;
(h) Promote and protect human and peoples' rights in accordance with the African Charter on Human and Peoples' Rights and other relevant human rights instruments;
(i) Establish the necessary conditions which enable the continent to play its rightful role in the global economy and in international negotiations;
(j) Promote sustainable development at the economic, social and cultural levels as well as the integration of African economies;
(k) Promote cooperation in all fields of human activity to raise the living standards of African peoples;

(l) Coordinate and harmonize policies between existing and future Regional Economic Communities for the gradual attainment of the objectives of the Union;

(m) Advance the development of the continent by promoting research in all fields, in particular in science and technology;

(n) Work with relevant international partners in the eradication of preventable diseases and the promotion of good health on the continent.

Article 4
Principles

The Union shall function in accordance with the following principles:

(a) Sovereign equality and interdependence among Member States of the Union;

(b) Respect of borders existing on achievement of independence;

(c) Participation of the African peoples in the activities of the Union;

(d) Establishment of a common defence policy for the African Continent;

(e) Peaceful resolution of conflicts among Member States of the Union through such appropriate means as may be decided upon by the Assembly;

(f) Prohibition of the use of force or threat to use force among Member States of the Union;

(g) Non-interference by any Member State in the internal affairs of another;

(h) The right of the Union to intervene in a Member State pursuant to a decision of the Assembly in respect of grave circumstances, namely war crimes, genocide and crimes against humanity;

(i) Peaceful co-existence of Member States and their right to live in peace and security;

(j) The right of Member States to request intervention from the Union in order to restore peace and security;

(k) Promotion of self-reliance within the framework of the Union;

(l) Promotion of gender equality;

(m) Respect for democratic principles, human rights, the rule of law and good governance;

(n) Promotion of social justice to ensure balanced economic development;
(o) Respect for the sanctity of human life, condemnation and rejection of impunity and political assassination, acts of terrorism and subversive activities;
(p) Condemnation and rejection of unconstitutional changes of governments.

Article 5
Organs of the Union

1. The organs of the Union shall be:
(a) The Assembly of the Union;
(b) The Executive Council;
(c) The Pan-African Parliament;
(d) The Court of Justice;
(e) The Commission;
(f) The Permanent Representatives Committee;
(g) The Specialized Technical Committees;
(h) The Economic, Social and Cultural Council;
(i) The Financial Institutions;

2. Other organs that the Assembly may decide to establish.

Article 6
The Assembly

1. The Assembly shall be composed of Heads of States and Government or their duly accredited representatives.

2. The Assembly shall be the supreme organ of the Union.

3. The Assembly shall meet at least once a year in ordinary session. At the request of any Member State and on approval by a two-thirds majority of the Member States, the Assembly shall meet in extraordinary session.

4. The Office of the Chairman of the Assembly shall be held for a period of one year by a Head of State or Government elected after consultations among the Member States.

Article 7
Decisions of the Assembly

1. The Assembly shall take its decisions by consensus or, failing which, by a two-thirds majority of the Member States of the Union. However, procedural matters, including the question of whether a matter is one of procedure or not, shall be decided by a simple majority.

2. Two-thirds of the total membership of the Union shall form a quorum at any meeting of the Assembly.

Article 8
Rules of Procedure of the Assembly

The Assembly shall adopt its own Rules of Procedure.

Article 9
Powers and Functions of the Assembly

1. The functions of the Assembly shall be to:
(a) Determine the common policies of the Union;
(b) Receive, consider and take decisions on reports and recommendations from the other organs of the Union;
(c) Consider requests for Membership of the Union;
(d) Establish any organ of the Union;
(e) Monitor the implementation of policies and decisions of the Union as well as ensure compliance by all Member States;
(f) Adopt the budget of the Union;
(g) Give directives to the Executive Council on the management of conflicts, war and other emergency situations and the restoration of peace;

(h) Appoint and terminate the appointment of the judges of the Court of Justice;

(i) Appoint the Chairman of the Commission and his or her deputy or deputies and Commissioners of the Commission and determine their functions and terms of office.

2. The Assembly may delegate any of its powers and functions to any organ of the Union.

Article 10
The Executive Council

1. The Executive Council shall be composed of the Ministers of Foreign Affairs or such other Ministers or Authorities as are designated by the Governments of Member States.

2. Council shall meet at least twice a year in ordinary session. It shall also meet in an extra-ordinary session at the request of any Member State and upon approval by two-thirds of all Member States.

Article 11
Decisions of the Executive Council

1. The Executive Council shall take its decisions by consensus or, failing which, by a two-thirds majority of the Member States. However, procedural matters, including the question of whether a matter is one of procedure or not, shall be decided by a simple majority.

2. Two-thirds of the total membership of the Union shall form a quorum at any meeting of the Executive Council.

Article 12
Rules of Procedure of the Executive Council

The Executive Council shall adopt its own Rules of Procedure.

Article 13

Functions of the Executive Council

1. The Executive Council shall co-ordinate and take decisions on policies in areas of common interest to the Member States, including the following:
(a) Foreign trade;
(b) Energy, industry and mineral resources;
(c) Food, agricultural and animal resources, livestock production and forestry;
(d) Water resources and irrigation;
(e) Environmental protection, humanitarian action and disaster response and relief;
(f) Transport and communications;
(g) Insurance;
(h) Education, culture, health and human resources development;
(i) Science and technology;
(j) Nationality, residency and immigration matters;
(k) Social security, including the formulation of mother and child care policies, as well as policies relating to the disabled and the handicapped;
(l) Establishment of a system of African awards, medals and prizes.

2. The Executive Council shall be responsible to the Assembly. It shall consider issues referred to it and monitor the implementation of policies formulated by the Assembly.

3. The Executive Council may delegate any of its powers and functions mentioned in paragraph 1 of this Article to the Specialized Technical Committees established under Article 14 of this Act.

Article 14
The Specialized Technical Committees

Establishment and Composition

1. There is hereby established the following Specialized Technical Committees, which shall be responsible to the Executive Council:
(a) The Committee on Rural Economy and Agricultural Matters;
(b) The Committee on Monetary and Financial Affairs;
(c) The Committee on Trade, Customs and Immigration Matters;
(d) The Committee on Industry, Science and Technology, Energy, Natural Resources and Environment;
(e) The Committee on Transport, Communications and Tourism;
(f) The Committee on Health, Labour and Social Affairs; and
(g) The Committee on Education, Culture and Human Resources.

2. The Assembly shall, whenever it deems appropriate, restructure the existing Committees or establish other Committees.

3. The Specialized Technical Committees shall be composed of Ministers or senior officials responsible for sectors falling within their respective areas of competence.

Article 15
Functions of the Specialized Technical Committees

Each Committee shall within its field of competence:
(a) Prepare projects and programmes of the Union and submit in to the Executive Council;
(b) Ensure the supervision, follow-up and the evaluation of the implementation of decisions taken by the organs of the Union;
(c) Ensure the coordination and harmonization of projects and programmes of the Union;
(d) Submit to the Executive Council either on its own initiative or at the request of the Executive Council, reports and recommendations on the implementation of the provision of this Act; and

(e) Carry out any other functions assigned to it for the purpose of ensuring the implementation of the provisions of this Act.

Article 16
Meetings

Subject to any directives given by the Executive Council, each Committee shall meet as often as necessary and shall prepare its rules of procedure and submit them to the Executive Council for approval.

Article 17
The Pan-African Parliament

1. In order to ensure the full participation of African peoples in the development and economic integration of the continent, a Pan-African Parliament shall be established.

2. The composition, powers, functions and organization of the Pan-African Parliament shall be defined in a protocol relating thereto.

Article 18
The Court of Justice

1. A Court of Justice of the Union shall be established;

2. The statute, composition and functions of the Court of Justice shall be defined in a protocol relating thereto.

Article 19
The Financial Institutions

The Union shall have the following financial institutions, whose rules and regulations shall be defined in protocols relating thereto:
(a) The African Central Bank;
(b) The African Monetary Fund;
(c) The African Investment Bank.

Article 20
The Commission

1. There shall be established a Commission of the Union, which shall be the Secretariat of the Union.

2. The Commission shall be composed of the Chairman, his or her deputy or deputies and the Commissioners. They shall be assisted by the necessary staff for the smooth functioning of the Commission.

3. The structure, functions and regulations of the Commission shall be determined by the Assembly.

Article 21
The Permanent Representatives Committee

1. There shall be established a Permanent Representatives Committee. It shall be composed of Permanent Representatives to the Union and other Plenipotentiaries of Member States.

2. The Permanent Representatives Committee shall be charged with the responsibility of preparing the work of the Executive Council and acting on the Executive Council's instructions. It may set up such sub-committees or working groups as it may deem necessary.

Article 22
The Economic, Social and Cultural Council

1. The Economic, Social and Cultural Council shall be an advisory organ composed of different social and professional groups of the Member States of the Union.

2. The functions, powers, composition and organization of the Economic, Social and Cultural Council shall be determined by the Assembly.

Article 23
Imposition of Sanctions

1. The Assembly shall determine the appropriate sanctions to be imposed on any Member State that defaults in the payment of its contributions to the budget of the Union in the following manner: denial of the right to speak at meetings, to vote, to present candidates for any position or post within the Union or to benefit from any activity or commitments, therefrom.

2. Furthermore, any Member State that fails to comply with the decisions and policies of the Union may be subjected to other sanctions, such as the denial of transport and communications links with other Member States, and other measures of a political and economic nature to be determined by the Assembly.

Article 24
The Headquarters of the Union

1. The Headquarters of the Union shall be in Addis Ababa in the Federal Democratic Republic of Ethiopia.

2. There may be established such other offices of the Union as the Assembly may, on the recommendation of the Executive Council, determine.

Article 25
Working Languages

The working languages of the Union and all its institutions shall be, if possible, African languages, Arabic, English, French and Portuguese.

Article 26
Interpretation

The Court shall be seized with matters of interpretation arising from the application or implementation of this Act. Pending its establishment, such matters shall be submitted to the Assembly of the Union, which shall decide by a two-thirds majority.

Article 27
Signature, Ratification and Accession

1. This Act shall be open to signature, ratification and accession by the Member States of the OAU in accordance with their respective constitutional procedures.

2. The instruments of ratification shall be deposited with the Secretary-General of the OAU.

3. Any Member State of the OAU acceding to this Act after its entry into force shall deposit the instrument of accession with the Chairman of the Commission.

Article 28
Entry into Force

This Act shall enter into force thirty (30) days after the deposit of the instruments of ratification by two-thirds of the Member States of the OAU.

Article 29
Admission to Membership

1. Any African State may, at any time after the entry into force of this Act, notify the Chairman of the Commission of its intention to accede to this Act and to be admitted as a member of the Union.

2. The Chairman of the Commission shall, upon receipt of such notification, transmit copies thereof to all Member States. Admission shall be decided by a simple majority of the Member States. The decision of each Member State shall be transmitted to the Chairman of the Commission who shall, upon receipt of the required number of votes, communicate the decision to the State concerned.

Article 30
Suspension

Governments which shall come to power through unconstitutional means shall not be allowed to participate in the activities of the Union.

Article 31
Cessation of Membership

1. Any State which desires to renounce its membership shall forward a written notification to the Chairman of the Commission, who shall inform Member States thereof. At the end of one year from the date of such notification, if not withdrawn, the Act shall cease to apply with respect to the renouncing State, which shall thereby cease to belong to the Union.

2. During the period of one year referred to in paragraph 1 of this Article, any Member State wishing to withdraw from the Union shall comply with the provisions of this Act and shall be bound to discharge its obligations under this Act up to the date of its withdrawal.

Article 32
Amendment and Revision

1. Any Member State may submit proposals for the amendment or revision of this Act.

2. Proposals for amendment or revision shall be submitted to the Chairman of the Commission who shall transmit same to Member States within thirty (30) days of receipt thereof.

3. The Assembly, upon the advice of the Executive Council, shall examine these proposals within a period of one year following notification of Member States, in accordance with the provisions of paragraph 2 of this Article.

4. Amendments or revisions shall be adopted by the Assembly by consensus or, failing which, by a two-thirds majority and submitted for ratification by all Member States in accordance with their respective constitutional procedures. They shall enter into force thirty (30) days after the deposit of the instruments of ratification with the Chairman of the Commission by a two-thirds majority of the Member States.

Article 33
Transitional Arrangements and Final Provisions

1. This Act shall replace the Charter of the Organization of African Unity. However, the Charter shall remain operative for a transitional period of one year or such further period as may be determined by the Assembly, following the entry into force of the Act, for the purpose of enabling the OAU/AEC to undertake the necessary measures regarding the devolution of its assets and liabilities to the Union and all matters relating thereto.

2. The provisions of this Act shall take precedence over and supersede any inconsistent or contrary provisions of the Treaty establishing the African Economic Community.

3. Upon the entry into force of this Act, all necessary measures shall be undertaken to implement its provisions and to ensure the establishment of the organs provided for under the Act in accordance with any directives or decisions which may be adopted in this regard by the Parties thereto within the transitional period stipulated above.

4. Pending the establishment of the Commission, the OAU General Secretariat shall be the interim Secretariat of the Union.

5. This Act, drawn up in four (4) original texts in the Arabic, English, French and Portuguese languages, all four (4) being equally authentic, shall be deposited with the Secretary-General of the OAU and, after its entry into force, with the Chairman of the Commission who shall transmit a certified true copy of the Act to the Government of each signatory State. The Secretary-General of the OAU and the Chairman of the Commission shall notify all signatory States of the dates of the deposit of the instruments of ratification or accession and shall upon entry into force of this Act register the same with the Secretariat of the United Nations.

IN WITNESS WHEREOF, WE have adopted this Act.
Done at Lomé, Togo, this 11th day of July, 2000.

APPENDICE C.
PROTOCOL ON AMENDMENTS TO THE CONSITUTIVE ACT OF THE AFRICAN UNION

The Member States of the African Union States Parties to the Constitutive Act of the African Union

Have agreed to adopt amendments to the Constitutive Act as follows:

Article 1
Definitions

In this Protocol, the following expressions shall have the meanings assigned to them hereunder unless otherwise specified:
"Act" means the Constitutive Act;
"Assembly" means the Assembly of Heads of State and Government of the African Union;
"Chairperson" means chairperson of the Assembly;
"Court" means the Court of Justice of the Union and Court of Justice has the same meaning;
"Union" means the African Union.

Article 2
Preamble

In the first paragraph of the Preamble to the Constitutive Act, the replacement of the words "founding fathers" with "founders"

Article 3
Objectives

In Article 3 of the Act (Objectives), the insertion of three new subparagraphs (i), (p) and (q) with consequential renumbering of subparagraphs:

The objectives of the Union shall be to:

...

(i) ensure the effective participation of women in decision-making, particularly in the political, economic and socio-cultural areas;

...

(p) develop and promote common policies on trade, defence and foreign relations to ensure the defence of the Continent and the strengthening of its negotiating positions;

(q) invite and encourage the full participation of the African Diaspora as an important part of our Continent, in the building of the African Union.

Article 4
Principles

In Article 4 of the Act (Principles), the expansion of subparagraph (h) and the insertion of two new subparagraphs (q) and (r):

...

(h) the right of the Union to intervene in a Member State pursuant to a decision of the Assembly in respect of grave circumstances, namely: war crimes, genocide and crimes against humanity as well as a serious threat to legitimate order to restore peace and stability to the Member State of the Union upon the recommendation of the Peace and Security Council;

...

(q) restraint by any Member State from entering into any treaty or alliance that is incompatible with the principles and objectives of the Union;

(r) prohibition of any Member State from allowing the use of its territory as a base for subversion against another Member State.

Article 5
Organs of the Union

In Article 5 of the Act (Organs of the Union), the insertion of a new subparagraph (f) with consequential renumbering of subsequent subparagraphs:

...

(f) The Peace and Security Council

...

Article 6
The Assembly

In Article 6 of the Act (The Assembly) and where-ever else it occurs in the Act, the substitution of the word "Chairman" with "Chairperson"; the deletion of the second sentence of subparagraph 3 and the insertion of new paragraphs 4, 5, 6 and 7.

...

3. The Assembly shall meet at least once a year in ordinary session.

4. At the initiative of the Chairperson after due consultation with all Member States, or at the request of any Member State and upon approval by two-thirds majority of Member States, the Assembly shall meet in Extraordinary Session.

5. The Assembly shall elect its Chairperson from among the Heads of State or Government at the beginning of each ordinary session and on the basis of rotation for a period of one year renewable.

6. The Chairperson shall be assisted by a Bureau chosen by the Assembly on the basis of equitable geographical representation.

7. Where the Assembly meets at the Headquarters, an election of the Chairperson shall be held taking into account the principle of rotation.

Article 7
Functions of the Chairperson of the Assembly

The insertion in the Act of a new Article 7 (bis):

1. The Chairperson shall represent the Union, during his/her tenure with a view to promoting the objectives and principles of the African Union as stipulated in Articles 3 and 4 of the Act. He/She shall also, with the collaboration of the Chairperson of the Commission, carry out the functions of the Assembly set out in Article 9(e) and (g) of the Act.

2. The Chairperson may convene the meeting of the other organs through their Chairpersons or Chief Executives and in accordance with their respective Rules of Procedure.

Article 8
The Executive Council

In Article 10 of the Act (The Executive Council), the insertion of a new paragraph 3:

...

3. The Chairperson of the Executive Council shall be assisted by a Bureau chosen by the Executive Council on the basis of equitable geographical representation.

Article 9
Peace and Security Council

The insertion in the Act of a new Article 20 (bis):

1. There is hereby established, a Peace and Security Council (PSC) of the Union, which shall be the standing decision-making organ for the prevention, management and resolution of conflicts.

2. The functions, powers, composition and organization of the PSC shall be determined by the Assembly and set out in a protocol relating thereto.

Article 10
The Permanent Representatives Committee

In Article 21 of the Act (The Permanent Representatives Committee) the insertion of a new paragraph 3:

...

3. The Chairperson of the Permanent Representatives Committee shall be assisted by a Bureau chosen on the basis of equitable geographical representation.

Article 11
Official Languages

In Article 25 of the Act (Working Languages), replace the title "Working Languages" by "Official Languages" and substitute the existing provision with:
1. The official languages of the Union and all its institutions shall be Arabic, English, French, Portuguese, Spanish, Kiswahili and any other African language.
2. The Executive Council shall determine the process and practical modalities for the use of official languages as working languages.

Article 12
Cessation of Membership

Article 31 of the Act (Cessation of Membership) is deleted.

Article 13
Entry into Force

This Protocol shall enter into force thirty days after the deposit of the instruments of ratification by a two-thirds majority of the Member States.

Adopted by the 1st Extraordinary Session of the Assembly of the Union in Addis Ababa, Ethiopia on 3 February 2003

And

by the 2nd Ordinary Session of the Assembly of the Union in Maputo, Mozambique on 11 July 2003

APPENDICE D.
LINKS TO THE AFRICAN UNION ORGANS, AGENCIES AND INSTRUMENTS

African Union Organs

African Union
http://www.au.int/

African Court on Human and Peoples' Rights
http://www.african-court.org/

Peace and Security Council, Situation Room
http://www.ausitroom-psd.org/

The Pan-African Parliament
http://www.pan-african-parliament.org/

New Partnership for Africa's Development
http://www.nepad.org/

African Peer Review Mechanism
http://www.aprm-international.org/

Regional Economic Communities

Arab Maghreb Union
http://www.maghrebarabe.org/en/

Common Market for Eastern and Southern Africa
http://www.comesa.int/

Community of Sahel-Saharan States
http://www.cen-sad.org/

East African Community
http://www.eac.int/

Economic Community of Central African States
http://www.ceeac-eccas.org/

Economic Community of West African States
http://www.ecowas.int/

Intergovernmental Authority on Development
http://www.igad.org/

South African Development Community
http://www.sadc.int/

Instruments of the African Union

OAU/AU Treaties, Conventions, Protocols and Charters
http://www.au.int/en/treaties

See on that page on the treaties, the following instruments:
1963 Charter of the Organization of African Unity (OAU)
1965 General Convention on the Privileges and Immunities of the OAU
1967 Phyto-Sanitary Convention for Africa
1968 African Convention on the Conservation of Nature and Natural Resources
1969 African Civil Aviation Commission Constitution
1969 OAU Convention Governing the Specific Aspects of Refugee Problems in Africa

1974 Constitution of the Association of African Trade Promotion Organizations

1975 Inter-African Convention Establishing an African Technical Co-operation Programme

1976 Cultural Charter for Africa

1977 Convention for the Elimination of Mercenarism in Africa

1980 Additional Protocol to the OAU General Convention on Privileges and Immunities

1981 African Charter on Human and Peoples' Rights

1985 Convention for the Establishment of the African Centre for Fertilizer Development

1985 Agreement for the Establishment of the African Rehabilitation Institute

1990 African Charter on the Rights and Welfare of the Child

1991 Bamako Convention on the Ban of the Import into Africa and the Control of Transboundary Movement and Management of Hazardous Wastes within Africa

1991 Treaty Establishing the African Economic Community

1994 African Maritime Transport Charter

1996 African Nuclear-Weapon Free Zone

1998 Protocol to the African Charter on Human and Peoples' Rights on the Establishment of an African Court on Human and Peoples' Rights

1999 OAU Convention on the Preventing and Combating of Terrorism

2000 Constitutive Act of the African Union (*See also* p. 525)

2001 Protocol to the Treaty Establishing the African Economic Community Relating to the Pan-African Parliament

2001 Convention of the African Energy Commission

2002 Protocol Relating to the Establishment of the Peace and Security Council of the African Union

2003 African Convention on the Conservation of Nature and Natural Resources

2003 Protocol to the African Charter on Peoples' Rights and the Rights of Women in Africa

2003 Protocol of the Court of Justice of the African Union

2003 African Union Convention on Preventing and Combating Corruption

2003 Protocol on Amendments to the Constitutive Act of the African Union (*See also* p. 543)

2004 Protocol to the OAU Convention on the Prevention and Combating of the African Union

2005 African Union Non-Aggression and Common Defence Pact

2006 Charter for African Cultural Renaissance

2006 African Charter on Democracy, Elections and Governance

2006 African Youth Charter

2008 Protocol on the Statute of the African Court of Justice and Human Rights

2009 Statute of the African Union Commission on International Law

2009 African Charter on Statistics

2009 Protocol on the African Investments Bank

2009 African Union Convention for the Protection and Assistance of Internally Displaced Persons in Africa

2009 Revised Constitution of the African Civil Aviation Commission

2010 Revised African Maritime Transport Charter

2011 African Charter on Values and Principles of Public Service and Administration

See elsewhere:

1991 Conference on Security, Stability, Development and Cooperation in Africa (CSSDCA): http://www.africa-union.org/Special_Programs/CSSDCA/cssdca-solemndeclaration.pdf (or) http://www2.ohchr.org/english/law/compilation_democracy/cssdca.htm

INDEX

A

AATUF, *see* All-African Trade Union Federation
ACOTA, *see* United States of America
ACP, *see* Africa Caribbean and Pacific States
ACPP, *see* Peacekeeping
ADB, *see* African Development Bank
Adjovi (R.), 143-158
Adoption, 477, 479, 485, 486, 492
Africa-Britain-China Conference on Agriculture and Fisheries, 221, 222
African Alternative Framework to Structural Adjustment Programmes for Socio-Economic Recovery and Transformation (AAF-SAP) 1989, 211, 212, 213
African and Madagascan Organization for Economic Cooperation (OAMCE), 15
African and Madagascan Union for Economic Cooperation (UAMCE), 15
African and Mauritian Organization (OCAM), 15
African army, 325
African Caribbean and Pacific Group of States (ACP), 246, 247
  ACP-EU, 246
  Cotonou Agreement, 246, 247
  Economic Partnership Agreements (EPAs), 246, 247, 248
  Lomé Convention, 246
African Central Bank, 19, 193, 199
African Centre for Study and Research on Terrorism, 148, 326
African Charter for Popular Participation in Development and Transformation (1990), 204, 211
African Citizens Directorate Organization (CIDO), 161, 176, 177
African Commission on Human and Peoples' Rights, 125, 128, 134, 136, 137, 420, 427, 428, 429, 432, 433, 437, 441, 442, 443, 449, 451, 452, 458, 459, 464, 465, 472, 473, 476, 488, 496, 517
  17th Session, 71, 300, 459
  Cases
    Civil Liberties Organization, 442
    Forum of Conscious, 435
    Jawara, 448
    Katangese Peoples' Congress, 432, 433
    Legal Resources Foundation, 420, 425, 429
    Social and Economic Rights Action Centre (SERAC) & Another, 432, 433

African Committee of Experts on the Rights and Welfare of the Child (ACERWC), 125, 128, 136, 137, 480, 487, 493
African Common Market, *see* African Economic Community
African Congress, 18, 19
African Council, 19
African Court of Human and Peoples' Rights, 70, 71, 119, 120, 123, 124, 125, 127, 129, 130, 131, 132, 134, 136, 139, 140, 141, 277, 444, 464, 473, 474, 489, 496, 513
   Advisory opinion, 136, 137, 138, 139, 140
African Court of Justice, 84
African Court of Justice and Human Rights, 106, 119-142
African Currency, *see* African Economic Community
African Customs Union, *see* African Economic Community
African Development Bank (ADB), 221, 240, 241
   President, 240
African Economic Community (AEC), 17, 35, 36, 38, 53, 72, 81, 95, 100, 102, 103, 112, 187-202
   African Common Market, 19, 189, 198, 234, 240, 241, 249
   African Currency, 193
   African Customs Union, 197, 198, 249

African Declaration on Cooperation, Development and Industry, 233
   Economic Development Strategy for Africa, 189
   Final Act of Lagos, 190, 211, 231
   Free Trade Areas (FTAs), 196, 197, 246, 248
   Lagos Plan of Action for the Economic Development of Africa, 190, 211, 231, 233, 234, 236
   Pan-African Economic and Monetary Union (PEMU), 193, 198
   See also African Alternative Framework to Structural Adjustment Programmes
African economic integration, 190, 196, 198, 200
African Energy Commission, 189
African Federal Union, 20
African fisheries, 221
African Investment Bank, 19
African Leadership Forum, 318
African Ministers of Finance and Economic Development and Planning, 208
African Monetary Fund, 193, 199
African Parliamentarian Network against Corruption (APNAC), 111
African Partnership Forum (APF), 220
African Peace Academy, 148, 326

African Peer Review
  Mechanism, see NEPAD
African security system, 154
African Standby Force, see
  Peace and Security Council
African Union Authority, 22
African Union Commission, 5,
  20, 22, 30, 71, 79-94, 143,
  144, 151, 152
  Chairperson, 21, 240
African Union Commission on
  International Law, 148, 326
African Union Peace Fund, 157
Agenda for Action
  Re-launching Africa's Socio-
  economic Transformation
  (1994), 294
Aggression, 501, 502
Al Bashir (O.), 370
Algeria, 16, 20, 21, 34, 205,
  208, 218, 225, 376, 411, 479,
  506
  Algiers, 34, 208, 254, 256,
    263, 264, 430
  Provisional Government of
    the Algerian Republic
    (GPRA), 14
Algiers Declaration on Peoples'
  Rights (1999), 263, 430
All-African Trade Union
  Federation (AATUF), 14
All-African Trade Union
  Federation, 14
Amate (C.O.C.), 92
America, 88
  See also Latin America
American Declaration of the
  Rights and Duties of Man
  (1948), 436
Amin Dada (I.), 419

Amr (M.S.), 159-183
AMU, see Arab Maghreb Union
Angola, 147, 162, 225, 306, 359
Annan (K.), 254, 309, 319, 349,
  352, 373
Apartheid, 479
Arab Maghreb Union (AMU),
  195, 219, 232
Arap Moi (D.), 357
Aristide (J.-B.), 268, 270, 271
Armed Forces Revolutionary
  Council (AFRC), see Sierra
  Leone
Arms
  Small arms, 380, 386
Arusha Accords, see Burundi
Asia, 88
Assembly of the Union, 27, 29,
  31, 33, 34, 37, 39, 41, 45, 47,
  54, 66, 71, 79-94, 106, 119,
  120, 121, 122, 123, 126, 128,
  135, 136, 144, 145, 146, 148,
  150, 152, 153, 154, 417, 445
Asylum, 463
Azikiwe (N.), 35

B

Banny (C.K.), 391, 392
Bedie (H.), 254
Bedjaoui (M.), 9-23
Belgium, 364, 372
  Brussels, 110
Benin, 15, 20, 225, 246, 511
  Cotonou, 246
Biko (S.), 11
Biswaro (J.M.), 79-94
Blyden (E.W.), 11

Botswana, 21, 208, 218, 359, 506
Bouteflika (A.), 205, 206, 207
Boutros-Ghali (B.), 153
Bozizé (F.), 256, 360, 361
Branco (R.), 257
Burkina Faso, 15, 20, 119, 225
 Ouagadougou, 119
Burundi, 20, 253, 262, 307, 339, 388, 397, 401, 439, 440
 Arusha Accords, 362, 363
 Conseil National pour la Défense de la Démocratie (CNDD), 362
 Forces pour la Défense de la Démocratie (FDD), 362
 ONUB, *see* Peacekeeping

C

Cairo Declaration (1993), 306, 337, 338, 339
Cameroon, 16, 206, 208, 218, 225
 Yaoundé, 206
Cape Verde, 20, 225, 448
 Praia, 448
Carter-Jonassaint Agreement, *see* Haiti
Cedras (R.), 268, 270, 271, 272, 273
CEEAC, *see* Economic Community for Central African States
CEMAC, *see* Monetary and Economic Community of Central Africa
CEN-SAD, *see* Community of Sahel-Saharan States

Central Africa, 195, 239
Central African Republic, 15, 20, 46, 256, 257, 339, 359, 360, 361, 370, 396, 397, 401, 403, 404
 Bangui, 359, 361
 Bangui Agreements, 403
 See also Peacekeeping
CEPGL, *see* Economic Community of the Great Lakes
Chad, 15, 20, 21, 356, 357, 358, 360, 361, 366, 369, 370, 420, 426, 428
 Aouzou Strip, 357
 GUNT, 356, 357
 Lagos Agreement, 356
 N'Djaména, 357, 407
Charter Review Committee (OAU), 27, 30
Child
 1979 African Union Declaration on the Rights, 478
 See also Conventions
Chile, 268
China, 205, 221, 222
 Beijing, 221, 458
 Chinese Academy of Fisheries Sciences, 221
 Ministry of Agriculture, 222
Clinton (W.), 271
Civil law, 101
Cold War, 143, 319
 Soviet Bloc, 228
Collective Security, *see* United Nations
Colonialism, 338, 419, 496, 501, 502, 506, 507

Commission on Mediation, Conciliation and Arbitration, 143
Committee on Unconstitutional Changes, *see* Unconstitutional Change of Government
Combatants, 503
COMESA, *see* Common Market for Eastern and Southen Africa
Common external tariffs, 197, 198
Common law, 101
Common Market for Eastern and Southern Africa (COMESA), 35, 44, 195, 201, 210, 219, 232, 237, 239, 247, 248
  Preferential Trade Area of Eastern and Southern States, 232
  COMESA/SADC Task Force, 239
Community of Sahel-Saharan States (CEN-SAD), 35, 195, 201, 210, 219, 232, 239, 256, 358, 359, 360, 383
Comprehensive Peace Agreement, *see* Sudan
Comoros, 46, 57, 75, 254, 263, 307
  Anjouan, 75, 254
  OMIC, *see* Peacekeeping
Conakry Declaration (1959), 14
Conference on Security, Stability, Development and Cooperation in Africa (CSSDCA), 148, 161, 162, 316, 317, 318, 319, 320, 325, 327, 329
Conference of Heads of State of Equatorial Africa, 15
Conflict(s), 503, 456, 463, 464, 484, 485, 496
Conflict Management Directorate, 153
Congo (Rep. of), 15, 225, 324, 478
  Brazzaville, 13
Congo, Democratic Republic of Congo (ex Zaire), 189, 233, 258, 306, 338, 357, 359, 389, 405, 406
  Kinshasa, 189, 233
Conseil de l'Entente, 15
Consensus, 479
Constitutional order, *see* Unconstitutional change of government
Continental Early Warning System, 152, 314, 321, 323
Conventions
  1948 Convention on the Prevention and Punishment of the Crime of Genocide, 341
  1950 Convention for the Protection of Human Rights and Fundamental Freedoms *or* European Convention of Human Rights, 126, 130, 136, 276, 280, 293
    Protocol No 1 to the European Convention of Human Rights (1952), 280

1951 Convention Relating to the Status of Refugees, 495, 498, 499, 500, 504, 507, 510, 514
  Protocol Relating to the Status of Refugees (1967), 495, 496, 498, 510
1951 Treaty establishing the European Commission, 106
1963 OAU (Organization of African Unity) Charter, 1, 27, 28, 30, 31, 32, 38, 41, 42, 45, 48, 49, 55, 57, 58, 59, 64, 66
  Protocol of Mediation, Conciliation, and Arbitration (1964), 336
1966 International Covenant on Civil and Political Rights, 70, 73, 428
1966 International Covenant on Economic, Social and Cultural Rights, 70
1969 OAU Convention Governing the Specific Aspects of Refugee Problems in Africa, 4, 495-518
1969 American Convention on Human Rights, 121, 126, 128, 129, 130, 132, 136, 137, 138, 139, 268
1977 Additional Protocols to the Geneva Conventions, 341
1979 Convention on the Elimination of all forms of Discrimination against Women, 460, 465, 466
1981 African Charter of Human and Peoples' Rights, 4, 43, 69, 73, 74, 204, 265, 277, 294, 297, 417-453, 477, 507, 496, 506, 507, 513, 516
  Protocol to the African Charter on Human Rights and Peoples' Rights on the Establishment of an African Court on Human and Peoples' Rights (1998), 70
  Protocol to the African Charter of Human and Peoples' Rights on the Rights of Women in Africa (2003), 4, 55, 63, 74, 286, 455-476
1989 Convention on the Rights of the Child, 479, 480, 481, 482, 483, 484, 485, 486, 489, 490, 491, 492, 493
1990 African Charter on the Rights and Welfare of the Child, 4, 70, 127, 477-493
1991 Treaty establishing the African Economic Community, 17, 34, 35, 36, 38, 39, 51, 82, 95, 96, 97, 98, 100, 191, 194, 196, 197, 198, 199, 200, 231, 233, 234, 235, 236, 238, 240, 241, 242, 243, 244, 245, 248

Index 559

Protocol on Relations between the African Economic Community and the Regional Economic Communities (1997), 236, 239, 241, 243, 244

Protocol to the Treaty Establishing the African Economic Community Relating to the Pan-African Parliament (2001), 39, 95, 97

1996 Inter-American Convention Against Corruption, 293

1997 OECD Convention on Combating Bribery of Foreign Public Officials in International Business Transactions, 293

1999 Council of Europe Criminal Law Convention on Corruption, 293

1999 ECOWAS Protocol relating to the Mechanism for Conflict Prevention, Management and Resolution, Peacekeeping and Security, 355, 358, 361, 363

2000 Constitutive Act of the African Union, 1, 2, 17, 18, 19, 20, 45, 47, 48, 54, 55, 58, 59, 63, 65, 66, 80, 81, 82, 83, 84, 85, 86, 87, 93, 94, 119, 132, 143, 144, 145, 180, 242, 243, 307, 310, 311, 312, 319, 320, 321, 322, 327, 328, 329, 525-542

Draft Constitutive Act of the African Union, 39

Protocol on Amendments to the Constitutive Act of the African Union, 543-548

2001 ECOWAS Protocol on Democracy and Good Governance, Supplementary to the Protocol relating to the Mechanism for Conflict Prevention, Management, Resolution, Peacekeeping and Security, 284

2002 Protocol relating to the Establishment of the Peace and Security Council of the African Union, 69, 144, 145, 158, 309, 337, 340, 341, 342, 345, 346, 348

2003 African Union Convention on Preventing and Combating Corruption, 4, 291-301

2003 United Nations Convention against Corruption, 293

2005 African Union Non-Aggression and Common Defence Pact, 148, 156, 321, 324, 327, 333, 384, 387

2006 United Nations Convention on the Rights of Persons with Disabilities, 470

2007 African Charter on
 Democracy, Elections and
 Governance, 4, 72, 73, 74,
 253, 265, 267, 275-290
Corruption, *see* Conventions
Côte d'Ivoire, 15, 46, 57, 75,
 99, 146, 254, 255, 263, 339,
 358, 388, 389, 390, 391, 392,
 393, 396, 397, 401, 402
 ECOFORCE, *see*
  Peacekeeping
 Front Populaire Ivoirien (FPI),
  255
 International Working Group,
  391, 392
 MINUCI, *see* Peacekeeping
 National Transitional Council,
  255
 ONUCI, *see* Peacekeeping
Council of Ministers (OAU)
 Resolution 464 (XXVI), 236
 Resolution 1279 (LII), 89
Council of Europe, 69
 Council of Europe law, 276
 See also European Court of
  Human Rights
Coup d'état, 340, 395
Crimes
 Crime against humanity, 309,
  322, 335, 340, 341, 343,
  347, 463, 503
 Crime against peace, 503
 Genocide, 309, 322, 335, 339,
  340, 341, 343, 347, 463
 War crimes, 309, 335, 339,
  340, 341, 343, 347, 463,
  503
Cross-Cutting Programs
 Committee, 175
Cuba, 205

Customary law, 101
Customs Union of Equatorial
 Africa, 15
Cyprus, 98

D

Dahomey, *see* Benin
Daqua (F.), 257
Déby (I.), 366
Debt reduction and
 cancellation, 386
Declaration Governing
 Democratic Elections in
 Africa (2002), 46
Declaration on a Code of
 Conduct for Inter-African
 Relations, and on Arms
 (1994), 148
Declaration on the Fundamental
 Changes Taking Place in the
 World and their Implications
 for Africa (1990), 294
Declaration on the
 Mechanism for Conflict
 Prevention, Management and
 Resolution (1993), 143
Decolonisation, 379
Democracy, 308, 316, 318, 329,
 331, 502, 503, 507
Department of International
 Development (DFID), *see*
 United Kingdom
Development
 Development of Africa, *see*
  Economic Commission for
  Africa *and* NEPAD

Right to Development, *see* United Nations General Assembly
DFID (Department of International Development), *see* United Kingdom
Diamonds, 393
  Certification or Kimberley Process, 393
Dias (D.), 257
Diop (C.A.), 11
Diouf (A.), 6
Disabled, 458, 470, 482, 483
Discrimination, 419, 422, 423, 426, 435, 453, 458, 507
Djibouti, 20, 162, 225, 360
Dlamini-Zuma (N.), 331
Domination (foreign), 501
Doumbé-Billé (S.), 53-75
Dubois (W.B.), 11, 12

E

EAC, *see* East African Community
EALA, *see* East African Community
EALC, *see* East African Community
Early warning, 380, 388
East Africa, 195
East Africa Federation, 15
East African Community (EAC), 35, 36, 195, 210, 219, 232, 239, 242, 248
  East African Legislative Assembly (EALA), 98
  East African Legislative Council (EALC), 116

East and Southern Africa, 239
ECA, *see* Economic Commission for Africa
ECCAS, *see* Economic Community for Central African States
ECHR, *see* European Court of Human Rights
ECOMOG, 253, 358, 359, 374, 405
Economic Affairs Committee, 174
Economic Commission for Africa (ECA), 190, 207, 208, 212, 213, 221, 240, 241, 244
  Conference of Ministers, 189
  Executive Secretary, 207, 240
Economic Community for Central African States (ECCAS), 195, 210, 219, 232, 239, 258, 383, 388, 516
  FACA, 360, 361
  FOMUC, 404
  MARAC, 388
Economic Community for West African States (ECOWAS), 35, 45, 98, 99, 102, 116, 146, 156, 195, 201, 210, 219, 232, 237, 239, 247, 253, 254, 259, 263, 275, 278, 280, 281, 282, 284, 285, 286, 288, 290, 328, 358, 377, 379, 380, 383, 388, 389, 390, 391, 395, 401, 402, 405, 502, 516
  Cease-fire Monitoring Group (ECOMOG), *see* ECOMOG
  ECOWAS & UEMOA, Single Monetary Zone for West Africa, 239

ECOWATCH, 388
Education, 461, 464, 466, 467, 468, 481, 483, 491, 492, 497, 498, 508
Economic Community of the Great Lakes (CEPGL), 232
Economic Partnership Agreement(s), *see* African Caribbean and Pacific Group of States
Economic, Social and Cultural Council of the African Union (ECOSOCC), 84, 136, 138, 159-183
  Rules of Procedures, 173
  Statute, 163, 176
Economic and Social Commission, *see* United Nations
Egypt, 16, 25, 119, 143, 168, 206, 208, 218, 225, 336, 337, 479
  Alexandria, 4
  Cairo, 143, 208, 294, 306, 312, 314, 318, 319, 323, 328
  Sharm-El-Sheikh, 22, 119, 168
EIPC, *see* Peacekeeping
Embargo, 390, 398, 399, 400
Environment
  Rio Conference (1992), 61
EPAs, *see* African Caribbean and Pacific Group of States
Equatorial Africa, 15
Equatorial Guinea, 20
Eritrea, 389, 397
Estonia, 98
Ethiopia, 14, 20, 21, 25, 26, 39, 97, 119, 162, 203, 207, 208, 218, 225, 234, 277, 358, 364, 389, 397, 399, 438, 478
  Addis Ababa, 13, 14, 16, 17, 22, 26, 39, 72, 74, 80, 88, 97, 119, 150, 156, 162, 182, 188, 203, 207, 234, 306, 311, 314, 320, 324, 404, 406, 407, 438, 478
EU, *see* European Union
Europe, 12, 88, 287
European Court of Human Rights (ECHR), 121, 123, 128, 130, 279
European Union (EU), 29, 38, 44, 49, 69, 98, 102, 105, 116, 117, 127, 130, 154, 157, 244, 246, 247, 324, 331, 332, 361, 364, 367, 369, 371, 373, 397
  European Commission, 84, 221
  European Court of Justice, 106, 127, 130
  European Parliament, 98, 99, 100, 102, 106, 110, 117
  EU-Egypt Euro-Mediterranean Agreement, 248
  EU-South Africa Free Trade Agreement, 248
  EU-Tunisia Euro-Mediterranean Agreement, 248
Executive Council of the African Union, 20, 22, 71, 79-94, 106, 121, 122, 135, 136, 144, 150
Expulsion, 510, 511, 512
Extradition, 507
Eyadema (G.), 75, 260
Eze (O.C.), 5, 495-518

F

Fahd (King), 260
Female genital mutilation (FGM), 465
Firmin (A.), 11
France, 12, 98, 254, 356, 359, 361, 368, 371, 373, 401, 406
  Linas-Marcoussis, 391, 402
  Paris, 12
  Strasbourg, 110
Franco-African Summit(s), 206
Francophonie, see International Organization of the Francophonie
Free Trade Area(s) (FTAs), see African Economic Community
Front Populaire Ivoirien, see Côte d'Ivoire

G

G77, 205
G8, 205, 217, 331, 332
Gabon, 15, 20, 21, 189, 208, 218, 225
  Libreville, 189, 360
Gambia, 15, 20, 22, 244, 418, 419, 421, 425, 438, 439, 448
  Banjul, 22, 244
Garang (J.), 365
Garvey (M.), 11, 35
GATT, see World Trade Organization
Gbagbo (L.), 255, 390, 392

General Agreement on Tariffs and Trade (GATT), see World Trade Organization
Genocide, see Crimes
Germany, 12, 98
  Berlin wall, 318
Ghana, 10, 13, 14, 16, 20, 34, 40, 99, 162, 225, 227, 253, 439
  Accra, 13, 14, 162
  Gold Coast, 10, 11
Governance, 308, 316, 325, 329, 331, 497, 518
Great Britain, see United Kingdom
Great Lakes region, 75
Gueï (R.), 75, 254, 255
Gueuyou (M.L.), 305-333
Guinea, 14, 16, 253, 258
Guinea Bisau, 20, 46, 254, 259, 263, 358, 388, 396
  Committee for the Restoration of Democracy and Constitutional Order, 259
Guinea-Ghana Union, 14

H

Haiti, 268, 270, 271, 272, 273
  Carter-Jonassaint Agreement, 271
Hansungule (M.), 417-453
HIV/AIDS, 386, 456, 467
Harare Declaration, 46, 263
Horn of Africa, 75
Human security, 325
Humanitarian law, 335, 342, 341
Hutu, see Rwanda

I

Ibengwe (M.G.), 108
ICAO, see International Civil Aviation Organization
ICC, see International Criminal Court
ICJ, see International Court of Justice
IGAD, see Intergovernmental Authority on Development
IGADD, see Intergovernmental Authority on Development
IGASOM, see Peacekeeping
Illy (O.), 187-202
IMF, see International Monetary Fund
Independence, 355
Indian Ocean Commission (IOC), 232, 239, 248
Inter-African and Madagascan Advisory Organization, 14
Inter-African Mission in Burundi (MIAB), see Peacekeeping
Interamerican Commission on Human Rights, 129, 268
   Case No 10.843 *Hermosilla et al.*, 268
Interamerican Court of Human Rights, 121, 123, 128, 129, 130, 132, 137, 138, 139, 276, 279, 287
Interference, see Intervention
Intergovernmental Authority on Development (IGAD), 195, 201, 232, 239, 311, 365, 380, 383, 388, 398, 399, 400, 516

Conflict Early Warning and REsponse Mechanism (CEWARN, 2002), 388
Internally displaced persons, 306, 463
   See also Refugees
International African Service Bureau, 11
International Atomic Agency, 221
International Civil Aviation Organization (ICAO), 221
International Commission of Jurists, 418
International Court of Justice (ICJ), 121, 123, 126, 127, 128, 130, 131, 132, 133, 134, 135, 136, 137, 138, 139, 140, 141, 142, 418
International Criminal Court (ICC), 70, 84, 341, 366, 370
International Monetary Fund (IMF), 210, 212, 213, 221
   Structural Adjustment Policies (SAP), 212
International Organization of the Francophonie, 4, 6
International Refugee Organization, 499
Intervention
   International Commission on Intervention and Sovereignty of States (ICISS), 341
   Non-interference, 307, 322, 335, 338, 339, 348, 350
   Non-intervention, 379
   Right to intervention, 325, 335-353

IOC, *see* Indian Ocean Commission
IRO, *see* International Refugee Organization
Islamic traditions, 101
Italy, 98

J

Jamaica, 11
Japan, 154
Jawara (D.), 418, 421, 425, 438
Jonassaint, *see* Haiti
Juvenile justice, 483, 489

K

Kabbah (A.T.), 253, 254
Kampang (H.), 10
Kannyo (E.), 203-229
Karangizi (S.), 231-249
Kenya, 15, 21, 225, 357, 369, 417, 431, 439, 442
  Nairobi, 357, 365, 369, 371, 380, 417, 431
Kenyatta (J.), 12
Kété (M.), 360
Khadafi (M.), 18
Kinshasa Declaration (1976), 189, 233
Kodjo (E.), 92, 261
Konaré (A.O.), 20, 87
Koroma (J.P.), 253
Kosovo, 68
Kuti (F.), 11

L

Landmines, 386
Latin America, 375
League of Arab States, 375
League of Nations, 25
Lesotho, 20, 163, 225, 359
Liberation, 419
  Liberation Movements, 496, 502, 503, 506, 507
Liberia, 13, 14, 16, 20, 25, 189, 306, 324, 338, 358, 377, 379, 389, 393, 394, 397, 403, 405, 417, 478
  Monrovia, 13, 14, 16, 189, 211, 417, 478
  UNMIL, *see* Peacekeeping
Libya, 16, 18, 19, 20, 22, 31, 33, 34, 39, 72, 96, 97, 134, 156, 163, 205, 208, 325, 340, 360
  Sirte, 18, 19, 21, 31, 33, 34, 37, 40, 72, 96, 97, 205, 207
  Tripoli, 39
Lome Declaration on Unconstitutional Changes of Government, *see* Unconstitutional Changes of Government
London, *see* United Kingdom
Lumumba (P.), 11
Lusaka Decision XXXVII (2001), 80, 93
Luxembourg, 98, 110

M

Madagascar, 20, 46, 75, 255, 256
Mahiou (A.), 187, 188, 195
Malaria, 386
Malawi, 20, 225
Mali, 15, 16, 20, 87, 208, 218, 225, 439
Mali Federation, 15
Malta, 98
Maluwa (T.), 25-52
Mandela (N.), 362, 363
Mano River, 503
Mano River Union (MRU), 232
Mauritania, 225, 260, 277, 315, 395, 422, 435, 443
Mauritius, 205, 208, 218, 225
  Grand Bay, 205
Mayanja (R.), 455-476
Mazimhaka (P.), 87
Mbeki (T.), 205, 206, 207
Mbenge (M.M.), 187-202
Mechanism for Conflict Prevention, Management, and Resolution (OAU, 1993), 254, 256, 337
Menzes (F. de), 257, 258
Mercenaries, 361
MERCOSUR (Common Market of the South, 1991), 44
Mexico, 457
MFN, *see* Most Favoured Nation
Millennium Development Goals, *see* United Nations
Millennium Partnership for the African Recovery Programme, *see* NEPAD
Mines, *see* Landmines

Ministerial Conference on Human Rights in Africa, 205
MINURCA, *see* Peacekeeping
MISAB, *see* Peacekeeping
Mohamed (S.L.), 95-117
Monetary and Economic Community of Central Africa (CEMAC), 196, 232, 239, 248, 256, 358, 359, 360, 361, 380, 383, 404, 405
Money laundering, 296
  See also Conventions
Monrovia Symposium / Strategy (1979), 189, 211, 233
Morocco, 14, 16, 479, 506
  Casablanca, 13, 14, 16
  Rabat, 189
Most Favoured Nation, 245
Mozambique, 53, 54, 87, 119, 163, 208, 218, 225
  Maputo, 54, 87, 119, 218, 256, 266, 324, 331, 397
MRU, *see* Mano River Union
Mubiala (M.), 355-374
Museveni (Y.), 40
Mwalimu (U.A.), 477-493

N

NAM, *see* Non Aligned Movement
Namibia, 204, 359
NATO, *see* North Atlantic Treaty Organization
Ndadaye (M.), 362
Ndulo (M.), 251-274
NEPAD (New Partnership for Africa's Development), 44,

111, 113, 148, 203-229, 294, 316, 317, 319, 320, 327, 329
African Action Plan (AAP), 220
African Peer Review Mechanism, 111, 203, 209, 222, 223, 224, 225, 227, 228, 440
   African Peer Review Forum, 223, 224
   African Peer Review Panel, 224, 227
   Comprehensive African Agriculture Development Programme (CAADP), 227
   Dakar-Ndjamena-Djibouti Transport Corridor, 226
   Declaration on Democracy, Political, Economic and Corporate Governance, 209, 222
   Draft National Plan of Action, 223
   Heads of State and Government Implementation Committee (HSGIC), 208, 218
   Millennium Partnership for the African Recovery Programme (MAP), 206, 207, 208
   NEPAD Fish, 221
   New African Initiative, 208
   Omega Plan, 206, 208, 226
   Planning and Coordinating Agency, 203
Neves (M. das), 257
New Agenda for the Development of Africa (1991), 212, 213

New International Economic Order, 188, 189
New Partnership for Africa's Development, *see* NEPAD
NGOs (Non Governmental Organizations), 418, 444, 449
Nguesso, *see* Sassou Nguesso
Nhasse (A.), 258
Niger, 15, 20, 21, 46, 263, 289
Nigeria, 5, 14, 16, 21, 99, 148, 156, 188, 190, 205, 208, 210, 211, 218, 225, 231, 234, 253, 258, 263, 272, 330, 357, 358, 364, 369, 421, 432, 435, 436, 438, 442, 506
   Abuja, 20, 21, 148, 156, 163, 188, 208, 210, 211, 231, 233, 234, 235, 236, 238, 240, 241, 242, 243, 244, 245, 248, 257, 311, 318, 324, 387, 406
   Lagos, 190, 356, 418, 419
   Lagos Agreement, *see* Chad
   Supreme Court, *Abacha v. Fawehinmi*, 421
Nkrumah (K.), 10, 11, 12, 13, 16, 18, 23, 34, 35, 188
Non-Aligned Movement, 206
   South Summit of the Nonaligned Movement, 205
Non Governmental Organizations, *see* NGOs
Non-discrimination, *see* Discrimination
Non-extradition, *see* Extradition
Non-interference, *see* Intervention
North Africa, 149, 163, 195

North Atlantic Treaty Organization (NATO), 68, 156, 157, 369
North-South Trade, 193
Nyerere (J.K.), 11, 35, 262, 362

O

OAMCE, *see* African and Madascan Organization for Economic Cooperation
OAS, *see* Organization of American States
OAU, *see* Organization of African Unity
Obasanjo (O.), 205, 206, 207, 261, 318
Observer Mission to the Comoros (OMIC), *see* Peacekeeping
OCAM, *see* African and Mauritian Organization
Occupation, 501
OECD, *see* Organization of Economic Cooperation and Development
Organization for Security and Cooperation in Europe (OSCE), 318
Organization of African Unity (OAU), 1, 2, 3, 4, 16, 17, 18, 19, 20, 85, 87, 88, 89, 91, 92, 93, 94
  Group of Neutral Military Observers (GOMN), *see* Peacekeeping
  Mechanism for Conflict Prevention, *see* Mechanism for Conflict Prevention,
  Management, and Resolution (OAU, 1993)
  Mediation, Conciliation and Arbitration Protocol, 338
Organization of American States (OAS), 44, 69, 268, 276, 278, 289, 350
  Interamerican Democratic Charter, 276, 279, 284, 285, 286, 287, 289
Organization of Economic Cooperation and Development (OECD), 221, 293
OSCE, *see* Organization for Security and Cooperation in Europe
Ouguergouz (F.), 1-6, 119-142

P

Padmore (G.), 12, 35
Pan-African Parliament, 71, 72, 84, 95-117
  Peace and Security Committee, 174
Panama, 272
Panel of the Wise, *see* Peace and Security Council
Patassé (A.-F.), 256, 257, 360
Peace and Security Council, 143-158, 260, 309, 310, 311, 312, 313, 314, 315, 320, 321, 322, 323, 324, 325, 327, 330, 331, 336, 337, 340, 341, 345, 346, 352, 355, 361, 363, 366, 368, 370, 371, 372

African Standby Force(s), 146, 152, 153, 158, 313, 321, 323, 326, 342, 380, 410, 413
Panel of the Wise, 152, 153, 157
Peace Fund, 152, 154, 157
Peace Facility for Africa / Peace Support Facility, 331, 397
Peacekeeping, 355-374
  African Conflict Prevention Pool (ACPP), 373
  AMIS (African Union Mission in Sudan), 146, 406, 407, 410
  AMISOM (African Union Mission in Somalia), 398, 399, 400
  BONUCA, 404
  ECOFORCE (ECOMOG in Côte d'Ivoire), 401
  Enhanced International Peacekeeping Capabilities (EIPC), 373
  GOMN (Group of Neutral Military Observers), 357
  IGASOM, 398, 399
  International Military Education and Training Program (IMET), 373
  MIAB (Inter-African Mission in Burundi), 401
  MINUCI (United Nations Mission in Côte d'Ivoire), 402
  MINURCA (United Nations Mission in Central African Republic), 360
  MINURCAT (United Nations Mission in Central African Republic and Chad), 403, 404
  MISAB (Bangui Agreements Implementation Mission), 359, 403, 404
  OLMEE, 358
  OMIC (Observer Mission to the Comoros), 357
  ONUB, 401
  ONUCI (United Nations Operation in Côte d'Ivoire), 402
  RECAMP (Reinforcement of Peacekeeping Capabilities), 373
  UNMIL, 397, 405
  UNMIS (United Nations Mission in Sudan), 397, 406, 407
  UNOSOM, 400
Peoples, see Algiers Declaration on Peoples' Rights
Permanent Consultative Committee of the Maghreb, 15
Permanent Representatives Committee (PRC), 84, 88
Peter (C.M.), 477-493
Ping (J.), xii-xvi
Pinochet (A.), 268
Plan of Action Against Impunity, 294
Political Affairs Committee, 174
Powell (C.), 366
Preventive diplomacy, 388
Provisional Government of the Algerian Republic, see Algeria

Public law of Africa, 2, 3, 5
Public order, 501, 506, 511, 513, 514, 515

R

Racism, 419
  Racist regimes, 507
Ratsiraka (D.), 255
Ravalomanana (M.), 46, 255
Rawlings (J.), 40
RECAMP, *see* Peacekeeping
RECs, *see* Regional Economic Communities
Refugees, 306, 463
  Committee for the Coordination, 515
  Division for Refugees, 516
  Non-refoulement, 507, 512
  Refugee Commission, 515
  See also Internally displaced persons
Regional Customs Unions, 197
Regional Economic Communities (RECs), 31, 35, 36, 38, 43, 103, 104, 159, 194, 195, 196, 197, 199, 200, 201, 202, 231-249, 317, 496
  Committee of Secretariat Officials, 201
  Coordinating Committee, 201, 202
Religions
  Animist, 365
  Christianism, 365
Revised Framework for Principles for the Implementation of the New International Order in Africa (1976), 211
Rosa (H.), 259
Rule of law, 308, 318, 331, 387, 395, 402, 404, 490
Rural Economy and Agriculture Committee, 174
Rwanda, 163, 208, 218, 225, 227, 262, 269, 307, 324, 338, 339, 341, 347, 349, 359, 369, 405, 406, 435, 440, 447
  FAR (Rwandan Armed Forces), 405
  Forces Démocratiques de Libération du Rwanda (FDLR), 405
  Gacaca, 464
  Hutu, 263, 362, 363
  Interahamwe, 405
  Tutsi, 263, 362, 363

S

SACU, *see* Southern African Customs Union
SADC, *see* Southern African Development Community
Sahel-Benin Union, 15
Sahrawi Arab Democratic Republic (SADR), 20, 389, 397, 446
Salim (S.A.), 254
Sangu (B.), 256
Sanctions, 379, 390, 393, 394, 396, 502
  Freezes on financial assets, 390
  Restrictions on international travel, 390

See also Unconstitutional Change of Government
Saõ Tomé and Principé, 208, 218, 225, 257, 258
SAPs, *see* International Monetary Fund
Sassou Nguesso (D.), 324, 325
Saudi Arabia, 260
Sciences and Technology Committee, 174
Seabra (V.C.), 258
Sectoral Cluster Committees, 167, 173, 175, 180
Self-defence, 342
Self-determination, 430, 433, 434, 502, 507
Senegal, 15, 20, 21, 22, 163, 206, 208, 218, 225, 357, 369, 418, 438, 479, 506
  Dakar, 208, 318, 418, 424, 458
Senegambia, 15
Seychelles, 163
Sharia Law, 365
Sharm-El-Sheikh, *see* Egypt
Sierra Leone, 20, 45, 147, 222, 225, 253, 254, 263, 272, 277, 338, 358, 377, 379, 389, 397, 403, 405
  Armed Forces Revolutionary Council (AFRC), 253
  Revolutionary United Front (RUF), 253
  Sierra Leone People's Army, 253
Sinjela (M.), 291-301
Sirte Declaration, 19, 33, 35, 38, 42, 50, 79, 83, 96, 244, 248, 521-524
Situation Room, 314, 321

Social Affairs and Health Committee, 174
Social justice, 497
Somalia, 306, 311, 324, 331, 338, 349, 355, 374, 389, 398, 399, 400
  AMISOM, *see* Peacekeeping
  IGASOM, *see* Peacekeeping
  UNOSOM, *see* Peacekeeping
South Africa, 11, 14, 25, 31, 96, 97, 110, 143, 204, 205, 206, 208, 209, 218, 222, 225, 227, 256, 263, 269, 294, 315, 330, 331, 359, 364, 369, 390, 401, 479
  Cape Town, 97
  Durban, 31, 47, 87, 97, 143, 209, 222, 294
  Kimberley, 393
  Midrand, 218
  National Party, 270
  Pretoria, 96, 208
  SANDF (South African National Defence Forces), 363, 364
  Truth and Reconciliation Commission, 464
Southern Africa, 195
Southern African Customs Union (SACU), 195, 196, 232
Southern African Development Community (SADC), 35, 109, 116, 156, 195, 201, 206, 210, 219, 232, 239, 247, 358, 359, 380, 383, 388, 516
  COMESA/SADC Task Force, *see* Common Market for Eastern and Southern Africa

Development Coordination Conference, 232
Organ on Politics, Security and Defence, 359
Parliamentary Forum, 109, 116
Spain, 192
Specialized Technical Committees, 162
Sudan, 15, 20, 22, 47, 146, 153, 155, 157, 225, 306, 389, 397, 398, 405, 406, 407, 411, 423, 434, 446
 AMIS, see Peacekeeping
 Comprehensive Peace Agreement, 365
 Darfur, 47, 57, 75, 91, 311, 315, 322, 329, 397, 398, 401, 406, 407, 410, 411
 Humanitarian Ceasefire Agreement, 366, 367
 Janjaweed, 322
 Joint Verification Commission, 358
 Khartoum, 21, 22, 407, 411
 SPLM, 365
 UNMIS, see Peacekeeping
Sullivan (L.)
 Leone Sullivan Summit of Influential African and African-American Leaders and Business People, 257
Summits of the African Union and the Organization of the African Unity
 8th Summit, 314
 16th Ordinary Session, 478
 26th Summit, 306, 478
 Abuja Summit, 311
 Accra Summit, 60

Addis Ababa Summit, 16, 17, 28, 188
Algiers Summit, 34, 254, 256
Durban Summit, 86, 256
Harare Summit, 264
Khartoum Summit, 21
Lomé Summit, 39, 41, 73, 256, 264
Lusaka Summit, 310
Maputo Summit, 86, 397
Monrovia Summit, 419
Sharm-El-Sheikh Summit, 22
Sirte Summit, 21, 37, 40
Togo Summit, 254
Sustainable development, 306, 308, 316, 319, 331
Swaziland, 163
Switzerland, 207
 Davos, 207
Sylvain (B.), 11, 12

T

Tanzania, 108, 124, 204, 208, 225, 438, 439, 506
 Arusha Accords, see Burundi
 Arusha, 124, 204
 Tanganyika, 15
Taya (M.O.S.A.), 260
Tehindrazanarivelo (D.L.), 375-413
Terrorism, 380, 386
Tiewul (S.A.), 337
Tigroudja (H.), 275-290
Togo, 16, 20, 31, 39, 75, 96, 146, 147, 163, 206, 225, 252, 254, 260, 261, 264, 265, 266, 395, 458, 459, 475

Lomé, 20, 31, 39, 40, 42, 96, 143, 251, 252, 256, 257, 264, 265, 266, 459
Togolese army, 260
Trade and Industry Committee, 174
Tuberculosis, 386
Tunisia, 21, 208, 218
Tunis, 14
Tutsi, *see* Rwanda

U

UAMCE, *see* African and Madagascan Union for Economic Cooperation
UDHR, *see* Universal Declaration of Human Rights
UEAC, *see* Union of Central African States
UEMOA, *see* West African Economic and Monetary Union
Uganda, 15, 21, 40, 208, 225, 359, 363, 399, 419, 440, 506
UMA, *see* Arab Maghreb Union
Unconstitutional Change of Government, 251-274, 328, 394, 395, 404
   Committee on Unconstitutional Changes, 251, 263
   Lomé Declaration on Unconstitutional Changes of Government, 251, 256, 257, 259, 264, 265
   Sanctions in Cases of Unconstitutional Changes of Government, 288

UNDP, *see* United Nations Development Program
UNDT, *see* United Nations Dispute Tribunal
UNESCO, *see* United Nations Education, Science and Cultural Organization
UNIDO, *see* United Nations Industrial Development Organization
Union of Central African Republics (URAC), 15
Union of Central African States (UEAC), 15
Union of Soviet Socialist Republics (USSR), 205
United Kingdom, 12, 98, 222
   Department of International Development (DFID), 222
   London, 12
   Manchester, 12
United Nations, 25, 26, 32, 57, 58, 66, 127, 131, 137, 148, 153, 155, 157, 213, 221, 268, 271, 272, 273, 305, 306, 307, 308, 313, 319, 320, 321, 323, 332, 337, 339, 342, 343, 344, 345, 346, 348, 349, 350, 355, 358, 359, 362, 364, 366, 370, 371, 372, 373, 374, 375-413, 428, 429, 430, 434, 450
   Charter, 26, 43, 58, 65, 66, 137, 132, 138, 145, 148, 159, 305, 308, 326, 336, 342, 343, 344, 345, 346, 348, 349, 350, 351, 352, 430
   Collective security, 305, 307, 310, 318, 319, 320, 323, 324, 326, 327, 330

Economic and Social Council (ECOSOC), 36, 505
Resolution 1503, 443
General Assembly, 71, 325, 347, 349, 377, 378, 379, 385, 409, 430, 499, 504, 505
Millennium Development Goals, 214
Millennium Summit, 213
Resolution 217 A (III), *see* Universal Declaration of Human Rights
Resolution 2625 (XXV), Declaration on Principles of International Law concerning Friendly relations and Co-operation among States in accordance with the Charter of the United Nations, 57, 65, 66, 67
Resolution 3314, 325
Resolution 32/130, 430
Resolution 41/128, Declaration on the right to Development, 430
Resolution 57/48, 379, 385
United Nations Standing Advisory Committee on Security Questions in Central Africa, 388
High Commissioner for Human Rights, 366
High Commissioner for Refugees, 366, 495, 496, 498, 499, 504, 505, 517, 518
Secretary-General, 154, 378, 382, 386, 391, 395, 396, 400, 407
Department of Economic and Social Affairs, 221
Office of the Special Adviser on Africa (OSAA), 221
Security Council, 71, 145, 146, 147, 154, 155, 259, 271, 305, 320, 322, 336, 341, 342, 346, 347, 349, 350, 351, 352, 355, 363, 370
Military Staff Committee, 321, 323, 326
Resolution 733, 398
Resolution 1125, 403
Resolution 1368, 70
Resolution 1528, 402
Resolution 1556, 407
Resolution 1574, 410
Resolution 1631, 382, 412
Resolution 1633, 392
Resolution 1706, 370
Resolution 1721, 392, 393
United Nations Program for Africa's Economic Recovery and Development, 211, 217
United Nations Conference on Trade and Development (UNCTAD), 193
United Nations Development Program (UNDP), 221
United Nations Dispute Tribunal (UNDT), 131

Index 575

United Nations Economic Commission for Africa, *see* Economic Commission for Africa
United Nations Education, Science and Cultural Organization (UNESCO), 221
United Nations Industrial Development Organization (UNIDO), 221
United States of Africa, 13, 18, 20, 22, 35, 37, 49, 63, 188
United States of America, 11, 12, 268, 271, 272, 331
  ACOTA, 373
  Dumbarton Oaks, 375
  New York, 12, 213
  San Francisco, 375
Universal Declaration of Human Rights (1948), 43, 58, 70, 73, 159, 262, 265, 424, 428, 429, 433, 436, 470, 512
Universal jurisdiction, 429
Upper Volta, *see* Burkina Faso
URAC, *see* Union of Central African Republics
USA, *see* United States of America
USSR, *see* Union of Soviet Socialist Republics

V

Vall (E.O.M.), 260
Vieira (J.B.), 254, 259

W

Wade (A.), 206, 207, 226
WAEMU, *see* West African Economic and Monetary Union
War crimes, *see* Crimes
Weapons, *see* Arms
Weddeye (G.), 356
West Africa, 149, 195
West African Economic and Monetary Union (WAEMU), 196, 232, 239, 247
Western Sahara, *see* Sahrawi Arab Democratic Republic
Williams (H.S.), 11, 12
Women
  First world conference for women, 457
  Women and Gender Committee, 174
World Bank
  Comprehensive development framework (CDF), 205, 210, 212, 213, 217, 221, 291
  Accelerated Development in Sub-Saharan Africa, 211
  See also International Monetary Fund
World Economic Forum, 207
World Fish Centre, 221
World Trade Organization (WTO), 193, 221, 245, 246, 247, 248
  Doha Development Agenda, 247
  General Agreement on Tariffs and Trade (GATT), 193, 245, 246

Regional trade agreements (RTAs), 245, 246, 248

X

X (Malcolm), 11

Y

Yala (K.), 258
Yugoslavia, 341
Yusuf (A.A.), 1-6, 335-353

Z

Zaïre, *see* Congo (Dem. Rep.)
Zambia, 20, 31, 49, 79, 208, 225, 294, 418, 425, 438, 439, 448
   Lusaka, 143, 208, 294, 306, 310, 359, 506
   Lusaka Ceasefire Agreement, 359
Zimbabwe, 45, 236, 253, 263, 359, 445, 446
   Harare, 17, 45, 236, 253, 263
Ziguele (M.), 257